THE FRAMEWORK OF
A CHRISTIAN STATE

The Framework of a Christian State

by Rev. E. Cahill, S.J.

*Author of "Freemasonry and the Anti-Christian
Movement," "Ireland's Peril," etc.*

*"When once men recognise, both in private and public life, that Christ
is King, society will at last receive the great blessings of real liberty,
well-ordered discipline, peace and harmony."*
— Pius XI in the Encyclical on the Kingship of Jesus Christ

$\mathcal{R}$oman $\mathcal{C}$atholic $\mathcal{B}$ooks
A Division of Catholic Media Apostolate, Harrison, New York
Business office: Post Office Box 2286, Fort Collins, CO 80522

De Licentia Sup. Ord.

        LAURENTIUS J KIERAN, S.J.

                        PRAEP. PROV. HIB.

DUBLINI, *die 26 Aprilis, 1932.*

Nihil Obstat:

        PATRICIUS DARGAN, S.T.D.,

              CENSOR THEOL. DEPUT.

Imprimi Potest:

      ✠ EDUARDUS,

          ARCHIEP. DUBLINEN.,

             HIBERNIÆ PRIMAS.

DUBLINI, *die 23° Maii,* 1932.

Dedication

to

Our Lord Jesus Christ,

King of the World,

and

of every State and Nation.

" Te nationum Paesides
Honore tollant publico
Colant magistri, judices,
Leges et artes exprimant."

" May rulers in their people's name
Thy Godhead solemnly proclaim,
Judges and teachers homage pay
Arts and the law accept Thy sway!"

(From the *Roman Breviary*—Office of Feast of Jesus Christ the King).

CONTENTS

PART II

CATHOLIC SOCIAL PRINCIPLES

CHAPTER XVI

CHAPTER XXII

CHAPTER XXIII

CHAPTER XXIV

CHAPTER XXV

CHAPTER XXVI

CHAPTER XXVII

CHAPTER XXVIII

CHAPTER XXIX

APPENDICES

APPENDIX I

APPENDIX II

APPENDIX III

PREFACE

THE matter of the present book was originally prepared in connection with the writer's duties as Professor of Social Science in Milltown Park, Dublin. The greater part of it has been already published in the *Irish Ecclesiastical Record* and the *Irish Monthly* between the years 1924 and 1930. The same matter has formed the basis of a series of lectures (of which summaries have appeared weekly in the *Irish Catholic*) which the writer has been giving to the Central Branch of *An Rioghacht* since the foundation of that association in 1926.[1] Grateful acknowledgments are due to the editors of the *Irish Ecclesiastical Record* and the *Irish Monthly* for their kind permission to republish in their present form the articles which appeared in these reviews.

. . . .

The book is intended primarily for students of Social Science who accept the Church's teaching. Its main purpose is to summarise and present in a consecutive and more or less scientific form the main elements of the teachings of the Roman Pontiffs (especially Leo XIII and our present Holy Father Pius XI), the Catholic Bishops and the standard Catholic authors on questions connected with social organisation and public life, including such topics as personal rights and duties, the privileges and position of the family in the social organism, the interrelations of capital and labour, the place of religion in public life, education, the functions of the State, its constitution, laws and administration, the due interrelations of its component parts with one another, its relations with the Church, etc.

Here and there in the book will be found suggestions borrowed mostly from approved Catholic writers, as to practical means of realising Christian principles and ideals in social and civic organisation. The principal non-Catholic

---

[1] *An Rioghacht* (the League of the Kingship of Christ) was founded in Dublin, October 31, 1926, on the occasion of the first celebration of the Feast of Jesus Christ the King. Its objects are the study and propagation of Catholic social principles and the promotion of Catholic Action.

theories on the subjects discussed, and modern non-Christian tendencies and movements are also dealt with ; and the well-being of the people under the Christian régime as illustrated from history is compared with their position in the non-Christian State.

.   .   .   .

Following the precedent of French, American and English writers on the same subjects, the author has striven to give special prominence to those aspects of the questions dealt with, which seem to have special importance in his own country ; and he naturally chooses his illustrations of principles and their application from existing circumstances in Ireland, the country with which he is most familiar. The main portions of the work, however, apply to all countries. Hence the writer hopes that the book may prove useful even to non-Irish readers. On that account he has relegated to Appendices the treatment of certain aspects of the social question which are rooted in historical causes peculiar to Ireland.

.   .   .   .

The writer wishes to thank very sincerely the kind friends whose invaluable assistance and patient collaboration have enabled him to complete much sooner than he could otherwise have hoped the tedious work of preparing the book for publication. He wishes also to thank those other friends whose helpful advice and friendly criticism have assisted him very much in the work of revision. Finally, he gladly acknowledges the great assistance he has received from the discussions carried on during the past five years at the meetings of *An Rioghacht.* These discussions have served especially to throw light on many practical questions, and have given the writer an insight into certain aspects of his subject with which he would be otherwise unacquainted.

E. C.

Milltown Park, Dublin.
Feast of Jesus Christ the King, 1931.

THE FRAMEWORK OF A CHRISTIAN STATE

(An Introduction to Social Science)[1]

PRELIMINARY CHAPTER

A CHRISTIAN State is one in which the laws and administration as well as the organised activities and general outlook
of the citizens are in accordance with Christian principles.
These principles, in so far as they are applicable to social
and public life, are practically identical with the dictates
of the natural law. It is with these principles and their
practical application in the life of the State that Social
Science has to do.

Term Sociology or Social Science.[2]—The term Social
Science or Sociology means etymologically the science of
Society or the science that deals with man in his social
relations. The subject, however, notwithstanding its great
importance at the present day, has scarcely yet secured full
recognition, at least among non-Catholic writers, as a distinct
science ; nor are men in agreement as to its complete object
and scope.

Although there are chairs of Sociology in very many of
the universities of the world, it does not appear that the

---

[1] Cf. Maritain—*Le Conflit de la Morale et de la Sociologie* (Paris, 1927) ;
Devas—*Political Economy*, 3rd edit. (London, Longmans, 1920), "Epilogue"
pp. 633–662 ; Cronin—*Primer of the Principles of Social Science* (Dublin,
1927) ; Antoine—*Cours d'Economie Sociale*, pp. 1–5 (6th edit., Paris, 1920) ;
Parkinson—*Primer of Social Science*, " Introductory " ; Macksey—*Argumenta Sociologica* (Romæ, 1918), cap. II. *See also* Gide—*Political Economy*,
chap. II, and *History of Economic Doctrines*, book iv, chap. I. (Both
books translated from the French, are published by Harrap & Co., London.)

[2] The Græco-Latin hybrid term *Sociology* which is sometimes used as
a synonym for *Social Science* was first brought into currency by the French
Positivist Philosopher, Auguste Comte (1789–1857). *See* Devas, Antoine,
Gide, *loc. cit.*

sciences taught under that name in the different universities are always founded on the same principles, or that the subject-matter dealt with is the same in every case. Most Catholic writers, however, now recognise social studies as a distinct science and are in substantial agreement as to its object and scope.

Non-Christian Sociology.—According to Auguste Comte and the writers of the Positivist School of Philosophy, the purpose of Sociology would be to collect and co-ordinate the facts of human history which bear upon the intellectual and social development of the human race, in order to found upon the knowledge thus obtained a complete scheme for the direction of individual and social conduct. Such a view, which would make custom and utility the sole rule of human actions, and eliminate completely God's eternal law, cannot, of course, be admitted by the Christian philosopher.

Herbert Spencer and other writers of the Evolutionist school, who deny human liberty, and reduce all the forces in the universe to the necessary transformation of matter and motion, adopt Comte's view regarding the scope of Sociology, but develop it in accordance with the Evolutionary theory. According to Spencer, the science of Sociology consists in a series of generalisations of the observed facts of social life, which exhibits, he says, a perfect analogy with the life of the individual. The structure of the moral body called Civil Society and the functions of its several parts are said to be quite similar to the organic structure and functions of individuals, including man ; and both exhibit alike their periods of growth, maturity and decay. Spencer and the writers of his school make the study of Sociology to consist mainly in the collection and co-ordination of facts to illustrate and prove this peculiar theory.

The Pantheistic philosophers of the Hegelian school of Evolution, who identify man with the Deity, and make all man's thoughts and actions to belong to the one eternal

Being evolving Himself towards a fuller and more perfect reality, regard organised civil society as the highest and most perfect manifestation of the Divinity. With them the scope of Sociology would be to expound and establish by abstract reasoning their theory of the nature of civil society, and to trace its gradual evolution towards the higher and better order to which, they say, it is tending.

With all these dreams and speculations we are not at present concerned. The theories of Positivism, Materialism and Pantheism, completely opposed as they are to common sense, and in flat contradiction of the practical experience of life, are referred to here merely to point out that Sociology or Social Science in the Catholic sense is something completely different from the so-called sciences which non-Christian philosophers designate by that name.

Christian Sociology.—But not even Christian or so-called Christian philosophers are in full accord as to the object and scope of Sociology or Social Science. Many English, especially non-Catholic, writers apply the term to all studies that relate to the social improvement of man. They often use the term Sociology or Social Science merely as a general heading under which to treat such subjects as social reform, ethics, charity, relief-work, statistics, criminology, politics, etc. Besides, with many of these writers, Social Science, or the collection of subjects grouped under that name, would be purely empirical or inductive. Christian teaching on the nature, objects and structure of society obtains little attention : nor are the civic rights and duties of men treated as portion of an immutable moral law.

The Catholic sociologist must reject such a method of treating his subject. He will, of course, utilise experience and induction in social studies. Conclusions drawn from statistics and history, showing the ascertained results upon human well-being of various political theories and economic methods, must form an important portion of the science. But Catholic Sociology rests, to a large extent, upon principles of the natural law, which are as uniform and unchanging as the essential nature of man. This will become clear from a consideration of the nature of society, which all admit to be, in some sense at least, the subject-matter of Sociology.

Meaning of Society.—Society is a moral unit made up of individuals associated together for a common purpose. A mere collection of persons, who, for instance, happen to be gathered in the same room, would not form a society. The individuals must have a common purpose, some object desirable for all and sought by all ; and some kind of intention or obligation of mutually assisting one another in its attainment. The idea of society requires, besides, that there be union of effort on the part of all towards securing for each and every individual of the body a due participation in the common object; for, if each one seeks the object by his own individual efforts or for himself alone, there is no moral union. Again, the union of effort that is required must not be the result of accident or physical necessity or blind instinct. It must come from the deliberate intention on the part of the members to co-operate for the common end ; or, at least, there must be a moral obligation to do so. Thus, a hive of bees do not form a society in the strict sense which we are assuming here. For although they are united in co-operating for a common objective, the bees, being devoid of reason and acting from blind instinct, cannot be subject to moral obligation, nor can they consciously aim at a common purpose. Hence, only rational beings such as human persons can form a society. Finally, the notion of society includes the idea of permanence, though not necessarily of perpetuity. A number of women who agree to take a day's outing together, or a dozen men, who form one side in a tug-of-war contest, and then separate, are not commonly called a society.

Hence a society may be described as *a permanent moral union of several persons for the purpose of attaining a common good by mutual co-operation.*

Governing Authority.—For the existence of such a union as is implied in the term *Society*, the element of social authority is essential. There must be some power present to direct the several members in their co-operation for the common good. For, considering the uncertain and fluctuating character of human opinion and human will, it is clear that the *permanent* co-operation of several persons for a special purpose is impossible without a directing and co-ordinating power to harmonise the discordant elements and direct the different forces towards a common end. This co-ordinating influence is nothing else than social authority, without which, therefore, human society is impossible.

Necessary and Conventional Societies.—The definition of Society which we have given includes, not only such great societies as the State and the Church, but numberless other types of social union. Families, municipalities, religious orders, commercial companies, relief committees, sporting clubs, etc., all are societies.

Now, of these different types, it will be observed that some owe their origin solely to the free choice of the individuals that compose them. The founders of the society constitute it after what manner they think well and the members are free to enter the society or not as they please. Such societies are called *free* or *conventional* societies. Examples of this type are religious orders, charitable societies, trading companies, sporting clubs, etc. There are other societies which in no way owe their origin to their members' choice. The Church, for instance, was founded by the direct intervention of God; and its constitution cannot be altered or interfered with by any human authority. Besides the Church, there are two—and only two—other types of human society whose existence and structure are not of mere human origin or liable to essential change. These are the Family and the State or Nation. The Family and the State are a necessary result of man's nature. They come into existence in response to essential human tendencies and character, and to provide for needs which spring from the very nature of man.

Hence there are three types of human association that form a class apart, namely, the Church, the Family, and the State or Nation. The existence and scope of these, the essential principles of their structure, the fundamental rights and duties of the members are determined by God's law, and cannot be altered by human authority. Of these, the Church differs from the family and the nation in that the two latter are *natural* societies. Their immediate object has to do with man's temporal interests ; and their existence and scope, as well as their fundamental structure, spring from the law of nature which was ordained by God in the very act of creating man. Hence the essential principles that govern their activities can be ascertained by the light of reason. The Church, on the other hand, is supernatural. Its object is to lead men to their supernatural destiny, which is direct union with God ; and its foundation and constitution depend upon God's positive revelation to man.

Perfect and Imperfect Societies.—Again, the Church and the nation differ from all other types of human association in that they are *perfect* societies. They—and only they— have within themselves all that is required for the complete and full realisation of the ends at which they aim. Neither can, within its own sphere, be validly subordinated to any human power outside itself ; while every other human society, even the family, is more or less dependent upon them. It is on this account that the Church and the State are called *Perfect* societies, while all the others, even the Family, are *Imperfect* societies.

Nature and Object of Social Science.—Bearing in mind these preliminary notions, we now come to consider the precise subject-matter and scope of Social Science. Understood literally and in its widest sense, Social Science would have to do with social organisation and social activities of every kind. Since, however, it is, like Ethics, a natural science, and refers primarily to man's temporal good, the Church's organisation and activities are outside its scope. Neither does it treat of free or conventional societies whether belonging to the natural or the supernatural order. Its scope is restricted by usage to the type of social union, which is natural and universal, namely, to the family and the State. Of these, the family, which, although of fundamental importance in the life of the nation, is not a perfect society, is treated only cursorily, and, as it were, indirectly ; in so far, namely, as is required to indicate its essential functions, its position in the social organism, and the attitude which the State is bound to assume in its regard.

Hence the proper subject-matter of Social Science is Civil Society, usually called the State or the Nation ; that type of society, namely, which is at the same time *universal, natural* and *perfect.* The ultimate object of the State is to secure the temporal happiness of its members, which, in practice, is the same thing as the fuller development of their physical, intellectual and moral powers. The proximate and immediate aim of the State's activities is to ensure peace and prosperity for all ; for these are means essential to man's temporal welfare, and can be secured only by the helps which the State affords. Social Science, taken in its widest sense, would include the speculative questions which concern the purpose, origin and constitution of the State, as well as those more practical questions which refer to social activity and the principles that govern the proper functions of the State. As the former class are usually treated at length in Ethics, Social Science, properly so-called, is confined mostly to the latter class. In other words, it is primarily a practical or normative science. Hence it may be defined as a *practical science, directing social co-operation towards the more perfect attainment of the ends and aims of civil society.*[1] In other words, it is the science which directs the different members of the State in the fulfilment of their civic duties.

---

[1] Garriguet—*Manuel de Sociologie,* chap. i.

From what has been said, it is plain that the science is partly analytical and partly inductive ; that is to say, the principles upon which its conclusions are founded are of two kinds, namely (1) *a priori* principles, founded upon the nature and end of man, and the purposes and essential functions of human society ; and (2) *a posteriori* principles which are generalisations taken from such sources as history and statistics, referring to actual or historical social conditions.

Its Relation with the Church.—Although Social Science is primarily a natural science, and its principles are ascertainable by the light of reason, the student cannot ignore or dispense with the Church's teaching. In the first place some of the principles of Social Science are illustrated and confirmed in the most striking manner by the truths of revelation. Thus the principles connected with the dignity and inalienable rights of the human person are confirmed in the strongest way by the mystery of the Redemption and man's elevation to the supernatural state. Besides, experience proves that social principles, although ascertainable by the light of reason, are in practice denied in large part or lost sight of wherever the Church's authority is rejected.

Furthermore, even when a social system is organised on true principles, its proper working has always to meet obstacles rooted in men's passions and ignorance and sin. These obstacles can be effectually overcome only by the forces of religion. Hence, if we are to look for a social system organised and worked in accordance with true principles, we shall find it only where the guidance of the Church prevails, and a strong sense of religion pervades the community. In other words, Christian civilisation is in practice the only type of civilisation in harmony with the principles of Social Science and the dictates of right reason.

Its Relations with Kindred Sciences.—Social Science, though closely connected with Ethics, Political Science or

Jurisprudence and Political Economy, still differs essentially
from all of these. It differs from Ethics, for the principles
of Ethics relate to human actions in their moral aspect,
distinguishing namely, the good from the bad, and aims at
leading men to their last end ; besides, Ethics has to do
with all the deliberate actions of men. Social Science, on
the other hand, relates only to acts that are external, and
is concerned merely with the bearing of these acts upon the
welfare of other members of the civil body. Social Science
is subordinate to Ethics, in so far that its principles must
be in conformity with ethical standards. In other words,
it cannot, for the sake of a supposed social advantage,
suggest a course of action that runs counter to sound moral
principles.

Social Science also differs from Jurisprudence. The purpose of the latter is to direct the rulers of the State in
framing laws and regulating their administration with a
view to the peace and prosperity of the citizens. Social
Science directs the citizens as well as the rulers, and includes
in its scope principles and conclusions which need not, and
should not, become the direct matter of civil law.

Finally, Social Science differs from Political Economy.
The latter refers only to the human activity that is employed about the production, distribution and consumption
of material goods. Social Science, having for its object the
entire temporal welfare of the citizen, includes in its scope
not only his material interests, but his intellectual and moral
development as well. If, however, Political Economy be
treated (as it should by the Christian economist) so as to
take full account of the influence upon social well-being
of the various methods of production, distribution and consumption, then Political Economy becomes practically
identical with one important branch of Social Science.

Its Origin as a Distinct Science.—Catholic Sociology as a
separate subject of study is of comparatively recent growth.
The *a priori* principles on which it is founded are, indeed,
contained in the works of St. Thomas and the great Catholic

authors of the 16th and 17th centuries. The proper application, however, of the general principles to many of our modern problems is not to be found in these writers, who did not foresee the peculiar conditions of present-day society. For in their time the modern social question had not yet arisen. Owing to the evils which have resulted from the disregard of civic duties in modern states (a legacy from the Protestant revolt against the Church in the 16th century), the whole question of social rights and duties has now assumed a position of paramount importance in almost every country.

The poverty and oppression that weigh upon the masses of the people ; the immense wealth and excessive power of the great financiers, mostly non-Christian ; the great trusts and monopolies ; the gambling on the Stock Exchange, productive of so much injustice and misery to the masses of the people ; the tyranny of the bureaucracy, masquerading under the cloak of popular authority ; the general unrest and widespread spirit of revolt ; the antagonism between the rich and poor ; the spread of irreligion among all classes and the general demoralization caused or promoted by the unchristian press and cinema ; the activities of the gambling agencies and numerous other influences more or less peculiar to modern society ; all these are prominent features of the social question, and a clear knowledge of Christian principles is essential for dealing effectually with them. This knowledge is what Social Science professes to offer. Hence, although the science, properly speaking, includes within its scope all kinds of social co-operation, it is usually confined in its practical treatment to the questions which bear more directly upon the social evils of our time.

History of Modern Social Science.—The two great names associated with the foundation of the science of Catholic Sociology and the Catholic movement to which it has given birth are Bishop Von Ketteler[1] of Mainz (1811–1877) and

---

[1] Cf. Metlake—*The Christian Social Reform of Bishop Ketteler* (Philadelphia, 1912).

Father A. Taperelli (D'Azeglio), S.J. (1793–1862) of Rome. Ketteler's contributions were greater on the practical side and Taperelli's on the doctrinal aspect.

Ketteler may be justly regarded as the founder of the Catholic schools of Social reform. Pope Leo XIII pays tribute to him as his great predecessor in social teaching. Pope Pius XI on the other hand has more than once extolled the work and writings of Taperelli and refers in his recent Encyclical on Christian Education to Taperelli's classical treatise on Natural Right[1] (which may be said to have laid the foundation of modern Social Science) as a "work never sufficiently praised, and never recommended strongly enough to the university student." Both these writers show how the teachings of St. Thomas and the principles of Catholic Philosophy contain the solution of the modern social question.

The great Encyclicals of Leo XIII, promulgated in the last quarter of the 19th century (1878–1901), contain a statement of the main principles of Catholic social philosophy and are generally accepted as the ground-work of Social Science. The teaching which they contain has been confirmed and in some particulars more fully developed in several Papal pronouncements of more recent date. The recent Encyclicals of our present Holy Father Pius XI, especially those on *Christian Education*, on *Marriage*, and on the *Social Order*, are of the first importance in this connection.[2]

Although several of the more important questions have

---

[1] *Saggio Teoretico di Diritto Naturale Appogiato sul Fatto* (Theoretical Essay on Natural Right from a Historical standpoint). *See Catholic Encyclopædia* for an account of Taperelli.

[2] In the following pages we quote the Papal Encyclicals (except where otherwise specified) from the English translation, entitled *The Pope and the People*, published by the English Catholic Truth Society (Edition, 1929). The page references are the pages of this book. A full collection of all Papal documents bearing on the present subject from those of Pius VII down to the present time (including the original text with French translation, biographical notices, complete indexes, etc.), is published by La Bonne Presse, 5 Rue Bayard, Paris. The volumes referred to, which form a cheap and convenient series are entitled *Actes de Leo XIII* (7 vols.), *Actes de Pius X* (8 vols.).

not yet been adequately studied, and although Catholic authors are not as yet in accord on all points of importance, the science has progressed steadily for the past thirty years owing to the labours of an ever-increasing number of Catholic writers, especially in Italy, France, Germany and Belgium. Writers in the English language, owing to their Protestant environment, have naturally been late in coming into the field. In recent years, however, the Catholic movement is making itself felt more and more, and excellent works on different phases of Catholic Social Science are constantly appearing in English.[1]

---

[1] General Bibliography.—The publications of the Catholic Social Guild, Oxford, established 1909, are worthy of special mention. Of these publications *A Code of Social Principles* (C. S. Guild, Oxford, 1929, price 6d.) is specially important. It is mainly a translation of the *Code Social* (" Edition Spes," 17 Rue Soufflot, Paris, 1927) prepared by the " Union Internationale des Etudes Sociales " (This union, founded 1920 at Malines by Cardinal Mercier, is made up of the leading European specialists in Social Science). The other C. S. G. publications include a small *Handbook for Social Study* (1923, price 1/–), containing a useful bibliography.

Antoine's *Cours d'Economie Sociale* (cf. *supra*, p. 1) is probably the best all round treatise on Social Science that has so far appeared. Among others may be mentioned : A. Belliot, O.F.M., *Manuel de Sociologie Catholique* (3rd edit., Paris, 1925) ; L. Garriquet—*Manuel de Sociologie et d'Economie Sociale* (Paris, 1924) ; V. Fallon, S.J.—*Principes d'Economie Sociale* (Bruges, 1923). This last book contains an excellent bibliography.

Of the standard books on the subject the following may be named :— Taperelli, S.J.—*Essai Theorique de Droit Naturel* (the work referred to above), translated from the original Italian, 1857 (3rd edit., Paris, 1883), 2 vols. ; also *Cours Elementaire de Droit Naturel* (Paris, 1864) ; Toniolo— *Trattato de Economia Sociale* (Florence, 1907) and *L'Odierna Problema Sociologica* (Florence, 1905) ; Devas—*Political Economy*, 3rd edit. (London, 1920) ; Castelein—*Droit Naturel* (Paris, 1903). Finally, both the *Catholic Encyclopædia* and the *Dictionnaire Apologetique de la Foi Catholique* (Beauchesne, 11 Rue de Rennes, Paris, 1911) contain, scattered under different headings, practically all the available matter on the subject of Catholic Social Science.

Of the English treatises on Catholic Philosophy, the following may be mentioned as specially useful for students of Social Science :—Rickaby, S.J. —*Moral Philosophy* (Longmans, London, 6/6) ; Coppens, S.J.—*Moral Philosophy* (Herder, London, 5/–) ; Cronin—*Science of Ethics*, 2 vols. (Dublin, 1917).

Of the Latin works on Catholic Philosophy the following treat social questions with special fulness :—Meyer—*Institutiones Juris Naturalis* (Freiburg, 1900), pars. 2, sectio iii. Macksey—*Argumenta Sociologica* (Rome, 1918) ; Donat—*Ethica Moralis* (Innsbruck, 1921), sectio iii ; Costa-Rosetti—*Philosophia Moralis* (Innsbruck, 1886), par. 3, sectio v ; Hickey—*Summa Philosophiæ Scholasticæ* (Gill, Dublin, 1923), vol. iii, pp. 447–517.

Division of the Subject-Matter.—Since modern Social Science has taken shape in reference to the social evils which now prevail more or less in every country inhabited by Europeans, it is necessary to set forth at the outset what these evils are, and how they have arisen. Hence, the First Part of our treatise will be devoted to a summary sketch of the history of social doctrines and social conditions in Europe from pre-Christian times to the present day. In criticising the different phases of doctrine and practice the Catholic teaching will be *indirectly* shown. In the Second Part we shall deal *directly* and explicitly with the fundamental principles of Catholic Social Science and their application to existing conditions.

PART I

HISTORICAL SKETCH

INTRODUCTORY NOTE

Bearing of European History on Social Science.—The purpose of civil society is to secure for the people the peaceful enjoyment of their rights ; and to promote morality, enlightenment, and sufficient material prosperity among all classes. Now it can be shown from European history that society as a whole failed to attain these objects before the advent of Christianity ; that they were best realized when the nations were under the influence and guidance of the Catholic Church, and that the masses of the people lost the civic advantages they had previously acquired when the State rejected the Church's authority. These conclusions, which go to show that Christian civilisation is the only civilisation suited to man's nature and that Christian social principles are the only true ones, are thus summarised by Pope Leo XIII.

" Although the Catholic Church . . . has for her immediate and natural purpose the saving of souls and the securing of our happiness in heaven ; yet in regard to things temporal she is the source of benefits as manifold and great as if the chief end of her existence were to secure the prosperity of our earthly lives. Wherever the Church has set her foot, she has straightway changed the face of things and has attempered the moral tone of the people with a new civilisation and with virtues unknown before. All nations which have yielded to her sway have become eminent for their culture, their sense of justice, and the glory of their high deeds. . . . It is clear that no better mode has been devised for building up and ruling the State than that which is the necessary growth of the teachings of the Gospel." [1]

The same fact is emphasised by Pius X :

" The Church has been the first inspirer and promoter of civilisation . . . preserving and perfecting whatever was good in pagan civilisation. . . . The civilisation of the world is Christian civilisation. The more frankly Christian it is so much is it the more true, more lasting and more productive of precious fruit ; the more it withdraws from the Christian ideal so much the feebler is it to the great detriment of society." [2]

---

[1] *Immortale Dei* (1885), pp. 45, 46.
[2] *Il Fermo Proposito* (June, 1905), p. 190.

I

It is not, of course, claimed that there is an exact and uniform correlation between the Catholic faith of the people and their social welfare. It has been truly said that " not everything on earth went wrong before the Incarnation, nor has everything gone right since." Still truer is it that a Christian régime cannot and in practice does not exclude all defects and abuses ; nor does a non-Christian régime necessarily imply the absence of all things that are praiseworthy and desirable. Social welfare is not the aim, but only an ordinary and natural consequence, of true religion ; and this consequence may be prevented from becoming actual through a thousand intervening causes. It is only when one considers the whole history of European civilisation that one is persuaded that for all the most precious elements of that civilisation we are indebted to the Catholic Church.[1]

Division of the Subject.—To deal adequately with so vast a theme is beyond our scope. It will be sufficient for our purpose to touch only on the main headings. We shall therefore first indicate briefly the principal features of social life in Europe[2] during each of the following periods :

(a) *The Early Roman Empire*, viz., the first three centuries A.D., when the European nations of the Empire had attained their highest development in non-Christian civilisation ; and before the influence of Christianity was yet much felt in public life. (Chap. I.)

(b) *The beginning of the Fifth Century A.D.*, when Christian principles and Christian teaching had largely permeated the laws and institutions as well as the social life of the Roman Empire ; and previous to the political and social upheaval caused by the Teutonic invasions. (Chap. II.)

(c) *The Early Middle Ages*, viz., the period from the sixth to the end of the eleventh century, when the Church had to undertake afresh the work of moulding the new

---

[1] *Letters on Social History* (Catholic Social Guild, Oxford, 1920), pp. 15, 16.

[2] We confine ourselves mainly to European history, as this exemplifies best the effects of the Church's influence. What we have to say, however, applies *mutatis mutandis* to the inhabitants of North and South America and of Australasia, who are predominantly European in race, and whose civilisation is wholly European. The history of the Philippine Islands also furnishes an excellent example of the elevating effects of Christianity.

barbarian nations to the principles and practice of Christian civilisation.   (Chap. III.)

(*d*) *The period lying between the twelfth and the fifteenth centuries,* which is the golden age of Christian domination in Europe.   As this period exemplifies Christian ideals in social life better than any other period of European history, we shall treat it at greater length.   (Chaps. IV–VII.)

Next, after dealing with the Protestant Revolt of the 16th century and the changes in social life which resulted directly from it (Chap. VIII), we shall treat of the modern social movements which have sprung indirectly from the same source, namely, Liberalism, unchristian Capitalism, Socialism and Freemasonry.   (Chaps. IX–XIII.)

Finally, after outlining the main social problems (commonly called " The Social Question ") to which these movements have given rise, we shall conclude our survey with a brief sketch of the modern Catholic Social Movement. (Chaps. XIV, XV.)

CHAPTER I

PAGAN SOCIETY IN THE EARLY ROMAN EMPIRE[1]

The Roman Empire.—In the first centuries of the Christian era, the empire of Rome included most of the known world. It extended from the Euphrates to the Atlantic, from Britain to Northern Africa, and from the Rhine and Danube to the Red Sea. Over all that vast area the institutions, customs, and, at least in the Western half of the Empire, even the language of Rome prevailed. The social customs and the moral views of the people, which were practically the same over the whole Empire, were a fusion of Grecian civilisation and ideals with those of the earlier Roman Republic.

Pagan Social Principles.—From the Christian and Pagan writings of the period, scholars are quite familiar with the main features of social life in the Early Roman Empire. Men centred their whole happiness in selfish gratification and mostly in sensual pleasure. Their moral code, which was founded upon the philosophy of Plato and Aristotle, rested upon the same worship of self. Its principles included contempt for the weak and hatred for one's enemies. Human dignity and personality as such were not recognised. It was formally admitted that the weaker members of society, such as women and slaves, were intended by nature for the utility of the strong, just as in the Christian law it is a principle that the lower animals are ordained for the benefit of man.[2]

---

[1] Cf. Balmes — *European Civilisation ;* Chateaubriand — *Génie du Christianisme* (tom. iii, liv. iii–iv) ; Ozanam—*La Civilisation au Cinquième Siècle* (tom. i and ii) ; Schmidt—*Social Results of Early Christianity* (London, 1907) ; Benevot—*Pagan and Christian Rule* (London, 1924) ; Devas—*Studies in Family Life ;* and *Key to the World's Progress ;* Allies— *Formation of Christendom* (Part I) ; *Catholic Encyclopædia*, art. " Charity " ; *Letters on Social History ;* Albers—*Manuel de l'Histoire Ecclesiastique,* " Introduction " ; Mourret—*Histoire de l'Eglise* (vol. i).

[2] The high ideals of natural virtue which one finds in many pagan writers, such as Plato, Cicero, Virgil, Horace, Seneca and others ; the praises of marital fidelity, patriotism, friendship, kindness, even of virginity, had little relation to actual life, at least in the period referred to here, whatever may be said of the earlier periods when the foundations of Rome's greatness were laid.

These principles had their logical effect in determining the functions and authority of the State, and the social position of women, children, slaves, and the poor.

The State, which in practice meant only the governing classes and included but a small fraction of the actual population, was regarded as an omnipotent power against which no personal or family rights were allowed to prevail. This absolute power of the State assumed concrete expression in the deification of the Emperor, who by law was regarded as a god. The Emperor himself was above all law and his sole will unfettered by any consideration of right and wrong or by any fundamental principle of the constitution, had in itself the force of law.

The Working Class.—The working class in the Roman Empire were slaves. In fact all the Pagan civilisations of Europe before the advent of Christianity reposed on slavery. The Roman slaves, who formed more than half the entire population, were practically deprived in law of all human rights and belonged, like chattels or cattle, to their masters. The slaves working in the fields usually had chains on their feet. Their food consisted of bread, water and salt. At night they were kept in damp underground cells with little or no ventilation. The old or weak were commonly allowed to perish like worthless cattle. If it occurred that a Roman citizen was killed in his own home, all the slaves were, or by a provision of the law might be, executed without enquiry or trial.

The Poor and the Weak.—The weaker members of society, such as women and children, were not allowed the enjoyment of their natural rights as human persons ; for human dignity as such was not recognised. " Degraded woman," writes Balmes, " was distinguished by the corruption of her morals, and debased by the tyranny of man ; infants were abandoned ; the sick and the aged were neglected." [1]

The lot of the millions of citizens that lived in abject poverty in all the cities of the Empire was little better than that of slaves. Rome alone had hundreds of thousands of hungry poor, who had come to look upon gifts of money and doles of bread from the State as their birth-right.

---

[1] *Op. cit.*, chap. xvi, p. 66.

Prevalence of Cruelty and Immorality.—Cicero quotes a contemporary as stating (although apparently with exaggeration) that there were only 2,000 owners of property in the city of Rome in his time,[1] whereas the total population is computed to have been more than 1,200,000. The great majority of the rest were slaves or proletarians.[2] Poverty was the one unpardonable sin in the eyes of the Roman who recognised nothing excellent in the human person apart from his goods or his power. Charity, love of the poor, even hospitality in the Christian sense and as we understand these virtues, did not exist.[3] Immorality of the grossest type was universal in both sexes and among all classes ; and cruelty and oppression reached a degree that is now scarcely conceivable.

We read of 400 slaves being put to death in one house in pursuance of the inhuman law that when a citizen was killed in his own house all the slaves were executed ; of a hundred free citizens of the poorer classes, many of them married and fathers of families, being mutilated in order to provide a train of eunuchs for a daughter of a noble about to marry ; of 3,000 Jews given to wild beasts to devour at a celebration of a feast ; of five, six or ten thousand people of all ranks and both sexes slaughtered on a mere suspicion of the Emperor ; of eighteen thousand gladiators compelled to slaughter one another as a public spectacle for the amusement of the populace ; of hideous scenes of sexual immorality enacted at the banquets of the nobles, which were further varied by the spectacle of gladiators massacring each other for the amusement of the revellers.[4] In a word, the horrors of life in the pre-Christian Roman Empire are inconceivable even in the neo-pagan immoral world of to-day.

---

[1] *De Officiis*, ii. 21.

[2] There was doubtless a small intermediate class of freemen such as shopkeepers, etc., who would not be classed as proletarians. But these did not form a notable element in Roman society.

[3] Cf. Lecky, *History of European Morals*, vol. i, pp. 40 ff, for many citations of pagan writers in commendation of universal brotherhood. These sentiments of the philosophers, however, had little or no relation to real life.

[4] For references and further examples, cf. Schmidt, *op. cit.*, book i, chap. iii ; also Chateaubriand, *loc. cit.*, and Ozanam, *loc. cit.*

CHAPTER II

Freedom of the Church.—After nearly three centuries of persecution the Church was at last allowed to emerge from the Catacombs. By the Edict of Milan, which was promulgated in 313 A.D. over the names of the joint Emperors, Constantine and Licinius, and the several supplementary edicts issued by Constantine himself when he became sole master of the Roman world, Christianity, which had by that time permeated every class of Roman society, got legal recognition and even official encouragement within the Empire. Nearly another century of varying vicissitudes had to elapse before it was established under Theodosius the Great (d. 395) as the religion of the State.

Society only Partially Christianised.—A considerable portion of the people were still pagan ; and even among large sections of the Christians many pagan customs and unchristian principles rooted in an unbroken tradition of a thousand years, continued to retain their hold. Even Roman law had not yet fully put off its Pagan characteristics. Still both laws and customs had already undergone a profound change in the early half of the 5th century : and the Theodosian Code which was compiled about 430 A.D. shows that Christian principles had then gained a definite mastery in the Roman world.

Supremacy of the Divine Law.—To begin with, the absolute supremacy of the State and the unchecked despotism of its ruler were no longer acknowledged even in civil law. By the fundamental principles of Christian teaching there is a higher law against which no human authority can prevail. The eternal law of God binds emperor, citizen and slave with the same force. This principle was now definitely recognised. Hence even slaves were now allowed rights of conscience with which slavery in the old sense was incompatible.

---

[1] References as for preceding chapter.

Rights Attaching to Human Personality.—Again, in opposition to the teaching of the Græco-Roman philosophy and the spirit of the old Roman law, the essential dignity and inalienable rights of the human person no matter how poor or weak were now at least partially recognised. According to Christian teaching, all, whether slaves or Romans, women or men, infants or adults, being children of the same Father, predestined to the same eternal end, and redeemed by the same Saviour, have by their nature indefeasible rights and inalienable responsibilities which no human law can make void. For under the Christian law there is, as St. Paul writes: *neither Jew nor Greek; there is neither bond nor free; there is neither male nor female. For you are all one in Christ.*[1]

In enforcing this principle not only was the Church confronted with prejudices rooted in the Pagan tradition; but the whole framework of the social organism, which was fashioned on a Pagan philosophy, had to be recast. Such a reform was necessarily slow. Still even the century after the freedom of the Church was first declared witnessed substantial progress. Thus in the case of women, minors, slaves, prisoners and the poor, the Church insisted from the very beginning that their essential rights be fully recognised, and she exerted her whole influence that all their other natural rights be gradually conceded.

Reforms in Roman Law.—The right of life and death which, by the old Roman law, the master had over his slaves, and the father over his children, is withdrawn in the Theodosian Code. Children are allowed emancipation from the parents' control when they reach a certain age. Girls over eighteen years of age can marry of their own free choice: and are allowed also the free disposal of their property. Slaves are allowed rights and facilities to acquire property; and many provisions are made protecting them against the injustice of tyrannical masters.

Many evidences also now appear of the more humane attitude of Roman law towards the poor and weak. Thus the bishops are accorded extensive powers of arbitration in disputes, and in several other ways are enabled to protect

---

[1] *Gal.* iii. 28.

the poor against oppression. When the parties to a dispute agreed to choose the Bishop as arbitrator, the civil judge was bound by law to enforce his decision. The Bishop also visited the prisons to see that the prisoners were properly treated. The provincial governors took their oath of office at the Bishop's hands, and after their period of office gave an account of their administration before him. Churches, and later on, even houses in the vicinity of the Church, were accorded rights of asylum where those accused of crime might take refuge and be thus safeguarded against precipitate punishment or personal vengeance. Hospitals endowed from public funds were established for the poor ; and special houses of refuge were opened for orphans, widows, and poor travellers.[1]

The inhuman custom of gladiatorial combats, in which hundreds and thousands of men slaughtered one another in the arena for the amusement of the people, was forbidden by Constantine about 313 A.D., but owing to the opposition which this measure aroused it was not enforced till 404 A.D. The abolition of gladiatorial combats was brought about by the heroic martyrdom of the monk Telemachus, who rushed into the arena to separate the combatants and was immediately stoned to death by the populace. Owing to the profound impression created by this incident, the Emperor Honorious was enabled to suppress finally these inhuman exhibitions in Rome.

The Example set by the Christians.—Among the Christians themselves, slaves and the poor were regarded, in contrast with the old pagan ideals, as the equals of the rich in human dignity and personal responsibility. They were treated with special kindness by the Church ; while in the Christian homes, all the members of the family, including the slaves, were united by close ties of charity and piety.

The principles regulating men's duties towards one another form another feature of Christian teaching which clashed with the social ideals of pagan Rome. In the latter, self-interest and self-gratification were recognised as the fundamental consideration, while the Christian ideal is summed up in the words of Christ : *Thou shalt love thy neighbour*

---

[1] Schmidt, *op. cit.* ; Benevot, *op. cit.* 73–91.

as thyself;[1] and again : *A new commandment I give unto
you that you love one another as I have loved you.*[2] The
practice of justice and charity which this law includes
marked the mutual relations of the early Christians ; and
extended itself even to those outside the Christian fold.
Such an example exerted an immense influence in the whole
social life of Rome and made itself felt in almost every
detail of life.

The New Concept of Ownership.—Finally, one of the most
important and revolutionary of the new principles introduced by Christianity was the Christian concept of
private ownership. This was directly opposed to the non-
Christian idea. According to Christian teaching the human
owner of material goods is merely a steward in the service
of the Supreme Owner Who is God. Hence, the wealthy
proprietor is bound by the law of Christ (and in those days
he fully recognised his obligations) to give for the relief of
the needs of others what remained over after his own
reasonable needs were satisfied. He was taught, too, that
his own wants were to be interpreted rather strictly, excluding luxuries and even unnecessary comfort and convenience.[3]

During the early centuries of Christianity, preachers and
writers were accustomed to emphasise these obligations
very strongly. They insisted a good deal upon the duties
and limitations of ownership and upon the fundamental
right of all to their due measure of access to the material
goods of the world. Although there is no proof that communism prevailed in the early Church, or that the teachings
of any of the early Fathers were opposed to the institution
of private property, the mere fact that many non-Catholic
writers can assert with a certain show of plausibility that
such was the case is sufficient to prove how strongly
Christian moralists and preachers insisted upon the limitations and responsibilities of ownership.

Among the Christians themselves the ideals of the Gospel
were very largely realised ; and as the Christians formed
in the fifth century the vast majority of the population,
their influence profoundly affected the whole tone of society.

---

[1] *Matth.* xxii. 39.   [2] *2 John* xiii. 34.
[3] Cf. *Catholic Encyclopædia*, vol. iii, art. " Charity," pp. 594, 595.

Marriage.—Among the Christians the marriage tie was then, as now, inviolable and perpetual ; and the marital obligations of husband and wife mutual. Even in Roman law, although divorce and concubinage still continued to obtain recognition, both were placed under strict limitations. Divorce was made very difficult. The law discouraged it ; and civil equality was established between husband and wife in all their essential marriage obligations.

The Social Status of Women.—The pagan idea of the essential inferiority of women was reprobated and a completely new ideal of womanhood was upheld. The Christian matron is a type quite unknown to the pre-Christian Romans. She is the close friend and companion of her husband to whom she is bound by ties which death alone can sever. She is the educator of the children and the mistress of the home in which her position is secure. The important rôle assumed by the Christian matron in all works of charity and benevolence was also a new phenomenon.

Finally, the special place set apart in the Christian law for virgins consecrated to God contributed to give to the Christian woman a dignity and a standing that were in striking contrast with pre-Christian ideas. So completely indeed had the influence of Christianity revolutionised the attitude of the Romans towards their women that we find Pulcheria, sister of Theodosius II, acting as her brother's regent and guardian and succeeding him as Empress after his death (450 A.D.).[1]

The Roman Slaves.[2]—The abolition of slavery was perhaps the greatest and most decisive triumph of Christianity in the social life of the people. That the disappearance of slavery among the European nations was a result of Christian principles is recognised by all historians. " As the morning rays of Christianity," writes Dr. Sigerson, " fell upon the nations, they first dispelled the darker clouds of slavery and then, as the light prevailed, bondage passed away. This happened more or less rapidly in different localities

---

[1] Cf. Ozanam, *op. cit.*, tom. ii (pp. 86–89).
[2] Cf. Paul Allard—*Les Esclaves Chrétiennes ; Dict. Apologetique*, art. " Esclavage " ; *Cath. Encyclopædia*, art. " Slavery " ; *Letters on Social History*, pp. 27–39.

as mountains may be seen illuminated with sunshine while the valleys at their feet are still in the shade." [1]

The slave question was the most troublesome and thorny of all the difficulties that the Church had to deal with. To liberate the slaves at once, even if it were possible, would mean a social upheaval the result of which no one could foresee ; and would have been fatal even to the interests of the slaves themselves. The numbers of slaves were immense, and the institution of slavery was deeply rooted in the manners, the ideas, and the whole social life of the people. Hence the Church had to proceed slowly and cautiously.

The Church's Mode of Procedure.—" Christianity," writes Lecky, " broke down the contempt with which the master regarded his slaves and planted among the slaves themselves a principle of moral regeneration which expanded in no other sphere with equal perfection. Its action in procuring the freedom of slaves was unceasing." [2] The Church reprobated the false idea that manual work is degrading. She insisted on the duty and the necessity of labour for all, and on the well-grounded self-respect which the practice of labour gives. She preached the equality of all in natural dignity, in personal responsibility, in the participation of heavenly graces and in the predestination to eternal happiness. While preaching to the slaves the duty of obedience to the master's just commands (because the master's authority at the time was necessary for the common good and consequently sanctioned by the Divine will) she also insisted strongly on the duties of masters towards their slaves ; and had her preaching sanctioned by canonical enactments and very severe penalties. [3]

Outside of what was essential for the needs of existing society, the Church acknowledged no distinction between slave and freeman. All had the same sacraments. The marriage of slaves among themselves had the same sanction as that of the free. Clerics of servile origin were numerous ; and so levelling was the Christian principle of personal

---

[1] Sigerson—*Land Tenure and Land Classes of Ireland* (Longmans, London, 1871), p. 228.
[2] *History of European Morals*, vol. ii, p. 69 (edit. 1913).
[3] Cf. Balmes, *op. cit.*, chaps. xv–xviii.

equality that the Chair of Peter was sometimes filled by men born of slaves, such as Pius in the second century and Callistus in the third.   In the Christian cemeteries there is no distinction between the tombs of slaves and those of the free.

Above all, the Church prepared the way for the eventual abolition of slavery.   The liberation of slaves was endowed with special ecclesiastical favour.   It was usual to perform the ceremony of manumission in the Church ; and the Bishop was accorded by civil law special powers to facilitate it. The Church also took liberated slaves under her special protection and strictly forbade that they should be in any way again reduced to servitude.   Under the influence of the Church, the State also made many other enactments to facilitate the manumission of slaves.   The movement was further supported by the example of Christian masters who frequently set free their whole households of slaves.   Besides all this the general attitude of the Christians towards their slaves and towards the poor set an example which profoundly affected the whole tone of Roman Society.

Results of the Church's Influence.—If the Roman State had been allowed to develop on the new lines thus marked out, the sixth century A.D. would probably have seen the complete liberation of the slaves, and the establishment of a fully developed Christian social régime.

The downfall of the Western Empire checked the development of Christian civilisation in Western Europe, although in the Eastern Empire the movement still continued. Enough, however, was already done even in the West to permeate the fabric of Roman law with Christian principles. This law became later on the groundwork of the legal systems of the European kingdoms which grew out of the Teutonic invasions that now swept over Europe.

CHAPTER III

Art. 1 *General Historical Survey* (*5th to 11th centuries*)

The Teutonic Invasions.—The period of the Early Middle Ages may be said to extend from about the middle of the 5th century to the Pontificate of Pope Gregory VII (*d.* 1085). The reign of the Emperor Honorius (395–423) had witnessed the beginning of the last struggles of the Roman Empire in Western Europe. From across the Danube the Goths over-ran Italy, Gaul and Spain. The Saxons, Jutes and Angles crossing the North Sea from the regions south of Denmark, swarmed into Britain. The Alemanni, Franks, Burgundians, and later on the Lombards, advanced from beyond the Rhine ; while from the plains of the Vistula, the fierce Vandals and the savage race of the Huns poured over Western and Southern Europe. Before the close of the 5th century, the Western Empire was finally dissolved. The Goths were ruling in Spain and the Vandals in Africa. The Franks had obtained mastery in Gaul and along the basin of the Rhine. Soon after, the Lombards definitely established their power in Northern Italy, and the Anglo-Saxons in Britain.

Many of these nations, including the Franks, Burgundians and Anglo-Saxons, were pagan. The Vandals, Lombards, Alemanni and Goths were Christian only in name. They professed Arianism, a debased form of Christianity, in which the mysteries of the Holy Trinity and the Incarnation of the Son of God were rejected.

Ireland and the Barbarians.—Meanwhile, during the second half of the 5th century, the Irish people, who had

---

[1] Besides the references already given, cf. Mourret—*Histoire Générale de l'Eglise*, vols. ii and iii ; Allies—*Formation of Christendom ;* Albers—*Histoire de l'Eglise*, tom. i, pp. 244 ff ; Kenelm Digby—*Mores Catholici ; Letters on Social History*, pp. 44, 45 ; Brown—*The Achievement of the Middle Ages* (Sands & Co., London, 1925), pp. 9–45.

remained outside the Roman Empire, and were not touched by the barbarian invasions, had been converted to Christianity ; and in a short time the Christian spirit had permeated the laws and social customs of the nation. During the three centuries that ensued, while confusion and turmoil reigned on the continent, Ireland became the principal depository in Europe of the Christian tradition. From Ireland most of the missionaries came that laboured during the 6th and 7th centuries for the conversion of the barbarian conquerors of Western Europe, both pagan and Arian, to Christianity.[1]

Conversion of the Barbarians.—By the end of the 8th century, the nations west of the Danube and Rhine, including Britain ; and two hundred years later, practically all Europe with the exception of the Moors in the southern half of Spain, had accepted the Christian faith. But the work of bringing the laws and social life of the converted nations into harmony with Christian principles was a more tedious and difficult task ; and much of the pagan spirit and outlook continued to live on among them for centuries after they had nominally embraced Christianity.

Eighth and two following Centuries.—The work of the Church was rendered more difficult by the disturbed state of Europe, and especially by the rise of the Mohammedan power and the invasions of the Norsemen, Hungarians and Slavs. In the early half of the 8th century, the Mohammedan Moors established their power in Spain and continued to push their way into France till the wave of invasion was finally broken by Charles Martel, on the field of Tours (A.D. 732).

Soon after, the pagan Norsemen and Danes began their wars of conquest in the North. These wars continued for

---

[1] More than two hundred and fifty saints of Irish birth and very many others who were educated in Ireland, all belonging to these centuries, are still venerated as local patrons, in Germany, Austria, Belgium, France, Britain and Italy. These were only the leaders of the crowds of Irish missionaries that evangelised these countries. Cf. B. Fitzpatrick— *Ireland and the Foundation of Europe* (New York, 1927), and *Ireland and the Making of Britain* (London, 1927) ; Lynch—*Cambrensis Eversus*, vol. ii, pp. 641–653 ; White—*Apologia Pro Hibernia*, pp. 14–45 ; Gougaud—*Les Chrétiéntés Celtiques* (Le Coffre, Paris, 1911), chap. v ; and *Gaelic Pioneers of Christianity* (Dublin, 1923).

more than two centuries and extended even to Italy and Sicily. The Norsemen broke up the civil and ecclesiastical organisation in Northern France, Belgium, Ireland and England, before they were themselves won over to Christianity in the 11th century.

Meanwhile, from the East the Slavs, still half pagan, carried on a fierce war against the Christian states on their borders ; while the fierce race of the Magyars or Hungarians began in the 8th century their terrible incursions into central Germany and Northern Italy. All these wars impeded the civilising influence of Christianity and delayed for more than two centuries the formation of Christendom.

Art. 2—*Social Regeneration of the Barbarians*

Influence of Ecclesiastics.—During the whole of this period the Catholic Church was the one power in Europe that stood for human right and liberty. As the nations became Christian, the Pope gradually gained recognition as the delegate of God who is the source of all legitimate authority. Hence he became the official adviser and ad-monitor of Christian rulers, the mediator between the rulers and the people and the arbiter in international affairs. The local bishops and abbots, and even individual priests, exercised, each in his own limited sphere, an influence similar to that which the Popes possessed in Christendom as a whole. For in those days intellectual training, at least outside of the Greek Empire and of Ireland, was practically confined to the clergy and the monks.[1] Thus it was from the Church's representatives—the Pope, the Bishops and the Clergy—that the serf, the slave, the poor and the weak sought and obtained protection against wrong.

And of Christian Teaching.—Historians generally recog-nise that it was as a result of Christian teaching and the Church's influence that the barbarian nations were gradually moulded to that sense of justice, charity and true liberty, which formed the basis of mediæval civilisation. Leo XIII strongly emphasises this fact :

" Christian Europe has subdued barbarous nations, and changed them from a savage to a civilised condition ; from

---

[1] Cf. Albers, *op. cit.*, vol. i, pp. 314–316.

superstition to true worship. It victoriously rolled back the tide of Mahommedan conquest ; retained the headship of civilisation ; stood forth in the front rank as the leader and teacher of all in every branch of national culture ; bestowed on the world the gift of true and many-sided liberty, and most wisely founded very numerous institutions for the solace of human suffering. . . . Whatever in the State is of chief avail for the common welfare : whatever has been usefully established to curb the licence of rulers, who are opposed to the true interests of the people, or to keep in check the leading authorities from unwarranted interference in municipal or family affairs ; whatever tends to uphold the honour, manhood and equal rights of individual citizens—of all these things, as the monuments of past ages bear witness, the Catholic Church has always been the originator, the promoter, or the guardian." [1]

It was the Church that checked the tyranny and absolutism of the ruler while teaching the subjects the duty of submission and obedience to lawful authority, thus pointing out to all the path leading to social happiness and peace. It was from the Church's teaching and admonitions that the wealthy and powerful baron learned his duties of justice and charity towards his vassals and serfs, while the latter from the same teaching became conscious of their dignity as children of God and realised the indefeasible rights they had, no less than the prince or the feudal baron, to a fair share even of temporal well-being. [2]

Formation of a Christian Civilisation.—All the complicated organisation which was gradually built up all over Europe in the interests of the poor, the aged, the infirm and the young—hospitals, asylums, orphanages, houses of refuge, etc.—was the work of the Church alone. " The Church," writes Lecky, " which seemed so haughty and overbearing in its dealings with kings and princes and nobles, never failed to listen to the poor and the oppressed ; and for many centuries their protection was the foremost of all the objects of her policy." [3] Again, it was the Church that

---

[1] *Immortale Dei*, 1855, pp. 55, 56 and 63.
[2] Cf. Ryan and Millar—*State and Church*, chap. v, for a valuable sketch of the process by which the Church introduced the ideas of law, of Christian constitutional government and of democratic freedom among the European nations.
[3] *Rationalism in Europe*, vol. ii, chap. 17.

purified the home and restored and safeguarded the dignity of the woman so closely identified with the purity and happiness of domestic life.

Restoration of the Arts and Sciences.—It was by Churchmen that the literary treasures of ancient Greece and Rome were preserved, and science and letters propagated among the people. The mechanical arts, too, such as masonry, carpentry, iron-work, etc., as well as agriculture, forestry, fishery, which are so essential for material prosperity, were restored throughout Europe principally by means of the Church. Even for the foundation of the great public utilities—schools, universities, banks, insurance companies, roads, bridges, etc.—which had practically disappeared over most of Europe as a result of the barbarian invasions, we are indebted to activities of the Church.

Special Christian Institutions and Achievements.—Among the Christian institutions and practices specially beneficial were the practice of Sacramental Confession, the discipline of the Penitential Canons,[1] the enforcing of the unity and perpetuity of the marriage contract, the institution of the Peace of God, and the prohibition of usury. It is outside our scope to treat these matters in detail. A few points, however, which refer directly to social well-being require special notice. These concern monasticism, the abolition of slavery and the charity of the Church. The question of usury will be dealt with later.

Art. 3—*Monasticism*[2]

Its Great Importance.—In the history of *Monasticism* during this period will be found perhaps the most striking

---

[1] According to the Penitential Canons, the penitent had to submit to long periods of penitential works, sometimes extending over several years, in expiation of the more serious social crimes, such as homicide, rape, adultery, etc. This universal practice of voluntary penance served to produce gradually in the minds of all a horror of crime which no merely civil sanction could bring about. The general use of Sacramental Confession in Western Europe, as well as the discipline of the Penitential Canons, were largely due to the influence of the Irish missionaries. The Irish Penitentiary Canons became prevalent in Europe before the middle of the eight century. Cf. Gougaud, *Chrétiéntés Celtiques*, chap. viii, sec. 4, pp. 267 ff ; also Watkin's *History of Penance* (London, 1920), vol. ii, part ii, " The Keltic System."

[2] Cf. Montalembert—*Monks of the Church ;* Albers, *op. cit.*, tome i, pp. 380–401. Mourret, *op. cit.*, vol. iii.

illustration of the Church's beneficient influence. It was largely through the medium of her monastic institutions that the Church evangelised the Teutonic nations and fashioned their social life to Christian ideals. From the 6th century onward the Benedictine and Irish monks spread over every country of Western Europe. In every district, on mountain and valley, near the sea-shore, and in inland regions their monasteries were to be seen. These formed the centres of the organised religion of the neighbourhood. It was the monasteries and convents of nuns that relieved the poor, reared the orphans, cared for the sick, afforded shelter to the traveller, and were havens of refuge for all who were weighed down by spiritual or corporal suffering.[1]

Its Influence on Social Customs.—The example of self-abnegation in the monk's life, the object lesson in human equality which the democratic spirit of their institute afforded, the ideals of co-operation embodied in their corporate organisation, their charity, their attitude towards their dependents and the poor, all exercised a profound influence on social customs.

The example of the monks gave a prestige to manual labour which, among the barbarians, as in pagan Greece and Rome, was previously esteemed unworthy of a freeman. Every Benedictine and Columbian monk, including the abbot, who in the people's eyes had the status of a feudal lord, was bound by rule to spend many hours a day in manual labour in the fields or in his workshop. As a result of the monk's example a lay artisan class of freemen was gradually formed, preparing the way for the subsequent city guild organisations.

On Agriculture, the Handicrafts and Art.—It was the monks, too, who introduced into Europe the art of agriculture and brought the land back again to cultivation.[2]

---

[1] " In the relief of the indigent it may on the whole be asserted that the monks did not fall short of their profession " (Hallam, *Middle Ages*, vol. iii, chap. ix, p. 302). This is the unwilling testimony of a prejudiced and hostile writer.

[2] Even such Protestant historians as Guizot and Hallam, both strongly prejudiced against the Church, assert this. Cf. Hallam, *loc. cit.*, p. 436 ; Guizot, *Histoire de la Civilisation*, ii, p. 75.

In the last centuries of the Roman Empire agriculture had fallen into disuse ; and it disappeared almost entirely as a result of the Teutonic invasions. Most of the lands given over to the monasteries were uncultivated and unappropriated at the time of the donation. The monks cultivated them with their own hands. In course of time immense tracts of country were thus reclaimed. Marshes were drained ; forests cleared ; roads made through the cultivated territory ; bridges built ; and all the equipment of civilised life gradually reappeared. A tradition of highly-skilled agriculture and of proficiency in handicraft as well as in fishery, forestry, horticulture, etc., was developed in the monasteries ; and from the monasteries these arts got diffused among the people. " Though agriculture and gardening," writes Lecky, " were the forms of labour in which the monks especially excelled, they indirectly became the authors of every other. For when a monastery was planted it soon became a nucleus around which the inhabitants of the neighbourhood clustered. A town was thus gradually formed, civilised by Christian teaching, stimulated to industry by the example of the monks and protected by the reverence that attached to them. At the same time, the ornamentation of the Church gave the first impulse to art." [1] Thus, not only agriculture, and the kindred arts, but architecture, also, as well as painting, sculpture and music, were renewed in mediæval Europe, by the initiative and example of the monks.

On Letters and Science.—Again, the monasteries were the schools of learning. In fact, outside of Ireland where, besides the monastic schools, a system of education existed independent of the Church,[2] the monasteries were, during all these centuries, the sole custodians of literary and scientific knowledge in Europe. It was in the monasteries, too, that historical records began to be kept.[3] It was by the monks, and especially by the Irish monks, that the people were taught to cultivate their own national languages,

---

[1] *History of Rationalism in Europe*, vol. ii, pp. 239, 240.
[2] Cf. *Joyce's Social History of Ireland*, vol. i, chap. xi (*See* sec. 3, *Lay Schools*).
[3] In this, too, Ireland is an exception. The Irish bardic class included hereditary historians as well as lawyers, doctors, poets, etc. Cf. *ib.*

thus laying the foundation of modern European literature.
The monasteries as well as the Carlovingian schools,[1] established by Charlemagne in the beginning of the 9th century
under the influence and inspiration of the Church, were the
parent stems from which the great mediæval schools and
Universities of Europe afterwards developed.

Art. 4—*Abolition of Slavery*[2]

Church's Efforts on behalf of Slaves.—The Teutonic
invasions had been calamitous for the slaves. Slavery now
became much more widespread, and slaves lost very
many of the privileges which had been secured for them
during the preceding century. As the nations became
Christian the Church again intervened in their behalf. It
procured the liberation of large numbers of slaves in every
country. Documents of the 5th, 6th, and 7th centuries
contain numerous records of captives who had been reduced
to slavery being redeemed by bishops, priests, monks and
pious laymen. Such redeemed captives were sometimes
sent back in thousands to their own country. During all
these centuries, enactments were constantly made in the
national and provincial Councils of the Church in the
interests of the slaves, providing for the protection of
maltreated slaves and for the help and patronage of those
that were liberated, securing the validity of the marriages
of slaves, enforcing in their interests rest on Sundays and
feast days, forbidding or limiting traffic in slaves and forbidding that freemen be reduced to slavery.

Development of Slavery into Serfdom.—But the Church's
beneficent influence is best illustrated in her treatment of
the slaves employed on the ecclesiastical estates, which
eventually led to the abolition of slavery in Christendom.
In the early centuries of this period the Church, owing to
several causes, found itself in the possession of immense

---

[1] For an account of the dominationg influence of the Irish scholars in
these schools, cf. Zimmer—*Ireland's Contribution to European Culture*
(translated from the German) ; Fitzpatrick, *op. cit.*

[2] Cf. Allard—*Esclaves, Serfs et Mainmortables ;* Brownlow—*Lectures on
Slavery and Serfdom in Europe* (reprinted from *The Month*, 1890–91) ;
Palgrave—*Dictionary of Political Economy*, arts. " Serfs," " Servus,"
etc. ; *Cath. Encyclop.*, art. " Feudalism and Land Tenure." ; Belloc—
The Servile State.

estates in every country of Europe. The immediate owners of these estates were the Pope himself, the bishops, the cathedral or collegiate chapters, and the monasteries. By virtue of a 4th century statute of Roman law, due to the influence of the Church, rural slaves could not be removed from the lands on which they worked even when the lands passed to another owner. This law was revoked after the barbarian invasions, except for slaves belonging to ecclesiastical estates. Hence the latter, whose numbers were immense, had the privilege of fixed work and permanent homes. By a whole series of canonical enactments the position of these slaves was gradually improved ; and the privileges enjoyed by the ecclesiastical slaves were gradually extended to those belonging to the lay-lords. The result was that about the 10th century European slavery had practically given way to serfdom.[1]

We shall see later how tolerable was the position of the mediæval serf as compared with that of the slave or of the modern proletarian labourer. Especially on the immense ecclesiastical estates, the serf or villein was treated with peculiar liberality. Here again the standard set up in ecclesiastical estates gradually spread to the lay-manors, preparing the way for the eventual development of serfdom into peasant proprietorship.

Art. 5—*Charity of the Church*[2]

Its Influence on Feudal System.—Besides the relief which the monasteries provided for the poor and weak, the Church which always regarded the *Corporal Works of Mercy* among her primary functions, made provision for their wants in several other ways. The feudal system, which had developed in Europe during these centuries and dominated the whole social life of the middle ages, became largely permeated by Christian principles, and the relations between lord, vassal and serf were strongly imbued with the Christian spirit. King, prince and feudal lord were constantly reminded that they held their offices from God and were responsible to God for the welfare of those under their charge. The poor, the weak and the helpless were, in theory and to a large

---

[1] Cf. Belloc, *op. cit.*, sec. iii, for a brief and graphic account of this process of transformation.   [2] Cf. *Catholic Encyclop.*, " Charity."

extent in practice, objects of their special care. Thus, by Charlemagne's legislation (*circ.* A.D. 800) the feudal lord was charged with the duty of caring for all the needy among his own vassals according to St. Paul's principle that everyone should attend to the needs of his own household.

The Patrimony of the Poor.—Besides the legal provisions in the feudal system in favour of the poor and the weak, there existed from the early centuries of the Church many other provisions for the relief of distress. All the Church revenues, even the sacred vessels, were regarded as subject to the demands of charity. Ecclesiastical property was referred to as " the Patrimony of the Poor," and a fourth part of all ecclesiastical revenue was always set apart for this object.[1]

Charitable Organisations and Institutions.—Collections were regularly made for the same purpose in the churches. The wealthy and the powerful constantly contributed large portions of their property.

The administration of charity was carried out by regular parochial organisations under the presidency of the bishops. Besides, there existed in almost every city from earliest times, parochial institutions called *Xenodochia*, which were under the control of the bishops. These, which had begun in the time of Constantine, were meant originally for widows, the poor, the homeless, abandoned children and other helpless classes. They were commonly managed by pious associations and were endowed from ecclesiastical property.

Conclusion.—Between the charitable work of the monasteries, the recognised duty of the feudal lords, and the parochial organisations to meet the needs of the poor, destitution and misery were always tolerably provided for. Hence it is certain that even during the darkest period of the Early Middle Ages, amid almost universal war and violence, pauperism never reached the appalling proportions which it assumed in England and Ireland in the 18th and 19th, and even the 20th centuries, although these countries then enjoyed peace, and England abounded in wealth.

---

[1] In the early ages of the Church, particularly during and after the reign of Constantine, ecclesiastical property gradually accumulated, as a result of grants and bequests made by the Emperor and other wealthy Christian proprietors. *See infra*, chap. xxvii, art. 4 ; cf. *also* Albers, *op. cit.*, vol. i, pp. 254–257.

CHAPTER IV

THE TWELFTH AND THIRTEENTH CENTURIES—HISTORICAL OUTLINE[1]

The Christian Age.—It is of this period, which is sometimes referred to as the Golden Age of Christianity, that Leo XIII writes :

" There was once a time when States were governed by the principles of Gospel teaching. Then it was that the power and divine virtue of Christian wisdom had diffused itself throughout the laws, institutions and morals of the people, permeating all ranks and relations of civil society. Then, too, the religion instituted by Jesus Christ, established firmly in befitting dignity, flourished everywhere by the favour of princes and the legitimate protection of magistrates; and the Church and State were happily united in concord and friendly interchange of good offices. The State, constituted in this wise, bore fruits important beyond all expectation whose remembrance is still and always will be in renown, witnessed to as they are by countless proofs which can never be blotted out or even obscured by any craft of any enemies." [2]

Again, the same Pontiff writes :

" Civil society was renovated in every part by the teachings of Christianity. . . . In the strength of that renewal the human race . . . was brought back from death to life, and to so excellent a life that nothing more perfect had been known before, or will come to be known in the ages yet to come."[3]

The time referred to is the period of the 12th and 13th centuries, when the influence of the Church in Europe was at its zenith. Christian principles then dominated social relations more fully than at any other period before or since ;[4] and the Christian State then approached most nearly its full development.

---

[1] Besides the works of Chateaubriand, Balmes, Allies, K. Digby and Devas already referred to, cf. Mourret, *op. cit.*, vol. iv., " La Chrétienté " ; Albers, *op. cit.*, tome i, pp. 423 ff ; *Letters on Social History* (C. S. Guild) ; Benevot, *op. cit.*, part iii, " Christian Rule at its Best " ; Browne—*The Achievement of the Middle Ages* (London, 1928) ; Walsh—*The Thirteenth, the Greatest of Centuries* (New York, 1924) ; Montalembert—*Histoire de Sainte Elizabeth de Hongrie*, " Introduction " ; Frederick Schlegel—*Philosophy of History* (translated by B. Robertson—Bohn's Standard Library), Lectures xiii and xiv, pp. 320–388.

[2] *Immortale Dei*, p. 55.   [3] *Rerum Novarum*, p. 148.

[4] This refers to Europe as a whole. Some few countries should be excepted. Ireland enjoyed the blessings of a Christian civilisation long

Its Outstanding Characteristics.—It was the age of great saints and churchmen like Bruno, Bernard, Francis of Assisi, Thomas of Aquin, Bonaventure, etc. ; of great rulers who were at the same time Christian knights and heroes, such as St. Ludwig of Poland (*d*. 1227), Rodolph of Hapsburg (*d*. 1281), St. Louis of France (*d*. 1270), and his cousin and contemporary, St. Ferdinand of Spain. It was the period, too, when the influence of Christian womanhood was most deeply felt in European life ; when the thrones of Europe borrowed lustre from such noble matrons as Matilda of Tuscany (*d*. 1114), St. Elizabeth of Hungary (*d*. 1231), St. Hedweg of Poland (*d*. 1245), Blanche of Castille, mother of St. Louis, Countess Sophia of Holland (*d*. 1176), and very many others. It was the age of the Crusades, of Gothic cathedrals, of Christian poetry and art, of Christian philosophy.[1] Finally, it was the epoch of true Christian democracy which was then realised under the control of the mediæval guilds, more fully than it has ever been before or since.[2]

Social System not Perfect, but Founded on True Principles. —We do not say that the mediæval State was perfect. No human institution can ever be so, as long as human passions and human ignorance remain. Besides, in mediæval Europe not a few characteristics inherited from paganism still survived, especially a certain helplessness among the masses of the people which was a heritage from centuries of slavery. Frederick Schlegel treating of this epoch when, as he says, great characters, noble motives, lofty feelings and ideas abounded more than in any other period of history, writes : " All that was then great and good in the State proceeded from Christianity and from the wonderful efficacy of religious principles. Whatever was imperfect and harmful was in the character of the men and of the age not yet fully

---

before. In her case the period extending from the 6th to the 9th century (before the Norse invasions) may be regarded as the truly Christian epoch. Again, the Christian State flourished in the Spanish Peninsula on to the 17th century and later still in Spanish-America, especially Mexico, where justice and liberty continued to flourish under a predominant Christian régime down almost to the 19th century.

[1] Cf. Walsh, *op. cit.*, chaps. xvi–xx ; Browne, *op. cit.*, pp. 161 ff.
[2] *Ib.*, chaps. ii–ix ; Brown, *op. cit.*, pp. 46 ff.

attuned to the ideals of Christianity." [1] Had the Christian State been allowed to develop in a normal way, there is little doubt, that many of these defects would be gradually eliminated, and a type of true democracy evolved in each country, suitable to the needs and character of the particular nation. This is substantially the evaluation of the mediæval social system which is conveyed in the moderate and carefully weighed words of Pius XI :

" At one time," he writes, " there existed a social order, which, though by no means perfect in every respect, corresponded nevertheless in a certain measure to right reason according to the needs and conditions of the times. That this order has long since perished is not due to the fact that it was incapable of development and adaptation to changing needs and circumstances, but rather to the wrong-doing of men. Men were hardened in excessive self-love and refused to extend that order, as was their duty, to the increasing numbers of the people ; or else, deceived by the attractions of false liberty and other errors, they grew impatient of every restraint and endeavoured to throw off all authority." [2]

Unity of Christendom.—Before the end of the 11th century practically all the nations of Europe, except those on the eastern shores of the Baltic, had embraced Christianity. The worst abuses in the discipline of the Western Church— the Eastern Church had at this time practically completed its separation from Rome—arising from the perpetual strife of the 9th and 10th centuries, were now mostly healed by the reforms associated with the name of Hildebrand or Gregory VII (*d.* 1085). With all the nations and all the rulers of Europe sharing a common Catholic faith, the Pope as the Vicar of Christ on earth, was accorded by unanimous consent a position of paramount influence. This reached its climax during the reign of Innocent III (1193–1216), when the sense of a common Christendom forming, as it were, one great European Empire, and held together by the ties of a common faith pervaded all classes.

The Crusades and Military Orders.—This union of the European nations was intensified by the great wars of the Crusades (1096–1273), including the protracted struggle with the Moors in the Spanish Peninsula. These wars, too,

---

[1] *Op. cit.*, lecture xiv, p. 364.
[2] *Quadragesimo Anno,* 1931 (C. T. S. edit.), p. 44.

gave occasion to the rise and spread of the great military Orders, the Knights of St. John, the Templars, the Teutonic Knights and the Spanish Knights of Calatrava and of St. James, which are a peculiar feature of Catholic life in this period. These Orders played an important part in the erection of the Kingdom of Portugal, in the suppression of the neo-pagan Albigenses of Southern France in the early half of the 13th century, and later on in the conversion to Christianity of the Eastern Baltic nations and the creation of the Prussian State. It was the Crusades, too, and the Christian spirit, of which they were an expression, that brought the Order of Chivalry to its highest development and enabled the clergy to enforce effectively in Europe the observance of the Truce of God.

Religious Institutions.—At the same time the Christian spirit of self-denial and prayer was exemplified and intensified by the rise and spread of the Cistercian Order,[1] in which the spirit of the early Benedictines was renewed. St. Bernard (d. 1153), the greatest of the Cistercians, whose attractive personality dominates the first half of the 12th century, may be regarded as the type and personification of his age.

The foundation of the great Mendicant Orders in the 13th century, namely, the Franciscans, the Dominicans, the Order of Mount Carmel and the Hermits of St. Augustine, marks a new development in the life of the Church. Unlike the earlier religious Orders, the Mendicant Friars bound themselves to absolute poverty, even as corporate bodies.[2] Besides, they did not confine themselves to their monasteries, but mingled with the people, devoting their energies to the work of leading others by their example and preaching to follow the teaching of the Gospel. Their influence can hardly be exaggerated. The Mendicant Friar moving about among the people, living upon the alms of the faithful,

---

[1] The Benedictine monasteries have been computed to number about 37,000 at the end of the 13th century (Cf. *Catholic Encyclop.* ii, p. 446). About the same time the Cistercian Congregation, which began in 1098, had more than 700 large monasteries of men in different countries of Europe and some 900 convents of nuns (Cf. Albers, *op. cit.*, tome i, p. 535.

[2] This rule of mendicancy was gradually modified by different Popes till finally the Council of Trent allowed all religious, except the Franciscans of the Strict Observance and the Capuchins, to hold corporate property.

clad in the habit of poverty, was a perpetual reminder to all of the ideals of Christ.

In the social sphere especially, the movement wrought by the spirit of St. Francis, renewed Christian life in Europe. The Third Orders of St Francis and St. Dominic, which were an adaptation for lay people of the Mendicant ideals of piety, detachment and charity, spread rapidly through Europe. The members included men and women of every rank, who bound themselves to carry out the obligations of religious perfection while following their ordinary avocations in the world. " The Third Orders," says Lacordaire, " produced saints in every walk of life from the palace of the monarch to the peasant's cot ; and that, too, in such teeming multitudes that even the desert and the cloister might well feel jealous." [1]

The Cities and Schools.—This period is also marked by the rise of the towns. In the preceding centuries there was comparatively little town life in Europe. The Roman towns were declining even before the barbarian invasions ; and these hastened their decay. The new German races loved the open life of the country ; and during all the period of the Early Middle Ages social activities centred round the manor or the monastery. Owing to various causes, however, such as the attacks of the Northmen, Hungarians and Saracens in the 9th and 10th centuries, against whom strong walls and a central government were the only effective bulwarks, towns began to assume importance. The growth of trade and commerce, which appeared in the following centuries as a result of the Crusades, caused their further development. The cities of Northern and Central Italy were the first to reap the fruits of the trade and commerce with the East, which developed with the Crusades ; and towards the close of the 13th century, Venice, Genoa, Florence and Milan were not only wealthy and prosperous cities, but had each become the centre of a powerful republican State. Northern and Central Italy was studded over with similar city-republics of a smaller type, all practically independent. The Italian cities became the centres of industry, learning and art, scarcely surpassed by the famous cities of early Greece. The Southern French towns

---

[1] *Vie de St. Dominique*, chap. xvi,

and Barcelona developed a little later. In the 13th century, numerous important centres of commerce and trade had been established in France, Flanders, Germany and England, some of which remain to this day among the great commercial towns of the world.[1]

The most important social development resulting from the rise of the towns was the formation of the great burgher class out of whose successful struggles for political emancipation arose the Third Estate or Commons which would most probably have grown into a full and real democracy had not the virus of modern Liberalism poisoned its later development.

Decline of Christendom.—It is outside our present scope to follow the course of the decline of the Church's influence, or to trace the sorrowful story of the events which led to the catastrophe of the Protestant Revolt—commonly called the " Reformation "—of the 16th century. The enforced exile of the Popes at Avignon (1309–76), the aggressive interference of the French kings, the great Western Schism (1378–1417), the neo-paganism intermingled with the revival of classical learning in the 15th century, the avarice and ambition of the German princes and, later on, of the English sovereigns and the Scottish lords, all had their share in bringing about the disaster. Abuses, too, in ecclesiastical discipline, owing principally to the above causes, were made the occasion and the pretext of robbing the people of their faith over large portions of Europe and preparing the way to their future enslavement.[2]

The social conditions, however, which had developed in the 12th and 13th centuries when the influence of the Church was at its height, did not change substantially till after the rise of Protestantism. The principles of Christian teaching which produced all that was good in these conditions, were not seriously questioned till the 15th century. We have now to analyse these conditions and principles a little more fully.

---

[1] Town-life in Ireland did not develop till the 14th century, when a considerable degree of peace and prosperity and a renewal of Christian civilisation were realised in proportion as the Norman and English invaders were beaten off or partically absorbed by the native element. Cf. Mrs. Green—*Making of Ireland and Its Undoing*, chaps. v and vi ; Ryan, S.J.—*Ireland from A.D. 800 to A.D. 1600*, chaps. vii, viii, xi and xii (Dublin, 1928).

[2] Cf. Pastor—*History of the Popes*, vol. v, " Introduction," and vol. vii, " Introduction."

CHAPTER V

Social Life permeated by the Christian Spirit.—The whole structure of mediæval society was founded upon Christianity. All the people were Catholic ; and ecclesiastical influence was very powerful. Christian principles were inculcated in the current literature, the pulpit, the schools, and the tribunal of Penance ; and were taken for granted, even when not faithfully followed, by all classes of society. The laws and their administration, the economic policy of the State, the recognised relations between the different classes, even international politics, were judged by Christian standards. So strong and deep-rooted was public opinion in the matter that it was difficult for individuals to disregard these standards openly.

Kenelm Digby mentions many interesting particulars illustrating the Catholic tone of public life. Thus : " A painting of the Crucifixion was usually to be seen in the great chambers of the parliaments . . . and over the seats of justice. The great, solemn, thirteenth century paintings of sacred subjects on the walls of the great hall at Sienna, in which the grand council of the Republic assembled, are an evidence of the tone of the government."

In the choice of public functionaries, fidelity and probity were the great qualities insisted on. The injunction contained in one of the Capitularies of Charlemagne gives an idea of the spirit which continued during mediæval times to dominate public administration.

" Let no count hold his *plaids* [viz., *placita generalia*—a kind of local council] unless he be fasting and fed with sense."

Again, Digby quotes the following from a mediæval collection of municipal laws :

" The town sheriff has to visit the round of the walls at night

to see that the watch has sufficient clothing.   He has to inspect
the provisions destined for the poor." [1]

Political Principles.—The fundamental principle of all
mediæval teaching upon public authority and civic rights
was that authority comes from God and is given to the
ruler solely for the people's good ; and that the people whose
good was to be promoted include all classes equally, rich
and poor, high and low, serf, burgher and feudal lord.[2]
Further, owing to the ingrained spirit of Christianity in
favour of the poor and weak, the principle was commonly
admitted that the humbler classes had the first claim upon
the consideration and solicitude of the ruling powers.   Thus
John of Salisbury[3] (d. 1180), a typical 12th century political
philosopher, writes :

" Then and only then will the health of the commonwealth
be sound and flourishing when the higher members devote themselves to the lower ; and when similarly the lower members co-
operate with the higher so that each and all are as it were
members of one another, and each believes his own interest best
served by what he knows to be most usefully provided for others."[4]

Again, the same author writes :

" All things are to be referred to the public good ; and whatever
is useful to the humbler classes, that is, the multitude should be
pursued in all things. . . . Christ will hear the poor when they
cry out, and it will be in vain to multiply vows, and to endeavour,
as it were, to bribe God by gifts." [5]

Hence, Henry II of England describes himself (and was
described) as the "Defender of the Poor and the Defenceless."

---

[1] *Op. cit.*, bk. iii, chap. iv.   Cf. also Otto Gierke—*Political Thought of
the Middle Ages* (1900), translated by F. W. Maitland.   For an interesting
and well-documented account of the Christian spirit which pervaded the
English mediæval law, *see* an article in *The Clergy Review* (March, 1931)
entitled " Christianity and the Common Law."

[2] Cf. St. Thomas, *De Rege et Regno* (*De Regimine Principum*), for a sketch
of the ideal Christian State.   Whether or not this book or the greater
part of it is really the work of St. Thomas, it certainly belongs to the
period of which we treat and summarises the then prevailing teaching.

[3] John of Salisbury, familiar to students of Irish history in connection
with the supposed Bull of Pope Adrian IV, was the friend of Adrian IV
and of Henry II of England ; and the secretary of Henry's Chancellor,
Thomas à Becket.   He was a prolific writer on political and other subjects.

[4] *Policraticus* vi. 20, cited by Rev. Paschalis Larkin, O.S.F.C.—*Property
in the XVIII Century* (Cork University Press, 1930), p. 3.

[5] *De Nugis Curialium*, lib. v, chap. xxvi (Rolls Series).

Vincent of Beauvais of the Order of St. Dominic (*d.* 1264), who was tutor to the children of St. Louis, writes in much the same strain as John of Salisbury on the duty of government :

" There must be mutual safety for the king and the people ; he errs who thinks that the king is safe when nothing is safe from the king.[1]

Tyrannical Rule Reprobated.—Another fundamental principle strongly insisted upon in the political teaching of that age is that the most absolute power is regulated by fundamental laws against which whatever is done is of its own nature null and void. This principle, at variance alike with the pagan principles of absolutism and the modern Liberalist view of the omnipotence of a majority, is frequently emphasised by St. Thomas (*d.* 1274). Thus he writes :

" One is bound to obey civil rulers, in as far as the order of justice demands. Hence if the power is not held justly, but is rather a usurpation, or if the laws are unjust, the subjects are not bound to obey, unless perchance in order to avoid scandal or danger."[2]

Again the same writer has :

" Those who defend the common good are not to be called seditious in resisting those who oppose it. . . . . The tyrant himself it is that is seditious, who encourages disunion and sedition in the people he rules, in order that he may more easily retain his control over them. For this is tyranny to aim, namely, at the personal advantage of the ruler to the detriment of the people."[3]

We find in Dante (*d.* 1321), whose work contains so faithful a picture of the mediæval spirit, many echoes of this attitude towards unjust rule. For instance a certain group in the infernal regions are thus referred to :

" Those are the souls of tyrants, who were given
To blood and rapine. Here they wail aloud
Their merciless wrongs."[4]

---

[1] *Speculum Doctrinæ* (Rolls Series), lib. v, chap. ii.

[2] 2ª. 2æ. Q. 104, a. 6 ad 3um.

[3] *Ib.*, Q. 42, a. 2 ad 3um. Cf. the words of the great English lawyer Coke to James I ; " Rex non debet esse sub homine sed sub Deo et lege " (a king ought not to be subject to man but to God and to the law)— (cited in *The Clergy Review, loc. cit.*, p. 257).

[4] *Hell*, c. xii. ll. 104–107 (Cary's translation). Cf. St. Thomas, *De Rege et Regno* (*De Regimine Principum*), cap. xi, for the same ideas.

Mediæval Christian Democracy.—Such doctrines commonly acknowledged, and the structure of a society fashioned under their influence, effectually secured a high degree of genuine democratic rule. Despotism, understood in the sense of irresponsible rule exercised mainly in the interest of the rulers and practically regardless of the people's rights—the system of government which obtained all over Europe before the rise of Christianity and was re-introduced as a result of the Protestant Revolt—did not generally prevail under the Christian régime of the Middle Ages. This fact, which is strongly asserted by the Catholic apologists,[1] is acknowledged even by historians hostile to the Church. Thus Lecky writes : "The balance of power produced by the numerous corporations which she [viz., the Church] created or sanctioned, the reverence for tradition resulting from her teaching which created a network of unwritten customs with the force of public laws, the dependence of the civil upon the ecclesiastical power, and the rights of excommunication and deposition [exercised by the ecclesiastical authorities] all combined to lighten the pressure of despotism."[2]

Hallam, while acknowledging the prevailing spirit of justice and democratic independence in the mediæval system, does not state that this was due to the influence of Christianity.

Decentralisation of Political Power.—Another very important safeguard against tyranny was the decentralisation of political power. In this the mediæval state contrasts strongly with the ancient pagan state as well as with the royal absolutism of the 17th and 18th centuries and the centralising tendencies of the modern bureaucracies. The extensive power conferred by royal charter on the city municipalities, which were organised on a democratic basis, and the fundamental laws and privileges of the provinces were all strong safeguards against centralised despotism.

---

[1] Cf. Ryan and Millar, *op. cit.*; also Chateaubriand, *op. cit.*, tome iii, chaps. vi, x and xi ; Balmes, *op. cit.*, chaps. xlix–lxiii ; De Maistre, *Du Pape*, liv. iii, chaps. ii, iv and v.
[2] *Rationalism in Europe*, vol. ii, chap. vi, pp. 216, 217. Cf. also Hallam—*Middle Ages*, vol. i, chap. ii, part ii.

3

So too was the guild organisation of the towns, to which Pius XI refers as

"The highly-developed social life which once flourished in a variety of institutions organically linked with each other."[1]

On the other hand the very real power of the king, which depended largely upon popular support, acted as a check against the abuses of local barons.[2]

Conclusion.—Hence, although wicked and unprincipled rulers are to be met with even in the period of which we write, their power to injure and oppress was much more limited than that of a modern bureaucracy. Widespread injustice and continued tyranny were scarcely possible ; and the oppression and tyranny which did exist here and there were partially counteracted by the resources which religion supplied.

---

[1] *Quadragesimo Anno*, p. 36.

[2] Concerning the attitude of the great mediæval theologians towards slavery, an attitude which some writers represent as out of harmony with the Christian principle of men's equality in essential rights and human dignity, see *infra*, part ii, chap. xvii, art. 4. On the whole question of mediæval political teaching, cf. four valuable articles by Professor A. O'Rahilly, M.A., published in *Studies*—viz., "The Catholic Origin of Democracy" (March, 1919) ; "The Sources of English and American Democracy" (June, 1919) ; "The Democracy of St. Thomas" (March, 1920) ; and "The Sovereignty of the People" (March and June, 1921).

CHAPTER VI

Division of Subject.—Christian principles dominated the economic no less than the political teaching in mediæval times. The responsibilities attaching to the ownership of property, the principles of justice and equity in wages and commercial dealings, the lawfulness or unlawfulness of charging interest upon borrowed money, are questions of conscience which find practical application every day of one's life. Hence it was inevitable that the Church's teaching upon such matters should exert a profound influence on social relations among Catholic and deeply religious communities as all the European nations then were. We shall, therefore, treat briefly of the three main principles of mediæval economy that clash most strongly with modern Liberal views. These relate to *Ownership of Goods*, the *Just Price* in buying and selling, and *Usury*. The contrast between social and economic life, as we know it to-day, and that of the Christian period is rooted mainly upon the difference between the Christian and the modern Liberal attitude towards these three questions.

Art. 1—*Ownership of Goods*

Before attempting to analyse the mediæval doctrine of ownership (which has always been the Catholic view) we shall first try to explain briefly the difference between *Private Ownership* and the *Communal Ownership* of goods.

Communal Ownership.—In communal ownership, the goods in question are held in common by the members of a certain group such as a corporation, a municipality, an industrial guild, or even the State itself. No individual member can claim exclusive ownership of any of the goods, although he may use them in common with the other members as far as his needs require ; or even may have certain portions of them—determined according to the nature and extent of his needs—assigned to him for his exclusive use.

Religious Communities and Socialists.—This type of ownership is familiar to us in the institution of religious

35

communities. The community or congregation owns property as a corporate body, but the individual members are excluded by their vow of religious poverty from personal or private ownership, or at least from the free exercise of it. Each member does the work assigned him, and each receives from the common store all he may reasonably require.

Such also is the system of ownership which the Socialists or certain sections of them, aim at establishing, at least to some extent, over the whole State. They would have the goods, or at least the productive goods, owned in common by certain groups within the State, or even by the whole State as one corporate body, while the individual members co-operate in the work of production and distribution, and each is enabled to use the property and to enjoy the fruits of the co-operative labour in accordance with his reasonable needs.

Communal Ownership and Co-Partnership.—We may note that communal ownership, as here defined, differs essentially from co-partnership as exemplified in trading companies. In the latter system, the extent of each member's claim upon the fruits of the industry is determined solely by the amount he has contributed to the common fund whether in capital or by labour ; while, in communal ownership, the individual member's claim is determined principally or solely by his reasonable needs.

Communism and Collectivism.—We may further note the distinction sometimes made between *Communism* and *Collectivism*. Both these terms imply common ownership of the means of production established as a regular system over the whole State. In the system known as *Communism* (which is characterised by *Communal Ownership* properly so-called), the distribution of the produce is made according to the principle : " To each according to his needs " ; whereas in the system known as *Collectivism*, the distribution of the produce is carried out on the principle : " To each one according to his merits." In other words, under the Collectivist system each is supposed to receive his share of the fruits of the work of production in proportion to the amount or efficiency of the labour he has contributed. Thus the system of ownership, which at present (1931) actually exists or is supposed by law to exist in Soviet Russia, seems to oscillate between Communism and Collectivism as here defined. Hence, Collectivism may be broadly described as universal co-partnership established compulsorily and by law as the prevailing system of ownership over the whole State.

Private Ownership.[1]—In opposition to the communal system of ownership is that of private ownership. In this the individual (or family) has exclusive rights over such property as appertains to him in virtue of certain recognised titles, such as occupancy, production, inheritance, contract, etc. ; and ordinarily, each individual or family depends for sustenance solely or principally upon such goods.

Unchristian Concept of Private Ownership.—We find this system *in its extreme form* in the old Roman Empire, before the rise of Christianity, and in modern states which have fallen under the influence of unchristian Liberalism. In these social systems communal ownership, though not illegal, did not and does not prevail to any considerable extent except in the public utilities (such as roads, public hospitals, the postal service, public libraries, etc.), and in the religious or charitable institutions organised by the Church. The individual owner may control property to an unlimited extent. He may do what he likes with this property and live in the highest degree of luxury *without any reference* to the needs of other members, even those of his own country or municipality.

This perverted conception of ownership, resulting from a non-Christian attitude of mind and belonging properly to an unchristian civilisation, was first introduced into the Christian States of Europe in the 14th and 15th centuries

---

[1] Cf. St. Thomas, 1a. 2æ, Q. 105, ; 2a. 2æ, Q. 66 ; a. 1, 2 and 7 ; Q. 32, a. 5 and 6 ; 1a, 2æ, Q. 94 ; a. 5 ad 3um and Q. 105 a. 2 (*corp.*). Ashley—*Economic History*, vol. i, chap. iii, pp. 126–131 (London, 1913) ; O'Brien—*Essay on Mediæval Economic Teaching*, chap. ii, secs. 1 and 2 (Longmans, London, 1920) ; Palgrave—*Dictionary of Political Economy*, art. " Aquinas." Dom Bede Jarrett, O.P.—*S. Antonio and Mediæval Economics* (Herder, London) ; Larkin, *op. cit.*, chap. i—A very valuable and well-documented sketch of the mediæval conception of property rights. Professor O'Rahilly —*St. Thomas' Theory of Property* (art. in *Studies*, vol. ix, p. 337, 1920) ; McLoughlin—*St. Thomas and Property* (*ib.*, p. 571) ; W. Sanderson— " Chaos in Industry "), a thoughtful and able article published in *The Nineteenth Century and After* (October, 1925, pp. 515–526).

with the introduction of Roman law.[1] It was, however, only after the rise of Protestantism in the 16th century that it gained general currency.

The most repulsive feature of this extreme system of private ownership is that many individuals, sometimes even the majority of the population, may be practically excluded from their natural right of access to the goods of the earth. This exclusion may be enforced by law as in case of the slaves under the old Roman régime. Sometimes it arises as a result of the actual working of the system as in the case of multitudes of the modern proletariat population.

Mediæval System of Ownership.—Mediæval teaching rejected completely this extreme form of private ownership, emphasising the limitations which the natural law, as well as Christian teaching, set to property rights. While not repudiating or even discouraging communal ownership where found practical and useful as a supplementary and corrective element within the prevailing system of private ownership, mediæval teaching and practice rejected communal ownership as the ordinary system of conducting human affairs. The mediæval doctors maintained that the only system compatible at the same time with man's temperament and with the teachings of Christianity, was a system of private ownership limited by obligations of justice and charity, subject in due measure to the *Higher Dominion* (*altum dominium*) of the State, and supplemented where useful and possible by a certain admixture of communal ownership.

St. Thomas' Teaching.—The Christian and mediæval teaching on ownership may be gathered from several passages in the *Summa* and other writings of St. Thomas. His doctrine, which is founded upon the Gospel teaching as interpreted by the early Fathers, summarises the current views of his time, and was adopted as the standard by all or practically all the mediæval writers. He has been followed also by the great Catholic theologians of the 16th

---

[1] Cf. Mourret, *op. cit.*, vol. v, chap. ii ; also Meyer and Ardant—*La Question Agraire*, 2nd edit. (Paris, 1887), Prém. Partie—" Introduction." Larkin, *loc. cit.* See *infra*, chap. xvii, art 3.

and 17th centuries. We may briefly summarise St. Thomas' doctrine as follows :

1. God, Who alone has the supreme dominion and ownership of material things, has ordained the latter for the use of all. Hence, such a practical access to these things as may enable man to supply his human needs is natural to him, and is each man's inalienable right.[1]

2. It is false and even heretical to say that all private or exclusive ownership of material things is against the natural law.[2]

3. The system of private as contrasted with that of communal ownership is not only lawful, but within certain limits is necessary for the due conduct of human life, at least as long as men retain their present normal characteristics. Hence it is imposed on man by the *Law of the nations (Jus Gentium)*.[3]

Proofs of the Necessity of Private Ownership.—This last proposition St. Thomas proves by three reasons—(a) Private ownership supplies a necessary stimulus to human endeavour. For men will not ordinarily put forth their best efforts in productive labour except the fruits of the labour are to be their own. (b) Private ownership facilitates the proper division and co-ordination of labour, whereas in communal ownership the distribution of labour would be very difficult or impossible. (c) Private ownership promotes peace and harmony. For in this system (when properly understood) each one has sufficient and is content with his own ; whereas

---

[1] 2a, 2æ, Q. 66, a. 1 and 7.

[2] *Ib.*, a. 3, *Sed contra.*

[3] Cf. *ib.*, a. 2 ad 1um and Q. 37, a. 3. For the precise meaning of the *Jus Gentium*, cf. St. Thomas 1, 2æ, Q. 95, a. 4, and Meyer, S.J., *op. cit.*, Pars. 1ma, n. 571, and Pars. 2a, n. 178. It differs from the natural law in that its obligations are not so urgently demanded by man's individual nature and destiny as the obligations of the natural law. Nevertheless given fallen man as he actually is, and with his social instincts and needs, the dictates of the *Jus Gentium* are morally necessary for him. Hence, whether the obligations of the *Jus Gentium* rest upon positive human law, as some seem to hold, or upon remote conclusions of the natural law, as others assert, all agree that it is in practice necessary for man's well-being and cannot be changed by human enactment. For such an enactment, as for instance a law abolishing the institution of private property, would be contrary to the common good and so intrinsically invalid.

disputes occur more frequently among those that possess things in common.[1]

Christian Concept of Private Ownership.—The system of private ownership, however, which St. Thomas defends as lawful, and in practice obligatory, is not to be understood in the extreme individualistic sense already referred to. It includes only the exclusive right of *dominion* and *the control of the production or exploitation and of the distribution of the goods* (*potestas procurandi et dispensandi*). It does *not* include the *exclusive* right to the *use* of them. This right is strictly limited and cannot be exercised without due consideration for the needs of others. In this regard the owner has only a priority or first claim as far as his needs require. St. Thomas's words are as follows :

" In regard to that [namely, the *use* of goods] one must not regard material things as one's own, but as common property, so that one freely shares them with others who need them."[2]

The limitation here implied to the lawful use of property rights is an obvious conclusion from the fundamental principle that God has ordained material things to satisfy the needs of all. The actual division of them by means of private ownership, which is a human institution, cannot validly contravene that decree, nor therefore prevent men from satisfying their needs by them. Consequently the property which people possess in excess of what they require should be used to satisfy the needs of those that are in want.[3]

Its Social Aspects.—Hence, according to mediæval teaching the rights of private ownership were subject to the following limitations :

(*a*) Anyone may in case of a clear and pressing need (*evidens et urgens necessitas*) lawfully disregard another's ownership and appropriate for his own use what he thus clearly and urgently requires ; nor can the owner who has no urgent and immediate need of the thing in question lawfully prevent him. He would violate charity and even justice by doing so.

---

[1] *Ib.*, Q. 66, a. 2 (*corp.*). St. Thomas apparently does not mention the reason which by some is regarded as the most convincing of all in favour of the system of private ownership, namely, that it is a necessary means of securing the individual's personal independence and responsibility.

[2] *Ib.* From other passages (such as *ib.*, a. 7) we know that St. Thomas implies that one's own reasonable needs are satisfied before the obligation arises of sharing the goods with others.   [3] *Ib.*, a. 7 (*corp.*).

(b) The owner is bound at least under an obligation of charity to distribute the goods he does not require for his own reasonable needs to those that do need them. Hence his exclusive right to *such* goods is confined to the control over the working or exploitation of the capital, and directing the distribution of the proceeds (*potestas procurandi et dispensandi*). These latter he is bound, in varying degrees and within varying limitations according to circumstances, to give to those in need.[1] But when all men's wants cannot be relieved, the owner may select the particular persons with whom he will share the goods.[2]

(c) Although outside the case of clear and pressing needs, an individual may not lawfully appropriate for his own use even the superfluous goods of his neighbour, he has a right in *Legal Justice* that the public authority, whether guild or municipality or State, should see to it that he *gets a fair opportunity* of providing for all his reasonable needs, even though it were necessary for that purpose to override another's ownership, in regard, that is, to his superfluous goods.[3]

Extension of Communal side by side with Private Ownership.—The tendency of mediæval teaching and practice was to encourage a reasonable and voluntary extension of the communal ownership of property, as an offset to the dangers and shortcomings of an exclusive system of Private ownership. For the Church has always recognised that private property alone is not sufficient to meet the needs of the masses of the people. There will always be numbers who cannot, or in practice will not, acquire private property sufficient for their security. Hence some type of communal or quasi-communal property is usually required to supplement private ownership.[4]

---

[1] Cf. chap. xxvii, art. 4, for a short exposition of the extent and urgency of this obligation.

[2] *Ib.*

[3] *Ib.*, Q. 58, a. 6 ; Q. 61, a. 1 ad 4um ; 1^{a} 2^{æ}, Q. 105. *De Rege et Regno* (*De Regimine Principum*), lib. i, cap. xv.

[4] *See* Meyer et Ardant, *op. cit.*, 2^{ieme} partie, chap. vi, pp. 279 ff. Compare also the words of Comte de Mun, leader of the Catholic social movement in France : "While proclaiming that the right of private property is a natural right we only demand that alongside of private property a certain amount of collective [or communal] property be freely

Owing to this attitude on the part of the Church, it gradually came about in nearly every country of Europe as a result of the voluntary gifts of Christian rulers and other pious benefactors, that a large portion of the wealth, including sometimes almost a third part of the whole property of the country, was held in trust by Christian corporations of various kinds to be administered for the benefit of the members and others in accordance with their actual requirements. Thus Church property and the corporate property of the guilds were applied and distributed, to a great extent in meeting the wants of those in need.

Especially in Land.—There were besides, in every country, large tracts of land called " Commons," which were held on the communal system. Again, turbary rights, fishing rights, hunting rights, etc., were also usually communal. It was in accordance with the general custom in mediæval times, if not a recognised principle, that *all the soil should not be appropriated, and even in what was appropriated that certain rights should always be reserved to the community.*

Conclusion.—All these customs and recognised principles, limiting property rights, and supplementing the system of private ownership, combined with the influence upon public opinion of the Church's teaching, had an immense effect during all this period in equalising the condition of the people and moderating extremes of poverty and wealth.

Art. 2—*The Just Price*

Application in Mediæval Times.—The mediæval law of Just Price is another example of the altruistic spirit which permeated the social and economic life of the middle ages. Individuals were not permitted to use freely the property they controlled in ways that might be detrimental to the common good. They were compelled, when the needs of others required it, to place the goods they had to dispose of at the service of the public *under equitable conditions.* The poor and weak were protected against unfair competition,

---

established to vest [for communal purposes] in free associations, municipalities and corporations " (cited by Garriguet, *op. cit.*, pp. 163, 164). Hence, too, the Church has always been so insistent on the conservation of ecclesiastical property, which is in large part the " Patrimony of the Poor." Cf. Meyer et Ardant, *loc. cit.*, and Sanderson, *loc. cit.*

so that all might be secured a fair access to the material goods of the community.

The laws of Just Price[1] had to be observed in wages, buying and selling and every contract of exchange ; otherwise the contract was accounted unjust and invalid in conscience, and the aggrieved party had a claim to restitution. " Whoever," writes Trithemius, a well-known fifteenth century author, " buys up corn, meat and wine in order to drive up their prices, and amass money at the cost of others, is, according to the laws of the Church, no better than a common criminal. In a well-governed community all arbitrary raising of prices in the case of articles of food and clothing is peremptorily stopped. In times of scarcity merchants who have supplies of such commodities can be compelled to sell them at fair prices ; for in every community care should be taken that all the members should be provided for, lest a small number be allowed to grow rich, and revel in luxury to the hurt and prejudice of the many."[2]

Contrast between Christian and Non-Christian Standpoint. In the old Roman law, just as in modern Liberal states, selfishness was assumed to be the dominating motive in every contract ; and the fullest liberty was allowed to both parties to decide the price and even to over-reach each other, provided nothing was done that the law regarded as fraud.[3] According to mediæval teaching on the other hand, the price of a commodity was supposed to be determined by objective value alone ; and could not be justly influenced by the special need or ignorance of buyer or seller.

Doctrine of the Just Price.—This doctrine, which was universally accepted in mediæval times, is thus summarised by St. Thomas :

" If the price exceeds the value of the thing, or if the thing is worth more than the price paid, the equality which justice requires is done away with."

---

[1] Cf. St. Thomas, 2ª, 2ᵃᵉ, Q. 77, a. 1 and 4 ; O'Brien, *op. cit.*, chap. iii, sec. i ; Palgrave—*Dict. of Pol. Economy*, art. " Justum Pretium " ; *Cath. Encyclop.*, art " Political Economy " ; Ashley, *op. cit.*, vol. i, chap. iii, sec. 16 ; Ryan—*Distributive Justice* (New York, 1915) sec. iv., chap. xxiii, pp. 332–336 ; Bede Jarrett, *op. cit.*, chap. vii ; Sanderson, *loc. cit.*
[2] Quoted in O'Brien, *op. cit.*, pp. 124, 125.
[3] St. Thomas, 2s, 2a, Q. 77, a. 1.

The seller cannot justly exact a higher price merely on account of the special need the buyer may have of the thing, or the accidental advantage that may accrue to him from it ; for in such cases he would be selling what is not his.[1] Hence the criterion of exchange value was something intrinsic to the commodity itself, not merely competition or the higgling of the market. Hence, too, the modern distinction between value in use and value in exchange was recognised only to a very limited extent.

How it was Fixed.—The objective value of a commodity was calculated mainly and primarily upon the cost of production. This latter, which was accounted the first charge upon every product, was itself determined on the basis of a becoming standard of living for the producers.

In the case of most commodities, the Just Price was usually fixed by the guilds or by the municipality, or even by the State. Even when the price was not legally determined, it was not left to the arbitrary decision of the buyer or seller, but was supposed to be fixed by what was known as the *common estimation* of the community. In this case, although prices might vary within certain limits, it was well understood that to pass these limits for accidental causes, such as scarcity or the special needs of the buyer or seller would be unjust.

Mediæval Attitude Towards Trade and Speculation.— Mediæval principles ordinarily approved only of two sources of wealth and profit, namely, the natural produce of the earth and labour.[2] The occupation of the speculator or trader, he, namely, who buys not in order to use but to sell again at a dearer price, was looked upon with disfavour ; and its morality was, for a long time, considered doubtful. " Such trading," says St. Thomas, " is justly condemned (*vituperatur*) because of its own nature it subserves the desire of gain which knows no limit and tends to indefinite increase." He goes on, however, to say that it is not neces-

---

[1] *Ib.*   [2] Cf. Dante :
　　　" These two, if thou recall to mind
　　　Creation's holy book from the beginning,
　　　Were the right source of life and excellence
　　　To human kind."
　　　　　　—Hell, c. xi, 118–121 (Cary's translation).

sarily vicious, and that moderate profits, which would be a just wage for one's labour, would be lawful." [1]

Although the prevailing attitude towards trading became more liberal in the following centuries, with the gradual expansion of commerce consequent upon the Crusades, it was always held to be less honourable in itself than productive labour, and of less solid utility to the State. Besides, it was recognised that the activities of the trader and the commercial dealer, owing to the numerous temptations to avarice and dishonesty, and the greater difficulty in insuring the observance of the law of Just Price, required to be carefully scrutinised and kept within the limits of justice. [2]

Effects on Social Life of the Principle of the Just Price.— The doctrine of the Just Price and the whole mediæval attitude towards trading profits imply a fundamental contrast between the Catholic economic outlook and the one that prevails in modern times. Although it may be difficult to determine with exactness the intrinsic value of a commodity or the just price at which it might be sold, it was universally admitted that all commodities had a certain value which common estimation could determine and which accidental circumstances, such as scarcity or the special needs of the buyer or seller, could not substantially change. Competition was thus confined within the limits of natural equity, and the unjust activities of the financier, the middleman and the trader were kept in check.

The Principle of the Living Wage.—The recompense of labour or the rate of wages was determined in accordance with the general rules relating to just price. Labour is the ordinary means by which, according to the law of nature, man supplies the needs of human life. Hence it was regarded as possessed of an intrinsic minimum value. This value was calculated on the principle that the worker should have wherewithal to support life in reasonable human conditions according to his capacity and state. The price of the labour expended in the production of an article or the worker's wage was regarded as the first consideration

---

[1] 2a, 2æ, Q. 77, a. 4.
[2] Cf. O'Brien, *loc. cit.*, pp. 136 ff.

in fixing the price of a commodity.[1] The actual rate of wages was usually fixed by the guilds.

Recognised but not Elaborated by Mediæval Writers.— The obligation of paying a just wage was so universally accepted that the matter is little discussed by the mediæval writers. St. Thomas refers to the just wage only accidentally here and there.[2] Albertus Magnus alludes to the same matter in his *Ethica*, where he implies that the human needs of the producer of the article, or, in other words, the amount of the labour expended on its production, is the main element to be considered in estimating its exchange value.[3]

But that question was not then by any means as urgent or important as it has become in our times. In those days the proletariat or class of unpropertied wage earners did not exist, or was very small. The peasant or serf had his own holding, the labour he had to give to the lord of the soil being regulated by custom, while the working classes of the towns were mostly independent producers who sold their wares instead of their labour.

Art. 3—*Usury*[4]

Prevalence and Destructive Effects of Usury.—Leo XIII, enumerating the main causes of the misery and wretchedness of which the working classes of modern times are the unhappy victims, mentions usury as one.

" Public institutions and laws have set aside the ancient religion. Hence by degrees it has come to pass that the working men have been surrendered, isolated and helpless to the hardheartedness of employers and the greed of unchecked competition. The mischief has been increased by rapacious usury, which, although more than once condemned by the Church, is

---

[1] Cf. O'Brien, *ib.* ; Ryan, *op. cit.*, p. 338.

[2] Cf. 1ª, 2æ, Q. 114, a. 1, where he takes for granted that the rate of wages comes under the law of Just Price ; also *In.* iii, Dist. 18, a. 2, where he implies that just wages or hire are to be measured not arithmetically, but proportionately.

[3] Cf. *Ethica*, lib. v, trac, ii, cap. ix and x.

[4] Cf. St. Thomas, 2ª, 2æ, Q. 78, aa. 1–4. Macksey—*Argumenta Sociologica*, cap. iv ; Vermeersch—*Quæstiones de Justitia, Quæstio Nona* ; Costa Rosetti—*Philosophia Moralis*, pp. 766–770 (note) ; Larkin, *op. cit.*, 178 ff—a well-documented historical sketch ; O'Brien, *op cit.*, chap. iii, sec. ii ; Bede Jarrett, *op. cit.*, chap. vii ; Ashley, *op. cit.*, vol. i, chap. iii, sec. 17 ; *Cath. Encyclop.*, art. " Usury " ; Palgrave, *op. cit.*, art. " Canon Law " ; Garriquet, *op. cit.*, 4ieme partie, chap. iii ; Antoine, *op. cit.*, chap. xvii, arts. 5 and 6 ; Belliot, *op. cit.*, pp. 162 ff.

nevertheless under a different guise, but with like injustice still practised by covetous and grasping men." [1]

Devas speaks of the prevalence of usury and the incalculable misery it has caused "from remote ages to the present day" as among the "saddest features of history"; and adds truly that "the prevention and punishment of this crime are among the first duties of Government." He quotes from the official *Report on Money Lending* issued by the British Government in June, 1898, instances of money being lent in England at an interest of anything between 60 per cent. and 3,000 per cent! "The law," he continues, "became a partner to outrageous injustice : for, except in the rare cases where *illegal* fraud could be proved, it inflicted no punishment on the usurers. . . . But in many countries besides our own the slackness or absence of usury laws gave such an impetus to similar misdeeds and ruined so many peasants in Europe and India [and Ireland], that the 19th century has been called the "Century of Usury." [2]

It is generally recognised that the "Rapacious Usury" of which Leo XIII speaks has been and still is, both in its naked form and "under a different guise," one of the radical causes of social misery in Ireland as elsewhere. Thus amid universal business depression, unemployment and poverty, the monied interests are allowed to control the distribution (and in a large measure the production) even of the necessaries of life, making enormous profits to the injury or ruin of both producers and consumers. [3]

Mediæval Attitude on Usury.—Such widespread abuse would not be possible in the mediæval times. Public opinion, formed under the guidance of the Church's teaching, justly regarded usurers and unjust profiteers as the very worst of criminals. Dante, voicing the sentiments of his age, puts the usurers in the lowest division of his seventh

---

[1] *Rerum Novarum*, p. 134.
[2] *Political Economy* (3rd edit., 1920), pp. 415, 416. Cf. also Antoine, *op. cit.*, pp. 601, 602.
[3] Cf. Shove—*The Fairy Ring of Commerce* (The Manchester Distributist League, 1930), chap. v and *passim* ; also Sanderson, *loc. cit.*, where the writer refers to the fact that coal sold at the pit head at 20/6 per ton costs 50/- per ton to the consumers.

circle in Hell, in company with the most degraded and unnatural sinners :

> " And thence the inmost round marks with its seal
> Sodom and Cahors,[1] and all such as speak
> Contemptuously of the God-head in their hearts."

Christian teaching, as we have already seen, emphasises the dignity of manual toil and the duty of labour for all. It condemns idleness as unnatural and degrading and as opposed to the divine ordinance that men should employ their God-given energies in suitable labour.[2] This doctrine, which was then accepted as a fundamental principle of social life, would alone be sufficient to render the calling of the usurer dishonourable. The practice was besides definitely condemned on other grounds.

The early Fathers protest against usury in the strongest terms ; and the Church always regarded it with disfavour.[3] It had been forbidden to clerics since the 4th century and to lay people as well as clerics since the 9th. This prohibition was again and again enforced in the 12th century. Of the numerous ecclesiastical decrees on the subject we may mention those of the two General Councils of Lateran (1139 and 1179), in which the penalty of excommunication with denial of Christian burial was decreed against usurers ; and that of Gregory X, a century later, who ordained, in the Council of Lyons (1274), that no community, corporation or individual, should permit foreign usurers to hire houses, but should expel them from their territories.

Church's Discipline at Present Day.—We may note that although the Church's prohibition of usury has been confirmed again and again in modern times, especially by Benedict XIV in the Encyclical *Vix Pervenit* (1745), there has been a certain relaxation of the law since the early years of the 19th century. This apparently modified attitude of the Church is confirmed in the recently issued Code of Canon Law which, in dealing with the matter, reads as follows :

" If a commodity which is consumed by its first use (such as money, bread, etc.), be lent on the stipulation that it becomes

---

[1] A city of Guinne much frequented by usurers.
[2] Cf. *Infra*, chap. xvii, art I.
[3] Cf. Vermeersch, *loc. cit.*, for a whole series of Patristic quotations on the subject.

the property of the borrower, who is bound to return to the lender not the thing itself but its equivalent only, the lender may not receive any payment by reason of the loan itself. In the giving or lending of such a commodity, however, it is not in itself unlawful to make an arrangement for the recovery of interest at the rate allowed by the civil law (*de lucro legali pacisci*) unless that rate is clearly excessive : One may even arrange for a still higher rate of interest, if there be a just title for doing so, in proportion to the amount of the excess." [1]

According to the terms of this Canon one may *without enquiry or solicitude as to the existence or not of extrinsic titles* (such as accidental loss caused by the loan, the risk of not being repaid, etc.) receive interest at the rate laid down by the civil law provided that rate be not clearly excessive. The reason for this change or apparent change in the Church's attitude towards usury is that in modern times, owing to the capitalistic organisation of economic life, money has practically become a form of capital,[2] and the Church follows her traditional policy in regulating her attitude towards it. As usual she temporarily adjusts her discipline as far as possible to the needs of the age, even when these needs are the result of a state of things of which she does not approve, and allows the faithful to act in accordance with social customs sanctioned by existing civil law, provided these customs are not manifestly immoral or unjust. Hence, in the present instance she allows the faithful to avail within certain limits of the civil law and custom regarding usury and interest. We have already seen how in a similar manner, owing to the needs of society and to avoid greater evils, the Church permitted masters in the early years of Christianity to retain their slaves even though the institution of slavery is opposed to Christian principles.[3]

Catholic Teaching on Usury.—Usury in the mediæval sense meant payment exacted for the use of borrowed money. The grounds for the Church's condemnation of usury as essentially unjust are expounded by St. Thomas,

---

[1] *Codex Juris Canonici*, c. 1543.
[2] Vermeersch, *loc. cit.*
[3] Cf. Costa Rosetti, *op. cit.*, pp. 772–786 ; also Belliot and Macksey, *loc. cit.*

whose teaching on the matter was universally adopted. Thus he writes :

"Money, like wine and wheat, is consumed by being used. Hence the use of the thing cannot be separated from the thing itself. Consequently he who, besides requiring back the thing [viz., the money lent], also exacts a price for its use, sells and gets paid for what does not exist, which is unjust." [1]

It may be objected to this argument that money, unlike bread or wine, may be used as capital, and that capital is, with labour, an element of production. Thus a man who lends his machine or beast of burden to another in order that the latter may utilise it in productive labour, may lawfully require in payment a certain portion of the produce. In the same way, one who lends his money to another for capital, or trading purposes may fairly exact a share in the profits. This objection refers only to *money borrowed for capital*, and would not in any case affect the question of money borrowed in order to procure goods of consumption such as food or clothing. Even as regards the former kind of loan, St. Thomas does not admit the validity of the objection. His answer is : The machine or beast lent to another still remains the property of the lender, hence the element it contributes towards the produce is his. In the case of money it is different. When one borrows money even for capital, the dominion or ownership of the money is transferred to the borrower. This is shown by the fact that the borrower may consume (or destroy) the money (which he does by using it). [2]

Besides, should the money get accidentally lost or mislaid while in the borrower's possession, the latter and not the lender is the sufferer. In the case of a borrowed instrument or animal, on the other hand, the borrower has no right to destroy the borrowed article seeing he is not its owner ; and should the article get lost or destroyed (when in his possession) through no fault of his, not he but the lender (viz., the owner of the article) suffers the loss. Hence, the element which the borrowed money contributes to production belongs not to the lender, who no longer is the owner of the money, but to the borrower, to whom the ownership has passed.

---

[1] 2a, 2æ, Q. 78, a. 1. For a fuller exposition of the argument, cf. Slater— *Manual of Moral Theology*, vol. i, pp. 513 ff.

[2] *See ib.*, a. 2, ad 5um, for St. Thomas' words, which the text summarises.

Extraneous Titles to Interest on Money Lent.—Although usury, that is payment for the use of money, was unlawful, neither St. Thomas nor the other mediæval writers deny that a certain modest payment may be exacted under other titles. If the lender suffered a positive loss by the loan, he might demand that the loss be recouped. If he himself would have utilised the money as capital had he retained possession of it, he might demand payment for the loss of opportunity he suffered by lending it.[1] If, finally, his lending endangered in any way the security of whole or part of the amount, he may justly charge such an interest as may be considered equal to the risk incurred. The lender, however, who would exact payment for the use of money beyond the moderate interest that may come under these headings was regarded as a usurer and fell under the penalties of the Church.

Effects of the Church's Prohibition.—The Church's legislation and teaching did not, it is true, succeed in completely preventing the practice of usury, especially on the part of the Jews. These laws and principles were, however, an immense check upon the unjust activities of money-lenders and speculators, so that anything approaching the systematised extortion and stock-gambling of modern times was impossible.

Conclusion.—It is commonly admitted that the undue concentration of wealth under the control of a few is one of the radical causes of the social misery and unrest that prevail at the present day. Individuals controlling great wealth have excessive power in almost every phase of social activity, and, following the tendency of human nature, they too often use their power unjustly and tyrannically. Those huge fortunes are usually amassed by unjust profiteering, artificially created monopolies, usury, unjust reduction of wages, the sudden fluctuations of the markets which play into the hands of greedy speculators. The mediæval economic doctrines and legislation and the public opinion they produced and fostered made impossible, or at least kept in check, such methods of accumulating wealth, and so were a potent safeguard against one of the worst types of social injustice.

---

[1] *Ib.*, a. 2 ad 1um and a. 3.

CHAPTER VII

SOCIAL CLASSES IN MEDIÆVAL TIMES

Introduction—Main Divisions of the Population.—In order to appreciate better the beneficient influence of the Church on social welfare, it is desirable to know something of the actual condition of the people during the period in which her power was at its height. Hence, before leaving the subject we shall sketch in brief outline the main features of social conditions in Europe during the 12th and 13th centuries. The task is all the easier, as there existed at the time a considerable uniformity of social organisation, and much similarity in social conditions throughout most of Christendom.[1]

There were three main divisions of the population, namely, the feudal nobility, the agricultural class, principally though not entirely serfs or villeins, and the townspeople, who were practically all organised in guilds. Slaves were comparatively few even in the 11th century, and slavery had practically disappeared before the opening of the 13th.[2] The clergy and the religious of both sexes were drawn from all classes of the population. The clergy performed, in addition to their ecclesiastical duties, most of the functions of our present professional classes, although there was a certain number of lay professional men whose social status is not clearly defined. Besides these there were the Jewish traders and moneylenders, and a considerable number of the nondescript type, who do not require special treatment. With the rise of commerce after the 13th century traders of all kinds, as distinct from those that manufactured the goods they sold, became numerous, but during the period with which we are here principally concerned that class was not considerable. Hence, to obtain a general idea of the social

---

[1] The case of Ireland, which stands apart, will be treated in Appendix I.
[2] Palgrave, *op. cit.*, art. " Servus."

conditions in mediæval times we may confine our attention to the three main classes of the population, of each of which we shall now briefly treat.

Art. 1—*The Feudal Nobility*[1]

Their General Functions.—The feudal nobility, which comprised the ruling and military class, formed only a small fraction, possibly less than one-twentieth of the population. The feudal lords were, at least in legal theory, the sole owners of the land. From this they derived maintenance and the means to meet their military expenses. They themselves, however, did not work on the soil. Their duties were those of administration and military defence. The productive work was carried on by the serfs and other agricultural classes, and by the free artisans of the towns, who were usually exempt from military duties.

The feudal organisation which we find firmly established among the Franks in the 8th century, got more and more widely diffused owing to the needs of the time. Before the opening of the 12th century nearly all the territory of Christendom, not even excluding the ecclesiastical estates, were held in one way or another under the feudal system. The lords and their retainers, all mounted warriors and all of the feudal class, formed, as it were, the standing army of the nation. (The attendants and footmen who belonged to the non-feudal class were not regarded as warriors.) It was these mailed horsemen, and the impregnable walls of their castle fortresses, that saved Christendom against the fierce invaders of the 9th and 10th centuries : and at the same time prevented domestic chaos. Feudalism declined after the 13th century according as the causes which produced it ceased to exist.

---

[1] Cf. Betten and Kauffmann—*Modern World* (Boston, 1919), book i, sect. ii ; *Letters on Social History* (C. S. Guild), pp. 50–55 ; Ashley, *op. cit.*, vol. i, part i, chap. i ; Robinson—*Readings in European History*, vol. i, chap. ix ; Bland, Brown and Tawney—*English Economic History* (Select Documents), secs. ii and iv ; *Encyclopædia Brittanica*—arts. " Feudalism " and " Knighthood and Chivalry " ; *Cath. Encyclo.*—arts. " Feudalism " and " Chivalry " ; K. Digby—*Mores Catholici* or *Ages of Faith*, vol. iii, chaps. vii–xii.

Nature of the Feudal Organisation.—The feudal organisation, although containing an endless variety of peculiarities in different places, had certain fundamental characteristics which were the same everywhere. Among these are the following :—Every holder of land was, or was supposed to be, a tenant and vassal of a higher lord, at least till the highest rank was reached. To this lord he owed service and loyalty, while the lord owed him justice and protection.

Hence in the theory of feudalism, even the kings held their dominions as fiefs from a higher suzerain. Some professed to hold from the Emperor, others from the Pope, while some acknowledged no supreme suzerain but God. The king parcelled out his dominions to his chief men, who held from him on conditions similar to those which existed between the king himself and the higher suzerain. The chief men in turn divided up their territory in the same way to sub-liegemen or vassals, whose relations to them corresponded with theirs to the king ; and so on through all the grades.

The whole organisation may be compared to a cone with the king or the Emperor at the apex, and the body of the lowest vassals forming the base. These latter might have only a very limited extent of territory, sometimes not exceeding a modern good-sized farm. But all were classed as nobles or gentlemen and all enjoyed social equality.

Rights and Duties of the Classes.—According to the common law recognised, at least in theory, throughout all Christendom, the conditions of the vassal's tenure included not merely loyalty to his suzerain, but also loyalty to God, probity and honour in his dealings with others, and fidelity to what is just and right. Hence, should any vassal become disloyal or rule unjustly or wickedly, he would thereby forfeit his fief, which his suzerain might take from him and give to a worthier liegeman. Even an independent ruler, like the Emperor, or the King of France, who acknowledged no suzerain but God Himself, would, according to common law, forfeit his realm if he remained for a whole year under the ban of the Church.

The privileges of the vassals and the services they owed the lord varied indefinitely according to the size and importance of their fiefs. Some vassals had most of the rights of independent princes ; others were little more than simple soldiers. Of the vassal's obligations towards his suzerain, the principal one was military service. He was bound to support his lord in the field, bringing with him for that purpose a specified contingent of fully-equipped warrior retainers in proportion to the extent of his fief. The vassals were bound, besides, to some other less important services, such as to act as jurors or judges in the lord's court, to furnish aids in money at specified times, etc.

The duties of justice and protection which the lord owed his vassal, and which then were very real and onerous, extended to all that lived on his lands, even to the serfs and other such dependents.

Pagan and Christian Elements in the Feudal System.— It is outside our scope to discuss the origin of feudalism, upon which there is a wide divergence of opinion. It is certain, however, that the clear-cut distinction of caste between the feudal landowners and the non-free or servile classes who worked as craftsmen or upon the soil, was wholly or in large part a survival of paganism. For according to the pagan ideals, which had prevailed equally among both the Roman and the Teutonic predecessors of the feudal warriors, servile or manual labour was inconsistent with the status of a freeman.

On the other hand, the moral elements in the feudal organism, such as the inter-relation of reciprocal rights and duties, the ideas of responsibility attaching to ownership and power, the obligations of fidelity and probity as conditions of vassalage, all were the results of Christian teaching. The military features of the system were a natural product of the needs of the time.

Critique of the Feudal Social System.— In estimating the character of feudal society and the relations of the feudal barons to one another and to their servile dependents one should bear in mind that even in the 12th century, Europe as a whole had only just emerged from a state of barbarism, social development having been arrested by the wars and partial chaos of the 9th and 10th centuries. Customs and principles inherited from Roman imperialism and Teutonic military ideals were not yet extinct. Again the continual invasions and shocks from without which retarded for a long time the normal development of the nations into fully organised political units, were frequently a source of much misery and disorder. Still, notwithstanding many defects and limitations, feudal society under Christian influence and the whole social organisation that was formed upon it had many advantages and, taken all in all, probably came nearer, at least in the 13th century, to an ideal State than anything that continental Europe had seen before, or has experienced since.

Prevalence of the Christian Spirit.—To begin with, the ruling classes frankly accepted Christian principles. Pride, avarice and sensuality were of course there, and cruelty and injustice were not unknown. But on the other hand, wondrous manifestations constantly appear of Christian humility, heroic self-sacrifice and charity which went far to counteract the results of human passion. Even the men whom ambition and uncontrolled anger betray into acts of cruelty or tyranny are constantly seen to repent and make reparation for the injustice done. The ministers of the Church exerted immense influence which was a constant check upon the absolutism of the feudal lords. We are familiar with the history of St. Bernard who, though a simple monk, was in his day probably the most powerful influence in European politics. Gregory VII by the exercise of his spiritual prerogatives compelled the submission of Henry IV of Germany (then the most powerful monarch in Europe), although the latter probably had little faith and less sense of conscience. The same is true of the dispute between Innocent III and King John of England, as well as that between Innocent III and Philip the Fair of France.

Social Justice Substantially Secured. –The ownership of the land and other privileges appertaining to the feudal class carried with them real duties and onerous responsibilities. In fact these rights and privileges rested essentially on the idea and obligation of service. They were allowed or granted not for the comfort or enjoyment of the person possessing them, but in order to enable him to perform the public services to which he was bound. The duties of vassal and suzerain rested upon definite legal relations which bound both parties equally. To break the feudal bond was dishonour as well as felony. A great respect for law and justice as well as a wholesome spirit of true liberty and independence were thus developed. No overlord could venture to act arrogantly or unjustly with his vassal ; for the latter stood upon his rights as a freeman. In the same way, though to a less extent, the relations between the lord and his serfs were regulated by definite laws founded upon immemorial custom.

The heavy expenses attaching to the lord's military duties, which were essential to the safety of the community, could not be met except through the productive labour of the serf. The lord's own life was laborious and simple. Extreme luxury and wealth, such as prevailed among the pre-Christian Roman aristocracy or the plutocracy of modern times, were then unknown. We see this exemplified in the feudal castles which were manifestly built not for luxury and comfort, but for protection—affording a strong contrast with the palatial manor-house of the post-Reformation period.

Besides, the barriers between the noble and servile classes were not altogether insuperable. Even a serf could by notable merit rise to the rank of the nobility. Add to this that the highest offices in the Church were always open to men of every rank ; and the Christian principles of charity, brotherhood and personal equality were then very living and real forces securing a large measure of real union among all.

Land Fairly Well Distributed.—Again, the feudal system secured a tolerably fair distribution of the land and made impossible the concentration of uncultivated ranches in the hands of wealthy owners, which is one of the worst abuses of the modern land system. Every territorial lord had to furnish a number of warriors proportioned to the extent of the lands he held. These he procured by making grants of land within his domain to a sufficient number of vassals. If the fiefs or holdings were too large, the requisite number of warriors could not be supplied. In the same way it was necessary for each feudal lord to have on his estate a sufficient number of labourers, for a manor was practically self-contained, in which everything the community needed had to be provided. And as the wage system was then unknown, at least for agricultural workers, the lord secured the needed workers by retaining a large body of agricultural labourers who, besides owning and working each his own cottier farm, did their share in cultivating the domain lands of the lord of the soil.

Horrors of War Moderated.—Finally, although the horrors of war were not unknown, war in those ages had redeeming features which religious faith and practice gave. In the first place, the only recognised motives of engaging in war were those of religion or justice. The modern Machiavellian principles of political expediency were still publicly reprobated ; and although hypocrisy and ambition did of course exist, the buccaneer type of military adventurer, devoid of religion and conscience, which we meet in the 16th and 17th centuries was then practically unknown. The awful trade wars of those and of later times were scarcely possible with the public opinion which then reigned in Christendom.

Order of Chivalry.—The influence of Christian principles over warring princes and even over freebooters is well illustrated by the institution of *Chivalry* as a kind of religious brotherhood, and by the *Truce of God*. The institution of Chivalry was one of the principal methods adopted by the Church to humanise the fierce Teutonic warriors and fashion their principles and habits to the requirements of justice and charity. A feudal soldier was not regarded as a fully-approved warrior till he was formally received into the ranks of knighthood. The knighthood was the great object of every young soldier's ambition. Although the privilege was normally confined to men of the feudal caste, individuals of a lower degree were not unfrequently raised to the knighthood, and thereby to the ranks of the nobility, as a reward for outstanding merit.

The knights formed a kind of religious brotherhood. A worthy knight, according to the ideals then taught, must show proof not merely of military prowess, but also of loyalty, Christian courtesy, charity and kindness to the weak. The Church shared in the ceremonial of conferring knighthood and thus gave its blessing to the warlike profession, when carried on in the spirit which the knightly character symbolised. The aspirant to knighthood prepared beforehand by Confession, Holy Communion, fasting, a vigil of prayer, and a symbolical bath to remind him of the purity of soul he should always preserve.

At his installation he bound himself by vow to use his weapons chiefly in defence of religion and for the protection of the weak and defenceless, especially women and orphans. In the ceremonial he was invested with a white robe to impress on him the need of keeping his conscience pure. The priest presented him with his knightly equipment and weapons one by one to the accompaniment of liturgical prayers.

All this illustrates the tendency of mediæval chivalry. Christian courtesy and kindness to all, truthfulness, honour and uprightness in social relations, justice and fair play even in dealing with an enemy, fearless self-sacrifice, were held up as the characteristics of the true Christian knight, battling for right and justice, with the blessing and under the sanction of the Church. The ideal, of course, was not often realised in its fulness, but the fact that multitudes, perhaps the majority, aspired towards it, must have had a profound effect upon the manners and character of the men and women of the time.

The Crusades.—The nature and ideals of Christian chivalry are perhaps illustrated most strikingly in the history of the Crusades. These wars were inspired by religious zeal. Notwithstanding the lamentable incidents by which their history is sometimes disfigured, and the individual cases of selfish ambition or foolish vanity which are met with all too frequently, it still remains true that the driving force behind the Crusades was the loftiest and purest idealism. Love of the Redeemer and the desire to rescue from the power of the unbeliever the places which had been consecrated by association with Him were the main forces that succeeded more than once in mobilising, amid the greatest religious enthusiasm, nearly the whole military resources of Europe against the enemies of the Church.

Godfrey of Bouillon, Bertrand of Guescelin, Tancred of Normandy, Richard Cœur de Lion and St. Louis were all real types, though, of course, types of the best kind. The age that produced men of that character in their thousands and tens of thousands amid all the violence of war ; and the social and military ideals that could make it possible for a young man of the lofty character and high principles of Francis of Assisi to seek after Christian perfection in the profession of arms, are something unique in the chequered history of Europe. It is from the Christian ideal of the true knight that the warlike profession still borrows whatever lustre is attached to it. The chivalry and mercy and sense of honour still often displayed amid the horrors of modern warfare are echoes of the principles and ideals of the rough warriors of mediæval Europe.

The Truce of God.—The *Truce of God* and the obligations of the *Peace of God* illustrate the same theme. The legislation of the Peace of God began long before the period of which we are treating. By this law persons dedicated to God (such as clerics, monks, and nuns), as well as churches, cemeteries and other consecrated places, were privileged and regarded as sacrosanct and inviolable at all times, under penalty of excommunication. It was also forbidden by the same law and under the same sanction to carry on warlike operations on Sundays and holydays. The protection of the Peace of God was gradually extended to pilgrims, to crusaders, and even to merchants on a journey ; and the obligation was ordinarily observed.

The Truce of God took its rise early in the 11th century amid an epidemic of private wars. It was the remedy put forward by the Church against the lawlessness, violence and private revenge which the lay authorities were unable to prevent. Certain days in every week, namely, from Wednesday evening till Monday morning, and long periods of the year, roughly corresponding to Lent, Advent, and the Paschal season, were by ecclesiastical law privileged or sacrosanct, so that no act of violent aggression, on the part either of private individuals or public authority, whether justifiable or not in itself, was lawful during these periods.

" Although," says Balmes, " the Truce was apparently only a testimony of respect paid to religion by the violent passions which in her favour consented to suspend hostilities, it was really a triumph of right over might, and one of the most admirable devices ever used to improve the manners of a barbarous people. The man who for four days of the week, and during long periods of the year was compelled to suspend the exercise of force was necessarily led to more gentle manners : he must in the end completely renounce it."[1]

The truce of God was universally enforced and substantially observed during the period of the Crusades.

Art. 2—*The Agricultural Class*[2]

Serfdom.—Prior to the rise of the towns the great bulk of the people of mediæval Europe (with the exception of a few small nations such as the Irish and the Basques) were agricultural serfs. As already stated, slavery had almost disappeared before the end of the 10th century and had given way to serfdom. Serfdom implies a condition intermediary between slavery and freedom ; and according to the different customs of various countries, and the varying grades of serfs in the same country, or the same manor, it approached more nearly to one extreme or the other.[3]

Its Origin.—As to the origin of serfdom, all agree that in France, Spain, and to a lesser extent in Britain, it developed from Roman slavery.[4] The gangs of rural slaves that cultivated the lands of the old Roman villas gradually acquired privileges and rights owing to the influence of

---

[1] *Op. cit.*, p. 150,

[2] Cf. Brownlow, *op. cit.* ; Allard—*Origines du Servage en France*, and *Esclaves, Serfs et Mainmortables ;* Seebohm—*English Village Community*, chaps. i, ii, iii, vi, vii ; Fustel de Coulanges—*Origin of Property in Land*, translated from the original French by Mrs. Ashley (4th edit., Allen and Unwin, London, 1927) ; Ashley—*English Economic History*, vol. i, chap. i ; Belloc—*The Servile State ;* Bland, Brown and Tawney—*English Economic History and Theory* (Select Documents), part i, sec. iv ; Robinson—*Readings in European History*, vol. i, chap. xviii, nn. 157–160 ; Husslein—*Democratic Industry*, chaps. v to x ; Palgrave—*Dict. of Political Economy*, arts. " Serf," " Services Predial and Military," " Servus " and " Villanus." Lecky—*History of European Morals*, vol. ii, pp. 61–72 ; Hallam—*Middle Ages*, vol. i, chap. ii ; *Cath. Encyclop.*—arts. " Labour and Labour Legislation " (pp. 720–722) ; " Slavery," " Land Tenure." *Dict. Apolog. de la Foi Cath.*—arts. " Esclavage " and " Droit de Seigneur." K. Digby—*Mores Catholici or Ages of Faith*, vols. i and ii.

[3] The term *serf* is merely a variant of the Latin word *servus*, slave. The alternative term *villein* comes from the Latin *villanus*, belonging to the villa or manor.

[4] Cf. Allard, *op. cit.*

Christian practice and teaching, and thus in course of time attained a status which was far superior to anything that could be properly termed slavery.

Whether the same process of development took place among the Teutonic nations is disputed. One school of historians put forward an opposite theory. They say that the earlier Teutonic communities held lands in common according to what these historians call the German " marc " system. In this system the cultivators were free-men and had from time immemorial certain indefeasible rights in the soil. During the centuries of continual wars, however, these free cultivators lost their privileges and fell almost completely under the control of the military chiefs. As a result, their position got assimilated after a time to that of the quasi-servile agricultural population on the Roman villas.

This theory, which is put forward by the German scholars, is rejected by Fustel de Coulanges[1] and other French historians and by some modern English writers, especially by Seebohm,[2] Ashley,[3] and Belloc.[4] These hold that mediæval serfdom in all countries was, in the main, a development of earlier slavery.[5] It is very improbable and contrary to the ordinary course of development, as known from uncontroverted history, that the state of any large section of the community should in Christian times deteriorate from freedom to partial slavery. It is true indeed that many free landowners, anxious to secure the protection of feudal chiefs during the centuries of turmoil, did here and there, under pressure of necessity, accept conditions which practically reduced them to the position of serfs. But that this occurred in the case of a large percentage of the population is very improbable. Hence it seems more likely that the vast bulk of the mediæval serfs

---

[1] *Op. cit.* In this classical work the writer seems to prove conclusively that there is no solid historical foundation for the German theory propounded by Mourer, Waitz, Brunner and others according to which the primitive Teutonic agricultural workers were freemen who owned the soil on a system of village communism. Cf. also Ryan—*Distributive Justice*, chap. ii.

[2] *Op. cit.*, chap. ix.

[3] Cf. *loc. cit.*, pp. 13 ff and the Introduction to the work of Coulanges, just referred to.

[4] Cf. *Catholic Encyclopedia*—arts. " Feudalism " and " Land Tenure."

[5] Cf. Brownlow, *op. cit.*, and the *Month*, 1891, pp. 537, 538.

of all European countries were the descendants of rural slaves.

The Mediæval Manor.—Whatever theory one holds as to the origin and development of serfdom in the various countries of Europe, the main facts which alone directly concern us are certain. More than three-fourths of the whole population of feudal Europe in the 11th century were serfs. Almost all the territory was divided out into large manors or villas, varying in extent, each ruled by a feudal lord. The lord dwelt in the baronial castle and was supported by the labour of the serfs, whose dwellings were usually gathered together in a village on the manor lands. These latter were partly domain lands, in the immediate ownership (*dominium*) of the lord himself, partly allotments held and cultivated by the serfs.

The amount held by each serf varied in different manors, or in accordance with the hereditary grade of the holder. In Britain the average amount was about thirty statute acres. Each holding consisted of numerous strips scattered about the great open fields of the manor, intermingled with the strips of the other serfs and of the lord himself.[1]   Of the whole manor land, the domain land usually amounted to about one-third or two-fifths, while the remaining two-thirds or three-fifths were held in villeinage by the serfs. Besides the divided lands there were usually some pasture and forest and different kinds of waste lands shared in common by all.

Obligations of the Serf.—The serf " was bound to the soil." He could not, without the lord's consent, migrate from the land he cultivated. Neither could he marry—at least he could not take a wife from outside the manor—without the lord's consent. Further, he usually could not, in default of direct heirs, dispose of his property at his death. It passed to the lord. The serf's rent was paid partly in kind and partly in personal services. Principal among the latter was a certain number of days' work on the domain—usually two or three in the week, with additional days at special seasons, such as ploughing time and harvest.[2] The rent

---

[1] For a minute description of a manor, cf. Robinson, *op. cit.*, pp. 399–405
[2] Cf. Palgrave, *op. cit.*, " Services."

paid in kind was sometimes fairly considerable ; not infrequently it was merely nominal, such as a few eggs at Easter time. All the produce of the domain lands belonged to the lord, though a daily wage in kind was allowed to the serf for his days of service. In many cases the lord had claims also to what was called the " heriot." This was a certain portion of the serf's property, such as the best animal or the best implement on the farm, which had to be handed over to the lord at the serf's decease before his son succeeded to the holding.

Seeing that the mediæval manor was almost wholly self-contained, everything needed being produced on the estate, the serf population included, besides the ordinary agricultural workers, artisans in all the necessary crafts. Each of these had certain specified duties and clearly-defined rights, all of which were determined by immemorial custom.

His Rights and Privileges.—Hence, even though the serf was in legal theory a slave, his actual position and privileges were far removed from those of slavery. All his essential family rights were secure. Given that the due services were fulfilled, he was his own master, and, within the limitations already implied, he was complete owner of his own farm and of whatever other property he might acquire. " The serf of the early Middle Ages," writes H. Belloc, " of the 11th and early 12th centuries, of the Crusades and the Norman Conquest, is already nearly a peasant. . . . It is easy and common for the members of the serf class to enter the professions and the Church or to go wild, to become men practically free in the growing industries of the towns." [1]

The rent or the services due to the lord could not be increased by the latter with the increased value of the holding, even though the enhanced value was in no way due to the serf's labour. Besides all this, the serf's right to the lands he held was indefeasible. He could not be evicted ; nor could his land or his working capital be distrained for debt. In addition to his land he had several very important claims on the communal lands of the manor, such as free grazing rights, forest rights, fishing rights, turbary rights, the use of waterways, of water-power, etc.

---

[1] *Op. cit.*, p. 47.

All these rights and the amount of each serf's and of the lord's own participation in them were regulated minutely by custom, and could not be altered by the lord. Hence, although in legal fiction the lord was considered the owner of the whole manor and of all the property upon it, his rights were in practice strictly limited ; and he was compelled to respect the privileges even of the lowest serf of the manor.

The Gradual Improvement of his Status.—The serfs on the immense ecclesiastical estates were treated with peculiar liberality in the matter of rights and services. This fact gradually influenced the status of the whole serf population ; so that for this reason and owing to the general tendency of Christian influence in favour of the poorer classes, the position of the serfs continued to improve steadily as long as the Church's influence prevailed. " With every passing generation," again writes Belloc, " the ancient servile conception of the labourer's status grows more and more dim, and the courts and the practice of society treat him more and more as a man strictly bound to certain dues and certain periodical labour within his industrial unit, but in all other respects free. As the civilisation of the Middle Ages develops . . . . the character of freedom becomes more marked."[1]

The French Companies.—A very interesting type of serf and peasant organisation, which was fairly common in parts of Europe, notably in France, during the Middle Ages, and which persevered in some places even to the 18th century, was that of *Companies* (*copani*). A certain number of serfs, not necessarily of the same kindred, formed a group or corporation, holding and tilling their lands in common. They also held in common much of the movable property on the land, such as the cattle, implements of agriculture, etc. They shared in common the services due to the lord, and supported themselves and their families from the common store of produce.[2] Besides the rights in the communal

---

[1] *Op. cit.*, pp. 47, 48.
[2] Hence the name *Company* (*panis*, bread ; *cum*, together), which etymologically means sharers in a common board.

5

property each one also had or could have his own private property. This consisted of the property he possessed before joining the association, and the personal gains that accrued to him later. Each, too, retained his independent responsibility for his own family. The association had a chief, usually elected, who was the head of the corporative administration. The chief regulated the laws of purchase and sale ; and decided each family's proper share in the common profits.

Among the many advantages of such corporate association was the obvious one that since a corporation does not die with the death of individual members, there is no danger of the lands held by these associated fraternities reverting to the lord in case of the failure of male heirs, nor was there any liability to the payment of the heriot. From many indications it is clear that these rural associations were amongst the most prosperous of the French peasant communities down to the 17th and 18th centuries.[1]

General Estimate of the Serf's Social Condition.—The mediæval serf enjoyed all his essential human rights ; and the more serious of the disabilities which he inherited from previous generations were gradually ameliorated under the Church's influence. In matters of security and provision for all essential needs he was far better off than the modern unprotected agricultural labourer or industrial employee. In contrast with the latter the serf had definite claims on the protection of the lord whose own interests were closely bound up with those of his serfs. He had his permanent home and farm from which he could not be evicted. The services toward the lord to which he was bound were probably much lighter than the rents exacted from very many free tenants in modern times, and could not be compared with the rents and services imposed upon the Irish peasants from the 17th to the 19th centuries. " The villeins," writes Ashley, " were indeed tied to the soil, but the soil was also

---

[1] Cf. Allard—*Esclaves, Serfs, et Mainmortables*, chap. xvii. The organisation of these co-operative communities reminds one of the interesting and partly successful experiment in rural communal organisation which was made in Co. Clare, Ireland, in the early half of the 19th century. Cf. Connolly—*Labour in Ireland*, chap. xi, and *An Irish Commune: History of Ralahine* (Dublin, 1917).

tied to them. No very great accession of wealth was possible
to them, but, on the other hand, they always had land upon
which they could live—and live, except in very occasional
seasons of famine, in rude plenty."[1]

Besides all this the mediæval serf lived amid all the consolations of an intensely religious society. If for any reason
poverty or misfortune came his way, religious institutions
of all kinds were within reach where help and consolation
could be found.[2] "Was it not better," writes K. Digby,
"to be one of the people then than to be so now in the
19th century [propertyless, unprotected and isolated] . . .
The serf held to something. A moral tie attached him to
the family of his master, to the castle whose old towers
protected him as they had protected his fathers ; to the
church at whose door he had assumed all the dignity of a
man and of a Christian, and which offered him an inviolable
asylum against the powers of the world. Around him all
was animated. His habits, his labours, his privations, his
perils were all connected with ideas in which he had faith
and for which he would have gladly died. . . . There was
then a unity of feeling, and even of taste, and a community
of enjoyments among the high and the low."[3]

Abolition of Serfdom.—We cannot follow in detail the
history of the improvements which took place in Catholic
times in the position of serfs, and shall cite only a few of the
outstanding facts connected with the principal countries
of Europe. In England under Edward I, in the second
half of the 13th century, most of the serfs, who at the time
of the Domesday Survey of 1086 comprised nearly four-
fifths of the whole recorded population,[4] got the privilege

---

[1] Cf. Ashley, *op. cit.*, pp. 17 and 53.
[2] *Mores Catholici*, vol. i, chap. ii, p. 25.
[3] *Op. cit.*, chap. i, p. 40. For proof and illustration of the same theme,
cf. Thorold Roger's *Six Centuries of Work and Wages*, chap. ii (15th edit.,
Fisher Unwin, London, 1923).
[4] Cf. Louis Veuillot—*Le Droit de Seigneur du Moyen Age* (Paris, 1878),
for an examination and refutation of calumnies concerning certain supposed mediæval customs and fabulous seignorial rights enjoyed by feudal
lords. These legends, which have their origin in anti-Catholic propaganda
in England and France in the 17th and following centuries, still find some
credence in these countries. Thus Canon Sheehan in " *The Queen's Fillet* "
utilises the legend of the French peasant compelled to spend the night in
a lake or pond to prevent the frogs croaking lest the lord's sleep be disturbed. Cf. also *Dict. Apol. de la Foi Catholique*—art. " Droit du Seigneur."

of commuting for a yearly money payment the most burdensome of their personal services to the lords. In the 14th century their condition was still further improved. Serfdom had practically disappeared from England before the 16th century. Of the Church's share in this transformation Macaulay writes : " Moral causes noiselessly effaced first the distinction between Norman and Saxon, and then the distinction between master and slave. It would be unjust not to acknowledge that the chief agent in these two great deliverances, the greatest and most salutary social revolutions that have taken place in England, was religion. . . . The benevolent spirit of the Christian morality is undoubtedly adverse to distinctions of caste. But to the Church of Rome such distinctions are peculiarly odious." [1]

In France serfdom was first abolished in Normandy and the other Northern provinces. In these it had mostly disappeared in the 12th century. The main emancipation was effected over the whole country before the beginning of the 14th century. The feudal rents, however, and some other payments to which the peasants were still bound, as well as a certain amount of obligatory labour on the roads, continued on to the period of the Revolution (1789). In Italy and the portion of the Spanish Peninsula that had been reconquered from the Moors, the process of liberating the serfs, which began in the 10th century, was practically completed before the beginning of the 15th century. In none of these countries was serfdom afterwards re-established.

Serfdom Under Non-Catholic Influences.—In Germany, on the other hand, as well as in Denmark and Sweden, the movement of enfranchisement, which had commenced somewhat later than in the Latin countries but was nearing completion before the rise of Protestantism, was checked in the 16th century, so that in the end of the century the position of the serfs was worse than before. This deterioration was the result of the Peasants' Revolt and of the

---

[1] *History of England*, vol. i, chap. i, pp. 22, 23. The statement of Hallam, who is followed by Lecky and other non-Catholic writers, that the liberation of the serfs on the Church lands was the last to be brought about and was opposed to Church law, is contrary to fact. Thus in the German States, the serfs on the ecclesiastical estates were the first to be enfranchised. Cf. *Dict. de la Foi Catholique*—art. " Esclavage," v. 2°.

new spirit introduced by Protestantism.[1] Serfdom was not finally abolished in Baden till 1783, nor in Prussia till 1809. It lingered on in Saxony and some other parts of Protestant Germany till 1832 or later, and in Denmark till 1804.

Serfdom continued longest of all in Russia. There the small farmers and other free peasants got gradually identified with the slaves, and all formed one class of serfs. From these the Tzar, Boris Gondulf (1598–1605), took away the right of migration. The position of the serfs once tied to the soil got gradually worse. They lost the right even of permanent homes ; and the power of the owner to sell them apart from the land became recognised late in the 17th century. A peasant revolt was suppressed ; and it was not till after the Crimean war (1856) that a real movement of emancipation began, which ended in the final abolition of serfdom in 1861.[2]

Conclusion.—The history of slavery and serfdom, and the gradual process of emancipation, which took place under Christian guidance, point unmistakably to the conclusion that the influence of the Catholic Church in every country tends strongly towards the freedom and well-being of the weaker members of the community. When that influence is withdrawn, the general trend of development inclines in the opposite direction.

Art. 3—*The Industrial Workers*[3]

Origin and Development of the Mediæval Cities.—Most of the old Roman towns suffered eclipse or were totally destroyed during the barbarian invasions. Hence between the 5th and the 10th centuries there was comparatively little town life in Europe. The early history of the great

---

[1] Cf. *Dict. de la Foi Catholique, loc. cit.*, p. 1504 ; and Brownlow, *loc. cit.*, pp. 540–545.

[2] Cf. Walsh, S.J.—*The Fall of the Russian Empire*, chap. ii (The Blue Ribbon Books, New York, 7th edit., 1931),

[3] Cf. Husslein—*Democratic Industry*, chaps. ix–xxiii ; Pastor—*History of the Popes*, vol. v, pp. 52 ff ; Gasquet—*Eve of the Reformation*, chap. xi ; Ashley—*English Economic History*, vol. i, part i, chap. ii, and part ii, chaps. i and ii ; Bland, Brown, and Tawney—*English Economic History* (Select Documents), part i, secs. v and vi ; Robinson—*Readings in European History*, vol. i, chap. xviii, nn. 161–165 ; *Historical and Municipal Documents, Ireland*, 1172–1320 (Rolls Series) ; Martin-Saint-Leon—

mediæval towns, most of which rose into prominence after the 11th century, is involved in obscurity. Some, especially in Italy and Germany, could trace their history back to the times of the early Roman Empire. Most, however, date only from the mediæval epoch. Of these many owed their origin to the monasteries which gradually became centres of population, or to the great Christian shrines which attracted ever-increasing crowds of pilgrims. Some resulted from the coalescence of several villages in a populous district. Others, again, developed from the forts erected by the military chiefs, round which families originally gathered for protection and safety. Not a few, especially in Italy and Northern Europe, grew up in the 10th and 11th centuries as centres of oversea trade, as did the Irish cities of Galway, Dublin and Limerick four centuries later.

For a long time agriculture must have been the main occupation of the inhabitants of the towns, who were still mostly in the position of serfs, under the neighbouring feudal chiefs. Agricultural produce was the principal or the only commodity of local trade. For this purpose markets were established under the protection of the lord. As time went on foreign traders began to bring their wares to these markets to be exchanged with the people of the neighbourhood for local produce. Heavy tolls were exacted by the feudal lords in return for their protection, and in virtue of their claims as lords of the soil.

As the towns and villages grew in size and importance and the inhabitants became better organised, they found the interference of the feudal lords burdensome ; and a movement for emancipation arose. In the 12th century this movement began to spread throughout all the countries of Europe. In some places the burghers openly revolted

---

Histoire des Corporations ; Madame Sabatier—*L'Eglise et le Travail Manuel* ; Levasseur—*Histoire des Classes Ouvrières en France ;* Janssen—*History of the German People at the Close of the Middle Ages* (Mitchell's translation), Book iii, chaps. ii and iii ; *Letters on Social History* (C. S. Guild), pp. 39–79 ; Walsh, *op. cit.*, chaps. xxi and xxiv ; *Cath. Encyclop.*, chap. vii, pp. 66–72— art. " Guilds " ; *Encyclop. Britt.*, vol. vii, p. 784—art. " Commune (Mediæval) " ; Brown—*The Achievement of the Middle Ages*, chap. p. 141 ff ; Shields—*The Evolution of Industrial Organisation* (London, 1931, 2nd edit.), chap. i. Some English non-Catholic writers usually *minimise* or *altogether ignore* the essential part played by the Church in the organisation and working of the guilds.

against the authority of the feudal rulers. As a result charters of liberty were granted, sometimes by the lord of the soil, sometimes by the king or Emperor. The charter, which was a kind of written contract between the lord or prince, on the one hand, and the commune or town merchants' organisation, on the other, served as a kind of legal certificate of the birth of the town, more or less defining its independent constitution.[1] The charters usually comprehended all dwelling within the precincts of the town, so that if a serf had for any reason lived in the town for a specified time—usually about a year—he became by that fact freed from the lord's control.

Origin of the Guilds.—The history of the social conditions of the townspeople centres round the associations or guilds in which they were organised. Even earlier than the period with which we are dealing, and long before the issue of town charters, there existed in the villages what were called *Peace Associations* or *Frith Guilds*.[2] The object of these associations was to maintain the public peace and to safeguard the person, property, and reputation of the members, for in those days the power of the governing authority, whether baron, tribal chief, or king, was usually quite insufficient for these purposes.

The religious element, however, had also a very prominent place among the activities of the Frith Guilds. Thus, provision was usually made in the guild regulations for the giving of alms by each individual of the association, for the celebration of Masses in aid of the soul of a lately deceased member ; for assisting and entertaining pious pilgrims, etc. These characteristics re-appear in the great Merchant and Craft Guilds that arose in the 12th century, with which we are principally concerned here.

With the rise of the great Merchant Guilds the history of urban life in the Middle Ages really begins. As to the origin of these great free associations historians are not in agreement. Some historians regard them as developments of the Frith Guilds. Others trace them back to the trade unions of ancient Rome (*Collegia Opificum*). Others, again,

---

[1] Cf. Robinson, *loc. cit.*, nn. 161–163 ; also Bland, Brown and Tawney, *loc. cit.*

[2] Cf. Husslein, *op. cit.*, chaps. ix and x.

derive them from the East. Many writers, however, with
perhaps more probability, seek no other explanation of their
origin than Christian influence and teaching as applied to
the circumstances of mediæval society. These hold as at
least very probable that the whole guild organisation
developed from the religious confraternities, which were
directly organised by the Church. Whatever theory one
may adopt as to the origin of the mediæval guilds, there
can be no doubt that it was the Church that impressed
upon them those marvellous Christian characteristics which
essentially distinguish them from every similar organisation
known to history.

Their Essentially Christian and Democratic Character.—
The *Livre des Metiers* of Etienne Boileau, Provost of Paris
in the reign of St. Louis of France (*d.* 1245), and the
numerous records of English and German mediæval town
life, including the charters of several guilds, reveal to
us the structure and character of the guild organisation.
Of that organisation an outstanding characteristic was the
spirit of true Christian democracy that permeated it through
and through. Here we find the highest conception of the
dignity of labour and the nearest approach hitherto made
to real democratic control of industry.

From these guilds developed the whole municipal organisation of the mediæval towns. Some of these towns, such
as the great cities of Northern Italy, grew into independent
republics ; while others, as in Flanders and Northern
Germany, became free cities with practical independence.
Furthermore, in most European countries it was through
the municipal communes which developed from the guilds
that the people were first represented in the national
government.

The Merchant Guilds.—The mediæval guilds were of two
types—viz., the Merchant Guild (or the " Guild Merchant "
as it was sometimes called) and the Craft Guild. The
Merchant Guild belonged to the earlier period, and attained
its highest development in England in the 12th century.
It was a union of the original townspeople more or less
emancipated from the control of the feudal lord and owning
some property within the town area. It was by means of

those unions that the burghers in the earlier stages of town development wrested their full emancipation from the feudal lords ; and then organised themselves for urban government and administration.

The Merchant Guild was in its original conception a labour union, for in those days every " merchant " was a craftsman who manufactured his own wares and sold directly to the consumer. In the guild all the town craftsmen, including at first practically all the inhabitants, were banded together for the common good. The principal objects of their union were to safeguard their privileges, to secure that no stranger should interfere with local trade nor any individual among themselves monopolise more than his fair share. Mutual assistance in almost all the details of life entered into the objects of the guild. Above all it was confessedly organised upon a religious basis and religious principles dominated all its activities.[1]

The Craft Guilds.—As the towns grew and trade and commerce increased the Merchant Guilds tended to degenerate into close oligarchies of comparatively wealthy traders, jealous of their privileges, and desirous to exclude others from them. This led to the formation by the poorer traders of the *Craft Guilds*, which began before the end of the 12th century. The members of each craft or trade organised themselves into separate associations more or less on the model of the original Merchant Guilds, but each association being confined to persons engaged in the same craft. For some time both types existed side by side ; but by the 14th century the Merchant Guilds had disappeared or had become identified with the central municipal government of the town. In the 14th century the Craft Guilds were at the height of their power in all the countries of Europe. It is in them that the mediæval spirit of Christian association is best exemplified.

The first Craft Guild to be formed in a town was usually a guild of weavers. It was these weavers' guilds that led the way in the contest of the poorer traders with the older Merchant Guilds. Soon we find guilds of butchers, of

---

[1] *Ib.*, chaps. xi–xiv.   Cf. also Gasquet, *loc. cit.*

bakers, of tailors, of leather-dressers, of dyers, of spurriers, of helmet-makers, etc. A town might have fifty or more different guilds. Just as the original Merchant Guild included, or was meant to include, all the traders of the town, so each Craft Guild aimed at gathering into itself all persons engaged in any way in the particular craft.

Their Relation to the Municipal Authority.—For the foundation of a guild a charter had to be obtained from the sovereign or the municipal authorities of the town. This charter of foundation usually conferred such extensive powers on the guild that the latter might be almost described as a kind of petty republic, subordinate indeed to the municipal government, but possessing very extensive control over its own members and over all matters pertaining to the trade or business of the guild. Each guild was in fact a kind of industrial fief organised on a democratic and religious basis, holding from the central municipal authority, which itself may be regarded, or in reality was, a fief of the sovereign. Hence by a natural process the municipal government itself was to a large extent in the hands of the guild authorities, or rather was a kind of imperial union made up of the different guilds as petty subordinate states. It was the guilds that in practice selected the municipal officials, furnished the town police, and carried on the whole municipal administration.

Their Wealth and Independence.—The Guilds were usually wealthy and powerful corporations. As a rule each guild had its own hall, its own hospital, its own chapel, its special emblems, its particular banner, its distinctive uniform. In the magnificent civic displays in which that age delighted, the guilds took a leading part and spared no expense. The principal sources of their revenues were :—(a) The annual subscriptions of the members, which were graduated according to the means of each. (b) The entrance fees paid by apprentices, assistants and masters. (c) Fines. (d) Donations and bequests, which often included lands or houses given for the purposes of the guild or for some specific object within the guild's jurisdiction.[1]

---

[1] Cf. Gasquet, *op. cit.*, chap. xi, pp. 326, 327.

The Organisation of the Guild.—The members of a Craft Guild were divided into three grades or classes, namely Apprentices,[1] Journeymen[2] and Masters. To each grade belonged rights and duties peculiar to itself. At the head of the guild administration stood the *Governing Council*, which usually consisted of four persons, chosen annually from among the oldest and most trustworthy of the Masters.

The Governing Council.—These were the accredited representatives of the Guild Corporation. They appointed the subordinate officials, administered the finances, and controlled the whole executive of the organisation. They watched over the interests of each member of the guild and were the official guardians of the apprentices. They were not paid. At the end of their term of office, they had to give an account of their administration before an assembly of masters.[3]

The guild authorities regulated the wages of journeymen, the hours of work, the conditions of purchasing raw material, and of marketing the produce ; and the prices at which the latter was to be sold. They arranged the numbers of apprentices and of journeymen that each individual master might employ and the duration and conditions of apprenticeship. They took measures to guard against fraud on the part of their members and to secure good workmanship.

The Apprentices.—The interests of the apprentices were well provided for. The period of apprenticeship was usually seven years. During that time the apprentice lived in the master's house as a member of the family and on terms of social equality. The master was bound to protect and exercise parental control over the apprentice committed to his care. He was responsible for his moral and religious conduct, as well as for his professional training. The master's duties and responsibilities in this regard were of a very solemn and serious kind. If he failed in his duties the guild authorities quickly intervened on the apprentice's

---

[1] From the French word *Apprendre*, to learn.
[2] From the French word *Journée*, day.
[3] Cf. Martin-Saint-Leon, *op. cit.*, pp. 83 ff.

behalf. The following extract from a guild document quoted by Janssen will convey some idea of the objects aimed at by the guilds in the training of the apprentices :

" No trade or profession can succeed honourably unless the apprentice is early taught to fear God and be obedient to his master, as if he were his father. He must morning and evening and during the week beg God for help and protection, for without God he can do nothing. . . . Every Sunday and holy day he must hear Mass and a sermon and read good books. He must be industrious and seek not his own glory but God. The honour of his master and of his trade he must also seek, for this is holy, and he may one day be a master himself, if God wills and he is worthy of it. . . . When the apprentice fails in obedience and the fear of God, he shall be punished, so that through the pain of the body, the soul may benefit." [1]

The Journeymen.—The apprenticeship completed, the young man sometimes became a master-craftsman immediately, with his own establishment and his own apprentices. More usually, however, he had to serve some years as an assistant or *Journeyman*. In the 14th century this was made compulsory, so that by guild law every craftsman had to serve a term of assistantship before he could be enrolled by the guild authorities as a master. The journeyman chose his own master with whom he arranged the terms of service. Like the apprentice, he usually lived as a member of the master's household. He often married the master's daughter, and thus became a permanent member of the family. The journeyman, though not eligible for the official positions of the guild, had a voice in the administration and in the election of the masters, and a share in all the ordinary privileges of the guild.

The Masters.—Higher than the journeyman in grade of dignity was the *Master*. The Master had his own establishment, either as his father's successor or otherwise. At that time it required no great capital to start an independent business ; and the guild was usually ready to advance money for the purpose on easy terms to a deserving member. But to be enrolled as a master other conditions were required.

---

[1] *Op. cit.*, book iii, chap. ii, p. 20.

The candidate had to be a practising Catholic. He was required to present satisfactory testimonials from the masters under whom he served as apprentice and journeyman. It was necessary besides to pass a satisfactory professional test. This usually took the shape of presenting what was termed a " masterpiece " of his own handiwork. Lastly, he had to pay a fee and in the presence of the council to take an oath promising fidelity to all the obligations of the association.[1]

Social and Economic Policy of the Guilds.—The general policy of guild law common to both Merchant and Craft Guilds, was that while each individual member was left free within certain limits to pursue his own interests as he thought best, the common interests of the whole trade were considered paramount. Hence every member was bound to submit, in the interests of the common good, to certain general regulations which limited his freedom. He was also bound to come to the assistance of his fellow-members when required.[2]

The guild regulations were aimed at preventing an undue absorption of the trade by any individual ; at checking profiteering (which was known as *Regrating*), trusts, or monopolies, and all commercial practices which savoured of excessive selfishness. Thus if a person attempted to " corner " some particular product by making excessively large purchases, he was compelled to share such materials at cost price with any guildman that might require them.[3] Again, no one was allowed to take part in any work that did not belong to his own craft. Separate unions of masters and journeymen were forbidden. To such an extent did the altruistic spirit prevail that in some places—as for instance at Florence—when a member was considered unduly wealthy he was bound to give his surplus wealth to the guild.[4]

Industrial Protection and Control.—Protection was a prominent feature of the economic policy of the guilds. Accord-

---

[1] Cf. Antoine, *op. cit.*, chap. xiv, art. 3. For some account of the Dublin Guilds, cf. Shields, *op. cit.*
[2] Cf. Ashley, *op. cit.*, part i, p. 74.
[3] Cf. Husslein, *op. cit.*, chap. xii.
[4] Cf. Belliot—*Manuel de Sociologie Cath.*, p. 32.

ing to the mediæval guild doctrine the natives of the place
had the first claim on local resources and trade. Hence
outsiders were excluded in so far as their interference or
competition might prevent the town traders from earning
a proper livelihood.

We have already referred to the doctrine of the Just
Price, on the strength of which the guild authorities fixed
the prices of products as well as of labour. The objects
aimed at were to secure a proper wage for the manufacturer
and at the same time to safeguard the interests of the
consumer. Thus every guildman (which practically meant
every worker of the town) was enabled to earn a fair living ;
and the weak were protected from the effects of unfettered
competition, in which they might be so far worsted as to
be deprived of the means of supporting life. If an individual had special ability or skill he was to employ it
not in accumulating a large fortune, but in producing for
the market the most perfect articles of workmanship.[1]
This policy promoted efficient workmanship. The artisan
had a great pride in his profession and usually a great
ambition to excel. Hence that age produced the greatest
triumphs of handicraft.

The guild regulations also aimed at securing the common
good of the town. The high standard of public spirit which
the guilds displayed was due partly to the Christian principles which then dominated social relations, and partly
to the democratic character of the community. The power
of one guild was kept in due check by the others, who could
retaliate on any association that acted unfairly. Hence
the guilds legislated to prevent scarcity on the one hand,
and over-production on the other.

They took efficient measures through their bailiffs and
inspectors to secure good workmanship in all the articles
produced by the craftsmen, as well as a high standard of
honesty and fair dealing. Their records contain numerous
instances of heavy fines being imposed for dishonestly
dyeing wool, for mixing bad wool with good, for selling at
more than the fixed price, etc.[2] Guild inspectors constantly
visited the merchants in their homes or workshops to ensure

---

[1] Cf. Husslein, *op. cit.*, chap. xi.
[2] Cf. Ashley, *loc. cit.*, p. 75 ; also Husslein, *op. cit.*, chap. xv.

that all things were honestly done. Members were sometimes expelled from the guild for repeated violations of honesty.

The Pervading Spirit of Charity.—The greatest spirit of solidarity and mutual help animated the whole guild organisation. Thus money was advanced on easy terms to members who needed it. Those suffering from sickness, old age, accidents, etc., were liberally provided for. Even a guildman who might get into trouble with the municipal or state authorities had a right to the protection of the guild. If, after investigation by the council, his case was considered a deserving one he was defended in the courts at the common expense. Sick members were visited ; and wine and food were sent from the public banquets to those whom illness or weakness prevented from attending. The dead, if the family was poor, were buried at the expense of their guild with all the honours befitting their position, and their daughters dowered for marriage or the convent.[1]

The Religious Character of the Guilds.—Another peculiarly Christian characteristic of these guilds was their practical recognition of the intimate connection of religion with commercial relations and with all the activities of life. Although the primary object of the associations was economic, the guilds made every effort to secure good conduct and fidelity to religious duties on the part of the members. Individuals were punished or sometimes expelled from the guilds for immoral or irreligious conduct.

Every guild was under the protection of a patron saint or was specially dedicated to the Holy Trinity or to the Blessed Mother of God under one of her titles. The portrait of the guild patron was painted on the banner of the guild which was borne in the public processions. Thus the guild of wood-workers was commonly under the protection of St. Joseph. The shoemakers usually had on their banner paintings of SS. Crispin and Crispinian. Bakers were often under the patronage of St. Honorius, and so on. The association of the heavenly patron with the trade that belonged to the guild intensified the craftsmen's pride in their work and the men's esteem for the nobility of manual

---

[1] Cf. Ashley, *loc. cit.*, p. 76.

labour. The Church Feast of the patron was always the occasion of the great annual banquet of the guild.

Many guilds had their own special chapels ; and we commonly find provision made in the guild statutes for the support of a chaplain and sometimes of several chaplains. Some of the most beautiful of the mediæval churches belonged to or were built by the guilds. Provision was also regularly made for the celebration of Masses for the intentions of the guild, and for the offering of candles at holy shrines. On the death of a member care was taken to have Masses offered and alms given for his eternal rest. Almsgiving, which was practised even towards the poor outside the guild, was an important item of the ordinary guild expenditure. Oftentimes a guild gave feasts in its buildings to the poor of the whole town.[1]

Destruction of the Guilds.—In the 15th century, owing to the spread of the spirit of the Renaissance, more or less unchristian, the guilds began to lose their religious character and to decline in utility and influence. After the Protestant Revolt of the 16th century they gradually developed into exclusive corporations of wealthy traders. In England, at the Reformation period, the religious confraternities that were attached to the guilds were suppressed as being superstitious associations, and most of the corporate property of the guilds was confiscated. When the supervision of the Church was withdrawn the guilds soon lost their Christian character as well as their social significance. In France, under the despotic rule of the French kings after the 15th century, the guilds ceased to be a means of protection for the journeymen, who were then a majority of the members. These formed associations of their own, regardless of all professional or even religious distinction. Something similar took place in the other European countries about the same period or a little later. Hence the guilds, as far as they survived after the 16th century, had a scope and character different from the mediæval guilds which we have described. They were suppressed in France at the Revolution of 1789.

---

[1] Cf. Pastor—*History of the Popes*, vol. v, Introduction i, pp. 35 ff; Gasquet, *loc. cit.*, pp. 327 ff.

Can the Mediæval Guilds be Revived ?—Modern industrial conditions are very different in many respects from those of the mediæval town. The population is much larger ; intercommunication with foreign countries greater ; the State organisation more highly developed. Above all, the industrial unit of the great factory, worked by expensive machinery, is much more difficult to organise than the simple workshop of the mediæval craftsman. Hence a renewal of the mediæval guilds in the shape that they had assumed in the 12th and 13th centuries may not be practicable. But the principle of co-operation and democratic control tempered and guided by Christian influence, and elevated by religious practice which underlay the mediæval organisation of industry, are always applicable ; and in a return to these principles lies the only real solution of the present " Social Question." Such a solution is quite feasible in a Catholic country, under a government animated by Christian principles and aided by the co-operation of the Church.[1]

[1] Leo XIII—*Rerum Novarum*, 1891, pp. 142–144 ; *Graves de Communi*, 1901, pp. 166, 177-179 ; Pius XI—*Ubi Arcano*, 1922, pp. 240-248, also *Quas Primas*, 1925, and *Quadragesimo Anno*, 1931, *passim*, especially pp. 36–44 (C. T. S. edit.). *See also infra*, chap. xv, art. 2 ; chap. xviii, art. 2 ; chap. xx, art. 6.

6

CHAPTER VIII

SOCIAL RESULTS OF PROTESTANTISM

Art. 1—*Introductory*

Summary of the Preceding.—In the foregoing chapters we have attempted to convey some idea of the effects upon social life of Christian as contrasted with non-Christian principles and methods.

The latter, which rest upon egoism and the glorification of brute force, held undisputed sway in Europe during the early centuries of the Roman Empire and were again partially re-established after the Teutonic conquests of the fifth and following centuries. In both cases they resulted in the oppression, pauperisation, or degradation of the weaker members of society, especially women, the poor, and slaves. On the other hand, the Christian régime which prevailed to a considerable extent over the Roman Empire immediately before the Teutonic invasions, and was gradually restored and perfected during the Middle Ages, secures respect for human dignity and protection for the personal rights of every member of society, even the poorest and weakest, and an effectual recognition in social relations of the essential brotherhood of men. Under the Christian régime, justice and charity are practised and co-operation and mutual help promoted ; so that every member of the community is usually attached to some organised body from which he can, when need requires, claim protection and assistance.

Hence mediæval society, notwithstanding its many short-comings, was on the whole the best the world had hitherto known. In that society there were protection and security for the poor and weak, and, as a rule, tolerable material conditions for all. Substantial happiness and contentment prevailed, the consolations of religion making up for many material hardships. The ideal of human brotherhood was in practice substantially realised, and there existed a sympathetic union between the different social classes ;

at least all of these traits are to be found in the mediæval Christian society in a larger measure than Europe had ever previously known or has experienced since.

End of Catholic Régime.—The change from the Christian régime first began to be seriously felt in the 15th century. After the capture of Constantinople by the Turks, in the year 1453, Greek scholars crowded into Italy, France and Germany, bringing with them the treasures of classical literature and art, which they had rescued from the fallen city. The sudden spread of pagan Greek learning and culture, combined with debased pagan ideals masquerading as " humanism," together with an unprecedented accession of wealth, consequent upon the discovery of the New World and the opening up of the maritime routes to the Far East, tended to produce a great deterioration of morals, especially among the leisured and privileged classes. All this combined with other causes already touched upon[1] prepared the way for the great catastrophe of the 16th century, commonly called the Protestant Reformation. This marks the turning point at which the history of modern Europe begins.

The New Phase in Social Conditions.—As a result of this fatal upheaval the unity of Christendom was broken and large portions of Europe were detached from the ancient faith. At the same time the influence of the Church was so seriously weakened, even in countries that remained Catholic, that non-Christian principles were gradually reintroduced into political and social life ; and many of the character-istics of the old pagan régime began to reappear.

Prominent among these characteristics are the absolutism of the government, whether the latter be a monarchy or a so-called democratic body ; an ever-growing tendency to bring domestic life under the despotic control of the secularist State ; a practical disregard for the human dignity and independence of a person who is without property or power ; a revival of the old pagan conception of the absolute rights of ownership in disregard of its responsibilities and duties ; the gradual disappearance of communal property and of the co-operative social organisations which did so

---

[1] Cf. *Supra,* chap. iv at end.

much under the Christian régime to safeguard the interests of the poor. Among the results of all this have been the concentration of the material resources of the nation under the control of a few individuals, and the practical enslavement and degradation of the unpropertied masses, with the consequent reappearance of the fierce antagonism between rich and poor.

Leo XIII, writing of modern errors and revolutionary movements, traces the great evils of modern life to the Protestant Revolt of the 16th century :

" Those venomous teachings [viz., the principles of the Protestant Reformers] like pernicious seed scattered far and wide among the nations have produced in course of time death-bearing fruit. . . . Deriving pretentiously its name from reason, this false doctrine . . . has pervaded the whole of civilised society. Hence . . . governments have been organised without God or His divinely established order being taken into account. It has even been contended that public authority . . . originates not from God, but from the mass of the people which, considering itself unfettered by all divine sanction, refuses to submit to any laws that it has not passed of its own free will. . . . The very Author and Redeemer of mankind has been forced slowly and gradually to withdraw from the scheme of studies at universities, colleges and high schools, as well as from all the practical working of public life. . . . The keen longing after happiness has been narrowed down to the range of the present life. . . . No wonder that tranquillity no longer prevails in public or private life, or that the human race has been hurried onward well nigh to the verge of ruin." [1]

Division of the Subject.—In order to convey an adequate idea of the effects upon social life of the 16th century revolt, we shall first sketch briefly the course of events by which Protestantism secured a firm foothold in Northern Europe, and then indicate under a few main headings, the most notable changes in political and social life, that followed as a direct result from the Protestant revolt. We shall next discuss the social and economic theories of unchristian Liberalism, which was the logical outcome of Protestant teaching. As modern capitalism has borrowed its ultra individualistic character from Protestant and Liberal principles we shall treat briefly of it and the deplorable social

---

[1] *Quod Apostolici Muneris*, 1878, pp. 13–14.

Predates the Prot. Revolt by 2 cent. and may be one of the causes of Prot. spreading in Society.

one of the results of modern capitalism

conditions which have resulted from it. We shall then discuss Socialism, which is at bottom merely a new phase of Liberalism, though differing from it in its economic doctrines. In a supplementary chapter we shall strive to show how all the anti-Christian and anti-social elements of modern society are more or less concentrated in, or rather are represented by, the doctrines and tendencies of an aggressive world wide organisation born of Protestantism and repeatedly condemned by the Vicar of Christ, viz., Freemasonry. After discussing briefly the main headings of the social evils resulting from all those modern doctrines and movements, we shall conclude our historical sketch with a short review of the Catholic social movement which has now spread into almost every country of Europe and America and aims at the re-establishment of Christian principles in political and social life.

Art. 2—*Rise and Spread of Protestantism*[1]

Its Beginnings.—Protestantism began in Germany. The main driving force behind the movement there as elsewhere was not religion, but personal ambition or avarice or lust or all these motives combined. The leader of the movement was Martin Luther, an apostate Augustinian friar, of remarkable ability, unbridled passions and boundless ambition. Luther launched the revolt against the Church on October 31st, 1517, when he posted his celebrated Ninety-five Theses on the church door at Wittenberg.

The Name Protestant.—The name *Protestant* is derived from the *Protest* presented by the German Lutheran princes at the Diet of the Holy Roman Empire, held at Speyer in the year 1529. In this protest they rejected and condemned as unjust and impious the imperial decree first promulgated at the Diet of Worms five years before, and now again renewed at Speyer, which prohibited the princes from forcing the new religion upon those of their subjects that

---

[1] Pastor—*History of the Popes* (English translation), vols. ix–xiii ; MacCaffrey—*History of the Church from the Renaissance to the French Revolution,* 2 vols (Gill, Dublin, 1915) ; Mourret—*Histoire Générale de l'Eglise,* vol. v (La Renaissance et la Reforme) ; Janssen—*History of the German People* (Mitchell's translation) ; Belloc—*How the Reformation Happened* (Cape, London, 1928).

wished to adhere to the old faith. The name was originally used to designate only the protesting princes, but it was gradually extended to include all the adherents of the new religion, whether Lutheran, Anglican, Calvinistic, or belonging to any one of the numberless sects into which Protestantism gradually broke up. The name has been accepted by Protestants themselves ; and is appropriate in so far as it is closely associated, both historically and etymologically, with opposition to Catholicism. For disagreement with Catholic doctrine and practice, and especially with the teaching authority and governing power of the Church, is practically the only point upon which all Protestants are at one.[1]

Nature of Protestantism.—Protestantism, as a system of religious practice and belief, is vague and indefinite, which it needs must be, when every man is constituted the ultimate arbiter of his own obligations and the deciding authority in regard to the truths of faith which he may reject or accept. For this tenet, which is called *the Right of Private Judgment*, is a fundamental principle in Protestantism. The system may be loosely described as resting on, or centering round three standard principles. These are as follows :

(a) The Bible, as interpreted by each individual for himself, is the sole rule of faith, Christian tradition being thus rejected.

(b) Man is justified by faith alone, so that good works are useless for salvation or merit.

(c) As a result of the foregoing principles, there is no room for a divinely-constituted priesthood, or hierarchy. For, since every man is his own supreme teacher, and is able to sanctify himself by an easy act of faith or trust in God without the aid of sacrament or sacrifice, the priesthood, if retained at all, is not to be considered an essential part of Church organisation.

These principles, however, were never fully accepted by all Protestants. In fact, the first, which confers on all the

---

[1] Hence the declaration of faith made by the King of England at his coronation : " I declare that I am a faithful Protestant," is in practice meant to convey only this meaning. Nobody pretends to define positively what a " faithful Protestant " means except that it is inconsistent with being a Catholic.

right of private judgment in religious matters, manifestly
excludes the possibility of a consistent system of practice
or belief.   The proclamation and propagation of the new
principles, however, attained the desired object of destroying
the authority and organisation of the Church over large
portions of Christendom.

Rapid Spread of Protestantism.—Within little more than
half a century from the commencement of Luther's revolt,
Protestantism had definitely gained the upper hand in
central and northern Germany, also in Holland, Denmark,
Scandinavia, and in a great part of Switzerland, as well as
in England and Scotland.   The new religion had also made
great progress in Austria, Bavaria, and other portions of
Germany, as well as in Hungary, Bohemia and Poland.
The fate of France, in which the Huguenots, a strong aggressive faction of fanatical Calvinists, were in open rebellion
against the king, was hanging in the balance.   Ireland,
where most of the Irish princes and Anglo-Irish barons, as
well as very many leading ecclesiastics had, as in England,
accepted the usurped ecclesiastical supremacy of the English
king, was also in imminent peril of being lost to the faith.[1]
Even in Italy and Spain the subversive movement had made
no little headway.

Its Causes.—The rapid progress of the new religion was
partially due to real abuses in the discipline and administration of the Church.   These abuses had existed for a considerable time ; and for more than a century before Luther's
time, all sincere Catholics had been striving in vain to
bring about a thorough reform of the Church in its head
and members.   Many of the clergy of all ranks were leading
very worldly lives.   Money was often extorted from the
people in unjustifiable ways or to an unreasonable extent.
Neglect of the sacraments was widespread in many places.
    The principal cause, however, of the rapid spread of the
revolt was the methods adopted by the innovators, whose
real aim was the complete overthrow of the Church, and

---

[1] Cf. Ronan—*The Reformation in Dublin*, 1536–1558 (Longmans, London,
1926) ; also *The Reformation Under Elizabeth*, 1536–1580 (Longmans,
London, 1930).

who mobilised in support of their movement all the worst instincts of men. In their code of morals they deliberately pandered to the most depraved human passions. Sin, according to the new doctrine, presented no obstacle to eternal salvation. Pride, lust, avarice, injustice, cruelty and the rest, were to be healed or covered over by an easy act of trust in God. The Lutheran doctrine rejecting the utility of good works was carried still further by Calvin,[1] according to whose teaching men are predestined to heaven or hell without any account being taken of their actions ; for in the Calvinistic doctrine the human will is not free, and so men's actions are not worthy either of reward or punishment.

Besides the strong appeal to men's depraved passions which such doctrines contained, many other inducements were held out to draw the people away from the ancient religion. " The immense fortune of the Church [the Patrimony of the Poor] was now to be the prize of apostasy ; political and religious independence allured the kings and princes ; the abolition of tithes, Confession, fasting, and other irksome obligations attracted the masses. Many persons were deceived into the new religion by outward appearances of Catholicism, which the innovators carefully maintained as in England and the Scandinavian kingdoms." [2]

Amongst the people that were not depraved, Protestantism made progress only as a result of deception or under pressure of coercive force. From the very beginning the innovators, after the example of the Mohammedans nearly a thousand years before, propagated the new religion with " the Bible in one hand and the sword in the other." Over the whole of Christendom, from Switzerland in the south, to Scotland and Scandinavia in the north, fierce and bloody wars were stirred up, which continued to desolate Europe for more than a hundred years. The long drawn-out civil wars in Germany (terminated only in 1649 by the Peace of Westphalia), the fierce struggle in the Netherlands

---

[1] The Protestants of Switzerland, Holland and Scotland are Calvinistic. So, too, were the Presbyterian planters of the north-eastern counties of Ireland and the original founders of most of the New England States of America. Even the Protestant church established by law in Ireland (" The Church of Ireland," as it was called) was and remained predominantly Calvinistic at heart.

[2] Cf. Cath. Encyclop., vol. xii, p. 449 (b).

between Philip II and the revolted provinces, the Huguenot
wars in France were but different acts in the long and terrible
drama. The fierceness and implacable cruelty which characterised the Tudor and Puritan conquests of Ireland,
during which about two-thirds of the population were cut
off by famine and the sword ; [1] and the oppression, robbery
and persecutions that followed borrowed much of their
intensity from the same religious hatred and fanaticism.

The progress of the new faith was thus marked almost
everywhere by a trail of desolation and blood, the material
effects of which (we shall speak later of the appalling deterioration of morals) weighed heavily on several countries
of Europe during the two succeeding centuries.

Turning of the Tide.—We have said that Protestantism
made very rapid progress during half a century or more
after the beginning of Luther's revolt, so that at one time
the Church would seem to be imperilled in almost every
country of Christendom. The early violence of the movement, however, did not last ; and the storm gradually began
to subside. Before the beginning of the last quarter of the
sixteenth century, the tide had definitely turned in favour
of the ancient faith ; and within the next fifty years the
Church had not only consolidated its position, but had regained much of the ground that had been lost.

One of the causes of the change was no doubt the
bitter dissensions and numberless divisions among the Protestants themselves ; but the root cause of the Catholic
recovery was the real reform which was wrought in the
discipline and administration of the Church. The inspiring
force in this counter Reformation was the work of the great
Council of Trent (1545–1563). A decisive element in carrying out the work of reform were the labours of the Society
of Jesus which was founded in 1540.

Austria, Bavaria, and the other portions of Southern and
Western Germany that were endangered, as well as Hungary

---

[1] The population of Ireland before the Tudor Wars is generally estimated
at about two millions. According to a census made in 1659 (viz., after
the Elizabethan and Puritan wars in Ireland) the population was 500,091
(Cf. O'Brien—*Economic History of Ireland in the 17th Century*, pp. 122–123,
also p. 12). According, however, to Sir W. Petty's estimate made in
1672, the Catholic population at that time (which would roughly correspond to the whole native population to the exclusion of the British
settlers that were introduced after the wars) was about 800,000,

and Poland, were thus substantially saved to the Church. Heresy was stamped out in Spain and Italy through the activities of the Inquisition. Spain's zealous championship of Catholicism did much to check the aggressive policy of the revolted states and strengthen Catholic resistance. The power of Calvinism was broken in France after a series of destructive civil wars which desolated the country for more than thirty years (1562–1598).

Saving of Ireland.—Ireland was saved to the Church partly as a result of the preaching and labours of the Franciscan Friars. Another important factor in the work was the coming of Father D. Wolfe, S.J., who arrived in the country as Papal Delegate in 1560 and succeeded in selecting worthy candidates for the vacant Episcopal Sees. Later on came the labours of the Jesuit Fathers who established a permanent mission in Ireland in 1598. Two other important elements in deciding the religious crisis in Ireland were the exceptional strength among the ordinary people of the Irish Catholic tradition and the long drawn-out struggle of the Geraldine wars. The dominant issue in the latter was the religious question. James Fitzmaurice, the Irish Catholic leader, with whom Fr. Wolfe was in close intimacy, was directly supported by the Pope and the King of Spain. These wars, and the war of the Irish Northern princes which succeeded it, by clearing the issues, forced the trimmers and the faint-hearted, whether Irish or Anglo-Irish, to espouse openly one side or the other ; and, although the Catholic Irish were beaten to the dust in the military contest, the war proved one of the most important elements in saving the country to the Church.

During the first quarter of the seventeenth century ecclesiastical seminaries for the training of Irish students were opened on the Continent, several of them having been endowed by the King of Spain. The constant supply of zealous and well-trained priests from these seminaries during the 17th and 18th centuries made the position of the Church in Ireland practically secure. The preservation of the faith in Ireland, which hung for many years in the balance, has had far-reaching consequences not only in the country itself but on the position of Catholicism in the whole modern world.

Art. 3—*Direct Consequences of the Protestant Revolt*[1]

Protestant View.—While historians of all schools generally admit that Protestantism produced results of immense importance on European society, they are not in agreement as to what these results actually were. Protestant historians generally strive to hold up the Protestant Revolt against the Church, not only as just and necessary in itself, but as the harbinger of numberless social blessings for the European races. They assume almost as a truism that Protestantism did, and by its very nature must, lead not only to a higher and purer moral life among the people, but to democratic freedom, increased intellectual activity resulting in great scientific progress, and, above all, to economic prosperity and a wider diffusion of material comfort and well-being. In discussing the truth of this view one may examine the character of the new forces which the Protestant Revolt set in motion, and infer what their effects must needs be ; and, again, the facts themselves as actually recorded in history may be summarised and weighed in the balance. In our brief discussion of the question in which both these methods will be utilised, we hope to show that no part of the Protestant view can be historically proved ; and that the greater portion of it is at variance with well-established historical facts.

Repudiation of Christian Principles and its Results.—The obligations of the Christian religion cover the whole range of a man's activities, extending even to his inward thoughts and the motives and springs of his actions. Baptism implies, as it were, a new creation which elevates the soul to a higher sphere. All the activities of the baptised Christian, and especially his domestic and social relations, which in Christian teaching hold a position of paramount importance, are expected to be in harmony with his new dignity as the adopted child of God. Hence it happened, as we have already seen, that when the nations were con-

---

[1] Cf. Baudrillart—*The Catholic Church, the Renaissance and Protestantism,* chaps. viii–x ; Balmes—*European Civilisation ;* Janssen, *op. cit.* ; O'Brien— *An Essay on the Economic Effects of the Reformation ;* Cobbett—*History of the Protestant Reformation ;* Pastor—*History of the Popes,* vol. x ; Mourret— *Histoire Générale de l'Eglise,* tome v (La Renaissance et la Reforme) ; Tawney—*Religion and the Rise of Capitalism* (London, 1926).

verted to Christianity the whole character of society gradually underwent a profound change in proportion as the domestic and civil life of the people became attuned to Christian ideals. " Religion became intimately bound up with the social life of the people animating it and penetrating it at every point " ;[1] so that the whole network of social relations and practices was built upon the foundations of Christianity. A repudiation of Christianity would thus lead necessarily to an upheaval affecting the very groundwork of society. Now, Protestantism, while not professing to reject Christianity, did repudiate several of its fundamental principles.

Repudiation of the Church's Doctrines.—The " Reformers " denied the value of good works and the transforming effect of sanctifying grace on the soul. They denied, too, the existence of an organised spiritual power independent of the State, with authority to take cognisance of all the activities of men, and even of their inmost thoughts and desires ; and to punish injustice and wrong. Hence, Confession was abolished, and all spiritual penalties and sanctions removed. The usurer, the fraudulent dealer, the oppressor of the poor had no longer to appear before the inexorable tribunal, from which there is no escape, of a divinely founded Church endowed by God with power to admonish, to judge and to condemn. The criminal was now his own admonitor and judge, except when he came formally within the coercive power of the civil law, which too often he could easily evade.

Where, as in England, the Protestant leaders did not formally reject the principle of a Christian hierarchy, they deprived that order of its influence on social life by confining its activities and authority to the sphere of public worship. Besides all this, their teaching tended to restrict the functions of Our Divine Lord to those of a Redeemer, so that He was no longer held up, at least to the same extent as before, as the Teacher and Model of men. In contrast with the old traditional ideals of Christianity, religious obligations were thus almost entirely confined to the duties of worship and prayer, and had little or no influence upon political and social life.

---

[1] Gasquet—*Eve of the Reformation*, chap. xiii, p. 393.

And of its Moral Code.—Having repudiated the teaching authority of the Church, round which all Christian practice and belief had previously centred, Protestant rulers and people were left to the vagaries of their own unaided judgment and the uncertain impulses of human prejudice and passion. Their moral code ceased to be a definite legal system covering all the activities of life. It became instead a set of more or less vague philosophical maxims and principles in the application of which every man was his own teacher and judge. One can easily understand how such a far-reaching revolt against traditional principles produced consequences of the first magnitude upon the political, economic and social life of European society. On this subject the Protestant author, Ingram, writes :

" It must be admitted that with the whole modern movement serious moral [or social] evils were almost necessarily connected. The general discipline which the Middle Ages had sought to institute, and had partly succeeded in establishing . . . having broken down, the sentiment of duty was weakened along with the spirit of *ensemble* [viz., the tendency towards mutual co-operation] which is its natural ally, and individualism in doctrine tended to encourage egoism in action. In the economic field this result is specially conspicuous. National selfishness and private cupidity increasingly dominate ; and the higher and lower industrial classes tend to separation and even to mutual hostility."[1]

These results were not confined to the revolted provinces. The " Reformation " weakened the Church's power as a social and civilising force even in the countries that remained faithful. This occurred, partly as a result of the fatal spread of the spirit of revolt through most of Europe during the early half of the 16th century, partly through the standing example of the new social ideals adopted in the Protestant countries, partly also by directing into the field of religious controversy the energies by which a united Church had during the Middle Ages built up a Christian civilisation in Europe.

Protestantism and Democratic Freedom.—The assertion that Protestantism has introduced into Europe, or promoted, democratic freedom or real liberty of conscience is still more

---

[1] *History of Political Economy*, chap. iv, p. 34 (Dublin, 1888).

patently untrue. It is a fact, indeed, that at the beginning of the revolt Luther's professions were radically democratic. He promised to benefit the people at large by curtailing the power of both Church and State. But he and his followers ended up by supporting an irresponsible despotism such as Europe had not known since the days of the pagan Emperors of Rome.

Incited by Luther's democratic professions and his denunciations of the " tyranny and oppression " of the rulers, the knights and lesser nobility of many of the German States, and, later on, the peasants rose in open revolt against the princes. When the revolution was crushed in blood (1525) the victorious princes, now without a rival, and no longer kept in check by the moderating influence of the Catholic Church, used their augmented power to establish a despotism which they exercised for their own personal advantage, in opposition to the interests of the people ; while Luther, with unscrupulous inconsistency, now proclaimed the doctrine of the unlimited power of rulers.

Soon even the Church in the Protestant States fell completely under the control of the ruling princes, who were thus established as absolute masters of both Church and State. The wealth of the Church, which hitherto had been the patrimony of the poor ; its authority ; all the ecclesiastical institutions, including hospitals, schools, homes of refuge, etc., passed into the hands of the kings, princes, and the town magistrates. At the Peace of Augsburg (1555), which ended the first phase of the revolution in Germany, the principle was formally adopted that the prince of each state was free to dictate the religion of each and all of his subjects.[1]

The example of the German princes was not lost upon the other European rulers. Within less than a century the principle of despotic and more or less irresponsible government had permeated almost every country in Europe, even those in which the religious tenets of Protestantism had made little progress. Hence, in the 17th century the King of France, equally with the King of England, claimed to

---

[1] This principle was expressed in the celebrated formula, *Cuius regio eius religio*. " The religion of a particular place is in the control of him who owns (or governs) that place."

rule by right divine, and, therefore to hold authority as limitless as that of God, whose plenipotentiary he was. The celebrated principle of Louis XIV, " *L'Etat c'est moi* " (I am the State), is only a logical inference from the principles of the Protestant reformers a century before.[1] We have already spoken of the effects of the Protestant Reformation upon the position of the serfs in Germany and the other European countries in which their liberation had not been completed before the " Reformation " had begun. Not only was any further amelioration delayed for centuries, but in most places the serfs lost, as an outcome of Protestantism, most of the privileges they had previously enjoyed.

The religious intolerance of Protestant Germany was imitated, or improved upon, in the other revolted countries— in Denmark, Sweden, Norway and England, and still more decidedly in the countries where Calvanism was established, such as Switzerland, Holland and Scotland. In each and all of these countries, though with varying degrees of severity, penal measures were enforced against all the dissenters from the State religion. In Ireland and England, under the Tudors and the Puritans, the most ferocious of all the penal codes were enacted against Catholics and others who were unwilling to conform to the established religion.

Protestantism and Intellectual Progress.—The assertion commonly made by Protestant writers that Protestantism stimulated intellectual activity and led to intensified scientific and literary progress is not true, or at least cannot be proved. It is true indeed that the physical sciences which correspond to one important phase of intellectual activity, have made remarkable progress among the European nations during the past four centuries, as the higher mental and moral sciences did during the preceding

---

[1] Cf. Bossuet—*La Politique tirée des Propres Paroles de l'Ecriture Sainte* : " As in God are united all perfections and every virtue, so all the power of all the individuals in a community is united in the person of the king "— cited in Carlton Hayes's *History of Modern Europe*, vol. i, p. 236. *See also* MacCaffrey, *op. cit.*, vol. i, chap. vii. In England after the 17th century, this false doctrine of the Divine Right of Kings gave way to the Divine Right of Parliament. On the whole question of the Catholic Origin of Democracy and the Protestant origin of modern Statolatry and bureaucratic tyranny, cf. Professor A. O'Rahilly's articles in *Studies* (1919–1921) already referred to (chap. v, p. 34).

four ; and that some great literature has been produced in Protestant countries, and even by Protestant writers. It is true also that some few nations, notably England and Holland, grew immensely in wealth and power during or after the 16th century, and that the beginning of their rise to greatness practically coincided with the change of religion. But it cannot be shown that the change promoted any one of these results.[1]

In the first place it cannot be shown that the intellectual achievements of Europe since the 16th century are on the whole greater, or even as great as those of the preceding four hundred years. If they have been greater in the field of physical science, they have been much less in the higher plane of philosophy, theology and mysticism. Again, most of the masterpieces of European literature, notably those of the Italian, Spanish and French writers, belong to the Catholic nations, and very many are of direct Catholic inspiration. Even the English Shakespeare, if not a Catholic, owes a good deal of his inspiration to purely Catholic ideals, and little or nothing to Protestantism. This applies still more decidedly to the great masterpieces of architecture, sculpture and painting. Since the rise of Christianity most of the great works of art have been directly inspired by the Catholic religion, or have been accomplished under Church patronage. Under Protestantism, art has, on the whole, not flourished, and it is commonly recognised that the loss of the Catholic faith by a nation is followed by a gradual deterioration of the artistic sense among the people and a lessening of the love of beauty. Even as regards the scientific achievements of the post-Reformation period or of the Protestant nations, no sound argument can be adduced to show that any portion of the best work has been inspired by Protestantism, or owes its success to the Protestant Revolt.

Protestantism and Economic Progress.—The like is true, though not to the same extent, of economic progress in the Protestant countries. Such progress has not been confined to them, as the example of Belgium shows, and, besides, the Catholic districts of the Protestant countries are, on

---

[1] Cf. O'Brien, *op. cit.*, chap. i ; Baudrillart, *op. cit.*, chaps. ix and x.

the whole, as progressive as the Protestant ones.[1] The foundations of England's commercial greatness were laid by the discovery of the New World, before the nation became Protestant. The success was promoted by the people's spirit of initiative and self-reliance, which was largely the effect of the free political institutions and the system of decentralised government which the country enjoyed. These existed in England before the Reformation. If they survived it to a certain extent,[2] it was not without a long and bitter struggle. They had existed in Germany before Luther's time, but were crushed out, as we shall see, as a result of the " Reformation."

Besides all this, it cannot be assumed that increased wealth and imperial expansion necessarily imply economic betterment. Economic progress in the true sense cannot be considered apart from the temporal prosperity, or material well-being of the people.[3] How completely the increased wealth and imperial expansion of Britain and other Protestant countries have failed to promote the temporal prosperity of the people at large we shall show when dealing with the modern social question.

Art. 4—*Protestantism and Pauperism*

Results of the Plunder of the Church.—Not only is the Protestant Revolt mainly responsible for the unsocial character of Britain's economic system but it was the immediate cause of much of the degrading pauperism that has disfigured British civilisation for the past four centuries. We have already alluded to the plunder of the Church and the alienation of the revenues[4] devoted to charitable and educational purposes, which took place as a result of the religious revolt. This led directly to dreadful hardship in the case of the poor, to whose benefit most of the ecclesiastical revenues had previously been applied. The confiscated wealth, which according to the law under which the confiscations were carried out should have been devoted to

---

[1] Cf. Baudrillart, *op. cit.*, chap. x ; and O'Brien, *loc. cit.*
[2] On this subject, see H. Belloc's illuminating continuation of Lingard's *History of England.*
[3] Cf. Devas—*Political Economy*, chap. i and Epilogue.
[4] Chap. vii, art. 3, p. 8o.

7

the service of the State, was in very large measure appropriated by lawyers, court favourites and other greedy and avaricious adventurers. These henceforth formed a new class of wealthy and unscrupulous plutocrats who in the following centuries dominated the political and social life of their several countries. Nowhere did this robbery of Church goods produce such disastrous results as in Ireland and Britain. In both these countries the Protestant Reformation laid the foundations, secure and deep, of extreme individualistic capitalism, with its hideous counterpart of pauperism and oppression of the poor, which forms one of the chief characteristics of their social history during the following centuries.[1] On this aspect of the question, Cardinal Gasquet writes :

" Viewed in its social aspect the English Reformation was in reality the rising of the rich against the poor. . . . Those in place and power were enabled to grow greater in wealth and position, while those who had before but a small share of the good things of this world came in the process to have less. . . . The supposed purification . . . of doctrine and practice was brought about . . . at the cost of driving a wedge well into the heart of the nation, which . . . established the distinction which still exists between the classes and the masses."[2]

The history of this lamentable revolution in England, by which the whole face of a great Catholic nation became permanently disfigured, the great majority of her once happy children plunged in ever-increasing degradation and misery, and her ideals and principles conformed to a non-Christian instead of a Christian standard, is graphically told by the Protestant writer, Cobbett, in his *History of the Protestant Reformation*.[3] " Never," he writes, " since the world began was there so rich a harvest of plunder." He tells how gold and silver, books and manuscripts, ornaments, paintings and statuary of priceless value equally with

---

[1] Cf. H. Belloc—*The Servile State*, sec. iv ; Tawney, *op. cit.*, chaps. iii and iv.

[2] Preface to Cobbett's *History of the Reformation*, p. 6.

[3] This classical work, written during the years 1824–27, has been re-edited, with notes by Cardinal Gasquet. The few historical inaccuracies and exaggerations which had existed in the original are eliminated or corrected ; authorities are quoted, so as to make the book, with all its startling disclosures a standard historical work.

church, monastery and convent fell a prey to the satellites
of Henry VIII and Thomas Cromwell :

" The whole country was thus disfigured : it had the appearance of a land recently invaded by the most brutal barbarians ;
and this appearance it has . . . even to the present day. Nothing
has ever come to supply the place of what has been destroyed." [1]

Explaining the social effects of the plunder of the Church,
Cobbett writes :

" The Catholic Church included in itself a great deal more
than the business of teaching religion . . . and administering
the Sacraments. It had a great deal to do with the temporal
concerns of the people. It provided . . . for all the wants of
the poor and distressed. . . . It contained a great body of land
proprietors, whose revenues were distributed in various ways
amongst the people upon terms always singularly favourable to
the latter. It was a great and powerful estate, and naturally
siding with the people. . . . By its charity and its benevolence
towards its tenants it mitigated the rigour of proprietorship,
and held society together by the ties of religion rather than by
the trammels and terrors of the Law."[2]

Dissolution of the Monasteries.—The dissolution of the
monasteries, with the resulting confiscation of their property, immediately produced overwhelming distress amongst
the multitudes who had been maintained by the resources
that the religious bodies had administered. It proved
disastrous also to the tenants on the monastic lands, which
were probably more than 2,000,000 statute acres in extent.
The tenants who had been accustomed to an easy and
sympathetic mode of treatment at the hands of the monks,
now passed under the power of harsh and exacting landlords.
Rack-rents were too often exacted and the numerous exemptions and privileges to which the tenants had been
accustomed were withdrawn.

Enclosures and Confiscations.—Again, the common lands,
in which the poor of the neighbourhood had from
time immemorial possessed common rights, were seized

---

[1] Cobbett—*History of the Protestant Reformation in England and Ireland.*
Edited by Cardinal Gasquet (Art and Book Co., London, 1899), chap. vii,
n. 182.
[2] *Ib.*, chap. viii, n. 206.

and enclosed in the lords' demesnes ; and numberless other hardships, hitherto unknown, now began to press upon the people.

The wanton confiscation of the property of the guilds, hospitals and almshouses, unjust and indefensible even from the Protestant standpoint, was also disastrous to the interests of the poor. The destruction of the religious schools and colleges, in which so many children were educated free of cost, was still another blow. Even the introduction of a married clergy, which diverted into another channel the energies and resources that would otherwise be expended upon charity, aggravated further the lot of the poor.

Vagabondage in England.—Hence it was that the destruction of Catholicism in England gave rise to the sordid pauperism which has since disfigured English civilisation. Cobbett describes in his own eloquent and vigorous style how England, " once happy, and hospitable, became a den of famishing robbers and slaves." As a result of the plunder of the Church and the destruction of the institutions which had grown up under its influence, the country quickly became filled with the destitute. Immense numbers of these were driven to live as professional robbers. " There were," writes Hume, " at least 300 or 400 able-bodied vagabonds in every county who lived by theft and rapine, and who sometimes met in troops to the number of sixty and committed spoil on the inhabitants." [1] As many as five hundred of this expropriated class were sometimes executed in a single year during the reign of Elizabeth. [2]

English Poor Laws.—This state of affairs—a direct result of the Protestant revolt—gave rise to the celebrated Elizabethan legislation on pauperism, " as novel as it was harsh," [3] which for the first time standardised pauperism as distinct from poverty. The former was henceforth the status of those who, being destitute of the prime necessaries of life, are maintained at the public expense in the parish

---

[1] *History of England,* vol. ii, p. 591.
[2] Cf. Strype—*Annals of the Reformation* (2nd edit.), chap. vii, quoted in Cobbett, *op. cit.,* chap. xi, n. 331.
[3] Gasquet, *ib.*

poorhouses. They are no longer " God's poor," to whom as the special representatives of Him Who became poor for men's sake, special sympathy and even reverence are due. They are now despised outcasts, the pariahs of society. They usually live, or are supposed to live, in the poorhouses, segregated from their wives and children, under a harsh discipline, deprived of the franchise and compelled to wear a special uniform.[1]

The following extracts from Palgrave will convey a general idea of the spirit which animated the English post-Reformation legislation on mendicancy and poverty :

" It was only towards the middle and end of the 16th century that measures against it [viz., mendicancy] were enforced, possibly in part owing to the sounder (sic) teachings of the Reformers on the subject. Then we find Southampton ordering that beggars should have their hair cut, and Parliament decreeing punishments on a progressive scale of severity. Whipping, branding, cutting off the gristle of the ear, even death, were the penalties assigned (!) . . . A Consolidating Act of 1713 lays it down that any person wandering about the country, on any one of a long list of pretences, is to be summarily arrested and removed to his settlement, or, if he have none, to be dealt with by the poor law authorities of the parish in which he is apprehended ; but previously he may be flogged or set to hard labour, or committed for seven years to the custody of any person who will undertake to set him to work in Great Britain or the Colonies. By the Act of 1744 even women are to be flogged for vagrancy, and as late as 1824 flogging is retained as punishment for " incorrigible rogues."[2]

Such was the spirit introduced by Protestantism into the legislative system of a country that was once the " Dowry of Mary."

---

[1] Cf. Palgrave—*Dictionary of Political Economy*, vol. iii, art. " Poor Law," p. 154 ; also art. " Pauperism," p. 81 ; cf. also Thorold Rogers— *Six Centuries of Work and Wages* (Fisher Unwin, London, 14th edit., 1923), chap. xv, " The English Poor Law " ; Webb—*English Local Government—English Poor Law History* (Longmans, London, 1928), part i, chaps. i and ii. A departmental committee appointed by the Minister of Health for Great Britain states in its report (issued Aug. 13, 1930) that the treatment of the poor in the " casual wards " of some of the British workhouses " might fairly be described as infamous and intolerable " (cited in the Belfast *Irish News*, Aug. 14, 1930).

[2] *Op. cit.*, vol. ii, art. " Mendicity," p. 725, chap. iv, sec. iv.

Art. 5—*Protestantism and Morality*

Immediate Effects upon Morality.—The assumption that Protestantism brought a higher and purer moral life to the nations that came under its influence does not need elaborate refutation. It is a fact of uncontroverted history that " public morality did at once deteriorate to an appalling degree wherever Protestantism was introduced. Not to mention robberies of church goods, brutal treatment meted out to the clergy, secular and regular, who remained faithful, and the horrors of so many wars of religion," we have the express testimony of Luther himself and several other leaders of the revolt, such as Bucer and Melancthon, as to the evil effects of their teaching ; and this testimony is confirmed by contemporaries.[1] Luther's own avowals on this matter are numberless. Thus he writes :

" There is not one of our Evangelicals, who is not seven times worse than before he belonged to us, stealing the goods of others, lying, deceiving, eating, getting drunk, and indulging in every vice, as if he had not received the Holy Word. If we have been delivered from one spirit of evil, seven others worse than the first have come to take its place." [2]

And again :

" Men who live under the Gospel are more uncharitable, more irascible, more greedy, more avaricious than they were before as Papists."[3]

Even Erasmus, who had at first favoured Luther's movement, was soon disillusioned. Thus he writes :

" The New Gospel has at least the advantage of showing us a new race of men, haughty, impudent, cunning, blasphemous . . . quarrellers, seditious, furious, to whom I have, to say truth, so great an antipathy that if I knew a place in the world free of them, I would not hesitate to take refuge therein."[4]

These Effects not Temporary but Permanent.—That these evil effects of Protestantism were not merely temporary— the accidental results of the excitement and confusion which

---

[1] Cf. Janssen, *op. cit.*, vol. v, pp. 278 ff, and Baudrillart, *op. cit.*, chap. viii, where numerous quotations and references are given.

[2] Quoted in Baudrillart, *op. cit.*, p. 244, from Luther's works (edit. Walch, vol. vii, p. 2727).

[3] *Ib.* (edit. Walch, vol. xiii, p. 2193).

[4] *Ib.*, p. 233 (quoted from Erasmus, Ep. lxviii, p. 503).

are peculiar to a stage of transition (although they were no doubt intensified thereby)—is shown from present-day statistics. The condition of domestic morality is usually best indicated by the statistics of divorce, and of illegitimate births,[1] and by the proportion of legitimate children to the number of marriages ; while statistics of general criminality, where they can be had, would convey a fair idea of the individual and public morality in any given place. According to these tests Protestant countries are at the present day much inferior to Catholic countries in domestic and public morality.

Protestant and Catholic Countries Compared.—The following examples will help to illustrate this :

Italy, Spain and Ireland are perhaps the most Catholic countries of the world, while Britain, the United States of America, with Denmark and Scandinavia, are the most Protestant. Legalised divorce does not exist at all (1930–31) in any country of the former group. It exists in all the countries of the latter group ; and the number of divorces is increasing year by year. In England and Wales there were 3,740 divorces in 1928, being about one divorce to every 114 marriages. In the United States of America the number of divorces in 1916 was 112,031, being one divorce to every 10 marriages. Ten years later (viz., in 1926), the number of divorces reached the appalling total of 181,000, being about one to every seven marriages.[2] The statistics of illegitimate births tell a similar tale. Thus in 1927 the proportion of illegitimate births was 44 per 1,000 for England and Wales, and 29 per 1,000 for the Irish Free State.

Again, the Irish Free State has a very high proportion of births to marriages, one of the highest in Europe. England, where the birth-rate has now fallen to nearly 16 per 1,000, has the lowest birth-rate in the world as compared with the marriage rate. While all Catholic countries have a fairly high birth-rate, the birth-rate is so low in some Protestant or non-Catholic countries that the

---

[1] The argument from statistics of illegitimacy, although not without value, is not in itself conclusive.

[2] Cf. *Encyclopedia Brittanica* (14th edit., 1929), vol. vii, pp. 458, 459, also the *Registrar General's Statistical Review*, 1927.

human race there is hastening to extinction. This is in fact what has occurred to the original Protestant settlers in the New England States of America, who have practically disappeared, being in large measure supplanted by the Irish, the Canadians and others.

Exact statistics of criminality are difficult to obtain; and trustworthy comparisons between different countries are more difficult still. Anyone, however, who remembers the constant recurrence of the ceremony of presenting " white gloves " to the judges of the criminal courts in Ireland owing to the complete absence of criminal indictments a few years ago, when the country was in its normal state, and contrasts this fact with the records of the criminal courts of Great Britain and U.S.A. may draw his own conclusions.[1]

Conclusion.—It has been not inaptly said that " greed, robbery, oppression, rebellion, repression, wars, devastation, depredation, would be a fitting inscription on the tomb of early Protestantism."[2] We shall see that the later effects of the new religion, though not so violent or dramatic, have fulfilled the promise of its earlier years.

---

[1] Cf. on this subject : C. Owen—*King Crime* (Benn, London, 1931), for an account of the apalling prevalence of organised crime in U.S.A. The author calculates that out of the 120 millions of inhabitants in U.S.A. at least one million are actively engaged in crime or directly dependent for their livelihood on criminal activities. *See* also *infra*, chap. xvi, art. 3.

[2] Cf. *Cath. Encyclop.*, art. " Protestantism," p. 501.

CHAPTER IX

LIBERALISM[1]

Art. 1—*What is Liberalism?*

Meaning of the Term.—The terms Liberal and Liberalism, derived from the Latin word *liber* (*free*) mean etymologically such personal qualities or style of acting and thinking as may be thought worthy of a freeman. Thus we speak of a "liberal education," a "broad-minded liberal disposition," etc. In one of its derived meanings Liberalism may also denote a political system or tendency that is opposed to centralisation and absolutism. Liberalism in this sense may be worthy of praise, and has nothing in it opposed to Catholic principles. The champions of unchristian Liberalism frequently utilize these meanings of the term to confuse issues and obscure the real character of their policy.

The term is used here, however, in quite a different sense. Since the end of the 18th century the word Liberalism has been generally applied, as we apply it here, to denote those tendencies and principles in intellectual, religious, political and economic life, which imply a partial or total emancipation of man from the obligations of the supernatural order and even from the authority of God.

Liberalism is the direct outcome of Protestantism[2] of which its principles and policy may be regarded as the ripened fruit. It is the root cause of the evils comprised in what is usually styled the "Social Question"; and is at present the greatest obstacle to social prosperity and peace.

General Character of Unchristian Liberalism.—Unchristian Liberalism, or rather the movement which it embodies, is not unfrequently referred to, especially by French Catholic writers, as the *Revolution*. It is also sometimes called the

---

[1] Cf. *Cath. Encyclop.*, vol. ix, art. " Liberalism " ; and *Dict. Apologetique de la Foi Catholique*, vol. iii, art. " Liberalisme."
[2] Cf. *Supra*, chap. viii, art 1, for the words of Leo XIII. *See* also Leo XIII *Immortale Dei*, p. 56.

Anti-Christian Movement. It is in fact essentially revolutionary and anti-Christian, and has been repeatedly
condemned as such by the Holy See during the past two
centuries.[1] Resting on an assumption of man's innate independence of any authority or rule of conduct or belief
outside himself, Liberal teaching rejects or ignores the whole
supernatural order, including divine revelation, a divinely
instituted Church, and man's predestination to eternal life.
Without formally committing themselves to a positive
denial of God's existence or His possible claims on men in
their individual capacity, Liberals repudiate all divine
authority in public and social life, which, according to their
ideals should be organised and conducted as if God did not
exist ; much less will they take account of the teaching
of Our Divine Lord, or acknowledge the authority of the
Church which He has founded. Absolute and unlimited
freedom of thought, of religion, and of conscience ; unchecked freedom of speech and of the press, freedom in
political and social institutions is, according to the principles of unchristian Liberalism, man's inalienable right.

These principles, which, by their repudiation of divine
authority are in opposition even to the natural law, are
applied by Liberals to moral, political and economic life.
Modern systems of state-craft, of civic organisation, of international relations, etc., have been shaped largely under their
influence. Hence Liberalism tends strongly to reproduce
in society the most repulsive features of pagan civilisation.
Liberal tenets and the consequences to which they lead
are in fact more unnatural than those of the pagans who,
although worshipping false gods, acknowledge the claims of
religion.

Relation of Unchristian Liberalism to other Social Forces.
—One of the strongest driving forces behind the Liberalist
movement during the past two centuries has been Freemasonry, permeated and reinforced as it is by international
Judaism. Socialism, which is opposed to many of the
economic and political principles of Liberalism, is in harmony

---

[1] Cf. *Cath. Encyclop.* and *Dict. Apolog. de la Foi Catholique, loc. cit.* ;
also G. Michon—*Les Documents Pontificaux sur la Democratie et la Société
Moderne* (Paris, Les Editions Ridier, 7 Place St. Sulpice, 1927).

with it in its materialistic view of life, and in its assumption
of man's emancipation from a supernatural or divine law.
The political and economic doctrines which now prevail in
Italy, under the Fascist régime, are in some respects a
reaction against Liberalism.

The Catholic Church, with its hierarchical constitution,
and its God-given power of authoritative teaching, forms
the only effective barrier against the progress of Liberalism.
This fact has always been frankly recognised by the Liberal
leaders Voltaire's impious cry : *Ecrasez l'Infame* (" Crush
the infamous monster," viz., the Catholic Church), has been
re-echoed down to our own day by Voltaire's disciples, who
openly proclaim it their aim to " put out the lights of
Heaven," and who would fain believe that Catholic principles and authority are everywhere, even in Ireland, doomed
to the fate of " icebergs in warm water." The words of
Charles Bradlaugh (*d.* 1891), a professed atheist and one of
the founders of the present secularist or extreme Liberalist
movement in Britain, are equally significant :—" One element
of danger in Europe is the approach of the Roman Catholic
Church towards meddling in political life. . . . There is
danger to freedom of thought, to freedom of speech, to
freedom of action. The great struggle in this country
(England) will not be between Free thought and the Church
of England . . . but between Free thought and Rome." [1]

Division of Subject.—In order to convey a general but
connected idea of unchristian Liberalism which, like Protestantism, is often vague and somewhat intangible, par-
taking more of the nature of a spirit permeating modern
society than of a definite and consistent system of social
organisation and thought, we shall give a brief sketch first,
of intellectual Liberalism, usually called *Rationalism* or
Naturalism, which forms the philosophic ground-work of
the Liberal movement ; secondly, of political Liberalism or
Secularism upon whose principles the constitutions of most
modern states are modelled, and finally of economic
Liberalism, which reached its apogee in the 19th century,
and is closely allied with modern capitalism.

---

[1] Quoted in *Cath. Encyclop.* in art. " Secularism," from *C. Bradlaugh's
Speeches,* ii, p. 412.

Art. 2—*Rationalism or Naturalism*[1]

Origin of Modern Naturalism.—The spirit and tendency of the unchristian " Humanism " of the 15th century, and still more the principle put forward by the 16th century Reformers that every individual has the right of interpreting divine revelation according to his own judgment without the aid of a teaching Church, opened the way, first to a repudiation of all supernatural revelation, and then to atheism and materialism.

During the second half of the 17th century there arose in England a school of freethinkers and Deists whose teachings without spreading, for the time being, to any great extent in England itself, exerted much influence in France and the Continental countries. A few of these Deists remained nominally Christian, but most rejected completely all supernatural religion ; and some threw doubt even on the existence of God. Among the best known were John Hobbes, author of the *Leviathan* (1651), John Locke author of the *Essay on the Human Understanding* (*d.* 1704) ; Collins, Roland, Tyndal, Charles Blount, Lord Bolingbroke, and later on, Hume and Berkeley.

Protestant Germany gave birth to a similar Rationalistic school, founded on the teachings of Leibnitz, Wolf and others, whose names were afterwards overshadowed by that of Emmanuel Kant, the greatest of German Rationalistic philosophers, and the real founder of the modern German Rationalistic School.

Its Spread in France.—France, however, was, or soon became, the real centre of the Naturalist movement. The ground had been prepared there by the Gallican and Janssenistic propaganda of the preceding generation and by the rationalistic tendencies of Descartes' philosophy. But the principal cause of the rapid spread of the movement was the moral corruption which had eaten, like a canker, into the wealthy classes, the aristocracy, and even a considerable portion of the clergy.

---

[1] Cf. Belliot, *op. cit.*, 1[iere] partie, chap. ii, sect. ii, pp. 47–54 ; *Catholic Encyclopedia*, arts. " Deism," " Liberalism," " Encyclopedists," " Materialism," " Secularism." MacCaffrey—*History of the Catholic Church from the Renaissance to the French Revolution*, vol. i, chap. viii, pp. 345–371, Mourret, *op. cit.*, tome vi, " Ancien Régime," pp. 470–480, and tome vii, " L'Eglise et la Revolution," pp. 426–442.

Voltaire brought from England the doctrines of the English freethinkers and Deists, and with Jean Jacques Rousseau, became the most powerful apostle of the new ideas. Soon a whole galaxy of brilliant writers appeared, filled with the spirit of Locke, Hobbes, Rousseau and Voltaire. Ecclesiastical authority, religion, revelation, all the cherished ideals and principles of Christianity were now persistently held up to ridicule in poetry, romance, drama, letters, historical and philosophical treatises, written mostly in a brilliant and attractive style.

The Encyclopédie.—The extreme rationalistic doctrine, which denies the existence of God, and the immortality of the human soul, rejects the moral law, and proclaims war against all authority, was summarised in the celebrated *Encyclopédie*. This monumental work, the first of its kind, appeared about the middle of the 18th century, under the editorship of Diderot and d'Alembert, and immediately secured unprecedented popularity. In the *Encyclopédie* all kinds of subjects were treated and discussed, sometimes with a certain appearance of fairness and impartiality, but always with the underlying purpose of discrediting Christianity. Diderot, in whose mind the virtue of chastity is only the result of ignorant prejudice, sketched an ideal society whose perfection lies in the complete gratification of the sexual passions, while the professed ambition of Naigeon, one of Diderot's disciples, was to " strangle the last of the priests with the entrails of the last of the kings."[1] This anti-religious campaign in France, resulting in the excesses and religious persecution associated with the French Revolution, was the first great effort of the Liberal anti-Christian revolt, which has continued to spread and gain strength down to our own day.

Modern Phases of Naturalism.—During the 19th century the Rationalistic movement manifested itself in the pseudo-philosophic theories of Pantheism, Materialism and Positivism, culminating in the Modernism, Neo-Gnosticism, Theosophism, Christian Scientism, etc., of the present day. The movement has gathered into its wake

[1] Cited in Belliot, *op. cit.*, p. 52.

most of the perverted intellectual forces of Europe. It
has spread more or less into every country, but has taken
deepest hold in France, Britain, the Protestant portions of
Germany, the United States of America, and the British
Dominions.

Pantheism, Materialism and Positivism.—The Pantheistic
philosophy of Kant and Hegel in Germany, tending to make
each individual a kind of god unto himself, and setting up
actual fact, the *fait accompli*, as the sole criterion of what
is reasonable and right, leads, when applied to social life,
to a glorification of brute force ; and contains besides a
philosophic ground-work for the most extreme and selfish
individualism.

The whole philosophy of Materialism, as propounded by
Haeckel, Huxley, Spencer and others, and especially the
theories of the Evolutionists, including those of the " struggle
for life " and " the survival of the fittest," as well as
Nietzche's theory of the " superman " for whose sake other
men are born to toil, have similar practical applications.

Positivism, which was first put forward by Auguste Comte
(*d.* 1857), was widely adopted by French and English
Rationalists, such as J. S. Mill, during the second half of
the 19th century. In this system a new deity is set up
for men to worship and serve. That deity is none other
than Humanity. Positivism, while encouraging a vague
and ineffective philanthropy or humanitarianism, has a
predominant tendency, like all forms of Rationalism, to
an extreme and unnatural individualism. For a Positivist
of the average type tends to regard himself as representing
Humanity, and consequently to consider himself, and not
God, as the summit and centre of the Universe, towards
whose glorification all his interests and efforts must
converge.

Modernism and Neo-Gnosticism.—Modernism, Neo-Gnosticism, Kabbalism, Theosophism, and Spiritism, are at
present perhaps the most dangerous and insidious forms of
Rationalism and Naturalism. The Modernists, who aimed
at remaining within the Church's fold while working to
undermine her teaching, were condemned by Pius X in

1907.[1] They deny, or strive to whittle down and explain away by specious reasoning, everything supernatural, including miracles, divine revelation, supernatural grace, etc. Neo-Gnosticism essays to get rid of a deity distinct from man and to whom man is responsible. Hence the votaries of the Neo-Gnostic theory deny the dogma of Creation. All things, according to their philosophy, are in some way or other emanations of the divine essence. Thus man is practically identified with the deity, with the result that whatever he thinks or does must be right and good.

The Neo-Gnostic philosophy is apparently the same as, or very similar to, that of the ancient Gnostics so often referred to in the writings of the early Fathers of the Church. This philosophy has reappeared at different times in the history of the Church, assuming various shapes, but remaining always substantially the same, and invariably tending to supply an apparent justification for the unrestrained gratification of man's worst passions. It was, under varying forms, the underlying philosophy of the Manichæans of the 5th century, of the Albigenses of the 12th century, of the Waldenses, etc., of later times. It was the heresy, too, of which the Templars of the 15th century were rightly or wrongly accused.

The doctrines of Gnosticism and Neo-Gnosticism are closely associated with the occult practices and beliefs of certain pre-Christian sectaries of the East which have always attracted minds of a certain perverted type, and seem to show strong indications of the direct influence of the evil one. Gnosticism and its different manifestations are not improbably the heresy or philosophy to which St. Paul is said to refer in his First Epistle to Timothy : *In the last times some shall depart from the faith, giving heed to spirits of error and doctrines of devils, speaking lies in hypocrisy, and having the conscience seared.*[2]

Kabbalism and Theosophism.—The Kabbalists and Theosophists are closely associated with the Neo-Gnostics, and their theories are only different manifestations of the same desire to free man from all supernatural law, and even from

---

[1] Litt. Encyl. *Pascendi Dominici Gregis* (Cf. *Juris Canonici Fontes*, vol. iii, p. 690).
[2] I *Tim.* iv. 1, 2.

the rule and authority of God. Kabbalism, which betrays the Jewish influence in the modern Naturalistic movement, would found its Rationalistic doctrines on ancient Jewish tradition, intermingled with Pagan and Gnostic philosophy. Theosophy relies for all knowledge, and especially for knowledge of the Deity, upon some kind of interior revelation or illumination, the result of the study and contemplation of secret rites and symbols. In some of its forms or teachings, Theosophy seems to contain a blend of Pantheism, Materialism and the doctrine of the transmigration of souls. It is closely allied to Brahminism and Buddhism, and tends to teach some kind of universal faith which would be, as it were, a common denominator in which all religions and creeds would be at one. For, according to the Theosophists, all religions of all times, including Christianity, are but different manifestations of the one true religion, which Divine Wisdom reveals under varying forms suited to different times, places and persons. The Theosophist sectaries are much addicted to spiritism, magic, unlawful hypnotism, etc., which they substitute for religious worship.

Their Profoundly Anti-Christian Character.—All these phases of Naturalism are closely associated with the intensive anti-Christian movement of to-day. The propagation of the Neo-Gnostic pseudo-philosophy, as well as that of the Kabbalists, the Illuminists, the Theosophists, the Spiritists, etc., is in fact the most dangerous phase of the war now waged throughout the world against the Church by the Masonic and Jewish sectaries. Their philosophy cuts deeper into Christian life and affects more fatally the Christian organisation of society than their purely political and economic activities, as it tends to destroy the very foundations of all Christian morality and belief.

Art. 3—*Political Liberalism*[1]

Introduction.—Before proceeding to sketch the nature and history of political Liberalism, or Secularism, as it is

---

[1] Cf. Pius IX—*Quanta Cura*, 1864 (*Juris Canonici Fontes*, vol. ii, p. 993) ; Leo XIII—*Immortale Dei* (Christian Constitution of States), 1885 and, *Libertas, Præstantissimum* (Human Liberty), 1888 ; *Cath. Encyclop.*, *loc. cit.*, especially art. " Liberalism," pp. 212–214 ; *Dictionaire Apolog.*

sometimes named, it will be useful to recall what we have already touched on in treating of the civil organisation, and political principles of mediæval Europe.[1] The whole political and social structure centred round, or rather reposed on, the principle that God was its Author; and His divine ordinance was recognised as the fundamental sanction of all valid rule and the basis of all social and civil obligations.

The general acceptance of this principle secured reverence and obedience towards the government while setting strict limits to its power, and affording safeguards to the subjects against oppression. When, on the other hand, this principle is ignored, or in other words, when God is eliminated from the political organism, and His rights rejected in favour of what are termed the " Rights of Man " (as occurs in the Liberal system), the foundations of legitimate authority are taken away ; there is no fixed principle to set limits to the competency and scope of the ruling powers ; and no real safeguard against tyranny and abuse of authority.

Principles of Political Liberalism. Leo XIII summarises as follows the main political principles of Liberalism :

" The Naturalists lay down that all men have the same rights and are in *every respect* of equal and like condition ; that each one is naturally free ; that no one has the right to command another ; that it is an act of violence to require men to obey any authority other than that which is obtained from themselves. According to this, therefore, all things belong to the free people ; power is held by the command of the people, so that whenever the popular will changes, rulers may be lawfully deposed ; and the source of all rights and civil duties is either in the multitude, or in the governing authority, when the latter is constituted according to the latest doctrines. It is also held that the State should be without God ; that in the various forms of religion

---

de la Foi Catholique, art. " Liberalisme," col. 1822–1841 ; Belliot, *op. cit.*, pp. 424–442 ; Castelein—*Droit Naturel*, Thèse 20, pp. 737–765 ; Riquet— *Sa Majestie la Loi* (reprinted from two articles in *Les Etudes*, April, 1925, and published by the Ligue des Droits du Religieux 36, Rue du Montparnasse, Paris) ; Robertson—*Readings in European History*, vol. ii, chap. xxxv, pp. 409–411 ; (Declaration of the Rights of Man) ; *Cambridge Modern History*, vol. vi, ch. xxiii (written from the Liberal and non-Catholic standpoint) ; Palgrave—*Dictionary of Political Economy*, arts. " Hobbes," " Locke," " Rousseau," etc.
[1] Cf. *Supra*, chap. v.

there is no reason why one should have precedence of another, and that they are all to occupy the same place." [1]

Hence Political Liberalism may be described as implying the following main principles :

I. Everyone has an inalienable right to freedom of thought, of speech, and of action, a freedom which may be curtailed only where its exercise would clash directly with the rights of other individuals. Besides, no one can be bound to submit to any authority in which he himself has no share.

II. Hence the rights of God over human society are rejected or ignored. Rulers must base their jurisdiction not on divine authority but solely upon a supposed delegation from the people. In other words, the " Sovereignty of the People " usurps the position of the sovereignty of God.

III. Religion is relegated from public life into the domain of each one's individual conscience. Hence there is no public and official recognition of God's supreme authority. The laws of Christianity as such are ignored ; and the Church is no longer a public and legal institution.

IV. Hence, too, the supposed " will of the people," may prevail against the law of God, as manifested in the divinely established organisation of the human family, or the God-given rights of the individual person or the constitution of the Church which God has founded. The epigrammatic phrase : " A nation has a right to do wrong," thus expresses a fundamental principle of political Liberalism.

V. As the people can exercise their authority only through representatives elected by a majority of votes, and as these representatives in turn usually function by the same means, this unlimited " sovereignty of the people " is in practice the sovereignty of a majority whether real or supposed. It is in fact the tyranny of brute force under a new guise— more dangerous than the tyranny of a military dictatorship,

---

[1] *Humanum Genus*, 1884 (Cf. *The Great Encyclicals of Leo XIII*, p. 96. Benziger, New York, 1913) ; cf. also Leo XIII—*Libertas, Præstantissimum*, pp. 78, 79, 88, 91.

because more easily veiled. Hence Leo XIII again refers
to the Liberal doctrine of authority as follows :
  " Authority is severed from the true and natural principle
whence it derives all its efficacy for the common good ; and the
law determining what is right to do is at the mercy of a majority.
Now this is simply a road leading straight to tyranny." [1]
  VI. The State having now acknowledged responsibility to
safeguard the eternal laws of God, no longer recognises its
duty to prevent the spread of false or irreligious doctrines
or to suppress public incentives to vice except in as far
as the interests of mere public order require.

Its History—Hobbes and Locke.

Its History—Hobbes and Locke.—The English philosopher,
John Hobbes, already referred to, may be regarded as the
founder of modern political Liberalism. He wrote at the
period of the Puritan Revolution against the Stuarts, and
in his two treatises, *De Cive* (1642) and the *Leviathan* (1651),
he upheld the theory of government's absolute and irresponsible power. John Locke, Hobbe's fellow-countryman, and
his successor in the same school of thought, maintained in
his *Letters on Toleration* (1689) and his *Essay on Civil
Government* (1690) that the governed possess a permanent and
inalienable right to rebel when they so wish. The foundation
of the error in case of both these writers was the same.
Both theorists eliminate from the civic union the essential
element of the authority and law of God.
  According to Hobbes, men are naturally free, and all seek
exclusively their own interests. Hence, men lived at first
in a state of perpetual war. Then, as a practical expedient,
they compacted to form society, to which, as represented
by its rulers, unlimited power over the individual members
was confided. This sovereign body Hobbes called the
Leviathan, the monster of limitless strength and power.
As a logical inference from his rejection of divine authority
in the constitution and government of states, Hobbes rejected
the distinction between the temporal and spiritual power
and denied the independent rights of the Church ; for " a
man cannot obey two masters, and a house divided against
itself cannot stand." Hence, whatever worship or religion
exists in a State must be completely subject to the civil

---

[1] *Libertas Præstantissimum*, p. 80 ; cf. *also* p. 79.

power, and no dogma can be appealed to against a law of the State.[1]

In Locke's theory the liberty which men had before the supposed original social contract remains with them and is inalienable, " for no one can ever be subjected to authority without his own consent." But as this *universal* consent can scarcely ever be had, the only remedy against anarchy is that the majority must include the rest. Hence it is a law both of nature and of reason that the act of the majority is the act of the whole." [2]

The principles of Hobbes and Locke were more fully elaborated by the 18th century founders of the French Liberal school and those of the German Aufklärung. Of the latter, Emmanuel Kant (*d.* 1804) has had the widest influence. In Kant's view, man, as a moral being, is " a law to himself and an end to himself, a cause but not an effect." [3] Hence the civil union whose object is to secure *liberty* for all must presuppose an implied contract as a necessary foundation of its authority.

Rousseau.—The principal founders of French Liberalism were Calvinists, mostly natives of Geneva. Jean Jacques Rousseau (1712–1778) the best known of these, wrote about half a century after Locke. His great work, *Le Contrat Social*, appeared in 1761. Like Locke and Hobbes, Rousseau was a Deist. He professed a vague belief in a " Being, whatever He may be, who moves the universe, and orders all things." Like his English predecessors, Rousseau bases civil authority upon a supposed social contract ; and, like Locke, he required the general consent of the governed as an essential condition of authority. Hence a republic is the best form of government, because it is the most sensitive to the desires of the people. Rousseau develops more fully than Locke the doctrine of man's inalienable independence of all authority outside himself. In his view all men are naturally free and good. In fact, all are by nature kings. And freedom, goodness and kingship are, according to him,

---

[1] *Cambridge Modern History, loc. cit.*, pp. 785–795.
[2] *Ib.*, p. 810 ; *see also* Palgrave's *Dictionary of Political Economy*, vol. ii, p. 633.
[3] Cf. Palgrave, *op. cit.*, vol. ii, p. 501 (Kant) ; and pp. 79 ff (German School).

incompatible with submission to rule, except as a result of previous free consent.[1] Since the beginning of the 19th century, Rousseau's theory of man's essential independence of all authority has been further developed. For, according to the Positivists, such as Auguste Comte and other modern sectaries to whom we have already alluded, all men are gods, or at least every man is a god to himself.

Mme. de Necker and Mme. de Stael.—Contemporary with Rousseau during the second half of the 18th century there arose among French literary circles a widespread movement of ideas inspired mainly by Calvinism and promoted and fostered in its more advanced forms in the Masonic lodges which were then spread everywhere over France. Mme. Necker and her daughter, Mme. de Stael, Calvinists and natives of Geneva, were the central figures in these literary circles. Mme. de Stael, who was closely associated with Mirabeau and the Constitutional Party of the French Revolution, is the connecting link between the Liberalism of the 18th and that of the 19th century. She rejects as absurd the Christian principle that human authority is derived from God ; as well as the doctrine of a divinely founded Church forming a perfect society independent of the State.

Declaration of the Rights of Man.—All these doctrines took definite political shape in the celebrated *Declaration of the Rights of Man* which was drawn up by the French National Assembly (1789) as the foundation of the new constitution. This document, which implies a definite abandonment of the Christian political ideals, has had immense influence in shaping the constitutions of modern States. According to the " Declaration of the Rights of Man," the principle of all sovereignty resides essentially in the people ; law is only the expression of the general will ; liberty, which is every man's inalienable right, consists in the freedom to do everything which injures no one, a limitation which can be determined in the concrete only by *the law* (which itself is only an expression of the will of the people) ; no one may be disquieted for his religious

---

[1] Cf. Palgrave, *op. cit.*, vol. iii, p. 330.

views, provided their manifestation does not disturb the public order established by law, etc.[1] Thus the divine authority, or the Will of God, upon which in the mediæval Christian ideal all legitimate rule must rest, is definitely eliminated ; and the people, fickle, ignorant, weak as they may be, are enthroned in God's place. The *Rights of God* are supplanted in the social order by the *Rights of Man*.

These principles manifestly imply a denial of all real authority (for men cannot be their own superiors). They are in fact the underlying philosophy upon which all the subversive movements of modern times are based. The destruction of the established order, which accompanied the French Revolution ; the confiscation of Church property ; the Civil Constitution of the Clergy, by which the Church in France was subjected to the civil power, were the natural outcome of the principles embodied in the " Declaration of the Rights of Man."

Prevalence of Political Liberalism.—Under the influence of France and England the Liberal movement spread during the 19th century over most of Europe and America. The political principles associated with it now prevail in France, Mexico, Portugal and Russia, and to a very large extent in the United States of America and the countries of the British Empire.[2] Upon these principles, too, the constitutions of the new States, which were set up as a result of the great European war, have been based. These same principles have, besides, impressed themselves more or less deeply on the laws and administrations of very many other States, such as Spain, whose constitutions still (1931) remain predominantly Christian.

Art. 4—*Effects of Political Liberalism on Public Life*

Revolutionary Movements.—Liberalism is essentially opposed to Christianity. In the case of governments which have fallen completely under its influence, this opposition shows itself in a contempt for the principles of Christian

---

[1] For the text of the document, cf. Robertson—*Readings in European History*, vol. ii, pp. 410–411.

[2] Cf. *The Clergy Review*, March, 1931, pp. 258 ff, for an account of the gradual de-Christianisation of the English Legal Code, which was finally accomplished in 1917.

morality, and sometimes even in a systematic persecution
of the Catholic Church. In the case of Catholic States, such
as Spain, Italy, Portugal and the States of Spanish-America,
which were not much affected by Protestantism, and where
the Catholic tradition was strong enough to resist the
peaceful penetration of the Liberal movement, the introduction of Liberalism, with its Masonic alignments has
always tended to produce Revolution and social upheavals.
In fact, most of the revolutions that have taken place in
Europe and America for the past century and a half have
been to a very large extent the offspring of Liberalism and
Freemasonry.

Degradation of Public Life.—Egoism and sordid ideals ;
oppression of the weak and a cynical disregard of social
justice ; the spread of corruption and vice by means of the
press ; a free and unscrupulous use of slander, corruption
and fraud in political life—these and such like traits invariably accompany the introduction of Liberalism into a
State.

That it should be so is inevitable. When once the claims
of God and the authority of God's law are refused their due
place in the legislature and administration of the State,
the very basis of public morality is removed ; and human
enactments or coercive force become the only, or the main,
principles of discrimination between right and wrong.
Laws and administrative activities injurious to family life,
or opposed to the rights of the Church, being no longer
regarded as essentially invalid and unconstitutional, sooner
or later force an entrance into the State. The obligations
of social justice, charity and Christian patriotism cease to
have a clear meaning and are gradually forgotten. The
principles of naturalism find expression in the current
literature, the press, the theatre, and the cinema, with the
result that the whole tone of social life is gradually lowered
to the non-Christian level. The administration of the State
falls under the control of unscrupulous political adventurers
who, while pretending to rule in the people's name, abuse
their power for personal aggrandisement, while the people
themselves are enslaved and ground down by exorbitant
taxes.

Hence, Leo XIII, speaking of the public evils which

result from the " widespread perversion of the primary truths on which, as on its basis, human society rests," refers in a special way to the

" Reckless mismanagement, waste and misappropriation of public funds ; and the shamelessness of those who, full of treachery, make semblance of being champions of country and freedom and every kind of right." [1]

Perversion of the Idea of Liberty.—(a) *The True Idea.*—

Another element in the demoralising influence of political Liberalism is the perverted idea of human liberty upon which the Liberals found their political system. According to Christian teaching and true philosophy, the liberty, to which everyone has a natural right, differs essentially from a licence to do evil. It implies, indeed, freedom from unjust constraint and the safe and unimpeded enjoyment of one's natural and acquired rights. [2] But it does not mean to imply a licence to act or speak or write falsely or sinfully, or a right to do anything injurious to the public good. Again, true Christian liberty is quite consistent with due submission to all lawful authority ; and authority may be lawful even though the subjects have no voice in its exercise. For while it is true that everyone has a right to be governed justly, and that civil authority should be exercised solely for the good of the people, it does not follow that everyone has a natural much less an indefeasible right to a share in the government.

Hence, too, the Church, which has always been the champion and upholder of true liberty, has no special pre-dilections regarding the form of government (viz., whether it be monarchical or democratic), provided the conditions required for just rule be fulfilled. Neither can it be shown that the democratic form of government (viz., that in which the actual rulers are elected from time to time by the popular vote) is always, or even usually, the best, or that it contains any sure guarantee against tyranny and the oppression of the masses of the people. [3]

---

[1] *Inscrutabili*, 1878, pp. 1, 2.

[2] Cf. Leo XIII—*Libertas Præstantissimum*, pp. 71 ff.

[3] Cf. Donat—*Ethica Specialis*, sec. iii, cap. iv. In this connection it may be noted that the term *Christian Democracy* does not at all refer to the *form* of the Government, but rather to its character. It implies that civil

(b) *The Perverted Liberal View.*—According to the Liberal teaching, on the other hand, liberty is bound up essentially with the political franchise as if it were against reason that one should submit to an authority in which he does not himself share. Furthermore, it includes the right of professing and preaching false religions ; of propagating false philosophy ; of speaking or writing what is false or injurious to public morals ; in a word, it implies a licence to do anything that does not directly disturb the peace or violate commutative justice even though it may injure the religious belief or morality of the people. And to liberty, thus falsely defined, the Liberals assert that every citizen has an inalienable right.[1]

Under cover of such principles as these, vice is freely propagated by means of an immoral literature, a licentious press, and a degrading cinema and theatre. The drink traffic and the sporting and betting syndicates are allowed to function freely under the protection of the law, to the detriment and degradation of the people. The principle is acted upon, and sometimes openly proclaimed, that, in a free country, the public administration must not interfere with the liberty of the subject, even while he is propagating ideas subversive of morality, or dangerous to the people's faith ; or while, in the pursuit of unholy gain, he is propagating the vices of drunkenness, idleness, gambling and unchastity.

Art. 5—*Liberal Catholicism*

What it Means.—A milder form of political Liberalism but one which has wrought much injury to the Church during the past century, is what is known as *Liberal Catholicism*.[2] This system was first formulated by the Abbé de Lamennais in *L'Avenir* early in the 19th century,

---

authority and social action are exercised, as Christian teaching requires, for the good of the masses of the people. In accordance with the Encyclical of Leo XIII—*Graves de Communi* (on Christian Democracy), January, 1901 (pp. 169 ff), the term *Christian Democracy* is now usually applied to indicate the great movement of Catholic Social Action (to be discussed in chap. xv *infra*), which is altogether non-political. Cf. *Cath. Encyclop.*, vol. iv, art. " Christian Democracy."

[1] Cf. Leo XIII, *ib.*

[2] The term *Liberal Catholic* is also sometimes applied in a loose sense to a Catholic who puts forward opinions favouring any of the false doctrines of unchristian Liberalism.

and was defended for a while by such illustrious men as Lacordaire, Montalembert, Dupanloup, etc.

The Liberal Catholics, while recognising that God is the ultimate source of civil authority, would regulate the relations between Church and State, and some other details in the social organism, in accordance with the more moderate Liberal principles as expounded by Benjamin Constant. In this system the Church and State would be completely divorced from each other. The civil power would profess no particular religion, and remain quite indifferent to religious interests, neither obstructing nor assisting the work of the Church. There would thus be a " free Church in a free State," and equal toleration for all religions whose tenets and practices do not interfere with the established social order.[1]

The system thus advocated as admissible, if not desirable and in complete accordance with Catholic principles, is practically identical with the system with which we are familiar in these countries since the cessation of the persecution of the Church.

Condemnation of Liberal Catholicism.—This system was condemned by Gregory XVI[2] and again by Pius IX.[3] Leo XIII, who confirms the condemnation of Catholic Liberalism previously made, assigns the reasons why it is opposed to the Church's teaching :

Since the State is a moral person created by God, it must formally acknowledge God's authority and give Him public worship in its corporate capacity. " Justice therefore forbids, and reason itself forbids the State to be godless or to adopt a

---

[1] Cf. *Dictionaire Apologétique de la Foi Catholique*, *loc. cit.*, col. 1824 ff.

[2] *Mirari Vos*, 1832. *Inter Præcipuas*, 1844.

[3] *Quanta Cura*, 1864. Pius IX also includes in the syllabus of *condemned propositions* (1864) the three following, which contain the central tenets of Liberal Catholicism :—

" 77. It is no longer desirable that the Catholic religion be considered as the only religion of the State to the exclusion of all others.

" 78. Hence in some Catholic countries provision is laudably made that immigrants coming into the country be allowed the free exercise of their own religion.

" 79. It is false to assert that freedom to practise any religion whatever and the full liberty to express openly and publish all opinions and ideas, tend to corrupt the morals and minds of the people or lead to religious indifference." Cf. Denzinger—*Enchiridion Symbolorum* (nn. 1777-1780).

line of action which would end in godlessness—namely, to treat the various religions (as they call them) alike, and to bestow upon them promiscuously equal rights and privileges."[1] For God must be worshipped in the manner which He Himself has ordered, and in communion with the Church which He has established. Hence the true religion is the only one that should be recognised or assisted by the State.

Toleration of False Religions.—Leo XIII, however, adds that Holy Church, allowing for human weakness, does not forbid public authority to tolerate error when a well-founded fear of a greater evil counsels such toleration :

" For while holding it unlawful to place the various forms of divine worship on the same footing as the true religion, the Church does not condemn those rulers who, for the sake of securing some greater good or of hindering some great evil, allow custom or usage to be a kind of sanction for each kind of religion having place in the State."[2]

He goes on, however, to say in another pronouncement on the same matter, that :

" The more a State is driven to tolerate evil, the further it is from perfection, and that the tolerance of evil which is dictated by prudence should be strictly confined to the limits which its justifying cause, the public welfare, requires."[3]

Hence, although existing false religions may be tolerated in a Catholic State, as far as may be necessary for the public peace, it does not follow that further false systems of propagation of unchristian or irreligious opinions or false or immoral teaching may be allowed. That would be contrary to the primary duty of the civil power, which is to safeguard the religious, moral and intellectual interests of the people as well as to promote their material well-being.

Art. 6—*Economic Liberalism*[4]

Not Necessarily Connected with Material Progress.—The false principles of unchristian Liberalism, which have

---

[1] *Libertas, Præstantissimum*, p. 83 ; cf. also *Immortale Dei*, p. 48.
[2] *Immortale Dei*, pp. 62–63.
[3] *Libertas, Præstantissimum*, pp. 89–90 ; cf. also *Immortale Dei*, p. 48. *Symbolorum*, nn. 1777–1780) ; cf. also *Immortale Dei*, p. 48.
[4] Cf. Antoine, *op. cit.*, 1iere partie, chap. viii (L'Ecole Libérale) ; Belliot— *op. cit.*, pp. 304–310 (Ecole Libérale) ; Gide—*History of Economic Doctrines*, chaps. ii and iii ; Devas—*Political Economy*, bk. iii, chap. viii (Liberty and

wrought such havoc during the past two centuries in the moral, intellectual and political spheres, have had in their application to economic life equally disastrous effects upon the material well-being of the people. In fact, all or most of the excessive poverty, insecurity and degradation which are outstanding features in our modern " civilisation " are traceable to these principles and the social organisation founded upon them.

It is sometimes assumed, especially by non-Catholic writers, that Liberalism has some kind of necessary connection with commerce and manufacture, as if these latter could flourish only under a Liberal régime. There is no foundation for such an assumption. Commerce and manufacture had already made great progress in Europe during the 14th and 15th centuries, under the financial predominance of the great Catholic republics of Florence, Pisa, Venice and Genoa. These and the Hanseatic cities of Germany and the Low Countries attained at that time a degree of wealth, power and culture which, in some respects, has never been surpassed or perhaps equalled at any other period of European history.

The invention of the mariner's compass and of printing, the discovery of America and of the new route to the East, the colonial expansion of Spain and Portugal : all these and other causes[1] led to an immense increase of industrial and commercial activity centuries before the rise of Liberalism, and while the Catholic economic principles founded on Christian teaching, as expounded by St. Thomas and the great scholastic authors, still held undisputed sway.[2]

Mercantile System of Economics.—After the rise of Protestantism, however, and especially under the influence of

---

Law), and par. ii, secs. 3–7 (pp. 648–655, 3rd edit.) ; Tawney, *op. cit.*, chaps. iii and iv ; O'Brien—*Economic Effects of the Reformation*, chap. ii ; Ingram—*History of Political Economy*, chap. v ; Palgrave, *op. cit.*, arts. " Turgot," " Gournay," " Dutch School of Economics," " Physiocrats," " Self-Interest," " Adam Smith," " J. B. Say," " Manchester School," " Free Trade," etc. ; Larkin, *op. cit.*, chaps. iii–v.

[1] Cf. Tawney, *op. cit.*, chap. ii (1).

[2] These Catholic principles were developed by different Catholic writers of the 14th and 15th centuries, and adapted to contemporary conditions. Thus Nicol Oresme, Bishop of Lisieux (*d.* 1382), wrote a treatise on Usury and Exchange (*Tractatus de Origine, Natura, Iure et Mutationibus Monetarum*), which can hold the field even to-day. (Cf. Ingram, *op. cit.*, p. 36).

Calvinism and of the new pagan ideals connected with the
" Renaissance," non-Christian principles began to exert an
ever-increasing influence in industrial and commercial
relations.[1] What is known as the *Mercantile System* of
economics arose in the 16th century. This system reached
its highest development about the middle of the 17th
century and continued to prevail till the rise of Liberalism.
The Mercantile policy is closely associated with the Elizabethan legislation and the English Navigation and Corn
Laws. Strafford and Cromwell in England as well as
Colbert, the Minister of Louis XIV of France, are usually
mentioned as the best-known representatives of the Mercantile economic policy. The prevalence of the system
coincided with the growth of the power of England and
Holland in the 17th century.

The purely economic principles of Mercantilism were
adapted to the building up of a strong military state. With
this end in view, manufacture and commerce were assi-
duously promoted, and the importance of protective tariffs
and state intervention in individual activities very much
emphasised. Each nation aimed at acquiring great quantities of the precious metals, which were regarded as
synonymous with wealth.

Such a view is manifestly false. Wealth cannot be conceived in an exclusively objective sense and apart from the
human persons, whose needs it is meant to satisfy. Besides,
gold and silver are only one form of wealth understood
even in its objective sense. There are numberless other
commodities more essential for human needs than the
precious metals, and these are also wealth which therefore
has no essential connection with money, much less with
silver or gold.[2]

The Mercantile economists erred, too, in another way. For
while they made military power, national aggrandisement
and colonial expansion the great objects of public endeavour,
the well-being of the multitude, which in Christian philosophy
is regarded as the primary end and purpose of all the State's
activities, was largely forgotten or neglected. Oppressive

---

[1] Cf. Tawney, *op. cit.*, chaps. iii and iv. O'Brien, *loc. cit.*
[2] Cf. Palgrave, *op. cit.*, vol. iii, pp. 660–661 ; Devas—*Political Economy*
(*see* index under word " Wealth ") ; Gide. *op. cit.* (do.).

taxes were imposed and inequitably distributed, the agricultural classes were impoverished, and the public finances became confused and chaotic.[1]

Rise of Economic Liberalism.—These evils helped to bring about the general abandonment of the Mercantile system ; and in the 18th century the system of economic Liberalism, which was still further removed from Christian ideals, began to prevail. In the Liberal system national aggrandisement was still regarded as the primary duty of the Government, which, however, now concentrated upon industrial rather than military power. The wealthy industrial and mercantile classes, which as a consequence of the Protestant upheaval had acquired excessive power, especially in Britain, found in the principles of Liberalism an excellent opportunity of exploiting the labour of the poor for personal and national aggrandisement.

The Physiocrats.—Some of the principles of economic Liberalism had been previously put forward by the French *Physiocrats.* This small group of writers appeared in the second half of the 18th century, and were the real founders of the modern science of economics. The term, " Physiocrat," adapted from the Greek, means one who advocates the *Rule of Nature.* The Physiocrats were much influenced by the unchristian philosophy of Voltaire, Rousseau and the Encyclopedists, and were the first to formulate the maxim (which the Liberal economists afterwards adopted as a fundamental principle) of the non-intervention of the State in industrial and commercial life (*Laissez faire, Laissez passer*). They also put forward the erroneous interpretation of the Natural Law which was afterwards adopted and developed by the Liberal economists. Of the Physiocrats the best known names are Quesnay (*d.* 1774), the founder of the school ; Turgot (*d.* 1778), financial minister of Louis XVI ; de Gournay (*d.* 1759), and Dupont de Nemours (*d.* 1768).[2]

---

[1] Cf. Palgrave, *op. cit.* (" Mercantile System ") ; Ingram, *op. cit.*, chap. iv ; Shields, *op. cit.*, chap. i, pp. 8 ff.

[2] Cf. Gide., *op. cit.*, pp. 1–5; *Cath. Encyclop.*, arts. " Physiocrats," "Turgot," etc. ; Palgrave, *op. cit.*, arts. "Physiocrats," " Turgot," etc. ; Ingram, *op. cit.*, pp. 57–70.

Classical School of Economics.—It was in Britain, however, that Liberalism was first formulated into a complete economic system. This was done by the writers of the so-called *Classical School* of which the Scotchman, Adam Smith, was the founder. Adam Smith's great work, *Enquiry into the Nature and Cause of the Wealth of Nations*, appeared in 1776. The other leading writers of the English Liberal school are Malthus, who published his famous *Essay of the Principle of Population* in 1789 ; David Ricardo, author of the *Principles of Political Economy and Taxation* (published 1817), and John Stuart Mill, whose *Principles of Political Economy* appeared in 1848.[1]

Materialism and utilitarianism are dominant characteristics in the works of these and the other English writers of the Liberal school. Most of them also show determined hostility to religion, and a profound opposition to the Christian principles of social and domestic life.[2] The principles of the classical school have dominated British economic policy and law down to our own time, although since about 1870 strong opposing currents have appeared both in doctrine and in legislative tendencies.[3]

Its Main Tenets.—We may summarise the principal tenets of the classical school as far as they concern us here in the three following propositions :

I. *Untrammelled liberty for the individual in economic action is the only sure foundation of economic progress and social harmony*, just as liberty in religious belief is the only foundation of true religion ; and liberty and equality in political action are necessary for good government.

II. *The material self-interest of the individual, which is always his only motive of action, and which supplies an unlimited stimulus to human endeavour, works out infallibly for the greater good of the whole social body.*

---

[1] Cf. Ingram, *op. cit.*, pp. 55–196 ; Gide, *op. cit.*, bk. i, chaps, ii and iii and bk. iii, chap. ii ; Palgrave, *op. cit.*, arts. " Classical Economists," " Adam Smith," " Malthus," etc. For a discussion of the dominating influence of Locke's teaching on the rise and progress of individualism, cf. Larkin, *op. cit.*, chaps. iii and iv.

[2] Cf. Devas, *op. cit.*, pp. 652–654 ; Antoine, *op. cit.*, chap. viii, art. 1.

[3] These opposing currents come from the Historical School of Political Economy, from the Socialists and from a partial revival of Christian principles. Cf. Gide, *op. cit.*, bk. iv, chaps. 1 and iv.

III. Hence, *free trade with foreign countries and free competition between individuals or corporations, each working exclusively for his, or its own material interests, implying the non-interference of the Government in the operations of finance, in the relations between employers and employed, etc., must be regarded as a fundamental principle in the constitution of the State.*

These principles have been in large measure the intellectual groundwork upon which the modern capitalistic system has been built up, and are accountable for some of the worst evils of modern industrialism. It was under plea of these principles that the Customs duties between Ireland and England were practically abolished in 1800 with disastrous effects upon Irish manufacturing industry. It was these principles, too, that formed the nucleus of the group of ideas comprehended in the term " Manchester School," of which Sir Robert Peel, Cobden and Bright were the best known representatives. The teachings of the Manchester School were the driving force behind the Free Trade movement in the 19th century. The Free Trade movement led to the repeal of the Corn Laws in 1848, a measure which was ruinous to Ireland and did much to destroy the agricultural life of Britain itself.[1]

Credit Reform Movement.—Partly as a reaction against some of the abuses to which economic Liberalism has led— namely, the dominance of the financial magnates and the private monopoly of credit, there came into prominence after the European war what may be described as a kind of new economic school, giving rise to what is sometimes described as the " Credit Reform Movement." A group of English writers, including Major Douglas, Orage (editor for some time of the *New Age*), Professor T. Loddy, M. A. Kitson and others (while emphasising the abuses and injustice associated with the present monetary system, which they say is even *technically unsound* and leads *necessarily* to poverty, unemployment and war),[2] propose an alternative system in which gold would be definitely abandoned as a

---

[1] Cf. Palgrave, *op. cit.*, arts. " Manchester School " and " Free Trade."
[2] Cf. An article by Rev. Dr. Coffey (of Maynooth College), published in the *Clergy Review*, March, 1931, entitled " Capital Ownership and Credit Control."

medium of exchange. In the proposed system the conduct of industry would be carried on under the control of professional or industrial syndicates or guilds enjoying a large measure of autonomy ; the currency (represented by coupons issued by State-controlled banks) would correspond to, and vary in symbolic value with the actual volume of production each year.[1] The scheme (the merits of which it is outside our scope to discuss) has not gained the approval, at least in its entirety, of any of the recognised economists, who condemn it as embodying or leading to State Socialism. On the other hand, *some* important elements in it, such as its rejection of the dominance of industry by the monied interest and the setting up of industrial corporations with an extensive measure of autonomy, seem to bear a certain resemblance to the orthodox Catholic ideal as outlined in the recent Encyclical of Pius XI.[2]

Art. 7—*Critique of Economic Liberalism*

Its Philosophic Ground-Work.—Without discussing in detail the purely economic tenets which distinguish the different schools of Liberal economic writers, we shall now indicate, in a general way, the main points in which economic Liberalism is at variance with Christian principles. In the philosophy of Liberalism, the science of Economics, no less than those of Politics and Jurisprudence, has been unnaturally divorced from the science of Ethics. Its whole scope is confined to the methods and means of producing and accumulating wealth. For in the doctrines of Liberalism wealth is regarded as an end in itself, instead of being a means to promote the temporal well-being of the people— as if the wealth or prosperity of a State could be justly estimated, apart from the prosperity and well-being of the individuals that compose it.

Again, as a result of their ignoring Divine authority and man's eternal destiny, the Liberals put forward an idea of the Natural Law which is radically false and misleading.

---

[1] Cf. Douglas and Orage—*Credit Power and Democracy ;* Douglas— *Economic Democracy* (Palmer, London, W.C. 1, 1921) ; Marshall Hattersley *This Age of Plenty* (Pitman, London, W.C. 2, 1929) ; Adams—*Real Wealth and Financial Poverty* (Palmer, London, 1925).

[2] *Quadragesimo Anno,* pp. 36–44.

Ignoring or denying original sin, they identify the Natural Law with the lower tendencies of man, his innate selfishness and his natural craving for wealth, power and pleasure, leaving out of consideration the dictates of his higher nature which subordinate these tendencies to God's law, and man's own eternal interests. Upon this false view of the Natural Law, coupled with the equally perverted concept of human liberty which we have already discussed,[1] the Liberals base their whole economic system.

" Nature," they say, " has provided for men's happiness by implanting in the human heart certain instincts which, when allowed full scope, work inevitably for the general harmony and the good of all.   Hence the path to prosperity and peace is found by allowing these tendencies free play." Hence, too, the State has no duty to regulate the use of property, to control free competition, or to safeguard the interests of the poor and the weak against the wealthy and the strong.[2]   As an inference from these principles, the so-called rights of ownership are regarded as independent of all limitations, even of such as may come from the fundamental rights of others to a reasonable means of livelihood.

Hence we may summarise the Catholic attitude towards Economic Liberalism in three sentences : Its main principles are false. Many of the inferences and assertions, which the system includes are contrary to experience. In its practical application it has proved disastrous to the temporal well-being of the people which it is the object of the State to promote.

(a) **Principles False.**—*The abstract principles upon which the Liberal economic system is based are contrary to Christian teaching and are ethically false.*   We have already pointed out the fallacy underlying the Liberal view of human liberty, which is one of the fundamental principles of the whole Liberal position.

The Liberal concept of the Natural Law, in which man's relations to God and to his own eternal destiny are ignored, and man is regarded as an isolated individualistic being, devoid of all natural social rights and duties, is equally mis-

---

[1] Cf. *Supra*, p. 106.
[2] Cf. Antoine, *loc. cit.* ; Ingram, *loc. cit.*

leading. Man's relations to God and to his own eternal happiness and misery lie at the very root of his being and dominate every activity of his life, and so are essentially included in the Natural Law.

Again, as man's nature has been fashioned in such a way as to need and to be suited for civil association with his fellow-man, the Natural Law also includes the duties and rights of Legal and Distributive Justice, as well as those of Charity and Patriotism, which form the bonds of social and civil life. Hence the " *Economic Man* " of Adam Smith and the Classical School of economists (in which the human being is considered as detached from all social ties and actuated solely by a desire to acquire wealth, with no spiritual or moral impulse, no ideals of charity or patriotism, no obligation of social justice, etc.) is not the man that actually exists. The *Economic Man* is a pure figment of the mind, and has no relation to real life.[1]

Finally, since God created the goods of the earth for the use of all, human ownership or one's right to one's property is only a stewardship, and carries with it an obligation (which may be, and, where necessary, should be defined by the civil law) of exercising one's ownership in accordance with right reason and the common good, and of taking account of the needs of others and their natural right to a fair opportunity of procuring a becoming livelihood.

Hence, although it is true, as the Liberals assert, that " Nature " and the " Laws of Nature " have made due provision for man's temporal happiness, Nature has to be understood in its true sense, as including man's relations to God and to the society of which he forms a part, and not in the one-sided and purely materialistic sense in which Liberal philosophers use the term.

(b) Inferences and Assertions Contrary to Experience.—

It is untrue and contrary to experience that material selfishness is the only motive of men's energy, and that this motive supplies an inexhaustible incentive to human endeavour. Such an assertion is derogatory to human dignity, and a libel upon man's nature. Besides his material needs and his

---

[1] Cf. Antoine, *loc. cit.*, art. 2 ; Palgrave, *op. cit.*, art. " Egoism," etc. (Cf. index, Palgrave's *Dict. of Pol. Econ.*, " Economic Man ").

natural desire for material betterment, man has also intellectual, moral and religious needs and tendencies. Although the former do supply a powerful incentive to human endeavour, religion, patriotism, and philanthropy also exert immense influence on man's activities. Besides, material wants and desires are not limitless ; whilst man's desire and longing after moral and intellectual excellence increase in proportion to his successful efforts to attain it.[1]

(c) **Injurious to the Well-being of the People.**—*The application to economic life of the Liberal principles of individualism and egoism cannot lead to social peace and prosperity ; and to expect it to do so is in contradiction to experience and history.* The assertion that the untrammelled liberty of the individual in economic activities can supply a sure foundation of peace and harmony need not be seriously discussed. Human society is unthinkable apart from social rights and duties and a due regard for the common good, all of which must limit individual liberty. Besides the limitations set by the natural law it is a matter of commonsense and experience that public authority must in many ways interpose its sanctions to secure that social rights and duties be respected, and the common good adequately safeguarded.

Hence, Pius XI, treating of economic Liberalism, writes :

"Free competition . . . though within certain limits just and productive of good results, cannot be the ruling principle of the economic world ; this has been abundantly proved by the consequences that have followed from the free rein given to these dangerous individualistic ideals."[2]

The freedom accorded by English law to the Irish landlords of the 18th and 19th centuries to rack-rent and arbitrarily evict their tenants did not lead to harmony or justice between the two classes concerned ; and, far from promoting material welfare or economic progress, resulted in the pauperisation and partial extermination of the agricultural population. Neither did the liberty which the British manufacturing employers enjoyed during the same

---

[1] Antoine, *loc. cit.*, art. 2.
[2] *Quadragesimo Anno*, 1931 (C. T. S. edition), pp. 40, 41 ; cf. also *ib.*, pp. 60, 61.

period to beat down the wages of their workers to a standard of bare subsistence and to subject them to inhuman conditions produce harmony between the classes or promote social progress so far as the overwhelming majority of the people were concerned.

Indeed, the indictment of history against the principles of economic Liberalism is quite overwhelming. It is the practical application of these principles that has led to Irish and British pauperisation, which in extent and intensity is unparalleled in Europe.[1] The same principles are accountable for the unchristian character of the British Poor Law System of the 19th century, for the horrors of the English factory system of the first half of the same century,[2] for such national crimes as the Irish famines of the 18th and 19th centuries, for the periodic famines in India,[3] for the evils connected with modern capitalism such as cornering, profiteering and gambling on the Stock Exchange, the consequent extremes of poverty and wealth, the class antagonism, the misery and moral degradation of the poorer classes.

Unlimited freedom of competition in economic matters sets up in fact a species of anarchy as a result of which the weaker members of the social body inevitably fall under the domination of the stronger and more ruthless. At the present day this economic dominance is realised and exercised through money and the monopoly of credit concentrated in the power of a few.

---

[1] Cf. Antoine, *op. cit.*, chap. xx.

[2] Cf. Devas, *op. cit.*, bk. iii, chap. viii.

[3] " The characteristic doctrine of classical political economy has caused, during the 19th century, not less than ten millions to perish of starvation in India and Ireland." Devas, *op. cit.*, bk. i, chap. vii, p. 145. Cf. also *Prosperous British India*, by Sir William Digby (London, 1902), in which the author shows the disastrous results of the British Indian policy (shaped in accordance with the principles of Economic Liberalism). Among these results have been the appalling increase of Indian famines. During the 19th century no less than 19 famines have occurred in India, accounting for a death-roll of 33,000,000 of persons (the complete death list of all the wars of the 19th century reached about 5,000,000 ; that of the recent Great European War about 7,000,000) : and all this notwithstanding the well-known fact that India produces more food than her people can consume, and that she is much less densely populated than most European countries. But, as with Ireland, the well-being of the people has been disregarded under the plea that Government measures for such a purpose " interfering with the course of trade " " would be contrary to the principles of Political Economy " (Cf. Antoine, *loc. cit.*).

" This accumulation of power," writes Pius XI, " the characteristic note of the modern economic order, is a natural result of the limitless free competition, which permits the survival of those only who are the strongest, which often means those who fight most relentlessly, and pay the least heed to the dictates of conscience." [1]

Hence, too, the enforcing of the principle of unlimited freedom of competition has had the effect of destroying all competition and producing unjust monopolies. This result, which the present day has seen substantially realised, is also deplored by Pius XI :

" Free competition is dead : economic dictatorship has taken its place. Unbridled ambition for domination has succeeded the desire for gain : the whole economic life has become hard, cruel and relentless in a ghastly measure." [2]

The logical development and practical tendency of economic Liberalism are towards a return to the economic system prevailing in Europe before the rise of Christianity, namely, the establishment of *the Servile State*. Where such development does not occur, the existence of Liberal capitalism inevitably causes a reaction towards Socialism. [3]

---

[1] *Quadragesimo Anno*, 1931 (C. T. S. edition), p. 47.
[2] *Ib.*
[3] Cf. Belloc—*Servile State, loc. cit.*

CHAPTER X

INDIVIDUALISTIC CAPITALISM[1]

Liberalism is justly regarded as the philosophic ground-work of modern Capitalism, of which we shall now treat. The term Capitalism is often used in a vague and undetermined sense. It is commonly understood to refer to an industrial system or régime in which the resources of the country are controlled by a comparatively small number of individuals, while the working population are property-less and more or less oppressed. How far these general ideas of Capitalism are accurate will appear from the following.

Division of the Subject.—In the present sketch, after explaining what the Capitalist Economic Régime is, and discussing briefly its moral aspects and the attitude of the Church towards it, we shall outline the main features of the form which it has assumed in modern times, and which we have in the title of the present chapter termed *Individualistic Capitalism*. We shall then sketch briefly the genesis and growth of the Capitalist Economic Régime, and of the type of capitalism which has got engrafted on it. In the third place we shall analyse the false principles upon which Individualistic Capitalism rests ; and describe briefly the main evils to which it has given rise.

---

[1] Cf. Antoine, *op. cit.*, chap. xiii ; Belliot, *op. cit.* 1iere partie, chap. ii, sec. ii ; and 2ieme partie, chap. ii ; Costa-Rosetti, *op. cit.*, pp. 512 and 762–833. O'Brien—*Economic Effects of the Reformation* (London, 1923), chap. ii ; Tawney—*Religion and the Rise of Capitalism* (London, 1926), and *The Acquisitive Society* (Bell, London, 1927, 8th edit.) ; Werner Sombart—*The Jews and Modern Capitalism* (translated from the German by M. Epstein. Dutton & Co., New York, 1903. The French translation of the same book is entitled *Les Juifs et la Vie Economique*, Payot, Paris, 1923), chaps. ii–xi ; Belloc—*Servile State*, secs. iv and v ; Devas—*Political Economy*, bk. ii, chaps. x and xi ; and bk. iii, chap. viii ; *Cath. Encyclop.*—art. " Monopoly " ; Watt, S.J.—*Capitalism and Morality* (Cassel, London, 1929) and *The Future of Capitalism* (C. S. G., Oxford, 1931) ; Adams—*Real Wealth, Financial Poverty* (London, 1925) ; Palgrave, *op. cit.*, vol. ii, art. " Industrial Evolution " ; Lingard and Belloc—*The History of England*, vol. xi (London, 1915), pp. 60, 65, 113, 127–137, 174, 175, 242–244, 429–436, 599–769 ; *Dict. Apolog. de la Foi Cath.*—art. " Socialisme," cols. 1441–1446. Cahill, S.J.—*Freemasonry and the Anti-Christian Movement* (Dublin, 1930, 2nd edit.), *see* index *sub verbo* " Capitalism."

Art. 1—*The Capitalist Régime and Individualistic Capitalism*

Capital and Capitalists.—In order to convey a correct idea of the meaning of the Capitalist Economic Régime and of the abuses which Individualistic Capitalism includes, we must first explain briefly the kindred term *capital.* Some authors define capital as *wealth which yields a revenue ;* others as *that part of wealth which is set aside for future production.*[1] Each of these definitions serves to emphasise a special aspect of capital. Economists draw a distinction between *goods of consumption* such as food and clothing, which serve for the purpose of directly satisfying one's immediate needs and are consumed by being used, and *productive goods,* such as land, machinery, railways, farm stock, which, although meant ultimately to satisfy human needs, are directly utilised rather for the production of other goods. We may for our present purpose understand Capital in the general sense of *productive goods,* to which each of the given definitions substantially applies.

Capital therefore is an essential element in the conduct of industry of whatever kind ; for " Capital cannot do without Labour, nor Labour without Capital,"[2] and as long as the social organisation is based mainly upon private property (which is the only system compatible with human well-being and peace), individual proprietors will always own the capital of a country, at least to a considerable extent. In other words there always have been, and always will be capital and capitalists.

The Capitalist Economic Régime.—The Capitalist Economic Régime is aptly described by Pope Pius XI as the economic system " in which the capital and labour jointly needed for production are provided by different people."[3] It is contradistinguished from the economic system in which the workers are also the owners of the capital. This latter system prevailed largely in mediæval times even among the industrial population ; and it still exists among the major portion of the agricultural classes. In industrial work, however, as distinct from that of agriculture, the

---

[1] Cf. Palgrave, *op. cit.,* vol. i, p. 217.
[2] Leo XIII—*Rerum Novarum,* p. 142.
[3] *Quadragesimo Anno,* C. T. S. edit., p. 45.

capitalist régime has now become almost universal, with the result that in some countries the ownership or control of most of the productive property is exercised by a relatively small section of the community, while the majority of the population possess no productive property of any kind, and are employed by the others as wage-earners. The former class are styled the Capitalists and the others the Proletariat —a term borrowed from the writers of pagan Rome, where the propertyless but free population was referred to as the *Proletarii*.

Moral Aspects of the Capitalist Régime.—We shall show in a later chapter,[1] when dealing with Employer and Employed, that the wage contract is not in itself essentially unjust. Neither would a régime be in which even the dominating portion of the labouring population earn their bread by working under equitable conditions, for capitalist owners or employers. For in such a system each party, employer and employee, receives a fair portion of the fruits of production to which both parties have contributed, the one by giving his labour and the other by supplying the capital, without which the labour would be impossible. Hence the Church does not condemn the capitalist economic régime as in itself unjust, nor does she find fault with the owner of capital who, while granting a just wage and due conditions of employment to his labourers, reserves a reasonable profit for himself as the just equivalent of the part played in the production by the capital which he owns.

" Surely," writes Pius XI, " it [viz., the Capitalist Economic Régime] is not vicious of its very nature ; but it violates right order whenever capital so employs the working or wage-earning classes, as to divert business and economic activities entirely to its own arbitrary will and advantage . . ."[2]

Church's Attitude towards it.—But although the capitalist régime is not essentially vicious, the Church's tendency has always been more in favour of a system in which the dominating portion of the workers are owners or part owners of the capital with which they labour. The Christian social

---

[1] *Infra*, chap. xxi, art. i
[2] *Quadragesimo Anno*, p. 48.

ideal, which emphasises so strongly the dignity and privileges of human personality, is more easily realised in a social system which includes the widest extension of ownership. Hence Leo XIII writes :

" The law should favour ownership, and its policy should be to induce as many as possible of the humbler class to become owners."[1]

The reason of the Church's policy in this regard is obvious. Labour has been constituted by Providence as the normal means of supporting life. Now, one cannot labour without something to exercise one's energies upon. Hence the man who lacks productive property is at the mercy of others in a matter which lies at the root of his temporal well-being. This is out of harmony with Christian ideals of reasonable liberty as a natural right of the human person.

Besides, it is a well-known fact that the possession of at least a reasonable amount of productive property tends to develop in the individual a praiseworthy spirit of self-respect and self-reliance, as well as a sense of responsibility. Thus the wide diffusion of ownership improves the general character of the people and communicates an element of stability to the whole social system.

" Every effort, therefore, must be made," writes Pius XI . . . " that . . . an ample sufficiency be supplied to the working-man. The purpose is . . . that wage-earners of all kinds be enabled by economizing that portion of their wage which remains after necessary expenses have been met to attain to the possessions of a certain modest fortune."[2]

A further reason why the Church favours the wide extension of ownership rather than the prevalence of the capitalist régime, is the fact that the latter is specially liable to grave abuse and tends to develop into the Individualistic Capitalism which is so prevalent at the present day.

Individualistic Capitalism.—Individualistic Capitalism is nothing else than the unjust and perverted form which the capitalist régime has assumed in modern times. It is to this form of capitalism Pius XI refers when he says that

---

[1] *Rerum Novarum*, p. 158.
[2] *Quadragesimo Anno*, pp. 30 and 34.

the capitalist régime though not vicious of its very nature " violates right order, whenever capital so employs the working or wage-earning classes, as to divert business and economic activity entirely to its own arbitrary will and advantage, without any regard to the human dignity of the workers, the social character of economic life, social justice and the common good."[1]

According to Christian teaching and the natural law, all men's activities must be exercised in harmony with proper order and the divine plan ; and they are faulty in so far as they recede from it.   Now since God created material goods to supply men's temporal needs, the process of manufacture and exchange by which these goods are made available for human use must be subordinated to these needs.   Hence it is a perversion of right order to make the productive and trading activities of the community completely subservient to the personal gain or ambition of a few capitalists even to the detriment of the people's well-being.   This is what has actually occurred in modern times.   Practically the whole economic system is being shaped and worked with a view to gratifying the avarice and ambition of the capitalist owners, or still worse of those who, though not the real owners of the capital, are enabled by means of the financial lever to control and mould to their own arbitrary will the economic life of the nation.   Hence have followed the oppression and exploitation of the working population, whose right to a fair opportunity of utilising the earth's resources for their human needs is not sufficiently upheld either by the law of the land, or in the public conscience.

Owing to the dominating role played by the financial magnates in this perversion and abuse, and the extent to which the modern economic system, founded as it is upon the Capitalist Economic Régime, has become subservient to the monied interests, modern or Individualistic Capitalism is sometimes defined *as a social system in which the bankers and masters of finance have unjustly seized the supreme control of production, consumption and exchange and practically dominate the whole social life of the nation.*

"On the one side," writes Leo XIII, " there is the party which holds power because it holds wealth, which has in its grasp the whole of labour and trade, which manipulates for its

---

[1] *Ib.*, p. 45.

benefit and its own purposes all the resources of supply, and which is even represented in the councils of the State itself. . . . On the other side there is the needy and powerless multitude, broken down and suffering and ever ready for disturbance."[1]

Art. 2—*Rise and Growth of the Capitalist Economic Régime*

Summary of the Subject.—The causes which have led to the rise and spread of the Capitalist Economic Régime are numerous and complex, and it is outside our scope to attempt an adequate analysis of them. Among these causes may be enumerated the rise into importance of liquid or fluid funds and the lowering of the prestige of immovable property, which began in the 16th century as a result of the expansion of commerce ; the Protestant revolt of the same century; the " Industrial Revolution " of the 18th century ; the Liberalistic Philosophy which began to prevail about the same time ; and finally the purely selfish and materialistic outlook derived especially from Calvinism and Judaism which is the very essence of the capitalistic spirit. The two last causes, namely, Liberalism, and the selfish and materialistic mentality of Judaism and Calvinism are the main sources of the anti-social abuses which we have designated by the term Individualistic Capitalism.

Growth of Liquid Wealth.—In mediæval times immovable property and its accessories, such as land and farm stock, mines, fisheries, factories and workshops, were practically the only type of wealth, and were mostly owned by individual proprietors, who depended on them for their support. Before the 16th century the volume of European trade, and consequently the amount of money in circulation, were comparatively small. As a result, however, of the discovery of America, South Africa and the sea route to the East Indies, new fields were opened up for enterprise and commerce, while at the same time immense supplies of the precious metals flowed into Europe. This greatly increased the desire and the need of money, and from this also arose a new form of wealth founded upon oversea trade and the different organisms of exchange. About the same

---

[1] *Rerum Novarum*, pp. 158, 159.

time the removal, under the Protestant régime, of the prohibition of usury gave money a new and additional value.
As a result of these causes, the ancient prestige of productive
property, as the one type of wealth, declined. Lands and
other forms of immovable property were mortgaged for
money, and large portions of the real property of Europe
passed under the control of money-owners and money-
lenders.[1] Later on, when, as a result of the industrial
revolution in the 18th century, the custom of mass production began to prevail, great sums were needed to equip
factories and organise the yearly-increasing volume of trade.
This led to the foundation of the great joint stock companies
in which shares were often held by persons who had no
other connection with the activities of the trading or manufacturing companies of which they were the part-owners.

Again, increasing trade supplied the occasion for speculation, thus opening a new field for easy profits without
labour. These tendencies continued to assume ever greater
proportions during the 16th and following centuries,
especially in Great Britain, till in our day speculation and
finance dominate the whole economic and social life of
many nations.

Formation of the British Capitalist Class.—An important
and indeed almost decisive element in the rise and extension
of the Capitalist Economic Régime was the course of events
in Great Britain and Ireland during the 16th and 17th
centuries. By the plunder of the Church in these countries
in the 16th century a very large proportion of the total
wealth (hitherto controlled by the guilds and the ecclesiastical corporations for the service of the people) passed into
the hands of a small clique of greedy adventurers, who thus
formed the nucleus of a capitalist class. Later on, in the
17th century, this class, now reinforced by the Puritan
and allied Jewish elements, made the Crown subservient to
them, and succeeded in establishing a political oligarchy
founded on the control of wealth.[2]

The two great movements, one agricultural and the other

---

[1] Cf. Belliot, *loc. cit.*
[2] Belloc—*Servile State, loc. cit.*, and *History of England* (Lingard and
Belloc), *loc. cit.* ; cf. also Pius XI, *ib.*, pp. 45-48.

industrial, which mark the social and economic history of Britain in the 18th century, enabled this dominant class to extend their power still further. They assumed almost complete control of the whole economic and political life of the nation, while the mass of the people, although nominally enjoying political freedom, were practically reduced to the condition of a helpless proletariat.

The improved methods of agriculture which were introduced into Britain during the first half of the 18th century were accompanied by the unjust seizure of the common lands by the landlord class, and the wholesale absorption of the small peasant holdings into the demesnes of the great proprietors.[1] Thus the possession of the land, which in every country is the foundation of political and economic freedom, passed from the people to the dominant class.

In the latter half of the same century, the invention of the steam-engine, the power-loom, etc., and the introduction of the smelting of iron by coal, brought about what is called the " Industrial Revolution."[2] The main characteristic of this new economic phase is mass production by means of machinery and steam or motor power. As it requires very considerable means to equip a factory, the wealthy class, already referred to, were enabled to anticipate and prevent any attempt at a co-operative development of the new industrial methods. They quickly gained control of the large factories, in which the mass of the propertyless workers were employed for wages ; destroyed the trade of the small independent artificers and thus dominated the whole industrial machine.[3]

The laws enacted in England and other countries for the formation of impersonal manufacturing and trading companies facilitated the growth of the power of the capitalist class, and the increasing exploitation of the workers.

" The regulations legally enacted," again writes Pius XI,

---

[1] Cf. Palgrave, op. cit., vol. i, p. 29 ; Seebohm—English Village Community, pp. 13–15. It is said that between 1710 and 1867, over seven and a half millions of statute acres in England and Wales (nearly a third of the whole cultivable area) passed from small holders into the hands of the large proprietors, thus displacing or drawing into the wage-earning and propertyless class hundreds of thousands of peasants.

[2] Cf. Palgrave, op. cit., vol. ii, p. 400, art. " Industrial Revolution."

[3] Cf. ib. ; also Belloc—Servile State, pp. 57–77, and History of England (Belloc and Lingard), vol. xi, loc. cit.

"for corporations with their divided responsibility and limited liability have given occasion to abominable abuses. The greatly weakened accountability makes little impression, as is evident, upon the conscience. The worst injustices and frauds take place beneath the obscurity of the common name of a corporative firm."[1]

Art. 3—*Rise of Individualistic Capitalism*

Individualistic Capitalism has developed from the Capitalist Economic Régime. It is not a necessary result of that régime which, as already stated, is not essentially vicious. The capitalist régime is, however, specially liable to abuse owing to the abnormal power it places in the hands of the capitalist section of the community and the weak position of the propertyless workers. Still, had the influence of the Church been as great in the 18th century when the capitalist economic régime began in Great Britain, as it was in the 11th century when feudalism was Christianised, it is certain that the development of industrial life would have followed a very different course. The influences which led to the rise of Individualistic Capitalism came from three main sources, namely, Protestantism, Judaism, and unchristian Liberalism. We touch briefly on each in turn.

Protestant and Calvinistic Mentality.—A very important element in the evolution of Individualistic Capitalism is the purely selfish and materialistic outlook on life which was inherited from the Protestant Revolt. This attitude of mind, which is fundamentally opposed to the spirit of Catholicism, appears in its worst form in the spirit of Calvinism and Puritanism. Calvinism is the type of Protestantism that prevailed in Holland, Switzerland and Scotland, and later on in the north-Eastern counties of Ireland. Puritanism, which exerted the greatest influence in England, is only an adaptation of Calvinism. The growth and triumph of Puritanism in England in the 17th century was the most fundamental factor in the formation and development of modern England, as we know it.[2] Now England and Holland were, so to speak, the homeland of

---

[1] *Ib.*, p. 60.
[2] Cf. Tawney, *op. cit.*, pp. 198, 199 ; O'Brien, *op. cit.*, chap. ii.

the Capitalistic Economic Régime and the breeding ground
from which the individualistic spirit of modern capitalism
has spread over a large part of the modern world.

Jewish Influence.—As in the case of Liberalism, Freemasonry, Bolshevism, and almost every modern movement
that is essentially unchristian and anti-Catholic, the formation and development of Individualistic Capitalism un-
questionably owes much to the Jews. The whole modern
system of finance, upon which modern capitalism pivots,
is practically a Jewish creation, and the world of finance is
to-day almost completely dominated by the Jews.[1] Again,
English Puritanism, which is so closely associated with the
rise of Individualistic Capitalism, seems to exhibit a certain
affinity with modern Judaism. The Jews were always
specially favoured by the Puritan leaders, and attained
much influence in England under Cromwell, the greatest
and most typical of the English Puritans. Again, the selfish
concentration upon material gain and the worship of worldly
success, which are characteristic of the modern individualistic
spirit, take the place of real religion with Jew and Puritan
alike.[2]

The Liberalist Philosophy.—We have already treated of
the rise of Liberalism in the 18th century, and especially
of the British school of Liberalist Economics. The prevalence of this philosophy with all it implies was to a large
extent the result of the causes already mentioned, and has
been a main factor in the evolution of Individualistic
Capitalism. It is to this element Pius XI alludes in the
following passage :

" A stern insistence on the moral law enforced with vigour
by the civil authority could have dispelled, or perhaps averted
these enormous evils [viz., the abuses and frauds connected with
speculation, finance and the constitution of the impersonal
Limited Liability Companies]. This, however, was too often
lamentably wanting. For at the time when the new social
order was beginning [viz., that of the industrial Revolution of
the 18th century] the doctrines of rationalism had already taken

---

[1] Cf. W. Sombart, *op. cit.*
[2] Cf. O'Brien, Tawney, Sombart, *loc. cit.* ; also Belloc—*The Jews.*

hold of large numbers and an economic science [viz., Economic Liberalism] alien to the true moral law had arisen, whence it followed that free rein was given to human avarice."[1]

The oppression and abuses proceeding from the principles of Economic Liberalism seem to have reached a climax in our own days when almost the whole economic and social life of many nations is dominated by the activities of the great financiers and the giant trusts. These now control in large measure even the production and distribution of the very necessaries of life. They too often divert the energies of the nation to the promotion of activities which are useless or harmful while the masses of the people are in want. Hence arise unnatural monopolies, cornering, dumping, industrial crises, caused by useless overproduction, enforced idleness, euphemistically termed unemployment ; the utilisation of the public credit to promote gambling, degrading cinema shows and sensational newspapers.

Art. 4—*Principles Underlying Individualistic Capitalism*

The principles which form the essence of the modern capitalistic spirit may be described as follows : a false concept of human ownership or control of property ; a perverted idea of the true aim of industrial activity ; an unqualified acceptance of usury ; and a false idea of the legitimate functions of government. We treat each in turn.

(a) **False Concept of Ownership or Control.**—According to Christian teaching, human ownership or control of property is only a stewardship, which the person is bound to exercise in accordance with God's laws, and with due regard to the needs and rights of others. Hence ownership or control of property, as we shall see later,[2] includes—according to Christian teaching—a social as well as an individual aspect : for its object according to the natural and divine law is not only to enable individuals to provide for their own needs and the needs of their families, but also to secure that the goods which the Creator meant for the human race may truly serve that purpose and serve it too in an orderly and stable manner. It follows from this twofold character of ownership, the individual and social character,

---

[1] *Ib.*, pp. 60, 61.   [2] Cf. *Infra*, chap. xvii, art. 3.

10

that the owner in utilising his rights and the State in exercising its functions of safeguarding the rights of all and promoting public prosperity, must take into account not only the individual owner's advantage but also the public good.[1] In this particular, above all, the individualistic outlook of modern Capitalism, in which the rights of ownership and control are regarded as independent of all social obligations and are in practice used for the sole object of increasing the power and wealth of a small class without due regard to the claims of social justice and charity, is in direct opposition to the Christian law. It is to this tyrannical abuse of wealth and power that Leo XIII refers when he speaks of a

" small number of very rich men who have been able to lay upon the teeming masses of the labouring poor a yoke little better than that of slavery itself."[2]

In another passage of the Encyclical quoted the Pope stigmatises the same abuse when he refers to

" the party which has in its grasp the whole of labour and trade, which manipulates for its own benefit and its own purposes all the sources of supply, and which is even represented in the councils of the State itself."[3]

(b) **Perversion of the True Aim of Industry.**—We have already shown that the natural law ordains that industry be conducted in the interests of the community, that is of the actual producers and consumers of the goods, which form the object of the industry. Christian ideals require besides, that in the management and control of industrial operations, the well-being and security of the workers should be a primary consideration. In the actual form, however, which modern capitalism has assumed, the ownership of the capital and supreme control of the industrial organisations are very frequently divorced almost entirely from the life of the workers, and from the interests of both producer and consumer. Thus the Rio Tinto Mines of Spain may be controlled by a British syndicate. The Irish, Roumanian, or Greek railway system or mercantile

---

[1] Pius XI—*Quadragesimo Anno*, pp. 20–22.
[2] *Rerum Novarum*, p. 131.   [3] *Ib.*, p. 159.

marine ; the diamond mines of Kimberley ; the tobacco factories of Ireland, etc., may be controlled by groups of London or American or Jewish financiers, whose policy is shaped only with a view to power or gain, and who have no personal connection with, and no interest in, the actual producers or in those whose needs these industries are meant to supply, except in so far as they may be utilised as a means to profit. This is the root cause of the chaos which reigns to-day in the industrial organisation of the civilised countries of the world, where the anomalous position exists that immense multitudes are unemployed and in want while natural resources from which all their needs could be supplied are left undeveloped.[1]

(c) **Modern Capitalism Essentially Connected with Usury.**—The Christian teaching on usury is practically disregarded in the working of modern Capitalism. The system in its actual working includes, according to Leo XIII, the practice of " rapacious usury " which, though appearing " under a different guise," is included in the Church's age-long condemnations.[2]

(d) **False Principles regarding the Functions of Government.**—Leo XIII, in a passage already quoted, writes, that as a result of the revolt against the Church and the dissolution of the industrial guilds, the workers were " surrendered all isolated and helpless to the hardheartedness of employers and the greed of unchecked competition." This was done in accordance with the false principles of economic Liberalism, which we have already described.[3] According to Liberalist principles the State has no duty and no right to interfere in economic activities even for the purpose of defending the rights of the poor and the weak. Consequently, the interests of these were left to the working of what the defenders of this theory call " Economic Laws." The inevitable result of such a policy was the oppression of the workers, the gradual increase of the wealth and power of the capitalistic class and the growing concentration of

---

[1] Cf. Adams and Devas, *loc. cit.*
[2] *Rerum Novarum, loc. cit.*
[3] Cf. *Supra,* chap. ix, arts. 6 and 7.

148   THE FRAMEWORK OF A CHRISTIAN STATE

power and control in the hands of the few who were able
to drive all other competitors from the field.

" This accumulation of power," writes Pius XI, " the characteristic note of the modern economic order is a natural result
of the limitless free competition, which permits the survival of
those only who are the strongest, which often means those who
fight most relentlessly, who pay least heed to the dictates of
conscience. . . . As the ultimate consequence of this individualistic spirit in economic affairs . . . free Competition is dead ;
economic dictatorship has taken its place, unbridled ambition
for domination has succeeded the desire for gain ; the whole
economic life has become hard, cruel and relentless in a ghastly
measure."[1]

Art. 5—Evil Results of Individualistic Capitalism

Widespread Insecurity and Pauperism.—Leo XIII, writing
in 1891 on the Condition of the Working Classes, speaks of
the " misery and wretchedness pressing so unjustly on the
majority of the working classes."[2] Pius XI in his recent
Encyclical on the social Order refers to the

" immense numbers of propertyless wage-earners on the one
hand and the superabundant riches of the fortunate few on the
other."[3] He speaks too of " the frightful perils to which the
morals of the workers . . . and the virtue of girls and women are
exposed in modern factories . . . of the disgraceful housing
conditions . . . and the insuperable difficulties placed in the
way of a proper observance of the holydays." " Bodily labour,"
he adds, " which was decreed by God's Providence for the good
of man's body and soul . . . has everywhere been changed into
an instrument of strange perversion ; for dead matter leaves the
factory ennobled and transformed where men are corrupted and
degraded."[4]

The wealth and power of modern Europe, the great
colonial expansion opening up new and almost inexhaustible
fields of enterprise for the energies of the European people,
the scientific discoveries and mechanical inventions of the
past two centuries by which the productive capacity of the
nations of the world has been multiplied many times over,
have not brought proportionate relief or improvement of
conditions to the masses of the people. In many ways the

---

[1] *Ib.*, p. 47.   [2] *Rerum Novarum*, p. 134.
[3] *Quadragesimo Anno*, p. 29.   [4] *Ib.*, pp. 61, 62.

condition of these is much worse than it was four centuries ago. Pauperism, insecurity, unrest, and material degradation are much more intense and widespread to-day than they were before the productive power of human labour had been reinforced by modern scientific and mechanical discoveries ; and the prevalence of these conditions in any given country corresponds broadly to the extent to which the modern individualistic capitalism has taken hold there. Thus at present in three of the most capitalistic and highly industrialised countries of the world (viz., the United States of America, Great Britain and Germany) there are more than twelve millions of workers unemployed, who with their families must needs be suffering dire need even as regards the prime necessaries of life ! That this unprecedented phenomenon is mainly a result of the modern capitalist system is generally admitted. Again, Pius XI, making special reference to the workings of the same system in the native and colonial States of Asia and Africa, in which European capitalistic methods have been introduced and the native social organisation supplanted, writes :

" After modern machinery and modern industry had progressed with astonishing speed and taken possession of many newly colonized countries no less than of the ancient civilisations of the far East, the numbers of the dispossessed labouring masses, whose groans mount to heaven from these lands increased beyond all measure."[1]

In the same passage the Pope speaks of the condition of the landless rural labourers of European countries. He recalls the words of Leo XIII, who refers to the same class as " the needy and powerless multitude sick and sore in spirit and ever ready for disturbance ! " and adds :

" There is the immense army of hired rural labourers, whose condition is depressed in the extreme, and who have no hope of ever obtaining a share in the land. These, too, unless efficacious remedies be applied, will remain perpetually sunk in their proletarian condition.[2]

Contrast with Mediæval Social Conditions.—The unsocial and unnatural character of the modern Capitalistic system

---

[1] *Quadragesimo Anno*, p. 29.   [2] *Ib.*

is still further illustrated, when present conditions are contrasted with the social conditions of mediæval times under a predominantly Christian régime. Although the average productive capacity of each man was then immensely less than it now is, owing to mechanical contrivances and scientific knowledge, the people as a whole had a greater abundance of the necessaries of life, greater contentment and security, than they now enjoy.[1] Nay, notwithstanding the primitive methods of agriculture and manufacturing which then prevailed, the workers had much more rest and leisure than at present. Thus, besides the Sunday rest, there was in most countries of Europe an average of one holyday of obligation every week, and in some localities nearly double that number. On these days all abstained from servile work. At present there are scarcely half a dozen days in the whole year besides Sundays in which the labourers are exempted from work ; and in many countries not even is the Sunday rest observed.[2]

Forcing of Women into Industrial Work.—A still further illustration of the chaos which now reigns in the economic world is the increasing participation of women (and sometimes even of children) in industrial and other work outside the home to the neglect of home duties, and other work which women alone can do and which is of greater import-

---

[1] Cf. *Supra,* chaps. v and vii.

[2] It is true that pestilence and local famines (resulting mostly from unscientific methods of agriculture and consequent failure of crops) were of frequent occurrence in mediæval times ; and that there was little organisation to cope with them. This state of affairs gave rise to petty wars, raids for food into neighbouring territories and consequent feuds. Much of all this has been eliminated owing to the progress of science, increased facilities of transit and intercommunication, and the higher development of governmental organisation. Again, modern society has made great progress in the wider diffusion of literary knowledge (as distinct from education) ; in the organisation of public utilities, such as roads, bridges, etc., and in hygiene with a consequent decrease of infant mortality (at least among the well-to-do classes) and the lengthening of the average duration of human life. It is true, too, that a certain, though altogether inadequate, participation in the advantages of modern material progress has flowed out to the poorer classes ; and that their condition is not as bad now as it was, for instance, in the first quarter of the 19th century (*See infra,* chap. xi, art, 4, p. 176 ; also Pius XI—*Quadragesimo Anno,* p. 29) ; but none of all this affects the general truth of the statements in the text.

ance for the public good. Pius XI refers frequently in his recent Encyclicals to this abuse.

" Intolerable, and to be opposed with all our strength, is the abuse whereby mothers of families . . . are forced to engage in gainful occupations outside the domestic walls to the neglect of their own proper cares and duties, particularly the education of their children."[1] Again, he writes : " The mind shudders if we consider the frightful perils to which the morals of workers . . . and the virtue of girls and women are exposed in modern factories."[2]

According to the manifest intention of the Author of nature the man is in normal circumstances the breadwinner of the family, while the primary function of the woman is to take charge of the home and of the children's upbringing. The root cause of the perverted custom which the Pope stigmatises is the chaos which has been permitted to reign in industrial life in pursuance of the Liberal principles of free competition and the non-interference of public authority in industrial organisation. Employers were allowed to reduce men's wages below the true standard of a living wage, thus making necessary the supplementary earnings of the wife and mother. Again, employers seeking their own personal gains often prefer women's labour, as it is usually cheaper. In default of any regulating authority, or the moderating influence of a Christian and well-informed public opinion, the abuse has been allowed to grow till the stability of the family and of home life is now seriously threatened.

Dictatorship of the Financial Lords.—Forty-one years ago (1891) Leo XIII referred in memorable words to " a small number of very rich men who have been able to lay upon the teeming masses of the labouring poor a yoke little better than slavery itself."[3] The dominance of the monied classes is much more absolute now than it was then. Now, not only the workers and the poor but also manufacturers, merchants, and even farmers are made to feel in a very effective manner

---

[1] *Quadragesimo Anno*, p. 33.
[2] *Ib.*, p. 61 ; also *Casti Connubii* (C. T. S. edit.), p. 62 ; and Leo XIII—*Rerum Novarum*, p. 156.
[3] *Rerum Novarum*, p. 134.

the despotic control of the great bankers and controllers of finance.

" It is patent that in our days," writes Pius XI, " not only is wealth accumulated, but immense power and despotic economic domination is concentrated in the hands of a few : and that those few are frequently not the owners, but only the trustees and directors of invested funds, who administer them at their own good pleasure."[1]

The control exercised by the banking syndicates over the people's money deposited with them has undergone a new development especially in our own times. Industry of all kinds is now largely financed by what is called credit or bank loans : and the bankers who control the allotment of the credit and can stipulate its conditions can thus practically control industry and trade. It is to this special characteristic of modern Capitalism that Pius XI refers in the following striking passage.

" This power," he writes, alluding to the control exercised by the Bankers and the Directors of companies over the people's deposits and the invested funds, " becomes particularly irresistible, when exercised by those, who because they hold and control money, are able also to govern credit and determine its allotment, for that reason supplying so to speak the life-blood to the entire economic body, and grasping, as it were, in their hands the very soul of production, so that no one dare breathe against their will."[2]

The dictatorship of finance is at present probably the most comprehensive and far-reaching evil of the capitalist system. It puts the financial magnates, who are mostly Masonic Jews and the inveterate enemies of Christianity,[3] in a position to exercise an immense measure of control over the public and private life of the whole people. These financial magnates—irresponsible, anonymous, almost impersonal—now largely control every department of industry and commerce, including even agriculture and fisheries as well as the agencies of distribution. The result is that they form a kind of irresponsible super-government. They can so manipulate the industrial machine that by their arbitrary

---

[1] *Quadragesimo Anno*, p. 46.   [2] *Ib.*
[3] Cf. Cahill, *op. cit.* (*See* Index under " Jews and F." and " Finance and F.").

decree, issued at New York, or London or Hamburg, millions of workers all over Europe and America can be deprived of all means of livelihood. They can increase or reduce the purchasing power of a given sum of money by freely issuing or withdrawing currency and financial credit. By this means productive industry may be held up, the current of trade may be stopped or reversed. The smiling countryside, with its waving crops and happy homesteads may be gradually converted into a tenantless expanse and the helpless people driven into exile or sent to swell the degraded slum population of the crowded cities.

The same half-hidden, anonymous influence controls the Press, the international newsagencies, the theatre, the cinema, the book market.[1] It practically arranges what the public shall eat and wear and read. Although injustice and tyranny have been all too common in every age of the world's history it is questionable if any tyranny ever before existed so widespread, so irresponsible and so callous as the tyranny over men's activities which is at present exercised by the masters of high finance.

Usurpation of Functions of Government.—Another phase of this abuse still more injurious to the public welfare is the unscrupulous manner in which the great capitalists and financiers have in modern times practically usurped the functions of the legitimate government in most countries of Europe and America. According to Catholic teaching, the State is a Perfect Society, the purpose of which is to promote the temporal well-being of its members. Hence it has within itself the duty, as well as the right, to take all the necessary measures for that end, which are consistent with the divine and natural law. The ruling power in the State cannot lawfully hand over its responsibilities to any outside power. Much less can it allow the economic life of the nation upon which the temporal well-being of the people so largely depends, to pass under the control of irresponsible individuals or foreign syndicates. This is what has actually occurred in very many modern states of Europe and America. In these the real power, controlling not only the economic life of the nation, but even its

---

[1] *Ib,*, pp. 165–167.

domestic and foreign policy is exercised by the banking syndicates and the great finanical magnates. On this aspect of modern capitalism, Pius XI writes :

" The intermingling, and scandalous confusion of the duties and offices of civil authority and of economics have produced crying evils, and have gone far to degrade the majesty of the State. The State, which should be the supreme arbiter, ruling in kingly fashion far above all party contention, intent only upon justice and the common good, has become instead a slave, bound over to the service of human passion and greed."[1]

It is the financiers and big capitalists who nowadays effectively control the domestic and foreign policies of states, make and unmake governments, set up and pull down dynasties, order wars and dictate the terms of peace. These matters are arranged not for the purpose of promoting the temporal or spiritual good of the nations, but solely with a view to safeguarding or increasing the power of certain individuals or groups, who have no legitimate right or claim to such control or to any special voice in these affairs.[2]

Modern Trade Wars.—It is now commonly admitted that most modern wars are at root trade wars, the issues at stake being principally the financial interests of certain groups rather than any real political or national question.

" This concentration of power," again writes Pius XI, referring to the great financiers, " has led to a threefold struggle for domination. First, there is the struggle for dictatorship in the economic sphere itself ; then the fierce battle to acquire the control of the State so that its resources and authority may be abused in the economic struggle ; finally, the clash between states themselves. This latter arises from two causes : because the nations apply their power and political influence, regardless of circumstances to promote the economic advantage of the citizens ; and because *vice-versa* economic forces and economic domination are used to decide political controversies between peoples."[3]

---

[1] *Quadragesimo Anno*, pp. 47, 48.
[2] For some interesting illustrations of the power of financiers in dictating policy, cf. Count Corti—*Reign of the House of Rothschild* (Gollancz, London, 1930).
Quadragesimo Anno, p. 47.

Threatened Ruin of European Civilisation.—Not only does this modern individualistic capitalism tend to produce the dreadful clashes netween nations of which the Pope speaks, but it also, especially at the present day, bears in its bosom the germs of revolution and social upheaval. Leo XIII, writing of capitalism forty-one years ago, refers in a passage already quoted to the labouring population who have been disinherited through its operation as " the needy and power-less multitude broken down and suffering and ever ready for disturbance." It is certain that the poverty and in-security, and in many cases degrading human conditions to which so large a proportion of the labouring population are at present subjected are unnatural, and preventible, as well as unjust ; and that there is in reality abundance for all, or at least an abundance of natural resources which could be developed, were it not for the tyrannical and unjust control exercised by the capitalistic magnates. Such con-ditions are in modern times incompatible with national stability. Hence it is generally admitted that European society, especially in the more capitalistic countries, cannot last long in its present state of unstable equilibrium.

" Is it surprising then," writes Pius XI, " that we should no longer possess that security of life in which we can place our trust, and that there remains only the most terrible uncertainty and added fears for the future. Instead of regular daily work there is idleness and unemployment. That blessed tranquillity which is the effect of an orderly existence . . . is no longer to be found, and in its place is the restless spirit of revolt."[1]

One of the possible results of revolution, or even of a great European war, would be an attempt or attempts in different countries to establish Socialism which we shall next discuss.

---

[1] *Ubi Arcano* (1922).

CHAPTER XI

SOCIALISM[1]

Art. 1—*Introduction*

Relations to Capitalism.—Socialism is in part a reaction against Capitalism, its economic theories being, at least in appearance, the reverse of the Liberal principles which form the philosophic groundwork of the capitalistic system. The socialist theories owe such attractiveness as they possess for the labouring population mainly to the opposition in economic doctrine between Socialism and Capitalism, and to the avowed purpose of Socialists to heal the evils which Capitalism has produced. In reality, however, the differences between Socialism and Capitalism are not so great as may seem on the surface. In both systems alike power is concentrated in the hands of a few (viz., the great financiers in one case and the political leaders in the other), and in both also the mass of the people are propertyless, helpless, and practically enslaved. Again, the moral and political principles on which Socialism rests are, like those of Liberalism and Capitalism, purely materialistic. Like Liberalism, too,

---

[1] Cf. *Dict. Apolog. de la Foi Cathol.*, cols. 1396–1446, art. " Socialisme." Gettelmann-Cathrein—*Socialism* (Benziger, New York, 1904) ; Elder— *A Study in Socialism* (Herder, London, 1919) ; Stang—*Socialism and Christianity ;* Kelleher—*Private Ownership* (Gill, Dublin, 1911), chaps. v and viii ; Antoine, *op. cit.*, chap. ix ; Belliot, *op. cit.*, pp. 310–363 (" Ecole Socialiste ") ; C. S. Devas—*Socialism* (booklet of the International Cath. Truth Soc., New York) ; *Cath. Encyclop.*—arts. " Socialism, " " Communism," " Collectivism," " Bolshevism " (Supplementary vol., 1922) ; Palgrave—*Dict. of Pol. Econ.*—arts. " Socialism," " Marx," etc. ; Cronin— *Science of Ethics*, vol. ii, chaps. v–viii ; Ryan—*Distributive Justice*, chaps. iii, iv and xi ; Nesta Webster—*The Socialist Network* (London, 1926) ; Gide and Rist—*History of Economic Doctrines*, bk. ii, chaps. ii, iv and v; bk. iv, chaps. ii and iii ; bk. v, chap. iv. Sydney and Beatrice Webb— *Problems of Modern Industry*, chap. ii ; Sydney Webb—*Socialism in England ;* Karl Marx—*Capital* (translated from the German by Moore and Aveling, 15th Edition, London, 1918) ; Karl Kautsky—*The Capitalist Class* (The Socialist Press, Glasgow) ; Riaznov—*Karl Marx and Frederick Engels* (Laurence, London, 1927) (Riazanov is the Director of the Marx-Engels Institute in Moscow. His philosophy is one of undiluted Materialism).

Socialism is in its origin and history closely associated with Freemasonry, and Talmudic Judaism, and is no less hostile to Christianity.[1]

Anarchism.—The close relations between Socialism and Liberalism are illustrated by the fact that the Anarchists are frequently classed with Socialists, although their doctrine and system, which are those of Naturalism and ultra-individualism, are definitely founded on the Liberalist conception of life. While Liberals would reduce the rôle of the Government to a minimum, the Anarchists would completely abolish all civil and religious authority as well as private property and class distinction which, they say, are the root cause of dissensions between men. They hope when these are removed that men will live together in harmony and peace without the aid of any governing authority. The principal means advocated by the radical or revolutionary Anarchists are the violent spoliation of the capitalists, the burning of title-deeds, the assassination of rulers, and the replacing of the existing social organism by a federation of groups. Another school of Anarchists, however, hold that the end in view will be better promoted by peaceful propaganda, education, co-operation, etc. The best known exponents of Anarchism are Bakunin (d. 1876) and Prince Kropatkin of Russia ; Eliseus Reclus and Proudhon (d. 1865) of France ; and J. Most of Germany.[2]

Syndicalism.—Syndicalism, founded in France (1895), is one type of Anarchism ; for the Syndicalists aim at eliminating completely the central government of the State. They would have the State made up entirely of industrial and perhaps other syndicates, each syndicate including all the workers engaged in the industry and owning and controlling it completely. The State would be a kind of free federation of syndicates. Again, the syndicalists aim at realising their ideal through the means of sabotage, the general strike, revolution and confiscation. The Industrial

---

[1] Cf. Cahill, *op. cit.* (*See* Index under " Jews," " Liberalism " and Communism ").
[2] Cf. *Cath. Encyclop. and Encyclop. Britt.,* art. " Anarchy " ; Antoine, *loc. cit.,* art. 4 ; Elder, *op. cit.,* second part, chap. iii ; Cathrein, *op. cit.,* pp. 14 ff ; Palgrave, *op. cit.* (*See* Index under " Anarchism ") ; Cahill, *op. cit.* (*See* Index under " Anarchy and F ∴.").

Workers of the World (T.W.U.) of U.S.A. (founded by
E. Debbs and W. Haywood in 1905), profess the syndicalist
doctrines.[1]

Division of Subject.—Before discussing Socialism we shall
first treat briefly of Idealistic Communism. For the latter,
although differing essentially from Socialism, contains some
ideals and principles which Socialists have utilized in
elaborating their theories. Russian Bolshevism, which is
a contemporary and relentless application of Socialist principles followed out to their logical conclusions shall be
treated in a separate chapter.

Art. 2—*Idealistic Communism*

Meaning and Use of Term.—The term *Communism* is
sometimes loosely applied to all types of economic organisation in which private ownership of property is either wholly
or partially excluded, whether voluntarily or by law.
Hence Marxian Socialism, in which the private ownership
of productive property is regarded as invalid and immoral,
while ownership of consumers' property is allowed, is sometimes referred to as Communism. Thus the Manifesto of
Marx and Engels (published in 1848) which began the
modern Socialistic movement was called by them the
" Communist Manifesto." Hence, too, Russian Bolshevism
is termed Communism.

The term Communism is also usually applied to the
historical schemes for establishing certain ideally arranged
communities, organised, like the family or religious orders,
on the basis of the members holding all their property in
common. The members, under the direction of a head,
labour and serve the community, each in proportion to his
or her capacity, while each receives from the common store
what he or she needs. This latter type of Communism we
term for the sake of clearness, *Idealistic* and the other
Revolutionary. In the present article we treat only of
Idealistic Communism.

---

[1] Cf. *Cath. Encyclop.*—art. " Syndicalism " ; Clay—*Syndicalism and
Labour* (New York, 1911) ; Hunter—*Violence and the Labour Movement*
(New York, 1914).

Ancient Pagan Communism.—In Crete as early as 1300 B.C., all civil institutions are said to have been organised on a communistic basis.

All the citizens were educated by the State in a uniform way, and all ate at the common tables. The constitution of the Greek city-state of Sparta (or Lacedaemon), said to have been drawn up by Lycurgus (about 900 B.C.), is supposed to have been similar.[1] The Empire of the Incas of Peru is also said to have been organised on a communistic basis.[2]

The Communism of Sparta, however (and probably also that of Crete), was far from being perfect or complete. The privileges of common ownership and civic equality were confined to the dominant or free class, which formed only a small minority of the whole population. Hence in Sparta, the Helots, who were a subject race, and did most of the productive work, were slaves in the worst sense of the term. The Communism described and advocated by Plato in his " Republic," in which there was to be a community of property, of meals, and even of wives, and in which the State was to control the education, the marriages and the occupations of the citizens,[3] is said to have been suggested by the Spartan constitution. Like the latter, Plato excluded slaves from the common privileges and rights.

Christian Communism.—There is, however, a more real, and genuine type of Idealistic Communism, the one, namely, that has been inspired by motives of religion, and especially by the teachings of Christianity.

Most of the religious, or quasi-religious Orders that have arisen within or without the Catholic Church exhibit some of the features of Communism.

The full ideal of the communal life is realised in the Religious Orders and Congregations of both sexes in the Catholic Church. According to the constitutions of these bodies, private ownership, or at least the independent use

---

[1] Cf. Plutarch's *Lives* (" Lycurgus "), and Thucydides' *History*, i, x ; also Myers—*General History*, chap. xiii. Whether or to what extent these States were really communistic is much disputed.

[2] This, too, is doubtful—cf. Gide—*Communist and Co-operative Colonies* (Harrap, London, 1930), chap. iii.

[3] Cf. Plato—*Republic* (London, 1892) ; also Elder, *op. cit.*, Second Part, chap. i.

of property, is completely excluded.   All the members work under the direction of a Superior, each according to his or her capacity, while each receives from the common store what he or she needs.

Many of the early Christians also, even while living in the world with their families, voluntarily adopted the communal life.[1] Further, as we have already pointed out, there existed a very notable communal element in the Christian mediæval social organisation. Indeed this element may be regarded as an essential constituent of the Christian social system.[2]

The Reductions of Paraguay (1608–1757), which were organised under the direction of the Jesuit missionary fathers, were on a partially communal basis, and form the most noted and successful communistic experiment hitherto known outside religious life.[3]

Again, some of the early and mediæval heretical sects, such as the Anabaptists, the Catharists, the Brothers and Sisters of the Free Spirit, proclaimed the necessity of Communism for all Christians. Finally in the 18th and 19th centuries, several non-Catholic religious associations organised on a communal basis, arose in the United States of America. Among these were the Ephratic Community (founded 1732), the Shakers (1787), the Harmonists (1805). One Community of the Shakers apparently still existed in 1925,[4] and is probably not yet extinct.

More's Utopia.—Blessed Thomas More's celebrated work, *Utopia*, which contains a romantic description in the form of a dialogue of an imaginary commonwealth organised on a communistic basis, is perhaps the most inspiring treatise on Communism ever written.[5] The work was meant as a protest against the oppressive practices (such as the unjust enclosure of the common lands, the raising of the rent, etc.) which some of the British landowners indulged in under the Tudors.   The result of these measures was to produce the

---

[1] Cf. *Acts of the Apostles*, ii. 44, 45 ; iv. 32–37, v. 1–4.
[2] Cf. *supra*, chap. vi, art 1.
[3] Cf. *Cath. Encyclop.*, art. " Reductions " ; also Gide, *op. cit.*, chap. v.
[4] Cf. *Cath. Encyclop.*, vol. iv, p. 181, " Communism " ; also Gide, *op. cit.*, chap. vi.
[5] The original of the *Utopia* is in Latin.   Robinson's translation was made in 1551, of which *cf.* Dibbin's edition (London, 1808).

beginnings of the poverty and insecurity which, later on, became so marked a feature of capitalistic England.

In "Utopia," as in Plato's Republic, all the goods are held in common, but there is no community of wives, and the sanctity of family relations is fully provided for. The advocacy of State Communism, however, which the book contains is put by More into the mouth of Raphael Hythoday his principal interlocutor. More himself rejects Hythoday's theories and advocates instead the practice of charity and the Church's traditional doctrines regarding private ownership.[1]

Among several other descriptions of ideal communistic states which owe their inspiration to More's *Utopia*, the best known are Campanella's *City of the Sun* (1625), Francis Bacon's *New Atlantis* (1629), and Harrington's *Oceana* (1656).[2]

Unchristian Communistic Reformers.—Gracchus Babeuf (guillotined 1797), Charles Fourrier (*d.* 1837), and Etienne Cabet (*d.* 1856), all advocated Communism in their writings.[3] Their inspiration came from the spirit of the French Revolution. Hence their ideals were those of Liberalism, so that religion had no place in their system. Again, Robert Owen of Wales (*d.* 1858), one of the great pioneers of the modern labour movement, which he has influenced deeply, and the first to call public attention to the wretched condition of the British factory workers (he introduced many salutary reforms in his own spinning factory at Lanark), elaborated also a type of Communism on a purely materialistic basis.[4]

These writings contained the principles, mostly materialistic and unchristian, on which several purely secular communistic societies (different from the non-Catholic but

---

[1] Cf. Campbell—*More's Utopia and his Social Teaching* (Eyre and Spottiswoode, London, 1930).

[2] Cf. Morley's *Ideal Commonwealths* (London), 1885 ; also Elder, *op. cit.*, Second Part, chap. i.

[3] Cf. Palgrave, *op. cit.*, arts. " Communism," " Babeuf," etc. ; also Gide, *op. cit.*, chaps. vi–viii. *See* also *ib.*, chaps. ix and x for an interesting and useful sketch of a number of agrarian communities, some cooperative, and others partially communistic, including some of the recently established Zionist communities in Palestine.

[4] Cf. Palgrave, *op. cit.*, vol. iii, pp. 46–52.

religious American communities already referred to) such as the Icarians and the New Harmony Community, all very short-lived, were founded in the United States during the 19th century.[1]

Critique of Idealistic Communism.—We may summarise as follows our criticism of idealistic Communism :

I. A social system in which " mine " and " thine " are practically excluded, and in which all the members of the community labour for the good of all in proportion to each one's capacity is an ideal which, from the beginning has inspired generous and noble souls. It probably would have been the normal system of society but for man's fall, and would be still possible at least for a large percentage of the human race were it not for human passions and ignorance and sin.

II. The complete equality between men, as they now are, which communist idealists insist upon and seek to realise, is a well meant but mistaken interpretation of the great truth that the *inalienable* rights attaching to human personality are the same for all. The source of the error lies in ignoring the fact that since the capabilities and circumstances of men vary indefinitely, their *acquired* or *accidental* rights will not be equal. Hence Pope Leo XIII writes :

" It is impossible to reduce society to one dead level. . . . There naturally exist among mankind manifold differences of the most important kind. People differ in capacity, skill, health, energy ; and unequal fortune is a necessary result of unequal conditions." [2]

III. Nevertheless, a very notable element of the communal ideal, at least as regards the use and to a certain extent the ownership of property, may be regarded as practically essential to the Christian concept of society, which is opposed to excessive individualism. The want of this essential element in the modern unchristian social organisation is accountable for most of the unjust and oppressive anomalies, which some well-meaning reformers

---

[1] Cf. Nordhoff—*Communistic Societies of the United States* (New York, 1857) ; Gide, *op. cit.*, chap. vii.
[2] *Rerum Novarum*, 1891, p. 187.

have observed without correctly analysing their causes and true remedies.

IV. The enforcement by law of absolute communism by which men would be excluded from acquiring or enjoying the ownership of property, would be unjust and immoral. Men have a natural right to acquire the ownership of property, at least within certain limits ; and even though individuals may, if they so wish, forego their right, they cannot ordinarily be deprived of it without their own consent.

Besides the system of private ownership is the only practical method upon which society can be successfully organised, as long as men retain their present character- istics. Hence that system is imposed by the Law of Nations (*Jus Gentium*),[1] as being essential for men's well-being.

V. Given man's natural tendencies and needs, a per- manent communistic society is normally possible only in the case of such as choose that type of life from religious motives, and live under strong religious influences. Even in such cases a permanent communal life is usually possible only for celibates, or for small communities living a simple life separated from outside influences.[2]

Art. 3—*Nature of Socialism*

Use of Term.—The term *Socialism* is often used vaguely to indicate any increase of collective or state control over individual action, and especially over economic activities. It is also sometimes employed invidiously to designate the lawful defensive movements of the poorer classes, or even the necessary measures of the government to curtail the privileges of the wealthy owners. Omitting these mis- leading applications of the term, and many others more or less inaccurate,[3] we treat here only of Socialism properly

---

[1] Cf. chap. vi, art i.

[2] Cf. *Cath. Encyclop.*, art. " Communism," p. 182 ; also Gide—*Political Economy*, bk. iii, chap. i, sec. 2, " Communism."

[3] For a sketch of several theories and movements sometimes incorrectly styled *Socialism* and the orthodox Catholic attitude towards them, and especially for some account of the important proposal called " Guild Socialism," cf. McEntee, *op. cit.*, chap. iii ; also Moon—*The Labour Problem and Social Catholic Movement in France* (Macmillan, New York, 1921), chap. xii.

so-called, namely, the theory and system of social organisation, which under the name of Socialism is definitely condemned by the Church. This implies essentially a negation or prohibition of individual ownership of productive property, and an excessive and unnatural degree of state control. It may be defined *as a system of social and economic organisation in which the State becomes sole owner of all the sources of production and means of distribution, and assumes to itself a despotic control of the chief activities of human life.*[1]

Fundamental Principle of the Socialist Economic System.— The avowed object of the socialist reformers is not so much to establish a system in which universal brotherhood is realised (which is the aim of Idealistic Communism), but rather one in which everybody receives the fruit of his or her own labour.[2] According to their theory the greater portion of the fruit of the hired worker's labour is, and in the present economic system must be, appropriated by the employer. Hence, they say, the system is *essentially*

---

[1] Cf. *Cath. Encyclop.*, vol. xiv, pp. 62 ff. (An excellent sketch of Socialism by Toke and Campbell) ; and *Dict. Apologet., loc. cit.*, for a still fuller and more up to date (1928) account. It should be noted that at present many people who call themselves Socialists have mitigated, in some cases they almost entirely reject, some of the fundamental principles of Socialism, at least as far as the practical application of these principles is concerned. This applies especially to the theories of class warfare, and the abolition of private property. They also condemn recourse to physical force. " It would seem," writes Pius XI, " as if Socialism were afraid of its own principles, and of the conclusions drawn therefrom by the [more logical] communists, and in consequence were drifting towards the truth which Christian tradition has always held in respect. For it cannot be denied that its programmes often strikingly approach the just demands of Christian social reformers. . . . Just demands and desires of this kind contain nothing opposed to Christian truth, nor are they in any sense peculiar to Socialism. . . . They are defended much more cogently by the principles of Christian faith ; and are promoted much more efficaclousiy by the power of Christian charity." (*Quadragesimo Anno*, 1931, pp. 50–52, C. T. S. edition).

[2] Most of the Socialist leaders have been wealthy, and very many are millionaires. Among these latter may be mentioned Vandervelde, in Belgium ; Bebel and Singer, in Germany ; Millerand, Jaures, Gerault-Richard, Bertaux, Vaillant and La Furgue, in France. Engels, the brother-in-law of K. Marx (who himself was far from poor), died in London in 1895, leaving his heirs 630,000 francs (£25,200). Cf. Belliot, *loc. cit.*, p. 359. Note also that the Continental Socialist leaders are mostly, if not all, Freemasons. *Ib.*, p. 360 ; also Cahill, *op. cit.* (Index, under Socialism and F.).

unjust,[1] and *necessarily* leads to the concentration of the
wealth of the State in the hands of a small capitalist class
of parasites. The abolition of the wage system is therefore
one of their primary objects.
Now the wage system and the private ownership of productive property are essentially connected with each other.
Hence, the latter, too, is unjust and immoral and must cease,
at least in so far as it needs the employment of hired labour.
Private individuals may indeed own property such as food,
clothing, dwellinghouses, gardens, vehicles, furniture, ornaments, books and musical instruments. They may even
accumulate wealth in gold, silver or precious stones. The
one all-important type of property from which they are,
at least partially, excluded, is what is known as productive
goods or capital, such as lands, mines and machinery.
These the individual cannot own, except in so far as he
can utilise or exploit them by his own personal labour. He
cannot employ wage labourers to work them, nor can he
trade in them for personal profit. The main outlines of the
socialist economic system are summarised in the following
passage of a contemporary writer :

" The people collectively is (in the Socialist system) sole proprietor not of all the wealth of the country, but of all the wealth
that may be lawfully employed for producing other wealth by
means of buying and selling or other contracts. A man may
thus own the house he lives in, the coat upon his back, the wine
in his cellar, even the garden that grows cabbages for his table,
but he may not hire hands to cultivate the garden and then sell
the produce ; he may not build houses and rent them ; he may
not import wine for the market. The State will be sole landlord, sole manufacturer, sole owner of shipping and railroads,
and all branches of the carrying trade, sole exploiter of mines,
sole practitioner of medicine (taking fees), sole educator, sole
keeper of wine and spirit vaults, sole merchant and sole retail
dealer—in a word, sole capitalist. The only way to wealth for
the individual will be his own personal labour ; he will get nothing
but the wage of his work . . . Mental labour will be rewarded
as well as bodily. . . . Everyone will receive pay who does work
useful for the community and no one else will receive anything.
. . . Labour will be paid . . . not in proportion to the ex-

---

[1] Cf. Pius XI, *Quadragesimo Anno*, 1931, pp. 30 ff. (C. T. S. edition
London, 1931).

cellence of the work, but in proportion to the time that the workman, manual or intellectual, may be supposed to have taken in acquiring his skill. The apprenticeship will be counted into the value of the labour." [1]

The Class War.—Further, since the wage-earners are con stantly being deprived of their just rights by the capitalist employers, and the interests of these two classes are dia metrically opposed, their normal relations to each other must consist in mutual hostility, distrust, and struggle till the capitalist owners are finally eliminated or destroyed. In other words, the *Class War* is assumed to be a necessary and normal characteristic of our present social and economic life.

From all this it is clear that the establishment of a full Socialist régime would involve a complete and probably violent transfer of all capital to the State, and that, too, apparently, without compensation to the present individual owners. (This is what actually took place in the Bolshevist Revolution in Russia in 1917.) And if some Socialist reformers such as the advocates of State Socialism are willing to make many concessions to the exigencies of the *status quo* such concessions are intended to hold good only during a transition period or until the time is ripe for the abolition of all private ownership of capital.

Philosophic Ground-work of the Socialistic System.— Closely connected with their economic principles and aims, or rather as a philosophic back-ground and basis for them, Socialist reformers put forward a definite all-round philosophy of human life. In the Socialist philosophical system, which like that of Liberalism is purely materialistic, no account is taken of moral or spiritual goods nor of any life beyond the present. All human wants and desires are centred on temporal benefits and animal gratification. Hence all human activities are dominated by economic relations and are to be viewed only from the economic standpoint.

Consequential Principles.—From these principles it follows that duties and rights in regard to family and country,

---

[1] Rev. J. Rickaby, S.J.—*Catholicism and Socialism* (Cath. Truth Society, London, 1905), pp. 2–3.

duties even toward God Himself cease to have any place or meaning ; and the virtues of filial piety, patriotism[1] and religion are eliminated from human life.

Again, seeing that no private individual can control productive property, no one can be primarily responsible even for the support of his own wife or children. For these, as for all else, the State is primarily responsible. The State, too, has supreme control in the education of the children. Consequently the family disappears as a divinely instituted and independent society, and the permanency of the marriage tie is no longer necessary or desirable.[2] Finally, since religion has no rational basis in the Socialist philosophy, the Church disappears as a public institution, and has no rights or standing in a Socialist State.

Such in brief are the main outlines of the system which the Socialists are determined to erect on the ruins of the existing civilisation ; and in which, as its votaries promise, "idleness or selfishness or sin will be unknown,' and "all will have plenty and be content ; and the sweet spirit of comradeship will blossom forth like the fabled rose of unchanging beauty."[3]

Art. 3—*Historical Sketch of Socialism*

Genesis of the Socialist Economic Theories.—Several of the ideas and principles of the system were borrowed originally from the Communist writers already referred to, such as Babeuf, Fourrier, and Robert Owen, as well as from other nineteenth century economists. Among these latter may be mentioned Henri St. Simon (*d.* 1825) and Louis Blanc (*d.* 1882) of France, Karl Robertus (*d.* 1875), and Ferdinand Lasalle (*d.* 1864) (founder of the "German Workman's Party") of Germany, Godwin (*d.* 1836), and C. Hall (*d.* 1825) of England.[4] In the writings of these are

---

[1] " The workers have no country. What they have not got cannot be taken from them." This is the reply given by Marx and Engels in the *Communist Manifesto* to the accusation that they " wish to abolish all national and patriotic aspirations." Cf. *Manifesto of the Communist Party* (Socialist Press, Glasgow, 1909), p. 19.

[2] Cf. *Ib.* ; also Cathrein and Elder, *op. cit.*

[3] *See* Elder, *op. cit.*, First Part, chap. i.

[4] Cf. Palgrave, *op. cit.*, under each name ; also Elder, *op. cit.*, Second Part, chap. iii. *See* also McEntee, *op. cit.*, pp. 96 ff, where the fundamental doctrines of Socialism are traced to the works of English writers of the first half of the 19th century. Cf. also Riazanov, *op. cit.*, chaps. i and ii.

to be found most of the principles and shibboleths, partly true, partly false, which are now commonly associated with socialist propaganda, such as " Property is Theft," " All men are equal by nature and by law," " Appropriation by individuals of the unearned increment is unjust," etc., etc. These writings also, especially those of the English economists, contain the substance of the theories of " Surplus Value," " the Exploitation of the Poor by the Rich," " the Class War," etc., which form the basis of Marx's great work, *Das Kapital.*

" Iron Law of Wages."—Lasalle's special contribution to the socialist structure is his celebrated theory of " The Iron Law of Wages," which, however, Marx did not adopt. The average rate of the labourer's wages, according to Lasalle's theory, cannot rise above the standard " which is necessary in order to secure to the labourer the possibility of existence and propagation," otherwise there would result from the easier and better conditions of the labourer an increase of the labouring population and of the supply of hands, which would again reduce the wages to the average rate or even below it. " Nor can wages permanently fall below the average necessary for the sustenance of life, for this would give rise to emigration, celibacy, prevention of propagation, and finally the diminution of the labouring population, which would . . . again raise wages to their former or even to a higher rate. . . . Actual wages, therefore, constantly oscillate about this centre of gravity to which they must always return, and around which they must revolve."[1]

Karl Marx.—Karl Marx (*d.* 1883) is the real founder of modern Socialism, athough Bakunin, the Anarchist leader, on the one hand, and Lasalle on the other, influenced the movement very considerably. All the different types of real Socialism, which are very numerous, are based on the Marxian system. Marx was a native of Treves, and although

---

[1] Cited in Cathrein, *op. cit.*, p. 196, from Lasalle's *Offenes Antwortschreiben* pp. 10–12. It should be noted that Lasalle's conclusion actually applies only to cases where the wage rate is controlled *completely* by supply and demand. The " Iron Law " should, and under a Christian régime would, be counteracted by wise protective legislation, and by the organisation of strong labour unions. Cf. Cathrein, *op. cit.*, pp. 196–200.

born of Jewish parents, became a Protestant. He and his friend Frederick Engels, also a German Jew, published in 1848 the *Communist Manifesto*, which, with *Das Kapital*, is referred to by the Socialists as the Charter of Freedom and the Bible of the working classes. The *Manifesto*, which is a brief and forcible exposition of the whole socialist doctrine, closes with the well known words : " The Communists . . . openly declare that their ends can only be obtained by the forcible overthrow of existing social conditions. Let the ruling classes tremble at a Communistic Revolution. The Proletarians have nothing to lose but their chains ! They have a world to win ! Proletarians of all lands Unite ! "[1]

International Workers' Association (L'Internationale).—As a result of the revolutions which occurred all over Europe in 1848, the revolutionary societies were suppressed in nearly every continental country, and the leaders banished. Most of the leaders, and Marx among them, took refuge in England. In London, Marx founded, in 1864, " The International Workmen's Association," which met annually in different European cities, such as Geneva, Brussels, London, and Basle. This organisation has given Socialism immense power and influence, by erecting it into what is almost a world-wide association, and thus bringing home to the organised working classes of Europe and America that their grievances and discontent are shared by their fellow-workers the world over. The object of the " International," as it is called, is to bring about the " Great Revolution " by means of simultaneous risings all over the world, in order that thus the government of one country would not be able to come to the assistance of another.

The first practical result of the " International " was the rising of the Paris Commune in 1871, in which the fierce anti-Christian and destructive character of Socialism was displayed. The " International " collapsed soon after 1871, principally owing to the failure of the Paris Revolution. In 1889 a second " International " was formed, being made up of Socialist and trade union delegates. This continued to meet till the beginning of the European War in 1914, when it again collapsed.[2]

---

[1] Cf. *Manifesto of the Communist Party*, p. 29.
[2] Cf. Webster, *op. cit.*, chaps. ii–iv ; Elder, *op. cit.*, Second Part, chap. iii.

It was again revived in 1918 after the War. Amsterdam is the centre of the revived organisation, which is called "The Third International." The Third International seems to have met little success partly owing to irreconcilable differences of opinion, regarding the attitude to be adopted towards the full Marxian policy of revolution, but mainly because the Amsterdam International is being gradually overshadowed by the "Komintern" (of which we shall treat later) or Communist International of Moscow, which is also called "The Third International."[1]

Das Kapital.—In 1867 Marx published the first volume of *Das Kapital*, the monumental work in which his whole system is elaborated, and which still remains the authoritative exposition of orthodox Socialism. The two remaining volumes which were published by Engels after Marx's death contain very little additional matter of importance.

The substance of *Das Kapital* is a dexterous combination of the evolutionism of Hegel, the revolutionary doctrines of the writers associated with the French Revolution of 1879, and the economic theories of the Liberal economist, Ricardo, combined with those of the unchristian Communists already referred to. The basic principles of Marx's system are contained in the *Materialistic Conception of History* and his theory of *Surplus Value*.

(*a*) **Materialistic Conception of History.**—This conception of human history, which is founded upon a philosophy of pure materialism, would have it that the whole structure of our present society both in its material elements and the principles and ideas that govern it, is the result of the existing system of production and distribution. Hence all our so-called fundamental truths and principles, such as the belief in God's existence, the idea that murder, theft, adultery, etc., are unlawful, have no objective reality. They are merely the reflection in the human mind of exterior ceonomic conditions. In this philosophy free-will disappears, the idea of God is eliminated, and all moral responsibility as well as all motives for religion or charity, honour or patriotism are taken away.

---

[1] Cf. *Encyclop. Brit.*, vol. 20 (14th edit., 1929), art. "Socialism," pp. 892, 893 ; also Gautherot—*Le Monde Communiste* (Edition "Spes.," Paris, 1925), pp. 50–55.

(b) **Theory of Surplus Value.**—Marx's theory of *Surplus Value* is as follows :—He first correctly distinguishes the two types of value, viz., *value in use*, which is measured by the utility of the object in satisfying human wants, and *value in exchange*, which depends upon the extent to which use-value may be purchased by the object. He next lays down, with some of the classical economists, the unproved and false principle that exchange value accrues to merchandise only on account of human labour.[1] From this doctrine of value he passes on to consider the nature of the modern wage contract : what the employer undertakes to buy from the labourer is the labour capacity of the latter. The price which the employer pays the labourer for his labour capacity corresponds, according to Marx, to its *exchange value*, whereas he (the employer) receives in return its *use-value*, which is very much greater than the exchange value. The excess of the use-value over the exchange-value is called the *surplus-value*.[2] This surplus-value which belonged to the labourer but was unjustly filched from him by the employer is the source of all the capitalist's profits and accumulated wealth. These gains are therefore essentially unjust and no better than theft.[3]

(c) **Marxian State.**—Marx then explains in accordance with his materialistic conception of history the coming in-evitable transformation of society into the future Socialistic State : society, as constituted at present, is unnatural and unjust, and therefore involves a constant mutual antagonism of class against class. As a result of the growing burdens of the people, the increasing number of crises, and the con-sequent class-war, revolution will be necessarily produced, and " the expropriators shall be expropriated." From this revolution the Socialist commonwealth will be evolved.

---

[1] *Capital*, chap. i. Besides the element of labour, several other elements have to be considered in reckoning the exchange value of a commodity, especially its utility, the degree of demand for it, its scarcity or the reverse. Cf. Cathrein, *op. cit.*, chaps. i and ii.

[2] *Capital*, chap. vii. This theory of surplus-value resting on the false theory referred to in a previous note regarding the foundations of exchange-value is also itself false. Cf. Cathrein, *Ib.* ; Elder, *op. cit.*, Part i, chap. i (*See* Pius XI, *Quadragesimo Anno* (1931), pp. 26–28 (C. T. S. edition, London, 1931).

[3] *Capital*, chaps. xxiv, xxv. Cf. also Cathrein, *op. cit.*, pp. 46–53, and Elder, *loc. cit.*

This will be a complete democracy[1] owning all the means of production and distribution. In this new type of social organisation all private property and class distinction will be unknown ; everyone will work, but, owing to education, labour will be a pleasure.[2]

Spread of Marx's Teachings.—Owing to the prevalent injustice and misery resulting from unjust social conditions the teachings of Marx were eagerly embraced by the disinherited proletariat. The movement was supported, especially by the Jewish element of the population in almost every country.[3] Thus Socialism rapidly spread, and subversive movements, more or less strong, were organised and promoted during the last quarter of the 19th and the first decade of the 20th century.

Meanwhile, simultaneously with the spread of International Socialism, there arose in various countries local socialistic organisations each borrowing its colouring from national character and conditions. In Germany, the fatherland of dogmatic or " scientific " Socialism, the socialistic movement was strongest up to the period of the European War. The first leaders, Marx, Engels, and Lasalle were followed and assisted by Liebknecht, Bebel and Singer, all Marxians. In 1874 socialist members were elected for the first time to the Reichstag, and a strong socialist political party was formed. A similar development took place in Belgium, France and Italy. In 1891, the " *Erfurt Programme,*" embodying Marx's principles, was formally adopted by the German Socialist Party, and still remains the official creed of the more advanced socialist parties in most countries.

Revisionist Movement.—In 1899, however, Edward Bernstein started the " Revisionist " movement which rapidly gained ground up to 1914. The " Revisionists " concentrated upon obtaining through the constitutional

---

[1] The fact that the Russian Soviet Government is not, and does not profess to be, a democracy, seems to be one of the principal reasons why they term their system *Communism* rather than *Socialism*. Cf. *Official Report of British Trades Union Delegation to Russia*, 1924, p. 3.

[2] *Capital*, chap. xxxii. Cf. also Cathrein, *loc. cit.*, for a fuller sketch of Marx's ideal commonwealth.

[3] Cf. Cahill, *op. cit.*, pp. 169 ff.

government definite social reforms. They " revise " (viz., change or depart from) several of the Marxian doctrines. The Social Democrats, who form a majority in the present (1931) German Government, are mostly of the Revisionist School, while the so-called " Spartikist " party form the more radical and revolutionary section. In other countries the same two tendencies, namely, the Parliamentary and the Revolutionary agitations, struggle for the upper hand, now one, now the other becoming predominant. Since the European War, however, and the great Russian Revolution, there has been a decided swing of the pendulum towards revolutionary Socialism. Nominally, the two types differ only in methods ; but in reality they frequently differ in principles.[1]

State Socialism.—The Parliamentary Socialists, while not rejecting completely the private ownership of productive property, deny that it is a natural right, and allow it only as a concession of the State. Further, they leave out religion from every effort to alleviate the sufferings of the masses. They aim at " nationalising " all the great financial and industrial enterprises of the country so that the State would become the universal treasurer and banker, the general agent of transport and commerce, the exclusive distributor of labour and of wealth, of means of education and of all social aid—in a word, the promoter and regulator of all national activity. That is what is commonly termed *State Socialism*, and is substantially the aim not merely of the Revisionist Socialists of Germany, but of the moderate socialists of England,[2] France, Belgium, America and Australia.

Revolutionary Socialism.—The Revolutionary Socialists on the other hand proclaim the essential invalidity of all private ownership of productive property, and hold that revolutionary methods, which have come to be called " Direct Action," are the only effectual means of securing the wished for reforms. The " General Strike " is the method of " direct " action commonly advocated, although others besides Socialists sometimes advocate this same method.

---

[1] Cf. Pius IX, *ib.*, pp. 49–51.   [2] Antoine, *loc. cit.*

The " Syndicalist Socialists "[1] of France and the more advanced parties in Belgium, Spain, Italy and other continental countries, as well as in America and England, are of the Revolutionary type. Since 1918 the Revolutionary Socialists have grown much stronger in most countries, especially in England. The same was true of Italy up to the time of the Fascist Revolution. It is also true of the industrial cities of Spain, such as Barcelona and Bilbao. What their power and prospects are at present (1931) it is difficult to determine.[2]

Socialism in Ireland.—The Socialist movement has so far made little progress in Ireland (owing to its anti-Christian character and the strength of the people's Catholic faith). Its doctrines, however, and propaganda have had a very disturbing effect on a considerable section of the labouring population. This is especially true in the cities, where the material conditions of the poor, resulting from an unchristian capitalistic régime of more than two centuries, are amongst the worst in Europe.

Besides, there are no Catholic Trades Unions or Labour Associations in Ireland such as now exist in Italy, France, Germany, Belgium, Holland and the other countries of Continental Europe ; and although nearly all the Irish workers (outside some of the North-Eastern counties) are Catholic, several of the official labour leaders are non-Catholics or non-believers.

A further element of weakness and danger in the position of the labouring population of Ireland is the affiliation of some of the Irish Trade Unions to corresponding British Unions. The members of the latter are mostly non-Catholic,

---

[1] Cf. *supra*, art. 1 ; also Cronin, *op. cit.*, vol. ii, pp. 160, 161 ; *Cath. Encyclop.*, art. " Syndicalism," p. 385. Also *Encyclop. Britt.*, vol. 32 (New Volumes), art. " Syndicalism."

[2] For a brief account of Socialism in America and other countries, cf. Cathrein, *ib.*, pp. 67–118 ; also Elder, *op. cit.*, Second Part, chap. iii. The object of the " Fabian Society of England," founded in 1883 by Sydney Webb (now Lord Passfield) and others, was to educate the public, especially the municipal bodies and the political parties, in socialist or " Collectivist " ideas, by means of literature, pamphlets, etc. Of late years, however, there has been a reaction against " Fabianism." Cf. *Cath. Encyclop.*, *loc. cit.*, p. 65 ; also *Fabian Tracts* (London, 1908).

and the needs and circumstances of the two countries are different. In that way the connection which apparently is meant to strengthen both the English and Irish unions is in reality a source of confusion and weakness in the Irish section.

Again, some of the leaders of the Irish Transport Union, of which we shall speak presently, profess to be affiliated to the Russian "Red International" (the Komintern). There are, besides, in Dublin and other centres organisers from the British Communist Party, some of whom have been trained in Russia ; and even some Dublin young men are undergoing a course of Communist training in Moscow with a view to Communist activities in Ireland. The present state of widespread unemployment and poverty (1931) undoubtedly supplies a very favourable occasion for Socialist propaganda, which is all the more dangerous owing to the want of a Catholic Workers' Union ; but otherwise the movement has little or no appeal for the Irish Catholic Worker.

The I. T. & G. W. U.—In the year 1908 the "Irish Transport and General Workers' Union" was founded in Dublin by James Connolly and James Larkin. In the great Dublin lock-out of 1913 this union sprang into importance ; and after the Easter Week rising of 1916, spread rapidly over the whole country, gathering into its ranks agricultural labourers, carters, and all classes of unskilled workers, men and women. It had affiliated to it also some of the skilled or professional unions. Up to 1922 it was by far the largest and most powerful Union in Ireland, and included some 150,000 workers.

The leaders and official personnel of the Irish Socialist Party, which was founded a few years later, but soon collapsed, seem to have been partially identical with those of the Irish Transport Union. How far that party's aims and principles correspond with those of real Socialism, is not clear. Their economic gospel seems to be that of James Connolly, as far as he had formulated a consistent system. In reality, Connolly, well-meaning and able in many ways as he was, had not thought out a complete system. The circumstances of his death prove that he was not a Socialist. His writings manifest no little inconsistencies and confusion of thought. The Constitution of the *James Connolly Workers' Club* of Dublin, an educational and propagandist organisation, is definitely Socialistic or Communistic, although many of the members are Catholics.[1]

A split occurred in 1923 in the ranks of the Irish Transport and General Workers' Union. Mr. James Larkin seceded and formed a new union called the " Irish Workers' Union." Besides, most of the rural members fell away. They had little sympathy with the revolutionary tendencies of some of the leaders, and found besides that the needs of rural and urban workers are different and could not be well provided for in the same union. Since then the strength of the I. T. & G. W. U. has steadily declined.

Influence of Socialism on Modern Legislation.—Although Socialists have not so far succeeded, except in Russia, in setting up a permanent socialist state, their influence has impressed itself deeply on modern legislation in very many countries. The pressure exerted by them on Liberal governments has helped to bring about much remedial legislation. On the other hand, however, that same influence has been largely accountable, in conjunction with Liberalism, for several of the worst features of modern legislative tendencies. Thus, the monopoly of education, now too often assumed by the State, and the tendency to share with the parents the care of the children, State usurpation of authority over the matrimonial contract, the tendency towards centralisation of civil authority, and undue interference in municipal administration are all features of the socialist régime.

Art. 4—*Non-Catholic Social Movements and Socialism*[2]

General Sketch.—Side by side with Socialism two other movements (besides the great Catholic Social Reform Movement of which we shall treat in a later chapter) have grown

---

[1] Cf. Rev. L. McKenna, S.J.—*The Teaching of James Connolly.* Connolly —*Labour in Irish History* (Dublin, 1917) ; Ryan—*The Irish Labour Movement* (Dublin, 1919).

[2] Cf. *Encyclop. Britt., loc. cit. ;* Antoine, *op. cit.,* chap. xiv, art. 4 ; O'Brien—*Labour Organisation* (Methuen, London, 1921), chap. i ; Sydney and Beatrice Webb—*History of Trade Unionism and Industrial Democracy* (Longmans, London, 1920).

up since the middle of the 19th century in Europe and America. These are Trade Unionism and the Co-operative Movement. Both have had their origin in Great Britain. Their rise dates practically from 1825, when the oppressive statutes, which had up to that time forbidden the combination of workmen in their own defence were repealed. Excepting the Christian religion these movements are the most powerful remedial agencies for counteracting the evils arising from unchristian Capitalism. As the interrelations between these movements and Socialism are now dominant considerations in Great Britain, Ireland, and many countries of Europe and America, we touch briefly on them here.

The Trades Unions.—The Trades Unions may at first sight seem to be the modern counterpart of the mediæval guilds. In reality, however, there are essential differences between the two types of union. The guilds included in their membership all classes of persons connected with the particular industry to which the guild belonged, employers and employees, rich and poor. The trades union, on the other hand, is an association of wage-earners alone. Again, the guild was organised and directed under strong religious influences ; and it concerned itself with all the interests of its members, including even their spiritual welfare. The primary objects of the trades union, (which in the English-speaking countries, including Ireland, and even in some non-English speaking and Catholic countries such as Spain, are quite secular in character) is to secure from the employers by means of collective bargaining just conditions for the labourer. There are, however, many great Catholic Trades Unions in some of the continental countries, such as France, Belgium, and Germany. These approximate more nearly to the mediæval guilds in their organisation and scope.

Trade Unionism has reached its highest development in Britain, the land of its origin. The Association of the " Knights of Labour " in U.S.A. is, however, the largest and most powerful single labour association in the world.

The Political Labour Parties. As a result of the Trades Union movement a political Labour Party came into being in Great Britain towards the end of the 19th century, and a similar party was formed in the Irish Free State in 1922.

12

The Labour Party of Great Britain has become an effective force in British politics since 1900. Its influence has increased immensely since the European War. Its leaders have already (1931) twice formed the Government of Great Britain, although the party has not so far (1931) secured an absolute majority in the House of Commons. The political principles of the Labour parties are not clear except that its leaders seek reform by constitutional rather than revolutionary methods.[1]

The Co-operative Movement.—The Co-operative movement, which is also of British origin, is one of the outstanding and most striking features of modern industrial history. It had its first weak beginnings in Rochdale, Lancs., England, in 1844, when the operatives of one of the factories began to contribute two pence a week to a fund for a co-operative store. From Lancashire it spread through Great Britain (making some progress also in Ireland) and the British Dominions. It has now penetrated into practically every country inhabited by Europeans. At present the number of people directly or indirectly involved in the movement would amount to close upon 200,000,000 (two hundred millions)— including over 6,000,000 (six millions) in Great Britain itself. Of the 1,364 co-operative societies which existed in Great Britain in 1929, ninety-nine were for co-operative production. The total capital of the British Co-operative Societies was then £205,131,379.[2]

The Co-operative Agricultural movement in Ireland, which in 1915 seemed prosperous and progressive, including 981 affiliated societies and 225 co-operative banks, has now only 305 affiliated societies, several of which are not prosperous, and practically no banks. The partial failure of the movement has been due partly to the tactics of the British army of occupation, which destroyed great numbers of the creameries (1919–21); partly to the fact that the Irish co-operative movement was too confined in its scope.

---

[1] Cf. *Cath. Encyclop.*, *loc. cit.*
[2] Cf. *The People's Year Book* (1931), published by The Co-operative Wholesale Society, 1 Balloon Street, Manchester, p. 20. The standard work on the modern co-operative movement is by Beatrice Potter (Webb), and is entitled *The Co-operative Movement in Great Britain* (Longmans, London).

The movement was also handicapped from the beginning by another circumstance : it was promoted, and to a large extent directed, by members of the Protestant ascendancy and Scottish or English officials, and so never won the confidence of the people at large. Such an organisation in order to be permanently successful must be organised and conducted in harmony with the Catholic and native traditions of the people.[1]

Relations with Socialism.—The attitude which Socialism ought to adopt towards the Trades Unions and the Co-operative movement has been a constant subject of discussion and dispute among the socialist leaders. Those of the revolutionary type tend strongly to discountenance them, except in as far as they may be useful instruments for revolutionary propaganda and organisation. Socialists of the Revisionist and Parliamentary type, on the other hand, regard Trade Unionism and the Co-operative movement with favour.[2]

In every country both the Trade Unions and the Co-operative societies are in constant danger of being captured and dominated by the socialists. This is especially the case since the Great War. Thus, in Britain before 1914 Socialism had made comparatively little progress.[3] Since 1918, however, the Trade Unions have become deeply impregnated with Marxian principles, and the British Labour Party seems to be, or at least to have been at one time, affiliated in some way or other to the "International," which now has its centre of energy in Soviet Russia.

Art. 5—*Critique of Socialism*

Socialism.—Socialism, no less than Liberalism, bears the stamp of irreligion, materialism, and active antagonism to Christianity. Indeed, these traits appear if anything more aggressive in Socialism as exemplified under the Russian Soviet régime. It is well known, too, that the Judæo-Masonic forces and the unchristian financial magnates favour

---

[1] For the best account of the movement in Ireland, cf. Smith-Gordon— *Irish Rural Reconstruction. See* also *infra*, chap. xxi, art. 5.
[2] Cf. Cathrein, *op. cit.*, pp. 74 ff, 85 ff, 92, 104.
[3] Cf. Elder, *op. cit.*, pp. 198–202.

Socialism as much, or almost as much, as they favour Liberalism.[1]

Many of Its Aims Commendable.—On the other hand, it is true that several of the aims professed by socialists, especially by those of the constitutional or " Revisionist " type, are lawful and excellent in themselves if detached from the general socialist system of which they are made to form a part. So true indeed is this that Pius XI does not hesitate to say :

" It would seem as if Socialism . . . were drifting towards the truth which Christian tradition has always held in respect ; for it cannot be denied that its programmes often strikingly approach the just demands of Christian social reformers."

The Pope then refers to the remarkable toning down so evident in recent years in the tenets and demands of many socialist leaders, even in regard to the central principles of Socialism, such as those concerning class-war and private ownership ; and he adds :

" If these changes continue, it may well come about that gradually the tenets of mitigated Socialism will no longer be different from the programme of those who seek to reform human society according to Christian principles."[2]

Thus it is essential in the interests of the public good that the excessive power of over-wealthy capitalists should be kept in check ; that unjust monopolies and " trusts " be prevented ; and that the control of currency and credit as now exercised by irresponsible banking and financial syndicates be radically reformed. The power of holding up the national resources which the capitalist proprietors now possess should be put an end to or counteracted by prudent legislation. Further, it should be regarded as a primary duty of the civil government to secure, as far as the natural resources of the nation will allow, that everyone has a fair opportunity in his own country of earning by his labour a suitable livelihood, including food, clothing and housing for himself and his family.

It may be desirable, too, that public utilities such as

---

[1] Cahill, *op. cit.*, pp. 169, 170 ; also *Révue Internationale des Sociétés Secrètes* (weekly review published at 8 Avenue Portales, Paris), *passim*.
[2] *Quadragesimo Anno* (C. T. S. edit.), pp. 50, 51.

railways and mines, the great electric plants, the waterways and water power should be at least partially controlled by some public authority for the service of the community ; [1] and that the " unearned increment " on the value of such property as urban building sites should belong at least in great part to the municipality. Reforms such as these, if carried out in the spirit of Christian teaching, would go far to eliminate the conditions that give Socialism its driving force.

But Its Basic Philosophy False and Irreconcilable with Christianity.—But although Socialists put forward many claims which are quite in harmony with the Christian law, Socialism as a whole is so fundamentally opposed to the teachings of Christianity that the two cannot be reconciled.

" Socialism," writes Pius XI, " whether it be considered as a doctrine, or as an historical fact, or as a movement, cannot, if it really remain Socialism, be brought into harmony with the dogmas of the Catholic Church . . . the reason being that it conceives human society in a way utterly alien to Christian truth. . . . Hence, ' Religious Socialism,' ' Christian Socialism,' are expressions implying a contradiction in terms. No one can be at the same time a sincere Christian and a true Socialist." [2]

The fundamental opposition between Socialism and Christianity is a necessary consequence of the materialistic philosophy upon which Socialism rests. In this philosophy the authority and even the existence of a personal God are denied or ignored ; the immortality of the human soul, free-will and human responsibility are eliminated. Thus the foundations of the moral law completely disappear.

Ideals Purely Materialistic and also Unattainable.—Even if we leave out of consideration the abstract philosophy on which Socialism is based and consider its direct teachings alone, it is still impossible to reconcile it with Christianity. In the first place Socialism, ignoring a future life, centres

---

[1] Cf. *Code of Social Principles* (C. S. Guild, Oxford, 1929), n. 132.
[2] *Ib.*, pp. 53, 54. Cf. also Leo XIII—*Quod. Apostolici Muneris*, 1878, pp. 12 ff ; *Rerum Novarum*, 1891, pp. 134 ff ; *Graves de Communi*, 1902, p. 167 ; also Pius X, in his Apostolic Letter to the Bishops of Italy on Catholic Social Action (Cf. Ryan and Husslein—*Church and State* (Harding and Hore, London, 1920), pp. 110 ff).

all of man's happiness and good in material well-being, to which every other duty and interest are subordinated. Hence socialists assume that the sole and ultimate purpose of human society is the material advantages which it brings to the members. Besides, they profess to aim at a state of material prosperity free from suffering, poverty, and irksome labour, and in which all enjoy social equality.

Now it is a fundamental principle in Christian teaching that temporal happiness, although a legitimate object of human endeavour, can never have more than a secondary place in men's aims. The temporal prosperity which is the end of Civil Society must be subordinated to man's ultimate end. For man's supernatural interests are always paramount, and being eternal must dominate his every action and desire. The degree of reward and punishment, of happiness and suffering, that is each person's due is not to be measured by this life alone. The even-handed justice, tempered with mercy, which the Christian confidently expects as an essential element in the moral order of the universe is not and cannot be realised unless man's complete life, of which his earthly career is only a preparatory phase, be taken into account.

Hence those who hold up before the people, as socialists do, visions of an earthly paradise free from suffering, poverty and irksome labour only delude men by promises which cannot be fulfilled. Labour (the punishment of our first parents' fall) and " the other pains and hardships of life will . . . accompany man as long as life lasts."[1]

False Interpretation of Human Equality.—Again, the doctrine that all have a right to social equality and that class distinctions are always based on tyranny and oppression, implies a false interpretation of the natural law and of Christian teaching. Justice and Charity, and the spirit of human brotherhood are indeed imposed as obligatory by the natural law, and are strongly inculcated in the teaching of Christianity as fundamental duties ; for all men have immortal souls ; all have free-will and personal responsibility ; all are the beloved children of God, made to God's own image and likeness ; redeemed by the sufferings of

---

[1] *Rerum Novarum*, 1891, p. 142 ; also Pius XI, *ib.*, pp. 53, 54.

His Divine Son, and created for supernatural union with God for ever in Heaven. But human society cannot function without lawful authority, which therefore has its sanction in divine law. This implies as a necessary correlative the duty of reverence towards lawful superiors and of obedience to just rule.

Moreover, inequality in social rank, inequality of opportunity and of material well-being, are necessary results of men's varying abilities and character, coupled with their right to acquire property and to utilise their various natural gifts each in his own way.[1]

False Doctrine of Class War.—Seeing that class distinction has been designed by the Author of nature as a necessary part of the social organism, and may exist without injustice or oppression of any kind,[2] it follows that the rising of one class against another could be justified or tolerated only as a very exceptional expedient against injustice or oppression. Hence class-war if ever justifiable cannot be lawfully undertaken as a means to do away with all class distinctions ; much less can such a war be described as socialists describe it, as a normal feature of human society.

Unjust Prohibition of Private Property.—In denying men's natural right to acquire and hold productive property, socialists infringe on an inalienable human right, and would destroy the individual's personal independence and his responsibility for his own future well-being. They would thus do away with rights which are essential to human dignity and personality, and would erect the State into a position of unnatural pre-eminence and power, as if it were prior to the individuals that comprise it.[3]

Besides in withholding from men the power of becoming

---

[1] Cf. Leo XIII—*Quod. Apostolici Muneris*, 1878, pp. 16, 17 ; *Immortale Dei*, 1885, pp. 46, 47 ; *Rerum Novarum*, 1891, p. 141 ; *Sapientiæ Christianæ*, 1890, p. 110. *See* also *infra*, chap. xvi, art. 2.

[2] Cf. Leo XIII, *Ib.*, also *infra*, chap. xxi, art. 1.

[3] Cf. Leo XIII—*Rerum Novarum*, pp. 138 ff. Cf. also the words of Pius XI : " They [the socialists] affirm that the loss of human dignity, which results from socialized methods of production, would be easily compensated for by the abundance of goods produced in common, and accruing to the individual, who can turn them at his will to the comforts and culture of life," *Ib.*, p. 54.

independent by their own labour and raising their families
in the social ladder, they would deprive them of a stimulus
to labour, initiative and inventiveness which is most useful.
if not indeed essential to the well-being of society.

Dismemberment of the Family.—In its attitude towards
the family and the permanence of the marriage tie Socialism
is also fundamentally opposed to the natural law and to
Christian teaching.[1] The socialist State in withholding
from its citizens their right to acquire productive property
and assuming full responsibility for the maintenance of all
its members undertakes the duties and usurps the right of
the father of the family ; and at the same time strikes at
the root of the doctrine of the essential permanence of the
marriage tie.   It even founds a claim, which would inevitably
(though perhaps only gradually) be enforced, of interfering
with the innermost and most sacred family relations.
Besides, in denying the natural subordination of wife to
husband in the details of domestic life Socialism destroys
the notion of permanent society.[2]

Elimination of Religion from Social System.—Finally, in
the socialist system there is no place for the Church.
Socialists are at one with Liberals in denying the Church's
authority and her independent place in human society.
They undertake, too, to find a remedy for social evils, without any aid from religion.   In all this they are opposed to
the Divine ordinance by which the Church is set up as a
perfect society independent of the State, and is made the
authoritative exponent of the fundamental laws that govern
the social as well as the individual life of man.

Again, in seeking to bring about human prosperity and
peace independently of the help of religion, they disobey
the Divine precept, " *Seek ye first the Kingdom of God and*

---

[1] Leo XIII—*Ib.*
[2] Cf. *Ib.*—*Quod Apostolici Muneris*, 1878, pp. 17, 18 ; Cathrein, *op. cit.*,
chap. iv, sec. vi, pp. 340–351. (Here the author shows that the ideals and
principles of Socialism as described by its authentic exponents are fundamentally opposed to the natural constitution of the family which is upheld and insisted on by the laws of Christianity).   Cf. also Cronin, *loc. cit.*
These socialistic principles regarding the family, are now actually put in
force in Soviet Russia.

His justice and all these things shall be added unto you."[1]
Religious motives alone can effectually curb human passions,
and thus secure a reign of social justice. Religion, and it
alone, can make men courageous and happy under pressure
of the ills in which human life will always abound.[2]

Historical Antagonism to Christianity.—Considered apart
from its teachings and viewed as a phase of human history
Socialism has always been profoundly hostile to Christianity.
Socialist teaching has its roots in the Protestant revolt of
the sixteenth century and the Liberalism of the following
centuries, which was the consummation of that revolt.[3]
The protagonists and leaders of the socialist movement have
always been closely associated with the anti-Christian secret
societies of which the Roman Pontiffs one after another,
since the beginning of the eighteenth century, have issued
the most severe and uncompromising condemnations.[4]

Hence in Catholic countries such as Italy, Spain, and
France the socialist organisations have always been aggressively anti-Christian in practice as well as in profession.
And if here and there the socialists of the rank and file
show a tendency to revolt against the Jews and Freemasons,
who utilise the socialist movement in their war against

---

[1] Matth. vi. 32, 33.
[2] Cf. Leo XIII—*Exeunt iam anno*, 1888, pp. 98 ff ; *Rerum Novarum*,
1891, pp. 141, 144, 147–150.
[3] Cf. Leo XIII—*Quod Apostolici Muneris*, 1878, pp. 13, 14.
[4] *Ib.*, p. 12. Cf. also *Humanum Genus* (1884) (See *The Great Encyclicals
of Leo XIII*. Benziger, New York, 1913, p. 99). See also Cahill, *op. cit.*,
in Index under words " Socialism and F ∴" For a very useful account
of the rôle played in Revolutionary Socialism by the Jewish leaders,
cf. L. Fry—*Le Retour des Flots Vers L'Orient*, published as a serial in the
Rev. Intern. des Soc. Sec., 1931, Nos. 23 and ff. (*See* especially chaps. iv.
and v in Nos. 30 and 31). To those who have not studied Freemasonry
it may seem strange (to some indeed it will appear almost incredible) that
Freemasonry is closely identified not only with unchristian Liberalism
and Capitalism—a fact which is generally recognised—but also with
Socialism even in its most revolutionary and subversive aspects. The
fact, however, is certain. Cf. Poncins—*Secret Powers Behind the Revolution*
(Boswell, London, 1929), p. 35 ; also pp. 100 ff, 127 ff, etc. ; also Cahill,
op. cit., pp. 169, 170. The real explanation of the seeming anomaly seems
to be that the real aim of Freemasonry in which the Jewish element is
the inspiring and driving force (cf. Cahill, *op. cit.*, chap. iv, and Poncins,
passim) is to change the present civilization, which is essentially Christian,
and set up in its place a Masonic system based upon naturalism or atheistic
rationalism. Socialism, Communism, Liberalism and Capitalism can all
be utilised for this end. Besides financiers can control Communist states
even more effectually than states in which private property prevails.

Christianity, the motives of such an apparent disagreement is not the anti-Christian nature of Freemasonry, but the predominance of capitalist interests among the Judæo-Masonic leaders.

In the non-Catholic countries, too—in Germany, Holland, Denmark, Britain, and the United States of America, not to speak of Soviet Russia—organised Socialism makes no secret of its inherent antagonism to Christianity. And even where such opposition is deprecated by socialist leaders, it appears plainly enough in the socialist programme and projects of legislation.

The German founders of Socialism—Marx, Engels and Lasalle—were notoriously anti-Christian. So, too, have been their successors—Bebel, Liebknecht, Kautsky, Dietgen, Bernstein and Singer. The same is true of the French, Belgian and Dutch socialist leaders—Lafargue, Jaures, Viviani, Sorel, Briand, Vandervelde, and Herriot, as well as those of Italy, Spain, Switzerland and Russia. This anti-Christian spirit, which is inherent in Socialism, has been clearly shown in the revolution of the Paris Commune (1871), in the Barcelona riots (1909), in the Bolshevist régime in Russia, in the Bolshevist risings in Hungary and Munich,[1] and in the recent Communist excesses in Spain (1931).

Even in the English-speaking countries, where Socialism, like Anglo-American Freemasonry, is perhaps not so openly aggressive, " a very slight acquaintance with the leading personalities of the socialist movement and with the habits of thought current among them, is sufficient to dispel the illusion "[2] that they are not equally anti-Christian. The great protagonists of the British Socialist movement, such as Aveling, Bax, Blatchford, Hyndman, Leatham, Morris ; the English Fabians such as Bernard Shaw and Pease ; the Independent Socialists, like Wells, are all more or less anti-Christian and naturalistic in outlook and tendency. The English political leaders, too, who profess the socialist creed, however strongly they may proclaim that their Socialism is " only Christianity in terms of modern

---

[1] Cf. *Cath. Encycl.*, *loc. cit.* ; also Elder, *op. cit.*, pp. 301–315 (a list of Socialist writings) and *passim* ; Cathrein, *op. cit.*, pp. 105–120.
[2] *Cath. Encycl.*, vol. xiv, p. 67.

economics," are ready to advocate or support measures which are anti-Christian at least in principle and tendency. This is still more true of the contemporary socialist writers and leaders of the United States of America, such as Abbot, Brown, Hilquit and Kerr.

Economic as well as Political Principles Unsound.— Apart from the philosophical errors of Socialism and its anti-christian character, its economic principles and conclusions are unsound and little calculated to promote the peace and prosperity which form the objects of civil society. Marx's fundamental error in assuming that labour is the sole foundation of value and that the wage system is consequently always unjust, has been already referred to.[1]

The statement that private ownership of productive property leads inevitably to the concentration of all industries in the hands of a few and the consequent pauperisation of the masses is exaggerated and misleading. It is notoriously untrue of agriculture in which small and medium-sized farms are in normal circumstances the most secure and stable. Even in the case of manufacturing industry carried on principally by machinery, although there has been, on the whole, a strong tendency towards concentration during the past two centuries, the direction of the current is not altogether invariable ; and it is impossible to show that the excessive concentration which has occurred is normal or a necessary consequence of private ownership, and not rather the result of the abuses already referred to in connection with modern capitalism.[2]

The remedy for the social misery connected with ownership or absence of ownership lies in correcting the abuses and not in attempting to abolish a right which is founded upon man's nature. The system in which private ownership is excluded is opposed to man's needs and his fundamental instincts. Such a system would take away the motives founded upon personal interest and the desire of

---

[1] Cf. *Supra*, art. 4.

[2] Marx's " law " of the inevitable and ever-increasing pauperisation of the masses can be proved by statistics to be a fiction. In fact, during the past forty years and at least up to the aftermath of the war, the conditions of the working classes showed on the whole a decided improvement upon the earlier part of the nineteenth century. Cf. Cathrein, *op. cit.*, pp. 150 ff; also Cronin, *op. cit.*, pp. 201 ff.

family advancement, which form at present the most powerful incentive to energy, resourcefulness, and invention ; and would lead besides to confusion, limitless corruption, idleness, and malingering. " Society as the Socialists conceive it," writes Pius XI, " is impossible and unthinkable without the use of compulsion of the most excessive kind." [1] The truth of these words of the Holy Father is exemplified in the present socialistic régime in Soviet Russia.

Above all, the socialist State would inevitably develop a bureaucratic tyranny as bad as, or worse than, the tyranny of the capitalist state. The individual and the family, devoid of private capital, and permanent means of subsistence, which form the real foundation of individual independence, would be completely at the mercy of the administration.[2] At best the minority in such a State would be at the mercy of the majority. Even in the doubtful hypothesis that the workers' material condition would be improved, their status would accord little with the Christian ideal of personal dignity which implies responsibility and freedom, and would be more akin to the status of the comfortable and well-fed slave or lower animal.

---

[1] *Ib.*, p. 54.
[2] Cf. *Quadragesimo Anno*, 1931 (C. T. S. edition), pp. 53, 54.

CHAPTER XII

REVOLUTIONARY COMMUNISM[1] (BOLSHEVISM)

Art. 1—*Historical Sketch*

General View.—The Russian Revolution of 1917, culminating in the establishment for the first time of a permanent socialist State for a third part of the whole
population of Europe, seems destined to rank side by side
with the Jacobin Revolution of 1793 among the most far-
reaching political events of modern times. The abuses and
oppression of the Tsarist régime against which Bolshevism

---

[1] Cf. *Cath. Encyclop.* (Supplement, 1922), arts. " Russia," " Bolshevism,"
" Soviet." *Encyclop. Brit.* (edit. 1929), arts. " Russia," " Soviet System,"
and " Bolshevism." G. Gautherot—*Le Monde Communiste* (" Edition
Spes," Paris, 1925), and *Le Communisme à l'Ecole* (Paris, 1929). Gautherot,
Professor of the History of the Revolution in the *Institut Catholique de
Paris*, is recognised as one of the best living authorities on the modern
anti-Christian movement. His books are fully documented, mainly from
Communistic sources, including the *Izvestia* (official organ of the Soviet
Government) and the *Pravda* (official organ of the Communist Party).
They are among the best summaries hitherto published on present day
communism. Also *La Vague Rouge*, a monthly review, edited by Gautherot,
and published at 134 Boulevard Haussmann, Paris (VIIIᵉ). (The matter
it contains is borrowed principally from the documentation collected by
the *Entente Internationale* first convoked at Paris in June, 1924, and including representatives of 26 nations. The objects of the *Entente Internationale* are " to defend against the subversive organisations of the *Third
International* (of Moscow) the principles of social order, private ownership,
domestic life and patriotism "). Vicomte Leon de Poncins—*Les Forces
Secrètes de la Revolution* (2nd edit., Paris, 1929). An English version of
the First Edition, entitled *The Secret Power Behind the Revolution*, was
published in 1929 (Boswell, Essex St., London). Nesta Webster—*The
Socialist Network* (London, 1926) ; also *World Revolution* (London, 1922,
chap. x), and *Secret Societies and Subversive Movements* (London, 1924) ;
L. Fry, *op. cit.*, chaps. iv and v ; Batsell—*Soviet Rule in Russia* (New York,
1929), edited under the auspices of the Committee of International
Research of the University of Harvard. *Official Report of the British
Trade Union Delegation to Russia*, 1924, published by the Trades Union
Congress General Council, 32 Eccleston Square, London, S.W.1. This
report, while professing to be impartial, manifestly aims at defending
Bolshevism. Maxin Litvinoff—*The Bolshevist Revolution*, published by
the British Socialist Party (London, 1919). *The Land Revolution in
Russia* (Socialist Labour Press, Glasgow) ; Bukarin—*The Programme of
the World Revolution* (Socialist Labour Press, Glasgow) ; Postgate—*The
Bolshevist Theory* (London, 1920). The writer is sympathetic towards
Communism. The Appendices contain reprints of : (*a*) *The New Communist Manifesto*, issued by the Congress of the Third International, held

is mainly a reaction, were far worse than the abuses
associated with the monarchist régime in France, and the
reaction has been even greater and more violent.[1] As a
result of the setting up of the Soviet Government in Russia
the extreme socialist party all over the world have now a
more or less unified organisation with a visible centre of
direction in Moscow ; so that a world movement of which
no one can foresee the issue has taken definite shape.

The Russian revolution, though fundamentally of the
same character and tendency as the French, differed from
the latter mainly in its economic doctrines, which are those
of Marxian Socialism. Besides, the anti-Christian and anti
religious virus which Bolshevism exhibits is even more
pronounced and extreme than that of the French Jacobins

at Moscow, March, 1919 ; (b) *Lenin's Nineteen Theses*, which were pre
sented to the same Congress, and (c) *The Appeal to the U.S.A. Industrial
Workers of the World* (I.W.W.) issued (January, 1920), by the Central
Executive Council of the *Third* (Moscow) *International*, over the name
of Zinoviev, the President of the assembly. J. Douillet—*Moscow Un
masked. A Record of Nine Years' Work and Observation in Soviet Russia*
(The Pilot Press, London, 1930). (Mons. Douillet has lived in Russia fo
35 years since 1891, first as Belgian Consul, and after the Revolution, a
member of the mission of the Supreme Commissioner of the League o
Nations ; as Assistant Director of the Catholic Mission in Rostov-on-Don
etc. The English translation of the book has been made by A. W. King)
Walsh, S.J.—*The Fall of the Russian Empire* (Blue Ribbon Books, Nev
York, 7th edit., 1928). (Fr. Walsh was one of the principal members o
the Papal Relief Commission in Russia, 1922–23). McCullagh—*Red Russia*
also *Bolshevik Persecution of Christianity* (1924). Mgr. D'Herbigny, S.J.—
Le Front Anti-Religieuse en Russie Sovietique and *La Guerre Anti-Religieuse
en Russie Sovietique* (" Edition Spes," 1930, Paris). (Mgr. D'Herbigny is
head of the Pontifical Russian Institute in Rome, and one of the bes
living authorities on the Soviet régime in its relation to the Church. Th
booklets are amply documented mostly from Soviet official sources)
Notæ Quædam de Persecutione Religiosa in Russia (Rome, 1930). Thi
is a Latin brochure, which has been compiled by a number of Roman
ecclesiastics, belonging to several different nationalities, who are attache
to the Russian Pontifical Institute in Rome, and who by order of th
Pope have made a systematic study for which they are specially equippe
of the whole Russian question. The Soviet official documents, the Russia
Press, the official Reports of the Catholic missionaries, etc., supply ampl
material for such a study. The brochure is fully documented. S. P
Melgounov—*La Terreur Rouge en Russie* (1918–1924), translated from th
original Russian by W. Lerat (Payot, 106 Boulevard St. Germain, Paris
1927). This book is made up almost entirely of extracts from officia
Soviet documents, and is justly regarded as one of the most importan
collections of contemporary documents on the period which it embrace
(1918–24). There is also an English translation. It contains perhap
the most terrible indictment yet published of the Soviet Régime.
[1] Cf. Walsh, *op. cit.*, chaps, i–iv.

In his great Encyclical on the Social Order Pius XI refers
to Bolshevism in the following passage :

"Communism teaches and pursues a two-fold aim : merciless
class-warfare, and complete abolition of private ownership ; and
this it does not in secret and by hidden methods, but openly,
frankly, and by every means, even the most violent. To obtain
these ends communists shrink from nothing and fear nothing ;
and when they have attained to power, it is unbelievable, indeed
it seems portentous, how cruel and inhuman they show themselves to be. Evidence for this is the ghastly destruction and
ruin with which they have laid waste immense tracts of Eastern
Europe and Asia ; while their antagonism and open hostility to
Holy Church and to God Himself are, alas, but too well known
and proved by their deeds. We do not think it necessary to
warn upright and faithful children of the Church against the
impious and nefarious character of Communism." [1]

Genesis of Bolshevism.—The term Bolshevist is derived
from the Russian word *Bolshinistvo*, which means "majority."
Ever since 1898 there had existed in Russia a Socialist
organisation called the *Social-democratic Party*, aiming at
the substitution of a republic for the monarchical government and the reorganisation of the economic and social
life of the country on a socialistic basis. At the second
congress of this party, which was held in London (July,
1903), a number of delegates (who formed the *majority* and
were consequently called the *Bolsheviki* in contradistinction
to the *Mensheviki* or Minority party) definitely determined
upon an effort to overthrow by armed rebellion the Imperial
Government of the Tsar. Thenceforward the *Bolsheviki*
and the *Mensheviki* formed two distinct revolutionary
parties, of which the former was the more advanced.

In the year 1905, after the Russian debacle in the Russo-
Japanese War, the Bolsheviki, under the direction of the
Jew, Bronstein (alias Trotsky), and other aliens, made their
first abortive attempt to establish a revolutionary Government in Petrograd. The failure of the attempt resulted in
the Bolshevik leaders being expelled and their organisation
driven underground. After 1905, while the Mensheviki
continued their socialistic propaganda openly, hoping to
attain their ends through the medium of the newly established Parliament or *Duma*, the Bolsheviki, who repudiated

---

[1] *Quadragesimo Anno* (C. T. S. edit.), pp. 49, 50.

all constitutional means, continued their secret preparations for a revolution.[1] Their principal leaders were Jews.[2] They were in league with the Masonic secret societies, and are said to have been financed with Jewish money.[3] Working in secret among the industrial masses, they preached hatred against the capitalist régime, against the monarchy which supported it, against the propertied classes, and even against the moderate Socialist Party as traitors to the people's cause.[4]

The Great European War precipitated the crisis. The misery and disorganisation of the people, the crushing military disasters, and the centralisation of political power produced by the war supplied a favourable opportunity for a band of revolutionary adventurers to gain possession of the govermental machine. In March, 1917, the monarchy was overthrown by the popular party, under the leadership of the Jew, Kerensky,[5] who took possession of one of the royal palaces. But some eight months later (October, 1917), the Bolsheviki, who were only a small minority, but were aided by Jewish finance, overthrew by a *coup d'etat* Kerensky's administration and seized the reins of government.[6]

The different states and provinces of the former Russian Empire (over thirty in number, including a few new states), with a total population of nearly one hundred and fifty millions, now form a kind of federal union of socialist states which is called the Union of Soviet Socialist Republics (U.S.S.R.). The different states of the union enjoy at least

---

[1] Cf. Walsh—*op. cit.*, chaps. iii–iv ; *Encycl. Britt.*, *loc. cit.*

[2] Cf. Fry, *op. cit.*, chap. v. Jewish organs, such as *The Maccabees* (New York), claimed as early as 1905 that the Russian Revolution was the work of the Jews.

[3] Cf. De Poncins, *op. cit.*, pp. 160 ff ; also *The Jews Who's Who* (published by The " Britons," 62 Oxford St., London, W.I., 1921) ; also Fry, *op. cit.*, chap. v.

[4] Gautherot—*Le Monde Communiste*, p. 23.

[5] Kerensky's revolution was supported by the British Government of the time. For the Tsar had determined, owing to the military disasters, to withdraw from the European War. Kerensky himself is said to have been a Jew, a Socialist, and a Freemason of the 32nd degree of the Ancient Scottish Rite. (Cf. *The Light*, an American Masonic Journal, Sept. 15th, 1927).

[6] Gautherot, *op. cit.*, pp. 21–24 ; Walsh, *op. cit.*, chaps. xiii–xvi (for a detailed and graphic account of the revolution). N. Webster—*The Socialist Network*, pp. 40–43. *Encycl. Britt.*, *loc. cit.*

nominally, varying degrees of autonomy ; but are all under the supreme control of the All-Russian Central Executive Committee.

The Term Communism.—Since their accession to power the Bolsheviki have been commonly referred to as Communists, and have themselves accepted the name.[1] Communism understood in the sense of Bolshevism differs in two special characteristics from ordinary Socialism. The Communists aim at establishing State Socialism by violence and terrorism rather than by constitutional means ; and the ideal State which they have organised in Russia and propose to set up elsewhere is not a democracy, but a dictatorship—the dictatorship, namely, of the class of unpropertied workers whom they term the Proletariat. This means in practice the dictatorship of the Communist party, or of the Communist leaders.[2]

Since the Russian revolution the division between the parliamentary or democratic socialists and those of the revolutionary type, now commonly called Communists, has become more clearly marked than before.

The Soviets.—The term *soviet* is a Russian word which means *council*. At the time of the first Bolshevik outbreak in 1905, the leaders organised local soviets or revolutionary councils of industrial workers, which were to send representatives to a central soviet in Petrograd. This central soviet was to control the whole revolutionary movement. These organisations, which collapsed after the outbreak of 1905, were again formed in 1917 on a more comprehensive system ; and soviets of the deputies of soldiers and peasants were added to those of the industrial workers.

According to the Soviet system, which was formally adopted at the Fifth All-Russian Congress of Soviets in July, 1918, the highest legislative and administrative authority of the State is the *All-Russian Congress of Soviets*. It is composed of representatives of the local, urban and provincial soviets. But as it does not meet oftener than twice a year, the real governing power, both legislative and

---

[1] Cf. *The New Communist Manifesto* (Postgate, *op. cit.*, p. 176).
[2] Cf. *Official Report of the British Trades Union Delegates*, pp. 2, 3. Gautherot, *op. cit.*, pp. 11–18, 29–31. Postgate, *op. cit.*, chap. iv ; also *New Communist Manifesto*, *ib.*, pp. 193–198.

13 *

executive, vests in the *All-Russian Central Executive Committee* and the *Council of the People's Commissaries*.[1] The personnel of both these bodies is in a large part identical, and both are dominated by the Communist party.[2]

Violent and Oppressive Methods of the Bolshevists.—How far the violence and massacres that marked the early stages of the Russian revolution (which in this regard presents a striking contrast to the revolution in Italy), and the destructive famines and pestilence that almost decimated the unhappy people are to be attributed to the Bolsheviks it is difficult to decide. It is certain, however, even from their own official statements, that the Communist leaders have established their dictatorship by the most ruthless methods,[3] and their régime is still marked by terrorism and repression,[4] Executions, imprisonments, and transportations still go on on a very large scale.[5]

---

[1] *Ib., Cath. Encycl.* (Supplement, 1922), pp. 701, 702.
[2] Gautherot—*Ib.*, pp. 27, 28.
[3] Cf. Postgate, *op. cit.*, chaps. iv and v ; also *New Communist Manifesto* (*ib.*, pp. 175 ff), and *Theses of N. Lenin*, pp. 201 ff.
[4] Gautherot, *ib.*, pp. 32–36 ; also *ib.*—*Le Communisme Contre les Paysans* (published 134 Boulevard Haussmann, Paris, 1931), *passim.*
[5] In the year 1927, on the occasion of the tenth anniversary of the first organisation of the " Ce-Ka," or Soviet Secret Police (now called the Ogpu), a Soviet official list was published of the victims whom they put to death. The list includes only those for whose death the " Ce-Ka " formally accepted responsibility. The total number given in this official paper is as follows :
1917 (Dec.) to 1921 (Sept.) :

Priests	1,243	
Students (i.e., " *Intellectuales* " or " *Intelligensia* ")	365,250	
Teachers	6,755	
Doctors	8,800	1,649,749
Soldiers and Army Officers ..	260,000	
Labourers	192,350	
Peasants	815,351	
1921 (Sept. to Dec.)		18,351
1922 (Jan. to Dec.)		38,000
1923 ,, ...		12,000
1924 ,, ...		?
1925 ,, ...		14,000
1926 ,, ...		3,000
1927 ,, ...		9,574

Total number of victims *officially* acknowledged   1,744,674

These numbers do not include those victims who were murdered or got rid of surreptitiously. These, according to the best informed authorities, would amount to over a million more. Hence the *actual* total of victims put to death in Russia by the Ogpu during the ten years 1917 to 1927 may be safely put down at least 3,000,000 ! ! (cf. *Nota Quædam*, p. 14) ; cf. also De Poncins, *loc. cit.*

Compared with the Protestant Persecutions in Ireland.—
Their methods bear a striking resemblance to the methods
adopted in the 17th and 18th centuries by the English
Protestant party in Ireland to break up the old Irish
Catholic civilisation, but are even more ruthless and cruel.
The expropriations and confiscations, the disfranchisement
of the opponents of Communism, the destruction of Christian
institutions, including the monasteries and seminaries for
the training of priests, the complete suppression of the
existing educational organisation, accompanied by a strictly
enforced ban upon all education that is not Communistic,
the massacre, banishment or impoverishment of the educated
classes—all these measures are in the main a repetition of
the means which were adopted by the English colonial
planters in Ireland for the complete conquest of the country
and the break up of its existing Catholic Irish organisation.

The aims of the Bolshevists, however, are more radical
and unnatural. They definitely reject and wish to destroy
all religion ; and they propagate principles directly opposed
to Christian morality. Furthermore, they *compel all the
children* of the nation to attend their schools in which these
irreligious and immoral principles are inculcated.

Art. 2—*Communist International Activities*[1]

Revolutionary Attempts in Hungary and Germany.—In
March, 1919, a socialist government was set up in Hungary
under Bela Kun and other Jewish leaders, but it lasted only
a few months.[2] The Socialist revolutionary party failed,
at least for the time being, in Germany[3] and Austria. The
movement was foiled in Holland mainly owing to the well
organised resistance of the Catholic forces. In Italy the
progress of the socialist forces has been definitely checked
under the new Fascist and Catholic reactions.

---

[1] Cf. On this subject an article in the *Irish Rosary*, Sept., 1931, by
G. M. Godden, pp. 677–684.

[2] Cf. *Cath. Encyclop.* (Supplement, 1922), art. " Hungary " ; also *Studies*
(Dec., 1922), pp. 541–558, art. " Bolshevik Revolution in Hungary," by
Rev. L. McKenna, S.J.

[3] Cf. *Studies* (Sept., 1923), pp. 361–377 (" The Bolshevik Revolution
in Munich," by Rev. L. McKenna, S.J.), for an account of the short-lived
Soviet régime in Munich in March, 1919.

World-wide Soviet Propaganda.—Propaganda, however, of unprecedented activity, and peaceful penetration of various kinds and degrees go on in most countries of Europe and America, and even in India and China, without intermission or relaxation. This propaganda is evidently supported by an unstinted supply of funds. A sustained attack is being made on identical lines in all countries. The object of this campaign of propaganda is to root out from the minds of the people the Christian faith and even the belief in God, and to overthrow the existing civilisation founded upon that faith. With this purpose organisations of immense variety are formed : meetings and conferences are held ; magazines, newspapers, leaflets, films, dramatic representations, sporting clubs, literary and academic societies, and so forth, are utilised to interpenetrate every social class, dominate every regional and national movement, and allure every type of mind. It is impossible within our available space to do more than indicate in a general way the main outlines of this unprecedented and portentous phenomenon which is essentially international and gives evidence of intense driving force, superb administrative organisation, and the command of almost limitless supplies of funds.

The Komintern.—In 1919 the Bolshevist leaders founded at Moscow *The Communist International*, commonly called the *Komintern*, which they term the (real) *Third International*, and to which the words of the Preamble to the Soviet Constitution may be truly applied that it " marks a decisive step in the direction of the confederation of the labouring classes of the world for the realisation of the *great world Socialist Soviet Republic.*" [1] The device of the league, printed in six different languages under the arms[2] of the U.S.S.R., is that of the Communist Manifesto, " Proletarians of all Countries unite ! " The personnel of the Executive Committee of the Communist International, comprising twenty members, belonging to fourteen different States (France, England, Japan, China, etc.), include for Russia itself the names of some of the leading Ministers of

---

[1] Quoted in Gautherot—*Le Monde Communiste*, p. 50.
[2] The arms of the Russian Soviet Social Union are made up of a sickle and a hammer surmounting a globe surrounded by rays, the whole dominated by a star with five rays. *Ib.*

the Russian Soviet State, such as Zinoviev (President)
Bukarin and Stalin.[1]
The avowed object of the Komintern is to bring about
revolutionary upheavals in the different countries of the
world with a view to the formation of a world socialist State
under the dictatorship of the Communist party. This policy
was clearly enunciated at the second congress (" World
Congress "), which was held in Moscow (July August, 1919).[2]
In the official account published in the *Communist International*[3] (the official organ of the Komintern), we read
that the following resolutions were passed at the Congress :

(a) That the Communist party must enter the different
national parliaments not for the purpose of organisation
work, but in order to blow up the whole bourgeois machinery
and the Parliament itself from within.

(b) That the policy of the Komintern is that of the
revolutionary Marxian doctrine. . . . " The working classes
cannot achieve a complete victory over the bourgeois by
means of the General Strike alone and by the policy of
folded arms. The proletariat must resort to an armed
rising."

(c) That " iron discipline [viz., perfect obedience to the
decrees of the Komintern] is to be the first commandment
of the Communists."

From these resolutions and numberless other evidences
it is clear that the Komintern is a distinctly revolutionary
and anti-national organisation, ruled from Moscow.
The Komintern has now spread its tentacles all over
Europe, Asia, and America. There is a central European
secretariate with headquarters at Vienna, a Western secretariate with headquarters at Amsterdam,[4] and an Eastern
secretariate for the Far East. In 1924 the total Russian

---

[1] *Ib.*, p. 52. Webster—*Socialist Network*, p. 139. Trotsky, while at
the head of the War Department, was also one of the Russian representatives on the Executive Committee of the Komintern.
[2] The Russian delegates at this Congress were Lenin, Zinoviev, Bukarin
and Trotsky, all Jews ; those from England were Quelch, Gallagher, Sylvia
Pankhurst and W. Macklaine.
[3] No. 13, pp. 2405–2454 (quoted in *The Socialist Network*, p. 139).
[4] It has been recently removed to London, from which Communist
organisers are attempting to exploit the unemployment and general
poverty in Dublin and other Irish cities in favour of a movement towards
Communism.

membership was officially put down at 699,689 (including 73,328 women),[1] and that of the non-Russian European affiliated branches at 656,090.[2] Besides the *Communist International*, which is published in several languages,[3] there are in the different countries special organs of Communist propaganda which the Komintern inspires or directly controls. Of these we may mention : *L'Humanite* in France ; *Die Rothe Fahne* in Germany ; the *Drapeau Rouge* (daily) and the *Roode Vaan* (weekly) in Belgium, etc.

The Profintern.—Another International Communist organisation is the *Red International Labour Union*, commonly known as the *Profintern* (from the two Russian words *Professionalye International*). This union is completely controlled by the Central Executive Committee of Moscow, which is itself, like the Executive Committee of the U.S.S.R. and the Komintern, dominated by the Russian Communist party.[4]

The British section of the Profintern is usually styled "The Minority Movement." Its organ is *The Worker* (weekly). It also publishes an English edition of *The Red International of Labour Unions* (monthly).

In 1923, two years after the foundation of the Profintern, the total European membership was set down at between twelve and thirteen millions of workers ;[5] but how far such figures represent anything approaching the reality and what is the real strength of the Red Labour movement it is difficult or practically impossible to determine.

---

[1] According to the *Izvestia* (official organ of the Soviet Government Party) of Feb. 15th, 1925 (quoted in Gautherot, *op. cit.*, p. 237).

[2] Official statistics presented at the Fifth World Congress of the Komintern, which was held at Moscow, 7th July, 1924 (*ib.*, p. 238).

[3] Another Bolshevist international organ is the *Inprecorr* (*International Press Correspondence*) which, like the *Communist International*, is also printed in several languages. The *Labour Research* is an English Communist monthly specially devoted to the collection and publication of matter in aid of Communist propaganda.

[4] Cf. *Socialist Network*, pp. 80, 81, and pp. 138, 139, where from the different lists of the leaders it appears that the leaders of the Red International are partly identical with the Communist leaders.

[5] *Le Bulletin Communiste*, Aug. 2nd, 1923 (quoted in Gautherot, *ib.*, p. 239).

Other International Communist Organisations.—The Komintern is seconded in its efforts by other allied associations, such as the *International Association for the Support of the Defenders of the Revolution*, apparently identical with *Friends of Soviet Russia*,[1] whose main business is that of propaganda by the Press, by brochures, leaflets, etc., which are scattered among the peasant industrial workers. Among the other numerous subsidiary international organisations dominated by the Komintern may be mentioned *The Young Communist League* or *International of Communist Youth* (which counts 700,000 members in Russia, 70,000 in Germany, etc., and whose congress, held at Moscow (1924) included 144 delegates from different parts of the world, all under 23 years of age);[2] the *League of International Sport ; The Workers' Theatre Union ; The International Association of Proletarian Freethinkers*[3] (to which the *Russian League of Militant Atheists* is affiliated) ; *The International Peasants' League (Krestintern)* ; the *Society for Cultural Relations between the People of the British Commonwealth and the U.S.S.R.*

Other instruments of Communist interpenetration are the Soviet *Trade Delegations*, now established in most countries, and enjoying full diplomatic immunity. The vast London Delegation, commonly called *Arcos*, has 800 departments, including those of trade, commerce, banking, etc. In real fact, however, it is an active world-centre of intensive Communist propaganda.[4]

All these and numerous other leagues and organisations, some open and some secret, inspired by the Bolshevist

---

[1] A branch of the " Friends of Soviet Russia " existed in Dublin, 1929–31, and carried on an active Soviet propaganda among the Catholic working-men. Its members were said to number over a hundred (1931), a large percentage of whom were women. Very many (probably most) of the Catholic members of the association had been deluded by the leaders into the belief that the economic and political principles of Communism can be detached from its essentially anti-Christian character. The association was suppressed by the Government in 1931.

[2] Gautherot, *ib.*, pp. 53, 54.

[3] It was this International League that organised and conducted the unspeakable anti-Christian Exhibition in Berlin which the Government was forced to suppress owing to the strong protests of the Catholics. See *Notæ Quædam*, p. 8.

[4] A Soviet publication allied to the activities of the *Arcos* is the *Moscow News*, printed in Moscow, of which copies are sometimes distributed in Dublin, where depôts of the *Arcos* were opened in 1931.

movement, directly or indirectly controlled from Moscow, and in some instances at least aided by the resources of Communist finance, are merely units in one great division of the army which is now waging a world-wide war against Christianity, and whose central objects of attack are the Church, the home, and the fatherland.

It is in reference to these organisations and the Communist interpenetration and propaganda of which they are the means that Pius XI has written the words of warning and rebuke to the rulers of States who allow such pernicious activities to go on in their territories, and who besides neglect to remove the causes which impel the suffering masses towards Communism :

" We cannot contemplate without sorrow," he writes, " the heedlessness of those who seem to make light of these imminent dangers, and with stolid indifference allow the propagation far and wide of those doctrines, which seek by bloodshed and violence the destruction of all society. Even more severely must be condemned the foolhardiness of those who neglect to remove or modify such conditions as exasperate the minds of the people, and so prepare the way for the overthrow and ruin of the social order." [1]

Art. 3—*The Soviet Governmental System*

Ideal Not National Or Patriotic.—The ideal aimed at in the Union of the Socialist Soviet Republics (U.S.S.R.) is not a Russian Empire but an international union intended ultimately to include the whole world. The fact that Sovietism has its present centre in Russia is accidental. The Bolshevist leaders would have initiated the movement just as willingly in London, Paris or Berlin, had the opportunity offered. The Communists do not admit the principle of the natural division of the human race into different nations and states, each state forming a supreme and independent society, to which its members are bound by ties of patriotism and legal justice. Instead of the Christian virtue of patriotism they substitute devotion to humanity and zeal in the prosecution of the class war. The object of the latter is to establish and maintain the

---

[1] *Quadragesimo Anno*, 1931 (C. T. S. edit., p. 50).

" Dictatorship of the Proletariat " until all class distinctions
and state boundaries are destroyed and governmental
authority automatically ceases.[1]
Consequently the army of the Union is not called the
Russian Army but the Red Army. The flag is not the
Russian flag but the Red flag of " Universal Brotherhood."
The design on the coins of the Union is not a national
one, but the sickle and the hammer, with the legend,
"Workers of the World, Unite !" A worker of any country
who happens to reside within the Union needs no ceremony
of naturalisation to possess all the rights of citizenship.

Governmental System.—In actual fact, however, the
All-Russian Central Executive Council and the smaller
Council of the People's Commissaries, both of which are
appointed by the *All-Russian Congress of Soviets*, govern
the Union. The All-Russian Congress of Soviets forms, as
it were, the apex of a pyramid of soviets. It is made up
of delegates from the soviets of the various republics in
the Union. These soviets are themselves composed of
delegates from the soviets of the Provinces, and so on
through the soviets of the cantons, the districts, the villages,
and the factories. There is a highly elaborated system of
representation,[2] in which the industrial or professional unit,
such as the factory, is substituted for the local constituency.
According to the written constitution, the delegates may be
recalled at any time by those whom they are supposed to
represent ; and there is no division such as exists in other
states between the executive and the legislative authority.

A Limited Franchise.—The government does not, however,
profess to be a democracy, except in a limited sense ; for
whole classes are excluded from the rights of citizenship.
These rights are confined to the proletariat or working class,
just as in the mediæval state they were confined to the
feudal class, or in the Irish State system of the 18th century

---

[1] The professed aims of the Communist Party are : " To end the domination of capital and make war impossible, *to wipe out State boundaries,
to transform the whole world into one co-operative commonwealth,* and bring
about human brotherhood and freedom." From the *New Communist
Manifesto* (Cf. Postgate, *op. cit.*, p. 191).
[2] Cf. Postgate, *op. cit.*, chap. xi ; Gautherot, *op. cit.*, p. 36.

to the Colonial Protestant class. Hence the government is called the "Dictatorship of the Proletariat," just as the early mediæval system of government in most European states might be called the "Dictatorship of the Feudal Class," or the 17th and 18th century British Government the "Dictatorship of the Propertied Classes."

All the working population who are over eighteen years of age have votes, irrespective of sex, nationality or religion. On the other hand, all are excluded from the franchise who employ others for wages or live on income not earned by personal labour, such as dividends on invested capital, interest on money, rent, etc. Priests, religious, traders, and commercial travellers, are also excluded. Hence the electors are mostly the poorer peasants, the industrial workers and the soldiers of the Red Army.[1] The skilled artisans and clerical workers also have the franchise, but on a much less favourable basis than the unskilled. The industrial workers are favoured beyond the peasants.[2] Thus the franchise is confined to the less educated and more unstable elements of the community, who (especially when the influence of the Church is eliminated and the Press completely in the hands of the administration) are easily controlled by the Communist leaders.

"The essence of the Soviet power," writes Lenin, "consists in the fact that the unique basis of . . . public authority is constituted by the mass organisation of exactly those classes which were oppressed by Capitalism—the worker and semi-proletarian and the peasants, who do not exploit hired labour, but are forced to sell a fraction of their own labour power."[3]

Soviet leaders profess that the system of limited franchise is intended only for the transition period ; namely, until the power of the "bourgeois" class is broken, and the

---

[1] Cf. *Official Report*, etc., pp. 9, 10 and 101.
[2] "The industrial proletariat is favoured . . . because it is the most aggressive, the best organised and politically ripest class under whose leadership the semi-proletarian and small farmers will be gradually elevated." *New Communist Manifesto* (Postgate, *op. cit.*, p. 195).
[3] Lenin's *Theses* (No. 14) presented at the Third International (Cf. Postgate, *op. cit.*, p. 212). Note the use of the term *exploit* in this citation. The term is here a propagandist word, implying the fallacy already referred to that the wage contract is *always* unjust and *necessarily* includes an exploitation of the wage-earner. This principle is condemned by Leo XIII and Pius XI (Cf. *Quadragesimo Anno*, 1931, p. 31).

State transformed into a "Classless Communist Common-wealth." [1]

The Communist Party.—Side by side with the official government there is the political organisation of the Communist Party, which is the parent body of the Komintern. In theory the Communist Party bears somewhat the same relation to the administration as an ordinary party organisation in England or the U.S.A. may bear to the actual government of the country. The Communist Party, however, completely dominates the government. It is a closely organised body of militant Communists, mostly soldiers, industrial workers, students and government officials, with a certain sprinkling of peasants. [2] Candidates for membership have to undergo a probation of six months and receive a recommendation from two existing members before being enrolled. The whole Communist Party, including the candidates, numbers, or numbered a few years ago, a little less than 700,000. [3] These form the nucleus and driving power of the whole Communist organisation. They are an active, enthusiastic and well-disciplined body. All must profess and follow the extreme Communist creed, any deviation from which, such as a religious marriage, circumcision as a religious ceremony, and so forth, entails expulsion from the party. [4]

Party Controls the Government.—The Communist Party utilises the machinery of government to keep the power in their own hands. By means of a highly organised press propaganda (the pressmen being specially selected and trained for the purpose at the public expense), [5] by rigging the elections and manipulating the results ; by terrorism and bribery ; by the activities of a whole network of Com-

---

[1] *New Communist Manifesto* (Postgate, *op. cit.*, p. 193).
[2] Cf. Gautherot, *op. cit.*, pp. 27, 28, for the relative numbers. The number of peasants in the Communist Party is given as 66,000 by the *Izvestia* (15th Feb., 1925). The total peasant population of the Union is over 100 millions.
[3] Cf. *Izvestia, ib.* (quoted, *ib.*, p. 237). Note that the total population of the Union of which the Communist Party is the real governing power, is about 150 millions, so that the Russian Communist Party is less than ½ per cent. of the whole population.
[4] *Official Report*, etc., pp. 13, 14.
[5] Gautherot, *op. cit.*, p. 36.

munist agencies[1] operating in the local soviets, the factories, and the villages they manage completely to control the elections, while still preserving some outward semblance of democracy.[2]

In the All-Russian Congress of Soviets, which is the supreme governing authority of the Union, more than 80 per cent. of the deputies are members of the Communist Party, which thus completely dominates the assembly.[3] Seeing that it is these Congresses that appoint the Central Executive Council and the smaller Council of the People's Commissaries, which are the actual governing bodies of the Union (the People's Commissaries being the heads of the several departments of State, like the members of the British Cabinet), one need not wonder at the fact that the personnel of these two councils are practically all members of the Communist Party and mostly identical with the personnel of the Executive Committee (*Polit-Bureau*) of the Communist Party itself.[4] Hence the Communist Party is at present the real governing power of Soviet Russia, just as it is the driving and directing force of the Komintern, the Profintern and the other subsidiary Communist organisations.

Its Jewish Element.—In order to understand the position more fully, one must keep in mind the predominating influence of the Jews in Russian Communism, a fact which is now generally recognised. The whole Socialist movement is largely a Jewish creation. The founders of Socialism— Marx, Engels and Lasalle—were Jews, as was also Ricardo, from whom some of the fundamental principles of Socialism[5] are borrowed. Even before the Great War the Socialist movement over the whole world was controlled almost

---

[1] *Ib.*, pp. 36, 37.

[2] *Ib.*, pp. 36–50. *Official Report*, etc., pp. 12–17.

[3] Thus of the 1,300 deputies present at the Congress of 1924, 1,100 were members of the Communist Party ; and at the Congress held in May, 1925, consisting of 1,244 deputies, 1,000 belonged to the same Party. Cf. Gautherot, *op. cit.*, pp. 30 and 32 (notes).

[4] Cf. Gautherot, *op. cit.*, pp. 31, 32 ; also Mrs. Webster's *Socialist Network*, pp. 138, 139, where the names of the members of the different bodies as they were in March, 1926, are given in full.

[5] Viz., Marx's *Theory of Value* and Lasalle's *Iron Law of Wages*. It should be added that both Marx and Ricardo, though Jews by birth, became Protestants.

entirely by Jews.[1] This was specially true of Russia, which contained a large portion of the Jewish population of the world, and where for the past century the Jews have usually been the centre of the subversive movements.

The predominance of the Jewish element in Russian Communism is strikingly illustrated in a brochure entitled *Who Governs Russia ?*[2] This brochure, which is carefully documented from Soviet official sources,[3] contains lists of the chief government officials of the Soviet Union as they were in 1919–1920, indicating the nationality of each. Of the 22 *Commissaries of the People* 17 were Jews, and the President, Oulianoff (Lenin), a Russian (Mongolian) born of a Jewish mother. Of the 43 members of the *Commissariat of War* 33 were Jews, including the President, Bronstein (Trotsky). Of the 64 members of the *Commissariat of the Interior* 45, including the President, Apfelbaum (Zinoviev), were Jews. Of the 30 members of the *Commissariat of Finance* 24 were Jews. Of the 21 members of the *Commissariat of Justice* 18 were Jews ; and so on through all the different departments of State. The names of 413 leading officials are given ; and of these 345 are Jews and only about two dozen are Russian, the remainder being of other different nationalities. Lists are also given of the members of the *Central Executive Council* as elected by the Fourth and Fifth All-Russian Congress of Soviets. Thirty-three out of the 34 members appointed by the Fourth Congress are Jews, the remaining one being Lenin himself ;

---

[1] Cf. De Poncins, *op. cit.*, p. 197, where a series of texts mostly from Jewish writers in support of this statement is quoted.

[2] Published 1920 by the American Association known as *Unity of Russia* (121 East 7th Street, New York). A summary of the brochure, including the lists of names, is given in Jouin—*Les Fidèles de la Contre Eglise*, pp. 109–136. Cf. also Poncins, *op. cit.*, pp. 160 ff, where the dominant rôle of the Jews in Bolshevism is shown from official documents of the French and U.S.A. Governments drawn up in 1919. Cf. also *La Documentation Catholique*, 1920, where the most important of these documents was published for the first time. Samuel Gompers, himself a Jew, published two articles in the *New York Times* (May, 1922, and Dec., 1923), revealing the support given to the Communists by certain very well-known and highly placed Jewish bankers of U.S.A. (two well-known bankers are mentioned by name). The name of a third, equally well-known, occurs frequently in the documents reproduced in Poncins (*loc. cit.* and pp. 132 ff of the English edition of the same work. Cf. also Fry, *op. cit.*, chap. v.)

[3] Viz., the *Izvestia, Golos Frouda*, the *Red Gazette* and others.

and of the 62 members appointed by the Fifth Congress[1] 43 were Jews and only 6 were Russians. In a further series of lists the writer gives the names of the leaders of the other so-called Russian Socialist parties who are opposed, or affect opposition, to the Communist Party. Of the 64 names enumerated 59 are Jews and only 4 are Russian.[2]

Although since the accession of Stalin to power (1928) efforts have occasionally been made by some of the native Russian Soviet leaders to rid themselves of the Jewish domination, with the result that several important Jewish leaders, including Bronstein (Trotsky), have disappeared from the public view, Jews still hold most of the key positions in the Soviet government. Thus we learn from the *Forwerts* (Sept. 16, 1931), a New York Yiddish daily,[3] that the following high placed Soviet officials are Jews : Litvinov, Commissar for Foreign Affairs ; Jakovlev, Minister for Agriculture ; Rosengoltz, Director of Foreign Commerce ; Ruchimowits, Commissar for Transport, Railways, etc. Raganowits, Stalin's right hand man and the real author as well as practical director of the " Five Years' Plan," is also a Jew. Again, we learn from the *Jewish World* (June 25th, 1931) that another Jew, Gurewitch, is Chairman of the most important commercial committee ; and that " Jews hold many other responsible posts." The *Jewish World* adds :

" In so far as the Communist Party (viz., practically the Government) are in a position to control the attitude towards the Jew everything possible is done to make no distinction between Jew and non-Jew. . . . But anti-Semitism is spreading in spite of the authorities. It is like a disease that has penetrated to the blood of the masses. Wherever one goes one observes this anti-Jewish feeling . . . in the factory, among the Communist workers, among the petty officials, and among certain sections of the peasants, who were formerly not ill-disposed towards Jews."[4]

The general conclusion from all the above seems to be

---

[1] This was the Congress that adopted the present Soviet Constitution.

[2] The Jewish Bolshevist leaders are apparently of the Rationalistic and Cabalistic type, who reject all real religion (cf. Cahill, *op. cit.*, chap. iv and *passim*). Orthodox Jews are in fact persecuted under the Soviet régime.

[3] Cited in *The Patriot*, Oct. 15th, 1931, p. 373.

[4] Cited in *The Patriot* (*ib.*).

that the Russian Revolution was not the result, at least in the shape it has assumed, of a genuine national movement ; and that the present régime is in reality a tyranny exercised by an oligarchy largely alien, who represent the real Russian people as little as the Protestant colonial oligarchy that governed Ireland after the Puritan conquest of the 17th century represented the Irish people.[1] The rising tide of anti-Jewish animosity referred to in the above extract seems to suggest the beginning of a Russian reaction which sooner or later is inevitable against the tyranny imposed upon the nation by a highly organised oligarchy largely alien in race, and un-Russian and anti-Christian in outlook and ideals.

Art. 4—The Soviet Internal Policy

General Character of Soviet Régime.—The Russian Revolution implies a radical change in the Christian organisation of society ; and the repudiation of several of the most sacred and fundamental principles of conduct in men's daily lives. The Soviet social system represents the natural outcome and, as it were, the ripened fruit of the Secularism, Naturalism and Modernism which are rampant to-day among the nations of the European races.[2] We can only touch briefly on some of the central points in which it is at variance with Christian principles.

Intensive Religious Persecution.—In pursuance of the materialistic principles of Karl Marx, the Soviet State in theory and according to its Constitution, excludes all consideration of religion, of the Deity, and of the moral law. In actual fact, however, the Soviet government and régime are positively and fanatically anti-religious, to a degree that would seem incredible, were not the facts established beyond all doubt. Thus by a Soviet decree of 1929 Atheism has

---

[1] Cf. Webster—*Secret Societies and Subversive Movements*, chap. xv ; *Revue Internationale des Sociétés Secrètes* (published weekly at Avenue Portalis 8, Paris VIIIe), *passim ;* also De Poncins, *op. cit.*, pp. 126–160.

[2] " The new Russia is a challenge to Christian society ; and the New Russia does not stand alone. The challenge comes from the whole modern world. Russia has revealed the strength and the possible outcome of the tendencies of the day in Western Countries, especially in England." (From an article entitled " Reflections after Visiting Russia," by H. Somerville, M.A., published in *Studies*, December, 1929, p. 357.)

been made a kind of State dogma : and the provisions of the Soviet Constitution allowing religious freedom were annulled. Atheists alone are allowed the right of teaching their " beliefs." The religious persecution which has been carried on with varying intensity since the establishment of the Soviet régime has of late years definitely assumed the character of an anti-God campaign. The sacrilegious outrages which are committed " go far beyond and even against the text of the revolutionary constitution although that was already very anti-religious."[1]

The persecution, though in many respects conducted along the traditional lines followed by the enemies of Christianity for almost 2000 years, is in some ways unique in history. Like the 18th century religious persecution in Ireland it is directed against the overwhelming majority of the people. But unlike every other religious persecution known to history the aim and object of the Bolshevik anti-religious campaign is not the establishment of some particular cult, such as paganism or Calvinism or Judaism, but the destruction of every form of religious worship and the elimination from the people's minds of all idea of a Supreme Deity or a moral law. In this particular, and in the subtle and comprehensive character of its anti-religious propaganda, the Soviet State would seem to be a foretaste of the rule of Anti-Christ.[2]

Pius XI and the Soviet Persecution.—Pius XI stigmatises and laments this inhuman persecution in a letter addressed (Jan., 1930) to Cardinal Pompili, the Cardinal-Vicar of Rome.

" We are deeply moved," he writes, " by the horrible and sacrilegious crimes that are repeated every day with increasing intensity, against God and against the vast population of Russia. . . .

" From the very beginning of Our Pontificate we multiplied Our efforts to put an end to this terrible persecution, and to avert the grievous evils that press upon these peoples. We were

---

[1] From the letter of Pius XI to Cardinal Pompili (Jan., 1930), referred to *infra*. For many details of the Soviet persecution, proved from Soviet official sources, cf. an article by G. M. Godden in the *Irish Rosary*, August 1931, pp. 587–599.
[2] Cf. Cahill, *op. cit.*, pp. 67–74. *See* also the booklet, *God and the Soviet*, by E. A. Amedingen (*Irish Messenger* Series, 1931).

also at pains to ask the Governments represented at the Conference of Genoa to make by common agreement a declaration,
which might have saved Russia and all the world from many
woes, demanding as a preliminary to any recognition of the
Soviet Government respect for conscience, freedom of worship,
and of Church property. Alas, these three points, so essential
above all to those ecclesiastical hierarchies unhappily separated
from Catholic unity, were abandoned in favour of temporal
interests, which in fact would have been better safeguarded if
the different Governments had first of all considered the rights
of God, His Kingdom, and His Justice. . . .[1]

" This sacrilegious impiety rages against all priests and the
adult faithful, amongst whom, in addition to other victims
faithful to the service of God, We hail in a particular manner,
our most beloved sons, Catholic priests and religious, imprisoned,
deported, and condemned to forced labour, with five other
bishops, our venerable brethren Boleslao Sloskana and Alessandro
Frison, together with Our representative for the Slavic rite, the
Catholic Exarch, Leonida Fiorrov. . . .

" But the organisers of this campaign of atheism and the
' Anti-God-Front ' wish above all to pervert youth, abusing
their simplicity and ignorance. For, instead of imparting instruction, science and culture, which, like honesty, justice and
goodness itself, cannot prosper or flourish without religion, they
organise the ' Militant No-God League.' They deceitfully hide
their moral, cultural, and even economic decadence by an
agitation as barren as it is inhuman, instigating children to
denounce their parents, to destroy and defile the religious buildings and emblems, and above all to contaminate their souls by
every kind of vice and the most shameful sins. . . . During the
recent festival of Christmas (1929) hundreds of churches were
closed and numbers of icons [viz., sacred images] burnt, and
servile work imposed for that day upon the workers and school
children. The Sundays also were suppressed by law. Things
have even come to such a pass that those employed in the workshops, both men and women, are compelled to sign a declaration
of formal apostasy and hatred of God, *under pain of being
deprived of their tickets for food, clothing and lodging, without
which [tickets] every inhabitant of that unhappy country must die
in cold, hunger and misery.*[2]

" In all the cities and in many villages infamous spectacles
were organised, similar to those which the foreign diplomatist

---

[1] The diplomatic efforts of the Holy Father here referred to took place
in 1922.
[2] Italics not in the original.

14

beheld last Christmas in Moscow, in the very centre of the capital city. They saw lorries pass by in which large numbers of young men were arrayed in sacred vestments, and holding Crosses upon which they spat. Other lorries carried large Christmas trees from the branches of which numerous dolls hung by the neck dressed to represent Catholic and Orthodox Bishops. In the centre of the city other youths performed every species of outrages against the Cross."[1]

Soviet Methods.—The policy of the persecutors is not to proclaim openly their anti-religious aims, but rather to make religious practice ridiculous and impossible, while nominally allowing it and to commit the direct work of destroying religion to apostate priests, and lay people, especially the young.[2] Hence the victims of the religious persecutions are never formally condemned for religious practice or profession, but under some such pretext as violating the laws, plotting against the Soviet Government, etc.

Meanwhile, however, religious teaching in public or private schools is forbidden. It is made a criminal offence punishable by hard labour of one year to teach religion to a person under 18 years of age ; churches are being gradually closed or confiscated for profane uses ;[3] a religious marriage is held invalid in law ;[4] Christian feasts, including Sundays, are abolished, and the clergy harassed in every available way and even deprived of the means of subsistence. The destruction of the monasteries and Christian schools has rendered impossible the training of a native priesthood, which seems therefore doomed to destruction. Of the Catholic priests in Russia about 50 per cent., including at least two bishops, together with the Catholic Exarch

---

[1] Cf. *Soviet Campaign Against God* (*Protest of Pius XI*) (C. T. S.). For original, *see Apostolicæ Sedis*, Feb. 22nd, 1930, p. 69.

[2] This policy is described in *Bezbojnik* (3rd March, 1929), one of the Communist organs, in the following terms : " To make not martyrs but apostates of the Christians, so that these latter may become champions of Atheism and impiety " (cited in *Notæ Quædam*, p. 4).

[3] Thus, according to the Soviet official statistics in the Republic of Russia proper alone, during the year 1929, there were closed or confiscated 1,119 churches (viz., 530 in the cities and 589 in the rural districts), 126 synagogues, and 124 mosques (Cf. *Notæ Quædam*, p. 5).

[4] This impious law prevails also at present in several other countries, in which also Christian festivals have been abolished.

Leonidas Fiodorov, are at present (1931) in prison or under-going sentence of hard labour.[1]

Besides all this there is a highly organised anti-religious propaganda carried on all over the Union. This, although not an officially acknowledged government activity is assisted and facilitated by the Government to such a degree that it may almost be described as the most important government function.

Anti-Religious Organisations.—The most prominent and aggressive of the anti-religious organisations is the " League of Militant Atheists," founded in 1922 ; and formally approved by Stalin, then General Secretary of the Communist party, in 1925. This league, whose membership is over half a million, directs and controls all the anti-religious activities all over the Union. It practically controls the whole Russian Press, which it makes an instrument of its propaganda.[2]

Since 1926 it has affiliated to it the " International Association of Proletarian Freethinkers " with its centre in Vienna destined for international anti-religious propaganda. For the same purpose was established a few years ago the association of " Young Russian Atheists." By means of these leagues the anti-religious propaganda is carried on in the Press, the Trade Unions Clubs, above all in the schools and colleges and all the public institutions.[3]

Family in the Soviet System.—The Soviet State does not recognise the family as a social unit. The Christian principle founded on the natural law (and hitherto more or less recognised in all types of social organisations, whether Christian or otherwise), according to which the married pair form one moral person, inseparably united and jointly responsible for their children's upbringing, is rejected.

---

[1] Cf. *Notæ Quædam.* According to more recent reports, especially that of Mgr. D'Herbigny, who travelled in Russia disguised as a workman (1931), almost all the Catholic priests have been put to death or imprisoned.

[2] The total roll of members of the League is about 600,000. The total number of professed atheists in the Union is estimated at about 2,300,000. *Ib.,* p. 9.

[3] Cf. An article entitled " The Anti-God Front in Soviet Russia," by Mgr. D'Herbigny, in *Studies*, March, 1930, for an account of the recent anti-religious laws of April, 1929, which are far more severe and searching than any that preceded them.

(a) **Family Rights and Duties not Recognised by Law.—** Under the Soviet system "a man has no dependents." The responsibility for the children's rearing and education is transferred to the State, to which the children are supposed to belong.[1] In industry and all social relations, men and women, whether married or not, are regarded in law as isolated individuals depending on the State, working as separate units and receiving individually their wages and State allowances, called "benefits." In order to prevent the accumulation of personal property, which is more or less bound up with the Christian principle of the parents or the head of the family being responsible for the future prospects of children, a man cannot leave to his heirs more than £1,000. The rest of his property, if he have such, goes to the State after his death.[2]

(b) **Marriage Practically Abolished by Soviet Law.—** Marriage in the Soviet State is merely a matter of witnessed registration. Divorce is still easier, and may always be had on application. Illegitimate children have in law exactly the same legal standing as those born in wedlock. In fact the principle of illegitimacy is not recognised in Soviet law.[3] Birth control is formally encouraged by the State. Abortion is legalised.

(c) **Family Life Positively Discouraged.—**Not only is the family not recognised as a social unit, but family life is positively discouraged. The whole tendency of the State policy is to transfer the social centre of gravity from the home to the club.[4] In the Communistic system of proprietorship (or rather the absence of proprietorship) as conceived in the Soviet State, the domestic privacy of a home that is one's own can scarcely be realised. Hence in the great centres such as Moscow and Leningrad, where the Soviet system is in full operation, there is little or no family life.[5]

---

[1] *Official Report*, p. 130.   [2] *Ib.*, pp. 101–104.   [3] *Ib.*, p. 124.   [4] *Ib.*, pp. 99 ff.
[5] The following passage from *Russia To-day and Yesterday* (a book favourable to Soviet principles and leaders), by Dr. E. J. Dillon (London, 1929), illustrates this :
"The Muscovites are huddled together like tinned sardines in rooms, corridors, cellars . . . corners of staircases. Cosiness, privacy and all the elements that constitute a home are eliminated. Only ten per cent. of the inhabitants reside in flats, about eighty per cent. vegetate in rooms,

(d) **Appalling Results.**—The results of the Soviet attitude towards the family and all it stands for may be imagined. Sexual vice has become rampant, wherever the Soviet system is in real operation. But the worst results are those that affect the children. Thus we learn from a Soviet official report that in the industrial district of which Moscow is the centre, 72 per cent. of the boys and 70 per cent. of the girls between the ages of seven and fourteen use alcoholic drink ; and that 20½ per cent. of the boys and 20 per cent. of the girls are habitual drunkards.[1] Immense numbers (computed by the million) of boys and girls promiscuously rove the country side and the streets of the cities in small bands, half naked, half famished, like fierce wild animals, ignorant, savage, drunken, eaten up with venereal and other diseases.[2] Some of these abandoned and unhappy little ones are no doubt the still surviving children of parents lost in the original Revolution or the succeeding famines ; but the majority are the products of the Soviet system, of the usurped guardianship of the State and the destruction of family obligations and ties.[3]

while the worst of all are those who have no roof to cover them, and are forced to stand in a queue outside a night refuge and wait there in the cold till they are let in or turned away. Most of the rooms are occupied by three or four persons, some have as many as five inmates. . . . I paid him [viz., a friend with his family of three] a visit a month or more later, and while we were talking in that stuffy reeking chamber, some carpenters came in with saws, hammers, planks and nails to make two rooms out of the one [which the friend and his family occupied], and worked away heedless of our presence " (pp. 50, 51).

[1] Report of the Lady Doctor Siminova in the *Teachers' Journal*, No. 5, 1929. Quoted by Gautherot—*Le Communisme à l'Ecole*, p. 36.

[2] Cf. *Les Etudes*, 5th March, 1930, in an article entitled " Change sur la Face de Russie." Cf. also Douillet, *op. cit.*, pp. 109 ff, and Dillon, *op. cit.*

[3] In further illustration of the matter of this section, cf. Gautherot—*Communisme à l'Ecole*, in which documentation from Soviet sources is given, describing conditions in much more lurid terms than given above. Cf. also Dillon, *op. cit.*, chap. viii, " Women," in which the Soviet ideal and practice are graphically described. The Soviet ideal of the " emancipated " woman is summarised in the words of a Soviet woman leader : " Away with the family, husband, pots and kettles, and hurrah for free women " (*Ib.*). Cf. also *Etudes* (20th Oct., 1931), pp. 129–158, for an exceptionally interesting article by Mgr. D'Herbigny, entitled " Une Campagne Sovietique Contre L'Egalitarisme." The article points out the recent abandonment by Stalin and the Soviet Government of the ideal of social equality and the inauguration of a new economic policy leading to class distinction. Most of the article is made up of citations from the official Soviet press, which demonstrate a state of widespread wretchedness among the people as regards food, clothing, and the prime necessaries of life.

Education in the Soviet State.—The Soviet government has usurped the complete control of education. No other rights (such as those of parents and Church) are recognised. According to Soviet law education is obligatory and completely secular. In actual fact it is naturalistic, materialistic and positively irreligious.[1] The full school programme, which, however, is apparently not carried out except in the great urban centres, includes clothing and food for all school and college children and even for University students.[2]

Irreligious and Immoral Character of the Schools.—There is no distinction made between the sexes in any of the schools or universities. The school curriculum includes detailed instruction in sex relationship. The results on the morality of the children and undergraduates, and even of the teachers themselves, both men and women, are appalling, to a degree that cannot be here described.[3] Furthermore, atheism and irreligion are systematically taught ; so that it is officially proclaimed that the Soviet School " must be the principal pulpit for the propagation of atheism." The school curricula are arranged with a special view to the anti-religious and atheistical formation of the pupils ; and numerous other activities are organised for the purpose with a thoroughness and shamelessness that would almost seem incredible.[4] The League of Militant Atheists have charge of the conduct of the anti-religious school propaganda.

The ideas and principles of the class war are also carefully inculcated in the schools. Thus the abuses and crimes of the ruling authorities throughout the centuries are strongly emphasied ; and every means is adopted to impress on the child's mind the need of class consciousness ; to break down the Christian tradition of reverence for

---

[1] Cf. W. T. Goode, M.A.—*Schools, Teachers and Scholars in Soviet Russia* (London, 1929). Mr. Goode, who writes as a frank admirer of the Soviet system, states that the whole educational system is founded upon the materialistic teachings of Marx, Engels, Darwin, Dietzgenmith and Lenin. Cf. also Godden—*The Soviet and the Child* (an article in the *Irish Rosary*, Oct., 1931), pp. 749 ff.

[2] Cf. *Official Report*, p. 112.

[3] *Ib.*, p. 105 ; also Gautherot—*Le Monde Communiste*, pp. 38, 39 ; and *Le Communisme à l'Ecole*, chap. iv ; also Godden, *loc. cit.*, p. 751.

[4] Cf. Mgr. D'Herbigny in *Studies* (March, 1930), pp. 46–48.

authority and lessen or destroy the prestige of the virtues of obedience, humility, meekness and purity.[1]

Soviet Economic Régime.[2]—In the first flush of the Revolution the nobles and the landed gentry were completely displaced, leaving the land entirely in the hands of the peasants. Industrial concerns of every kind were confiscated to the State : the Church property, landed and otherwise, was also confiscated ; and private ownership of all kinds of capital was abolished by law.

" New Economic Policy."—Soon, however, the economic principles of undiluted Socialism were found unworkable. This was especially true of the agricultural holders who form approximately 85 per cent. of the whole Russian population and who, like the peasants all over the world, are essentially small-property men. When they learned that they had to grow grain not for the market, but for the State, and that only a certain allowance would be assigned them for their own needs, they stopped sowing, so that the grain crop of 1920 fell to half the normal amount. The result was the dreadful famine of 1921 in which, some six millions of people died of starvation.[3]

Hence Lenin found himself compelled to abandon at

---

[1] Cf. Gautherot—*Le Communisme à l'Ecole, loc. cit.* ; also *Official Report ;* also Goode, *op. cit.,* p. 22. Our object, as already indicated, is only to point out the aspects of the Soviet system which are at variance with Christian teaching. That the Soviet theory of education and general social organisation does also contain some principles which are in themselves good if detached from the false system of which they form a part is not denied. Thus we read : "The educational authorities exercise a large measure of control over the cinema, the wireless and theatres, all of which are national property. . . . The films in the U. S. S. R. are supervised by education authorities, and not by the police as in Capitalist countries. . . . There are also special theatres run for children " (Unfortunately, however, the educational authorities mostly belong to the League of Militant Atheists. Cf. Gautherot—*Communisme à l'Ecole,* passim, *Notæ Quædam,* etc.).

Again, we find among the Soviet ideals such principles as the following : " Life and livelihood depend on work. Hence the schools and other educational institutions are brought into the closest contact with the life of the people around them." " Children and teachers take part as workers in collective activity of all kinds."

These ideas are excellent, but not new. They are an echo of principles of education which are as old as Christianity ; but too often disregarded in modern pedagogic systems.

[2] Cf. Gautherot—*Le Communisme Contre les Paysans,* also *Le Communisme Contre les Œuvriers* (Paris, 1931).

[3] Cf. Walsh, *op. cit.,* " Introduction."

least partially the Communist system. In 1921–22 what
was called the New Economic Policy was inaugurated.
Nume·ous changes or " concessions " of far-reaching importance were made so that the economic régime was no longer
socialistic in the full Marxian sense.[1] Thus, although in
the original revolution all the land was nationalised (or
" socialised ") and rent and hired labour abolished, there
was a few years later no less than 96 per cent. of the land
in the possession of the peasantry, who had practically
become peasant proprietors paying an annual tax to the
State.[2]

The smaller industries and the home handicrafts, as well
as the smaller trading depots, were also " de-nationalised "
and freedom of private enterprise restored. The same
occurred in regard to many of the larger industries, although
many, too, continued to be carried on by the State or under
a mixed management.[3] But all the larger industries, even
those conducted under private management, were subject
to many legal restrictions limiting their complete freedom ;
and their operations were overseen by State inspectors
recruited from the working classes.[4]

Marxism in Agriculture.[5]—Since the accession of Stalin
and his party to power in 1928 there has been a return in
what is called the " Five Years' Plan " to the Marxian
economic régime both as regards land and the manufacturing
industries. The " Five Years' Plan " is mainly an attempt
to " industrialise " agriculture, and organise rural operations
on the system of mass production on a gigantic scale. It
was calculated that the transition period from the old
system would cover about five years (1928–33). Hence the
name given to the scheme.

The land is to be taken over from the peasants (who are
thereby transformed into " proletarian " agricultural
labourers) and laid out in immense farms to be worked
directly by the State under the supervision of State stewards.
The work is organised on a military basis and the workers

---

[1] Cf. *Official Report*, etc., pp. 3, 4.   [2] *Ib.*, pp. 63–65.
[3] *Ib*, etc., pp. 50, 51.   [4] *Ib.*, pp. 42–51.
[5] Cf. Gautherot—*Le Communisme Contre les Paysans ;* also Walsh, S.J.—
The Last Stand (Little, Brown & Co., Boston, 1931). This latter book
contains a fully-documented analysis of the Five Years' Plan, and the
policy underlying it,

are under military discipline. The supervisors are mostly Trade Unionists members of the Communist Party who have received a summary agricultural training for the purpose. Tractors replace for the most part beasts of burden. Some 60,000 of these farms are already (1931) organised. The farms comprise a very considerable percentage of the whole arable land of the more fertile regions, such as the Volga basin, the Ukraine, and some of the northern portions of the Caucasian regions.

The object aimed at by the Soviet leaders in the " Five Years' Plan " is twofold.[1] In the first place, they hope to render the Russian peasant population amenable to the will of the Soviet oligarchy. For this purpose the peasant is deprived of his independent ownership of land (and thereby of his real freedom of which ownership is the foundation), and reduced again to the position of practical serfdom. The second object is to increase production with a view to world-wide domination and a coming war.

The *Kulaks* (the more prosperous type of peasants), who number about five millions, and the *Serendiaki* (small cottiers of moderate, but what would be under normal circumstances, sufficient means), who form about one-half of the whole population of Russia (their numbers are estimated to be over 76,000,000), are being forced into the system against their will by the imposition of impossible imposts and taxes. Those who venture to resist openly are imprisoned, deported to Siberia or shot offhand.[2] As a consequence the conditions of smouldering or suppressed war which have existed over large areas of the country since 1920 have been itensified.[3]

---

[1] Cf. Gautherot, *op. cit.*, pp. 26–29, where the official Soviet declaration is cited.

[2] *Ib.*, pp. 33–37 ; Walsh, *op. cit.*, chap. iv.

[3] Cf. Gautherot—*La Monde Communiste*, pp. 28–29, 36, 37 ; also a valuable series of articles in the *Osservatore Romano*, Dec., 1931, for some account, drawn from Soviet official documents of the state of discontent and smouldering rebellion which prevails among the Russian peasantry under the Soviet régime. Even before the inauguration of the Stalin policy of agricultural mass production and forced labour, the settled policy of the Government seems to have been (as it needs must be) to keep the peasantry helpless (cf. Walsh, *loc. cit.*). The prevailing conditions show, in some respects, a striking analogy to the 18th and 19th century conditions in Ireland, where a somewhat similar policy was followed by the ruling oligarchy. Cf. O'Brien—*Economic History of Ireland in the 17th Century* and *Economic History of Ireland in the 18th Century* (Maunsell, Dublin, 1918–1919).

Besides the *Kulaks* and the *Serendiaki* there are (or were) two other types of peasant class in Russia. First come the *Batraki* (agricultural labourers), whose lot was very miserable before the Bolshevist revolution : their number was estimated at about five millions in 1925, but showed a considerable increase in 1927. The other type is that of the *very poor* cottiers, whose number was estimated at twenty-two millions in 1927. These two classes have had little or nothing to lose by the imposition of the Communistic régime, and probably welcome the change, at least in its purely economic aspects.[1]

As to the probable outcome of the " Five Years' Plan," it is difficult to form a judgment at the present stage, especially as the position is far from clear in many of its details. It is likely that the Soviet leaders will succeed to a considerable extent in their main object—viz., in breaking up the peasant life and rural organisation of Russia. That production will be, or can be, *permanently* increased, or even maintained at its previous level by the methods put in force is very doubtful : and the statistics so far available seem to point to the ultimate failure of the " Plan " in its economic objectives.[2]

Payment of Workers.—In all enterprises controlled directly or indirectly by the State, the worker's wage, which varies according to the category of his profession or trade, is intended to cover only the actual necessities for which he has to pay cash. The rest of his requirements—recreation, travelling, yearly holiday, medical and insurance benefits, the education and upbringing of the family, housing, etc.— accrue to him in the form of " Benefits " supplied by the State, in whose power therefore he entirely is.

Prospects of the Bolshevist Régime.—How far the Soviet system is in real operation throughout the Empire, or is likely to permeate the great masses of the immense population of the Union, it is very difficult to estimate. Even if one were to accept as substantially true the statement of the British Trades Union delegates of 1925, that the system has, or then had, the support of the whole industrial population, it would not mean that it was accepted by the

[1] Cf. Gautherot—*Le Communisme Contre les Paysans*, pp. 23, 24.
[2] Cf. Gautherot, pp. 38 ff, and *La Vague Rouge*, July-Sept., 1931 ; also Walsh, *op. cit.*, chap. vii.

Russian people. For it must be borne in mind that the Russian people are mainly agricultural. The whole industrial population, men, women and children, is not much over 20 millions, of whom only " 25 per cent. are members of the Trade Unions " and directly involved in the system.[1] Whereas the peasants number about 110,000,000. Again, the aboriginal tribes, which exist in some parts of the Empire, are quite untouched by Communist ideas.

The worst danger is the aggressively atheistic and immoral character of the schools which all the children between the ages of seven and sixteen years are legally bound to attend,[2] and which it is feared may with time destroy the faith and morals of the people of the whole Soviet Union. As a fact, however, the law of compulsory school attendance has not so far been, and cannot be, effectually enforced, owing to the resistance of the peasant population : so that the number of school children actually show a steady decrease.[3]

The perils which the Soviet propaganda contain even for countries outside the Union can scarcely be exaggerated. This propaganda is evidently maintained with all the resources that money can command. The restoration of Christian principles and just conditions in social life, together with Catholic organisation, are the only effective safeguard against the Soviet menace.

Conclusion.—We shall conclude our sketch of Revolutionary Communism by citing the warning words of two authorities separated from each other by a space of more than four centuries, both of whom inculcate the same salutary lesson. The first is Trihemius, whose warning words penned at the end of the fourteenth century are so apposite to-day as almost to seem prophetic :

" If the duty of right use and management of property, whether material or spiritual is neglected ; if the rich think that they are the sole lords and masters of what they possess, and do not heed the needy as their brethren, there must of necessity arise an internal disruption of the State. False teachers and deceivers will then gain influence . . . by preaching to the people that earthly property should be equally distributed among.

---

[1] *Official Report*, pp. 109, 110.
[2] Gautherot—*Le Monde Communiste*, p. 38.
[3] Cf. *Ib.*—*Le Communisme à l'Ecole*, pp. 41 ff.

all, and that the rich must be forcibly condemned to a division of their wealth. Then follow lamentable conditions and civil wars ; no property is spared ; no rights of ownership any longer recognised ; and the wealthy may then justly complain of the loss of possessions, which have been unrighteously taken from them : but they should also seriously ask themselves whether in the days of peace and order they recognised in the administration of those goods the rights of their superior lord and owner ; the God of all the earth." [1]

Our next citation shall be from the recently issued Encyclical of Pius XI *On Christian Marriage*, in which the Holy Father speaking of the duty of the public authorities in regard to poor families, emphasises the same warning :

"If families," he writes, "have not suitable dwellings ; if the husband cannot find employment and means of livelihood ; if the necessities of life cannot be purchased except at exorbitant prices ; if even the mother of the family, to the great harm of the home, is compelled to go forth and seek a livelihood by her own labour ; if she, too, in the ordinary, or even extraordinary labours of childbirth is deprived of proper food, medicine, and even the assistance of a skilled physician, it is patent to all . . . how great a peril can arise to public security and to the welfare and very life of civil society itself, when such men are reduced to that condition of desperation, that having nothing which they fear to lose they are emboldened to hope for chance advantage from the upheaval of the State and established order." [2]

---

[1] Cited in O'Brien—Essay on " Mediæval Economic Teaching," p. 86 ; from Janssen's *History of the German People* (English Translation) vol. ii, p. 91

[2] *Casti Connubii*, Dec., 1930 (*See* C. T. S. booklet, *Christian Marriage*, by Pius XI.) Appeals for social reconstruction, official and otherwise, from the representatives of the Church are becoming more and more insistent and urgent in recent years. As one typical example we quote the following from a country of Eastern Europe no less Catholic than our own : Rev. Jan Urban, S.J., editor of the Polish monthly, *Przeglad Powszechny*, in the number for Dec., 1930, points out the need, especially from the religious point of view, of a radical change in economic conditions and methods ; " The people," he writes, " who are still Christian at heart, should be made to feel assured that the Church for its part will leave nothing undone to further the victory of social justice. Unless they can be persuaded of this, all our efforts to save them from Bolshevism will be in vain ; for as Bishop Kubina of Czenstochau says : ' social misery and unjust oppression of the masses are arguments in favour of Bolshevism stronger than any reasons we can bring against it.' He also cites the following sentences from the same Bishop : ' Unless we effect the needed economic modifications by peaceful means, we may rest assured that sooner or later against our will, an overwhelming alteration will be forced on us which will establish on earth the kingdom of Satan instead of the longed for Kingdom of Christ.' " (Cited in the *Stimmen der Zei*, Feb., 1931, pp. 377, 378.)

CHAPTER XIII

FREEMASONRY AND ALLIED SOCIETIES[1]

Introductory Remarks.—The modern anti-Christian movement, which centres round Liberalism, owes much of its rapid progress to the secret society of the Freemasons, who are, as it were, the advance guard of the forces of Liberalism. Leo XIII describes the purpose of Freemasonry to be the " utter overthrow of the whole religious order of the world which Christian teaching has produced, and the substitution of a new state of things . . . based on the principles and laws of pure Naturalism."[2]

Freemasonry is to-day the central enemy of the Church and of every Catholic government and Catholic institution in the world. It is closely associated with modern Judaism (including the Rationalistic Jews, as well as those of the Talmud and the Cabala)[3] ; and is largely under Jewish influence and guidance. In pursuing its ideal of a universal, naturalistic Masonic State, Freemasonry aims at, or rather tends necessarily towards the destruction of religion, morality, family life, and of all national and patriotic ties. In the present sketch we can do no more than give the outlines of the subject under a few main headings.

Art. 1—*The Rise and Spread of Freemasonry*

The Pagan " Mysteries."—The claim that Freemasonry is a continuation of certain pre-Christian religious associations of Egypt, Palestine, Greece and Rome, is devoid of

---

[1] The matter of this chapter is mainly a summary of the writer's book, *Freemasonry and the Anti-Christian Movement* (Gill, Dublin, 2nd edit., 1930). The book is referred to in the notes as, " Cahill, *op. cit.*" See also Poncins, *op. cit.*, also Deschamps—*Les Sociétés Secrètes* (Paris, 4th edit., 1881), and Belliot—*Manuel de Sociologie Catholique* (Lethielleux, Paris, 2nd edit., 1911), pp. 381–391—an excellent summary).

[2] *Humanum Genus.* The term *Naturalism* means the complete rejection and contempt of the supernatural, including faith, grace, and the sacraments, and the elimination of all reference to a future life.

[3] Cf. Cahill, *op. cit.*, chap. iv ; also Index, *ib.*, sub verbo " Jews."

all historical foundation ; all these associations were founded on a religious basis. They presupposed a priesthood of some kind, and were essentially connected with the idea of theocracy and the privileges of an aristocratic or governing class. Freemasonry, on the other hand, implies or aims at the elimination of all religious organisation and the establishing of a type of human liberty and equality which are inconsistent not only with the ordinary arrangement of society, but even with the supreme authority of a personal God distinct from man himself. Some, however of the tenets and practices of these pagan associations, such as the doctrine of Pantheism, the deification of the principle of generation and the shameful rites connected with the phallic worship, do reappear in certain sections of Free-masonry, which may therefore claim, at least to that extent some real connection with pre-Christian doctrines and practices.

The Templars.—Many writers, Masonic and otherwise associate the origin of Freemasonry with the Order of the Templars suppressed in the 14th century, and with some other anti-Christian sectaries of earlier periods. Among these sects are the Gnostics, the Manicheans, and the Albigenses, whose doctrines and ritual the heretical section of the Templars were supposed to inherit. The Templars before their suppression in 1308, were accused of heresy the systematic practice of blasphemy and certain other abominable and nameless rites. Masonic historians hold that the order continued to subsist as a secret society especially in Scotland, after its legal suppression ; and that through this secret society the spirit and doctrines of the original heretical Templars have been transmitted to modern Freemasonry.[1]

The Humanists.—Some again find the definite beginnings of the Masonic movement in certain revolutionary and anti Christian secret associations which sprang up in the 15th century under the influence of the pagan Humanism, resulting from the so-called Renaissance.[2]

---

[1] Cf. Deschamps, *op. cit.*, p. 300 ; also Cahill, *op. cit.*, in Index, *sub verbo* "Templars." Any historical connection of Freemasonry with the Templars has not been, and probably cannot be, proved.

[2] Cf. Belliot, *op. cit.*, pp. 371 ff ; also Deschamps, *op. cit.*, vol. i pp. 318-28.

English Origin.—England, however, was the real cradle and nursing ground of modern Freemasonry. The history of the early developments of English Freemasonry, of its connection with the revolutionary and occultist forces on the one hand and with the old guilds of operative masons on the other, is obscure. The main facts, however, are as follows : The framework as well as the name of the new society were adopted from the old guilds of operative masons which, after the Protestant Revolt, had lost their Catholic character. Some of these, and especially the great London Masons' Guild, gradually dropped their professional character and received into their body members who had no connection with the building craft. Among these non-professional members received into the London guild in the 17th century were Jews, Deists and Freethinkers, under whose influence strong anti-Christian elements got embedded into what was originally an exclusively Christian body.[1]

Masonic Constitutions.—Early in the 18th century (Masonic historians usually fix the date at 1717, when the first Grand Master of the English Lodges was appointed) the Freemason Society dropped completely its professional character, and formally assumed the rôle of a philosophic and religious (or anti-religious) association, with a definitely propagandist purpose. About five years later James Anderson, a Scotch Presbyterian minister, assisted by John T. Desaguliers, a Huguenot refugee who also became a minister, drew up the constitutions and ritual which remain to this day the groundwork of the Masonic organisation all over the world.

Anderson's constitutions retain a portion of the framework of the old operative Freemason guilds, such as the grades of Apprentice, Associate (or Companion) and Master, while adapting them to the exigencies of the new society. But the soul and spirit of the old Catholic constitutions were so fundamentally altered that in their new form they ceased to be Christian or even Theistic.[2] God and Christ, to

---

[1] Cf. Cahill, *op. cit.*, pp. 1–6 ff ; also Deschamps, *op. cit.*, pp. 281 ff.

[2] The usual distinction between Deists and Theists is, that the latter acknowledge a supreme *personal* God, distinct from the created universe, though they may deny the mysteries of the Holy Trinity and the Incarnation ; while the so-called God of the Deists may be merely some force of nature, or attribute of matter, or something which they describe as the soul of the world, or which Freemasons term the " Grand Architect of the Universe."

whom the old Catholic masons promised service and loyalty, were replaced by the vague and intangible being who is called "The Grand Architect of the Universe."[1]

For the old Catholic charge made to the working-mason, "Be true to God and Holy Church and use no error or heresy," Anderson substituted a rule which implies naturalism and religious indifference. According to this rule the Freemasons were obliged only *to follow the religion in which all men agree, leaving the particular opinion to themselves, that is, to be good men and true, or men of Honour and Honesty, by whatever denominations or persuasions they may be distinguished . . . being as Masons only of the Catholic religion above mentioned.* In other words, the Catholicity and religion of the old Mason's guilds is supplanted by a new Catholicity which is some kind of vague Deism or naturalism, and embraces in one universal religion the cult of pagan, Mahommedan, Buddhist, etc.

Again, the old charge of the Catholic guild to its members regarding loyalty to their country, is radically altered in Anderson's constitutions. The old charge was : " You shall be good liege men of the King without treason or falsehood ; and you shall come to know no treason, but you shall mend if you may, or else warn the King or his council thereof." Anderson's text reads :

" If a Brother should be a Rebel against the State, he is not to be countenanced in his rebellion, however he may be pitied as an unhappy man ; and if convicted of no other crime . . . they [the Brethren] cannot expel him from the Lodge, and his relations to it remain indefeasible."

The reason given by Anderson for this alteration is that Freemasonry is cosmopolitan, and transcends all national distinctions :

"We are resolved against all politicks ; we, being only as Masons of the Catholick religion . . . we are also of all Nations, Tongues, Kindreds and Languages."[2]

These two fundamental characteristics of Freemasonry,

---

[1] The Masonic Deity (the " Grand Architect of the Universe ") is not necessarily a personal God much less the true God of the Christian religion. Cf. Cahill, *op. cit.*, chaps. ii and iii and *passim*. (*See* Index, *ib.*, *sub verbo* " God ").

[2] Cf. *Ib.*, pp. 62, 63 ; also *Cath. Encycl.*, vol. ix, pp. 777, 778.

namely, indifference in matters of religion, which means
absence of all real religion, and a tendency towards cosmo-
politanism and a false and exaggerated internationalism
remain to this day, outstanding features of the Masonic
spirit even in its least disruptive manifestations.

Freemasonry in Ireland.—Speculative Masonry thus
organised spread rapidly in England and Scotland, and
within a few years after its foundation was introduced among
the English colony in Ireland. The sect took strong root
among the latter. Indeed, down to the present day, Freemasonry and Orangeism (an off-shoot of Masonry, and controlled by it),[1] which was founded in 1795 dominate the
inner councils of the Protestant and pro-British party in
Ireland. How much this party and the British Government
relied and still rely on Freemasonry and Orangeism for their
hold on the country is well known ; and may be illustrated
by numerous significant facts. Thus the oath prescribed
by law to be taken by the Royal Irish Constabulary and
Dublin Metropolitan Police excluded them from all political
organisations or secret societies, *" unless the Societies of
Freemasons."* In the two Home Rule Acts for Ireland,
those of 1914 and 1920, the Irish Parliaments were
definitely precluded from any power to *" abrogate or pre-
judicially affect any privilege or exemption of the Grand Lodge
of Freemasons in Ireland, or any lodge or society recognised
by the Grand Lodge."*[2] Again, that the " Curragh mutiny "
and " Ulster rebellion " of 1912–13, as well as the Belfast

---

[1] The constitution, ritual, and oaths of secrecy, of the Orange society
are almost identical with those of Freemasonry. The objects of the two
are substantially the same except that Orangeism is regional. The Orange
leaders are, of course, Masons. For a detailed account of Orangeism,
cf. *The Orange Society,* by Rev. H. W. Cleary (afterwards Bishop of
Auckland, New Zealand), 7th edit., 1899 (C. T. Society, London, 1899).
A Masonic handbook entitled *Ahiman Rezon,* published in Belfast 1804,
is dedicated by the author, L. Dermott (the well known Masonic organiser
of the time), to the Masters and Brethren of the Orange Lodge of Belfast,
who had, he says, reorganised Freemasonry over all the Province of
Ulster (Cf. *Ahiman Rezon,* Belfast, 1804, pp. vii, viii).
[2] At the present time, according to the current law in the Irish Free
State, the police and the members of the Free State army, are precluded
by the oath they have to take, from belonging to secret societies. This
clause, however, which was inserted to meet the difficulty caused by a
secret organisation existing within the Free State army, is omitted in the
oath prescribed for members of the Free State judiciary, by a law passed

15

Orange riots and pogroms of 1919–1922 were engineered through the medium of the same societies, is also commonly believed, not without good foundation.

Spread of Freemasonry.—During the first half of the eighteenth century, Masonic lodges were founded from England and from Ireland in France (1721), and in the English colonies, as well as in Spain, Holland, Russia, Turkey, Germany, Hungary and Poland. Later on, lodges were formed in New England (North America), India, China, Africa, Central and South America.

In France, especially, where the ground was prepared by the Gallican and Janssenistic movements of the preceding generation, Freemasonry spread very rapidly, and gained immense influence. The Masonic lodges became the meeting-places in which every type of impiety, immorality and revolt found a safe refuge, and where all the anti-religious and anti-social elements of French society, as well as the profligate, religiously indifferent and worldly-minded both laymen and ecclesiastics, met on common ground. This spirit of revolt soon bore fruit all over Europe and America in the anti-religious persecutions, the expulsion of the Society of Jesus from various countries, the complicated intrigues which culminated in the suppression of the same Society (forced on the Holy See through Masonic influence), and later on, in the excesses connected with the French Revolution (1789).

The Illuminists.—About the middle of the 18th century, the irreligious and disruptive elements in Freemasonry received a new impetus from the secret societies of the German Illuminists and the French Martinists which were merged in it. The unchristian and anarchical ideals of these societies had come into Northern Germany from England and France early in the century, and had spread south into the Catholic portions of the country. In 1776 Adam

---

about the same time ; and no such stipulation appears in the oath prescribed for members of the Free State Executive Council, Dail, or Senate. Cf. "The Soldier and the Judge," by Lex (*Irish Rosary*, October, 1926).

For a full account of the legal position of Freemasonry in Ireland under the British régime (a position which has not so far been altered even in the Irish Free State) cf. a series of articles in the *Irish Rosary*, April and May, 1930, entitled "Freemasonry and the Law," by M. J. Lennon, B.L.

Weishaupt, a professor of the University of Ingolstadt, became the leading spirit of the movement. The Illuminists and the other kindred secret societies were suppressed by the Bavarian Government in 1784 ; but their principles and methods have continued even to our own day to infiltrate through the medium of Freemasonry into European society, and to spread more and more into every part of the known world. They are in fact practically identical with the principles and ideals of Revolutionary Communism, now commonly called Bolshevism.

Masonic Activities for Past Two Centuries.—Freemasonry supplies the key, and at least a partial explanation of the extraordinary progress of the spirit of infidelity, irreligion and revolt against lawful authority which has characterised the history of the European races during the past two centuries. The constantly recurring revolutions, political upheavals, assassinations, and religious persecutions, which loom so large in the modern history of Europe and America have been, for the most part, the work of Freemasonry. The network of secret societies—irreligious, anarchical, and communistic, which now almost cover the face of the globe, are practically modelled upon and inspired by Free-masonry, and are in large measure controlled by it.

This is true of the Jacobin excesses of the French Revolution of 1789, of the French Revolutions of 1830 and 1848, as well as of the revolutions which took place about the same time in several countries of Europe. It is equally true of the Italian Revolution (1870) with the accompanying spoliation of the Papal States ; and of the rising of the Paris Commune (1871), in which the fierce anti-Christian spirit of the insurgents rivalled that of the Jacobins eighty years before. The modern anti-Christian persecution in France dating practically from 1870, the Mexican Revolution with all its anti-Christian virus, as well as the revolutions and anti-Christian movements in Spain itself and the South American States; the Portuguese Revolution of recent times; the Young Turk Movement of the early years of the present century with the unspeakable Armenian massacre that accompanied it ; all (or at least the fierce anti-Christian spirit which all alike display) have had their source and inspiration in Masonic teaching and intrigue. All have been supported, approved or glozed over where open approval was impossible, by the Mason-controlled press of Great Britain and U.S.A., as well as by the non-Catholic press of the continental countries. The Nihilists of Russia (progenitors of the present Bolshevists), the Carbonari of Italy, the Orange Society of Ireland and the British Colonies, the American Ku Klux Klan, and the six hundred or more secret societies of the United States of America, all more or less disruptive and anti-Christian, are all offshoots of Freemasonry, modelled upon and largely controlled by it.[1]

Varying Masonic Tactics.—In order to understand the working of Freemasonry in its varying manifestations, one must bear in mind that it is essentially anti-Christian. Its activities, revolutionary or otherwise, and the support it accords to political and other parties, are only a means to an end. Hence it usually exhibits openly its revolutionary virus only in Catholic countries or where the government and social organisation are more or less under the guidance of Christian principles. In non-Catholic states or in a social organism which is already largely dechristianised, or where the governing powers are mainly under Masonic influence, it affects the pose of constitutionalism and loyalty to the established government.

This is the real key to the apparent contrast between the Grand Orient Masonry of France, Mexico and Portugal, and the Freemasonry of the Anglo-American and Anglo-Irish type. The difference is rooted in the varying circumstances of the different countries and the resulting need for varying tactics.

Statistics of Freemasonry.—According to its official statistics Freemasonry numbers at present some four and a half millions of registered members, besides a million or so of " Negro " Freemasons in U.S.A. who are not officially recognised. Of this four and a half millions only about 300,000 (or less than one-fourteenth of the whole) belong to the so-called Latin or continental sections, while over 4,000,000 belong to the English-speaking countries. These

---

[1] Cf. Preuss—*A Dictionary of Secret and other Organisations* (Herder, London, 1924) ; also Stevens—*The Encyclopedia of Fraternities* (New York, 1901).

latter form the real strength and centre of the Masonic organisation. The United States of America have over three million registered members ; Great Britain over 400,000 ; Canada about 200,000, and Ireland over 50,000. More than half of the so-called Latin or continental section—including the Grand Orients of Italy, Spain and Portugal, the Grand Lodges of Greece, Denmark, Holland, France, Brazil, and Egypt, as well as the Grand Lodge York of Mexico—are in close official relations with Anglo-Irish Freemasonry.

The remaining small section of " Latin " Freemasonry (including probably over 100,000 members), such as the Grand Orient of France and some of the Mexican and South American Lodges, are not at present (viz., since 1878) *officially represented* in the London and Dublin Grand Lodges owing to certain domestic differences of terminology and tactics. All, however, are linked up in the " World Chain of Freemasonry " through numerous liaison bodies such as the Grand Lodge Alpina of Switzerland ; through international congresses, etc., and still more by a unity of purpose and of spirit.[1]

Strength of Freemasonry in Ireland.—The Freemasons in Ireland are practically identified with the imperialist and non-Catholic portion of the population. The ostensible number of Freemasons in Ireland (about 50,000) although very much greater[2] in proportion to the population than

---

[1] That Freemasonry forms one body the whole world over is in fact officially recognised by the Freemasons themselves ; although individual Freemasons frequently deny the fact for purposes of controversy. All sections, both continental and Anglo-Saxon, are equally enumerated in the official Masonic Year Books. Irish, English and American Freemasons supply statistics of their members, etc., for publication in the continental Calendars. They send their representatives to the international Masonic congresses. Even in the Dublin Grand Lodge there are official representatives of Portugal, Italy and Spain, and of the Grand Lodges of France, Belgium, Mexico and Brazil. Bro. A. Pike, the great prophet and leader of Anglo-American Freemasonry of the 19th century, publicly avowed that the pretence of diversity between British and Latin Freemasonry was futile and could not be maintained. Cf. Cahill, *op. cit.*, chap. ii ; also pp. 223, 224 ; also Appendix ii and *passim.*

[2] Some 1,050 Irish Masonic lodges, of which 140 are in Dublin, are mentioned in the *Irish Freemasons' Calendar* of 1929. It seems probable that the vast majority of the whole non-Catholic population of Ireland belong directly or indirectly (viz., through husband, father, etc.) to the Freemasons' or Orange Society or both.

the number of Freemasons in any country of continental Europe or South America, is not an adequate measure of their effective strength. The Masonic party inherit the fruits of the British domination. They control very much of the economic life of the country, including the banks and railways, several of the more important academic and educational institutions, such as the Queen's University, Dublin University (or Trinity College) with its allied medical schools, and a large section of the Press. Besides, they have at command, for the purposes of their anti-Catholic and anti-Irish activities, the Orange Society which is practically a Masonic body. In addition to all this, it may be truly said that in Ireland as elsewhere, Freemasonry wields more influence and power through its allied associations and organisations than by its own personal membership.[1]

Art. 2—*Masonic Aims, Character and Policy*

Masonic Secrecy.—" One of the first . . . obligations," writes John H. Cowles, ' Sovereign Grand Commander ' of the Southern Jurisdiction, U.S.A., of the A. and A. Scottish Rite of Free-masonry, " assumed by every initiate of the Masonic Fraternities is that he will in no manner reveal any part of the secrets that are imparted. The solemnity of this obligation is impressed upon him in explicit detail. . . . The *Wisdom of Secrecy in Regard to Esoteric Masonry* has been long established, is based upon sound reasoning, and its value has been proven through the many years of the Fraternity's existence. . . ."[2]

Freemasonry, the child of darkness, is essentially secret. Its secrecy does not lie merely in the fact that its membership is partly unknown and its counsels and doings kept from the knowledge of the public. The essential nature of the society itself, its real aims, even its moral and philosophic teaching, are all shrouded in mystery. All these are unknown even to the vast majority of the members ; and are fully communicated only to a select few, belonging to the

---

[1] See *infra*, art. 3, " Imperfect Freemasonry " and " White Masonry."

[2] *The New Age*, official organ of the Supreme Council 33° of the Ancient and Accepted Scottish Rite of Freemasonry, July, 1931, p. 388. (The italics are not in the original.)

inner circles, whose mentality and moral outlook are supposed to be sufficiently attuned to Masonic ideals. For the rank and file of the Craft, all these matters are veiled in allegory and symbolism whose real significance they do not understand, and concerning which they are in fact deliberately misled.[1] By that means immense multitudes are induced to lend their names to an institution and to promote purposes from which, if they knew the full truth, they would recoil with horror. Hence it is that at every stage of Masonic initiation, the candidate renews the impious oaths of secrecy, and that secrecy is so much insisted upon in every portion of the organisation and working of the society.

Nevertheless, a society cannot, any more than a person, permanently conceal its real character. Hence, not a few enquirers, both Catholic and Protestant, who have made a systematic study of Freemasonry from the abundant materials that have accumulated during the past two centuries, have succeeded in lifting, at least partially, the veil that covers it and in laying bare for those who wish to learn the real nature of Freemasonry and the framework of its secret organisation.[2] Besides, even from the very beginning, the Popes, with the unerring vision which the guidance of the Holy Spirit confers, saw clearly and denounced in no doubtful terms the wickedness of Freemasonry and its designs against Christ's Kingdom on earth.

Essence of Freemasonry.—Freemasonry is the soul and centre of the whole modern anti-Christian movement. It is in other words the "Counter Church." A modern Catholic writer commenting on the well-known words which occur in two different letters of Pius IX, where the Pope signalises Freemasonry as "the Synagogue of Satan," describes the sect as "a synthesis of all the heresies and the rallying point of all the uprisings of man against God."[3]

Freemasonry sets up a code of morals and a principle of human virtue and beneficence *independent of God*; and

---

[1] Cahill, *op. cit.*, chap. iii, where the texts bearing on Masonic secrecy are quoted.

[2] Cf. Cahill, *op. cit.*, pp. 95 ff.

[3] Gautherot in the *Dictionaire Apologétique de la Foi Catholique*, vol. ii, col. 95.

while it affects to ignore Our Divine Lord, or where circumstances require, pays a homage of lip service to His sacred Name, its very essence is opposition to Him and to His mission on earth. Underlying the whole Masonic system, colouring all its teaching and all its activities and ceremonial, there is a steady current of antagonism to Christianity. The Church's ideals are held up to derision ; its teaching misrepresented ; its ministers and religious, when occasion serves, are calumniated and persecuted. Even its most sacred mysteries and rites, such as the Incarnation, the Mass and the Sacraments, are fantastically and blasphemously caricatured in some of the Masonic ceremonial and teaching.

Immediate Objective of Masonic Policy.—Naturalism and Hermeticism or Occultism (including Theosophy, Spiritism, Christian Scientism and Satanism) are characteristic of the Masonic cult and philosophy. These are put forward as a substitute for real religion, and are in fact to-day perhaps the most powerful solvent of the elements of true Christianity which still survive among the non-Catholic communities of the English-speaking world.

With the object of making the principles of Naturalism effective in the lives of the people, Freemasonry everywhere strives to de-Christianise as completely as possible the educational system and the public life of the State. Hence its political and social programme includes :

I. The banishment of religion from all departments of government, and from all public institutions ; and, as a mark of the triumph of this policy, the removal of the Crucifix and all religious emblems from the legislative assemblies, the courts of justice, the public hospitals, the schools and university colleges, etc.

II. The secularisation of marriage, and the introduction of divorce facilities.

III. The establishment of a state system of education which, at least in its primary stages, will be obligatory, gratuitous and conducted by the laity.[1]

---

[1] This is the professed object of the Masonic *League of Instruction,* which was established in France in 1866.   Cf. Deschamps, *op. cit.,* vol. iii, pp. 427 ff ; also Mgr. Jouin—*Le Péril Judaeo-Maçonnique,* vol. xii (*Le Loi d'Enseignment*), pp. 99 ff.

IV. Complete freedom of worship (at least for all religions except the true one).

V. Unrestrained liberty of the Press even in the propagation of irreligious doctrines and of principles subversive of morality ; similar freedom for the stage, the cinema, and for all manner of public activities, even when most injurious to the public interest, such as the operation of the betting and gambling agencies, and of agencies for debasing amusements, the drink traffic, the traffic in drugs and instruments of unnatural vice, etc.

VI. The elimination of all distinction between the sexes in education and in all departments of public life, and the promotion or encouragement of radical feminism.

The same programme usually includes or favours a constitution or government which is nominally Democratic or Republican, but is so organised as to be easily dominated by the Masonic press, and the masters of high finance ; indiscriminate universal suffrage ; and the centralisation of political and administrative authority in the hands of a bureaucracy. It is opposed on the other hand to the national distinctions which are associated with the Christian virtue of patriotism, to the ideal of strongly organised rural communities settled permanently on the land ; and finally to the organisation of society in classes bound together by ties of common interest and mutual service. Hence its policy tends towards commercialism, a false internationalism and extreme individualism.[1]

Papal Condemnations.—The Church forbids Catholics under pain of excommunication, to be incurred by the very act (*ipso facto*) to enter the Masonic society, or to give it any assistance or support. Furthermore, the papal condemnations of Freemasonry are so severe and so sweeping in their tenor as to be quite unique in the history of Church legislation.

During the last two centuries Freemasonry has been expressly anathematised by at least ten different Popes, and condemned directly or indirectly by practically every Pontiff who sat on the chair of Peter. The Popes charge the Freemasons with occult criminal activities with " shameful

---

[1] Cf. Cahill, *op. cit.*, pp. 156 ff.

deeds " ; with acting under the direct inspiration of the
devil, if not actually worshipping Satan himself (a charge
which is hinted at in some of the papal documents) ; with
infamy, blasphemy, sacrilege, and the most abominable
heresies of former times ; with the systematic practice of
assassination ; with treason against the State ; with anarchical and revolutionary principles and with favouring and
promoting what is now called Bolshevism ; with corrupting
and perverting the minds of youth ; with shameful hypocrisy
and lying, by means of which Freemasons strive to hide
their wickedness under a cloak of probity and respectability,
while in reality they are a very " Synagogue of Satan,"
whose direct aim is the complete destruction of Christianity,
and the universal restoration of paganism in a form more
degraded and unnatural than the world has hitherto known.

The Popes again and again remind Christian rulers of
their urgent duty, in the interests of religion and morality,
and for the sake of the peace and safety of the State, to
suppress all the secret societies in their dominions.[1]

The Popes do not accuse all individual Freemasons of
participating actively in the crimes and shameful deeds of
the Masonic body. But, since all members lend their names
and at least their moral support to the condemned sect, all
come under the censures and are held to share its responsibility and guilt. Thus Pope Pius IX writes :

" It is not alone the Masonic body in Europe that is referred
to [viz., in the Papal condemnations] but also the Masonic
associations in America and in whatsoever part of the world
they may be. "[2]

Hence the whole Order and all sections and divisions of
Freemasonry are condemned indiscriminately.

Art. 3—*Masonic Organisation*

Although the main outlines of Masonic organisation are
fairly well known, very many of the details are still obscure

---

[1] For a series of citations (in English) from the texts of the Papal pronouncements on Freemasonry, cf. Cahill, *op. cit.*, chap. vi (pp. 118–135).
For a more complete and exhaustive series of references and citations from
the papal documents on Freemasonry, cf. *Revue Internationale des Soc.
Sec.* (1929–1930), in a series of articles by Rev. Dom Baucher, O.S.B.,
entitled " Les Papes et la Franc-Maçonnerie."

[2] *Etsi Multa*, 1873.

and doubtful. We touch here only on points that are well ascertained.

The Duplicate Personality.—Freemasonry has, so to speak, a duplicate personality. There is the outer Freemasonry, whose personnel, organisation and activities are more or less openly acknowledged. This Freemasonry publishes its rituals, holds its festivals, edits its calendars, etc. Besides this there is what we may call the inner or *esoteric* Freemasonry, which forms the real centre and soul of the society and in which the Jewish influence usually predominates.

The outer Freemasonry stands ostensibly for toleration, liberalism in religion, and humanitarianism. It contains multitudes of members who do not know the aims, the activities, or even the existence of the inner body. Many of the members of the outer circle are wealthy or influential men. These serve as useful figureheads who promote the prestige of the Masonic body and give it a reputation for moderation ; but in reality they exert little influence over its activities, and are merely utilised as tools by the inner circles. Thus Louis XVI of France, as well as Marie Antoinette, belonged, at one time, to the Masonic body, which later brought about their execution. So, too, in England and Ireland, men like the Duke of Norfolk (1730), Lord Coleraine, the Earl of Ripon, the Earl of Inchiquin, Lord Byron, many Protestant Bishops, and even members of the royal family have held from time to time the highest rank in the Masonic body.

Outer Administrative Organisation.—When a person enters the Masonic body he is first of all received into an apprentice lodge. When his mind is judged to be sufficiently receptive of the Masonic " light," he is initiated into a lodge of *Companion* Masons. After a further period of observation and trial he will, if judged satisfactory, be promoted and initiated into a Master's lodge. Every Mason can enter any lodge of a degree similar or inferior to his own, but is strictly excluded from a higher lodge. These three degrees, viz., those of Apprentice, Companion and Master, which form the lower or Blue Masonry, are the fundamental elements of the society. The members of these degrees are the ordinary " faithful " of the Masonic counter-church.

Freemasonry is divided into several groups or federations which are administratively independent of one another. Most of these groups, while corresponding mainly to one country, have affiliated branches (colonial settlements as it were) in several other countries. Again, in the same country there may exist side by side several independent jurisdictions.[1] All the several groups or federations although nominally independent, are usually linked up or interlocked with one another through the medium ot permanent representatives, or liaison bodies or members who hold at the same time important positions in two or more independent federations.

The lodge (which in some groups is called the *Chapter* or the *Preceptory*) is the fundamental unit in each group. It is directed by officers who are elected for one year. These have no jurisdiction outside the lodge. The supreme governing authority of the group or federation is a kind of parliament (or *convent* or *congress*) made up of delegates from the lodges. It meets at stated times usually about twice a year. This assembly appoints by election an executive council, at the head of which there is a smaller council or board, presided over by the Grand Master (in some federations called the President and in some again the Sovereign Grand Commander).

From all this it is evident that the outer administration or government is organised on a democratic basis. But this outer democratic administration, which the majority of the rank and file believe to be the real governing authority, has in actual fact very little power. Its position and authority correspond broadly to the position and authority of the nominal government of those modern states which have fallen under the baneful influence of Freemasonry. The real government of these states is the hidden forces which operate behind the scenes and which are mostly identified with the great leaders of high finance.

Secret Organisation of the Degrees and Inner Circles.— Of the details of the secret organisation of Freemasonry

---

[1] Thus there are in France *at least* two well-known jurisdictions—viz., the Federation of the Grand Orient of France and that of the Grand Lodge of France. In Ireland there are apparently four. Cf. Cahill, *op. cit.*, pp. 138 ff.

little is known with certainty. The Masonic oaths and the dreadful penalties attached to them have proved in practice substantially efficacious. One thing is, however, established beyond doubt. Between Freemasonry, whose administrative system we have sketched (and which appears on the surface as a philanthropic and mutual aid society), and the immense revolutionary and anti-religious part which Freemasonry has played and still continues to play in the world, there is a striking contrast. The *visible* organisation of the Masonic body, and the results which that body has obtained show a manifest disproportion with each other. Again, why should a simple philanthropic society, organised in the manner just described, exact from all the members the terrible oaths of inviolable secrecy, each oath accompanied by unspeakable curses and threats against him who should violate it ? There is clearly something evil and sinister behind the façade. The following well ascertained facts will help to throw light on the matter.

Superimposed on the outer Freemasonry, with its three degrees and its democratic constitution, there is the Freemasonry of the higher degrees for which the members are carefully *selected* (not *elected*) from the ranks of the Blue Masonry. The Members of the higher degrees (sometimes the existence of the degrees themselves) are frequently unknown to the rank and file. These degrees are governed by secret Committees, the number on each Committee diminishing progressively as the higher and inner circles are reached. The secret Committees form the real governing body.

In a lodge meeting of any degree there are always present one or more Masons of the higher degrees often unknown as such. It is an essential duty of these to inspire the lower members with the ideals and principles they have received from above and to guide, usually by suggestion and collaboration with one another, the plans and counsels of the lower lodges. Thus while the more or less open administrative organisation is directed democratically from below, the higher and inner groups and committees which are appointed not by election but by selection from above, are the power that really matters. They can secure that their decisions and arrangements pass in an invisible manner through the whole Masonic pyramid, so that the activities of the whole association are ordered more or less in accordance with their will.[1]

Imperfect Freemasonry.—What is usually known (among non-Masonic writers) as Imperfect Freemasonry, includes numerous secret and other societies mostly founded and controlled by Freemasons and modelled in large part upon the Masonic system. The object of these quasi-Masonic societies is partly to reach special classes which Freemasonry itself cannot reach and partly to concentrate upon some special item or aspect of the Masonic programme.

Familiar examples of Imperfect Freemasonry are the *Orange Society, Adoptive Masonry* or *Co-Masonry* (which admits women), the *American Protective Association* (A.P.A.), the *Knights of the Ku Klux Klan*, the *Loyal Order of Buffaloes*, the *Loyal Order of Moose of the World*, the International Socialist Organisations (*l'Internationale*), the *Theosophical Association*, some of the Feminist associations, the *League of Instruction*, etc.[2] These associations form in fact the real strength and the active fighting army of Freemasonry, which is truly said to have its most numerous and efficient supporters outside its own body.

White Masonry.—Another type of Imperfect Freemasonry is what is sometimes called *White Masonry*. The term is applied (again by non-Masonic writers) to the numerous associations which have sprung up in modern times (and still continue to multiply) ostensibly for the promotion of objects good in themselves, or at least not unlawful, but which, owing to their character or practical tendencies, are utilised to promote Masonic ideals, such as secularism, indifferentism in religion, and false internationalism. Among such associations may be mentioned *The Rotary International*, the *Esperanto Association*, the *Friends of Israel*, many associations of Journalists, Doctors, Jurists, etc., which are organised by Freemasons for the Masonic interpenetration of Christian society.[3]

---

[1] Cf. Cahill, *op. cit.*, chap. vii ; also De Poncins, *op. cit.*, pp. 23 ff.
[2] Cf. *ib.*, pp. 147–149, and Appendix iii.
[3] Cf. *ib.*, pp. 149–151, and Appendix iv.

Art. 4—*Masonic Methods and Means*

Leo XIII on Masonic Methods.—Freemasonry strives to re-fashion the civil and social life of the people after its own naturalistic ideals. It utilises men's passions to undermine Christian social customs. Of the activities of Freemasonry in this regard Leo XIII writes :

" The Freemasons deny that our first parents sinned, and consequently that man's free-will is in any way weakened or inclined to evil. . . . Wherefore we see that men are publicly tempted by the many allurements of pleasure ; that there are journals and pamphlets without moderation or shame ; that stage plays are remarkable for licence ; that designs for works of art are shamelessly sought in the laws of a so-called realism . . . and that all the blandishments of pleasure are diligently sought out by which virtue may be lulled to sleep. . . . There have even been in the sect of Freemasons some who have . . . proposed ARTFULLY AND OF SET PURPOSE that the multitude should be satiated with a boundless licence of vice ; as when this had been done it would come more easily under their power and authority." [1]

In pursuance of its purpose Freemasonry strives above all to influence the legislation and administration of the State, so as to make the latter subservient to its will. On this again Leo XIII writes :

" Including almost every nation in its immense grasp it [Freemasonry] unites itself with other sects of which it is the real inspiration and the hidden motive power. It first attracts and then retains its associates by the bait of worldly advantage which it secures for them. It bends governments to its will sometimes by promises, sometimes by threats. It has found its way into every class of society, and forms an invisible and irresponsible power, an independent government, as it were, within the body corporate of the lawful state. . . ." [2]

The Master Weapons of Freemasonry.—The most potent instruments used by the Masonic body in compassing its ends are financial control, the Press and Cinema, and the revolutionary movements.

We have already referred, when treating of Capitalism, to the usurped power exercised at present by the great masters of finance over almost the whole life of the people.

---

[1] *Humanum Genus* (Cf. Cahill, *op. cit.*, p. 129).
[2] *Parvenu à la Vingt-Cinquième*, 1902 (Cf. Cahill, *op. cit.*, p. 160).

It is generally recognised that the financial magnates are in great part Masonic Jews ; and that very much of the general demoralisation of social life is traceable to the baneful influence of the monied interest.[1]

We have also touched already on the intimate connection which is strongly emphasised by Leo XIII between Freemasonry and Socialism, especially in its revolutionary aspects. The recent rise of Bolshevism, in which Masonic Jews have had a predominant part, represents the ripened fruit of the revolutionary and anarchical movements inspired and fostered by Freemasonry, which have kept portions of Europe and America in spasmodic turmoil during the past century and a half.

The Press and Cinema.—It remains to refer briefly to the Press and Cinema as instruments of Masonic propaganda. From several Masonic documents it appears that the leaders of the anti-Christian movement rely very much on the public Press as one of their most effective instruments. The great capitalistic Press of the United States, England, Germany and France, is now almost entirely controlled by the great Jewish International financiers. Of the papers not directly owned by Jews, Jewish influence usually predominates in the management. In such cases the editor or art critics or principal foreign correspondents, or all of these, usually are Jews.

Apart from the direct control or ownership of the Press, exercised by Jewish syndicates or individuals ; and apart also from the Jews who take a leading part in the actual work of journalism, it is a recognised fact that practically the whole secular Press of Britain and America is effectually dominated through the medium of the advertising pages by the great financial and trading interests which Jews largely control. Not only what is called the Capitalistic Press, but even the Socialistic Press of the world, is in large part owned and controlled by Jewish financiers.[2]

Again, the great news agencies of the world, such as those of Reuter and of Wolff, which are the leading British and

---

[1] For an interesting example of the dominant influence of Jewish finance in the political life of the 19th century, cf. Count Corti—*Reign of the House of Rothschild* (Pollancz, London, 1928).

[2] Cf. Cahill, *op. cit. (See* Index, *sub verbo, Press and F ∴).*

German news agencies, as well as that of Havas, the principal French agency, are owned or controlled by Jews. Besides these news agencies, the recently founded J.T.A. (Jewish Telegraphic Agency) supplies news items *gratis* to most of the big dailies. Even Catholic journalists or editors, tend to accept uncritically the news circulated from these sources, although such news is often misleading and too frequently insidiously hostile to Christianity.

Without holding that all the Jewish newspaper owners or journalists are Masonic, one is forced to the conclusion, especially in view of the consistent and insidious propaganda against Christian ideals and Catholic interests which characterises the Jew-controlled Press, that this Jewish control is, broadly speaking, exercised in the interests of naturalism, and, on the whole, is definitely anti-Catholic and Masonic.

What is said here of the Press applies with equal or greater force to the Cinema ; practically all of which over the two continents of Europe and America is in the hands of the Jews.[1]

Methods Adopted.—We are familiar with the methods employed by the Press and the Cinema of permeating the body politic with unchristian or anti-Christian principles and ideals. The dose administered on each occasion is usually tempered .to suit the actual dispositions of the readers or the audience, while insensibly preparing the mind and character for something stronger. Little by little, the public mind gets accustomed to scenes and views of life, which a few years previously would shock and produce reaction. In this way public opinion is gradually demoralised and weaned from the old Christian tradition and outlook ; and after a certain time public life becomes practically dechristianised.[2]

---

[1] Cf. *Rev. Internat. des Soc. Secrètes*, December 16th, 1928, p. 1169, for a complete list of the great firms (all controlled by Jews) which supply most of the film and cinema markets of the English-speaking world.

[2] Cf. Cahill, *op. cit.*, pp. 167 ff.

16

CHAPTER XIV

THE SOCIAL QUESTION[1]

Meaning of the Term.—In the chapters on Protestantism, Liberalism, Capitalism and Freemasonry, we have sketched briefly the genesis of the social system which now prevails in the countries of the British Empire, in the United States of America and, to a certain extent, in every country of the European Civilisation. We have also touched here and there, and especially in the chapters on Political Liberalism and Capitalism, upon the main evils which are inherent in that system, and the moral and material degradation to which it inevitably leads. These evils and the social problems to which they have given rise constitute what is commonly termed the *Social Question*.

Genesis of the Social Question.—Leo XIII and the succeeding Pontiffs repeatedly insist that the main social evils of modern times are due to the revolt of the nations against the authority of the Church ; and the abandonment of Christian principles in men's mutual dealings and in the general organisation of society. In the first year of his pontificate, Leo XIII, dealing with the evils affecting modern society, referred especially to

" the widespread perversion of the primary truths on which, as on its foundations, human society is based, the obstinacy of mind that will not brook any authority however lawful, the endless sources of disagreement whence arise civil strife and ruthless war and bloodshed ; the contempt of law . . . . the insatiable craving for things perishable with complete forgetfulness of things eternal . . . . the reckless mismanagement, waste and misappropriation of the public funds, the shamelessness of those who, full of treachery, make semblance of being champions of country, of freedom and of every kind of right. . . ."

---

[1] Cf. Leo XIII—*Inscrutabili*, 1878 ; *Rerum Novarum*, 1891 ; *Graves de Communi*, 1901 ; Pius XI—*Ubi Arcano*, 1922; Antoine, *op. cit.*, 2e section, chap. vii ; Belliot, *op. cit.*, pp. 172–190, 219–230, 442–475 ; Parkinson—*Primer of Social Science*, Introduction i, ii and iii ; Garriguet—*Question Sociale et Ecoles Sociales* (Bloud and Gay, Paris).

" The enemies of public order," the Pope goes on to say, " have thought nothing better suited to destroy the foundations of society than to make an unflagging attack upon the Church of God, to bring her into discredit and odium by spreading infamous calumnies, and accusing her of being opposed to genuine progress. . . . From these causes have originated laws that shake the structure of the Catholic Church, the enacting of which we have to deplore in so many lands : hence, too, have flowed forth contempt of episcopal authority . . . . the dissolution of religious bodies ; and the confiscation of property that was once the support of the Church's ministers, and of the poor. . . . Thence, also, have arisen that unchecked freedom to teach and spread abroad all mischievous principles, while the Church's claim to train and educate youth is in every way outraged and baffled." [1]

That these words, penned more than fifty years ago, remain true to-day may be seen from the example of such countries as Portugal, Mexico, Russia and Spain ; for the enemies of the Church and of social order work on a consistent plan, which is always substantially the same.

Economic Evils—(a) Words of Leo XIII.—Thirteen years later the same Pontiff, in his great encyclical on the Condition of the Working Classes, sketches the material evils affecting them in a masterly passage which has come to be regarded as the classical description of the Social Question in its economic aspects. The Pope associates these evils and the growing perils which they include with the

" vast expansion of industrial pursuits and the marvellous discoveries of science . . . the changed relations between masters and workmen . . . the enormous fortunes of some few individuals, and the utter poverty of the masses, and finally the degeneracy of morals which characterises all classes. . . ."

" All agree," the Pontiff continues, " and there can be no question whatever that some remedy must be found and found quickly for the misery and wretchedness, pressing so heavily and unjustly at this moment on the vast majority of the working classes. For when the ancient workingmen's guilds were abolished . . . no other organisation for the workers' protection took their place, public institutions and the very laws having set aside the ancient religion. Hence, by degrees it has come to

---

[1] *Inscrutabili* (1878), pp. 1, 2.

pass that the working men have been surrendered all isolated and helpless to the hard-heartedness of employers and the greed of unchecked competition.

" The evil has been increased by rapacious usury, which although more than once condemned by the Church, is nevertheless under a different guise but with the same injustice still practised by covetous and grasping men.

" To this must be added the custom of working by contract, and the concentration of nearly all branches of trade under the control of a few individuals, with the result that a small number of very wealthy men have been able to lay upon the teeming masses of the labouring poor a yoke little better than that of slavery.[1]

(b) **Rooted in Unchristian Capitalism.**—In the chapter on Modern Capitalism we have already discussed the main evils here referred to and others closely connected with them. The two outstanding economic evils of the present day are :

I. The prevalence of an unpropertied class (constituting in some cases nearly one half of the population more or less helpless and oppressed. These, while personally free and nominally enjoying the franchise are, owing to their want of productive property, without security or any real independence, and are liable to unemployment and consequent distress even in regard to the prime necessaries of life.

II. The dominance of an irresponsible monied interest represented by the masters of high finance, who in very many countries have practically usurped the control of industry and even of agriculture. The latter evil has been so much intensified since the great European war, that it may be regarded to-day as the great fact which underlies the whole social question at least in its economic aspects. For, in the financial system that has come to prevail, employers as well as workers are exposed to the " rapacious usury " (in its new guise) and the slavery imposed on the world by " the small number of wealthy men " who control international finance.

The Political Evils.—Our present Pontiff Pius XI, in his great Encyclical on the Peace of Christ, issued during the first year of his pontificate, insists mainly on those aspects

---

[1] *Rerum Novarum*, 1891, pp. 133, 134. *See* also the Latin original with French translation in the series *Lettres Apostoliques de Leon XIII*, tom. iii, pp. 18–21 (issued by La Bonne Presse, 5 Rue Bayard, Paris, viii[e]).

of the social question which have become especially marked since the European war. He speaks of the rivalries and jealousies between states :

" sometimes hidden under the manipulation of politics or concealed beneath the fluctuation of finance " and the " dense fog of mutual hatreds and grievances " by which " public life is so enveloped . . . that it is almost impossible for the common people even to breathe freely." He alludes ·to the " state of armed peace which is hardly better than war itself, and which tends to exhaust national finances, to waste the flower of youth and to muddy and poison the very foundation of life, physical, intellectual, religious and moral." [1]

Another element to which he refers is the contests between political parties :

" Many of which do not originate in a real difference of opinion concerning the public good, or in a quest for what should best promote the common welfare, but in the desire for power or for the protection of some private interest, which inevitably results in injuring the citizens as a whole." [2]

The Class War.—Leo XIII treating of the advantages to society of a multiplication of small proprietors writes :

" For the result of civil change and revolution has been to divide Society into two widely differing castes. On the one side there is the party which holds power because it holds wealth. . . . On the other side there is the needy and powerless multitudes, sick and sore in spirit and ever ready for disturbance."[3]

One of the worst results of these unjust conditions which are being exploited for purposes of violent and radical upheavals is the modern class war, preached and promoted by the Socialists. Pius XI refers to it as

" the chronic and mortal disease of present day society, which like a cancer is eating away the vital forces of the social fabric : labour, industry, the arts, commerce, agriculture—everything in fact which contributes to public and private welfare.

" From this class war there result frequent interruptions of work . . . revolutions, riots, and forcible repression of one side or other by the Government, all of which cannot but end in general discontent and in grave damage to the general welfare." [4]

---

[1] *Ubi Arcano,* 1922. Cf. Ryan, *Encyclicals of Pius XI* (Herder, London, 1928), pp. 10, 11.
[2] *Ib.*   [3] *Rerum Novarum,* pp. 158, 159.   [4] *Ubi Arcano,* 1922. *Ib.*

The Moral and Domestic Evils.—Finally, Pius XI bewails above all the evils which now threaten the peace, integrity and purity of family life—the dissensions, disobedience and looseness of morals, resulting often in infidelity to the sanctity of the marriage tie. He laments, too, the

" morbid restlessness which has spread among people of every age and condition of life ; the general spirit of insubordination and unwillingness to live up to one's obligations, which has become so widespread as almost to seem the customary mode of living . . . the destruction of purity among women and young girls which is evidenced by the increasing immodesty in their dress and conversation, and by their participation in shameful dances." [1]

Besides these moral evils the Pope refers in another Encyclical to other evils which are rooted more directly in the prevailing economic régime :

" The mind shudders," he writes, " if we consider the frightful perils to which the morals of workers (of boys and young men particularly), and the virtue of girls and women are exposed in modern factories ; if we recall how the present economic régime, and above all, the disgraceful housing conditions prove obstacles to the family tie and the family life : if we remember the insuperable difficulties placed in the way of a proper observance of the holy days. . . ." [2]

Urbanism.—Another evil more or less peculiar to modern times is what is termed *Urbanism.* The rural population seeking for excitement and change tend to abandon the land and crowd into the cities. On the other hand, it is a fact of experience that an urban population is short lived. [3] It is only the rural families that survive and maintain the race. If these fail the nation is doomed. Besides, the land is the ultimate source of all the nation's wealth, and of everything that the people need for the support of life. Hence the only stable prosperity of a nation is the one that rests on agriculture. [4] The following extract from a remark-

---

[1] *See* Shove, *op. cit.*, chaps. i to iv, where this principle is elaborated with remarkable clearness.
[2] *Ib.*   [3] *Quadragesimo Anno* (1931), pp. 61, 62.
[4] It is well known that families living in towns soon die away, seldom reaching the fourth generation, and very frequently die out much sooner.

able article written by Mussolini (the Italian Premier) illustrates this :

" . . . At a given moment the city shows a marvellous increase due not to its own vital force but to accretion from outside. But the more the city increases the more sterile its people become, the progressive rate of sterility being in direct proportion to its rapid growth. While the metropolis attracts to itself the rural population, these latter also lose their fecundity and become as sterile as the city population in which they are merged. . . . And when the country is deserted the city itself is near its doom. . . .

" This is the oft-repeated process recorded in history of the decay of nations. . . . The whole European race can become submerged, and be supplanted by the coloured races,[1] whose numbers are multiplying at a rate quite unknown to our people." . . .[2]

Declining Birth-Rate.—Closely connected with the preceding is another ominous indication of the general corruption prevailing in European and American society. This is the swift decline of the birth-rate in Middle and Western Europe, and Anglo-America.

In England and Wales, the decline which has been going on since 1875 has attained unprecedented rapidity since 1920. The birth-rate for 1927 was only 16.6 per 1,000 inhabitants, which is the lowest record of the world, and the decline still goes on. In some districts of Great Britain the birth-rate has actually fallen to .10 per 1,000 ! In France, where the birth-rate has fallen to 18.2 per 1,000 inhabitants, the population is kept up only by immigration from Italy and other countries. At present two and a half millions, or about six per cent. of the whole French population, are immigrants. Large numbers of these have been settled on the land as peasant proprietors. The birth-

---

[1] It has been calculated that the population of Japan (which in 1892 was about 40,000,000) will have reached 100,000,000 in 1960 at its present rate of increase.

[2] Mussolini's article was published in the Fascist monthly review, *Gerarchia* (Oct., 1928), and reprinted (Nov. 10th, 1928) in *La Documentation Catholique* (a Catholic weekly published at " Maison de la Bonne Presse," 5 Rue Bayard, Paris). The article is founded upon a booklet by the German writer, Dr. R. Korherr, entitled *Failure of the Birth-Rate— Death of the Nations*, which has been re-edited in Italian and published by La Libreria de Littorio, 52 Piazzo Montecitoria, Rome.

rate in Germany is now even lower than that of France
In Belgium, too, the birth-rate is declining, and the rate
of decline is becoming progressively more and more rapid
In Switzerland the birth-rate, which in 1901 was 29 per
1,000 inhabitants, had fallen in 1926 to 18.2, being then the
same as in France.

Even in Italy itself, which up till lately was remarkable
for the fecundity of the people, the birth-rate is declining
fast. . . . The rate which during the years 1881–1885 was
38 per 1,000 inhabitants had declined in 1915 to 30.5, and
in the year 1927 to 26.9.

This general movement of decline seems to be accelerated
year by year. Europe is fast approaching the tragic stage
at which the cradles are empty and the cemeteries grow
larger. In other words, the European races, as a result of
their abandonment of Christianity, are hastening to
extinction.

The Ruinous Results Actual and Threatened.—Pius XI
after bewailing the general corruption of the present day
goes on to detail its results on social life and the still worse
evils which are to be feared :

" Is it surprising then," the Holy Father continues, " that we
should no longer possess that security of life in which we can
place our trust and that there remains only a most terrible uncertainty ; and from hour to hour added fears for the future ?
Instead of regular daily work there is idleness and unemployment. . . . As a consequence industry suffers, commerce is
crippled, the cultivation of literature and the arts becomes more
and more difficult ; and, what is worse than all, Christian
civilisation itself is irreparably damaged. In the face of our
much-praised progress we behold with sorrow society lapsing
back into a state of barbarism." [1]

---

[1] *Ib.*, pp. 10–14. For a sketch of social question in Ireland and its
genesis, cf. Appendices ii and iii.

CHAPTER XV

THE CATHOLIC SOCIAL MOVEMENT [1]

Art. 1—*Its Nature*

A Reaction Against Anti-Christian Forces.—In the earlier chapters of the present work we have given a short sketch of the Church's action up to the 16th century in building up the fabric of European civilization. As already shown, the decay of that civilization, which is so marked a feature of European society to-day, began with the Protestant revolt in the first half of the 16th century. Rationalism, political and economic Liberalism, Freemasonry, unchristian Capitalism and Socialism, which are now undermining the foundations of the old Christian organisation of Europe, are the natural consequences of that revolt. The modern Catholic social movement, which began about the middle of

[1] Cf. *La Hierarchie Catholique et la Problème Social*, compiled by the Malines " Union Internationale D'Etudes Sociales " in 1931, and published by the " Edition Spes " of Paris. This invaluable work, issued on the occasion of the fortieth anniversary of the *Rerum Novarum*, is a bibliography and summary (specially referred to by Pius XI in the *Quadragesimo Anno*) of Pontifical and Episcopal pronouncements on the Social Question made beteen the years 1891 and 1931. Cf. also Leo XIII, *Rerum Novarum* (1891), pp. 147–166 ; *Graves de Communi* (1901), pp. 169 ff ; Pius X, *Fin Dalla Prima* (1903), pp. 182 ff, and *Il Fermo Proposito* (" Christian Social Action ") (1905), pp. 189–201 ; Pius XI—*Ubi Arcano* (1922) (*see* Ryan—*Encyclicals of Pius XI*, pp. 2 ff, Herder, London, 1927), and *Quas Primas* (1925), instituting the Feast of Our Lord Jesus Christ the King (*see Ib.*, pp. 129 ff) ; *Quadragesimo Anno* (1931) (The Social Order : Its Reconstruction and Perfection. *See* C. T. S. pamphlet, London, 1931) ; *Quæ Nobis* (Nov. 13th, 1928), Apostolic Letter to Cardinal Bertram on the Fundamental Principles of Catholic Action (cf. the *Irish Ecclesiastical Record*, Feb., 1929, pp. 212 ff) ; Plater, S.J. *The Priest and Social Action* (Longmans, London, 1914), pp. 1–150, and *Social Work in Germany* (Sands, London, 1909) ; Ryan and Husslein—*The Church and Labour* (Harding and Moore, London, 1920) (*see* pp. 207–219 for a reprint of the *Pastoral Letter of the Irish Bishops on the Labour Question*, Feb., 1914) ; Antoine, *op. cit.*, chap. x ; Nitti—*Catholic Socialism* (translated from the Italian, *Il Socialismo Catholica*, Turin, 1890) (Macmillan, New York, 1895), chaps. vii–xii (Nitti uses the word *Socialism* in a sense now obsolete, as including Catholic social reform. He traces the Catholic movement up to 1890) ; Metlake—*Ketteler's Social Reform* (Dolphin Press, Philadelphia, 1912) ; Moon—*The Labour Problem and the Social Catholic Movement in France* (Macmillan, New York, 1921) ; McEntee—*The Social Catholic Movement in Great Britain* (Macmillan, New York, 1927) ; Crawford—*Switzerland To-day—a Study in Social Progress* (Sands, London, undated, *circa* 1913) ; Monti—*International Handbook of Catholic Organisations*, published in the five principal European languages by the International Office of Catholic Organisations, Rome (" Edition Spes," Paris, 1924), chaps. ii to vii,

the last century, represents the vital reaction of Christianity against these principles and tendencies. It aims at repairing or reconstructing Christian civilization where it has been injured or destroyed.

Such a movement is not a new phenomenon in the life of the Church. The Catholic faith is a living force, which tends to affect profoundly, and even to transform the character of the individual or the society that has adopted it. Hence Catholic Action, of which a Catholic social movement is the result, or rather the embodiment, is as old as the Church itself. It is in fact the main source of all that is best in European civilization.

" The Church," writes Pius X, " while preaching Jesus cruci-fied . . . has been the first inspirer and promoter of civilization. She has spread it wherever her apostles have preached, preserving and perfecting what was good in ancient pagan civilizations ; rescuing from barbarism and raising to a form of civilized society the new peoples who took refuge in her maternal bosom [viz., the Teutonic invaders of the period between the fourth and sixth centuries A.D.], and giving to the whole of human society, little by little, no doubt, but with a sure and onward march, that characteristic stamp which it still everywhere preserves.[1]

Scope and Aims.—The movement, although inspired by religion, and carried on under the immediate guidance of the Pope and the Catholic hierarchy, is not confined to the religious and moral interests of the people. Besides these it includes in its scope all that may affect their social, in-tellectual and material well-being ; and it seeks to promote these by means which are in harmony with Catholic tradition, and the moral and dogmatic principles of Christianity.

" No practical solution," writes Leo XIII, " of this question [viz., the modern social question] will be found apart from the intervention of religion and the Church. . . . The Church improves and betters the condition of the workingman by means of numerous organizations ; she does her best to enlist the services of all classes in discussing and endeavouring to further in the most practical way the interests of the working classes ; and considers that for this purpose recourse should be had in due degree to the intervention of the law, and of State authorities." [2]

---

[1] *Il Fermo Proposito* (1905), p. 190. Cf. also Leo XIII—*Immortale Dei* (1885), p. 54.
[2] *Rerum Novarum*, pp. 141–148.

Hence the immediate objects of the movement are :

I. To disseminate among the masses of the people a better knowledge of Catholic social principles and ideals.

II. To reorganize the public life of the nation in accordance with Catholic standards, and

III. To counteract by suitable measures, in harmony with the teachings of the Church, the poverty, insecurity and material misery of the labouring population.

Essential Characteristics[1]—(a) **Active Participation of the Laity.**—A special characteristic of the movement is the active co-operation of the laity (of both sexes), under the guidance of the Bishops, in the social activities of the Church. This trait is in large part an outcome of the Church's traditional policy of accommodating her methods as far as possible to the customs and ideals of the society in which she is operating. In contrast with the civic organization of mediæval times, when the political power was mostly in the hands of one class, the mass of the people now take an active part in the duties of legislation and administration. Hence the Church, adapting herself to this democratic tendency, invites, and indeed urges, the laity of all classes, and of both sexes, to take an active part in the work of building up again the shattered fabric of Christian civilization.

" Catholic action," writes Pius XI, " does not merely consist in each one striving after one's own Christian perfection, although this, it is true, is everyone's primary and principal duty, but it means a very real apostolate, in which Catholics of every rank and order take part. In this work the outlook and activities of each and all are linked up with and borrow their character from certain central institutions duly constituted with episcopal sanction, which supply the guiding principles, and direct and co-ordinate the varied activities."[2]

Further down in the same letter occurs the well-known phrase in which Catholic Action is authoritatively defined as " the participation and collaboration of the laity with the Apostolic Hierarchy."

---

[1] Cf. A useful booklet—L'Action Catholique, by Chanoine L. Picard—one of the series entitled Etudes Religieuses, published by " La Pensée Catholique " (Quai Mativa, 38 Liège, Belgium).

[2] Quæ Nobis (1928). (Cf. Irish Ecclesiastical Record, loc. cit., p. 213).

On the same subject the late Cardinal Vaughan writes :

" The Catholic layman has, perhaps, a more distinguished part to play now in the service of Christ than at any former time. . . . He is invited by the authorities of the Church to co-operate in a hundred ways and to take part in a hundred works, which are essentially and intimately connected with public life and with the salvation of souls. Rich and poor, learned and unlearned, are united in groups and associations which aim at securing the claims of Christianity and souls." [1]

(b) **Unity and Endless Variety.**—The movement, which has now spread into every country that has a notable Catholic population, embraces an endless variety of organisations, and aims at influencing the moral, intellectual and social lives of the people in almost every detail. Yet, amid all its various aspects and manifestations, the whole movement is marked by a wondrous unity of spirit and of aim, and is besides in perfect harmony with the traditional principles and aims which have inspired Catholic Action for almost two thousand years.

The principle of this essential unity is, in the first place, the moral and dogmatic teachings of the Church, upon which the whole movement is founded, and which never vary. Thus, in every phase of the movement, religion, justice, charity and piety are accorded primacy of place among the forces that are to solve the social question. Again, in dealing with the material miseries of the people, all Catholics are united in opposition to the exaggerations and false principles of Liberalism, Collectivism, Communism and the ultra-nationalistic and secularist aspects of Fascism. Catholics seek a solution in harmony, at the same time, with the instincts of human nature and the exalted ideals of Christianity.

A second source of the uniformity of which we speak is the fact that all the Catholic social activities of which the movement is composed are carried on under the guidance of the Bishops and the Supreme Pontiff, so that, in all its phases and organisations, it is directed by the same guiding hand. The recent Encyclicals of Pius XI on *Marriage* and *Christian Education*, and, above all, the Encyclical on the *Social Order* (*Quadragesimo Anno*, 1931) are outstanding

---
[1] Cited in Plater—*The Priest and Social Action*, pp. 22 ff.

examples of the authoritative and unifying guidance of the Sovereign Pontiff.

(c) **Solidarist Ideal.**—This last Encyclical was issued, as is expressly stated in the document itself,[1] to secure this unity especially among Catholic writers on social science. The Encyclical practically embodies the principles and conclusions of the present day German Catholic School of Sociology and Social Reform. The writers of this school include such names as Pesch,[2] Nell-Breuning, Otto Schilling and Grundlach. These and other workers in the same field have elaborated the system known as *Solidarismus*, which in reality is nothing else than the concrete expression of the Catholic traditional ideals as applied to modern conditions. The central idea of the Solidaristic social philosophy is the *organic* conception of the State functioning in accordance with the dictates of Legal Justice and Charity as contrasted with the " individualistic " ideal of the Liberals, the ' class-war " of the Socialists, and the excessive bureau-racy of Socialists and Fascists alike. This organic con-ception is realised by means of local units such as munici-palities and professional corporations (including both employers and employed), all enjoying each within its own sphere a large measure of autonomy.[3]

(d) **Strictly Non-Political.**—The movement, although some-times termed " Christian Democracy " (a name which has received the official sanction of Leo XIII and Pius X),[4] is strictly non-political. In other words, like the Church itself which is affiliated to no political party, and has no special predilection for any particular form of government, provided only that the functions of government are duly fulfilled), the Catholic movement is outside and above all party

---

[1] See *Quadragesimo Anno* (C. T. S. edition, London, 1931), p. 70.

[2] Cf. H. Pesch, S.J.—*Lehrbuch der Nationalökonomie* (5 vols.) (Herder, Fribourg, 1915–23), and *Neubau der Gesellschaft* (Flugschriften der Stimmen edition 1919) ; Teschleder und Weber—*Socialethik* (2 vols.) (Münster, 1931).

[3] *Quadragesimo Anno*, pp. 38–41. For a very brief outline of this tra-ditional Catholic conception of civil organisation, *see infra*, chap. xx, art. 5 ; chap. xxii, arts. 5 and 6 ; chap. xxvii, arts. 2 and 3 ; and chap. xxvi and xxvii.

[4] Cf. Leo XIII—*Graves de Communi* (1901), pp. 170–172, and Pius X—*Fin Dalla Prima* (1909), pp. 185–186.

politics. It may and does aim at promoting legislatior
and administration in accordance with Christian principles
and even may, when necessity arises, use pressure for tha
purpose on governing authorities ; but it is never allied t
or identified with any pol.tical party. On this subjec
Leo XIII writes :

"Although Democracy, by its very name and by philosophica
usage, denotes popular rule, yet in this application it must b
employed altogether without political signification. . . . For
the precepts of the natural law and the Gospel, for this ver
reason that they transcend the chances of human existence, mus
necessarily be independent of any form of civil government an
adapt themselves to all, *so long as these are not opposed to wha
is right and just.* They are, therefore, and remain in themselve
completely outside party rivalries and political changes. . .
This has ever been the morality of the Church ; by it Roma
Pontiffs have constantly dealt with States, what ever might b
their form of government."[1]

This direction of Leo XIII has been formally confirme
by Pius X, who writes :

"Christian democracy ought never to mix in party politics
and ought never to be made use of for party purposes or politic
objects ; that is not its province ; but it should be a beneficier
activity in favour of the people, founded on the natural la
and the precepts of the Gospel."[2]

We shall now sketch briefly the rise and development (
the Catholic social movement in the Catholic countries (
Europe. In a separate article a brief account shall be give
of some of the more important and characteristic organis
tions which have taken shape under its influence.

Art. 2—*Historical Sketch*

Precursors—Taparelli and O'Connell.—Father Aloysiu
Taparelli, S.J. (1793–1862), a native of Turin, and for man
years Rector of the Roman College of the Society of Jesu
may be considered as the precursor of the modern Cathol

[1] *Graves de Communi*, p. 172.
[2] *Fin Dalla Prima*, pp. 185, 186. The same direction is again strong
insisted on by our present Holy Father Pius XI (*Quæ Nobis*, 1928. (
Irish Ecclesiastical Record, loc. cit., pp. 213, 214), and again still mc
definitely in the Encyclical on Catholic Action—*Non Abbiamo Bisog*
(1931) (C. T. S. edit., pp. 15–17).

social movement, especially in its doctrinal or theoretical side. His works have had a profound influence upon Catholic social teaching and Catholic action for the past eighty years. His main work, *Theoretical Essay on Natural Right from the Historical Standpoint*,[1] which appeared about ninety years ago, still remains as one of the best expositions of Catholic principles and ideals regarding social and civic organisation.

Again, the career and work of Daniel O'Connell in Ireland, and the great popular movement of which he was the leader, had great influence in Continental countries ; and inspired ideas which prepared the way for a Catholic popular revival.

Ketteler, Windthorst and the Catholic Movement in Germany.

—The actual movement, however, began in Germany, and Baron Von Ketteler (1811–1877), Bishop of Mainz, was its real founder. Ketteler recognized the danger to the Church from the apathy of the wealthier Catholics, and even of large numbers of the clergy, in face of the misery and material degradation of the labouring population. In 1847 appeared the *Communist Manifesto* of Marx and Engels, heralding the birth of the Socialist movement. Ketteler was one of the few men of his generation that recognized its significance ; and to him belongs, in the words of another great Catholic leader, Gaspard Decurtins, " The undying honour of having met the manifesto of the Communists with a programme of Christian social reform that stands unsurpassed to this day."[2]

It was at the first Catholic Congress held at Mainz, 1848, two years before Ketteler's consecration as Bishop of Mainz, that he delivered the famous address which was really the beginning of the Catholic social movement in Germany. " The task of religion, the task of the Catholic societies in the immediate future," he said, " has to do with social conditions. The most difficult question—one which no

---

[1] *Saggio Teoretico di Diretto Naturale Apogiatto Sul Fatto* was first published about 1840. An abridgement of the book, entitled *An Abridged Course in Natural Right*, appeared in 1860, of which a French translation was published in Paris (1864). Among Taparelli's other works, one of the most important is his critical examination of Representative Government in Modern States (*Esame Critica degli Ordini Representativi della Societa Moderna*, Rome, 1854). Cf. *supra,* " Introduction."

[2] Metlake, *op. cit.,* p. 31.

legislation, no form of government has been able to solve—
is the *social question*. The difficulty, the vastness, the
urgency of this question fills me with the greatest joy ! ''
The cause of the joy he explains to be the fact that " It
must now become evident which Church bears within it
the power of divine truth. The world will see that to the
Catholic Church is reserved the definite solution of the
social question ; for the State, with all its legislative
machinery, has not the power to solve it.''[1]

It was largely as a result of Ketteler's labours and in-
cessant exhortations, continuing over a period of nearly
thirty years (1848–77), that German Catholics were stirred
into vigorous action on the social question. Since his time
the Catholic clergy of Germany have taken a prominent
part in social reform, and have produced from their own
ranks a succession of able writers and social leaders. Among
these latter may be mentioned Canon Moufang, who succeeded Ketteler in the leadership of the movement, and
later, on Canon Hitze, who succeeded Moufang.

Besides Ketteler's numberless sermons and addresses,
pamphlets and books poured from his pen. Even to-day
his two books, *Liberty, Authority and the Church*[2] and
Christianity and the Labour Question,[3] as well as his work
published under the title of *A Christian Labour Catechism*,[4]
remain a classical expression of the Church's position.

When, in 1870, the German Centre Party was formed
under the leadership of Ludwig Windthorst (1812–91), to
oppose Bismarck's *Kulturkampf*, the promotion of the
Catholic social programme became a central item in its
policy. After the death of Bishop Ketteler in 1877,
Windthorst became the predominating figure at every one
of the great German Catholic Congresses.[5] He fitly closed
his great career with the founding of the *Volksverein*—The
People's Union for Catholic Germany—the constitution of
which he drafted on his death-bed. We shall refer to it
again.

Precursors of the Social Movement in France.[6]—In the
first seventy years of the nineteenth century many French
Catholic publicists and economists of different political views

---

[1] *Ib.*, p. 26.   [2] Metlake, chap. ix.   [3] *Ib.*, chap. x.   [4] *Ib.*, chap. xii.
[5] Plater, *op. cit.*, p. 59.   [6] Cf. Moon, *op. cit.*, pp. 13–120.

wrote strongly in favour of social reform legislation, and advocated also Catholic organisation to combat the evils resulting from industrial liberalism. Among these may be mentioned Chateaubriand, author of the *Le Génie du Christianisme* (1802) ; Philip J. B. Buchez (1796–1865) ; Louis Veuillot (1813–1883) ; Lacordaire (1802–1861), the great Dominican preacher ; Vicomte J. P. A. Ville-neuve-Burgemont (1784–1850) ; Vicomte Arnauld de Melun (1807–1877) ; and Frederick Ozanam (1813–1853).

Ozanam, besides writing a good deal on social subjects and on the great rôle played by Christianity in promoting social well-being,[1] is perhaps best remembered as the founder of the Society of St. Vincent de Paul. This work, and indeed Ozanam's whole life, might be regarded as a reply, and not a wholly unconscious reply, to the well-known challenge to the Holy See which Saint-Simon, the Socialist writer, puts into the mouth of Luther.

" Your predecessors," he says in a supposed address to the Holy Father, " have sufficiently perfected the theory of Christianity ; they have sufficiently propagated that theory. . . . It is the general application of that doctrine must now be your concern. True Christianity should make men happy not only in heaven but also on earth. . . . The clergy will always exercise a predominant influence on the temporal institutions of all nations when it sets to work in a positive manner to ameliorate the condition of the poorer class, which is always the most numerous class of the community."[2]

Frederick le Play[3] (1806–1882) and Henry C. X. Perin (1815–1905), Professor of Law in the Catholic University of Louvain, both wrote extensively on social subjects ; and

---

[1] His best work is *La Civilisation Chrétienne Chez les Francs* (" Christian Civilization among the Franks ").

[2] Cited in Moon, *op. cit.*, p. 26, from Saint Simon's book, *Le Nouveau Christianisme* (1852). We may note in passing that although earthly happiness is not the object aimed at by Christian morality, the nation that is true to its precepts normally obtains the largest measure of true happiness that earthly life can afford (*see* chap. xxix, art. 3, *infra*).

[3] Le Play's most remarkable works are *Les Ouvriers Européens* (1855) and *Le Reforme Sociale en France* (1864). The former work, which is of permanent interest and importance, is a series of thirty-six monographs on the social condition of the working class families in as many different countries of Europe through which he had travelled for the purpose of investigating social conditions. Cf. Moon, *op. cit.*, p. 421. For an account of Perin and his writings, cf. *Ib.*, pp. 59 ff and p. 422.

17

258   THE FRAMEWORK OF A CHRISTIAN STATE

both exercised great influence on French Catholic thought during the third quarter of the 19th century. Their views, however, were more conservative than those of the Catholic writers of the preceding generation and of the school of social thought that arose after 1870. Unlike both these latter groups they were opposed to State interference in the relations between employers and workmen.

Count Albert de Mun.—The real founders, however, of the Catholic social movement in France were two young Catholic noblemen, officers in the French army, who made each other's acquaintance while prisoners of war (1870) in the German internment camp at Aix-la-Chapelle. These were Count Albert de Mun and the Marquis Réné de la Tour du Pin.

De Mun tells the whole story in his memoirs, which were published thirty-seven years later (1908).[1] He and his companion, returning to France after their release from prison, witnessed the dreadful scenes of the Paris Communist insurrection in 1871, and took part in the operations against the insurgents. When the fighting was over and De Mun and others were shocked by the ruthlessness of the measures adopted against the defeated Communists, a certain Vincentian lay-brother, Maurice Maignen, with whom De Mun accidentally came into contact, made a deep impression on him. Maignen one day pointed dramatically to the charred ruins of some of the great palaces, declared with emphasis that it was the rich and noble and not the pro-letarian insurgents who were fundamentally responsible for the ruined streets and the charred and mangled corpses with which they had been so recently strewn.

"It is you," he said, "who have amused yourselves within these palaces now in ruins ; you who pass by without seeing the people, without knowing them or their character or thoughts, or caring for their needs and their sufferings, it is you are the real culprits."[2]

Catholic Workingmen's Clubs.—Towards the end of the year 1871 the foundations of the new movement were laid, when De Mun, Maignen, La Tour du Pin, and several other

---

[1] *Ma Vocation Sociale* (Paris, 1908).
[2] *Ib.*, p. 62 (cited in Moon, *op. cit.*, p. 82).

leading Catholic gentlemen of Paris issued the famous
" Appeal to Men of Good Will," and sketched their social
programme. The latter included such items as the multiplication of Catholic Workingmen's Clubs on a huge scale
(*Oeuvres de cercles Catholiques d'Ouvriers*) :

"To subversive doctrines [the appeal continued] and dangerous
teachings, we must oppose the holy teachings of the Gospel ;
to materialism the notion of sacrifice ; to the cosmopolitan spirit
the idea of country ; to atheistical negation Catholic affirmation.
. . . The privileged classes have duties to fulfil towards their
brethren, the workingmen ; and society, though it has a right
to defend itself with arms, must know that shot and shell do
not cure, and that other measures are needed." [1]

De Mun and his party relied too much on the leadership
and patronage of the wealthier and better educated classes,
and did not believe in associations made up exclusively of
the working classes, which Leo XIII later on and his successors have so strongly recommended. However, the
Association of Catholic Workingmen's Clubs expanded
rapidly, and in 1884 had 400 Committees, with 50,000
members. But its importance and significance were out
of all proportion to its actual numbers, for it was the means
of initiating a national movement, which aroused the
Catholic upper classes to a sense of their social obligations.
It also became, through De Mun himself and the political
party called the Popular Liberal Party (which he founded
in 1899 in conjunction with Piou and others), an important
factor in influencing social legislation.

Another outcome of this Association was the Catholic
Association of French Youth (*Association Catholique de la
Jeunesse Francaise*), which was founded by De Mun in
1886 as a kind of preparatory school for the Catholic workingmen's clubs. The Association of French Youth has now
over 140,000 members,[2] and serves as a recruiting bureau
for the Action Populaire (of which we shall speak later),
and the other social popular organisations which sprang
up later on.

In France, as in Germany and Belgium, Bishops and
priests threw themselves whole-heartedly into the social

---

[1] *Ma Vocation Sociale*, pp. 67–75 (Moon, p. 83).
[2] Cf. Moon, *op. cit.*, pp. 347 ff.

movement.   In France especially there is a very voluminous social literature written mostly by the priests.[1]

De Mun and the Socialists.—Perhaps it was the Chamber of Deputies that witnessed De Mun's greatest efforts.   There he fought, with all his great oratorical powers, during a period of some thirty years, for remedial social legislation. The definiteness of the programme which he consistently but all too unsuccessfully advocated formed a striking contrast to the vague demands of the Socialists.   Hence he could declare, as he did during a debate on April 30th, 1894, addressing Millerand, the Socialist leader :

" For twenty years past I have demanded, here in this tribune, the most precise social reforms.   It is not my fault if hardly a single one of them has been achieved.   My responsibility is absolutely cleared.   It is yours that is in question.   You teach the people to expect nothing, to hope for nothing from the progess of ideas, of institutions, of laws, and to seek in their labour organizations, not the means of defending their rights, but a weapon of combat, preparing by means of continual violence for civil war. . . . I say, with profound conviction, you have cruelly betrayed the cause of the people."[2]

The   Movement   in   Switzerland,   Belgium,   etc.—From Germany and France the Catholic movement gradually spread into all the countries of Western and Central Europe, including Switzerland, Belgium, Holland ; and later on Italy, Spain and England.   The beginnings of the movement in Switzerland are associated with the names of Cardinal Mermillod and Gaspar Decurtins.   Mermillod filled in Switzerland somewhat the same position as Ketteler in Germany.   Decurtins was a disciple of Ketteler and a friend of Cardinal Manning.   It was he who, like De Mun in France, led the political agitation for social reform.

It was under Decurtins' auspices, too, that the first

---

[1] Cf. Plater, *The Priest and Social Action*, chap. v.

[2] Cited in Moon, *op. cit.*, p. 199.   Cf. *ib.*, pp. 113–120, for a very interesting and suggestive account of Leon Harmel, and the remarkable Catholic industrial guild (in which the mediæval Catholic principles are successfully adapted to modern needs) formed by the Harmel family at the Harmel Cotton Mills at Val-des-Bois.   *See* also the two volume *Vie de Leon Harmel*, par Père Guitton, S.J. (" Edition Spes," Paris, 1927).

" International Federation of Catholic Social Workers " was formed, in 1884, at Fribourg, under the presidency of Cardinal Mermillod. The social code and programme which was drawn up as a result of the conferences of the Federation was presented by Cardinal Mermillod to Leo XIII in 1888, and was probably one of the causes that finally resulted in the publication of the Rerum Novarum three years later.

The Malines Union.—The Fribourg Union discontinued its sittings after 1891. Another international Union on a wider basis was established at Malines in 1920 under the presidency of Cardinal Mercier. The Malines Union, which is called " The International Union for Social Studies," includes in its membership several of the most distinguished Catholic scholars in the social and economic sciences, drawn from all countries of Western Europe, France, Germany, Belgium, Holland, Italy, Spain, and England. After the death of Cardinal Mercier in 1924, his place as president of the Union was taken by Archbishop Van Roly, his successor in the See of Malines. The most important achievement, so far, of the Malines Union has been the issue, in 1927, of a compendium of Catholic principles and conclusions applicable to the present post-war conditions in Europe and America.[1] This little book summarizes and brings up to date the conclusions and recommendations of the best Catholic authorities concerning contemporary social problems.

The Movement in other Countries.—Space will not permit us to follow the developments of the Catholic movement in the different countries of Europe and America. In Italy Catholic action is very highly organised, and is under the immediate patronage of the Pope himself. There are regularly recurring local and national congresses, and a network of diocesan and national councils, which control associations of various kinds, covering almost every phase of human activity. Spain, in which the movement is organised partly on the model of Italy, held its first Catholic

---

[1] *Code Social* (" Edition Spes," Paris, 1927). An English edition entitled *A Code of Social Principles*, has been published by the Catholic Social Guild, Oxford, 1929.

congress in 1929, under the presidency of the Cardinal Archbishop of Seville.[1]

In Holland the movement is particularly strong and is very highly organised, being under the guidance of a number of priests specially devoted to the work, under the leadership of Mgr. Poels, a dignitary of the diocese of Limburg. It was the Catholic organisations that were mainly instrumental in saving Holland from the Bolshevist peril in 1919. Even in the United States of America, in which the Catholics form less than twenty per cent. of the population, the beginnings of a strong Catholic movement have appeared.

The Movement in Ireland.—In Ireland a Catholic social movement in the ordinary sense was practically impossible up to very recent times. The land struggle, the fight for educational freedom, the national contest, the work of church building and religious organisation, engaged the energies of the priests and people during the nineteenth and the first quarter of the twentieth century. It is certain, however, as Nitti acutely observes,[2] that it was principally owing to its Catholic faith, and the strenuous efforts and leadership of the Catholic clergy, that the Irish nation has been so far saved from destruction.

The time has now, however, arrived, when a movement for social reconstruction on a definitely Catholic basis is possible. That such a movement is urgently needed is admitted on all hands ; and in several different ways efforts are being made to promote it. Thus a regular course of social study has been inserted by the Irish Bishops in the programme of Religious Knowledge for the secondary schools. A whole series (nn. 233–249) of the Decrees of the Maynooth Synod of 1927 are devoted to the subject of " Catholic Action." The Society of St. Vincent de Paul, which is year by year becoming more active, especially in the principal towns, is now carrying on several activities of a social reconstructive character. The number of Catholic

---

[1] What may be the effects on the *Catholic Movement* of the Spanish Revolution of 1931, and about the same time the Fascist attack upon the Catholic societies in Italy, is not yet known (1931). Cf. the Encyclical of Pius XI—*Non Abbiamo Bisogno*, 1931 (C. T. S. edition).

[2] *Catholic Socialism*, p. 330.

social activities of different kinds, rescue societies, boys'
clubs, etc., is increasing.[1] The work of professional organisation on definitely Catholic lines has been begun. Thus the
" Irish Guild of Catholic Nurses," founded in 1922, has
received the formal approbation of the Bishops (1927).[2]
The " Legion of Mary," a union of Catholic women for
social work, which was founded in Dublin in 1925, is
gradually extending over the whole country. The " Catholic
Boy Scouts " was founded in 1928, under the patronage of
the Bishops, and is growing fast. The foundations of a
Catholic press are being gradually laid. *An Rioghacht* (the
League of the Kingship of Christ) was founded in Dublin
on October 1st, 1926 (the first celebration of the Feast of
Jesus Christ the King), with the object of promoting social
study and Catholic social propaganda and initiating social
reconstruction. Efforts are also being made to reunite and
co-ordinate for similar purposes the already existing
" Catholic Young Men's Societies." The Central Catholic
Library, founded in Dublin (1921), and the growing activities
of the Irish Catholic Truth Society are all evidences of a
nascent national movement for Catholic social reconstruction.

In England.—In England Cardinal Manning wrote strongly
during the second half of the 19th century in favour of
social reform. In innumerable letters to the Press and in
articles and periodicals he supported the workers in their
demands for protective legislation.[3] His efforts were ably
seconded by Bishop Bagshawe, of Nottingham, who advocated a programme of social reform even more thorough
than that of Cardinal Manning. In reality, however,
Manning as well as Bagshawe had more lasting influence
on the Continent than in England itself where a Catholic
movement on a large scale was at the time scarcely possible.

The foundation of the Catholic Social Guild, in 1909, by
a group of Catholic social workers, of whom Father C.

---

[1] Cf. The booklet published by the St. Vincent de Paul Society, entitled
Handbook for Catholic Social Workers in Dublin (1929), for a full list of
these.

[2] Cf. *The Irish Nursing News*, published monthly, which is the official
organ of the Guild. A Catholic Guild of Medical Doctors, to be called
the " Guild of SS. Luke and Damien," is also in process of formation, as
well as a Catholic Guild of Chemists (1931).

[3] Cf. McEntee, *op. cit.*, pp. 68 ff, and Nitti, *op. cit.*, chap. ii.

Plater, S.J., was the leading spirit, marked the beginning of a definite movement which continues to make steady progress. The main activities of the Guild are the establishment over the whole country of circles of social study, the publication of handbooks for the students, the organisation in Oxford of a Catholic Workers' College, for the higher education of carefully selected men of the working class, with a view to further propagandist work among workingmen ; and the conducting of an annual summer school in Oxford. The organ of the Guild is *The Christian Democrat*, which appears monthly.[1]

The Popes and the Catholic Movement.—The German associations which marked the definite beginnings of the modern Catholic movement, were called *Piusvereine* after Pius IX. It was due in no small part to his great influence with the people that the widespread Catholic consciousness was formed, which led gradually to a reaction against Liberalism, and to the general movement towards Catholic reconstruction which we have described.

The Encyclicals of Pope Leo XIII, and especially the Encyclical *Rerum Novarum* (1891) on the condition of the working classes, began a new phase in the history of the Catholic social movement. These pronouncements of the Supreme Pontiff, which have since been confirmed and enforced by the Encyclicals of Pius X and our present Holy Father Pius XI on the same subject,[2] besides containing the strong and cordial approval of the Holy See for the movement, are essentially an authoritative exposition of the Church's teaching on social matters. They are full of urgent appeals to the Bishops, the clergy and the faithful, to devote themselves zealously to the great work

---

[1] Cf. McEntee, *op. cit.*, pp. 173 ff. *The Christian Democrat* (a very valuable publication for all interested in the Catholic movement) is published by the Catholic Social Guild, Oxford.

[2] Most of these are published in English in *The Pope and the People* (new edition, 1929). Cf. also *The Great Encyclicals of Leo XIII* (Benziger Bros., New York, 1903), and *The Encyclicals of Pius XI*, edited by J. H. Ryan (Herder, London, 1927). The Encyclical *Quadragesimo Anno*, 1931, of Pius XI is, with the *Rerum Novarum*, the most important document hitherto published on the Catholic Social movement. This Encyclical and those on Marriage and the Christian Education of Youth, which are not contained in the collections just referred to, are each published in booklet form by the English Catholic Truth Society.

of Catholic social reconstruction.[1] Above all, the Encyclicals of Pius XI and the new phase of the movement which has developed under the name of Catholic Action, as a result of his influence, have given fresh life and renewed vigour to the Catholic Cause.

It is due mainly to the exhortations and guidance of the Sovereign Pontiffs that the movement has steadily gathered strength for the past forty years, and has spread so widely, while still preserving its unity of character and aim.

Art. 3—The Catholic Organisations

As it is outside our present scope to follow out in detail the several phases and developments of the Catholic Social Movement, we shall only indicate briefly some of the principal organisations to which it has given rise, and to which it mostly owes its steady progress.[2]

German Catholic Congresses.—The German Catholic Congresses had their origin in the society called the *Piusverein*, already referred to, founded by Professor Kaspar Riffel and his friend Lennig for the defence of religious liberties.[3] A general meeting of the delegates from the various centres was arranged to take place at Mainz in 1848. This was the first of the great Catholic congresses. It was at this gathering that Bishop Ketteler delivered his historic address, previously mentioned, which began the great social movement in Germany and in Europe. In 1858 not only were representatives of local branches of the *Puisverein* invited, but also representatives of other Catholic associations, as well as leading Catholic journalists, publicists, and professional men, so that the meetings took on the character of a Catholic parliament.

Their Utility.—These general meetings of Catholic Germany were found to have extraordinary utility in encouraging and co-ordinating the efforts of the Catholic social workers

---

[1] Cf. Leo XIII—*Rerum Novarum*, 1891, pp. 141–148 ; Pius X—*Fin Dalla Prima*, 1903, pp. 193 ff ; Pius XI—*Ubi Arcano*, 1922, pp. 247 ff, and, above all, *Quadragesimo Anno*, 1931 (C. T. S. edit.), pp. 61–70.

[2] Besides the reference already given, cf. *Catholic Encyclop.*, vol. iv, pp. 242–251, art. " Congresses, Catholic."

[3] Plater—*Social Work in Germany*, p. 39.

and propagating Catholic thought. They encouraged
Catholic workers by giving them a sense of solidarity, and
bringing home to each individual worker the fact that he
had tens of thousands of fellow labourers in the same cause.
The congresses were an encouragement, too, in another way.
Where the Catholics of a particular district needed strengthening, there the congress went to strengthen them, as
happened at Neisse, in Silesia (1899). Local effort was
stimulated by the presence, for a whole week, of the picked
forces of all Catholic Germany. The Catholics, disheartened,
perhaps, by the sneers of their Socialist fellows, could thus
again hold up their heads and glory in their faith.

Again, the congresses co-ordinated Catholic endeavour.
Windthorst called them the "Autumn Manœuvres," and a
hostile paper referred to them as "The Review of the
Catholic Troops." Practically all the German Catholic institutions are now represented at these congresses, and many
take the opportunity supplied by the congress to hold their
annual meeting and publish their reports. Different
societies profit by thus getting into touch with one another,
learning local needs and essaying fresh developments.
Thus the efforts, aims, methods and results of the various
associations are made known to the whole country, and
when fresh needs arise the congresses call into being new
organisations to meet them.

Especially as a Means of Propaganda.—Finally, the congresses propagate Catholic thought. In the first place wide
publicity is given to the proceedings of the congresses by
an army of reporters, representing every newspaper of
standing, including non-Catholic papers. An illustrated
volume is always published, giving a full account of the
meetings, including those of the various societies represented
at the congress. Besides all this, the congress issues a
number of resolutions embodying some Catholic principle
suited to the time. These resolutions are repeated by the
Press, and serve as mottoes for Catholic speakers. They
form the watchwords, for the year, of the Catholic associations, and so create a sound public opinion on questions of
the day.

It was in no small measure due to these congresses that
Catholic Germany stood so firm under the pressure of the

Kulturkampf. There was even an advance in some directions. For, whereas, before the Kulturkampf, there were but four or five Catholic papers in Prussia, the number had increased, in 1873, to one hundred and twenty, including many dailies.[1]

The Volksverein.—Of the permanent Catholic organisations of Germany, the *Volksverein*, or " People's League," is the most important. Father Plater, S.J.,[2] has described it as the most successful association ever devised for the promotion of the social sense among a people. Founded by Windthorst in 1890 to defend the Catholic position against the Social Democrats, the society spread very rapidly. In 1904 it had 400,000 members, and in 1924, after the havoc wrought by the war, it had again attained to 588,902, of whom 130,000 were women. The Volksverein has evolved a definite social programme, and educated the people in Catholic social principles. Besides its social teaching and propaganda, it also provides the people with an abundance of excellent yet cheap literature on Christian Apologetics.

The Central Bureau is at München-Gladbach. Here thirty-five men are employed. Of these, nine are scientific and literary collaborators, some being ecclesiastics and doctors in theology, others laymen and doctors in political economy. There is also a publishing-house with a press ; a section for lantern-slides ; a library of Social Science and Apologetics (70,000 volumes) ; a service of social information. In the country there are seven branch libraries, sixteen regional secretariates with nineteen employees, of whom ten are university graduates.

The *Volksvereinsverlag* publishing-house at München-Gladbach has published over 700 books and pamphlets ; and countless leaflets have been distributed free. Every two months there appear *Der Volksverein*, a review for men ; *Die Frau im Volksverein*, a review for women ; *Führerkorrespondenz*, a review for directors of organisations. Then there is a bulletin for representatives, a bulletin for propagandists or " Confidence-men " ; and the *Sozialpolitische Korrespondenz*, which appears every three weeks and is sent free to 350 Catholic newspapers.[3]

---

[1] Plater, *op. cit.*, p. 60.   [2] *Ib.*, p. 81.
[3] *International Handbook of Catholic Organisations*, p. 65.

Besides this abundance of excellent literature which comes pouring out from the München-Gladbach every year about 5,000 popular meetings are held where lectures are given on topical subjects. In various districts special courses are given in practical sociology, lasting from eight to fifteen days. At the central headquarters there are vacation courses of eight days ; special courses for workmen, artisans, business-men, agriculturists, commercial employees, school-masters, etc., social and apologetic courses for propagandists as well as for the leaders of Catholic and interdenominational professional organisations. This is but a very imperfect outline of one of the fifty-eight great Catholic organisations of Germany.

The " Semaines Sociales de France."—In France the *Semaines Sociales*[1] are the national congresses of the Catholic social movement. Even seventeen years ago a French publicist could truly write :

" All courses and all classic works treating of economic doctrines give a large space to the study of social Catholicism. And all signalise the *Semaines Sociales* as the most characteristic and most notably scientific manifestation of this sociological school."[2]

The *Semaines Sociales* are sessions of social study which take place in a different French city every year, gathering the directors of organisations around the most eminent masters of Catholic social science. " To attend as a student," says a contemporary writer, " is no sinecure. From eight in the morning until eleven at night, the student has hardly time to breathe. In the morning, he attends two lecture courses, each lasting an hour and a half ; after lunch, he is taken to visit neighbouring factories, co-operative societies, trade unions, or workingmen's gardens ; late in the afternoon there is another lecture course ; and finally, in the evening there is a general lecture, open to a more popular audience as well as to real students."[3]

---

[1] The institution of *Semaines Sociales* has been extended to other countries, such as Belgium, Canada, Chile, Spain, Italy, Holland, Poland, Switzerland, Uruguay, etc.

[2] *Revue Hebdomadaire* (Aug., 1913), pp. 522–531.

[3] Moon, *op. cit.*, p. 342.

Their Activities and Affiliated Organisations.—During the fifteen sessions which took place between 1904, the year of foundation, and 1923, more than 100 professors or lecturers have delivered over 300 courses or lectures, of which the reports *in extenso* are a store-house of learning.

Besides their own direct work, the *Semaines Sociales* have led to the creation of several organisations destined to extend their field of influence. Among the more important of these are : *Les Semaines Sociales Regionales* ("Local Social Weeks"), *Les Semaines Rurales* ("Rural Weeks"), and the *Union d'Etudes des Catholiques Sociaux* ("Catholic Social Study Unions").

The second of these organisations is of special interest to Irish social students. The purpose of the "Rural Weeks" is the education of social leaders for the rural districts. In a house of retreats, a monastery, or a school during the holidays, suitable young persons from 18 to 30 years of age are brought together. For a week religious courses are held, as well as courses of agricultural technique, but, above all, social courses (treating of such matters as trade unions, co-operation, rural credit, mutual insurance). In 1923 more than twenty "Rural Weeks" were held in various regions of France.[1]

The "Action Populaire."—If the *Semaines Sociales* of France correspond somewhat to the German Catholic congresses, the *Action Populaire*, which is conducted by the Jesuit Fathers, corresponds to the *Volksverein*, and was in fact, inspired by it. It was founded in 1902, and up to the European War had its headquarters at Rheims. During the War all its books, documents, etc., were lost owing to the bombardment of Rheims, and other causes. It resumed work in 1919, establishing its new headquarters in Paris.

The *Action Populaire* is an editorial and distributing centre for social literature, as well as an information bureau and a centre for organising study courses and popular conventions. Thus it is in a manner the heart and centre of the Catholic social movement in France. Even in 1912 the central office at Rheims employed sixteen editors—ten priests and six laymen—besides twenty-seven secretaries.

---

[1] *International Handbook*, pp. 62–63.

A large staff kept busy sending out the mass of literature daily dispatched from the bureau. This literature, produced by the most prominent Catholic social writers and by non-Catholic economists, is sold very cheaply. The association has recently brought about the foundation of a Joint Stock Company ("Edition Spes," Paris), which includes a publishing office, and has charge of the distribution of the pamphlets and other publications of the association.

Its Publications.—From the outset the *Action Populaire* has been publishing a series of thirty-page pamphlets (called *Brochures Jaunes*) on such subjects as old age pensions, co-operative associations, labour unions, mixed industrial boards, housing problems, accident compensation, socialism, workingmen's gardens, child labour, etc. To this series was added later on another called *Les Actes Sociaux*, which is a very cheap edition of the principal laws, papal pronouncements, and other documents on social matters. A third series, *Les Plans et Documents*, comprise documentary and doctrinal monographs, designed for social study clubs. A very notable publication is the *Année Sociale Internationale*, which is a monumental work of reference on the whole social movement.

The *Action Populaire* has also six periodicals. Of these we may mention *Dossiers de l'Action Populaire*, a fortnightly review, composed of detachable articles for study, documentation and action ; *Peuple de France*, a monthly review for popular education ; and *L'Action Populaire*, a quarterly of social and religious propaganda.

Its other Activities and Departments.—Again, the *Action Populaire* is an information bureau, where thousands of inquiries are answered every year. These inquiries are on all sorts of religious and social questions—how to found a mutual aid society ; what employment young girls leaving their home village should seek ; what authority should be consulted on social insurance, etc.

Finally, the *Action Populaire* has engaged increasingly in the work of organising study courses, participating in social conferences, organising popular conventions, etc.[1]

---

[1] Cf. *International Handbook*, p. 61 ; also Moon, *op. cit.*, pp. 321–339.

The Belgian " Boerenbond " (Farmer's Union).—Of very
special interest to the Irish reader is the Belgian *Boerenbond*.[1]
It was founded in 1890 by M. L'Abbé Mellaerts (a parish
priest of a rural parish in Flanders), assisted by M. Helleputte
and M. Schollaert. To-day it is a social force of the first
order among the Flemish peasants, answering in the highest
measure to the needs of the farming population. It caters
principally for small cottiers whose holdings consist usually
of some ten statute acres.[2]

The union comprises about 1,200 guilds, each guild including about 150 cottiers. The parish priest is usually
the hon. secretary of the guild ; and he with a few of the
more intelligent and better educated of the peasants form
the local executive committee. Every member must be a
practising Catholic. The president of the union is a priest—
a dignitary of the Archdiocese of Malines. In the head
office at Louvain about 500 men are employed, of whom
about seventeen are priests. All these are paid officials.
The officials of the local guilds are not paid.

Its Activities.—The functions of the Union are to watch
over the interests of its members in the public legislature
and administration, and to supply them with all the services
(and many more) which are in other countries committed
to a State Department of Agriculture. Amongst the advantages which the member enjoys the following are note-
worthy :

(*a*) All that the peasant requires to buy, such as seeds,
artificial manures, implements and machinery, etc., may
be procured through the *Boerenbond* depôt. The most
important advantages of this privilege are that the farmers
are ensured the best quality of seeds and manures, and when
selling the produce are assured a just price.

(*b*) An excellent, cheap and safe system of insurance of
cattle, hay, etc., as well as of life insurance, is brought
within reach of all the members through the *Boerenbond*
Insurance Department. This belongs to the farmers themselves and is self-contained.

---

[1] The Head Offices are in Louvain (Rue des Recollets 24).
[2] On this farm the Boerenbond peasant now keeps five or six milch
cows (whose average annual yield of milk is at present 800 gallons each),
rears two or three calves, keeps a sow and some fat pigs and much poultry.

(c) Every guild has a local bank which is affiliated to the Central *Boerenbond* Bank at Louvain. This latter is one of the strongest and most important banks in Belgium. Thus the union has complete control of its own financial affairs ; and can accommodate its members with loans at a very cheap rate. Advances are made to the individual cottier on the recommendation and *guarantee* of the local guild to which he belongs.

(d) Some forty inspectors are employed for the help of the members. All of these are skilled in organising and each is besides a specialist in some particular branch of agricultural science or work, such as Veterinary Science, Engineering, Building, etc.

(e) Several journals and reviews are published for the education of the members in agricultural and other matters.

The *Boerenbond* has transformed the whole agricultural life of West Flanders ; and since its rise the cottiers have become quite independent and prosperous. Associations like the *Boerenbond*, combined with the excellent social legislation of the Catholic government that held power for so many years previous to the War (1884–1914), places Belgium in a foremost position in social reform.[1]

Press Organisations.—Another class of Catholic social organisation which has been making much headway in Catholic countries since 1920 is the Catholic Press Association. The object of this association is to organise and propagate amongst the people reading matter of good quality, treating of all subjects of interest, including religion education, politics, economics, finance, sport, etc., but handling them from the Christian standpoint, and with a

---

[1] Cf. Vermeersch, S.J.—*Manuel Social*, for an account of the great series of laws for social and industrial reform passed by the Catholic Government of Belgium during these thirty fruitful years.

Among the several other types of Catholic associations which now flourish in Belgium the Association of Catholic Youth (" Association Catholique de la Jeunesse Belgique," or " A. C. J. B.") holds a foremost place. These include associations of boys, of girls, of boys of the labouring class (" Jeunesse Ouvrière Catholique " or " J. O. C."), of boys of the agricultural class (" J. A. C."), etc. Cf. Picard and Hoyois—*L'Association Cath. de la Jeunesse Belgique*, published at the Secretariat General de l'A. C. J. B., 126 Rue de Tirelemont, Louvain, 1924 ; also *Les Documents de la Vie Intellectuelle* (Monthly Review), Sept. 20th, 1931, published at 11 Rue Quentin-Bauchart, Paris viiie.

Catholic tone and outlook. The Catholic Press is thus meant to supplant the unchristian capitalistic Press, or at least to counteract its influences.

Some fifteen different Press Associations belonging to Germany, France, Italy, Spain, Holland, Hungary, etc., are enumerated[1] as existing in 1923. The number is probably very much greater at present. Some of these, such as the *Oeuvre du Franc de la Presse*[2] (founded in Paris, 1919, by Canon Couget), aim at providing funds for the founding of Catholic papers or for subsidizing those already in existence. The object of others is to unify and co-ordinate the activities and efforts of all the Catholic newspapers and pressmen of the country. Others again aim at forming a body of zealous workers who would devote their energies to extend the circulation of the Catholic Press.

" Ora et Labora."—The object of the *Institucion Internacional Ora et Labora*, which was founded in the Pontifical Seminary of Seville, 1905, and has now a membership of over 15,000, is to train seminarists for Catholic propaganda in all its forms ; to carry on a crusade on behalf of the Catholic Press ; and to propagate among all the nations the institution of the " Press Day."[3] It has sections in seventy-four Spanish seminaries, and correspondents in most of the chief cities of the world.

The " Maison de la Bonne Presse."[4]—The *Maison de la Bonne Presse* of Paris is the most powerful institution for Press propaganda that exists in France. It is organised as a Joint Stock Company, and unites in a single establishment a mass of newspapers, magazines, books and writings of all kinds, including works of information and organs of propaganda of the first order of excellence. It has special

---

[1] Cf. *International Handbook*, chap. iii. An excellent and very comprehensive account of the Catholic Press as it was twenty years ago, will be found in the *Catholic Encyclopedia*, art. " Periodical Literature, Catholic," vol. xi, pp. 369–396.

[2] The title in English would perhaps be " *Society of the Press Shilling.*"

[3] The " Press Day," which takes place all over Spain every year on the feast of SS. Peter and Paul, is celebrated by a General Communion, a solemn ceremony in the church, including a sermon on the Apostolate of the Press, and a collection for the Catholic Press. The collection yields over £6,000 a year (1931).

[4] The Head Office is at 5 Rue Bayard, Paris viii⁰.

18

staffs for all its papers and magazines, which numbered thirty before the war. It has branches and committees over all France, and a governing administration in Paris.[1]

Conclusion.—The associations which we have briefly described are a few typical examples of the multitudes of social organisations which exist and continue to increase. Very many of the people's needs in such matters as education, insurance, banking, agricultural and industrial training, public libraries, the Press, etc., which in other countries are provided by the State at great expense, and too often very inefficiently, or are in the hands of non-Catholic or neutral bodies, to the injury and peril of Catholic interests, are in many continental Catholic countries now supplied by these Catholic associations.[2]

---

[1] Cf. *International Handbook*, p. 23.

[2] If the framework of the social organism in Ireland is to be refashioned in accordance with Catholic ideals (and only such a refashioning can save the Catholic nation of Ireland from extinction) a strong Catholic Press must be built up, and a network of Catholic associations, such as we have described, gradually formed under the guidance of the Church. A strong and widespread movement for such a purpose is probably at present the country's most urgent need.

PART II

CATHOLIC SOCIAL PRINCIPLES

INTRODUCTORY NOTE

From the brief examination of the social doctrines and social conditions of Europe during the past two thousand years, which form the matter of the First Part of the present work, one may gather that the whole system of Christian civilisation centres round a few fundamental principles. If these or any of them are disregarded, the temporal happiness of the people will not be realised. These principles refer to the practical recognition of God's supreme authority in public as well as private life ; the essential dignity and rights of human personality ; the sacredness and integrity of family life, and the natural and therefore divinely ordained institution of the State.

In actual fact the principles set out above have not been followed, for any long period of time, except under the authority and guidance of the Catholic Church. They are in large part ignored among non-Christian nations, and in countries which have rejected the Church's authority, the fruits of Christian civilisation which previously existed tend to disappear in proportion as the Catholic tradition is lost.

In the Second Part of our treatise we shall try to analyse these principles more fully and examine some of their more important applications in the public life of the State. For it is with the State that Social Science has primarily to deal. We shall therefore first discuss the material elements of which the State is made up—viz., the human Individual and the Family. In connection with the latter we shall also discuss the relations of Employer and Employed and the Social Status of Women. In the next place we shall deal with the State itself, its natural constitution and functions ; and the ties which unite its members into one moral whole—viz., Justice, Charity and Piety (or Patriotism). Finally, we shall treat briefly of the Church and its functions in reference to social well-being and the due relations between Church and State.[1]

---

[1] To complete the treatise a Third Part would be required which, however, is not included in the present work. In that part certain questions of special importance which are touched on only briefly or incidentally in the present volume would receive fuller and more detailed treatment. Such questions would include the Distribution of Property, Municipal Organisation, Industrial Unions, Wages, Co-operation, Interest and Usury, Money, Taxation, and Catholic Social Action.

CHAPTER XVI

THE INDIVIDUAL

Although it is true that the natural and primary unit in the State is not the individual, but the family, the family itself is made up of individual persons; moreover, there are in the State, many men and women, emancipated from parental control and still unmarried. Hence the individual person is the fundamental element in all civil society. The institution of the State as well as that of the family is founded ultimately upon men's individual needs and natural attributes. The individual and the family are both prior to the State, which has been ordained by Nature to supplement individual weakness, and to assist the family in providing for the temporal happiness of the persons that compose it.

Hence, in order to understand the natural constitution and functions of the State, and of the family, one must first understand the nature of human personality; and the essential rights and duties attaching to it. These we shall now discuss.

Art. 1—*Human Personality*[1]

The Civic Body and the Human Body Compared.—In these days of materialistic philosophy and false individualism, when the dignity and rights of human personality are so often ignored, it will be helpful to keep before the mind the idea of the Christian State as conceived and largely realised in mediæval times under the guidance of the Catholic Church, and put forward in our day by the Supreme Pontiff[2]

---

[1] Cf. Castelein—*Droit Naturel*, Theses 3, 4 and 5; Meyer—*Institutio Juris Naturalis* (Fribourg, 1906), part i; Rickaby—*Moral Philosophy*, part i, chap. ii; Donat—*Ethica Generalis* (Innsbruck, 1921). Costa-Rosetti—*Philosophia Moralis*, par. ii; Brouad—*Petit Catechisme Social du Democrate* (Bloud and Gay, Paris, 1908).

[2] Cf. Pius XI—*Quadragesimo Anno*, p. 41, 42; also Leo XIII—*Rerum Novarum*, p. 142.

as the model upon which the modern States must be re-organised, if the chaos of the class war is to be remedied. The ideal Christian State may be compared in some ways to the organism of the living body. Every portion of the living body, every organ and nerve and muscle, has its peculiar function in providing for the support and development of the whole body, which in turn contributes from its vital stores all that each organ or part requires for its own upkeep and healthy action. The functions of no two parts are precisely the same, nor do any two organs require an equal expenditure of vital energy for their support. Each part contributes according to its nature and capacity to the maintenance of the bodily vitality, and each receives supplies of blood and vital energy in proportion to its needs.

So it is to a certain degree in the organism of the Christian State, whose parts and members are the different individuals, families and larger civic units that compose it. These are united into one whole by the moral bonds of Social Justice and Charity. Each contributes to the common good according to his or its capacity and receives from the common store assistance and protection in proportion to need.

The Essential Difference Between Them.—Between the organism of the human body, however, and that of the State there is one fundamental difference, which pagan philosophy and the philosophy of many modern schools ignore ; and this is the point of the comparison that immediately concerns us here.

The organs and parts of the human body belong essentially to a greater whole. They have no special end or purpose of their own, distinct from those of the body to which they belong ; and therefore no rights independent of the rights of the human person that owns them. The claim, if we may speak analogically, which the eye or the hand possesses to its due share of blood and vital energy from the body, rests solely upon the need of preserving that body in a state of healthy efficiency. Hence, no limits can be set to the demands which the human being may make, should need require, upon any part or faculty of his bodily organism. Even a limb may be amputated or an arm worked till it become permanently useless.

It is quite otherwise in the State, whose ultimate purpose

is not the good, or seeming good, of the body politic, but that of the individual members that compose it. These latter being persons, and having each a destiny of his own and a purpose in life far transcending his position in the social organism, can never be made into mere instruments for promoting the interests of any other person or thing in the created universe. Hence the *State is meant wholly and entirely for the good of the individual members, not the members for the State.* The sole end and purpose of the State is to assist each and every person within it in his efforts to attain to perfection and temporal happiness.[1]

Non-Christian Attitude towards the Individual—(a) The Pagan Attitude.—The wide divergence of view between Christian and non-Christian jurists in their conception of the State is rooted in their different views of the nature and rights of the human individual. The pagans of ancient Greece and Rome, whose teachings have partially reappeared in the non-Christian philosophy and jurisprudence of our own days, measured a man's dignity and rights principally or solely by the amount of material goods he controlled. The man himself, despoiled of his belongings, was little better than nothing. Hence the slave was regarded as a mere chattel, devoid of personal rights, and meant essentially for his master's good. Even the freeman, if poor, was treated with supreme contempt, and, in practice, reduced almost to a state of servility. Infanticide and abortion were freely practised, and were formally recommended even by such philosophers as Plato and Aristotle, in the interests, as they understood it, of the public good.

Many of these doctrines are revived in our own times. Thus non-Christian philosophers of the Aristocratic school, such as the German Nietzsche, openly reject the essential independence of human personality, in their doctrine of the " superman," for whose leisured well-being other men are bound to toil. Again, abortion is formally legalised in Soviet Russia. In the unchristian social theories of Eugenics and Euthanasia, and in several tendencies of the modern unchristian state, the inalienable rights of the human person are violated or made subservient to the

---

[1] Cf. Castelein, *op. cit.*, p. 666,

supposed good of an all-absorbing entity called the State
or Humanity.

(b) **The Liberals' Attitude.**—The Liberals, while upholding
in theory their doctrine (which, as explained by them, is
false and exaggerated) of liberty and equality for every
individual, disregard in practice the dignity and rights of
human personality ; and have in fact reduced the vast
majority of the people to a state of misery and dependence,
which Pope Leo XIII describes as " little better than
slavery." For, in the capitalist system of economy, which
is the natural outcome of Liberal philosophy, most of the
activities of the State are made subservient to the production of wealth. The worker, bereft of productive
property, and thus left without an opportunity of labouring
for his support except with the consent of the capitalist
proprietor, is handed over to the almost unchecked control
of men, often unscrupulous and unchristian, whose only
interest in him is as a producer of wealth.

According to the capitalist ideal, that State is accounted
most prosperous and most civilised which can show the
greatest amount of production, the mightiest hoard of
accumulated millions, the largest fleet and the strongest
army. But what of the human individuals that compose
the State ? Do they, each and all, enjoy the peace and
prosperity to which they have a natural claim, or are they,
through no fault of theirs, debarred from a fair opportunity
of happiness and self-development ? Such questions do
not trouble the financial magnates or the bureaucratic rulers,
too often the mere creatures of the financiers, in a system in
which economics and government are divorced from
Christian teaching, and the claims of God and the dignity of
the human person ignored.

(c) **The Socialists' Attitude.**—The Socialists, while professing to provide fully for man's material interests, would,
by making him the slave of an all-absorbing State, rob him
of his natural independence, and of some of his most sacred
personal rights. Ignoring, no less than the Liberals, the
laws of morality and the claims of the Creator, they would
also destroy or fatally lower man's natural dignity. For
in their social system even if it could attain the success at

which they aim, the individual, no longer responsible for his own well-being, would be degraded almost to the level of the well-fed, contented, irresponsible animal.

Christian Concept of Human Personality.—The Christian, differing from all these, sees in man and, above all, in man's immortal soul, incomparably the most precious thing on earth, and the one for whose good all other things on earth living and inanimate are ordained. Stamped with the image of the Godhead, redeemed by the Precious Blood of the Son of God, predestined to an eternal life of intimate union with God, clothed (in fact, or, at least, in God's intention and desire) with sanctifying grace, which makes man a sharer in God's nature and heir to God's kingdom, the human soul gives to man a place of dignity in the created universe with which nothing material can compare. This dignity, which gives him a worth that is almost divine, belongs inseparably to every human individual of both sexes and every age and every country and race. As a natural attribute of his spiritual soul, man enjoys freedom of will, which makes him master of his own actions, and personally responsible for the attaining of his own end.

From man's nature, and especially from his eternal destiny and the freedom of his will, spring the great prerogatives which are inherent in the human individual, giving him his dignity and essential independence, and forbidding that he be ever made a mere instrument for promoting another's good. Man is a *person*. He has *rights* and *duties*.

Foundation of Rights and Duties[1]—(a) **Man's Eternal Destiny.**—Each man's soul is created directly by God ; and each and every man is destined by his Creator for a life of happiness to be found in the perfect development and activity of all his faculties. This life of happiness will be realised in the intimate, supernatural union of his soul with God for ever.

This essential destiny and purpose of man's life belong

---

[1] Cf. Castelein, *loc. cit.* ; Meyer, *op. cit.*, pars. ii ; Costa-Rosetti, *loc. cit.* ; Donat—*Ethica Specialis*, sec. i ; *Cath. Encyclop.*, arts. " Right," " Duty," etc. ; Ryan and Millar—*The State and the Church* (London, Macmillan, 1924), chaps. xiii–xiv,

inalienably to every human being. Every one has to attain
to it by his own personal efforts aided by the divine grace,
and by the co-operation which society affords. Hence, every
man is bound by obligations, to which all other considerations are subordinate, and against which not even the closest
human ties can prevail, to fit himself by his actions for that
eternal life.

(b) **His Human Perfectibility.**—Meanwhile man has to
live also a human life on earth. His natural faculties and
powers are eminently capable of activity and higher perfection, even in this life ; and he finds his temporal happiness
in the due development and well-ordered exercise of these
powers. To this human happiness man has a natural
claim, with the essential limitations that his eternal
interests must always receive first consideration, and that
the similar claims of others must not be unduly interfered
with.

" The natural capabilities of every individual consist in
the powers of body, sense, intellect and will. The body
under proper conditions will grow to the full vigour of man
or woman, with a persistence of force in successive generations, which is one of the splendours of natural providence.
The intellect, though its quality may vary in no small
degree in different persons, is yet capable under favourable
circumstances of a good average of attainments and real
culture, such as we meet in well-educated men and women.
The will—notwithstanding the lower impulses, the constant
drag of indolence, the blind impulse of sense, the attraction
of harmful example, and the handicap of ignorance—is
capable, under suitable circumstances, of reaching a standard
of moral rectitude which, even when not heroic, should
compel the admiration of all."[1]

(c) **His Innate Desire of Well-being.**—Besides the instinct
of self-preservation, which man has in common with all
animals, nature has given to him an active, indestructible
tendency and instinct, included in his desire of happiness
and well-being, to develop all these natural faculties and
powers. And to their development and well-ordered

---

[1] Parkinson, *op. cit.*, pp. 31, 32,

exercise reason tells us man has a natural claim ; and that
he is the victim of wrong if this claim is not respected by
others.

(*d*) **God's Ordinance in Creating the Earth for Man's Use.**—
Again : God has given to all men the earth and all that
it contains, in order that by their labour upon it they may
each and all have a means of developing their natural
powers and of living a becoming human life.   Hence every
man has a natural claim to his due place on the earth's
surface, and cannot be legitimately excluded from access
to his fair proportion of the goods of nature.

Art. 2—*Rights and Duties*

From all these considerations there emerge the notions
of *right* and *duty*.   Rights and duties are the natural
attributes of personality, and can belong only to persons.
The lower animals, being created solely for man's use and
benefit, cannot have rights,[1] and, being bereft of free will,
are incapable of duties.

Meaning of Right.—A *right* means something that is due
to a person to complete, as it were, and round off his
personality.   It is defined by the philosophers as *a moral
power which a person has and which other persons are bound
to respect, to do something, or retain something, or exact something from another (Personæ facultas moralis, inviolabilis,
faciendi, retinendi, exigendi aliquid)*.   By the expression,
moral power, philosophers mean to convey that the person

---

[1] Although the lower animals have not rights and are ordained by God
for man's use and benefit (Gen. i and ix. 3), it would be a violation of God's
law to destroy animal life or to inflict pain on animals *without sufficient
cause*.   Our Divine Lord says of the sparrows that " *not one of them is
forgotten before God* " (Luke xii. 6) ; and several of God's saints were very
remarkable for tenderness towards the animal creation.   It betrays, however, an absence of the sense of proportion and suggests a want of
realisation of the dogma of the Redemption to make a fetish (as non-
Catholics often do) of kindness to animals or to confound one's duties of
charity towards one's fellowmen with the obligation of not abusing the
animal creation.   Animals at worst, owing to the absence in them of the
power of reflection, are incapable of suffering comparable to the sufferings
of rational beings, and the Christian who realises the worth and dignity
of the human soul, the mysteries of the Incarnation and Redemption will
never forget the infinite difference between the lower animal and the
human person.

may, without violating any law or obligation perform the action or retain in his possession the thing in question or exact it from another. The term, however, does not imply that he is physically capable of doing so. Hence although a person may be impeded by another in the exercise of his right, the right itself remains, appealing as it were, to the moral conscience of men that the unjust obstacle be removed.

A right implies an obligation on the part of others not to impede its exercise, but does not necessarily include an obligation on the possessor's part to exercise the moral power which the right confers. For some rights may be resigned even perpetually.

Meaning of Duty—Personal Duties.—Akin to rights are duties, which are another attribute of personality. *Duty is a moral obligation of doing or not doing something.* The term, *moral obligation,* may be explained by saying that the person on whom the obligation lies, while physically able to disregard it, violates the natural law, and disobeys God if he does so.

Man may be regarded as an independent person or as a member of a family, or as a member of the State ; and in each of these capacities he has rights and duties. We treat here only of the rights and duties which belong to man in his individual capacity. The consideration of his domestic and civic relations will come later. Again, we are concerned here only with the rights and duties which are founded on the natural law. We have nothing to say of those coming from the positive law, whether of Church or State.

Juridical and Non-Juridical Duties.—Although every right implies a duty upon all others not to interfere with the exercise of the right, the converse is not true. For even of men's duties towards one another, with which the science of Sociology is primarily concerned, only some imply that the person towards whom the duty lies has a right to its fulfilment. These latter are called *juridical* duties. The duties that do not imply any such right are called *non-juridical* or purely *ethical* duties. Thus a man's duty to pay his lawful debts is juridical ; while duties of charity, such as the obligation to give alms to a person in need, are non-juridical duties ; because the person who is the object of the act of charity cannot complain that any right of his is violated, if the duty is disregarded.

We shall see later that social duties, such as the duties of citizens to co-operate for the common good, and those of rulers to secure by just laws, impartially and efficiently administered, a due proportion of peace and prosperity for all are juridical ; and that their neglect implies real injustice. Hence the cry of the disinherited calling upon the rulers and proprietors to fulfil their social duties, " We demand justice and not charity," is founded upon true philosophy.

Perfect and Imperfect Rights.—Some rights are so closely bound up with man's nature and personality that they are quite indispensable for the attaining of his end. The exercise of such rights cannot be suspended or curtailed without the person's free consent. Nay, in the case of some perfect rights the right cannot be validly surrendered even by the free will of the person that possesses it. In this connection Leo XIII writes :

" To consent to any treatment which is calculated to defeat the end and purpose of man's being is beyond his right ; he cannot give up his soul to servitude ; for it is not man's own rights which are here in question, but the rights of God." [1]

Thus a man cannot give to another the right to take his life, nor can he make a valid contract binding himself to some course of action unworthy of his human dignity. Neither can any law validly impose upon him conditions which in the concrete are unjust or inhuman. The following passage from Leo XIII further illustrates this principle :

" In all agreements between masters and work people there is always the condition expressed or understood that there should be allowed proper rest for soul and body. To agree in any other sense would be against what is right and just ; for it can never be just or right to require on the one side, or to promise on the other, the giving up of duties, which a man owes to his God and to himself." [2]

Hence Tennyson's conception of the ideal soldier would

---

[1] *Rerum Novarum*, p. 155.   [2] *Ib.*, pp. 156, 157.

not bear analysis as a description of the true Christian warrior :

> " Theirs not to make reply ;
> Theirs not to reason why ;
> Theirs but to do and die."

For no one can fully surrender personal responsibility for his acts ; and no obligation, military or otherwise, can deprive a man of all personal rights. In other words, men have rights (implying duties) that are inalienable. These are sometimes called *perfect* rights.

There are, on the other hand, several classes of natural rights, which, although in normal circumstances helpful to man for the attainment of his end, are not quite indispensable for that purpose. The legitimate exercise of such rights is limited by the equal rights of others, and may, if the public good requires, be curtailed by civil law. Thus the exercise of a person's natural right to manufacture a certain type of food or drink, to wear clothes of a peculiar fashion, to publish or even express certain opinions or views, may be justly forbidden by law, should it cause injury or unfair temptation to others. In the same way, limits may be set to a man's natural right to acquire property, when the unchecked exercise of the right becomes a danger to the community.

It is clear, however, that the interference of public authority must be kept within reasonable bounds ; for the lawful[1] exercise of one's natural liberty cannot be justly curtailed without a proportionately grave cause founded upon the greater good of the community. Those rights which are natural to man, but whose exercise may be curtailed or partially suspended, owing to their apparent clash with the rights of others, are sometimes called *imperfect* rights.

It is often difficult to decide in practice what particular rights are perfect and what imperfect, and when the exercise of imperfect rights may be lawfully suspended. We shall touch further down on some of the problems connected with

---

[1] Liberty must not be confounded with licence *to do wrong*. No person and no moral body has or can have the *right to do wrong*. From the definition of right given above it is clear that the clause in question involves a contradiction in terms.

this question. It is, however, necessary to understand, even at this stage, that the mere fact of a person being unjustly defrauded of his rights does not always imply that he may, in disregard of existing civil laws, proceed straightway to exercise the rights which are unjustly withheld. For such a course of action would frequently cause, at least indirectly, still greater injustice to others. The sufferers may, and should, unite to secure remedy by peaceful means. And no one may legitimately oppose reforms which justice—even legal or distributive justice—requires.

Inborn and Acquired Rights.—Again, men's natural personal rights may be *inborn* (congenital) or *acquired*. The former class, which are derived from man's nature, belong to all. The latter are the natural result of some contingent fact, such as the exercise of human activity. Thus, one's right to life and freedom is inborn ; so is one's right to acquire property. On the other hand, a person's right to the ownership of his own particular property is an acquired right. For it is the natural effect of some historical fact, such as the actions of himself or another, which connects that property with him in such a way that the natural law now ordains it for his exclusive use.

Human Equality and Inequality.—In their inborn or congenital rights, as well as in the dignity of their human personality, and in all the attributes attached to that personality, all men are equal. For human nature, with its supernatural destiny which is the origin of these rights is the same in all men. But because of the diversity of men's natural capabilities and needs, and the varying nature of the facts and circumstances that affect them, men's acquired rights are very unequal. Leo XIII, treating of this subject, writes :

" It is impossible to reduce society to one dead level. Socialists may in that intent do their utmost, but all striving against nature is vain. There naturally exist among mankind, manifold differences of the most important kind ; people differ in capacity, skill, health, strength ; and unequal fortune is a necessary result of unequal conditions."[1]

---

[1] *Rerum Novarum*, p. 141.

On the same subject Pius X writes :

" Human society as God established it, is composed of unequal elements, just as the members of the human body are unequal. To make them all equal is impossible, and would be the destruction of society itself. . . . Consequently it is conformable to the order established by God, that in human society there should be princes and subjects, masters and men, rich and poor, learned and ignorant, nobles and plebeians, who, united by a bond of love, should help one another to attain their final end in Heaven, and their material and moral well-being on earth." [1]

This inevitable inequality in human life is an admirable dispensation of Providence on men's behalf. For it makes men need one another's help, and so serves to strengthen the social body, making it easier for the members to merge into a compact whole.

Duties and Rights in Relation to God, to Others and to One's Self.—Men's individual rights and duties may be classed under the three following heads : Men's duties (including rights) in relation to God ; their duties towards each other ; and the rights and duties of self-preservation and self-improvement. Men's duties towards each other comprising the obligations of *Justice* and *Charity* we shall treat at length later on, when dealing with the State. The duties and rights relating to one's self (viz., those of self-preservation and self-improvement) we reserve for the following chapter. We shall conclude the present chapter with a brief treatment of men's duties in relation to God, which are included under the general heading of Religion.

Art. 3—*Duty of Religion*[2]

Man's first and most important duty, including inalienable rights in regard to its fulfilment, is the duty of religion, which in practice is identical with man's right and duty to tend towards his last end.

" Of all the duties man has to fulfil," writes Leo XIII, " that, without doubt, is the chiefest and holiest, which commands him to worship God with devotion and piety. . . . No true virtue

---

[1] *Fin Dalla Prima* (1903), p. 183.
[2] Castelein, *op. cit.*, Thesis i ; *Cath. Encyclop.*, art. " Religion " ; Godts— *Scopuli Vitandi*, cap. xiv–xxiii ; Cuthbert—*Catholic Ideals in Social Life*, part ii.

19

can exist without religion ; for moral virtue is concerned with
those things that lead to God as man's supreme and ultimate
good ; and therefore religion, which (as St. Thomas says) ' per-
forms those actions, which are directly and immediately ordained
for the divine honour,'[1] rules and directs all virtues." [2]

Its Meaning and Foundation.—Religion includes all the
obligations that spring from man's relations with God
God is man's Creator and the source of his being ; He is
man's last end and the object of his perfection and happiness ; He is man's continual support and mainstay
without which, man, incapable of all activity or power
would immediately lapse into nothing. The natural duty
of religion, which corresponds to all these different relations
includes the knowledge and worship of God, and the
observance of the natural law as a divine ordinance.

Religion as a Moral Duty.—Man is bound to know his
duties to God ; and has an indefeasible right, valid against
all who may oppose it, to be allowed or enabled to acquire
that knowledge. Thus, children have an inalienable right
to be taught their religion as the most important of all
subjects of education.

Man is bound to worship God by prayer and other interior
acts of adoration ; and, because man's nature is composite
including body as well as soul, exterior worship, such as
vocal prayer and bodily acts of reverence, is also of
obligation.

In the third place, man is bound to observe the moral
law, as the ordinance of God. For God is the Author of
nature, and therefore the source and sanction of the natural
law.

We may add that the family and the State, both natural
units, are also bound by the natural law to give worship to
God in their social or corporate capacity,[3] and the rulers
of the State are bound to make its laws and administration
in harmony with the natural and divine law. For, as
Leo XIII again writes :

" Society, no less than individuals, owes gratitude to God
who gave it being and maintains it, and whose ever-bounteous
goodness enriches it with countless blessings."[4]

---

[1] *Summa*, 2ª, 2ᵃᵉ, Q. lxxxi, a. 6.   [2] *Libertas, Præstantissimum* (1888), p. 82.
[3] *Ib.*, p. 83.   [4] *Immortale Dei* (1885), p. 48.

Finally, seeing that God has established on earth a society, called the Church, to direct and assist man in matters appertaining to religion, with the precept that all men become members of that society and obey its laws, every one has a duty and an indefeasible right to belong to the Church of Christ and to obey its laws.[1]

Its Influence upon Temporal Well-being.

—The private and public worship of the Creator has been, down almost to our own times, a fundamental principle in the laws and customs of all great nations known to history ; it has permeated and dominated their public life as well as the private life of the citizens. This is true of the non-Christian as well as the Christian nations—of the Chinese, the Persians, the Hindus, the ancient Greeks and Romans, the Mohammedans, as well as the Christian nations of Europe and the East.

In the case of the non-Christian nations and of those that have lost, wholly or in part, their Christian faith, their religious worship is indeed intermingled with much error and superstition, and not unfrequently, even disfigured by immoral practices. These go far to counteract the effect which religion naturally has in elevating the people's lives. Still, history, when carefully read, conveys no more striking lesson than the influence of religion on the life of man. When due allowance is made for counteracting causes, which may interfere for a while with the working of the general law, the great fact stands out that nations are prosperous and happy in direct proportion to the living influence of religion among the people ; while the decay or weakening of religious observance and belief inevitably brings in its wake the loss of the nation's prosperity, the sterility of its genius, and the gradual enslavement of its people. Examples of this truth may be found in the history of the Romans under the Empire, in the rise and fall of the Mohammedan nations, and in the state of European society to-day.

Hence, even if we abstract from the eternal interests of the individual (which are always supreme) and regard merely his temporal prosperity, nothing can make up to a people for the loss of religious influence. It is a more important factor in temporal happiness than political

---

[1] *Immortale Dei*, p. 49.

liberty or national wealth or imperial power, or all these combined.

" Religion," writes Leo XIII, " of its essence is wonderfully helpful to the State. . . . It charges rulers to be mindful of their duty, to govern without injustice or severity. . . . It admonishes subjects to be obedient to lawful authority as to the ministers of God, and it binds them to their rulers not merely by obedience but by reverence and affection. . . . We need not mention how greatly religion conduces to pure morals, and pure morals to liberty. Reason shows, and history confirms the fact, that the higher the morality of states, the greater are the liberty and wealth and power which they enjoy." [1]

Examples of the Foregoing.—As an example of this beneficent influence, compare the Irish peasant of the 19th century with the Englishman of the same social class, as he then was, and still is, in those districts where religious belief and practice have died out. The Irish peasant, practically deprived of civic rights, robbed well-nigh of everything that human tyranny could take from him, ill-clad, insufficiently fed, without secure tenure even of the miserable hovel that sheltered him, was then probably the most oppressed and impoverished human type in Europe. The English peasant, on the other hand, had full political rights, fair material conditions, and the status of a free man in a nation that ruled one of the most powerful and extensive empires that history has known. Yet, in all the best things of life, domestic happiness, contentment, consciousness of his human dignity, moral and intellectual culture, those who have studied the conditions of both do not hesitate to decide that the Irish peasant enjoyed immeasurably the greater share of temporal happiness ; and that his advantage in that respect over his English neighbour was due almost entirely to his Catholic faith. [2]

Another familiar illustration of the same matter may be found in the present state of the people of the United States of America. The nation has practically all the elements that should make for its temporal happiness, except religion. It is probably the wealthiest nation in the world. It enjoys full political freedom ; and all the people possess equal

---

[1] *Libertas, Præstantissimum*, p. 84.
[2] See *Studies of Family Life*, by C. S. Devas (Burns and Oates, 1886).

rights before the law. But, with the exception of the Catholic portion of the population—about a sixth of the whole—the nation is very irreligious.

The result is that crime and human misery have reached appalling proportions. The percentages of divorces, murders and suicides are by far the highest in the world, the latter percentage (viz., of suicides) having reached the unprecedented figure of 19 per 100,000.[1] There is comparatively little domestic life or family affection. Extreme corruption prevails in public life. Most of the nation's wealth is controlled by an inconsiderable fraction of its citizens, with the result that immense numbers (which tend to increase year by year, and in recent years seem to have sometimes reached about 7,000,000 workers) are deprived of an opportunity of remunerative labour. Hence, although the country abounds in wealth, many millions, including indeed a large percentage of the total population, are insufficiently fed, badly clad and badly housed.[2]

Hence, any action of a civil government tending to lessen the influence of religion upon the people is to be reprobated, not merely because it is opposed to the duty of the State towards the Creator and violates besides the subjects' indefeasible rights connected with eternal happiness, but also because it tends to the ruin of their temporal happiness, which it is the primary duty of the State to promote.[3]

---

[1] Cf. *America* (Aug. 9th, 1930), pp. 410, 411, where Dr. H. Emerson, speaking at the International Congress on Mental Hygiene, held at Washington (May, 1930), is recorded to have stated that suicides in U.S.A. had increased from 5 per 100,000 in 1860 to 19 per 100,000 in 1930. This latter figure would mean about 800 suicides per year for a population of the size of the present population of Ireland !

[2] Cf. *Studies* (June, 1930), for an article by Dr. J. A. Ryan of Washington University, entitled " Poverty in the United States," in which the writer shows that the normal wage there is far below the level of a living wage. Cf. also Belliot, *op. cit.*, pp. 176 ff. In an address delivered at Yale University, U.S.A., May 26th, 1927, by Sir George Newman, Chief Medical Officer of the British Ministry of Health, the lecturer stated that in the year 1925, 22,000 deaths had occurred in U.S.A. from suicide and murder ; and about as many more as a result of motor accidents. A Committee of the American Bar, appointed to investigate existing conditions, reported in 1928 that the "criminal statistics in U.S.A. are, as far as crimes of violence are concerned, worse than in any other civilised country " (cited in *The Irish Times*, June 11th, 1929).

[3] On the whole question of the influence of religion on society and social well-being, *see* Castelein, *op. cit.*, pp. 36–39.

CHAPTER XVII

DUTIES AND RIGHTS REGARDING ONE'S SELF[1]

From a well-ordered love of one's self, which natural instinct and right reason teach to all, springs a third class of individual rights and duties. These comprise the rights and duties of *self-preservation*, and those of *perfection* or *self-development*.

Under the former are included the right and duty of self-defence, while such crimes as suicide, duelling, and the unnecessary exposure of one's life to danger are forbidden. The duty of self-preservation also implies the right and the duty to secure for one's self the goods, both material and spiritual, which are essential for human life. These comprise knowledge, personal liberty, a good reputation, and material possessions. A certain amount of all these is ordinarily indispensable for living a becoming human life.

The duties of perfection or self-development include, in the first place, the obligation of subordinating, by the practice of temperance, meekness and fortitude, the inferior appetites to the control of reason and will ; and secondly, the duty and right of developing more and more fully one's natural powers—physical, intellectual and moral.

Of these manifold rights and duties, which it is outside our present scope to discuss fully, we shall delay only upon three, which are of special importance to the student of Social Science. These are : (*a*) The duty and right of work or labour ; (*b*) the right of acquiring property ; and (*c*) the right of freedom in chosing one's work and state of life.

Art. 1—*Duty and Right of Labour*[2]

Duty of Labour Proved from Man's Nature.—All are bound by a precept of the natural law to exercise their powers by work ; and no one can be justly excluded from a

---

[1] Cf. Meyer, *op. cit.*, vol. ii, Theses v–ix ; Costa-Rosetti, *op. cit.*, Theses 86–96 ; Hickey, *op. cit.*, pars. ii, cap. iii.

[2] Castelein, *op. cit.*, Thesis 5 ; Sabatier—*L'Eglise et Le Travail Manuel* (Bloud and Gay, Paris, 1919) ; Koch-Preuss, *op. cit.*, vol. iii, chap. ii ; Cuthbert, *op. cit.*, pp. 74–84.

fair opportunity of doing so. That labour is a precept of
the natural law, obligatory upon all, is clear from the nature
of man and the circumstances of human life. The lower
animals have comparatively few needs, and the means to
satisfy the few they have are supplied by nature, ready to
hand. Their faculties develop spontaneously, and without
conscious effort on their part. They have no desires except
that of satisfying their animal propensities, which they do
under the impulse of blind instinct.

Man, on the other hand, is born with many needs which
cannot be supplied without labour. His best powers are
developed only by sustained and painful effort. With in-
activity and idleness, every human faculty languishes and
tends to decay. To supply the body with food and clothing,
to nourish the mind with truth, to maintain the will in the
way of righteousness, to save the soul from *ennui* and
despair, to perfect and develop all his God-given powers,
labour is a first essential for man. "Man," writes Pius XI,
"is born to labour as the bird to fly."[1]

Labour Essential to Satisfy Men's Needs.—Besides, God
has assigned to man the earth and its hidden treasures, and
the living things that dwell on it to satisfy his needs.
"*Fill the earth and subdue it*,"[2] God has told him ; and
again, "*Everything that moveth and liveth shall be meat for
you ; even as the green herbs, I have delivered them all to
you.*"[3] But nature has so arranged that all these treasures
are made available for man only by human toil. Hence,
Leo XIII treating of private property and the dignity of
labour, writes :

"That which is required for the preservation of life, and for
life's well-being, is produced in great abundance from the soil ;
but not until man has brought it into cultivation, and expended
upon it his solicitude and skill."[4]

Earth's rich harvests of fruits, the mineral resources and
precious stones hidden in its depths, the living things that
people its plains and its seas, and fill the air around it, all
necessary or useful for man's life, can be obtained only by
the exercise of human intelligence, the efforts of the human

---

[1] *Quadragesimo Anno*, 1931 (C. T. S. edit.), p. 30.
[2] *Genesis*, i. 28.   [3] *Ib.*, ix. 3.   [4] *Rerum Novarum*, p. 137.

will, and the stress of bodily toil. " *In the sweat of thy brow thou shalt eat bread*,"[1] has been spoken as the universal law for all.

Even such things as poetry, music and art and the great products of human genius are each and all the fruits of long and tedious effort. No great cause ever attained success without much human suffering and toil.

Imposed as a Duty by the Christian Law.—Again and again the inspired writer denounces in the holy scriptures the folly and crime of idleness, " the mother of all vices." Thus we read in the *Book of Proverbs ;* " *Go to the ant, O sluggard, and consider her ways, and learn wisdom ; which although she hath no guide nor master nor captain, provideth meat for herself in the summer, and gathereth food for herself in the harvest. How long wilt thou sleep O sluggard ?* "[2]

The life of the Son of God on earth was one of continual labour ; and during most of that life He worked as an artisan, thereby giving by His divine example a new dignity to the manual worker's calling. The Gospel history, as interpreted by Christian tradition implies that in the home of Nazareth where the Christian ideal of domestic life was realised, everybody was busy. Consequently, no duty is more stressed in Christian teaching than that of labour. " *If any man will not work neither let him eat*," says St. Paul.[3] In the rules of all religious congregations, which the Catholic Church puts forward as containing a model of the more perfect Christian life, the obligation of constant labour and even precepts of manual work are always prominent features.

Thus, labour is a duty of every individual ; and no State can prosper in which a considerable portion of the citizens shirk their duty of work : for as Pius XI writes :

" Universal experience teaches that no nation has ever yet risen from want and poverty to a better and loftier station, without the unremitting toil of all its citizens, both employers and employed."[4]

In an organised society, composed of different social classes, the nature of the work will vary, but there is no place in the Christian State for a purely parasitical class

---

[1] *Gen.* iii. 19.   [2] *Prov.* vi. 6–9.   [3] *2 Thess.* iii. 10.
[4] *Quadragesimo Anno*, p. 25.

who live upon the labour of others without themselves making any adequate contribution to the common good.

Special Value and Dignity of Manual Labour.—The Church defends and upholds in a special way the worth and dignity of manual labour. In fact, her attitude towards manual work, its dignity and its value, is a kind of counterpart of her attitude towards the institution of private property. The great encyclical *Rerum Novarum*, of Leo XIII, which is the classical defence of private property, is also in large part a eulogy of the dignity of manual labour. The Pope insists strongly on the important place the manual worker holds in the social organism, and on the indefeasible claim which he has to the special protection and assistance of the ruling authorities. Thus he writes :

"Labour is not a thing to be ashamed of, if we lend ear to right reason and to Christian philosophy, but is to a man's credit enabling him to earn his living in an honourable way." [1]

Pius XI writes on the same matter :

"Is it not apparent that the huge possessions which constitute human wealth are begotten by and flow from the hands of the workingman, toiling either unaided or with the assistance of tools and machinery, which wonderfully intensify his efficiency ? "[2]

The exercise of manual labour is of such fundamental importance for all the best interests of the community that one must regard that nation as diseased and ripe for decay in which the practice and esteem of manual toil have been lost or are on the decline. Hence, the ruling authorities are bound to encourage and emphasise the prestige of the manual labourer's calling, and by protecting his interests encourage the younger generation to adopt manual labour as their profession in life. They should take means to multiply suitable homes for the workers with plots of land attached. The activities of speculators of all kinds which are unproductive, and which tend to lure the workers with the hopes of quick and easy gains, should be discouraged and as far as possible prohibited. Finally, in the educational system of the country every means should be adopted to inspire the children with the esteem of work and with a

---

[1] *Rerum Novarum*, p. 143.   [2] *Quadragesimo Anno*, p. 25.

due appreciation of the dignity and need of manual labour and of the solid happiness and content it brings.

Right to Opportunity of Labour.—Seeing that labour is obligatory upon all, and has been appointed by God as a necessary means for securing one's self-preservation and development, it is an obvious conclusion that all have a right to an opportunity of labour. Besides, since God has given the earth and its treasures to men that they may each and all satisfy their human needs therefrom, everyone has an inborn right to such access to the earth and its goods as is required to enable him to obtain the necessaries of life by working upon them. Consequently, if any are precluded through no fault of theirs from the exercise of that right, they are victims of injustice.[1]

Unemployment.—The modern phenomenon, called unemployment, which in reality means enforced idleness, is the product of a social system which, though not in itself necessarily vicious, has, in its working, led to gross injustice. The earth's resources are more than sufficient to supply the needs of all. They can be made available for man's needs only by labour. Multitudes who are willing and anxious to work are in want of the necessaries of life ; and are denied a fair opportunity of securing by their labour these necessaries for themselves and their families.

" Unemployment," writes Pius XI, " particularly if widespread or of long duration . . . is a dreadful scourge : it causes misery and temptation to the labourer, ruins the prosperity of nations, and endangers public peace, order and tranquillity the world over."[2]

The root of this fatal anomaly lies in the practical repudiation of the teachings of Christianity and the principles of the natural law by those who control the industrial life of the nations. For, according to these teachings and principles, economic activity should be organised with a view to provide adequately for the human needs of the population, not to minister to the avarice or ambition or luxury of the

---

[1] Cf. Brouard, *op. cit.*, pp. 7–10 ; Macksey, *op. cit.*, cap. iii.
[2] *Quadragesimo Anno*, p. 35.

few. In actual fact, however, it occurs all too commonly
that in the words of Pius XI :
  " Capital diverts business and economic activity entirely to
its own arbitrary will, without any regard to the human dignity
of the workers, the *social* character of economic life, social
justice and the common good." [1]
  Thus, the natural resources of the country are held up
and left undeveloped while the public are in want. Labour
and energy are diverted from the production of the necessaries to promote activities that are useless or even degrading.
Finance and the monetary system, which should be instruments to help and serve men, have become in large
measure the masters of men's activities, so that the
happiness and lives of multitudes are sacrificed to the
ambition or caprice of the financial rulers. It is a primary
duty of the civil authorities to check these abuses, and
secure by suitable legislation and administrative measures,
that all the citizens are afforded a fair opportunity of
securing a decent livelihood by their labour.

Art. 2—*The Right to Acquire Property*[2]

Importance of the Question.—The desire to acquire property is a fundamental instinct of human nature.
  " The practice of all ages," writes Leo XIII,[3] " has consecrated the principle of private ownership as being pre-eminently
in conformity with human nature, and as conducing in the most
unmistakable manner to the peace and tranquillity of human
existence. . . . The authority of the Divine Law adds its
sanction, forbidding us in the severest terms to covet that which
is another's : *thou shalt not covet thy neighbour's wife ; nor his
house nor his field, nor his man servant, nor his maid servant, nor
his ox, nor his ass, nor any thing that is his.*"[4]

The history of the human race proves that human personality develops best, and true liberty and independence
are realised most fully among a population of proprietors.

---

[1] *Quadragesimo Anno*, p. 45.
[2] Cf. Meyer, *op. cit.*, vol. ii, Theses xxiv, xxv ; Costa-Rosetti, *op. cit.*,
Theses 123–128 ; Donat, *op. cit.*, sec. i, chap. iv ; Kelleher—*Private Ownership* (Gill, Dublin, 1911) ; Castelein, *op. cit.*, Thesis 8 ; Ryan—*Distributive
Justice* ; Garriguet, *op. cit.*, 2ième Partie, chaps. i–ix ; *Cath. Encyclop.*,
arts. " Property," " Agrarianism," " Socialism."
[3] *Rerum Novarum*, p. 138.
[4] *Deuteronomy*, v. 21.

Hence the ideal, at which great statesmen from Solon of Athens to Leo XIII and Pius XI have aimed, is a State made up principally of flourishing and self-contained communities of small proprietors, and especially of small farmers or peasants.[1] To this ideal the Liberal economists, the financial overlords and the socialists of all shades of opinion are equally opposed.

Its Precise Meaning.—In order to understand the precise meaning of the Right of Property, the reader must have a grasp of a few preliminary ideas. To begin with, there is question only of *personal* or individual rights; such, namely, as belong to one in virtue of one's human personality. We have already referred[2] to the system of Private ownership as essential, according to mediæval teaching, for the efficient and peaceful working of society. Hence, the individual's right to acquire property is assured by what the Scholastic philosophers call the "Law of the Nations" ("*Jus Gentium* "), which ordains that the social organisations be founded on the system of Private, rather than of Communal, ownership. Our present purpose is to show that independently of social needs, prior to man's becoming a member of any civic body or being subject to social laws, he has an inborn right to acquire by occupation, labour, or otherwise, the ownership of material goods. For, as Leo XIII and Pius XI lay down in almost identical terms : " The right to possess private property is derived from nature, not from man."[3]

Meaning of Ownership.—Individual ownership may be explained as implying such a relation or connection between an individual person and certain goods that the person may not only legitimately use the goods for himself, but also within certain limits exclude all others from the use of them. Everybody has an inborn right to *use* the goods of nature for his needs, seeing that God has ordained these goods for all ; but that does not imply that any individual has an

---

[1] Cf. Shove—*The Fairy Ring of Commerce* (Birmingham Distributist League, 1930).

[2] Cf. *Supra*, chap. vi, art. i.

[3] *Rerum Novarum*, p. 159 ; cf. also Pius XI—*Quadragesimo Anno*, (C. T. S. edit., p. 20).

inborn right to the *ownership* of such goods or of any particular portion of them. So much is evident from the fact that although all men have an inborn right to the use of air and sunlight, nobody possesses or claims an *exclusive right* to any portion of them, seeing that they are unlimited in amount and incapable of being divided.

The *actual* ownership of particular property does not come directly from nature, but from some contingent fact, such as occupation, labour, or inheritance. Hence, when we assert that man has a natural, inborn right to acquire ownership, we mean that it is a natural consequence of man's personality that he should be able to establish such a connection between himself and certain external goods such as food, land, implements of labour, that in virtue of the natural law he has henceforward a *right to their exclusive use*. Apropos of this matter, St. Thomas writes :

" Community of property is said to belong to the natural law, not in the sense that the natural law prescribes that all things are to be held in common, and nothing by private ownership ; but rather in the sense that the [actual] division of property does not come from the natural law . . . consequently private ownership of property is not contrary to the natural law but is superadded to it by man's arrangement." [1]

Socialists' Theory.—Marxian Socialists, whose theories we have already discussed, while usually allowing that men may acquire valid ownership of *consumable* goods, assert that individual ownership of *productive* property is immoral and invalid. Taking occasion of the appalling abuses to which political and economic Liberalism has led, and some, no doubt, really exasperated or alarmed by the capitalists' monopolies, which in practice tend to nullify the inborn rights of great numbers of the people, the Socialist reformers propose that the ownership of all productive property should vest in the State or the municipalities or quasi-governmental bureaux. It would then be the duty of these latter to see that every individual has access to whatever may be necessary or reasonably useful for him.

Theory of Henry George.—Henry George (1839–1897), the American economist and author of the celebrated work,

---

[1] 2ª, 2æ, Q. 66, a. 2.

Progress and Poverty[1] (1879), although a vigorous opponent of Marxian Socialism, has put forward a theory concerning the ownership of land, which is sometimes called by the rather misleading term *Agrarian Socialism*. George held that the ownership of the soil belongs inalienably to the community as a whole, seeing that it was created by God for all. He will, however, allow the individual to enjoy the usufruct (with security of tenure and the right of transmitting to others) of any portion of the soil provided he pays to the community (viz., to the State) in the shape of taxes a rent representing the *natural* productivity of that particular piece of land *plus* the extra value it may have acquired owing to adventitious causes other than the labour of the occupier.

The natural productivity must be paid for (according to George), since by the divine decree it belongs inalienably to the community ; and the adventitious increase of value must be paid for, because it too belongs to the community : in most cases it is actually produced by the community which, for instance, have built a town or a railway in the neighbourhood of that piece of land, or in some other way have increased its natural value. Even should the increase in value come from some natural cause independent of the action of the community (such as the change of the course of a river caused by an earthquake or a landslide), such increase, too, belongs by right to the community. For the latter (viz., the community) is the real owner and by the natural law *res crescit domino* (the natural increase of anything is the property of its owners).

Economic Rent and the Single Tax System.—The annual amount corresponding to this natural productivity and the unearned increment of value, both of which in George's view belong essentially to the community, are called the Economic Rent. According to his theory the huge sums (£35,000,000 or thereabouts) annually paid in rent to some eight thousand British landlords, are pure class robbery, and are the fundamental source of all the misery of the labouring classes. *This Economic Rent should be taken over by the*

---

[1] Kegan Paul, London, 1883. Cf. also the edition published by Dent & Sons in " Everyman's Library " series (London and Toronto, 1921).

*State, and should take the place of all other State taxes, which
would consequently be abolished.*

The system thus advocated is consequently termed the
Single Tax System. We are not concerned here with the
Single Tax System in itself as an economic proposal which
shall be discussed later. We deal at present only with
George's principle (of which the Single Tax as a method of
taxation is in reality quite independent), that the *dominion*
of the soil belongs *inalienably* to the State and that no
individual can ever acquire such dominion by a valid title,
nor consequently ever have a just claim to the Economic
Rent.[1]

**Proofs of Man's Right to Acquire Ownership of Capital
even of Land.**—We come now to the proofs of the Catholic
doctrine. The classical treatment of this subject is to be
found in the Encyclical of Leo XIII on the Condition of
the Working Class.[2] Leo XIII establishes man's right to
acquire ownership of productive property by proofs drawn
(*a*) from man's individual nature, (*b*) from the family, and
(*c*) from consideration of the public good. We summarise
each in turn :

(*a*) **Proof from Men's Nature.**—Suppose that a man fences
in and tills a piece of land (which up to that time was wild
and was neither claimed or owned by anybody), and thus
brings it from its prairie wildness to a state of productivity
(as Robinson Crusoe is related to have done when marooned
on a lonely island). In such a case, reason and common
sense proclaim that the cultivator by thus imprinting his
personality upon the thing hitherto unowned has made it
his own. This is all the clearer since the improvements
which his labour has imparted to the land and which undoubtedly belong to the labourer, are inseparable and in
great measure indistinguishable from the land itself.[3]

---

[1] For a critique of George's theory, cf. Garriguet, *loc. cit.*, chap. ii ;
Ryan—*Distributive Justice*, chaps. iii and iv ; also *Cath. Encyclop.*, art.
" Agrarianism." For a good summary of the several systems of land
tenure (six in number) known in historical times, cf. Garriguet, *loc. cit.*,
chap. i, pp. 68–71.

[2] *Rerum Novarum*, pp. 135–139.

[3] This argument is given by Leo XIII probably as a reply to the
assertion of H. George that *first occupancy* can never be the foundation
of a valid title to ownership.

Again, suppose a worker lives sparingly, saves money from his wages, and for greater security invests his savings in land or capital of any other kind. In such case the capital is only his wages under another form ; and consequently should be as completely at his disposal as the wages themselves.

Thirdly, as we have already seen, it is by labour that man has to provide for his needs and secure his self-preservation and self-development. Now a man cannot work without material goods to exercise his activity upon ; nor can he produce wealth without the use of productive property as land, tools, and such like. It is only the Creator who can work upon nothing. Hence, the moment a man is precluded from the control of productive property, that moment he loses his personal independence. His own life, his future well-being, the interests of those that are dear to him, depend on the fiat of a bureaucracy.

This becomes clearer if we consider the nature and extent of man's needs. Unlike the lower animals, man has a rational nature, which enables him to look forward to the future. His wants are not merely those of the day. He cannot help being solicitous for the morrow ; and he feels impelled by a law of his nature to seek provision even for the distant future. This he can effectually do only through the medium of productive property.

" Men's needs," writes Leo XIII, " do not die out but for ever recur. Although satisfied to-day, they demand fresh supplies to-morrow. Nature accordingly must have given to man a source that is stable, and remaining always with him, from which he might look to draw continual supplies. And this stable condition of things he finds in the earth and its fruits."[1]

In other words, it is in accordance with man's nature and its essential needs that he should be able to become the owner of permanent productive property and especially of land.

(b) **From the Family.**—A man has a right to marry, if he so wishes, and become the father of a family ; in such case reason and instinct teach him that he is personally responsible—and the responsibility is inalienable—for the

---

[1] *Rerum Novarum*, p. 136.

the well-being of his helpless children. How can he secure a home, a competence and a secure future for those whose interests are as dear to him as his own ? These can be secured only on condition of his owning productive property. On this point again we quote the words of Leo XIII :

" For it is a most sacred law of nature that a father should provide food and all the necessaries for those whom he has begotten, and similarly it is natural that he should wish that his children, who, so to speak, carry on and continue his personality, should be by him provided with all that is needed to enable them to keep themselves decently from want and misery amid the uncertainties of this mortal life. Now in no way can a father effect this except by the ownership of productive property, which he can transmit to his children by inheritance." [1]

The truth of this reasoning we see exemplified in the Soviet State of Russia, in which the prohibition of the private ownership of capital has carried with it the break up of the natural family organisation and the sundering of the family ties. The children in Soviet Russia are by law no longer dependents of the father but of the State. The deplorable results of this unnatural system we have already seen.

(c) **From Consideration of the Public Good.**[2]—The absorption by the State of the ownership of all productive property would dry up the sources of wealth by removing the most powerful incentives to effort and labour. For in such a system men would have little or no interest in exercising their talents or energy. Besides, it would throw open the door to envy and endless discord, and introduce confusion and disorder into the Commonwealth.

Reply to Opponents.—Henry George's main argument against the validity of private ownership of land, viz., that God gave the earth for the use and enjoyment of all, is easily answered. Every one, indeed, has an inborn right to a fair opportunity of getting a decent livelihood from the earth. The question is how can that right be best secured to each. Is it through private ownership or by

---

[1] *Rerum Novarum*, p. 139.
[2] This argument, which has already been given in treating of the mediæval Economic doctrines (chap. vi, article 1) proves a social right rather than a personal right.

20

some species of communal ownership, or by a due inter-mingling of both according to the Catholic tradition ? We have already shown that God's decree, by which all have the right of living from the earth's bounty, is best secured by the system of private ownership, limited as to use by obligations of Social Justice and Charity, and supplemented by a subsidiary system of communal organisation and communal reservation.

Art. 3—*Christian Concept of Property Rights*

" There are some," writes Pius XI, " who falsely and unjustly accuse the Supreme Pontiff and the Church as upholding . . . the wealthier classes against the proletariat . . . and launch against the Church the odious calumny that she has allowed a pagan concept of ownership to creep into the teachings of her theologians, and that another concept must be substituted which in their astounding ignorance they call Christian." [1]

How false and ill-informed are the assertions and accusa-tions, to which the Supreme Pontiff here alludes, is clear from a study of the activities and traditional attitude of the Church in favour of the poor and oppressed, which have been outlined in the First Part of this work. The calumny is founded upon a one-sided and inadequate presentation of the Church's teaching.

Two-fold Aspect of Ownership.—The Catholic teaching on the rights of ownership does not imply that one has a natural right to acquire property to an unlimited extent, or that one has *unlimited* rights as to *use* over the property one owns. A man has, indeed, a natural right to what he may lawfully acquire by his personal labour. [2] Furthermore, no authority may prevent him from obtaining by just means what is required for his present and future needs, including the needs of a family. But beyond these limits the rights he may claim rest upon social laws, whether natural or positive, which themselves are founded on consideration of the public good.

---

[1] *Quadragesimo Anno*, pp. 20, 21.

[2] If a man works as his own master on material of which he is himself the owner, he manifestly has a right to whatever new form or value is thereby produced; if he works as the employee of another and on material which another owns he has a right to a just wage for his toil. See *infra*, chap. xxi, art. 3.

There are, besides, certain limitations to the lawful use of property rights, acknowledged by all recognised Catholic authorities, and implied in the principles already laid down. These limitations (which we have already touched on in dealing with mediæval economic teaching),[1] rest upon the rights of all to acquire property for their necessary use, and on the general decree of Providence assigning the goods of nature for all men's needs. In other words, ownership in the Christian conception has a twofold aspect, namely, the *individual* aspect which refers to the rights of the individual owner, and the *social* aspect, which concerns the common good.

" The right to acquire property," writes Pius XI, " has been given to man by nature, or rather by the Creator Himself, not only to enable individuals to provide for their own needs and those of their families, but also in order to secure by that means that the goods which the Creator has destined for the human race may truly serve this purpose. There is therefore a double danger to be avoided . . . if the social and public aspect of ownership be denied or minimised the logical consequence is *individualism :* on the other hand, the rejection or diminution of its private and individual character necessarily leads to some form of *collectivism* [viz., Socialism]."[2]

We have already discussed the error of Collectivism or Socialism, which comes from disregarding the private and individual aspect of the natural right of ownership. It remains now to treat briefly of the other and opposite error which is rooted in the denial or practical disregard of the social and public aspect which is equally essential to the true and Christian concept of property rights.

Contrasted with Pagan and Liberal View.—In the First Part of the present work[3] we have dealt briefly with the contrast between the old pagan view of property rights and the conception of ownership first introduced into Roman society under the influence of Christian teaching : and more fully developed later on in the Christian states of mediæval Europe. Ownership under the old Roman law implied absolute and irresponsible control, which would include a right of abuse as well as of enjoyment and use. In the

---

[1] Chap. vi, art. 1.   [2] *Quadragesimo Anno*, pp. 20, 21.
[3] Cf. *Supra*, chaps. i and ii, and chap. v, art. 1.

Christian law ownership is understood in a different way. The human owner is not the absolute master ; but is regarded as the administrator of a Supreme Owner ; and hence the powers of the human proprietor are essentially limited and hedged round by the eternal laws of God. These latter are usually summarised under the heading of Justice, Charity and Piety ; which we shall discuss more fully later on.

Christian Feudal Law.—When the Roman Empire became Christian in the 4th and 5th centuries A.D., the old Roman law regarding property and civic rule, was considerably modified, especially in its administration and application owing to the influence of the Church ; but in many particulars the old *written* code remained unchanged, still retaining a large measure of its pagan character.

The new states of Europe which came into being after the break up of the Western Empire in the 5th and 6th centuries had developed each its own legal system which, however, remained for many centuries in a rather crude state. These systems were founded partly on the Roman law, partly on the old Teutonic customs of each nation, and to a very considerable extent on the feudal customs and law which grew up in Europe after the 7th century. But the whole system or systems of European law of this period were profoundly influenced in all details by Christian principles. For it was under the guidance of the Catholic Church that these nations were being gradually civilised. Hence, Christianity may be said to be the soul of the mediæval law of feudal Europe.[1]

Supplanted by Roman Law.—From the beginning of the 14th century, however, a strong movement began (owing largely to the influence of the French legists or jurists) to unify the European laws ; to abolish the feudal customs ; and to make the Roman law the prevailing type. Among the manifestations of this tendency are the increasing despotism of the rulers and the growing absolutism in the ideas of ownership.[2] This movement was powerfully strengthened by the pagan tendencies associated with the Renaissance ;

---

[1] Cf. Meyer et Ardant—*La Question Agraire* (Paris, 1887), vol. ii, Introduction.
[2] Cf. Mourret, *op. cit.*, vol. v., chap. ii.

and it reached its acme after the Protestant revolt, which sowed the seeds of modern Liberalism and Capitalism. Hence it is that many principles and ideas which are current in modern European states regarding property rights are fundamentally opposed to the teaching and principles of Christianity. Thus, of the several systems of land tenure known in different parts of Europe in historical times, the modern individualistic system, which exempts ownership of land from all responsibility to the community, is the only one recognised by the modern Liberal economists. In the individualistic system the proprietor is regarded as the complete and irresponsible master of the estate, no matter how extensive it may be. He can hand it over to the control of a foreign syndicate if he so wills ; can work it or allow it to lie untilled or altogether idle according to his good pleasure. Such a concept of the ownership of the landed property of the country was quite foreign to the economic principles of mediæval times. It is unchristian and unnatural. It has never been admitted by the Church ; and, although nominally upheld in some instances by civil law, has never been consistently followed out in practice.[1]

Limitations and Duties Attaching to Property Rights.[2]— The limitations and responsibilities which attach to property rights, and especially to the ownership of land, are rooted in the prerogatives of human personality, in man's subordination to the Divine Law, and in the natural institution and purposes of civil society already summarised.[3]   As

---

[1] Cf. Garriguet, *loc. cit.*, pp. 197–203.

[2] The doctrine stated here on the nature of private ownership, which is that of Leo XIII, Pius XI, St. Thomas, and of all " those theologians who have taught under the guidance and direction of the Catholic Church " (Pius XI, *Quadragesimo Anno*, p. 20), must be carefully distinguished from the theory put forward by the School of Saint Simon, Comte and others, who have apparently been followed in this matter by Gide and a few other Catholic authors.   According to this latter theory the individual's right or claim rests *solely* upon the needs and interest of the community or State, which is the *real owner*, and which commits to individuals the rôle of exploiting and administering a certain portion of the goods of the earth, as the most effective means of utilising them for the needs of all. Cf. Gide—*Political Economy*, book iii, chap. i, sec. iii, pp. 461, 462.   The theory is vague and dangerous and is opposed to the doctrine already proved of an *inborn natural right* to acquire property.   Cf. Garriguet, *loc. cit.*, chap. viii.

[3] Chap. vi, art. 1.

these will be dealt with again more fully under the heading of Justice and Charity, we here touch only on a few points of special relevancy to our present purpose.

Rights of ownership cease or are over-ridden in face of the superior right of another to preserve his life or safeguard interests which are regarded as belonging to the same category as life. Again, the principle that " one may do as he likes with his own," understood as including the right to use one's property for other than reasonable needs, is contrary to Christian teaching.[1]

The prerogatives of ownership are also limited or set off at least in regard to what is known as superfluous goods by the duties of Charity and Piety. Finally, rights of ownership (in regard again to superfluous goods) are subject to obligations of Legal Justice. Hence, should the public good require it, the State has the power and sometimes a duty to over-ride vested rights in regard to superfluous goods, and especially to prevent the natural resources of the country being withheld from the people by owners who are unwilling to develop them.[2]

Another Aspect of Man's Natural Right to Acquire Property.—From the right which men have from nature (and which human law cannot justly or validly take away) to acquire private property, a further inference of far-reaching importance must be drawn. It is not alone under a socialist or communist régime that men's natural right to acquire ownership may be violated. This is done no less effectually in a social system in which immense multitudes, while *nominally and legally* free to become owners, are in practice *excluded from the moral possibility* of doing so. Thus, if the bulk of the productive property of a country (land, mines, fisheries, waterways, wharves, etc.) is under the control of a comparatively small section, who do not or cannot exploit it, or worse still, is controlled by persons or syndicates belonging to another country, the result often is that the bulk of the people, or a large section

---

[1] Garriguet, *loc. cit.*, pp. 192, 193.

[2] Cf. Garriguet, *op. cit.*, chaps. viii and ix, especially pp. 199–203 ; *see* also *infra*, chap. xxv, art. 3, for an account of the drastic action of the Popes in dealing with the uncultivated ranches of the great landowners in the Papal States. Cf. also Meyer—*Institutiones Juris Naturalis*, pars. ii, nn. 220–224.

of them, are practically excluded from the possibility of becoming independent owners. Such an economic system is out of harmony with Christian principles.

Hence, the right which every individual has to a *fair chance of acquiring property by his honest labour*, and of thus realising an independence becoming his human dignity must not alone be recognised in *law* as against the Socialists' theories, but should be made secure in *fact* against the monopolies of the overgrown capitalist, the rancher, or the financial magnate. Consequently, Catholic teaching, which has always upheld the right of private ownership, also insists on the poor man's claim to a fair opportunity of actuating that right. Thus Leo XIII, after proving man's right to private ownership, goes on to say :

" The law therefore should favour ownership, and its policy should be to induce as many as possible of the people to become owners. Many excellent results will follow from this; and first of all property will certainly become more equitably distributed. . . .

" If the working people can be encouraged to look forward to obtaining a share in the land, the consequence will be that the gulf between vast wealth and sheer poverty will be bridged over and the respective classes brought nearer to each other.

" A further advantage will be a greater abundance of the earth's fruits. . . . And a third advantage would spring from this ; men would cling to the country in which they were born : for no one would exchange his country for a foreign land if his own afforded him the means of decent living and a happy home."[1]

The social anomalies and injustice which the capitalist régime in its present form involves are not only oppressive but are now recognised as the main element of the danger which at present threatens the stability of social order. It is only by removing the injustice through a wide distribution of the land and other natural sources of wealth and by the fostering of religious influence that the danger can be averted.

Art. 4—*Right to Personal Freedom*[2]

Its Nature and Limitations.—Seeing that man's end and purpose in life concern only himself and his Creator, and

---

[1] *Rerum Novarum*, p. 159.
[2] Castelein, *op. cit.*, Thesis 5 ; Meyer, *op. cit.*, pars. ii, nn. 85–87 ; Cuthbert, *op. cit.*, pp. 1–21.

that in personal dignity all men are equal, there is no reason
in the nature of things why one man should have a right
to interfere with another's freedom of action. Hence,
everyone has a natural right to order his life in his own
way, as long as he observes God's law and does not violate
the rights of others. In some cases, however, as already
pointed out, the exercise of this freedom may be limited,
when the public good requires ; although such limitations
cannot apply to the exercise of such rights as are perfect
or inalienable.

The reason why, in some cases, the public need may over
ride natural rights is not far to seek. The rights or needs
of society are founded on the rights of the individuals that
compose it ; and when one man's right of freedom clashes
with the collective rights of other members of the community, it is reasonable that the stronger and more urgent
claim should prevail. Hence, although no social needs can
be strong enough to rob the individual of such rights as his
right to his own life (which is indefeasible as long as he is
innocent of crime), or his right to liberty of conscience,[1]
or, at least in normal circumstances, his right to acquire
property, there are some other natural rights to which
limitations may legitimately be set. As the right of freedom
in choosing one's work and one's state of life is especially
important in this connection, we will treat briefly of a few
matters relating to these points.

Liberty in the Choice of a State of Life.—The question as
to whether one is to marry or not ; whether one is to serve
God and seek one's happiness and perfection amid ordinary
secular pursuits, or by following the evangelical counsels in
the priesthood or the religious life, is a question whose
decision dominates almost every activity of one's whole
life ; and is closely bound up with one's most intimate
personal interests. Hence, freedom of choice in such matters
is the individual's inalienable right.

---

[1] As the conscience of each one is his natural guide, no one may be
forced to act against it. If, however, an external act or omission, which
is dictated by a *false* conscience, violates the rights of others, it may be
prevented, or even punished, by public authority, even though the person
misled by the false conscience be quite honest and sincere in his convictions. Cf. Meyer, *ib.*, nn. 88–90 ; also Devas—*Key to the World's
Progress*, chap. vii.

" In choosing a state of life," writes Leo XIII,[1] " it is indisputable that all are at liberty to follow the counsel of Jesus Christ as to observing virginity, or to bind themselves by the marriage tie. No human law can abolish the natural and original right of marriage, nor in any way limit the chief and principal purpose of marriage ordained by God's authority from the beginning. *Increase and multiply.*" [2]

For the legitimate exercise of the right, the person must of course have reached an age when he or she is capable of making a prudent choice. One is bound also to give due consideration to the counsels of those who are one's natural advisers and guardians, and to any claims of justice or piety that should influence one's choice. But when the young man or woman has reached the proper age, any undue interference from outside with his or her freedom of choice in the matter of marriage or of selecting a state of life, is a violation of personal rights.

It is not, indeed, beyond the competence of the civil authority, should the public interest make it advisable, to accord special privileges to married people, such as special facilities to acquire land, exemption from certain taxes, etc., and, on the other hand, to subject bachelors to certain legal disabilities or to a larger share of the public burdens such as taxes or military service. Such measures may be quite equitable, and even desirable, in view of the fact that those who bring up children to be future citizens are fulfilling a most useful and necessary public function, which the others are not doing. For similar reasons and with a view to check selfishness and extravagance and to foster the domestic virtues, it may be desirable to graduate the salaries paid to public functionaries in accordance with their domestic responsibilities. But, for the State to attempt to enforce or prevent marriage in normal circumstances would be an unwarranted interference with personal freedom and a violation of inalienable personal rights.

Eugenics. [3]—The so-called science or theories of " Eugenics " must be touched on in this connection, Eugenics may be

---

[1] *Rerum Novarum* (1891), p. 138.   [2] *Gen.* i. 28.
[3] On the whole subject of Eugenics, cf. *Cath. Encyclop.* (Index vol.) ; also Davis, S.J.—*Eugenics* (Burns & Oates, London, 1930) ; Gerrard— *The Church and Eugenics* (C. S. G., 1921) ; Bruehl—*Birth Control and Eugenics* (Wagner, New York, 1928)—an excellent and comprehensive treatment of the subject.

defined as " the study of agencies under social control that
may improve or injure the racial qualities of future generations either physically or mentally." The Eugenic movement took its rise in England in the last quarter of the 19th
century, being mainly promoted by the writings and efforts
of Sir Francis Galton (1822–1911), a friend and relative of
Charles Darwin (1802–1882), author of the *Origin of Species*
(1860). The methods of the Eugenists are scientific research, propaganda and legislation. As a result of the
movement in U.S.A., laws have been passed in very many
of the States enforcing, for various classes of defectives,
artificial sterilisation, segregation, or prohibition of marriage.
These laws, however, have usually been left a dead letter,
or soon fallen into desuetude.

Church's Attitude towards Eugenics.—The science of
Eugenics in itself and in so far as it is a true science, is
quite in accord with Catholic principles. " The Catholic
Church," says a contemporary writer on this subject, " is
in favour of a healthy life, healthy offspring, clean living,
temperate habits, continence before marriage, temperance
in marital relations, care of the pregnant mother, elimination
of venereal diseases and of alcoholism, improvement of the
slums, avoidance of over-crowding and of the scandalous
herding together of growing children, suitable conditions of
labour, appropriate work for women and children, who
have to work, and, in fact, of everything else not contrary
to moral principles, which an enlightened people through
its government or municipal councils aims at securing for
the community. All this is eugenical in the best sense,
and in its highest degree."[1]

If the Church's laws (which are in the main only a re-
assertion or application of the natural law) were generally
observed, as they would be in a really Christian society,
the problems with which the modern Eugenist strives to
deal would be already practically solved, or would not arise
to any great extent. The Church's methods, however,
demand a measure of self-restraint which the spirit of an
unchristian public opinion is opposed to or despairs of
realising.

---

[1] Davis, S.J., *op. cit.*, p. 59.

Another source of the disagreement between the Church and the non-Christian Eugenist is rooted in the fact that the Church makes bodily health and mental culture *subservient* to the moral law and to man's spiritual interests. Hence, she will not even for an assured, and much less for a problematic, social or temporal advantage approve of any measure that may be harmful to one's eternal or spiritual welfare.

And Towards the Special Methods Proposed.—Regarding some of the methods advocated by modern eugenists the following may be said :

I. It has always been the common teaching of Catholic theologians that it would be a violation of inalienable personal rights, and, therefore, immoral and unjust to enforce for the good or convenience of others mutilation or sterilization on one who though mentally or physically defective is guilty of no crime. Besides, seeing that only a small fraction of the defective are born of defective parents, sterilization would do little to check the increase of the defective. This teaching has been authoritatively confirmed by Pius XI in his recent Encyclical on Christian Marriage :

" Public magistrates have no direct power over the bodies of their subjects. Therefore, when no crime has taken place and there is present no cause for grave punishment, they can never directly harm or tamper with the integrity of the body either for the reason of Eugenics or for any other cause. . . . Furthermore, Christian doctrine establishes, and the light of reason makes it most clear, that private individuals have no other power over the members of their own bodies than that which pertains to their natural ends ; and they are not free to destroy or mutilate their members, or in any other way render them unfit for their natural functions except when no other provision can be made for the good of the whole body." [1]

II. Some Catholic authors were of opinion that segregation of the unfit and defective in suitable homes would be permissible, on the ground that one's personal freedom may be limited when the public good requires it, and that such persons being quite unfit to fulfil the duties of parents could

---

[1] *Casti Connubii* (1930), p. 33 (London, C. T. S. booklet, entitled *Christian Marriage*).

not lawfully marry. This doctrine, however, has been authoritatively rejected by Pius XI, who writes :

" The family is more sacred than the State, and men are begotten not for the earth or for time, but for heaven and eternity. Although often these individuals are to be dissuaded from entering into matrimony, certainly it is wrong to brand men with the stigma of crime because they contract marriage on the ground that despite the fact that they are in every way capable of matrimony, they will give birth only to defective children even though they use all care and diligence." [1]

III. The method of dealing with the defective which the Church most strongly favours is what may be described as " Socialisation." It refers only to cases in which the defectives are capable of being trained so as to become self-supporting. Suitable homes are provided in which they are educated under religious influences, and in accordance with the ideals of family life. They are allowed to return to the ordinary life of the community, when they can live and earn their livelihood with their own people.

Freedom in Choice of Work.—Freedom in the choice of one's work is also closely connected with one's temporal and spiritual interests. Hence, as the individual alone is responsible for these interests, he has the natural right to choose the type of work to which he will devote himself. As this matter, however, does not affect one's life so deeply as the preceding, the individual's right to complete freedom of choice is not ordinarily considered perfect or absolutely inalienable. But to what extent public authority may justly override the natural right is often difficult to decide in concrete cases.

That the State could as an ordinary policy arrange the profession and work of its members, as one school of Socialists propose, would certainly be an unwarranted violation of individual rights. That the State could do so, temporarily on occasion of severe public stress, as in time of a defensive war or a plague, few would deny. That certain sections of the community, such as the slaves in the early Christian states or the serfs in mediæval Europe, who were bound to the soil (*adscripti glebæ*) should be compelled, as they

---

[1] *Casti Connubii* (1930), p. 33 (London, C. T. S. booklet, entitled *Christian Marriage*).

were by the fact of their slavery or serfdom, to follow professions not of their own choosing, is not in accordance with Christian ideals.

Slavery and Serfdom.—Nevertheless, owing to the peculiar social needs in the early Christian times, and afterwards in mediæval Europe (needs which were a heritage from the previous non-Christian social system), a mitigated slavery and serfdom had to be tolerated for the time being ; and the individual's natural claim to freedom of choice in work had to yield to the exigencies of the public good.

Attitude of the Church.—The Church, while exhorting the slaves and serfs to obey existing laws, always insisted that their inalienable rights be safeguarded, and that they be not subjected to any inhuman or over-oppressive conditions. Hence, she never approved, nor even tolerated, absolute slavery of the type that prevailed in Europe in pre-Christian times. Such slavery implies disregard of men's inalienable rights, and is essentially unjust and immoral.[1]   In mediæval slavery, on the other hand, at least in the circumstances in which it was tolerated by the Church, the essential personal rights of the slave population were safeguarded,[2] and in

---

[1] Cf. *Supra*, chaps. i and ii.

[2] The attitude of some of the great mediæval theologians such as St. Thomas, Scotus, Albertus Magnus and others, towards slavery has given rise to discussion and some misunderstanding.   On this matter the following may be said with certainty :

(a) The slavery (*servitus*) of which these authors treat is not slavery in the modern and usual sense, but mediæval serfdom in which the serf (*servus*) enjoys all his essential personal rights.

(b) They definitely reject the doctrine of Aristotle (revived by some modern philosophers) that men differ in *essential dignity of nature* and that some are born to be the slaves of others,   For, as St. Thomas says : " One man is not intended by nature for the good of another as the end and purpose of his existence " (" *Unus homo natura sua non ordinatur ad alterum sicut ad finem* " in IV *Sent.*, dist. 44, Q. 1, a. 33 c).

(c) They do assert, however, that it is in accordance with the natural order and with men's different characters and abilities that some command and others obey, that some rule and others serve ; but they imply that the rights of ruling and commanding must be exercised for the good of the subject and not of the master.

(d) They definitely allow serfdom (*servitus*) in certain cases, viz., if the *servus* freely consents, or if the state of *servitus* is imposed in punishment of crime.   They hesitate and are not in agreement as to whether a victor in a just war can justly reduce captive enemies to this state. (Cf. *Dict. Apolog. de la Foi Catholique*, art. " Esclavage," cols. 1495–1496 ; also *Studies*, vol. 9 (1920), pp. 15 ff, in an article by Professor A. O'Rahilly, entitled " Democracy of St. Thomas ").

proportion as the nations came more fully under the influence
of Christian principles the lot of the slaves improved ; so
much so that when they reached the stage of serfdom their
condition was very much better than the conditions of large
sections of the poorer classes in present-day Europe and
America. Meanwhile, however, the Church worked un-
ceasingly for their complete emancipation.

Results of Her Influence.—The disappearance of serfdom
from Europe was due almost entirely, as we have already
seen, to the influence of the Catholic Church. On the other
hand, serfdom reappeared during the 16th century in
Germany, Sweden and Denmark, as a result of the Protestant
revolt.

After the discovery of the New World, slavery was
partially revived. Large numbers of the native Indian
population were reduced to slavery ; and an inhuman traffic
in African Negro slaves was carried on, in which England,
Spain, France and Portugal participated. The Catholic
Church never ceased to protest against the immoral practice,
and, wherever her influence prevailed, slavery gradually
disappeared.[1]

Conscription Laws.—As to whether the conscription laws
of modern European states can be reconciled with men's
inalienable rights the following may be said : These laws,
in as far as they impose compulsory military service upon
the men of the State, are founded upon pagan precedent,
and are abhorrent to the spirit of Christianity. The modern
conscription laws (which date from the period of the French
Revolution) and the political ideals that have given rise
to them, are an outcome of the revolt against the Church
in the 16th century and the subsequent spread of non-
Christian philosophy in Europe. It is clear that these laws
tend to override men's personal rights in matters of the
highest importance. Man's natural right to free choice of
work and to personal liberty of action is suspended, and
other rights still more sacred are violated or endangered.
Besides, owing to the immense power which the conscription
laws put into the hands of a bureaucracy, one can easily

---

[1] Cf. *supra*, chap. vii, art. 2, for references and fuller details.

understand how almost every human right of the individual citizen is imperilled.

Hence it seems certain, from the principles already laid down, that compulsory military service could be justified only in circumstances which would make compulsion absolutely essential for the safety of the State. Such circumstances may arise in a country on occasion of a *necessary war of defence*, or the *certain* danger of such a war. Given such circumstances, it is not clear, notwithstanding the extreme nature of the measure, that compulsory military service for *defence of one's own country* is unlawful or unjust, when all other means have failed.

The reason is that the destruction of the liberty or independence of a nation by a foreign power is a calamity of such colossal magnitude, bringing invariably in its wake a whole train of degrading evils, that the nation's right to freedom from foreign aggression is strong enough to outweigh any individual rights that are not clearly inalienable.[1]

---

[1] Cf. Meyer, *op. cit.*, nn. 617–620 ; Donat, *op. cit.*, sect. iii, cap. v, art. 7 ; Costa-Rosetti, *op. cit.*, Thesis 165, pp. 680 ff.

CHAPTER XVIII

The family in its wider signification means an assemblage of individuals, dwelling in the same house under a common superior or head, and united by ties founded on the natural law. In this sense, the family is a composite society, which may be composed, at least potentially, in all or any of three ways—the union, namely, of husband and wife, of parents and children, and of master and servants.

The foundation of the family is the union of husband and wife, and, as a consequence of this union, the duties and rights of parents and children. The relations of the head of the family with others who may form a portion of the household, such as servants, are on a different plane, and have not the same intimate connection with the fundamental needs of man. Hence, we shall first of all discuss the essential elements of family life, namely, husband, wife, and children. But as the relations between masters and servants are also founded upon the natural law, and usually constitute an important factor in the social organism, we shall treat of these in a separate chapter.

Art. 1—*General Principles*[1]

The State a Union of Families.—Although the individual is the fundamental unit in the State, as in all human associations, it is not of individuals as such that the State is immediately composed. Between the individual and the State the family comes in as an intermediary unit. The State is essentially a union of families, for being a permanent organisation it must, in its essential constitution, provide for its own continuance, which, according to the natural law, can be realised only through the medium of the family. If individual persons sometimes form direct units in the

---

[1] Cf. *Cath. Encyclop.*, art. " Family " ; *Dict. Apologetique de la Foi Catholique*, art. " Famille " ; Devas—*Political Economy*, bk. i, chap. viii ; and *Studies of Family Life*, part ii.

social organism, as occurs in the case of men and women who do not happen to be members of a family, this is an accidental circumstance, and such cases are comparatively few.

In a properly organised State there will, it is true, exist other intermediary combinations, such as the parish, the municipality or the province, but these latter are not absolutely essential like the family unit, without which the continuance or, indeed, the existence of the State is impossible.

Family Prior to State.—The family, like the individual, is prior to the State. It comes into being in response to human needs and tendencies that are more urgent and more deeply rooted in human nature, and more necessary to all the best interests of the individual and the race than the needs for which the State has immediately to provide.

" The family," writes Leo XIII, " is a society limited, indeed, in numbers, but no less a true society, anterior to every kind of State or nation, invested with rights and duties of its own, totally independent of the civil community . . . governed by a power within its limits, that is, the father."[1]

Functions of the State in Its Regard.—Hence, generally speaking, the functions of the civil power are concerned directly and immediately with the family, and not with individuals as such. The State cannot interfere in any way with the unity and integrity of the family, nor override any of the essential obligations of domestic life, nor usurp the functions which the natural law has assigned to the parents. Any action of the governing power in violation of those principles would be tyrannical and invalid ; and laws tending, even directly or remotely, to the prejudice of domestic interests are opposed to the primary duty of the civil power.

On this subject Leo XIII writes :

" The contention that the civil government should, at its option, intrude into and exercise intimate control over the family is a great and pernicious error. True, if the family finds itself in exceeding distress . . . it is right that extreme necessity be met by public aid, since each family is a part of the common-

---

[1] *Rerum Novarum*, pp. 139–140.

21

wealth. In like manner, if, within the precincts of the house-hold, there should occur grave disturbance of mutual rights, public authority should intervene to force each party to yield to the other its proper due ; for this is not to deprive citizens of their rights, but to safeguard and strengthen them. But the rulers of the State must go no further : here nature bids them stop." [1]

When the governing power of the State keeps in view only individual interests, ignoring those of the family, the invariable result is a tendency, more or less strong, towards the weakening of the family and the disintegration of family life. This is one of the worst dangers now threatening European civilisation. The purpose of the civil law must be to secure as far as possible that family ties are kept strong and vigorous ; that the laws ordained by the Author of nature be allowed to function with efficiency and ease ; and that all avoidable temptation to the violation of them be removed.

Healthy Family Life Essential to the State.—Although the family is not meant primarily for the good of the State, nor can its essential interests be made subservient to any supposed public good, it is true, nevertheless, that the public good is best promoted by securing and safeguarding domestic life. For the family is to society what the heart and lungs and digestive organs are to the living body. Where family life is pure and domestic ties strong, the condition of the body politic is fundamentally sound, and such weaknesses and irregularities as may creep in can be remedied with comparative ease. But if family life be once undermined, everything in the social organism goes wrong, and the nation is on the road to decay.

(a) For the Family is the Nursing Ground of the Citizens.—The family is, in fact, the source from which come all the elements that go to form the State, and ensure its strength and stability. A citizen—man or woman—is not, like the lower animals, equipped for life as the result merely of generation and birth. One cannot become an active member of society till many years after being born. Years of patient nursing and training and the exercise of ceaseless

---

[1] *Rerum Novarum*, p. 139.

care and endless love and sympathy are required to bring
out the latent possibilities of the human faculties and fit the
person for the duties of citizenship. These needs can be
met only in the home, and in the bosom of the human
family. Hence Leo XIII writes :

" Each Christian family presents a likeness of the heavenly
home ; and the wondrous benefits thence resulting are not
limited simply to the family circle, but spread abroad abundantly
over the State at large."[1]

And in another place the same Pontiff writes :

" When domestic society is fashioned in the mould of Christian
life, each member will gradually grow accustomed to the love
of religion and piety, to the abhorrence of false and harmful
teaching, to the pursuit of virtue, to obedience to elders, and
to the restraint of that insatiable seeking after self-interest alone,
which so spoils and weakens the character of man."[2]

(b) And the School of the Civic Virtues.—Again, the family
is the training-ground of all the social and moral virtues.
" It is," as the Protestant writer, Lessing, has expressed it,
" the school founded by God Himself for the education of
the human race." Justice, charity, patriotism, which are
the bonds of social life, depend for their vigour, and almost
for their existence, upon the teaching of the home, and upon
fidelity to domestic duties. The example given within the
family circle of domestic affection and solicitude for the
rights and interests of others will bear its natural fruit in
the broader sphere of social relations ; while the qualities of
obedience, self-restraint, generosity, courage, discipline,
fidelity to duty, gentleness of manners, all of which go to
make up the character of the worthy citizen, are best
acquired in the home, and can scarcely be otherwise
obtained.

Again, the family is the depository of the local and national
traditions of the people, and the ordinary channel through
which these are passed on from generation to generation.
Love of country is thus the natural development of love
of home.[3]

---

[1] *Apostolici Muneris*, 1878, p. 19.   [2] *Inscrutabili*, p. 9.
[3] *Dict. Apolog.*, *loc. cit.*, cols. 1874, 1875.

(*c*) **And the Mainstay of a Sound Economic System.**—
Finally, even from the economic standpoint the help of the
family organism is practically indispensable for the prosperity of the State. The average man will put forth his
best endeavours in productive work only under the pressure
of domestic responsibilities. Besides, everyone interested
in economic matters is aware that the best and most efficient
work is usually done through family co-operation; and,
above all, by the multitude of small proprietors, where
almost every member of the household, old and young, contributes his or her share to the promotion of the family
business or profession.

Hence, to bring about the final ruin of a State, it is not
enough to overthrow a government, or to destroy the material
goods of the people, or to bring the nation under a foreign
yoke ; for governments return, and wealth can be again
restored by labour, and even a foreign usurper may in time
be driven out. But if family ties be once loosened, or the
mass of the people forget their reverence for domestic
obligations ; if homesteads are recklessly broken up, all
the best interests of the State will suffer ; industry will flag ;
the population will begin to fall off ; patriotism will languish ;
the young, no longer fashioned in a pure home to the discipline of justice, obedience and self-restraint will grow into
a generation ready to break through all social obligations.

Notable Examples of the Christian Family.—In Devas's
Studies of Family Life, published in 1886, may be read descriptions of domestic life, both Christian and non-Christian,
as it was to be found in several countries of Europe and
America in the second half of the 19th century.[1] The
author gives pathetic and depressing accounts of family
life as it existed at the time in places where religious faith
and practice had ceased. The examples of the non-
Christian family are taken from among the French peasantry,
the English labouring class, and the Americans of the United
States.[2] The types he describes are unfortunately much
more widespread now than they were fifty years ago ; and
the worst and most depressing features of his descriptions—

---

[1] Devas's sketches are founded mainly upon Le Play's great work,
Les Ouvriers Européens, already referred to (chap. xv, art. 2).
[2] *Op. cit.,* part ii.

the degrading immorality, the absence of piety and affection, and the human misery—are more pronounced than when Devas wrote. Omitting these, however, we transcribe two extracts containing descriptions of family life as it appears under the guidance of strong religious influences :

" Who, for example, has not heard of Ireland, and how there a vast population, suffering the extremities of economic and political oppression . . . showed a shining example of Christian family life, sins of the flesh being scarcely known among them, the reverence for parents and dutiful care for their brethren being universal. Nor were these virtues the product of the race, or of the land, but of religion. . . . The same race when transplanted among the After-Christian[1] population of English and American cities, frequently lose in a single generation the characteristics of chastity and dutifulness. . . ."

Another example of admirable family life is taken from Mexico (in 1870), which the author describes as a "land of mixed races and revolutions," where "if family life is good the goodness can only be ascribed to religious influence."

" As a rule the control of parents over their children never fully ceases save with death, and after death their memory is cherished, it seems to me, with more fondness than elsewhere in the world. . . . The children in Mexico strike you with surprise and admiration. You see no idle, vicious, saucy boys running around on the streets, annoying decent people by their vile language and rude behaviour. . . . I never saw a badly-behaved child in Mexico. In the family circle the people are models for the world. The young *always* treat the old with the deepest respect, and the affection displayed by parents for their children, and children for their parents, is most admirable. . . . The same causes have produced in many other lands and races the same effects. . . . Where the Christian religion is practised in its integrity, the reader will find the Christian family flourishing, as in Ireland and in Mexico, with its two great characteristics of chastity and dutifulness."[2]

In another work, the same author gives several examples borrowed from Le Play's monographs, of these typical Christian families, among the Catholic Hungarians, the

---

[1] The term "After-Christian" is used by Devas in reference to the nations that were once Catholic but have lost their faith.
[2] *Ib.*, pp. 175-177.

Rhinelanders, the Basques, the Tuscans, and the French. Of these latter he writes :

" Let France, conspicuous to-day as the sad parent of the After-Christians, give an example from her brighter past. . . . M. de Ribbe in his book on the families of France in the olden times . . . has found (from hitherto unpublished family records) in the 15th, 16th and 17th centuries a deeply religious spirit among rich and poor, filial piety, parental devotion, reverence to the mother and the widowed mother, the traditions of the past handed down from one generation to another, a family house for poor as well as for rich (not a lodging or a tenement), cultivation of the intellect among women as well as men, charity to the poor, edifying deaths, pious legacies (notably there were foundations in almost every village to enable poor girls to marry), wills a source of union, not of disputes, peace among brethren ; in a word, the Christian family."[1]

Duty of State to Protect and Assist the Family.[2]—From all that has been so far said it follows that a first duty of the State in providing for the common good is to protect and strengthen family life.

" Those who have the care of the State," writes Pius XI, " and of the common good cannot neglect the needs of married people without bringing great harm upon the State and upon the common welfare. . . . Not only in those things which regard temporal goods is it the concern of public authority that proper provision be made for matrimony and the family, but also in matters pertaining to the good of souls : namely, just laws should be made for the protection of chastity, for reciprocal conjugal aid, and for similar purposes ; and these laws must be faithfully enforced ; for, as history testifies, the prosperity of the State and the temporal happiness of its citizens cannot remain safe and sound where the foundations upon which they are established, which is the moral order, is weakened, and where the very fountain-head from which the State draws its life, namely, wedlock and the family is obstructed by the vices of its citizens."[3]

Ruinous Policy of Modern Governments.—Unfortunately the policy and tendencies of many modern governments are exactly the reverse of this ; and hence the perilous state of European society to-day.

---

[1] *The Key of the World's Progress*, p. 50.
[2] Cf Devas—*Pol. Economy* (*see* Index, " Family ").
[3] *Casti Connubii* (Dec., 1930), pp. 62, 63 (C. T. S. edit., London).

(a) **In Their Positive Legal Enactments.**—The laws of
divorce (which are essentially immoral) now existing in
the United States of America, in most countries of the
British Empire, and in practically all the countries of Europe,
except Ireland and Italy, strike at the very foundations
of family life. In like manner laws interfering with the
parents' control over their children ; laws of property or
inheritance tending to divide or break up the family homestead ; or to lessen unduly the authority of the parents ;
or to make the parents independent of each other, are out
of harmony with the natural organism of family life, and
tend strongly to injure and weaken it.

In the same category must be included the educational
systems in which the State assumes to itself the control of
the children's education, defraying the cost, specifying the
educational programmes, and in some cases even appointing
the school to which the child must go. These systems,
which have already wrought unspeakable havoc in America
and several European States, are an outcome of the baneful
influence of Liberalism. They are subversive of the natural
organism of the family, and so are opposed to the natural
and Divine law.

(b) **In Neglecting Their Duty to Protect Family Interests.**—
But it is not alone by positive laws and administrative
action that modern governments fail in their duties towards
the family. Their sins of negligence and omission are no
less serious. Led astray by the principles of unchristian
Liberalism, they tend to regard the State as a society
composed of isolated individuals towards whom the Government's primary duties lie. Hence, while the special claims
of the capitalists, the workers, the industrial and professional classes, the agricultural portion of the community,
the women, are more or less recognised, the rights of the
father of the family as such are largely ignored. The claims
of the family to special protection and assistance from the
Government, so that its unity and integrity be preserved
and strengthened, the purity of its domestic life safeguarded,
its fecundity encouraged and promoted—these claims receive
little or no recognition in legislation, administration or
programmes of social reconstruction.

Many States place no legal restraint upon the propagation

of doctrines or practices advocating or facilitating the unnatural vice of birth-control, or race-suicide, although this, like divorce, is directly subversive of the principles of family life, and opposed to the primary domestic obligations.[1] The activities of a more or less immoral press and a still more immoral cinema, the tendency of which is to make light of, or even turn into ridicule, the most sacred domestic ties—the relations between husband and wife and those between parent and child—are allowed to go on without sufficient censorship or restraint.[2]

" Now, alas," writes Pius XI, " not secretly or under cover, but openly, with all sense of shame put aside, at one time by word, at another by writings, by theatrical productions of every kind, by romantic fiction, by amorous and frivolous novels, by cine-matographs portraying in vivid scene, by addresses broadcast, by radio and telephony, in short, by all the inventions of modern science, the sanctity of marriage is trampled upon and derided : divorce, adultery, all the basest vices are extolled, or at least depicted in such glowing colours, as to appear to be free of all reproach and infamy.   Books are not lacking, which dare to call themselves *scientific* . . . in order that they may more easily insinuate their ideas. . . .

" These thoughts are instilled into men of every class, rich and poor, workers and employers, lettered and illiterate, married and single, the godly and the godless, old and young ; but for these last, as being easier prey, the worst snares are laid. . . .

" There are those who, striving as it were to ride a middle course, believe, nevertheless, that something should be conceded in our time, as regards certain precepts of the divine and natural law.   But these likewise, more or less willingly, are emissaries of the great enemy who is ever seeking to sow cockle among the wheat."[3]

The writings and propaganda here stigmatised by the Pope, and the opinions and practices to which they lead, are in reality more harmful to the good and stability of the State than the preaching of sedition or the advocacy of highway robbery ; and under a really Christian government,

---

[1] Even in Ireland (1931) there exists no legal restraint to the import and open sale of contraceptives.

[2] Very many, if not most of the British non-Catholic newspapers which even now (1931) are allowed to circulate freely in Ireland, propagate directly or indirectly not only infidelity, but immoral or degrading practices of various kinds, such as excessive gambling, and sensual vice.

[3] *Casti Connubii* (Dec., 1930), pp. 22, 23.

they would be prevented as effectively, and punished with no less severity.

Changes Urgently Needed.—Divorce laws should be abolished. The crime of seduction and all kinds of public incentives to the vice of unchastity, whether within or without the married state, should be kept in check by the arm of the law. The so-called "White Slave Traffic," one of the most hideous and shameful features of modern neo-pagan civilisation, should be strenuously hunted down and destroyed. The work of married women in factories, so injurious to the character of the home, where the mother's presence is usually necessary, should be abolished or kept within very strict limits.[1]

"Intolerable," writes Pius XI, "and to be opposed with all our strength, is the abuse whereby mothers of families, because of the insufficiency of the father's salary, are forced to engage in gainful occupations outside the domestic walls, to the neglect of their own proper cares and duties, particularly the education of their children."[2]

While the wife, and still more the widow, should get adequate protection, the law should not (as modern English law now tends to do) excessively favour independent proprietorship between husband and wife, whose interests, according to Christian principles, are, and should be, inseparable.[3] The earnings of sons and daughters during their minority should be left by law under the control of the parents. In every detail of the educational system the interests of the family should be made a primary consideration.[4]

In the distribution of the franchise, and in the allotment of the public burdens, everything possible should be done to enhance the prestige of the family and the privileges of

---

[1] Cf. Leo XIII—*Rerum Novarum*, p. 156 ; also Ryan and Husselein— *The Church and Labour*, pp. 174, 175.

[2] *Quadragesimo Anno* (C. T. S. edit.), p. 33.

[3] Cf. the words of Pius XI on this subject : " It is part of the duty of the public authority to adapt the civil rights of the wife to modern needs and requirements, keeping in view what the natural disposition and temperament of the female sex, good morality and the welfare of the family demand, and provided always that the essential order of domestic society remain intact, founded as it is . . . on the authority and wisdom of God, and so not changeable by public laws, or at the pleasure of private individuals " (*Casti Connubii*, p. 37).

[4] Cf. Devas, *loc. cit.*

the head of the family. In the land laws, the laws of inheritance, the schemes of social reconstruction, the main
object to be kept in view should be family interest.

All public activities which may either directly or indirectly prove dangerous to the interests of the home or the
purity of domestic life, such as the immoral press and
cinema, the drink traffic, betting and gambling activities,
the publication of betting and gambling news, should be
suppressed or kept within strict control by the arm of the
law, for all these are a manifest and acknowledged source
of danger to domestic interests, and can be effectively kept
in check only by public authority.

Art. 2—*The Family Homestead*

Material Conditions of the Family—Christian State Policy.—
Not only should the State safeguard the moral interests of
the home, but it should take measures to protect and promote
the material interests also. The aim of its policy should
be to secure that each and every family within the State
should have, or be in a position to acquire, secure possession
of a suitable homestead, and should have also a fair opportunity of acquiring sufficient material prosperity. For
family life cannot flourish nor duly function without a
suitable homestead and sufficient means for a modest
maintenance. This matter touches on the primary functions
of the governing authority. Every one has a right to live
on the earth's bounty, and no head of a family can be
justly denied *a fair opportunity of securing* for himself and
those depending on him a suitable home and means of
livelihood, which would be sufficiently permanent and secure.

" Since it is no rare thing," writes Pius XI, " to find that the
perfect observance of God's commandments and conjugal integrity encounter difficulties because the married parties are
distressed by straitened circumstances, their necessities must be
relieved as far as possible. . . . In the State such economic and
social conditions should be set up as will enable every head of
a family to earn as much as according to his station in life is
necessary for himself, his wife, and the rearing of his children
. . . If families particularly those in which there are many
children have not suitable dwellings : if the husband cannot find
employment . . . it is patent to all how great a peril can arise to
public security : and to the welfare and the very life of civil
society itself."[1]

---

[1] *Casti Connubii* (C. T. S. edit.), p. 62.

The Town Family.—There is no need to stress the point that neither the slum dwellings of the modern cities nor even lodgings or flats meet these requirements. Hence, there is need of a broad and far-reaching state policy which would aim at the gradual elimination of the slum dwellings and the formation round the towns of great city gardens in which each family would own a permanent home, with a suitable plot of land attached. In matters such as these, where elementary human rights are at stake, the so-called " vested rights " of property owners, must yield, as far as is necessary, before the claims of social justice.

The Rural Family—(a) Its Fundamental Importance.— Even of greater urgency and importance for all the best interests of the State are the claims of the rural population. Few things are more important for the stability and security of the State than the existence within it of a dominating number of small village and rural proprietors, each enjoying means for a modest but sufficient livelihood, and each secure in the *permanent* possession of his own small homestead. We have already referred to the well-known social phenomenon that urban families die out after a few generations, and that the urban populations survive only by means of constant supplies from the country. Hence the rural population is the real mainstay of the nation.

Besides, as a rule, it is only in the country that the family is attached to a particular locality and a hereditary home. It is this stable[1] rural population whose interests and traditions are intimately associated with the very soil of their country, that form the core and strength of a nation. It is from them that the most vigorous type of citizen comes, and among them that the best fruits of true patriotism are

---

[1] The family that is attached to an ancestral home and estate, which pass on within the same stock from generation to generation more easily preserves the ancestral family traditions and ideals, and thus becomes what is called the *stable* family (cf. the law of *Entail* in English legal system). The family, on the other hand, in which there. is no hereditary home belonging to the family as such, usually loses the family tradition, as the members all scatter or migrate. This type is called the *unstable* family. Thus the families of the feudal classes and of the agricultural population of mediæval times were stable families ; so, too, were the families of the Gaelic rural population of Ireland before the 17th century. Town dwellers, the trading and professional classes, floating populations of all kinds belong mainly to the category of the unstable family.

to be found. Hence it has always been the policy of enlightened statesmen to strengthen and stabilise the rural population.[1]

(b) **Its Loss Irremediable.**—There is a further consideration which makes this policy specially important. It is comparatively easy to produce an industrial population or a professional class. But a permanent rural population cannot be created to order. Town dwellers cannot, as a rule, be successfully transplanted into the country. A peasant population must be the result of a growth of generations. Hence, Goldsmith's well-known words are true :

" A brave peasantry, the country's pride,
When once destroyed, can never be supplied."

(c) **Special Protection Essential.**—The mediæval serf and his family, although enjoying little or no political rights, were secure (being protected by custom which had the force of law) in the possession of a modest estate which neither the serf nor the feudal lord had power to alienate. This custom, besides maintaining the stability of the rural population, also secured that the serf and his family were always certain of shelter, clothing and plenty of substantial food. Similar protection is afforded by law to small proprietors in some of the countries of Europe where Christian ideals of government still retain their hold.

The Homestead Exemption Laws of very many of the States of the American Union afford an example of the form which such protection may assume. According to the general trend of these laws, which differ in detail in various States, the homestead, including the farm and the buildings thereon up to a certain moderate value, cannot be seized or sold for any debt except taxes and money due for purchase or improvements. Neither can the homestead be mortgaged without the written consent of both parents ; and, even when the homestead is alienated, the householder still retains certain essential claims upon it for some time. When the householder dies, the widow cannot be disturbed during her life, nor any of the children till they attain their majority. Other provisions give the family inalienable

---

[1] Cf. Shove, *op. cit.*, chaps. i to iv.

rights to certain necessary goods such as tools, the implements of the family profession, personal belongings, etc.,
of which they cannot be deprived for any kind of debt.[1]

Destruction of Rural Homes.—In Ireland the destruction
of rural homes, the dispersion of families, and the uprooting
of family traditions have gone on steadily for over a century.
Between 1841 and 1901, what with famines, evictions and
the activities of village usurers, all created or protected by
the "law," more than half a million Catholic rural homesteads were destroyed, and the families scattered or driven
into exile.[2] The movement of rural depopulation still
(1931) goes on. Unless it be effectually checked and the
tide turned, the practical extinction of the old Irish nation
seems inevitable.

Stablising the Irish Rural Population.—At present nothing
is more urgently needed in Ireland than to stabilise and
increase the rural population. This seems to be still quite
feasible. For although the peasant population are (or
were up to 1931, when the industrial conditions in U.S.A.
checked the movement, at least temporarily) emigrating at
the rate of tens of thousands each year mainly as a result
of economic pressure, a very large percentage of those that
go could still be saved to their own country if only they
had means of an adequate livelihood. There are in Ireland
immense tracts of uncultivated and mostly uninhabited
land, some of which is very fertile. To replant under suitable conditions the sons and daughters of the disinherited
peasantry who now emigrate, on the uncultivated lands
is generally recognised as an obvious and urgent need, and

---

[1] *See* Devas—*Political Economy*, bk. ii, chap. xi. Old Irish law afforded
similar protection for tools and some other necessaries.
[2] According to Mulhall's *Dictionary of Statistics* the total number of
inhabited houses in Ireland in 1841 was 1,328,000 ; and the average size
of the family in each house was 6.2. In 1901 the number of inhabited
houses was reduced to 858,158. The decrease (469,842) in the number
of inhabited houses does not convey an adequate idea of the extent of
the destruction of rural homes ; for although the bulk of the disinherited
families went into exile, a considerable proportion migrated to the cities,
some of which as a consequence grew in population during the same
period : hence the exceptionally large slum population of the present day.

should be the aim of an Irish government. The acquisition of the land (without confiscation) can be facilitated by suitable land laws and a national financial system in harmony with the country's needs.

A New (or Newly Settled) Peasant Population.—The new peasant population should be, broadly speaking, of two types, viz., agricultural labourers and small farmers. The former are essential if the more extensive farmers, as distinct from the ranchers, are to remain, and to cultivate their land. The condition of these labourers can be made quite comfortable, if each labourer have a cottage and a plot of land sufficient to maintain a milch cow, a pig and some poultry, and to supply the family with vegetables. Probably about three statute acres would be the amount required.

The cottier or smaller holdings should be large enough to maintain the cottier family in comfort, and small enough to necessitate diligent and continuous work. The proper size would be somewhere between twelve and twenty-four statute acres of arable land of average fertility.

Restrictive Laws Essential.—Peasant proprietorship of itself, however, will not produce a stable rural population. The history of all nations tends to show that for the preservation of a peasant population the *cottier must not have the power freely to sell, mortgage or unduly subdivide* the holding. If he have, the peasant holdings will sooner or later become absorbed by the large owners, or by the moneyed interest.[1] Hence, although the cottier and the

---

[1] For an excellent and illuminating historical review of this whole question, cf. Meyer et Ardant—*La Question Agraire* (Paris, Retaux-Bray, 1887). *See* also Devas—*Political Economy* (Index *sub verbo* " Family "). The following passage from Devas's *Studies of Family Life* (p. 178) in reference to the Hungarian peasantry is interesting and instructive in this connection : " There were also [viz., before 1848, the year of the first Revolution, which led eventually to the setting up of the Liberal Constitution] great prosperity and security among the rural population being protected by a feudal constitution. The land was mostly held on a tenure of service (tilling the lord's soil) ; the peasant's holding was not divisible beyond a certain limit . . . no mortgaging was possible. By the changes that followed the troubles of 1848, completed after 1866 [viz., the Liberal movement and revolution under Kossuth], the peasants, now become independent proprietors, were left defenceless, and a swarm of Jewish usurers descended upon them, and filled the land with desolation and woe. . . .

labourer should *own* their holdings, certain restrictions should be imposed withholding power to sell, mortgage or subdivide at least beyond certain specified limits. The family should, besides, be protected by a suitable type of Household Exemption laws. The owner should have testamentary rights at least within the limits of his own family. But in no case should any one be allowed the ownership of a holding except he actually live on it.

New Scheme Suggested.—Possibly the best way to replant the uncultivated lands would be by settling *rural colonies of cottiers* around some kind of central institution which would conduct a model farm and by means of which all the cottiers would be linked up into a co-operative community. If, in addition the future cottiers had to spend a few years apprenticeship in the central institution before being qualified for an allotment, matters would be still further facilitated, and the prospects of success increased.

During the years of apprenticeship the young men could by their own co-operative labour fence off and erect the necessary buildings on their future holdings. On these they would be settled in turn and get full control after a few years, according as the initial expenses had been liquidated.

If laws were passed facilitating the formation of such *voluntary* institutions, and also facilitating the acquisition by them of lands, for the purpose of distribution ; and conferring besides on the rural colonies thus formed certain statutory privileges, including a municipal charter for independent local administration, the needed organisations, religious or otherwise, for conducting the scheme, would gradually spring up, and as a result of experience would soon evolve suitable methods. Thus a corporative rural organisation would in time develop forming the base of a stable and substantially self-contained peasant State—

In ten years over five hundred thousand farmers and over thirteen hundred thousand farm labourers were swept away ! ! In the single year, 1878, the compulsory sales of lands numbered 15,285, and the proceeds of these sales fell short by over eight million florins of the debts they were meant to cover." Cf. also *Rev. Internat. des Soc. Secrètes* (1931, No. 5), pp. 105 ff, for some account of the destructive influence of the Jewish usurers and financiers on the land question in Austria-Hungary.

the ideal at which the world's best statesmen have always aimed. It seems certain that it is only by means of voluntary and free organisations, assisted from State sources, and self-contained rural co-operative colonies coalescing into a co-operative civic organisation, that the Irish rural population can be saved.[1]

---

[1] Cf. *Land for the People*, a Scotch quarterly, edited by Rev. J. McQuillan, D.D., Bearsden Seminary, Glasgow, for an account of a scheme for initiating Catholic rural Colonies in Scotland on lines somewhat similar to those here indicated. For the success of any such scheme, however, the impossibility of turning town dwellers, at least on a large scale, into peasant farmers cannot be lost sight of.

CHAPTER XIX

HUSBAND AND WIFE

Art. 1—*The Marriage Contract*[1]

Meaning and Purpose of Marriage.—The conjugal society is the foundation of the family. The term *marriage* is sometimes used to denote the contract upon which the union is founded ; sometimes to mean the union itself as a permanent state. In the latter sense it may be described as *the permanent union between man and woman, made under contract, and having for its object the birth and education of children, and mutual help and companionship.*

The primary end of marriage is the birth and education of children. Thus marriage is absolutely necessary for the good, and even for the existence of the race. For, according to the natural and Divine law, the propagation of the human race cannot be attained or attempted outside the married state. The other purpose of marriage indicated in the definition, namely, mutual help and companionship between husband and wife, though not so essential to the human race as the primary purpose, also responds to needs of human nature. Hence it is assigned by the natural law as a secondary end of the conjugal union, and in practice is very often the principal motive that impels the parties to contract the marriage.

The sexes are intended to be complementary of each other, one possessing in capabilities and needs what the other lacks. And so as each sex is incomplete in itself, not representing human nature in its fulness, the Deity has implanted in both a mutual attraction for each other ; and in the intimate union of two persons of opposite sexes

---

[1] The classical Documents on Marriage are the Encyclical of Pius XI, *Casti Connubii* (Dec. 31, 1930), already referred to, and that of Leo XIII—*Arcanum Divinæ* (1880) ; cf. also *Rerum Novarum* (1891) and *Inscrutabili* (1878). See also Castelein, *op. cit.*, Theses 16 and 17 ; Donat, *op. cit.*, sect. iii, cap. ii ; Costa-Rosetti, *op. cit.*, Theses 141–143 ; Balmes—*European Civilisation*, chaps, xxiv–xxvi ; Gannon—*Holy Matrimony* (London, 1927) ; Cronin—*Science of Ethics*, vol. ii, chaps. xiii and xiv ; *Cath. Encyclop.*, arts. " Marriage," " Divorce," etc.

22

in one closely-knit society, such as nature has ordained in the married state, each party finds greater happiness and content, and realises, as it were, a greater and more complete fulness of life.

"Not only was marriage intended for the propagation of the human race," writes Leo XIII, "but also that the lives of husband and wife might be better and happier."[1]

Marriage Contract a Divine Institution.—The marriage compact upon which the union of husband and wife is founded, results, like other contracts, from the free consent of the parties concerned. The marriage contract is, however, peculiar in this that it has been directly instituted by God ; and all its essential features arranged by Him at the first creation of man. This is clearly conveyed by the inspired writer in the Book of Genesis, where the first marriage, between man and woman is described : "*But for man there was not found a helper like himself. Then God cast a deep sleep upon Adam ; and when he was fast asleep, He took one of his ribs, and filled up flesh for it. And the Lord built the rib which He took from Adam into a woman ; and brought her to Adam. And Adam said . ' This is bone of my bone, and flesh of my flesh . . . wherefore a man shall leave father and mother and shall cleave to his wife ; and they shall be two in one flesh.'*"[2]

Hence the character of the matrimonial union, and the mutual rights and obligations of the married pair, being founded upon man's nature and ordained by the Divine law, must continue unchanged as long as human nature remains as it is. Marriage has not been inaptly compared by Christian writers to the Tree of Knowledge in Paradise with which human interference was forbidden under pain of death. For history amply proves that respect for the marriage tie, and for all that it implies, is a question of life and death for human society ; and no nation can long survive which attempts to withdraw or change any of the essential attributes which the Deity has attached to the institution of marriage.

And a Foreshadowing of the Incarnation.—Not only was marriage instituted directly by God, but even from the

---

[1] *Arcanum Divinæ*, p. 35.   [2] *Genesis* ii, 1-24.

beginning it was a kind of foreshadowing of the Incarnation. The close union between husband and wife was intended by God to be a type of the union between His Divine Son and human nature. Accordingly, from the creation of man, there always was in the matrimonial union an element of religion and holiness, " not extraneous but innate, not derived from man, but implanted by nature."[1] Not only among the Jews, but even among the pagan nations of the Gentiles, this element of religion was commonly acknowledged; and marriage was usually celebrated " with religious ceremonies, under the authority of pontiffs, and with the ministry of priests."[2]

It is only in our own days, and as a result of the un-precedented revolt of the nations against the authority of God and the teachings of the natural law, that men have attempted to degrade the marriage compact into a merely human institution, and to subject it in its very essence to the arbitrary control of human laws.

And a Sacrament.—By reason of the transcending importance of the marriage contract for all the highest interests of the human race, Our Lord elevated it to the dignity of a sacrament. Hence Christians cannot validly marry without receiving a sacrament. In other words, the marriage contract itself is a sacrament for them. It confers grace, consecrating the perpetual union of the married pair, and ensuring them special supernatural aids to fulfil their obligations, and even to acquire holiness.

Furthermore, the mystical significance of the matrimonial union, which existed from the beginning in a fainter and less developed degree, has become under the New Law a definite figure and representation of the mystical union of Christ with His Church. Thus, under the Christian dispensation, the union and natural love between husband and wife have been raised to a higher plane by the addition of supernatural motives and the infusion of supernatural grace. For the husband should love and honour his wife even as Christ loves His Church.

Christianity has, besides, ennobled marriage by assigning to it " a higher and nobler purpose than was ever previously

---

[1] Leo XIII—*Arcanum Divinæ*, p. 31.   [2] *Ib.*

given to it"; [1] for, according to the law of Christ, marriage
has for its object not merely the propagation of the human
race, but the bringing forth of children for the Church, who
are to be the " fellow-citizens of the saints, and the domestics
of God " ; [2] so that " a people may be born and brought
up for the worship and religion of the true God and our
Saviour Jesus Christ." [3]

Attributes of Christian Marriage.—The Christian ideal of
marriage, which, in fact, only develops and defines more
clearly the ordinances of the natural law, is sometimes expressed in the formula, " One with one, exclusively and
for ever." Hence marriage, according to Christian law,
possesses the following five essential attributes :

(a) **Strict Unity.**—Christian marriage excludes *Polygamy*
of any kind. Polygamy may take the form of *Polygyny*
where a man has more than one wife, or that of *Polyandry*,
where a woman would have more than a single husband.
Polyandry is clearly opposed to the primary ends of
marriage, and so is evidently forbidden by the law of nature.
Polygyny is not so clearly opposed to the natural law as
polyandry ; for in polygyny, the primary purposes of the
matrimonial union, namely, the birth and education of
children, are still attainable. Thus it was that by a special
dispensation of God, the Mosaic law, while upholding the
marriage of strict unity and perpetuity as the type accepted
by the nation, and the one desired and aimed at by God,
made such concession to the ingrained prejudices and habits
of Eastern peoples, as to tolerate among the Jews polygyny
and divorce in certain cases, till the people would be so far
elevated and trained as to allow of their complete abolition.
Under the Christian law all such concessions are withdrawn ;
and polygyny is regarded like polyandry and complete
divorce as essentially unlawful and immoral. Nothing is
more striking in the history of the Catholic Church than
the uncompromising attitude which she has always maintained on this question, even when the most far-reaching
interests would seem to be involved, and when all the

---

[1] Leo XIII—*Arcanum Divinæ*, p. 28.   [2] *Eph.* ii, 19.
[3] Catech. Rom., c. viii.

dictates of human prudence would urge concession and toleration.

Polygyny is an outrage on the dignity of the woman, who by it is necessarily placed in an inferior position, contrary to the natural law which claims for her equal personal rights with the man. It leads inevitably to dissensions and jealousy. A plurality of wives would render impossible the mutual help and companionship and close friendship between husband and wife, which is one of the ends of marriage proposed by the natural law. Again, without promoting the propagation of the race—for experience teaches that the population does not increase more rapidly with polygyny than with monogyny—polygyny renders more difficult the education of the children, for whose proper up-bringing the close co-operation of both parents is essential. The energy, enterprise, and moral and physical strength of the European races, as contrasted with the decrepit and effeminate character of those of the East, furnish a striking example of the effects of monogyny upon the character and morals of a people.

(b) **Perpetual Stability.**—This attribute excludes all possibility of divorce, at least when the marriage contract is consummated. Our Divine Lord expressly withdrew the concession granted to the Jews regarding divorce which had been made temporarily, but by Divine authority, owing to their " hardness of heart." Divorce is destructive of the primary end of marriage, which is the good of the offspring. For when the union between the parents is severed, their due co-operation in the up-bringing of the children becomes impossible, and all the interests of the latter suffer. The possibility of divorce tends to obstruct fatally the secondary end of marriage, which implies the most intimate and perfect friendship between husband and wife. Divorce or its possibility, as experience only too clearly shows, opens the floodgates to immorality. Finally, divorce is specially injurious to the woman, whose dignity and secure position in the home inevitably suffer where divorce prevails.

(c) **Perfect and Permanent Fidelity.**—This obligation binds both parties equally. This law of Christian marriage is in striking contrast with the principles of pagan philosophy

and pagan law, and with the civil law of many modern
states. Neither Christian teaching nor the natural law
condones infidelity to matrimonial obligations in the
husband any more than in the wife.

(d) **Equality in Primary Rights.**—In respect of the primary
marital rights and obligations, husband and wife are equal.
The rehabilitation of the woman in the natural position in
which she was first created, as the companion of her husband,
and his equal in all essential personal rights, his "helper,
like himself,"[1] is one of the great glories of Christianity.
This natural equality follows from the fact that both are
equally persons, possessing immortal souls and destined
to eternal happiness.

(e) **Inequality, Tempered with Love in Ruling the
Family.**—Though husband and wife are equal in dignity
and essential rights, nevertheless, since they (with the
children, if there be such) form a society, and since a society
is impossible without a recognised head, there must be some
head to the family. For this purpose the natural law has
marked out the man rather than the woman ; seeing that
nature has given to him qualities which, generally speaking,
render him more suitable than her for the duty of ruler.
And so, although the wife, as a human person, is equal to
her husband, she is subject to his authority as a wife and
a member of the domestic society, just as a citizen in the
state is subject to the authority of the ruler to whom, nevertheless, he is equal as a human person.[2] The natural law,
which ordains the submission of the wife to the rule of the
husband, also ordains that that rule be tempered with love

---

[1] *Genesis* ii, 20.

[2] The classical passage of St. Thomas in which this principle is elaborated
runs as follows :

"There are two kinds of subordination. One is that of the slave. In
this the one who commands (*præsidens*), utilises for his own benefit the
persons subject to him. Such subordination came into the world as the
result of sin. The other type of subordination is economic or civil. In
this the person that commands others, does so for the good or utility of
the subject. This type of subordination existed even before sin came into
the world. . . . It is in virtue of such subordination that the wife is by
the natural law made subject to her husband ; nor is it true that such
inequality was absent even in the state of innocence" (I. Q. xcii, a. 1,
ad 2um). Cf. also *infra*, chap. xix, art. 4,

and reverence for the dignity of the wife, whom nature marks out as the manager of the household and her husband's most intimate friend.

" The man," writes Leo XIII, " is the ruler of the family and the head of the woman ; but because she is flesh of his flesh and bone of his bone, let her be subject and obedient to the man, not as a servant but as a companion, so that nothing be lacking of honour or of dignity in the obedience which she gives."[1]

This duty of conjugal obedience, its nature and limitations are more fully explained by Pius XI in the following important passage of his Encyclical on Christian Marriage :

" This subjection, however, does not deny or take away the liberty which fully belongs to the woman both in view of her dignity as a human person, and in view of her most noble office as wife and mother and companion ; nor does it bid her obey her husband's every request, if not in harmony with right reason or with the dignity due to wife ; nor, in fine, does it imply that the wife should be put on a level with those persons who in law are called minors, to whom it is not customary to allow free exercise of their rights on account of their lack of mature judgment, or of their ignorance of human affairs. But it forbids that exaggerated liberty which cares not for the good of the family ; it forbids that in the body which is the family, the heart be separated from the head to the great detriment of the whole body and the proximate danger of ruin. For if the man is the head the woman is the heart, and as he occupies the chief place in ruling, so she may and ought to claim for herself the chief place in love.

" Again, the subjection of wife to husband in its degree and manner may vary according to the different conditions of persons place and time. In fact if the husband neglect his duty, it falls to the wife to take his place in directing the family. But the structure of the family and its fundamental law, established and confirmed by God, must always and everywhere remain intact."[2]

The last sentence of the above passage is manifestly added by the Pope in order to reassert the principle from which he had set out and in support of which he quotes St. Paul[3] and Leo XIII, that " the husband is the ruler of the family, and the head of the woman." The Holy Father concludes by quoting a passage from Leo XIII, which summarises the whole doctrine, and at the same time

---

[1] *Arcanum Divinæ*, p. 28.
[2] *Casti Connubii* (Dec. 31, 1930), pp. 13, 14.   [3] 1 *Cor.* vii, 3.

indicates the only effectual means that can ensure its realisation :

" Since the husband represents Christ, and since the wife represents the Church, let divine charity be the constant guide of their mutual relations, both in him who rules and in her who obeys, since each bears the image, the one of Christ, and the other of the Church."[1]

Church's High Esteem of Marriage.—Although, according to Christian teaching, the union of man and woman in marriage is partly designed to satisfy human needs and tendencies, it must not be supposed that in the Christian ideal marriage is regarded in any way as a mere concession to human weakness, allowed by God in order that worse evils may be avoided. In contrast with the Manichean and other heretical sects, and the errors of Buddhism, the Christian law regards marriage as a good thing in itself, and the married state as a holy state, and one peculiarly blessed by God, and commended in the strongest terms by Our Lord Jesus Christ. It is, in fact, the state to which the vast majority of the human race are called.

No characteristic is more remarkable in the life of Our Divine Lord than His reverence for the married state. He begins His life on earth by blessing, through the visit of His Mother, the home of St. Elizabeth, from whose married life He had by miracle removed the reproach of sterility ; and He sanctified her infant son while still in his mother's womb. Later on, He opens His public life by blessing with His Divine presence the marriage feast of Cana ; and He works His first miracle in favour of the praiseworthy and natural rejoicing which the marriage celebration had called forth. The three miracles recorded in the Gospel in which families gathered together on the sanctuary of the home ; and the three miracles recorded in the Gospel in which Our Lord restored the dead to life were all performed by Him in sympathy with that sacred family affection which is so closely connected with the married life.[2] Hence St. Paul lays down that marriage " is a great Sacrament,"[3] and that " It is honourable in all."[4]

---

[1] *Ib.*, and *Arcanum Divinæ.*   [2] Cf. Castelein, *op. cit.*, pp. 533–536.
[3] *Eph.* v, 32.   [4] *Heb.* xiii, 4.

Excellence of Celibacy Practised from Supernatural Motives.—All this is quite consistent with the fact that the Church regards a life of perpetual virginity, dedicated to God, as a better and higher state even than marriage, and a state to which many are called. For though marriage is obligatory on the race as a whole, the precept does not fall upon every individual ; and no particular person is bound by it, as long as the object of the precept, namely, the propagation of the race, is sufficiently attained. This reasoning has all the greater force if, as is the fact, a greater and higher good is secured for the human race when some individuals abstain from marriage *from supernatural motives*.

The reasons for the higher excellence of virginity dedicated to God are easily understood. A life of religious celibacy, undertaken from supernatural motives, implies a more complete self-denial, and, therefore, a closer imitation of the Divine Founder of Christianity ; for in such a life the lower tendencies of human nature are more completely subject to the higher. Furthermore, such a life affords a better opportunity for prayer and close union with God. The celibate, besides, can devote himself more completely to the service of others ; for " charity will hardly water the ground, when it must first fill up a pool."[1] And last, but not least, the higher example of self-control given by the large number of Catholics who lead a self-denying life in the celibate state makes it easier for the mass of men to observe the chastity that is obligatory within the married state. The celibate lives of the Catholic priests and religious of both sexes have influenced deeply the character of Christian society. They have especially served to raise the general moral standard. Also the religious life of virgins consecrated to God has been a very important factor in raising the social standing and prestige of the Christian woman ; for it gives her an important function in Christian society quite independent of the other sex.

Art. 2—*Non-Christian Attitude Towards Marriage*[2]

Usurpation of Control by Civil Power.—An unchristian attitude towards marriage is often adopted not merely by

---

[1] " Bacon's Essays "—Marriage.
[2] Cf. Devas—*Studies of Family Life,* parts i and iii,

the pagan and Mohammedan nations but also by many of those which are still nominally Christian.

A necessary consequence of the Divine dispensation which makes marriage between Christians a sacrament, and of its higher religious significance as typifying the union of Christ with the Church, is that the marriage contract has been taken entirely from under the control of the civil power. The attitude assumed by so many governments in Europe and America towards the marriage contract implies a usurpation of powers quite outside their jurisdiction. Ignoring the conditions laid down by the Church (which is the only competent authority) for the validity of marriage between Christians, the State has instituted what are commonly called " civil marriages." Such unions, at least in the case of Catholics, are not marriages, but simple concubinage. In the same spirit of usurpation these states establish matrimonial impediments, and refuse to acknowledge as valid the marriages in which their unauthorised laws are disregarded. They have, besides, set up matrimonial courts,* which presume to give decisions affecting the marriage contract, deciding questions of disputed validity, or allowing the married pair to live apart, to the violation or detriment of matrimonial duties.

In all this the action of the State, at least in so far as it is devoid of any authority or delegation from the ecclesiastical rulers, is invalid and immoral, being a usurpation of authority entirely reserved by the Divine law to the Church. But these states go farther, and " worst scandal of all, and most injurious to public morality,"[1] they presume, in defiance of God's law, to issue decrees of complete divorce, thus usurping a power which God has expressly reserved from the jurisdiction of any human tribunal— for " *What God has joined let no man put asunder*,"[2] is a divine command.

The legitimate extent of civil authority in regard to Christian marriage is limited to two functions, namely, to safeguard, and, when necessary, to enforce the rights of the parties, and, secondly, to regulate and define certain civil consequences or accompaniments of marriage, con-

---

[1] Leo XIII, *Ib.*   [2] Matt. xix. 6.

cerning such matters as property and inheritance. Any unauthorised action of the State beyond these limits is an act of tyranny and usurpation, and tends directly to the degradation and ruin of human society.

Marriage among Pagans.—Although marriage, as originally instituted by God, possessed all the essential characteristics which now belong to Christian marriage, this ideal got obscured in pre-Christian times in proportion as the morals of human society became corrupt. Polygamy, in one form or another (sometimes, as among the ancient Romans, taking the form of legalised concubinage), and divorce have been always very common among non-Christian nations, both before and after the beginning of the Christian era. The facility of divorce among the ancient Greeks and Romans of the classical period, and the universal immorality of the grossest kind, of which that custom was an indication and a partial cause, are among the most repulsive features of the ancient pagan civilisation.

Again, if we except the Jews and a few pagan nations, among which are to be numbered the very early Egyptians, with whom the woman seems to have had a position of exceptional dignity and independence, the wife's social status was generally very low before the Christian era ; as it still is among the non-Christian nations of the world. Among the barbarians, she frequently became a wife through captivity or purchase. Even among the most civilised nations, such as the Greeks and Romans, the wife was generally regarded as the husband's property, and had little or no personal rights secured her by law. Nowhere was the husband bound by the same laws of fidelity to the marriage obligations as the wife.

Among Mohammedans.—The outstanding feature of marriage among the Mohammedans is polygyny and, as a consequence, the low status of the woman. The woman is looked upon as belonging to a lower degree of humanity. She is accounted higher, indeed, than the brute creation, but lower than man, and meant by nature to minister to man's wants and pleasures. Hence the Mohammedans consider the woman as deficient in judgment, and as no rational companion for her husband. Between the husband and his wife, or wives, there rarely exists genuine mutual affection, which essentially implies esteem and equality. As a consequence the character of the Mohammedan woman has become more or less debased. She is usually quite uneducated, is rarely devout, and often cunning and vicious— the very antithesis of the typical Christian woman.

Among the " After-Christians."—Marriage among the Protestant nations, or those that have abandoned Christianity wholly or in part, presents substantially the same leading features in all countries, whether in Europe, North America, Australasia, or Africa. Differences exist only in the degree to which in a particular country or at a particular period marriage and family life have been degraded. It is true that among these nations, districts and communities are sometimes found in which the people retain substantially the Christian ideals of family life, even for centuries after they have lost the integrity of the Christian faith. Among such types were the Puritan settlers in the New England States of America at the beginning of the 19th century, the English gentry, and in some places the better-class English farmer up to the middle of the same century. The same type survived in many of the districts of Holland, Saxony and Sweden down to our own day. A notable example of the non-Catholic but Christian family is that of the Russian peasant, at least as he was up to the Great War.

But the prevailing tendency of nations which have lost the Catholic faith is to fall away from the true Christian ideals of marriage and family life. This tendency becomes more apparent in proportion as the memory and influence of the Catholic tradition grow faint. Thus, in France, North America, throughout the British Empire (except among the Irish and the French Canadians) divorce is becoming dreadfully common, with its inevitable results of a general lowering of the moral standard, a fatal lessening of the intimacy and cordiality of the union between husband and wife, and a growing habit of infidelity to conjugal duties.

Birth Control or Race Suicide.—Again, the unnatural vice of race-suicide is becoming more and more common, and is sapping the very life of the non-Catholic nations of the

European civilisation.[1] The spread of this vice is due partly to the decay of the Christian spirit of self-sacrifice, which is needed to undergo willingly the burden of parenthood, partly to the spread of the false and unchristian theories of Political Economy which the writings of J. S. Mill and his school have made popular in the English-speaking countries, partly, as in France, to bad laws regarding inheritance. It seems clear that the only path to national security for these nations is their return to the fold of the Catholic Church, and the re-establishment of the Christian standard of morals in the civil, the domestic, and the individual life of their people.[2]

---

[1] Birth control is now openly approved of in Britain, even by the leaders of the Church of England. Thus a resolution of the Bishops of the Protestant Church of England and Ireland, at the Lambeth Conference, 1930, was carried by 193 votes to 67 justifying the immoral practice of birth control, provided it be practised " in the light of . . . Christian principles ! " and " not from motives of selfishness, luxury or mere convenience." Cf. *Lambeth Conference*, 1930 (Society for Promoting Christian Knowledge. Macmillan, London, pp. 43, 44). The same vice is also openly advocated by most of the non-Catholic British papers, which are till (1931) allowed to circulate in Ireland.

[2] Cf. the Encyclical of Pius XI on Christian Marriage, *Casti Connubii* (Dec., 1930), where the subject of Birth Control is fully treated. *See* also Sutherland, M.D.—*Birth Control* (Edinburgh, 1927) ; Devas—*Political Economy*, bk. i, chap. ix ; Castelein, *op. cit.*, Thesis 17, appendice ; Cronin— *Primer of the Principles of Social Science*, part i, sect. v ; *Science of Ethics*, vol. ii, pp. 479–486.

CHAPTER XX

Art. 1—*Introduction*

Parental or Filial Society.—As already stated, the primary object of the conjugal union is the birth and education of children. For the purpose of the child's education nature ordains not only that the union between the parents should continue after the child's birth, but also that parents and children should form one closely-knit society. Hence the *filial* (or *parental*) *society,* made up of parents and children, and having for its object the education of the latter, is an integral part of the family organism, and the natural complement of the conjugal union. Unlike the conjugal society, however, which of its own nature is perpetual, the filial society undergoes essential alterations, or ceases altogether, as soon as the primary object of the union has been secured. When the child is fully grown and his education complete, he[1] may, consistently with the dictates of the natural law, cease to be a member of his parents' family and be entirely emancipated from their control.

Permanence of Parental and Filial Duties.—Even after this has taken place, however, some of the rights and obligations as between children and parents (all of which are included in the virtue of piety) still subsist. The mutual offices of parents and child, continuing during all the years of the child's infancy and upbringing, produce close mutual ties and consequent obligations, which remain through life. With these, however, we are not directly concerned here, as they belong to the science of Ethics and Moral Theology. Suffice it to say that these duties include a permanent obligation on the parents' part to love the child and to assist him when necessary in his spiritual and corporal needs.

---

[1] Throughout the chapter the masculine forms *he* and *him* are to be understood as referring to children of both sexes except the context clearly requires the contrary.

They include on the child's part the duties of love, reverence, and gratitude towards his parents, inasmuch as they are the authors of his being, and have been his protection, guide and support during the period of his infant helplessness, and the long years of his education.

Special Reward of Filial Piety.—It is to this virtue of filial piety—the love and dutifulness of the child towards his parents, continuing during the life of the latter, and showing itself even in honouring their memory, and assisting their souls by prayer and sacrifices after their death—that God has promised a very special reward even in this life : " *Honour thy father and thy mother, which is the first commandment with a promise,*" says St. Paul, " *that it may be well with thee, and that thou mayest be long-lived upon earth.*"[1] The temporal reward here promised is, of course, meant to be a pledge and a foreshadowing of the eternal recompense to come.

Setting aside, therefore, the parental and filial duties which belong to the period when the education of the child has been completed, we confine ourselves to the relations that exist between parent and child while the child is still a minor. These relations involve rights and duties founded on the fact of parenthood and on the child's essential need of the assistance of others during the period of his upbringing.

Education—Its Nature.[2]—Man comes into the world in a state of helplessness which is more absolute and continues for a longer time than in the case of the offspring of any

---

[1] *Eph.* vi. 2, 3.

[2] The classical document on the subject of Education is the recently issued Encyclical of Pius XI, *Divini Illius* (1929), " On the Christian Education of Youth "—of which official versions were issued from the Vatican in all the principal European languages. The pages referred to in quoting the Encyclical are those of the English Catholic Truth Society booklet entitled *Christian Education of Youth* by His Holiness Pius XI. Cf. also Leo XIII—*Immortale Dei* (1885), pp. 45 ff ; *Sapientiæ Christianæ* (1890), p. 131 ; and *Inscrutabili* (1878), pp. 7, 8 ; *Cath. Encyclop.*, arts, " Education " and " Schools " ; Meyer, *op. cit.*, vol. ii, nn. 103–115 ; Costa-Rosetti *op. cit.*, Theses 144, 145 ; Koch Preuss, *op. cit.*, part ii, chap. ii, pp. 511–548. Cf. also Dupanloup—*The Child* (translated from the French by K. Anderson (Dublin, 1875). *See* Pastor—*History of the Popes*, vol. v, pp. 25 ff, for a useful summary of the matchless treatise— *On the Direction of the Family*, by Bl. Giovanni Dominici, published early in the 15th century.

of the lower animals. For the preservation of the child's life and the due development even of his bodily faculties, diligent care and nursing are required extending over a period of many years. The faculties of the soul also, namely, the intellect and will, have to be developed by long and assiduous training. The mind needs to be fed with knowledge and furnished with sound principles ; the reasoning faculties to be gradually formed to the perception of truth ; and the will and all the higher instincts to be moulded little by little to habits of rectitude and a love of virtue.

The whole process of nursing, bringing up, and training the child till he is fit to take his place as a fully-equipped member of civil society, is designated in scientific language by the term *education*. Education, as understood in this technical sense, denotes *the sum of all those cares and activities by which the life and growth of the child's body are safeguarded and promoted, and the due development of all his faculties, physical, mental and moral, is secured.* The work of education, therefore, begins at the child's birth, and is fully completed only when he has reached the mature age at which he can fully take care of himself.

Its Importance.—It is almost a truism to say that the question of education dominates the whole life of the body politic, and that the due up-bringing of the children lies at the very foundation of the welfare of the human race. For as the Wise Man says in the sacred Scriptures : "*A young man according to his way; even when he is old he will not depart from it.*" [1] In every climate and country, and in every age of recorded history, men and women remain through life mostly what their education has made them. Above all, the traits and dispositions that are developed in early years under the influence of family ideals and of the teachers with whom the children come into contact are rarely, if ever, eradicated.

The more advanced stages of education also, say between the ages of thirteen and twenty, exert an immense influence upon the after life and character of the man and woman ; for during that period, which is the transition stage from

---

[1] *Prov.* xxii. 6.

youth to maturity, the character is particularly impressionable.[1] All this tends to prove the supreme importance of education not merely for the individual person, but for the family and the whole State whose perfection comes from the perfection of the elements that compose it : For, as Pius XI writes :

" It [Education] aims at securing the Supreme Good, that is God, for the souls of those who are being educated and the maximum of temporal well-being for human society."[2]

This is why the Church has always so strongly emphasised the ultimate importance of Education. Thus Leo XIII writes :

" Where the right of educating youth is concerned no amount of trouble or labour how great soever can be undertaken, but that even greater still may not be called for."[3]

To Whom the Duty of Education Belongs.—Although the duty and the right of educating the child belong by the natural law to the parents, the positive law of God has assigned to the Church essential and even primary functions in it. The civil society also amid which the child is born and brought up has certain interests and duties in regard to the education of its future citizens. These duties, although secondary and supplementary, have also to be considered.

Aggressive Policy of Modern States.—The policy of controlling and, as far as possible, secularising education initiated by the British Government in Ireland and by the Republican Government of France, was adopted in the 19th century, though in varying degrees, by the governments of several countries of Europe and America. It is pursued at present in its most extreme form by the Soviet Government of Russia. This fatal policy, the outcome of unchristian Liberalism, is perhaps the worst evil of the present day ; and constitutes the greatest menace to the spiritual and temporal welfare of the European races. State authorities strive under one pretext or another to

---

[1] Cf. a valuable article in *The Irish Ecclesiastical Record*, July, 1930, by Rev. R. Devane, S.J., entitled " Adolescence and the Vocational Bill."

[2] *Divini Illius*, 1929.

[3] *Sapientiæ Christianæ*, p. 13.

usurp the parents' right of educating the child ; and, in addition, refuse to acknowledge the control and authority of the Church in any department of education.

" As for the State schools," writes Leo XIII, " it is well known that there is no ecclesiastical authority left in them ; and during the years when the tender minds should be trained carefully and conscientiously in the Christian virtues the precepts of religion are for the most part left untaught."[1]

In order to convey a comprehensive idea of rights and duties in the matter of education, and to place in its true perspective its essential connection with the family, we shall treat the subject as a whole, taking into account the functions of the Church and the State as well as those of the parents.

Art. 2—*Functions of Parents in Education*

Dictates of the Natural Law.—The main headings of Catholic teaching regarding the function of parents in the work of education are as follows : The natural law has assigned to the parents the right and the duty of educating the child. Although the parents may, where necessary, delegate the execution of the duty to others, they cannot lay aside their own responsibilities, which are inalienable.

All this follows from the fact that education is the natural complement of generation and birth—which are in a sense incomplete till the child's faculties are developed by the work of education. Hence the parents, who are responsible for the child's birth into the world, have the duty of completing by education the work they have begun.

" It is certain," writes Pius XI, " that both by the law of nature and of God this right and duty of educating their offspring belongs in the first place to those who began the work of nature by giving them birth, and they are indeed forbidden to leave unfinished this work and so expose it to certain ruin."[2]

Besides, the parents are by nature the most intimately connected with the child, who is, as it were, a portion and continuation of their own life and personality. They are consequently bound to administer to his essential needs almost as they are bound to attend to their own.[3]

---

[1] *Exeunte Jam Anno*, 1888, p. 97.
[2] *Casti Connubii*, Dec. 31, 1930, p. 9.
[3] Cf. St. Thomas, 2ª 2æ, Q. 10, a. 12.

Teaching of the Church.—The Canon Law lays down :

" Parents are under a grave obligation to see to the religious and moral education of their children, as well as to their physical and civil training as far as they can, and, moreover, to provide for their temporal well-being."[1]

Consequently, the unchristian idea which has been gaining ground in modern times under the influence of Liberalism that the children belong to the State rather than to the family, and that the State has an absolute right over their education is contrary to the natural law and the teaching of the Church.

" The children," writes Leo XIII, "are something of the father, and as it were, an extension of the person of the father. . . . They enter into and become a part of civil society, not directly by themselves, but through the family in which they were born . . . and therefore the father's power cannot be destroyed or absorbed by the State, for it has the same origin as human life itself."[2]

In another place the same Pontiff adds :

" It is the duty of parents to make every effort to prevent any invasion of their rights in this matter, and to make absolutely sure that the education of their children remain under their own control in keeping with their Christian duty."[3]

So jealous is the Church of the parents' inviolable right to educate the children that, notwithstanding her earnest desire that all should belong to the true Church and be instructed in its laws, she never consents save under peculiar circumstances, and with special precautions to baptise the children of infidels, or provide for their education against the will of their parents, till the children have attained the age at which they can choose for themselves.[4]

Extent of Parental Authority.—The parents' duties towards the child necessarily involve authority over him during the period of his education and the reciprocal obligation of obedience on his part. These mutual rights and duties, which continue till the child's education is complete, are the bonds uniting parents and children into one family.

---

[1] *Codex Juris Canonici*, C. 1113.   [2] *Rerum Novarum*, 1891, p. 140.
[3] *Sapientiæ Christianæ*, 1890, p. 131.   [4] Cf. Pius XI., *ib.*, pp. 17, 18.

The parents' authority over the child is, like all human authority, subordinate to the natural and divine law. Its extent is limited by the end and purpose of the authority itself, namely, the due education of the child and the ruling of the household. Consequently, it would not include such a power as that of life and death or the right to sell the child into slavery, or to impose on him any unjust or inhuman conditions. Consequently, the parents cannot interfere unduly with the child's inborn right to select freely his own state of life, after he has arrived at an age when he is capable of making a prudent choice. In that matter it is the parents' right and duty to advise and direct, not to command.

Finally, parental authority becomes less stringent, or rather, less comprehensive in its scope, as the work of education goes on, and the child becomes more and more capable of taking care of himself ; but it does not cease till the child has attained his majority, or, in other words, reached the full age of maturity. What that age precisely is may vary according to climate and circumstances, and is usually defined by the civil or ecclesiastical law.

Importance of Home Training.—The importance of the home training in the education of the child, and the parents' responsibility and influence in his religious, moral and civil formation, cannot be too strongly emphasised. Pius XI calls special attention to the

" present day lamentable decline in family education," and he deplores the fact that " many parents immersed as they are in temporal cares, have got little or no preparation or training for the fundamental duty and obligation of educating their children. . . . The declining influence of domestic environment is further weakened by another tendency, which . . . causes children to be more and more frequently sent away from home even in the tenderest years."[1]

The Pope also emphasises strongly the need of discipline and correction where necessary : for " just punishment is not to be described as despotism or violence " ; and as the Wise Man says in the Holy Scriptures : " *Folly is bound up*

---

[1] *Ib.*, p. 35.

in the heart of the child, and the rod of correction shall drive it away."[1]

"Disorderly inclinations," he writes, "the result of original sin from which all suffer, and which can never be ignored with safety, must then be corrected ; good tendencies encouraged and regulated from tender childhood ; and above all the mind must be enlightened and the will strengthened by supernatural truth, and by the means of grace, without which it is impossible to control evil impulses.[2]

It is the parents' first duty to see that their child is properly instructed in religious knowledge, and habituated from his earliest infancy to the practice of his religious duties. They must secure that he is safeguarded from contact with evil example, and from all other kinds of dangerous influence, and that the home itself, as well as the school which the child frequents, and the school-books he uses, are filled with the atmosphere of religion. For it is only by such means that the religious spirit will grow and deepen with the development of the child's mind and character.

Art. 3—*The Church's Function in Education*

Pre-Eminence of the Church's Rights.—Man has been raised by God's free ordinance to the supernatural state the perfection and culmination of which are to be founded in the eternal union of man's soul with God Himself in Heaven. Now, the Church has supreme control of everything connected with man's supernatural state, the interest of which must necessarily outweigh all others. It is an inference from these truths that in the present order of God's Providence the Church's rights and duties in the education of the children are pre-eminent and superior to all others, seeing that these others are founded on nature alone.

This pre-eminence of the supernatural over the natural order and the consequent superiority of the Church's authority and rights are not opposed to any rights founded

---

[1] *Prov.* xii. 15. "Teach a child its duty," says the late Dr. Hedley, "and then enforce it. . . . It is no use beating a child, if you cannot persuade it also " (cf. Wilson's *Life of Dr. Hedley*).

[2] *Ib.*, p. 29.

merely upon nature, for both orders come from God Who cannot contradict Himself. Hence the Church's prerogatives and rights, and their pre-eminence over all merely natural rights and duties, far from colliding with the legitimate authority and rights of the family and the State tend to safeguard and secure them, in accordance with the words of Jesus Christ : " *Seek ye first the Kingdom of God, and His Justice, and all these things shall be added unto you.*"[1]

Foundation of the Church's Title to Educate.

—The Church's authority in the matter of education is made clear by the express words, of her Divine Founder : " *All power is given to me in heaven and on earth. Going therefore teach ye all nations : baptising them in the name of the Father, and of the Son, and of the Holy Ghost . . . and behold I am with you all days, even to the consummation of the world.*"[2]

From these words it follows, as Pius IX writes, that :

" the Church has been set by her Divine Author as the pillar and ground of truth in order to teach the divine faith to men . . . to direct and fashion men, in all their actions individually and socially, to purity of morals and integrity of life in accordance with revealed doctrine."[3]

The Church's right to control and direct education also follows from her supernatural motherhood, in virtue of which she " the spotless Spouse of Christ, generates, nurtures and educates souls in the divine life of grace, with her sacraments and her doctrine."[4] In other words the Church being the parent of the Christian as to his spiritual life, has a primary right to educate the Christian child just as his natural parents have.

Comprehensiveness and Independence of Church's Function.

—Furthermore, the Church being a perfect society is independent of any earthly power in the free use of the means conducive to the end for which she was founded, Now every form of instruction has a necessary connection with men's eternal salvation, and is therefore subject to the

---

[1] *Matth.* vi. 33.   Cf. also Pius XI, *ib.*, pp. 12, 13.   [2] *Ib.* xxviii. 18–20.
[3] *Quam non sine*, 1884.   (Cf. *Fontes Jur. Can.*, vol. ii, p. 984, cited by Pius XI, *ib.*, pp. 6, 7).
[4] Pius XI, *ib.*, p. 7.

dictates of the divine law of which the Church is the interpreter and the guardian.[1] From these principles the
following inferences may be drawn:

(a) **Church's Authority Supreme in Teaching Faith and
Morals.**—In the moral and religious education of the child,
the parents, and those to whom the child's education may
be entrusted act as the mandatories of the Church, and
are directly subject to the Church's control and guidance.
Besides, in all matters which may affect the child's spiritual
interests *even indirectly*, they are bound by the divine law
to abide by the Church's decisions.

Consequently, the Bishop of the diocese, in the first
instance, or, in cases referring to the whole country, the
higher ecclesiastical authorities such as a Plenary Synod,
or, in the last resort, the Holy See can give authoritative
decisions, which Catholics are bound to obey, as to the
suitability or non-suitability for Catholic pupils of a certain
system of education, of a particular college or university,
or even of a special text-book.

(b) **Can Found Schools and Universities.**—The Church
has an inalienable right independent of all State authority
to found schools of all kinds, not only for the teaching of
matters which directly affect faith and morals, but for the
teaching of any or all subjects whatsoever.

"With full right," again writes Pius XI, "the Church promotes letters, science and art, in so far as necessary or helpful
to Christian education in addition to her work for the salvation
of souls, founding and maintaining schools and institutions,
adapted to every branch of learning and culture. Nor may even
physical culture, as it is called, be considered outside the range
of her maternal supervision, for it also is a means which may
help or harm Christian education."[2]

---

[1] *Ib.*, pp. 7, 8.
[2] *Ib.*, p. 9. Cf. also *Cod. Jur. Can.*, C. 1375. "The Church has the
right to found schools for every class of education, whether elementary,
secondary or higher." Hence the dissolution or expulsion by the civil
authority of the religious congregations, or the suppression of the ecclesiastical or monastic schools, colleges or universities, such as took place
in Ireland and Britain in the 16th and 17th centuries, and in recent times
in France, Portugal, Mexico, and Russia, and is now (1931) threatened
in Spain, is unjust, tyrannical, and a direct violation of the divinely-given
prerogatives of the Church.

(c) **Her Great Educational Resources.**—We have in another place[1] seen how the Church has been the inspirer and promoter of education and of all branches of science both sacred and profane ; and how the whole civilisation and true culture of the European races are founded upon the Church's efforts and the Church's teaching. The means of education, which the Church has at her disposal are countless. They include the Sacraments—those divinely instituted means of obtaining the helps and graces which the child needs to acquire virtuous habits and overcome unruly passions. There are besides the philosophical formation and mental culture which a knowledge even of the essential religious truths imply. Included also are the sacred ritual and liturgy which are so wonderfully instructive and inspiring. Even the material fabric of the Churches and other ecclesiastical buildings, as well as the treasures of art which they contain, have an immense educational value. Finally must be reckoned the great number and variety of schools, associations and institutions of all kinds, which the Church has established for the training of youth not only in Christian piety but also in literature and science, as well as her various institutions for recreation and physical culture.[2]

As a result of all this the ordinary Catholic boy or girl has at command in the institutions of religion an opportunity of education and culture, including intellectual training, which is far superior to anything that the children of the non-Catholic of the same social class possess.

Hence the State has no right to obstruct or interfere with the teaching activity of the Church or to refuse the fullest recognition to the Church's schools, universities, diplomas, and academic degrees. Nay the State is bound to encourage and assist in due measure the Church's schools as being most of all in accord with Christian tradition and the spirit of the Divine law.

(d) **Her Teaching Authority Extends to All, even Non-Catholic Nations.**—The Church's mission as educator embraces every nation without exception ; and in its ful-

---

[1] Cf. *Supra,* chaps. iii to v.
[2] *Ib.,* p. 36.

filment her God-given authority is subject to no earthly power.

" The extent of the Church's mission," writes Pius XI, " in the field of education is such as to embrace every nation without exception, according to the command of Christ, ' *Teach ye all nations*,' and there is no power on earth that may lawfully oppose her or stand in her way. . . . Her mission to educate extends equally to those outside the fold, seeing that all men are called to enter the Kingdom of God and seek eternal salvation."[1]

(e) **Can Supervise All Teaching of Catholics.**—The Church is bound in virtue of her office, and, consequently, has an inalienable right to supervise secular teaching and even the pupil's whole training as far as may be found necessary in order to safeguard him against all danger to faith or morals. This right of supervision extends to all manner of schools and institutions, whether religious or otherwise, in which Catholics are educated.

" It is," writes Pius XI, " the inalienable right as well as the indispensable duty of the Church to watch over the entire education of her children, in all institutions public or private, not merely in regard to the religious instruction there given, but *in regard to every other branch of learning*, and every regulation in so far as religion and morality are concerned."[2]

The rights and authority of the Church in these matters are thus summarised in the Sacred Canons :

C. 1381. " The religious education of the children in all schools whatsoever is subject to the authority and inspection of the Church. " The Ordinaries [viz., the Bishop of the diocese and his official representatives] have the right and the duty to take care that nothing contrary to faith or morals be taught, or any unlawful custom or conduct tolerated in *any school* within their diocese.

" The teaching of religious knowledge and the books used are also subject to their approval. Furthermore, for the purpose of safeguarding religion and morals, they have the power to demand the removal of any teacher from the school, or to forbid the use of any book.

C. 1382. " They have also the right of visitation and inspection, to be exercised personally or by their delegates, of all schools whatsoever, as well as all institutions for recreation, protection, patronage, etc., with a view to the religious and moral interests there concerned."[3]

---

[1] *Ib.*, pp. 11, 12. [2] *Ib.*, p. 10. [3] *Codex Jur. Can.*, Canons 1381, 1382.

Art. 4—*Functions of the State in Education*

Not Founded on Parenthood.—The rights and duties of the State in education, not being founded upon a title of fatherhood, are on a completely different plane from those of the Church and the family. The State, unlike the Church, is in no sense the parent of its members, who exist before it and whose rights are prior to those of the State. The end and object of the State's existence is to secure for its members the free exercise of their rights, and to assist them to attain to the highest spiritual and temporal well-being. From this we may gather what its proper functions in education are. These may be summarised as follows :

(*a*) **Should Protect and Assist the Work of Parents and Church.**—The first duty of the State in education is to safeguard and enforce the God-given rights of the parents and the Church, in carrying on and controlling the education of the children. In matters which need the assistance of public resources or the support of the arm of the law, the State is bound under this heading to supply that assistance as far as it can. Hence, it is a primary duty of the civil government to remove the public dangers and impediments, which may obstruct or counteract the religious and moral formation of the rising generation ; for the State alone can effectually deal with such matters. Consequently, it is the duty of the State and the municipal authorities to take effective measures against youth being exposed to the degrading influence of the modern unchristian press and cinema and improper public amusements and shows, which so often lead to the undoing of the best efforts of the Church and of Catholic parents.

" Snares and temptations to sin abound," writes Leo XIII; " impious and immoral dramas are exhibited on the stage ; books and the daily press jeer at virtue and ennoble crime ; and the fine arts themselves, which were intended for virtuous use, and rightful recreation are made to minister to depraved passion. Nor can we look to the future without fear ; for the seeds of evil are continually being sown broadcast in the hearts of the rising generation."[1]

As to the schools themselves the State should begin by encouraging and assisting good private schools, due to the

---

[1] *Exeunte Jam Anno,* 1888, p. 97.

initiative of the Church or the parents. State schools are to be set up only where private schools and those of the Church are found to be insufficient.

" It (viz., the State) should begin," writes Pius XI, " by encouraging and assisting of its own accord the initiative and activity of the Church and the family whose successes in this field have been clearly demonstrated by history and experience. It should, moreover, supplement their work whenever it falls short of what is necessary even by means of its own schools and institutions."[1]

The State may, where necessary, force the parents by means of suitable legal sanctions to fulfil their duties towards their children but it cannot, at least in normal circumstances, legitimately deal with the child except through the parents. On this subject Pius XI again writes :

" The State can exact and take measures to secure that all its citizens have the necessary knowledge of their civil and political duties, and a certain degree of physical, intellectual and moral culture, which, considering the circumstances of our times, is really necessary for the common good."[2]

(b) And in Exceptional Cases even Assume Direct Control.—

The State can assume direct control of the child's education only in the comparatively rare cases, when, the parents being dead, the child has no other suitable guardians; or when unnatural parents completely and invincibly neglect their parental duties. In such cases the civil power may, *in default of suitable agencies organised by private charity* (which is the preferable, and in a Christian country should be the normal alternative), assume the parents' place, taking care, however, that the religious and moral training of the child be carried out under the direction and guidance of the Church. Pius XI, treating of this phase of the subject, writes :

" It also belongs to the State to protect the rights of the child itself, when the parents are found wanting . . . whether by default, incapacity or misconduct. . . . In such cases, exceptional no doubt, the State does not put itself in the place of the family, but merely supplies deficiencies, and provides suitable means, always, however, in conformity with the natural rights of the child, and the supernatural rights of the Church."[3]

---

[1] *Divini Illius,* p. 20. [2] *Ib.,* p. 20. [3] *Ib.,* pp. 19, 20.

(c) **May Reserve to Itself a Certain Type of Higher Schools.**—The State may legitimately reserve to itself the establishment and direction of schools intended to prepare candidates for certain civil duties, connected with the due administration of public affairs and especially with military service. The reason assigned for this is that these functions call for special aptitudes and special preparation, and are directly concerned with the public good, which it is the special duty of the State to safeguard and promote. Even in such schools, however, care must be taken that the rights of the Church and of the parents are safeguarded and respected.[1]

(d) **Should Carry on Civic Education.**—It is also a portion of the functions of the State to provide what may be called civic education not only for the youth, but for all ages and classes. This is described by Pius XI as consisting

" in the practice of presenting publicly to groups of individuals information having an intellectual, imaginative and emotional appeal, calculated to draw their wills to what is upright and honest and to urge its practice by a sort of moral compulsion, positively by disseminating knowledge and negatively suppressing what is opposed to it."[2]

It is in accordance with the principle here laid down that in some countries the State assumes practical control of the cinema, as well as the radio, which it utilises for educational purposes.

State Monopoly Unlawful and Perilous.—Finally, regarding the functions of the State in education, the following words of the Pope are of special importance :

" Unjust and unlawful is any monopoly educational or scholastic, which physically or *morally forces families to make use of government schools,* contrary to the dictates of the Christian conscience, or contrary even to their legitimate preferences,"[3]

State monopoly of education (which, even at its best, is contrary to the whole tendency of the natural law) is always full of the greatest danger to the public good, and to the spiritual interests of the people. It places in the

---

[1] *Divini Illius*, p. 21.   [2] *Ib.*, p. 22.   [3] *Ib.*, pp. 10–20.

hands of a bureaucracy the power, which will inevitably be sometimes abused, of moulding the character and the ideals of the whole people. Such a monopoly, though not asserted in theory, is in practice brought about where the State, by confining its patronage and its subsidies to the State schools, or by dictating school programmes, which all schools must follow in order to obtain State subsidies, virtually crushes out private schools. For it thus directly forces most parents to send their children to the schools controlled by the State, or at least to adopt the State programme of education. Voluntary schools whose programme and administration are in no respect under State control have an equal claim, and, as their constitution is more in accord with the dictates of the natural and the Divine law, a far *greater claim* upon the patronage and the subsidies of the State. Hence, it will be the policy of a really Christian government to assist and multiply efficient and suitable voluntary schools. Such a government will also avoid the pernicious practice of forcing schools under the penalty of forfeiting the State subsidies to follow a uniform programme fixed by the State.

The imposition of a uniform programme and system which all the schools must adopt in order to obtain State subsidies, and which all the pupils, whether urban or rural, are practically forced to follow no matter what their individual needs or future intentions may be, is manifestly unnatural and unsound, and is especially so in a country whose population is largely rural. Moreover, the consequent competition of the schools and of the children in public written examinations tends to pervert the true idea of education, and degrade it to a commercial level.

Art. 5—*The Moral and Religious Elements in the Schools*

Religious Teaching at Every Stage.—To ensure the due moral and religious education of the young generation it is not sufficient that the schools in which the youth are trained recognise the control of the Church and that all harmful influences be eliminated. Positive religious teaching should form an important element in the child's education at every stage, so that the religious spirit may grow and deepen with the development of the child's mind and character. The degree of religious knowledge and religious training that may suffice for an illiterate man would be inadequate for one of moderate literary attainments ; and what may do sufficiently well for the latter would fall far short of the standard necessary for the university graduate, the journalist, the scientist, or the statesman.

Hence, the Catholic Church ordains that religious doctrine and religious training must, in every system of education, *form an essential part of the programme* in the primary, the vocational or technical, the secondary or intermediate and the university and professional schools.

" The school," writes Pius XI, " must not be in opposition to, but in positive accord with, the . . . family and the Church, and constitute as it were one sanctuary of education with them. Otherwise it is doomed to fail of its purpose and to become instead an agent of destruction.   For as a layman [Nicholas Tommaseo], famous for his pedagogical writings, says ' . . . The school, if not a temple, is a den,'   And again, ' when literary, social, domestic and religious education do not go hand in hand, man is unhappy and helpless.' " [1]

The precepts of the Canon Law on this subject are as follows :

C. 1372. " All the faithful are to be so trained from their childhood that not only nothing be imparted to them contrary to the Catholic faith or good morals, but that religion and moral training be given a foremost place in their education.

C. 1373. " In every elementary school the children must receive religious training suited to their age.   Young people attending intermediate or higher schools [such as university colleges or professional and vocational schools] must receive a fuller religious training ; and let the ecclesiastical authorities take care that this be done by priests who are distinguished for learning and zeal." [2]

Catholic Environment in Every School and Educational System.—But mere religious instruction is not sufficient. Religion cannot be treated as a subject apart like mathematics or literature or physical drill.   It must enter into every detail of the child's training.

" It is necessary," writes Pius XI, " that all the teaching and the whole organisation of the school as well as the teachers, the

---

[1] *Ib.*, p. 37.   [2] *Cod. Jur. Can.*, Canons 1372, 1373.

syllabus and the text-books in every branch be regulated by
the Christian spirit, under the direction and maternal supervision
of the Church, so that religion may be in very truth the foundation and crown of the youth's entire training, and this in every
grade of school, not only the elementary but also the intermediate and higher institutions of learning."[1]

The Pope here only repeats and confirms the precepts
already strongly insisted on by Leo XIII who, treating of
the same matter, writes :

" It is necessary not only that religious instruction be given
to the young at certain fixed times, but also that *every other
subject taught be permeated with Christian piety*. If this is
wanting, if this sacred atmosphere does not pervade and warm
the heart of masters and scholars alike, little good can be expected from any kind of learning and considerable harm will
often be the consequence."[2]

" Neutral " or " Mixed " Schools.—It is principally in
order to ensure that the atmosphere of the school, the programme of study, the general spirit and tone of the teaching
should be permeated with the spirit of religion and Catholic
piety, that the Church forbids the faithful to frequent neutral
or mixed schools, or any others except those which are
definitely and entirely Catholic. Thus the Canon Law lays
down :

C. 1374. " Catholics must not frequent non-Catholic schools
nor such as are open to non-Catholics or have no particular
religion. It belongs solely to the Ordinary of the diocese to
decide, in accordance with the rules made by the Holy See, in
what particular circumstances the attendance of Catholics at
such schools may be tolerated ; and [in case their attendance is
permissible] what safeguards are to be applied to avoid danger
of perversion."[3]

Pius XI treating of the same subject writes :

" The so-called ' neutral ' or ' lay ' school from which religion
is excluded is contrary to the fundamental principles of education.
Such a school, moreover, cannot exist in practice : it is bound
to become irreligious. . . . Neither can Catholics admit that

---

[1] *Ib.*, p. 38.
[2] *Militantis Ecclesiæ* (1897). (*Fontes Jur. Can.*, vol. iii, p. 520). Cf. also
Actes de Leon XIII, vol. v, p. 198 (Maison de la Bonne Presse, Paris).
[3] *Cod. Jur. Can.*, C. 1374.

other type of mixed school [least of all the *école unique*—obligatory on all] in which the students are provided with separate religious instruction, but receive other lessons, in common with non-Catholic pupils, from non-Catholic teachers."[1]

These regulations of the sacred canons by which the " neutral " or " lay " schools are definitely condemned are only a repetition of prohibitions already repeatedly issued by Pius IX and Leo XIII ever since the middle of the last century when these schools began to arise in Britain, Europe and America under the influence of Liberalism and Freemasonry.[2]

The compulsory education of children free of charge in the State schools without regard to religion has been one of the most important items of Masonic policy all over the world for the past seventy years. The following citation from the official declaration of the Supreme Council of A. and A. Scottish Rite, Southern Jurisdiction, U.S.A., issued

---

[1] *Divini Illius*, pp. 37, 38. Cf. also Leo XIII—*Militantis Ecclesiæ* (1897). (*Fontes Jur. Can.*, vol. ii, p. 519).

The primary or " National " Schools of Ireland have never been approved by the Holy See or the Irish Bishops. They are only tolerated ; for in their conception and legal constitution, they are " neutral " or " mixed " schools. Although in their practical working they have, in the course of time, approximated more and more to the standard and character of Catholic schools, they still remain only tolerated as being sufficiently " safe for Catholics " (*tutas pro Catholicis*), especially as the reading books are not always definitely Catholic, but of such a character as to suit non-Catholics equally well. The Maynooth Synod specifies the conditions upon which the limited approbation given to the National Schools may be continued. These are—that :

(*a*) The present Managerial System by which the school remains under the management and control of the Parish Priest or some other priest approved by the Bishop be maintained.

(*b*) That the school buildings remain under the control and ownership of the ecclesiastical authorities, and,

(*c*) That the appointment and dismissal of teachers remain in the hands of the clerical Manager and subject in each case to the express approval of the Bishop.

In what are called the " Model Schools " the above conditions still remain unrealised : and hence these schools remain under the Church's ban as being, in the full sense, " neutral " and " mixed," and therefore unsuitable for Catholic children. The Synod adds, however, that if certain conditions be fulfilled, the Bishop of the particular diocese in which one of these schools is situated, may allow Catholic children to attend it. (Cf. *Concil. Plen. Maynut.* (1927) *Acta et Decreta*, Tit. xxxviii, n. 386—Dublin, 1929).

[2] Cf. Pius XI, *ib.*, p. 37, where references are given to the preceding condemnations.

in 1921, is worth quoting, as it defines the Masonic aim accurately and definitely :

"We approve and reassert our belief in the free and compulsory education of the children of our nation in public primary schools supported by public taxation, which all children shall attend and be instructed in the English language only, without regard to race or creed ; and we pledge the efforts of the membership of the Rite to promote by all lawful means the organisation extension and development to the highest degree of such schools and to continually oppose the efforts of any and all who seek to limit, curtail or destroy the public school system of our land."[1]

Concerning countries where there are different religious beliefs, Pius XI writes :

"In such a case it becomes the duty of the State . . . to leave free scope to the initiative of the Church and the family, while giving them such assistance as justice demands. That this can be done to the full satisfaction of families and to the advantage of education . . . is clear from the actual experience of some countries comprising different religious denominations."[2]

Non-Catholic Schools and Universities.—It is in accordance with the general principles of Catholic discipline that the Plenary Synod of Maynooth (1927) renews in such strong terms its precepts against Catholics attending Trinity College, Dublin, or any other non-Catholic college, and forbids priests and clerics of all grades, even *under pain of grave sin*, to advise or recommend in any way, parents or guardians to send the youth under their charge to Trinity College, or to recommend the youths themselves to attend it.[3] The Fathers of the same synod also expressly and definitely forbid Irish parents to send their children, whether boys

[1] See the front page of *The New Age*, official organ of the A. & A. S. R., in which this declaration regularly appears printed in heavy type. *The New Age* is published monthly at 1735 16th Street, New York. The Ancient and Accepted Scottish Rite of Freemasonry is probably the most dangerous and the most profoundly anti-Christian section of Freemasonry. Its centre is in the United States of America. It has affiliated sections in most countries of America and Europe. It is very strong in Great Britain and Ireland. Cf. Cahill—*Freemasonry*, etc. (2nd edit., 1930), pp. 18, 38, 44, 45, 140, etc.

[2] *Divini Illius*, p. 39. On this subject, cf. a very useful and interesting series of articles in *The Irish Monthly*, vols. 57 and 58 (1929–1930), by N. Umis, M.A.).

[3] *Concil. Plen. Maynut.* (1927), *Acta et Decreta*, Tit. xxxix, n. 398. In this prohibition and by the injunctions regularly repeated in their pastorals, the Irish Bishops decide in accordance with Canon 1374 quoted above, that the circumstances which may make it necessary

24

or girls, to non-Catholic schools.[1] The Colleges of the present National University on the other hand, although "neutral" or "mixed," are allowed as being, owing to special circumstances and certain precautions adopted, "sufficiently safe for Catholics as far as faith and morals are concerned" (*quoad fidem et mores satis tuta*).

The Synod of Maynooth also allows Catholic youths to attend "neutral" day technical or agricultural schools *at which only these arts or sciences are taught and no further cultural education given.* The Synod, however, adds the injunction that the parish priest should personally, or through his curate, give to the pupils attending these schools, a fuller course of religious instruction.[2]

The Synod strictly forbids Catholics to live as boarders in any of these technical or agricultural schools, with the proviso, however, that the Bishop of the diocese may, for special reasons, give permission to do so in any particular case.

Art. 6—*Some Further Points Regarding Christian Education*

The following additional matter having reference to the general subject of Education may be useful, as illustrating more fully the Catholic standpoint and ideals.

Safeguarding Parents' Control over their Children.—The civil authority should by suitable laws co-operate in securing for parents full power to control and correct their children (whereas in many countries, especially in France, the United States, and, to a growing extent, in England, the civil laws tend in the opposite direction). Thus the State should make it illegal to employ any boy or girl under age without the express consent of the parents ; and, in case such boys

---

or justifiable *in some countries* to *tolerate* temporarily the attendance of Catholic children at non-Catholic schools, do *not exist* in Ireland. In face of these prohibitions and of the inevitable harm which must result for the children themselves, not to speak of the public scandal, it is difficult to see how Irish parents sending their children to non-Catholic schools can be excused from grave sin.

[1] *Concil. Plen. Maynut.* (1927), *Acta et Decreta*, Tit. xli, nn. 403, 404.

[2] *Ib.*, Tit. xl, n. 402. The permission here given to attend "neutral" technical schools would not apply to technical schools which include cultural courses such as literature, history, etc., in the programme. Catholics, therefore, could not frequent such schools, according to the Church's discipline, except the schools are exclusively Catholic.

or girls are employed, the wages should be placed by law under the parents' control.[1]

" Free Education for All."—The principles implied in the shibboleth, " Free Education for all," which have been gaining ground in modern times, under the influence of Liberalism and Socialism, are full of danger to the interests of family life, especially where the free education is to be given at the public expense in State schools. The danger becomes greater when the State or the municipal authority supplies books, stationery, and medical attendance, and sometimes even free meals,[2] to the children.

This system, suggesting as it does that the children belong to the State rather than to the parents, tends to withdraw both teachers and children from the parents' control. Besides, parents do not, under a system of the kind, take the same interest in the child's education as they do when they themselves defray at least some portion of the expenses. Hence it seems most desirable, in the best interests of both child and parent, that the latter should in all cases pay *directly* at least a small portion, and, where possible, even a considerable portion of the educational expenses.[3]

Selection of Teachers.—In the selection of teachers, especially for the primary and secondary stages of education, the moral character and religious training of the teachers are of the first importance. Thus it is that, according to Catholic tradition and practice, priests, nuns and members

---

[1] Cf. Devas—*Pol. Economy*, bk. i, chap. viii " Family and Law " ; also blt. iii, chap. vi.

[2] If free meals be needed owing to the extreme poverty of some of the parents, the expedient should be regarded as abnormal and temporary ; and the meals should, where at all possible, be supplied through the medium of the parents themselves or some religious or charitable organisation ; and every effort should be made by the rulers of the State to adjust the economic life of the country in such a way that the abnormal state of destitution which makes such an expedient necessary, should cease or be very rare.

[3] The custom which obtained in Ireland up to about the end of the 19th century, of supplying school books to the children on very cheap and special terms, while on the other hand the parents paid certain " tuition " fees to the National school teachers, has been dropped greatly to the loss of both parents and children, and even of the teachers themselves, whose authority with the child carries greater weight when supported by the active interest of the parent. It would seem very desirable that this laudable custom be again revived.

of religious orders and congregations are usually preferred
to all others ; and it should be the policy of a Christian
government to encourage and multiply efficient schools
under religious control.

Teachers not Civil Servants nor Ordinary Workers.—

Although teachers should be generously remunerated and
the teaching profession very highly esteemed by reason of
its excellence and importance for all the best interests of
the community, teachers should not be regarded as civil
servants ; for they are not such, even when they are paid
wholly or in part by the State.   They are no more to be
classed as civil servants than are the parochial clergy in
the countries in which the clergy are maintained by State
subsidies.   Just as the priest in the performance of his
sacred office is, and by the Divine law must remain, the
mandatory of the Church, so also the teacher of the child
is, according to the natural and Divine law, the mandatory
of the Church and of the parents in his dealings with the
child.

Hence, too, in the appointment, the retaining and dismissal of a teacher, the authority of the Church and the
parents must be supreme, and in deciding such matters the
good of the child must outweigh all other considerations.

For similar reasons it is manifestly incongruous and
improper that teachers' associations should be in any way
affiliated to the ordinary Labour Unions.   Such an affiliation
suggesting that the office of teacher is exercised (like that
of productive labour) principally for the personal gain and
advantage of the teacher, and not for the nobler motives
which should inspire him, tends to injure in very many ways
the teacher, the child and the profession itself.   These
reasons are all the more powerful in Ireland as the causes
which may have at one time justified or partially justified
the affiliation referred to have now ceased to exist.

Teachers' Guilds.—

All the reasons which have caused the
Holy See to set its face against Catholic workers belonging
to neutral or mixed Labour Unions[1] (viz., those which admit
non-Catholics) apply with much greater force to neutral or

---

[1] Cf. Chap. xxii, art. 5.

mixed organisations of teachers. The Catholic teacher is, as we have shown, primarily and essentially the mandatory of the Catholic Church and the assistant of the Church's sacred ministers in the great work of training and fashioning the little ones of Christ to become true sons and daughters of Christ's Kingdom. Such an office and profession cannot be reconciled, without perverting its nature and degrading its ideals, with the principles and general outlook of the non-Catholic teacher, seeing that the religion of the latter, if he have any, is irreconcilable with the Catholic faith, and the whole Catholic outlook on life.

Consequently, it is most urgently needed with a view to the refashioning of the social organism in accordance with Catholic principles, that Catholic Teachers' Guilds be organised upon the traditional principles of the Church. With the aid of the Catholic Preparatory Colleges and Training Colleges and the exceptionally good material for such an organisation among the Irish Catholic lay teachers both men and women, the formation of such a Catholic Teachers' Guild in Ireland should present no insuperable difficulties.

Naturalism in Education—(a) New Pedagogic Methods.— On this subject, the following extracts from the great Encyclical of Pius XI, already so often referred to, are of special importance :

" Every form of pedagogic naturalism which in any way excludes or weakens supernatural Christian formation in the teaching of youth, is false. Every method of education founded wholly or in part on the denial or forgetfulness of original sin and of grace, and relying on the sole powers of human nature is unsound.

" Such, generally speaking, are those modern systems bearing various names, which include a pretended self-government and unrestrained freedom on the part of the child, and which diminish or even suppress the teacher's authority and action,[1] attributing to the child an exclusive primacy of initiative and an activity independent of any higher law, natural or divine, in the work of education . . . as if there existed no decalogue, no Gospel law, no law even of nature stamped by God on the heart of man, promulgated by right reason and codified in positive revelation by God Himself in the ten commandments . . .

---

[1] " Having . . . sought by the most profound reflection to discover what the two fundamental rules in education were, I have found them to be *authority* and *respect* " (Dupanloup—*The Child*, p. 9, " Preface.")

" If any of these terms are used less properly to denote the necessity of a gradually more active co-operation on the part of the pupil in his own education ; if the intention is to banish from education despotism and violence, *which, by the way, just punishment is not*, this indeed would be correct but in no way new. It would mean only what has been taught and reduced to practice by the Church in traditional Christian education."[1]

(*b*) **Co-Education.**—The following citations from the Encyclical of Pius XI are of special and practical importance in connection with the question of the intermingling of boys and girls in the same school. Co-education which has wrought and is now working such havoc in the United States and some other countries, and has become in its most extreme form one of the prominent characteristics of the new educational system of Soviet Russia, is being gradually introduced into Ireland during the past thirty years. It now obtains in the University Colleges, in some of the Technical schools, and to an increasing extent even in the Primary or National schools :

" False and harmful to Christian education is the so-called method of " co-education." This, too, by many of its supporters is founded upon Naturalism and the denial of original sin ; but by all upon a lamentable confusion of ideas that mistakes a levelling promiscuity and equality for the legitimate association of the sexes. . . . There is not in nature itself which fashions the two sexes quite different in organism, in temperament, in abilities, anything to suggest that there can or ought to be promiscuity, and much less equality in their training. . . . These principles . . . must . . . be applied to all schools, particularly in the most delicate and decisive period of formation, *that namely of adolescence ;* and in gymnastic exercises and deportment, *special care must be had of Christian modesty in young women and girls* which is so gravely impaired by any kind of exhibition in public."[2]

---

[1] *Divini Illius*, pp. 32, 33. Cf. also the resolution passed by the Bishops in Ireland at a Special General Meeting, held May 26th, 1926 : " Mixed Education in public schools is very undesirable, especially among the older children." See *Concil. Plen. Maynut.* (1927), Appendix, p. 287.

[2] *Ib.*, pp. 29, 30. Cf. also Dupanloup, *loc. cit.*, pp. 14, 15. " The child is a moral being endowed with liberty and capable of action. It is necessary that he should labour to develop, to ennoble, to elevate himself : otherwise his education is not accomplished. . . . In education what the teacher *does himself* is a trifling matter ; what *he causes to be done* is everything."

(c) **Sex Instruction.**—Although the subject of sex education is of less practical importance in countries where the Catholic tradition in such matters is still strong, it may be useful to give the following citations from the Pope's Encyclical :

"Another very grave danger is that naturalism which nowadays invades the field of education in that most delicate matter of purity of morals. Far too common is that error of those who with dangerous assurance and under an ugly term, propagate a so-called sex-education, falsely imagining that they can forearm youth against the dangers of sensuality by means purely natural, such as a foolhardy initiation and precautionary instruction for all indiscriminately ; and worse still, by exposing them at an early age to the occasion, in order to accustom them, so it is argued, and as it were to harden them against such dangers. Such persons grievously err in refusing to recognise the inborn weakness of human nature . . . and also in ignoring the experience of facts from which it is clear that evil practices, particularly in young people, are the effect not so much of ignorance as of the weakness of a will exposed to dangerous occasions and unsupported by the means of grace. In this extremely delicate matter, if, all things considered, some private instruction is found necessary and opportune, from those who hold from God the commission to teach, and who have the grace of state every precaution must be taken. Such precautions are well known in traditional Christian education."[1]

(d) **Glorification of Athletics.**—We conclude with the following extract, concerning an abuse which is an obvious danger in a highly developed material civilisation, such as that of the English speaking world :

" In these days there is spreading a spirit of nationalism which is false and exaggerated. . . . Under its influence various excesses are committed in giving a military turn to the so-called physical training of boys (sometimes even of girls contrary to the very instincts of human nature) ; or again, in usurping unreasonably on Sundays the time which should be devoted to religious duties and to family life at home.

" It is not our intention to condemn what is good in the spirit of discipline and legitimate bravery . . . nor the noble sentiments of military valour in defence of country and of public order. . . . We condemn only what is excessive, as for example, violence which must not be confounded with courage ; and again, the exaltation of athleticism which, even in classic pagan times, marked the decline and downfall of genuine physical training."[2]

---

[1] *Divini Illius*, p. 31.   [2] *Ib.*, pp. 21, 22.

Conclusion.—The Irish educational system regarded from the standpoint of Christian principles (with which alone we are concerned) has been in many respects gradually improved during the past half century or more ; and its present state, considering the strength of the forces that have been pitted against it during the past three and a half centuries, may well arouse in the heart of the Catholic Irishman sentiments of gratitude to God, mingled with a certain legitimate pride and joy.

It would, however, be an error to suppose that the system as it stands is perfect or free from danger. Neither the present system of primary education, nor the technical or vocational schools, nor (indeed much less) the Irish University system, nor even the Secondary system (owing to the state programme, etc., practically obligatory on all the schools), realise the ideals of Catholic education. All have been more or less the result of a forced compromise with the aggressive policy of Protestantism and unchristian Liberalism, and all, or nearly all, have originally been forced on the Irish Catholic nation from outside. Hence, one may hope that they will now be gradually refashioned in accordance with the full Catholic ideal. Above all it is to be hoped that Catholic Philosophy will be restored to its rightful place in our secondary and higher educational programmes.

CHAPTER XXI

MASTER AND SERVANT (EMPLOYER AND EMPLOYED)[1]

Art. 1—*General Principles*

The relations between master and servant are or may be an integral part of the family organism. Although not essential for human life like the conjugal and parental society, the institution of master and servant is in itself, and apart from the abuses and injustice of which it is too often the occasion, quite in accordance with the natural law, and, indeed, necessary for the efficient working of a fully organised State.

Meaning of Term.—In every period of history—at least since the human race attained to considerable numbers on the earth—there has been a distinction of social classes more or less strongly marked. Certain individuals or families, who control more property than they can utilise with the work of their own hands, employ others to assist

---

[1] The classical documents on this subject are the great Encyclicals of Leo XIII, especially the Encyclical on the condition of the Working Classes (*Rerum Novarum*, 1891, pp. 133 ff), and the Encyclical on Christian Democracy (*Graves de Communi*, 1901, pp. 168 ff). To these are to be added several Encyclicals and other Papal pronouncements issued by succeeding Pontiffs in which the teaching and precepts of Leo XIII are confirmed and developed. Among these we may specially mention the letter of Pius X addressed to the Bishops of Italy on Social Catholic Action (*Fin Dalla Prima*, 1903, pp. 182 ff), and his Encyclical on the same subject (*Il Fermo Proposito*, 1905, pp. 189 ff) : his letter addressed to the Bishops of France condemning Sillon Notre Charge Apostolique, Aug. 25th, 1910. (Cf. Ryan and Husselein—*The Church and Labour*, pp. 118 ff ; and *Actes de Pie X*, vol. v, pp. 124 ff, published by La Bonne Presse, Paris) : his letter to the German Hierarchy on the question of Christian syndicates and Catholic Unions—*Singulari Quadam* (1912). (Cf. Ryan and Husselein, *op. cit.*, pp. 127 ff). Finally, must be mentioned the decree of the Sacred Congregation of the Council to the Bishop of Lille, containing the recent decision of the Holy See on the labour dispute between the Catholic Employers and Employees of the French district of Roubaix-Turcoign near Lille. (Cf. *Acta Apostolicæ Sedis*, vol. xxi, 1929, pp. 494 ff). An English translation of this important document with a short introduction has been published by the Catholic Social Guild, Oxford (C. S. G., 1929). The volume (336 pp.) entitled *La Hiérarchie Catholique et le Problème Social*, issued 1931 by the Malines Union on the occasion of the 40th Anniversary

them. Again, some sections of the community, belonging
usually to the wealthier class, devote all their energies to
intellectual or artistic pursuits, to the work of public administration, to religious activities, or even to a life of
pleasure and dissipation, while servants or workpeople or
slaves are maintained to wait upon them, cook the food,
keep the house in order, and attend to most of their daily
wants. Hence, arises what is known in Catholic philosophy
as the *Herile Society* (*Societas Herilis*), or the Association
of Master and Servant.

This society may be defined as *the moral union between a
person owning property and another, in which the latter works
for the former and under his direction, receiving from him
what he needs to supply his own wants.* The term as thus
defined includes not only the union of master and servant
and that of employer with his workpeople, which come from
contract, but also the union between master and slave,
which usually arises from causes other than contract.

Servants, Labourers and Slaves.—Labourers or workpeople
differ from servants in that the latter live in the master's
house, forming part of the family, and apply their whole

---

of the *Rerum Novarum*, and published by the " Editions Spes," Paris, is
a complete bibliography and summary of the Papal and Episcopal pro-
nouncements on this subject during the forty years, 1891–1931.
    Cf. also Ryan—*The Living Wage* (New and Abridged Editions, Macmillan,
New York, 1920) and *Distributive Justice* (do., 1919) ; C. Macksey, S.J.—
Argumenta Sociologica, cap. iii (De Labore) ; Donat, S.J.—*Ethica Specialis*,
cap. iii, art. 1 (De Societate Herili), and cap. x, art. 5 (De Operariis) ;
Cronin—*Science of Ethics*, vol. ii, pp. 334 ff ; Ryan and Husselein—*The
Church and Labour.* (This volume contains besides much other valuable
matter, the Encyclicals and letters dealing with the present subject by Popes
Leo XIII, Pius X, and Benedict XV, as well as some of the more important
Episcopal documents, including the important Pastoral letter of the
Bishops of Ireland on the Labour Question, issued Feb., 1914) ; Metlake—
Ketteler's Social Reform, chap. x, " Christianity and the Labour Question,"
pp. 97–145 ; McKenna, S.J.—*The Church and Labour* (a series of six
articles on the Labour Question originally delivered as lectures, and now
published in one volume in the " Irish Messenger " Series, 1913–14) ;
V. Crawford—*The Church and the Worker* (C. S. G., Oxford. Booklet) ;
Garriguet, *op. cit.*, 3iéme Partie (Le Travail) ; *Code of Social Principles*
(C. S. G.), chap. iii, nn. 68–71, 91–102, and 114–120 ; Devas—*Political
Economy*, bk. iii, chaps. iv–ix ; Husselein, S.J.—*The World Problem :
(Capital, Labour and the Church)* (Washbourne, London, 1918) ; *Les
Nouvelles Conditions de la Vie Industrielle*—Compte Rendu in Extenso
de XXIe Session (Besançon, 1929) de Semaines Sociales de France
(Gabalda, 90 Rue Bonaparte, Paris, 1929).

labour to the service of the master ; while labourers do not form portion of the master's family, but contract to perform certain specified services in return for definite remuneration. Slaves differ from both servants and labourers. They are bound to give their whole labour to the master's service and in obedience to his direction, but the relations are not founded upon contract ; nor are the slaves free to withdraw from the master's control. Their status as slaves was forced upon them in punishment of crime, real or supposed, or as a result of captivity in war, or merely by reason of their servile birth.

Herile Society Sanctioned by Natural Law.—The union of master and servant (in which term we include here the labourer and even the slave) is a real society ; for the different parties are united by the moral ties of mutual rights and obligations ; and co-operate for the attainment of a common good. The good aimed at is the carrying out of certain industrial or domestic operations which immediately or remotely redound to the advantage of both, or are supposed to do so.

In its fundamental conception, and abstracting from the unjust and oppressive forms which it too often assumes, the union of master and servant is a *natural* union, not, however, in the same way or to the same extent as the conjugal or parental society. For the two latter are required for the very existence of the human race, and would be essential to man even in the state of innocence ; whereas men could live and multiply upon the earth, and realise a certain degree of social well-being, even if every individual or family did its own work, and nobody worked for another. Such a social system, however, could never reach any high level of perfection.

At Least in Man's Present Fallen State.—Nor is the union between master and servant demanded by the natural law even as imperatively as the civic union. Civil society, namely, the union of men in separate nations and states, for the purpose of promoting their temporal well-being, would probably have existed even in the state of innocence ; for the mutual co-operation which the civic union implies does not necessarily include anything derogatory to the

dignity or happiness of man. But the relations of master
and servant, although necessary for the well-being of man
as he now is, could most probably be dispensed with, were
it not for the inherent weakness of human nature resulting
from man's fall. Besides, the position of partial dependence,
which the status of servant implies, is less in accordance
with the ideal life that men would enjoy had they remained
in the state of original innocence.

Hence, we conclude that the union of master and servant
is a natural society only in a secondary sense. In its
relations to the natural law it is analogous to the social
system of private property, which, according to the
Scholastic philosophers, is ordained by what they call the
" Law of the Nations " (*Jus Gentium*). In other words
the institution has existed among all nations from the
beginning of recorded history, and is practically necessary
for the due progress and well-being of man as he now is.

Proofs of Foregoing.—That the relations of master and
servant and the social inequality which these relations
imply are necessary and inevitable in man's present state
is easily shown. Men differ in their capabilities, their
natural tastes, the degree of energy they possess, the good
or bad fortune that attends their efforts. Some excel in
physical strength and endurance, others in mental or
artistic gifts ; some are naturally fitted for direction and
rule, others need guidance and help. As a result of these
inequalities, differences in men's social status would inevitably arise after a little while even if all were to begin life
on the same footing.

But in fact all men do not begin life on the same footing
or within reach of like opportunities. For once granted
the individual's right to acquire the ownership of productive
property—a right which is natural to man—men will be
born under very varying conditions. The parents of some
are poor or even destitute ; those of others have independent
means. Some parents are wicked or careless or incom-
petent ; others are quite the reverse. These and such like
circumstances, more or less inherent in the life of fallen man,
co-operate to produce varying types and classes of men,
and to cause the widest differences in the initial opportunities
of temporal well-being within the reach of each. Some

will be highly cultured, others rude and ignorant. Some will have virtuous habits and instincts, carefully instilled and fostered from their infancy ; others inherit from their parents, or acquire from the surroundings of their child- hood, inclinations and principles which handicap them while life lasts. Finally, some begin life with abundant means which relieve them to a large extent of the necessity of earning their daily bread ; while others experience more or less from their infancy the constant pressure of poverty. Hence it is that Leo XIII writes :

" It is impossible to reduce society to one dead level. . . . There naturally exist among mankind manifold differences of the most important kind. People differ in capacity, skill, health, energy ; and unequal fortune is a necessary result of unequal condition."[1]

Now, difference of social condition leads to or necessarily implies the institution of master and servant. The wealthy owner cannot exploit or utilise his property without the assistance of others working under his control. One cannot enjoy the leisure that is needed for high intellectual or artistic work or for application to public administration except by employing servants to attend to one's ordinary wants. Besides, in a society made up of such various elements as we have described many will have no suitable opportunity (some even have no desire) of procuring the food, clothing and shelter which they need, or of enjoying the advantages of domestic life except by attaching them- selves to another family and working under the direction of its head.

Social Inequality Beneficial to Society.—This inequality of condition, resulting as it does in the institution of master and servant, at least in so far as it proceeds from a variety of talents and tastes, and from moderate degrees of difference in the goods of fortune, has been wisely permitted by Providence for the good of man ; for it is quite indispensable for the attainment of any high level of progress and social well-being. Though all cannot be wealthy and leisured, yet it is well that some should be so, and that there should be no insuperable barrier to prevent others attaining to that

---

[1] *Rerum Novarum*, 1891, p. 141.

position. For, in the first place, the hope of attaining to wealth and independence is a useful spur, which most men need, to stimulate energy and enterprise and to promote inventiveness and resource. Without such a motive, given human nature as it is, industry would languish ; progress in invention and organisation would be slow ; and the development of the earth's resources, so needful for man's temporal welfare, would be delayed.

Again, intellectual progress, artistic culture, the production of beautiful literature, the cultivation of music, painting, sculpture, architecture, and of all the ornamental side of life, would be well-nigh impossible, without the co-operation of a more or less leisured class. The same applies to elaborate civil organisation. Without a multitude of men, highly educated and trained and free to devote their whole energy to public administration, there can be no great political development. And such a class cannot exist without leisure and independent means and the co-operation of servants and labourers.[1]

Finally, the virtues of reverence, obedience, loyalty, resignation, and submission to the dispositions of Providence on the one hand, and those of kindness, generosity and liberality on the other—all so singularly fitted to develop the moral capabilities of men—would have less scope for their exercise, were not society made up of rich and poor, ignorant and learned, powerful and weak. On this subject Leo XIII again writes :

" Inequality is far from being disadvantageous either to the individual or to the community. Social and public life can be maintained only by means of various kinds of capacity co-operating for business and the playing of many parts ; and each man as a rule chooses the part which suits his own domestic condition.[2]

---

[1] An excellent example of this is to be found in the Irish social system, which continued to prevail over most of the country down to the end of the 17th century. The whole class of *literati*, including historians, poets, musicians, teachers, doctors, and lawyers, formed a kind of hereditary caste. They were leisured and wealthy, having in each principality lands specially set apart for their maintenance. The members of this class were the mainstay of the civic life and the custodians of the national tradition, and from them came the ministers and advisers of the ruling families. Consequently, the extermination of the *literati* was, from the very beginning of the English wars of conquest, one of the first objects of the invaders.

[2] *Rerum Novarum*, 1891, p. 141.

Wage Contract Not Necessarily Unjust.—Here it may be well to examine the objection put forward by socialists, or those imbued with communistic opinions, against the wage contract, as entered into for the purpose of industrial production. Relying on the principle (which can be interpreted in a true as well as a false sense) that one has a right to the full fruit of one's own labour, socialists say that the industrial wage-contract is in practice always unjust. For if the hired operative gets what is his due, (viz., the full value of the fruit of his toil), his work cannot bring any profit to the employer, who would therefore cease to employ him. The Capitalist, they say, continues to employ the labourer only on the condition that the latter surrender to the employer a portion of what in justice belongs to himself (viz., to the labourer). In other words the employer cannot make any profit from industrial operations carried on by employees except by unjustly *exploiting* (as the communists put it) the poorer members of the community.

That the communist conclusion is false, will become clear to one who applies the principle to certain individual cases. Suppose, for example, a labourer who, after a few years of regular work and frugal living, has saved a little money with which he purchases a small garden for the growth of fruit and vegetables. While continuing his own calling he engages a gardener for a just wage to do all the work in connection with the newly-acquired garden, (viz., to cultivate the garden and market the produce). If at the end of the year a certain moderate profit is realised, does the owner of the garden act unjustly in retaining it ? Common sense will decide that he does not : for this profit corresponds to the part contributed by himself (or rather by the garden which he had bought by his earnings) to the production from which the profit was made. Capital, therefore, does contribute something towards production, and hence the owner of the capital can justly claim a share in the profits. It follows that the wage-contract between employer and employed for industrial production is not essentially or always unjust.[1]

Social Inequality no Obstacle to Peace and Harmony.—That the different social classes can live together in harmony

---

[1] Cf. Pius XI—*Quadragesimo Anno,* pp. 28–31.

and contentment, and that such a union of various elements produces a well-ordered and prosperous society, is proved from the testimony of history. We have already shown in sketching the social conditions of the mediæval period how mutual harmony, contentment and widespread social well-being were realised at that period under the influence of Christian principles.

Class War Unnatural and Destructive.—The natural and Divine law, which ordains differences of gifts and talents and a consequent distinction of social classes, reprobates the repulsive theory of the Socialists—a product of an unjust and oppressive social régime—that the different classes are naturally hostile to each other, and are meant to live normally in mutual conflict. In fact, the very contrary is true ; for each class needs the other, and each is meant to assist the other ; and in a just and well-ordered social régime this mutual co-operation can be realised. For, as Leo XIII writes :

" Just as the symmetry of the human frame is the resultant of the disposition of the organs, so in a State it is ordained by nature that these two classes should dwell in harmony and agreement, and should, as it were, groove into each other, so as to maintain the balance of the body politic. . . . Mutual agreement results in pleasantness of life and the beauty of good order, while perpetual conflict necessarily produces confusion and disorder."[1]

Strikes and Lockouts.—A strike or a lockout is a kind of declaration of war. Both parties in the dispute, as well as the community at large, suffer loss. Not infrequently the families of labouring men on strike are exposed to cruel suffering and privation. In many cases, and especially when there is a cessation of a public service, even the interests of the whole community may be seriously affected. Besides, the victory in the struggle does not necessarily lie with the side whose cause is just but rather with the party that is the stronger or can endure the more. Hence a strike or a lockout is, like war, justifiable only in an extreme

---

[1] *Rerum Novarum*, p. 142.

case,[1] and it is essential to the public good that industrial life be organised on such a basis that the need or the temptation to use so dangerous a weapon be eliminated. Thus Pius XI writes :

" It is the primary duty of the State and of all good citizens to abolish conflict between classes with divergent interests and thus foster and promote harmony between the various ranks of society. . . .[2]

Italian Law of Corporations.[3]

—It is worthy of note before concluding our general remarks on the question of Employer and Employed, that a very interesting effort is being made in Italy to realise the ideal we have put forward of organising the productive forces of the country in such a manner as to make private interests coincide more easily with the general interest of the community ; to put an end to class-warfare ; and bring about the needed harmonious co-operation between the various classes and the different factors of production. For one may learn much from some aspects of the Fascist experiment without approving or sympathising with the excessive centralisation bureaucracy and statolatry which disfigure the Fascist régime in much of its actual conduct. By the Italian *Law of Corporations* (first passed in 1926, and afterwards considerably expanded by a number of explanatory regulations), strikes and lockouts have been made illegal, and are liable to heavy penalties. On the other hand, the workers and the unions are secured such a status and such privileges that strikes have been rendered unnecessary : and will probably soon be as antiquated as duelling or faction fighting. Since the passing of the Law of Corporations, and the Promulgation of the Fascist " Labour

---

[1] A strike or lockout is never justified except for a cause that is just and proportionately grave : that is, the interests at stake must be serious enough to justify a decision which is sure to cause so much bitterness, suffering and loss as a strike or lockout invariably causes. Even where such a cause is present, a strike or lockout cannot be lawfully resorted to until every other means of settling the case amicably has been tried and have failed. Neither may violence be used either to force others to take part in the lockout or strike, or to inflict injury on the opposing party. Again, certain services are so indispensable to the community that their cessation by strike or lockout could be justified only in very rare and extreme cases, if at all. Cf. *Code of Social Principles*, p. 44, also *Decrees of Maynooth Synod*, 1927 (C. T. S. edit.), n. 243.
[2] *Quadragesimo Anno*, p. 39.   [3] See *infra*, art. 5.

Charter " (1927), whose provisions have been made a norm or standard for the courts in Labour disputes, Italian industry has entered upon an era of tranquillity and substantial harmony such as had been unknown for more than half a century.[1]

Art. 2—*The Modern Labour Problem*

Its Gravity and Importance.—More than forty years have gone by since Leo XIII issued his great Encyclical on the condition of the working classes, which still remains the most important document on that subject. Among the opening sentences of the Encyclical we read :

" The momentous gravity of the state of things now obtaining fills every mind with painful apprehension ; wise men are discussing it ; practical men are proposing schemes ; popular meetings, legislatures and rulers of nations are all busied with it—and actually there is no question that has taken a deeper hold on the public mind. . . . There is general agreement that some opportune remedy must be found quickly for the misery and wretchedness pressing so unjustly on the majority of the working classes.[2]

These words are as true to-day as when they were first written. Although Social Science and the present day Catholic social movement include in their scope a multitude of other important questions besides those of labour and capital, it may be truly said that the need of solving the problems connected with these has been the main driving force behind the Catholic social movement in both its theoretical and practical sides.

Its Genesis.—As a consequence of the Protestant Revolt of the 16th century (the effects of which were felt more or less deeply in every country of Europe), and especially owing to the influence of Calvinism and Judaism, the greed for material gain began to prevail more and more as time went on especially among the mercantile and monied classes. The Christian teaching on the value and dignity of human

---

[1] Cf. Barnes—*Universal Aspects of Fascism* (Williams and Nordgate, London, 1928), pp. 203 ff ; also *Survey of Fascism*—Year Book (1928) of the *Cinef* (*Centre Internationale d'Etudes Fascistes*) (Benn, London, 1928), pp. 136–147.

[2] *Rerum Novarum*, 1891, p. 133.

personality was also gradually lost sight of. This attitude of mind gained fresh strength with the rise of Liberalism in the 18th century. The principles of individualism which had prevailed under the old pagan régime were reintroduced into the social life of Europe, and the Christian ideals of Justice and Charity lost their hold. It was accounted each one's sole duty to provide for his own interests, and the fullest freedom of competition was allowed one in doing so.

Under the guidance of Liberal teaching the only limit set by the civil law to the individual's freedom was to refrain from violence and to observe his contract. Neither the law nor the public conscience took cognisance of the principle that a contract to be just or binding must be free on both sides, and that there are human rights and fundamental laws which no contract and no human law can override. The limitations set by Christian teaching to the power of rulers and of owners were alike disregarded. Governments became despotic and iresponsible ; and the exaggerated principle that " a man may do what he likes with his own property " was openly upheld.

Furthermore, owing to the plunder of the Church's property (which had previously been to a great extent the patrimony of the poor) and the system of unchecked competition, introduced under the influence of the " Classical School " of Economics,[1] most of the wealth got concentrated in the hands of a minority, who freely exploited and oppressed the poor. The guilds were broken up and their property confiscated ; and down to the 19th century there was no other organisation to take their place.

The working classes were thus left at the mercy of the capitalist employers, especially in the non-Catholic countries, and were compelled to labour under inhuman conditions, with insufficient pay, excessive hours of work, and exposed to all the risks of uncertain employment, accident, sickness and unprovided old age.[2]

" Hence by degrees it has come to pass," writes Leo XIII, " that the working men have been surrendered, all isolated and helpless, to the hard-heartedness of employers, and the greed of

---

[1] Cf. *Supra*, chap. ix, art. 6.

[2] Cf. Devas—*Political Economy* (3rd edit., pp. 532, 533), for a brief account of the awful condition of the industrial workers in England during the first half of the 19th century.

unchecked competition . . . so that a small number of very rich men have been able to lay upon the teeming masses of the labouring poor a yoke little better than slavery itself."[1]

The Present Position.—It is true that in some respects the position of the workers has improved in many countries during the past fifty years. The improvement has been the result of the rise of the workers' unions in the second half of the 19th century and of the vigorous movements of social reform already discussed which began about the same period. The improved position, however, cannot be regarded as anything like a satisfactory solution. The masses of the population, especially in the English speaking countries, are devoid of all productive property and have no security against periods of unemployment. Hence although the wages of those who are actually employed may be usually sufficient[2] or nearly so, the general condition of the labouring population, in view especially of the bad housing and the uncertainty of employment, is beneath the standard required for a becoming livelihood. Thus, Pius XI refers to the "number of the dispossessed labouring masses, increased beyond all measure, whose groans mount to heaven;" and also to the "immense army of hired rural labourers whose condition is depressed in the extreme, and who have no hope of ever obtaining a share in the land," and he adds:

"The immense number of propertyless wage-earners on the one hand, and the superabundant riches of the fortunate few on the other is an unanswerable argument that the earthly goods

[1] *Rerum Novarum*, p. 133. For a fuller treatment of this subject, cf. Thorold Rogers—*Six Centuries of Work and Wages* (Fisher Unwin, London, 15th edit., 1923), chap. xv.

[2] Unfortunately they are not always so. Thus Dr. J. A. Ryan, author of *The Living Wage*, etc., asserts in an interesting article which was published in the *Catholic World* (July, 1930) that the average wage of unskilled labourers in U.S.A. is far below the standard of a living wage even when they have regular employment. For with money values, as they are in U.S.A. a working man would require at least from 1,600 to 1,800 dollars (£320 to £360) a year, whereas the unskilled worker's average wage is not over 1,000 dollars (£200). He adds that the conditions of work in the factories are so exacting that the men are usually worn out at the age of 45, when they are ruthlessly dismissed. In U.S.A. there is neither Unemployment Insurance nor Old Age Pensions. Hence the condition of the unemployed or age-worn worker is deplorable. (For a summary of Dr. Ryan's article, cf. *The Irish Rosary*, Aug., 1930, pp. 633–37).

so superabundantly produced in this age of industrialism are far from being rightly distributed or equitably shared among the various classes of men."[1]

The general position has become very serious in recent years in the United States of America, Germany and the British Isles owing to the unprecedented increase of unemployment. Hence the class antagonism is more bitter than ever ; and internal unrest threatens the stability of the whole fabric of European civilisation. The peril of a destructive socialistic revolution in which all things would be engulfed, is in many countries far more imminent now than it was forty years ago ; so that to-day, even as in 1891, the minds of thoughtful people are laden with doubt and apprehension ; and it is becoming daily more evident that unless effective measures be taken without delay to right social wrongs, " the peace and tranquillity of human society cannot be effectively defended against the forces of revolution."[2]

The Position in Ireland.—In Ireland, the military conquest of the 16th and 17th centuries ; the unchecked power of the Protestant ascendancy class ; the enforcement of social and economic principles at variance with the teachings of Christianity, have combined to produce a labour problem of a special character.[3] Among its outstanding features are emigration,[4] rural depopulation, enforced idleness, enforced celibacy or bachelorship, the unnatural and unparallelled poverty of a large proportion of the population especially in the towns and the seaboard; and all this, notwithstanding the facts that the poorer classes in Ireland are as a rule excellent citizens and quite willing to work, that the natural resources of the country are more than sufficient for the population, and that there is no insurmountable obstacle, such as a heavy national debt or a depraved public morality, to placing fair material well-being within the reach of all.[5]

---

[1] Pius XI—*Quadragesimo Anno*, p, 29.   [2] *Ib.*, p. 30.
[3] *See* Appendices II and III.
[4] Owing to the anti-immigration measures recently adopted in U.S.A., and the prevalent unemployment all over the English-speaking countries, Irish emigration has been brought to a standstill (1931).
[5] *See* Appendix III.

Division and Treatment of Subject.—In the following pages we shall lay down the general principles which, according to Catholic teaching, regulate the rights and duties of the different parties concerned. We shall then touch briefly on the lines of a practical solution which have been traced by Leo XIII and his successors, especially Pius XI, as well as by the Bishops of different countries.

Some of the principles we assume as already well known and accepted. Thus while private ownership of productive property is a natural right which no civil government may abolish, ownership in the Christian sense has many limitations, and implies various obligations founded upon Legal Justice, Charity and Piety regulating its use.

On the other hand, as we have already shown, the essential relations of master and servant, and the social inequalities which such relations imply, are in accordance with the natural law, and are useful to society provided they are animated by the Christian spirit which produced in previous ages such fair fruits of prosperity and social peace. The further principles which we shall discuss are little more than inferences from the Christian concept of ownership, the rights of human personality and the natural and divinely ordained structure of civil society.

Art. 3—*Duties and Rights of Employers and Employed*

Christian Attitude Towards Poverty and Subjection.—The general principles which, according to Christian teaching, should govern the attitude of employers and employed and their mutual relations with each other, are contained in the Encyclical, *Rerum Novarum*, of Leo XIII. Poverty is no disgrace, nor, except when it is excessive, is it any hindrance to real happiness and true prosperity. Neither is *reasonable* subjection to another's authority, in any way derogatory to human dignity. Our Lord, Who proclaimed that the " poor in spirit " were blessed, was Himself *actually* poor and was subject to St. Joseph. Neither do material riches and power confer greater personal worthiness on the possessor, or necessarily promote his happiness, or exempt him from the pain and sorrow and uncertainty which are the lot of all.

" Labour for wages," writes Leo XIII, is not a thing to be ashamed of, if we lend ear to right reason and Christian philosophy ; but is to a man's credit, enabling him to earn his living in an honourable way."[1]

Hence the wealthy and powerful have no right to despise the poor, who are their equals in human dignity; who are bound to them by the ties of Christian brotherhood, and may be their superiors in all the best things of life.[2] Neither have the poor—the servants and labourers—any reason to envy the rich and powerful, or to covet unduly their position for themselves. The real good of both is promoted by mutual co-operation under the Christian laws of social order, justice, charity and liberty.

How Christian Ideals Can be Realised.—The two main factors which are needed to secure this harmonious co-operation are the influence of religious principles on both sides and the reign of social justice in the economic organisation, so that all reasonable grounds for discontent may be as far as possible removed. The Catholic worker who is true to the teachings of his religion will be faithful and loyal in his duty towards his employer. He will work diligently and conscientiously, recognising his obligation of justice to give a fair day's work for a fair wage.

"Religion," says Leo XIII, "teaches the labourer and the artisan to carry out honestly and fulfil all equitable agreements freely entered into ; never to injure the property nor to outrage the person of the employer ; never to resort to violence in defending their own cause nor to engage in riot or disorder ; and to have nothing to do with men of evil principles who work upon the people with artful promises . . . and excite foolish hopes which usually end in useless regrets and grievous loss."[3]

In order, however, to realise the peace and concord which are so much desired, Christian principles must be observed on bóth sides. The worker has rights as well as duties ; and these rights must be respected by the employer, and duly upheld by the civil government as well as by the Church.

The Personal Rights of the Poor Must be Safeguarded.— The natural law which ordains for the common good the distinction of social classes forbids that any class should

---

[1] *Rerum Novarum*, p. 143.   [2] *Ib.*, pp. 146, 147.   [3] *Ib.*, p. 143.

oppress or exploit another class for its own selfish interests,
or that any individual be deprived of natural rights, the
first of which is freedom to live and develop one's faculties
as nature has ordained.   Moreover, He who created the
earth and all it contains, that men might satisfy their needs
by labouring upon it, ordained by that very act that a fair
opportunity of remunerative labour be allowed to all ; and
that the normal return from the reasonable labour of a
willing worker should be at least sufficient to satisfy his
normal needs.   Hence " *sweated labour* " (in which the poor
have to work for an insufficient remuneration or under unfair conditions) and enforced idleness (euphemistically termed
unemployment) in the presence of undeveloped natural
resources are unjust, or the results of social injustice.[1]

A Just Wage.[2]—It is by human labour that wealth is
produced.   Labour, however, would be impossible or must
needs remain ineffective, " had not God, the Creator of all
things, in His goodness bestowed in the first instance the
wealth and resources of nature, its treasures and its powers."
Labour or work essentially means the application of one's
energy whether of soul or body to the gifts of nature, in
order to make them available for man's use, or develop one's
faculties by means of them.   Now the natural law, or rather
God's will manifested by it, demands that in the process of
making nature's gifts available for men's needs, right order
be observed ; and this order, as already shown,[3] can be
normally realised only by everything having its proper
owner.   When a man works upon material or with capital

---

[1] The rights that are here referred to and the duties which correspond
to them come under the head of Legal and Distributive Justice, although
in case of " sweated labour " Commutative Justice is also frequently
violated.   It is not alone a question between employer and employed,
but also between the individual and the governing authority in the
municipality or State. Cf. *infra*, chaps. xxv and xxvi ; also Macksey,
op. cit., cap. iii, Thes. v ; Ryan—*Distributive Justice*, chap. xxiii ; Husselein,
S.J., *op. cit.*, chaps. xii–xiv ;   Kitson—*Unemployment* (Cecil Palmer,
London, 1921).

[2] What is put down in the remaining portion of the present article on
the question of a Just Wage is merely a summary, with a few explanations
added here and there, of the teaching of Pius XI in the recently issued
Encyclical *Quadragesimo Anno* (1931), pp. 24–35 (C. T. S. edit.).   Cf. also
Leo XIII—*Rerum Novarum* (1891), pp. 157, 158 ; also Dr. Ryan—*The
Living Wage*, pp. 3–108.

[3] Cf. *Supra*, chap. xvii, art. 2 ; also chap. vi, art. 1.

or machinery, of which he is himself the owner or which are not owned by anyone, all admit that he has a right to whatever wealth or new value his labour has produced. If, however, a man applies his labour to material owned by another, or utilises another's capital or machinery, the case is different : for the man's toil and his neighbour's property both concur in producing the new value, each being helpless without the other. In such a case it is, as Pius XI lays down,

" entirely false to ascribe the results of their combined efforts to either party alone, and it is flagrantly unjust that either should deny the efficacy of the other, and seize all the profit."[1]

From this arises the important question (specially important at the present day owing to the prevalence of hired labour) as to the just and equitable distribution of the fruits of labour, when that labour is applied to or is aided by the property of another. In other words, how is an equitable wage standard for employees to be determined ?

False Theories.—Under the influence of unchristian Liberalism, the false principle was held, or at least too often enforced in practice, that *all the profits* should go to the owner of the capital and only " the barest minimum (what is usually called a ' subsistence wage ') should be allowed to the labourer—namely, as much as would enable him to repair his strength and ensure the continuation of his class." In this theory the labourer is condemned to perpetual and inexorable poverty, while all accumulation of wealth belongs to the capitalist alone.

As a reaction against the injustice and oppression resulting from this policy, the opposite extreme, equally false, has been proposed. According to this latter theory all the profits and products of labour, excepting those required to repair and replace invested capital, belong by right to the workman. We have already shown the falseness of the principle upon which this latter theory is founded.[2]

Catholic View of a Just Wage.—The Catholic teaching, which rejects both the foregoing theories, rests on the principle that the private ownership of goods is ordained by

---

[1] *Quadragesimo Anno*, p. 25.   [2] Cf. *Supra*, art. 1.

nature in order to secure that created things may minister to man's needs in an orderly and stable fashion. For this purpose it is necessary that not merely the claims of the individual, but also the common good of all, be kept in mind in determining how the standard of a just wage is to be fixed. Hence just as in the case of ownership, so also in labour (which is closely connected with ownership) there is a social as well as a personal or individual aspect to be considered ; and neither aspect can be disregarded if one is to arrive at a right estimate of the proper distribution of the fruits of labour. In illustrating what this social aspect of labour means, Pius XI returns again to the great traditional Catholic principles which form the key-note of the whole Encyclical :

" Unless human society forms a truly social and organic body, unless labour be protected in the social and juridical order ; unless the various forms of human endeavour dependent one upon the other, are united in mutual harmony and mutual support; unless above all, brains, capital and labour combine together for common effort, man's toil cannot produce due fruit."[1]

Neither Class to Absorb All the Profits.—If society is to be organised upon such principles as these, so that harmony and mutual co-operation take the place of mutual distrust, hostility, and class war, the reign of social justice must be established. With a view to this the Pope writes :

" One class is forbidden to exclude the other from a share in the profit. Now this law is violated by an irresponsible wealthy class, who in the excess of their good fortune deem it just that they should receive everything [viz., all the profits], and the labourer nothing [viz., none of the profits]. It is violated also by a propertyless wage-earning class who demand for themselves *all* the fruits of production as being the work of their hands. . . . These attack and seek to *abolish all forms of ownership and all profits not obtained by labour*, whatever be their nature and significance in human society, for the sole reason that they are not acquired by toil."[2]

Labourers Gradually to Become Owners.—The Pope then goes on to develop the broad lines which a just distribution of profits must follow. The aim must be not merely to

---

[1] *Quadragesimo Anno*, p. 32.   [2] *Ib.*, pp. 27, 28.

secure a living wage[1] (sufficient to maintain the worker and his family in frugal comfort) but also to enable him by means of thrift and honest labour to better his condition, rise above the level of a mere wage earner and acquire a certain amount of independent property. The Pope further recommends a wider extension of the custom already initiated "to the no small gain both of the wage earners and the employers " of modifying the wage contract by the addition or substitution of a contract of " some type of partnership," by which the wage earners are made sharers in some measure in " the ownership or the management or the profits." All this, however, is to be brought about not by a revolutionary change, but through the instrumentality of corporative organisations to which employers as well as employed belong ; and with the aid of the legislative and administrative powers of the State when the help of the State is needed. The Pope writes :

" Every effort must therefore be made that, at least in future, only a just share of the fruits of production be permitted to accumulate in the hands of the wealthy and that an ample sufficiency be supplied to the working men . . . so that these latter may by thrift increase their possessions, and by prudent management of the same may be enabled to bear the family burden with greater ease and security. . . . Thus they will be in a position not only to support life's changing fortunes, but will also have the reassuring confidence that when their own lives are ended, some little provision will remain for those whom they leave behind."[2]

The Standard of Wages.—In order that this result be brought within the possibility of realisation, a first need is that the standard of the labourer's wages be properly adjusted ; for " the wage-earner has nothing but his labour by which to obtain the necessaries of life " ; and it is usually only by a frugal management of wages that are adequate

---

[1] The principle of the Living Wage to which the worker has a right even in *Commutative Justice* is contained implicitly in the writings of the great Catholic authors of mediæval times, such as St. Thomas, Albertus Magnus, etc. It was formulated in express terms for the first time by Leo XIII in *Rerum Novarum* (1891) (cf. *Pope and People*, pp. 157 ff). The principle means that the scale of remuneration for a normal full-time worker should never fall below the standard required to enable him to maintain himself, his wife and family in conditions of frugal comfort.

[2] *Quadragesimo Anno*, p. 30.

that he can ever secure by thrift the means which may
enable him to attain to the moderate degree of ownership
which is so desirable. In determining the proper scale of
wages many considerations have to be kept in mind. Of
these the Pope specially stresses the following :

(a) **Living Wage for Family Essential.**—" The wage paid to
the working man must be sufficient for the support of himself
and his family. . . . *If in the present state of society this is not
always feasible, social justice demands that reforms be introduced
without delay,* which will guarantee every adult worker such a
wage."[1]

In another place the Pope had already written :

" In the State such economic conditions should be set up as
will enable every head of a family to earn as much as according
to his station in life is necessary for himself, his wife and the
rearing of his children."[2]

(b) **Particular Circumstances to be Taken into Account.**—" The
condition of any particular business and of its owner must also
be considered . . . for it is unjust to demand wages so high
that an employer cannot pay them without ruin, and without
consequent distress amongst the working people themselves."[3]

In developing this principle the Pope lays down that if
the inability of the employers " to pay the workmen a just
wage," comes from causes that are remediable, such as want
of enterprise, etc., the workmen's wages cannot be justly
reduced. If the cause lies in the fact that the taxes or other
burdens are excessive, or that the owners are forced to sell
the produce at too low a price, the workmen in such case
are made the victims of injustice, and those who are responsible (civil rulers, financiers, or middlemen), " are
guilty of grievous wrong." To deal with cases such as these
the Pope directs that employer and employed must unite

---

[1] *Ib.*, pp. 32, 33.
[2] Cf. *Casti Connubii* (1930) (C. T. S. edit.). In laying down this principle
of a *family* wage for the head of the family, the Pope does not leave out
of consideration the possible supplementary aid from the labour of the
labourer's wife and children. Indeed he manifestly implies that such
aid should be forthcoming " especially in the rural home or in the families
of many artisans and small shopkeepers." But he insists, nevertheless,
that the labourer's normal wage should be of itself " sufficient to meet
the ordinary domestic needs." The additional revenue from the efforts
of his family will thus be available to enable him to attain to independent
ownership, better the family condition and provide for their future needs.
[3] *Quadragesimo Anno*, pp. 32, 33.

their efforts " in a spirit of mutual understanding and Christian harmony," and that public authority should bring its assistance and protection where needed ; for in modern times protective measures of the government are oftentimes quite essential to enable the industries of the nation to be carried on on lines compatible with Social Justice. In the last extreme, counsel must be taken (manifestly by the guild or " Corporation " to which the particular industry belongs) as to " whether the business can continue or *some other provision be made for the workers.*" In all this the Pope visualises or implies the existence of co-operative organisations or guilds (which we shall discuss later), including representatives of employers and employed, and formally recognised by the civil administration.[1] It is to be noted that he does not contemplate even as worthy of discussion, the alternative (which is too often the solution actually adopted in modern times and is the product of an unchristian social system), of closing down the business and turning the employees adrift on the world without any means of support and with no responsible organisation able and ready to safeguard their essential rights.

(c) **The Common Good to be Considered.**—"The wage-scale must be regulated with a view to the common interest of the whole people."

The Pope in developing this principle keeps in view two main considerations, namely (1) the need, in view of the common good, " that wage-earners of all kinds be enabled, by economising that portion of their wages which remains after necessary expenses have been met to attain to the possession of a certain modest fortune," and (2) that " opportunities for work be provided for all those who are willing and able to work." For " a scale of wages that is too low, no less than a scale excessively high, causes unemployment." Hence Pius XI concludes :

" To lower or raise wages unduly, with a view to private profit, and with no consideration for the common good, is contrary to social justice, which demands that by union of effort and goodwill such a scale of wages be set up if possible as to offer to the greatest number opportunities of employment and of securing for themselves suitable means of livelihood."[2]

---

[1] See *infra*, art. 6.   [2] *Quadragesimo Anno*, pp. 34, 35.

Conclusion.—The Pope concludes his brief but pregnant treatment of this question by recalling again under another aspect the fundamental principle upon which his whole system is built up. The various economic activities of the state " should combine and unite into one single organism and become members of a common body lending each other mutual help and service." For this purpose there must be

" a reasonable relationship between different wages and (what is intimately connected therewith) a reasonable relationship also between the prices obtained for the product of the various economic groups, agrarian, industrial, etc."[1]

It is clear that if, for instance, the prices obtainable for agricultural produce are too low, and the cost of tools, machinery and clothing is high, agriculture (which is and always must remain the basic industry of every healthy and stable civil society) must languish, to the peril of the whole nation. It is only when due harmony and well-ordered proportion are maintained that the economic and social organism will be established on a secure basis ensuring

" for all and each those goods which the wealth and resources of nature, technical achievement and the social organisation of economic affairs can give. These goods should be sufficient to supply all needs and an honest livelihood, and to uplift men to that higher level of prosperity and culture which, provided it be used with prudence, is not only no hindrance, but is of singular help to virtue."[2]

Art. 4—*Implications of an Equitable Wage Contract*

A Becoming Livelihood.—Employers ordinarily are bound under an obligation of Commutative Justice to give their employees a wage sufficient for the support of the worker and his family in becoming conditions. The worker's right to such a just wage is prior to the capitalist's claim to a dividend on his investments. Hence the employer or capitalist owner cannot justly appropriate from the industry anything more than a just wage for his own personal labour until the claims of the worker to a just wage are satisfied.

Proper Food, Clothing and Shelter.—Under the heading of subsistence alone are included good food, suitable clothing

---

[1] *Ib.*, p. 35.   [2] *Ib.*

and housing for the worker and his family. Thus, sufficient milk is a prime necessity for young children, and should be within reach of the poorest worker. The worker should also be in a position to provide for himself and his family clothing such as the climate requires, as well as a home commodious enough to furnish decent comfort and privacy for all the family. Three sleeping apartments besides a living room, with some little surrounding space for a garden may be taken as the very least accommodation required.[1]

Furthermore, it is manifestly desirable that the worker have inviolable security of tenure in his homestead. This could be ensured him by laws such as exist in many of the States of the U.S.A., called the " Household Exemption Laws.[2]

Further Necessary Facilities.—In addition, a father should have the means of providing his children with education suitable to their state ; of securing the proper medical treatment, special food and care for the member of the family who may be delicate or ill ; and even of meeting to a reasonable extent such needs as have become, owing to custom, social environment and the circumstances of modern times, more or less necessaries of life.

" If," writes Pius XI, " families, particularly those in which there are many children, have not suitable dwellings : if the husband cannot find employment or means of livelihood : if the necessities of life cannot be purchased except at exorbitant prices : if even the mother of the family, to the great harm of the home, is compelled to go forth and seek a living by her own labour : if she, too, in the ordinary, or even in the extraordinary, labour of childbirth is without proper food, medicine, and the assistance of a skilled physician any one may see, especially since the husband and wife may lose heart, how difficult home life and the observance of God's law become for them."[3]

---

[1] " What chance is there for health or comfort, temperance or thrift, home education or a Christian life, if a married man has not a sanitary dwelling of three or four rooms to shelter his family ? " *Pastoral Letter of the Bishops of Ireland on the Labour Question*, Feb., 1914 (Cf. Ryan and Husselein, *op. cit.*, p. 213).

[2] These laws have been already briefly described in chap. xviii, art. 2. Cf. also Devas—*Political Economy*, pp. 420 ff.

[3] *Casti Connubii*, p. 62.

Security Against Obvious Risks.—Again, the working man should have the means of securing himself and his family, not indeed against all dangers, for that would be impossible, but against such obvious risks as periods of unemployment, sickness and old age, or the premature death or disablement of the bread-winner. It is not in accordance with the Christian ideals but rather with the ideals of Socialism that the State should guarantee the worker against these risks.[1]

Finally, over and above all this, such a margin should be allowed that a hard working and frugal family could share to a fair degree in the culture and easier conditions which flow from civilisation—fair hours of work, means of reasonable recreation, and a certain opportunity of mental improvement ; while, as has been already said, the industrious and thrifty family should be normally able to better their social position.[2]

Further Rights of the Workers.—Besides all that has been said, there is contained in every agreement between employers and workers the implied condition that all natural human rights are to be respected and safeguarded. Thus Leo XIII treating of this matter writes :

" Man's soul is made after the image and likeness of God. . . . In this respect . . . there is no difference between rich and poor, master and servant, ruler and ruled. . . . No man may with impunity outrage the human dignity which God Himself treats with great reverence, nor stand in the way of that higher life which is the preparation for the eternal life of heaven. . . . To consent to any treatment which is calculated to defeat the end and purpose of his being is beyond any man's right ; he cannot give up his soul to servitude, for it is not man's own rights which are here in question, but the rights of God. . . ."[3]

Under the heading of the rights here referred to, Leo XIII insists especially on the following :

(a) **Rest on Sundays and Holydays.**—The obligation and right of cessation from work and labour on Sundays and

---

[1] Cf. Husselein—*World Problem*, chap. viii and xvii. " Provision should be made," writes Pius XI, " in the case of those who are not self-supporting for joint aid by private or public guilds." *Ib.*, p. 61. Cf. also The Italian " Labour Charter," nn. 26, 28, for the Fascist aims and ideals regarding insurance (*See* J. S. Barnes, *op. cit.*, pp. 215 ff).

[2] Cf. also Macksey, *op. cit.*, cap. iii, art. 2.

[3] *Rerum Novarum*, p. 155.

certain holydays should be respected and observed. But the rest from work must be rest combined with religious observance. Thus the Pope again writes :

" The rest from labour is not to be understood as mere giving way to idleness ; much less must it be an occasion for spending money for vicious indulgence . . . but it should be rest hallowed by religion . . . which disposes a man to forget for a while the business of every-day life, to turn his thoughts to things heavenly and to the worship which he strictly owes to the eternal Godhead."[1]

It may be noted in this connection that in mediæval times when the social and economic life was organised after Christian ideals there was besides the Sundays an average of more than one holyday of obligation every week. When, as a result of unchristian influences, the Church's holydays were abolished, the labourers had to work every day, in some cases even on Sundays. Later on when the demand of the organised workers for more relaxation could no longer be refused and the holidays had to be, at least partially restored, the same unchristian forces were still at work to prevent the Christian holydays from being chosen ; and so purely civil holidays were established, while the Christian holydays are not recognised. Such a state of affairs is manifestly incongruous in a Catholic country.[2]

(b) **Hours and Conditions of Labour.**—There should be reasonable regulations regarding the hours and conditions of labour. These would " save the unfortunate working people from the cruelty of men of greed, who use human beings as mere instruments for money making," for as Pope Leo XIII again writes :

" Man's powers are limited . . . and it is neither just nor human so to grind men down with excessive labour as to stupify their minds and wear out their bodies."[3]

In determining what are reasonable conditions and reasonable hours, many things have to be taken into account, such as the severity of the work, and the season of the year.

---

[1] *Ib.*, p. 155.
[2] See *Decrees of the Maynooth Synod*, 1927, nn. 33–36, on " Holydays of Obligation." . . . (Cf. Dr. Browne's booklet entitled *The Synod of Maynooth*, 1927, C. T. S. I., Dublin, 1930, p. 16).
[3] *Rerum Novarum*, p. 155. Cf. also *ib.*, p. 143.

As a general principle it may be laid down that a workman ought to have leisure and rest in proportion to the wear and tear of his strength, for " waste of strength must be repaired by cessation from hard work."[1]

(c) **Regard for Age and Sex of Workers.**—There should also be proper regard to the age and sex of the worker : for what is quite suitable for a strong man cannot rightly be required of a woman or a child.   Thus :

" great care must be taken not to place children in workshops or factories until their bodies and minds are fully developed. . . . Again, women are not suited for certain occupations.   A woman is by nature fitted for home work, and it is that which is best adapted at once to preserve her modesty and to promote the good upbringing of children and the well-being of the family."[2]

On the same subject Pius XI writes :

" It is wrong to abuse the tender years of children or the weakness of woman.   Mothers will above all devote their work to the home and the things connected with it.   Intolerable and to be opposed with all our strength is the abuse whereby mothers of families, because of the insufficiency of the father's salary, are forced to engage in gainful occupations *outside the domestic walls*, or to neglect their own proper cares and duties, particularly the education of their children."[3]

This abuse, so widespread at the present day, is one of the worst features of the modern industrial system, and is among the forces now tending so strongly towards the destruction of family life, which is a fundamental element in the Christian concept of society.   Therefore, the abuse should be kept in check where necessary even by the arm of the law.

Duties of Government.—Where the efforts or the power of private enterprise fail or are inadequate to secure just and fair conditions of the workers, it is the duty of the State to intervene.

" The foremost duty," writes Leo XIII, " of the rulers of the State should be to make sure that the laws and institutions the general character and administration of the commonwealth should be such as of themselves to realise public well-being and

---

[1] *Ib.*, p. 156.   [2] *Ib.*   [3] *Quadragesimo Anno*, p. 33.

private prosperity . . . and amongst the rest to promote to the utmost the interests of the poor."[1]

Hence, the government is bound gradually so to re-adjust the laws and their administration, as well as the distribution of the national resources that suitable and becoming conditions of life be within reach of all willing and honest workers in their own country. It should take strong measures to prevent pauperism, unemployment, and the need of emigration. For as Leo XIII again writes :

" Justice demands that the interests of the working classes should be carefully watched over by the administration, so that they who contribute so largely to the advantage of the community may themselves share in the benefits which they create, that being housed, clothed and fed, they may find life less hard and more endurable. . . . The richer class stand less in need of help from the State, whereas the mass of the people having no resources of their own to fall back upon . . . should be specially cared for and protected by the Government."[2]

Seeing that the employers and owners of property are the most powerful members of the community, and exert most influence on legislation and administration, every individual among them shares in a special way the responsibility for any negligence or injustice of which the governing powers may be guilty.

Italian Labour Charter.—It should be noted here that in the " Labour Charter " signed by the Italian Premier, Signor Mussolini, April, 1927, several of the rights to which we have just referred are guaranteed by law to the Italian workingmen. The aim of the Labour Charter (which, like the " Law of Corporations," to which we shall refer later, is one of the most notable efforts made in modern times to co-ordinate the just claims of capital and labour and bring both into harmony with the common good) is to protect the worker against exploitations by the capitalist, to protect the employer against " slacking," and to secure that the interests and activities of both capital and labour be in

---

[1] *Rerum Novarum*, p. 150. Cf. also Pius XI—*Quadragesimo Anno*, pp. 33-35.
[2] *Rerum Novarum*, pp. 152, 154. Cf. also Pius XI—*Casti Connubii*, where these principles are still more strongly emphasised. *See* also *infra*, chap. xxv, art. 3.

harmony with the paramount interests of the State. The labourers are secured the right of collective bargaining and the right to a just wage, corresponding to the normal conditions of life and to the actual value of their labour. The Labour Charter further secures for labourers the right to the Sunday rest and to exemption from work on religious and civil holidays ; to an annual paid holiday under certain reasonable conditions ; to an indemnity in case of discharge without fault, and finally to security against dismissal should the business pass to a new owner.[1]

Obligations of Charity and Piety.—Besides the obligations of social justice of which we have so far treated, employer and employed have additional duties towards each other under the heading of Charity and Piety. A man's employees are in a certain sense members of the family of which the employer is the head. The life and work of employer and employed are interwoven and the interests of both are largely identical. Hence, since true charity and true piety begin at home, the labourer on his side, over and above his obligation in justice of giving a fair day's work for a fair day's pay, is bound besides under the virtues of charity and piety to be zealous for all the interests of his employer, which he should guard and promote in every reasonable way. The employer, on the other hand, is bound to guard and promote as far as he reasonably can the ordinary interests of his workpeople ; and this obligation is shared by the members of his immediate household, his wife, his sons and daughters ; for these latter, sharing in the advantages of the head of the family, have also their due share of his duties and responsibilities.[2]

---

[1] Cf. Barnes, *op. cit.*, pp. 215–228, for the full text of the document ; also *Survey of Fascism*, pp. 136 ff.

[2] Cf. T. Meyer, S.J., *op. cit.*, pars. ii, sec. 11, lib. i ; cap. iii. art. 1 ; also J. Donat, S.J., *op. cit.*, cap. iii, art. 1, p. 85 (2nd ed.) The obligations and ideals here referred to are realised to a very considerable extent in some of the great factories on the Continent owned by Catholics. A notable example of this is the great Harmel silk factory at Val des Bois in France, founded by Léon Harmel some sixty years ago ; and still owned and conducted by the Harmel family. Cf. *The Christian Democrat* (C. S. G., Oxford), Jan., 1929, pp. 4–8, for an account by Mons. Harmel (the proprietor) of the system adopted and the remarkable results obtained. Cf. also Père Guitton, S.J.—*Vie de Léon Harmel*, 2 vols (" Edition Spes," Paris, 1927).

Practical Suggestions.—Even though it may be impossible for individual employers to secure for all their workers wages and general conditions such as we have described, the spirit of Christian charity will still find many ways of alleviating their condition.

" Christian charity towards our neighbours," again writes Pius XI,[1] " demands that those things which are lacking to the needy, particularly in the case of a large and poorer family, should be provided : hence it is incumbent on the rich to help the poor, and that those who possess superfluous goods should not expend them fruitlessly or completely squander them, but should employ them for the support and well-being of those who lack the necessaries of life. . . . They who act to the contrary will pay the penalty. Not in vain does the Apostle warn us : *" He that hath the substance of this world and shall see his brother in need and shall shut up his bowels from him, how doth the charity of God abide in him.' "*[2]

A Special Type of Employers' Unions.—The following suggestions may be useful in this connection : If the wealthy Catholic owners of a particular city or district formed an association, not with a view to resist the demands of labour or to fight the workmen's unions, but in order to secure their workers just and fair conditions, and to bring pressure upon other employers to do the same, such a step would undoubtedly react favourably upon both classes ; all the more so as it is well known that within reasonable limits, shorter hours of work, higher wages and better conditions of life for the worker usually result in higher efficiency in his labour, and a consequent increase of production.

Pius XI commends the movement (which is already very widespread in continental Europe, especially in the Catholic states) of co-operation amongst employers for the purpose of promoting this object at least in one of its aspects.

" We might utter a word of praise," he writes, " for various systems devised and attempted in practice by which an increased wage is paid in view of increased family burdens, and special provision is made for special needs.[3]

In France and other continental countries there is a growing movement (to which the Pope here refers) to form associations of Catholic employers for the purpose of equal-

---

[1] *Casti Connubii*, p. 61.   [2] I *John* iii.   [3] *Quadragesimo Anno*, p. 33.

ising the task of giving special assistance to those workers whose families are more than usually numerous. Each employer contributes to the union in proportion to the total number of the workers he employs. The union then disburses these contributions to the *married* workers *pro rata* for the *number of children* each worker has to support ; so that, for instance, a worker with eight young children will receive four times as much as a worker with two. The recently-founded *Family Endowment Society* of England has for its object the general adoption of this scheme.[1] Similar methods could be applied in initiating housing schemes, with plots for workingmen ; in establishing insurance funds to be administered under sympathetic and paternal administration ; and providing marriage portions for the daughters of the poor.

Christian Attitude of Employers.—Again, if members of the wealthier classes commonly adopt a really Christian attitude towards the workers and the poor, they can alleviate the hardships and brighten the lives of the latter to an extent not to be measured in terms of money.

" There are no figures yet invented," writes Devas, "that will enable us to quote the price of domestic order, peace and affection; of the joyful sports of children ; of friendly social relations ; of good morals and the worship of God."[2]

How much of all these could be created or promoted by the activities of the wives and daughters of well-to-do employers working under enlightened guidance among the families of their own workpeople ! How far would such activities go to elevate the character of those engaged in them, to improve the lot of the workers, and to reintroduce the true Christian spirit into our whole social organism !

Art. 5—*Further Means to be Employed in Solving the Labour Problem*

Religion an Essential Element.—Reason and experience prove that no social or economic system no matter how well conceived will produce general well-being unless aided

---

[1] Cf. E. F. Rathbone—*The Disinherited Family* ; also M. T. Waggaman—*Family Allowances in Foreign Countries* (issued by the U.S.A. Bureau of Labour Statistics, 1926).

[2] *Political Economy*, bk. iii, chap. vi, p. 501.

by the help of religion and administered under religious influence. A civilisation or a social system from which religion is absent is usually founded upon the oppression and exploitation of one class by another. Hence Leo XIII constantly insists on the essential need of religion in order to produce or restore social well-being.

" No practical solution of the question [viz., the Labour problem] will be found apart from the intervention of religion and the Church. . . . Doubtless this most serious question demands the attention and the efforts of others besides Ourselves —to wit, of the rulers of the States, of employers of labour, of the wealthy, aye even of the working class themselves. . . . But We affirm without hesitation that all the striving of men will be vain if they leave out the Church."[1]

Ten years after writing the above the Pope repeats again the same warning in his Encyclical on Christian Democracy :

" It is the opinion of some . . . that the Social Question . . . is merely ' economic.' The precise opposite is the truth. It is first of all moral and religious ; and for that reason its solution is to be expected mainly from the moral law and the pronouncements of religion."[2]

It is in fact only the influence of religious teaching that can draw the employers and the working classes together, reminding each of its duties towards the other. It is religion too that effectually checks the unchristian greed for gain and inspires respect for justice, charity, piety, loyalty to duty, thrift and self-denial, which are the foundations of social peace and general prosperity. Hence, industrial associations should include in their scope, after the manner of the mediæval guilds, not merely the material interests of the members, but also their moral, spiritual and intellectual well-being and improvement. Manifestly, neutral associations of employers or of workmen from which religion is excluded and in which the Church has no part, will not bring about social peace or succeed in remedying existing abuses.[3]

---

[1] *Rerum Novarum*, p. 141.
[2] *Graves de Commune*, 1901, p. 174.
[3] Cf. Plater, S.J.—*The Priest and Social Action*. Ryan—*The Catholic Church and the Citizen* (Burns & Oates, London, 1928). Lugan—*Social Principles of the Gospel* (Macmillan, London, 1928).

The Italian *Law of Corporations*, to which we have already referred, offers a useful example in this matter. One of the provisions of the law runs as follows :

" No association whatever may be juridically recognised unless the Articles of Association include among its objects not only the general furthering of the economic and *moral interest* of the members, but also the taking of an active part in their technical, religious, moral, and national education and the support of charitable foundations open to them. Furthermore, no association may be juridically recognised unless its directors and staff of employees can give guarantees of capacity, morality and a firm national faith."[1]

Catholic Action.—Much can be done through organised voluntary action inspired by supernatural charity and directed by the Church, to relieve the pressing needs of the labourers and the poor—through the medium of building societies, co-operative stores, co-operative banks, etc.[2] Important results might also be obtained in the direction of class reconciliation by a well-organised propaganda of instruction through the medium of the press and other agencies, directed

" to infuse a spirit of equity into the mutual relations of employers and employed ; to keep before the eyes of both classes the precepts of duty and the laws of the Gospel, which by inculcating self-restraint keep men within the bounds of moderation, and tend to establish harmony among the divergent interests and various classes."[3]

For the purpose of permeating the civic body with the principles of social justice, Christian charity and true patriotism, and making these principles effective in social life, it is essential that there always be a large number of the laity well grounded in the social teaching of the Church and filled with zeal for its realisation. It is one of the functions of Catholic Action to train up and prepare such members under the guidance and direction of the Church, " which cannot forget or neglect its God-given mandate as

---

[1] Cf. Barnes, *op. cit.*, pp. 206–207.
[2] Cf. Husselein, S.J.—*The World Problem*, also *Democratic Industry*, chap. xxvii ; O'Grady—*Introduction to Social Work* (Century Co., New York, 1928).
[3] Leo XIII—*Rerum Novarum*, p. 163.

custodian and teacher of the truth in every sphere in which moral questions are discussed and regulated."[1]

A Wider Diffusion of Ownership.—One of the roots of the present labour troubles is the fact that immense multitudes are bereft of all productive property, and therefore wholly dependent upon wages for support. Such a state of affairs is opposed to the ideals of the Church, which is always in favour of the widest possible diffusion of ownership.[2] We have already, when treating of the Family Homestead,[3] suggested some practical means of mitigating this evil. The important and comprehensive question of economic co-operation has been also referred to.[4] As economic co-operation is amongst the most important practical means of realising the much-needed diffusion of some type of ownership among the industrial masses, we shall here treat the question at somewhat greater length.

Economic Co-operation.—It is generally admitted that economic co-operation in one shape or another must form an important element in the solution of the modern social question. Peasant agricultural holdings should indeed be multiplied and home industries encouraged in every practicable way.[5] Handicraftsmen who make their livelihood by the production of highly skilled or artistic types of work should also be protected and encouraged. But when all this is done, mass production and the employment of concentrated quantities of capital, including factories, and expensive machinery, will probably still remain an important element in the industrial system of any modern State with a growing population ; and the workers in these factories will still form a large percentage of the citizens. Are the ownership and control of these great enterprises to remain permanently in the hands of a few, while the multitudes of the workers are propertyless, living only on wages,

---

[1] Pius XI—*Quadragesimo Anno*, p. 44.
[2] Cf. *Supra*, chap. xi, art. 1.
[3] Chap. xviii, art. 2 ; also Daltha—*An Irish Commonwealth* (Talbot Press, Dublin, 1920), chaps. iii–xi.
[4] Cf. *Supra*, chap. xii, art. 4.
[5] Even as regards these, it would seem that peasant rural life cannot flourish, or even survive to any great extent in modern times, except by means of agricultural and industrial co-operation.

exposed more or less to the risks of unemployment, without any effective voice in the control of the industry, and consequently without much real personal interest in the work to which they devote their lives ? The only practical alternative seems to be some system of co-operative control or ownership.

Hence it is that the question of co-operation among the workers is so strongly insisted on in several pronouncements of Leo XIII, Pius X, Pius XI and the Hierarchy of different countries.[1] Even the socialist theories and programme contain the idea, although vaguely and incorrectly conceived, of co-operative ownership and co-operative labour. It is perhaps their only constructive contribution towards the solution of the modern labour problem.

Reconstruction Programme of American Bishops.—*The Social Reconstruction Programme* issued after the Great War by the four American Bishops who were chosen to represent the Hierarchy of the U.S.A. in the committee of the National Catholic War Council, contains the following important passages which practically summarise the Catholic attitude towards industrial co-operation.

(a) **Co-operative Stores and Banks.**—After insisting on the desirability of preventing by adequate laws and governmental action the " extortionate practices of monopoly " which unjustly raise the cost of living, the Bishops go on to say :

" More important and more effective than any government regulation of prices would be the establishment of co-operative stores. The enormous toll taken from industry by the various classes of middlemen is now fully realised. The astonishing difference between the price received by the producer and that paid by the consumer has become the scandal of our industrial

---

[1] Cf. Husselein—*Democratic Industry*, chap. xxvii. Cf. also Ryan and Husselein, *op. cit.*, p. 212, for the words of the Bishops of Ireland on the same subject : " An opportunity [viz., for the workers] to share in the profits or to acquire a co-partnership, or at least to benefit in some permanent way by the continued prosperity of the undertaking, might with great advantage be embodied in a scheme of employment. . . . The Church in the interest of mankind has ever desired a wider distribution of property, and in her days of greatest social power sanctioned a large control of industry by the worker."

system. The obvious and direct means of reducing this discrepancy and abolishing unnecessary middlemen is the operation of retail and wholesale mercantile concerns under the ownership and management of the consumers."[1]

(b) **Co-operative Management of Industry.**—Treating of the due participation of Labour in industrial management the Bishops write :

" It is to be hoped that the right of labour to organise and deal with employers through representatives will never again be called in question. . . . In addition to this, Labour ought gradually to receive representation . . . in the industrial parts of business management, viz., ' The control of processes and machinery, and of the nature of product, the engagement and dismissal of employees, hours of work, rates of pay, bonuses, etc., welfare work, shop discipline, relations with trade unions.' The establishment of *Shop Committees* working where possible with the Trades Union is the method suggested . . . for giving the employees the proper share of industrial management. There can be no doubt that a frank adoption of these means and ends by employers would not only promote the welfare of the workers but vastly improve the relations between them and their employers and increase the efficiency and productiveness of each establishment."[2]

---

[1] Cf. Ryan and Husselein—*The Church and Labour*, pp. 237 ff, where the Bishops' statement is reprinted. On the whole subject of Co-operation, cf. also "Æ"—*The National Being* (Maunsel & Co., Dublin, 1917); Husselein—*World Problem*, chaps. xix–xx, also *Democratic Industry*, chap. xxix. For a very interesting and suggestive account of the co-operative banks in Italy and Germany, cf. *World Problem*, pp. 214 ff and 326 ff. The business transacted by one and only one of the co-operative banks in Germany amounted to nearly £1,000,000,000 (one thousand million sterling) in 1910. Co-operative distribution and marketing and co-operative banks have made comparatively little progress in Ireland so far ; many of the co-operative stores have been closed during the past ten years ; and the 225 co-operative banks that existed before the war have practically disappeared. The temporary failure of this all-important branch of co-operation has been due partly to the want of proper leadership and of, an educated public opinion ; partly to the steady opposition of the traders and the press. It is a strange fact, too, that the Irish Agricultural Organisation Society (I.A.O.S.), which is the principal propagandist body associated with the co-operative idea in Ireland, has discouraged co-operative distribution, although this is an essential element of a healthy and successful co-operative movement.

[2] On this subject, cf. Ryan—*Social Reconstruction* (Macmillan, New York, 1920), chap. viii. Husselein, *loc. cit.* ; Shields—*Evolution of Industrial Organisation* (Pitman, London, 1928), chap. ix ; also a valuable and suggestive pamphlet by Dr. J. Ryan, entitled "*Capital and Labour*"— *Methods of Co-operation and Harmony* (published by the *Sunday Visitor*, Huntingdon, Ind., U.S.A., and reprinted in Ryan and Husselein, *op. cit.*, pp. 272 ff).

(c) **Co-operative Production.**—Finally, in what is perhaps the most important and far-reaching portion of the programme, the Bishops refer to co-operative production in the following terms:

" The full possibilities of increased production will not be realised as long as the majority of the workers remain mere wage-earners. The majority must become owners at least in part of the means of production. They can be enabled to reach this stage gradually through co-operative productive societies and co-partnership arrangements. In the former the workers own and manage the industry themselves; in the latter they own a substantial part of the corporate stock and exercise a reasonable share in the management. However slow the attainment of these ends, they will have to be reached before we can have a thoroughly efficient system of production or an industrial social order that will be free from the danger of revolution."

The difficulty in securing efficient management is one of the obstacles to the success of workers' productive co-operation, but this obstacle can be overcome, and will probably disappear, as a result of experience and in proportion as the co-operative tradition gets established. The initial difficulty in finding the necessary capital is more serious, although that too can be overcome once it can be proved from experience that co-operative industry is feasible and can succeed under proper conditions.

That the difficulties in the way of successful co-operative production are not insurmountable is shown by the continued success of co-operative agricultural enterprises in several countries and the partial success of other types of productive industry.

Thus in Ireland co-operative creameries owned by the farmers worked very successfully up to 1919,[1] and many do so still, as do also some co-operative bacon factories. In Great Britain there are at present no less than 99 co-operative productive societies, whose *gross* output value

---

[1] The Co-operative Agricultural movement in Ireland, which in 1915 seemed prosperous and progressive, including 981 affiliated societies and 225 co-operative banks, has now only 305 affiliated societies, several of which are not prosperous, and practically no banks. The partial failure of the movement has been due partly to the tactics of the British army of occupation, which destroyed great numbers of the creameries (1919–21); partly to the fact that the Irish co-operative movement was too confined

for 1929 totalled over £86,000,000.[1] In Italy, Denmark
and Holland rural co-operative industry has taken even a
much deeper hold.[2] In Italy a very remarkable co-operative
enterprise called the " Federated Co-operative Glassworks "
succeeded so far that in 1918 one half of the entire output
of bottles in Italy were produced by this company, in which
the workers owned the whole plant and business.[3]

" There is something so grand," wrote Bishop Ketteler nearly
a century ago, " in the idea [viz., of Workmen's Productive
Associations again owning and controlling the bulk of the productive industry] that it deserves our sympathy in the highest
degree. . . . The certainty and the hope spring up within me
that the forces of Christianity will take hold of the idea and
realise it in a grand scale."[4]

Ireland offers a specially favourable opportunity for the
initiation of co-operative industry, as the industrial field
has not been already occupied to any considerable extent
by the capitalist owners. Hence it is to be hoped that the
coming Irish industrial revival to which all look forward
will develop mainly on co-operative lines.[5] That such a
development is possible once the financial system is under
native control, and with the asisstance which the forces of
religion can give cannot be doubted.

An essential preliminary to a workmen's co-operative
industrial movement would be the organisation of the industrial workers in associations formed and conducted in
accordance with Christian principles. The general formation
of such associations would lead almost inevitably to the

---

in its scope. Again, the movement was handicapped from the beginning
by the fact that it was promoted and to a large extent directed, by
members of the Protestant ascendancy and Scottish or English officials,
and so never won the confidence of the people at large. Such an organisation in order to be permanently successful must be organised and conducted in harmony with the Catholic and native traditions of the people.

[1] Cf. *The People's Year Book*, 1931, *loc. cit.*, p. 28.

[2] Cf. *World Problem*, chap. xx ; Ryan, *op. cit.*, chap. ix ; also *The People's
Year Book*, pp. 129, 142, and 149.

[3] Cf. *Democratic Industry*, chap. xxx. In Holland the four great coal
mines are worked successfully under the direct management of the
Government.

[4] Cited in Metlake, *op. cit.*, pp. 129, 130, from Ketteler's great work,
Die Arbeiterfrage und das Christentum (Christianity and the Labour
Question), of which Metlake gives a useful summary, pp. 107-113.

[5] Cf. Daltha, *op. cit.*, chap. v. " Towards a Co-operative Commonwealth " ; also Smith-Gordon—*Irish Rural Reconstruction*.

settlement of the whole labour problem on the lines of economic co-operation. Hence we shall devote a special article to the important question of Industrial Associations.

Art. 6—*Industrial Associations*

General Nature of Industrial Associations.—Association with his fellows is natural to man. The consciousness of his own weakness impels him to call in aid from without, for, as the Wise Man says in the Holy Scriptures : *It is better that two should be together than one. for . . . if one fall, he shall be supported by the other*;[1] and again : *" A brother that is helped by his brother is like a strong city."*[2] Similarity of interests, occupations, training, habits of life and of participation in the world's goods, creates a tendency for members of the same class to join together with greater intimacy in order to defend and promote the particular good they have in common.[3] Such associations are lawful when their objects are in harmony with the general interests of the community ; and when they behave as constituent elements of the wider organisation of the municipality or State to which they belong. For thus they naturally tend to be united with the other classes or equally lawful associations, in that way forming an organic and consistent whole.

Subject to these reservations, it is quite in accordance with the natural law and the Christian organisation of society that private associations be formed for such purposes as mutual aid, collaboration, distribution, insurance, co-operative production, etc., and that the several classes of which the community is made up be organised in accordance with their various interests and tendencies.

Men's Right to Form Them.—So essential indeed to man is the right to form associations for such just and lawful purposes, that it is beyond the competence of the State to withdraw it. Thus Leo XIII writes :

" If the State forbids its citizens to form associations, it contradicts the very principle of its own existence ; for both they and it exist in virtue of the like principle, namely, the natural tendency of man to dwell in society.[4]

---

[1] *Eccles.* iv. 9, 10.   [2] *Prov.* xviii. 19.
[3] Cf. *Code of Social Principles*, p. 30.   [4] *Rerum Novarum*, p. 161.

Hence, the legal prohibitions of "combinations of wage-earners" which were enforced in England and still more severely in Ireland up to their repeal in 1824, were unjust and oppressive. These laws were in fact a characteristic expression of the capitalist mentality which has produced the class-war.[1] Similar unjust and oppressive laws existed in the United States of America until about the end of the 19th century. On the other hand, it was mainly through the instrumentality of associations such as the mediæval guilds, which were organised and conducted under the guidance of the Church, that the wonderful fruits which then appeared of prosperity, peace and fidelity to religious obligations were produced.

Strongly Advocated by the Church.—Consequently the Holy See strongly recommends and urges the formation and strengthening not only of mutual aid societies, craft organisations, private insurance societies, in which employers as well as workingmen are represented, but also of separate associations of the workers and of the employers in each trade.[2]

This policy, formulated by Leo XIII, has been consistently urged by the Holy See down to our own time. It has been strongly asserted in the important judgment recently given by the Sacred Congregation of the Council (June 5th, 1929), in favour of the workmen of the Roubaix-Tourcoing district in the diocese of Lille. Disputes had arisen there between the Catholic employers and workers, and the matter was finally referred to the Holy See. The judgment given contains an authoritative summary of the policy and wishes of the Holy See on the whole labour question ; and in it the formation of Catholic industrial unions is very strongly urged.

In this historical document[3] the Holy See lays down six leading principles, viz. :

1. The Church recognises and affirms the right of employers and workers to form industrial associations whether

---

[1] Cf. Webb—*The History of Trade Unionism*, chap. ii (Revised edit., Longmans, London, 1920).

[2] Cf. Leo XIII—*Rerum Novarum*, p. 60.

[3] An English translation of it has been published by the Catholic Social Guild (*Trades' Unions and Employers' Associations—the Catholic View*, C. S. G., Oxford, 1929).

separately or together, and sees in them an efficacious means towards the solution of the social question.

2. She even considers that under existing circumstances these industrial associations are morally necessary : and so she strongly urges their formation.

3. She emphasises the teaching of Leo XIII, that these unions should be founded and conducted in accordance with the principles of Christian faith and morals ; and that their purpose must be not to set class against class but rather to promote harmony and mutual co-operation of the classes.

4. She accordingly suggests the institution of Joint Committees as bonds of union between the associations of employers and those of the employees.

5. While recognising that special circumstances may, in certain cases, necessitate a different course, she desires that industrial associations should be constituted which are organised by Catholics for Catholics.

6. She recommends the union of all Catholics for combined work in the bond of Christian charity, emphasing the need for this purpose of the moral and religious training of the members of the unions. The clergy are exhorted in the document to strenuous exertion in their efforts to bring about a satisfactory solution of the Social Question. Finally it is suggested to the Bishops to appoint certain priests in each diocese who would be " Missionaries of Labour."

Catholic and Neutral (or " Christian ") Unions.—The fifth principle given above insisting on the formation for Catholics of exclusively Catholic unions, which would be under the guidance of the Church, is in accordance with repeated pronouncements of Leo XIII, and especially with the Encyclical, *Singulari Quadam* (1912) of Pius X. The reason why the Church sets her face as much as possible against Catholics belonging to neutral or non-Catholic Labour unions, or Employers' unions, is that the problems with which these associations have to deal, such as just wages, proper conditions of labour, strikes, lock-outs, and so forth, are moral questions, or at least involve moral issues, on which the Church is the authoritative and only safe guide. Besides, as Leo XIII points out :

" there is a good deal of evidence that many of these societies [viz., non-Catholic industrial associations] are in the hands of secret leaders and are managed on principles ill-according with Christianity and the public well-being."[1]

As in the case of neutral schools, however, the Church does not ignore the fact that in the special circumstances of some countries " it is impossible for Catholics to form Catholic unions," and consequently " they seem to have no choice but to enrol themselves in neutral unions."[2] On this subject Pius XI writes :

" It belongs to the Bishops to permit Catholic workingmen to join these [viz., neutral] unions, where they [viz., the Bishops] judge that circumstances render it necessary, and there appears to be no danger for religion, observing, however, the rules and precautions recommended by Our saintly Predecessor Pius X.[3] Among these precautions the first and most important is that, side by side with these [neutral] trade unions there must always be associations which aim at giving their members a thorough religious and moral training, in order that these may in turn impart to the labour unions to which they belong the upright spirit which should direct their entire conduct. Thus will these unions [viz., the Workers' Associations] exert a beneficent influence far beyond the ranks of their own members."[4]

---

[1] *Rerum Novarum*, p. 162.

[2] Pius XI—*Quadragesimo Anno*, p. 15. It should be noted that the term *neutral* does not include *Socialist* unions which are altogether forbidden to Catholics. Cf. Pius X—*Singulari Quadam* (Sept. 24th, 1912), reprinted with historical Introduction in Ryan and Husslein—*The Church and Labour*, pp. 122–132. Cf. also Pius XI—*Quadragesimo Anno*, pp. 15 and 54.

[3] In the Encyclical *Singulari Quadam*, above referred to.

[4] *Quadragesimo Anno*, p. 15. For a fuller account of the legislation on this important matter, cf. Ryan and Husselein, *loc. cit.* The legislation refers to Employers' Unions as well as those of workers. In Holland and Germany both types of union—viz., Catholic unions and Christian unions (*i.e.*, those open to Catholics and Protestants, but not to Socialists or Jews) are in operation, besides the Socialists' unions. In France, Belgium and Italy there are also strong Catholic unions. In Holland the advance of Socialism is kept in check by the collaboration of the Catholic with the Christian unions. It is generally recognised that it was mainly owing to the strength of the Catholic unions that Holland was saved from Communism after the European War (1919). In Spain there are (1931) no (or very few), Catholic industrial associations. Hence its peril at the present time in view of the anti-Christian efforts of the Communists and Freemasons. In Ireland, although the overwhelming majority of the people, especially of the working classes, are good Catholics, there are no Catholic unions. Both employers and labourers are organised in neutral unions, much to the prejudice of the labourers' interests and the injury of the whole industrial life of the country.

27

Different Types of Industrial Associations.—There are three distinct types of industrial associations ; and a fully organised industrial system would include all three. These are the Craft Organisation, the Employers' Association and the Trades Union or Workers' Association.[1]

The Employers' Association and the Trades Union should include associations of all the different trades which appertain to the Craft. Thus the Building Craft would include associations of Masons, Carpenters and Plumbers. The Craft organisation itself (or the Vocational Group, or Corporation as it is sometimes called) would include all, or the representatives of all, who co-operate in the industry either as directors or employers, or operatives of any kind. It should be mainly composed of representatives from the two classes of associations, viz., the Employers' Associations and the Trades Unions. In practice it may be a kind of permanent Joint Committee of these representatives.

It is the Craft Organisation which represents the whole craft before the public authorities. It gives to all the different trades and interests—to employers as well as employed—a bond of union and a point of contract by means of which harmony may be secured. To it naturally belong all matters which have to do with the common good of the craft, such as the settlement of internal disputes that may arise, the drafting of rules which are to direct the different services, the hours of labour and the rates of wages.

It is mainly upon the formation of Vocational Groups, of which the Craft Organisation would be one of the most important types that Pius XI insists in his great Encyclical on the Social Order. Indeed, the vocational organisation of society may be described as the basis or pivot upon which his whole scheme rests ; and he considers this vocational organisation essential for obviating the class-war and bringing order once more out of the chaos which reigns at present in the social system.[2] Thus he writes :

" The aim of social legislation must be the establishment of vocational groups. Society to-day still remains in a strained and therefore unstable and uncertain state, being founded on

---

[1] Cf. *Code of Social Principles*, nn. 91–96, from which the matter of this and the following section is borrowed.

[2] Cf. Taylor—*The Guild State* (Allen, London, 1919), for an account of the traditional ideals of Guild state organisation.

classes with contradictory interests, and hence opposed to each
other, and consequently prone to enmity and strife. . . . To
this grave disorder, which is leading society to ruin, a remedy
must evidently be applied as speedily as possible. But there
can be no question of any perfect cure except this opposition
be done away with; and well-ordered members of the social body
come into being anew, vocational groups namely, binding men
together, not according to the position they occupy in the labour
market, but according to the diverse functions they exercise in
society. For as nature induces those who dwell in close
proximity to unite in municipalities, so those who practise the
same trade or profession, economic or otherwise, combine into
vocational groups. These groups, in a true sense autonomous,
are considered by many to be, if not essential to civil society,
at least its natural and spontaneous development."[1]

Function of the State—Labour Courts.—Seeing that the
State is the supreme authority in temporal affairs, it is its
duty to prevent anarchy and confusion in industrial activities,
to enforce social justice, and give effective assistance in the
work of rebuilding a social order animated with the spirit
of Justice and Charity. For this end one of its duties will
be to set up Industrial or Labour Courts, so composed that
all parties could have confidence in their impartiality.
These would be, as it were, high courts of appeal to which
a Labour Union or an Employers' Association might resort
against the decisions of the Craft. It would be the duty
of these courts to give decisions in accordance with the
fundamental rights and duties of labourers and employers
which we have summarised in the preceding article.

The New Corporative Constitution of Italy.—After outlining the main features of the ideal Christian State ao
organised on the basis of vocational groups, largely autonomous, duly interrelated for the purpose of the common good,
and subordinate to the supreme control of the civil government, Pius XI makes special allusion to the new Italian
constitution. This he commends for its vocational organisation (although he points to serious drawbacks in the
organisation as actually realised under the Fascist régime)
as being calculated, if properly administered, to promote
the peaceful collaboration of the classes, and neutralise
Socialist organisations and efforts. The portion of the

[1] *Quadragesimo Anno*, pp. 37–38.

Italian constitution to which allusion is made is that connected with the Law of Corporations and the "Labour Charter" already referred to.

The Law of Corporations and the Labour Charter merit careful study ; for they are by far the most important constructive effort of modern times to supply a basis of harmony and co-operation among the different interests in the State. Their promulgation marks a definite break with the false theories of economic and political Liberalism : and their aim is to put an end to the unnatural divorce which had previously existed (and which still exists in many states of Europe and America) not only between employers and employed, but to a certain extent between the productive organisation of the country and its political institutions. In Italy the professional associations (including Trade Unions, Employers' Unions and Co-operative Guilds) are not only juridically recognised, provided they fulfil certain specified conditions, but they are made the basis of representation in the Italian Parliament.

Although there is no prohibition against forming unions that do not fulfil the conditions required for statutory recognition, it is only the juridically recognised unions that can represent workingmen or employers ; and it is they alone that can conclude labour contracts and labour agreements. No individual is bound to belong to the juridically recognised union : but everyone, whether workingman or employer, belonging to that branch of the trade, must pay his contribution to the union whether he joins it or not ; and he is bound by the contracts and labour agreements which it makes.

The "Corporations" (corresponding to the Craft associations mentioned above) are composed of representatives of the unions of workingmen and employers of the same trade or profession ; and "as true and genuine organs and institutions of the State, they direct and co-ordinate the activities of the unions in all matters of common interest. Strikes and lockouts are forbidden. If the contending parties cannot come to an agreement public authority intervenes."[1]

---

[1] Cf. Pius XI—*Quadragesimo Anno*, p. 42 ; also Barnes, *op. cit.*, pp. 203 ff, and *Survey of Fascism*, pp. 83–135.

The Italian system of industrial organisation is far from perfect. It falls short of the full Christian and democratic ideal, especially owing to its excessively bureaucratic and political character, by reason of which there is danger that the general interests of social order and the public good may be sacrificed to special political ends. The fundamental conception, however (which the Pope so strongly recommends), is excellent, and in accord with the true principles upon which a sane civic organisation should be built up.

CHAPTER XXII

THE SOCIAL STATUS OF WOMEN[1]

Introductory—Division of Subject.—Closely connected with the Christian concept of family life is the Christian ideal of womanhood. Owing to the influence of Liberalism and the anti-Christian movement, that ideal has become obscured, especially in the countries in which public life has been wholly or partially dechristianised. Hence in order to supplement our treatment of the Christian family, of which the Christian wife and mother is the centre and mainstay, we shall devote a chapter to the important subject of the social status of women. We shall treat first of the position and functions of women in the social organism as ordained by the natural law and confirmed by the teachings

---

[1] Cf. *Cath. Encyclop.*, vol. xv, pp. 687–698, art. " Woman " (a well-balanced and comprehensive sketch of the whole question, including a bibliography, by Rev. A. Rosler, C.S.S.R.) ; *Semaines Sociale de France, Nancy*, XIXe, Session, 1927 (Gabalda, 90 Rue Bonaparte, Paris). This, the 19th session of the Congress, was devoted exclusively to an examination of the question *What Society Owes to the Woman, and the Woman Owes to Society*. (The volume referred to (*circ.* 500 pp.) contains reprints of 25 separate papers read at the Congress by as many different lecturers— Bishops, priests, women and men—in which almost every aspect of the question is discussed.) Vermeersch, S.J., *op. cit.*, questio xiii, pp. 657–673 (an excellent summary of the question and of the Church's attitude in its regard) ; Donat, S.J., *op. cit.*, cap. v, art. 4, pp. 267–270 ; Garriguet, *op. cit.*, chap. xi, pp. 521–564 ; Taparelli, S.J., *op. cit.*, vol. ii, nn. 1550–1554 (a brief but illuminating sketch of the place assigned by the natural law to the woman in domestic life). Castelein, S.J.—*Droit Naturel*, Thesis 16, pp. 540 ff. Cf. also N. Fletcher—*Christian Feminism* (King, London, 1914) ; Cuthbert, *op. cit.*, pp. 42–58 " The Education of Women " ; Anderson—*The Catholic Girl in the World* (Burns and Oates, London, 1901) ; D'Azambuja—*What Christianity has Done for Women* (C. T. S., London) ; Keating, S.J.—*Christianity and Woman's Rights* (C. T. S., London) ; McMahon, S.J.—*Bebel's Libel on Women* (C. T. S., London) ; Rev. H. T. Hall—*Woman in the Catholic Church* (C. T. S., London, 1930). (This little booklet contains the substance of a very remarkable and inspiring discourse preached in the Church of Notre Dame at Geneva on the occasion of the International Congress of Women's Societies, Jan., 1920.) Rosler, C.S.S.R. (writer of the article on " Woman " in the *Cath. Encyclop.*), *Der Frauenfrage* (*The Woman Question*). (This is a standard work, and has been translated into French. An enlarged edition appeared in 1907.)

of Christianity. We shall then show briefly how women have fared in historical times under the Christian and non-Christian régimes. Next we shall give a brief account of the modern Feminist movement ; and finally indicate the Church's attitude in regard to certain practical issues connected with the social status of women.

Art. 1—*Sphere of the Two Sexes in the Social Organism*

Sexes Equal in Essential Attributes.—Men and women have all the essential attributes of human nature. Hence, men and women equally are persons. Both are endowed with liberty and responsibility ; have been redeemed by the merits of our Divine Lord, and are destined to eternal happiness. Consequently, women as well as men have all the inalienable rights and duties which attach to human personality.

All this is implied in the Holy Scriptures. From the history of the Creation as given in the book of *Genesis*, it is clear that the first woman was created not as man's slave like the lower animals, nor on the other hand as his mistress, but as his companion and his helper " *like himself.*" Thus we read : " *God created man to His own image and likeness . . . male and female He created them ; and God blessed them saying increase and multiply . . .*"[1] And again, "*It is not good for man to be alone ; let us make him a helper like to himself.*"[2] St. Paul, too, while upholding the authority of the man and the subordination of the woman in the marital union, expressly affirms the personal equality of the sexes as one of the principles of Christian teaching : " *For as many of you as have been been baptised in Christ have put on Christ. . . . There is neither male or female ; for ye are all one in Christ Jesus.*"[3]

Special Role of Women in the New Testament History.— The doctrine of Aristotle, that the woman is a kind of inferior man (*mas occasionatus*) is devoid of foundation, and is specially repulsive to the Catholic, who has been taught from childhood to honour the Mother of God next to God Himself. We know from the New Testament that

---

[1] *Gen.* ii. 27, 28.   [2] *Ib.* ii. 18.   [3] *Gal.* iii. 28.

the execution of the divine decree of the Incarnation was
made by God to depend on the fiat of a woman and that
the Divine Saviour anticipated the opening of His public
mission at the request of a woman. The manner in which
our Divine Lord honoured women during His mortal life
and after His Resurrection ; the rôle played by women in
contrast with the men during the last scenes of our Saviour's
life ; and the association of " the women and Mary the
Mother of Jesus " with the twelve Apostles in the Upper
Room[1] during the solemn days of preparation for the coming
of the Holy Ghost (the birthday of the Church), are facts
which cannot be ignored in considering the due status of
women in Christian society.[2]

Men and Women Different in Many Characteristics.—
Neither man or woman, however, is endowed with the
plenitude of human qualities and powers. Therefore, neither
can represent human nature in its entirety ; nor can either
be taken as the absolutely perfect one or the standard
of value for the other. In fact human personality manifests
itself in a different way in each sex. The structure of the
body is different. The physiological instincts and tendencies are not the same. The prevailing qualities of mind
and character of the normal man are different from those
of the normal woman. Some of these differences, especially
those of intellect and character, can be diminished by
custom and education ; but they cannot be totally eliminated.
The sexes are complementary of each other and form when
united an organic whole. Hence men and women are not
intended by nature to be rivals ; nor can one correctly say
that women or men as such are either superior or inferior

---

[1] *Acts* i. 13, 14.
[2] Cf. A. Christitch—*The Women of the Gospel* (Washbourne, London,
1929) ; Hull, *op. cit.*, pp. 5, 6. *See* also *Dict. Apologetique de la Foi Cath.*,
vol. i, cols. 1897, 1898 (" Femmes, Ames des "), and Vermeersch, *op. cit.*,
pp. 672, 673, for an account of the absurd and unfounded calumny that
the question as to whether women had rational souls was discussed by
some of the Bishops at the Council of Macon (A.D. 581). Not to speak
of the cult of the Blessed Virgin, then very strong and widespread in the
Eastern Church, and the multitude of Christian virgins already honoured
as Saints, the great St. Pulcheria had reigned as Empress over the Eastern
Roman Empire a century and a half earlier, having owed her elevation
to the purple in no small measure to the influence of the Church, of whose
rights she was so devoted and able a champion.

to each other ; just as the eye and the ear as human faculties with essentially different functions cannot be mutually compared with or set up in rivalry to each other.

" The sexes," writes Pius XI, " in keeping with the wonderful designs of the Creator are destined to complement each other, in the family and in society, precisely because of their differences, which therefore ought to be maintained and encouraged."[1]

The woman's natural qualities fit her especially for the activities and life of the home ; and the common sense of the human race has always regarded the home as the woman's most important sphere. If she is a mother, her constant presence in the home is needed ; and domestic duties which no one else can accomplish will absorb most of her energies. Her natural gifts of sympathy and love combined with her keener sensitiveness give her a special aptitude to promote the happiness of domestic life, which means so much both for man and woman. Hence it is that the Church insists so strongly on the woman's great duty and prerogative as mistress and queen of the Christian home :

" If the woman," writes Pius XI, " descends from her truly regal throne to which she has been raised within the walls of the home by means of the Gospel, she will soon be reduced to the old state of slavery . . . and become, as amongst the pagans, the mere instrument of man."[2]

Differences Cannot be Disregarded.—We have said that some of the innate differences between men and women may be diminished, though not eliminated, by custom and education. On account of these differences common sense and experience, confirmed by Christian custom and tradition, lay down certain fairly well-defined limitations and broad principles of propriety for the conduct of each sex in social intercourse. These cannot be disregarded with impunity. Thus, although some concessions may, perhaps, be allowed to the circumstances of modern life in some countries, the ideals and characteristics of the " emancipated " woman of the modern type, who repudiates some of the specially feminine excellencies in favour of a foolish and unnatural

---

[1] *On the Christian Education of Youth*, 1930 (C. T. S., London), p. 32.
[2] *Casti Connubii* (C. T. S. edit.), p. 36.

imitation of men, cannot be reconciled with Christian principles. Again, the action of the British War Office in enlisting women and girls during the European War for war-work in foreign countries, where, in some cases, they mingled almost indiscriminately with the men, was out of accord with Christian traditions of propriety. Such a departure from Christian precedent was bound to produce effects upon the morals of the whole nation, which no possible military necessity nor any supposed national good could outweigh.

Again, although it may, perhaps, be held that owing to national tradition and racial temperament, Irish boys and girls may' be allowed more freedom in social intercourse than is considered suitable or becoming for young people in the Latin (viz., Catholic) countries of Europe, it is certain that the almost unchecked intermingling of the youth of different sexes, away from the supervision of parents or guardians (a custom which, unhappily, has, as a result of the European War and contact with non-Catholic civilisation, become very prevalent in Ireland in recent years) cannot be reconciled with Catholic ideals or Christian tradition. Thus, Pius XI condemns the

" deplorable confusion of ideas that mistakes a levelling promiscuity and equality for the legitimate association of the sexes. The Creator has ordained and disposed perfect union of the sexes only in matrimony and with varying degrees of contact in the family and in society."[1]

Rights and Duties of Men and Women.—The fundamental rights and duties of the sexes, corresponding to the end for which each has been created, are determined by the natural law, and are manifested by the innate characteristics, the normal needs and capacities of each. This is seen most clearly in the marital union. The man becomes a father with paternal rights and duties, including the support of the family and, when necessary, their protection. Hence man's general functions in the social organism correspond

---

[1] *On the Christian Education of Youth* (C. T. S. edit.), p. 32. In illustration of the woeful results of this confusion of ideas and departure from the Christian tradition, cf. two important articles published in the *Irish Ecclesiastical Record*, January and February, 1931, entitled respectively " The Legal Protection of Girls " and " The Dance Hall," by Rev. R Devane, S.J.

broadly to those of the father of the family. The woman, on the other hand, receives with motherhood a whole series of maternal duties ; so that her part in social life may be described (broadly also) as the exercise of motherhood. This motherhood must not, however, be limited to its physiological aspect. The maternal sense and activities which represent the highest development of noble womanhood should precede marriage and can be realised without it.[1] Both men and women fulfil their end in life, and acquire moral perfection by developing and exercising their several natural powers in the manner which nature has assigned. The most perfect man will be the most manly ; and the most perfect woman will be she who is most womanly. Any effort to identify the functions of the sexes either in civil or domestic life, is against the intentions of the Creator, and must prove injurious to society as well as to the persons concerned.

Church's Attitude Towards " Women's Rights."—The general attitude of the Church towards the question of the civic rights of women, their education and their work, may be thus briefly summarised : Woman's most important sphere is the home ; and her primary social duties are those of wife and mother. The Church's teaching regarding woman's position in the home and in relation to her husband has been already explained.[2] The purity and virtue of womanhood lie at the very foundation of Christian society ; and no consideration of real or apparent public good can justify any custom or any law by which these may be seriously endangered.

Apart, however from these fundamental principles and in dealing with non-essentials, the Church pays a wise regard to the sentiments and customs of different nations and to the social needs and circumstances of particular times. She contents herself with proclaiming the essential doctrines that secure the dignity and safeguard the virtue and true interests of women. Hence, no work and no study, for which women are not physically unfit, is discouraged by the Church, provided always that there be nothing in either contrary to Christian modesty, or prejudicial to the order

---

[1] Cf. *Cath. Encyclop.*, *loc. cit.*, p. 688.
[2] Chap. xix, art. I—*The Marriage Contract.*

and discipline and interests of the Christian family. These latter conditions are to be regarded as essential. On this subject Leo XIII writes :

" Women are not suited for certain occupations : a woman is by nature fitted for home work ; and it is this which is best adapted to preserve her modesty and to promote the good bringing up of children and the well-being of the family."[1]

The work of women under-ground in mines and the employment of girls and young men mixed together in modern factories would violate the requirements of Christian modesty,[2] while the employment of mothers, day after day, and all day away from home, would be contrary to the interests of the family.[3] But neither condition would be violated by women, who are not prevented by domestic duties, undertaking rough, open-air work, or on the other hand, by their reaching the highest excellence in literature, science and art.[4]

---

[1] *Rerum Novarum*, p. 156.
[2] Cf. Pius XI—*Quadragesimo Anno* (C. T. S. edit.), p. 61.   [3] *Ib.*, p. 33.
[4] Cf. C. S. Devas—*Studies of Family Life*, pp. 154, 155. " What is injurious to women is not hard muscular work, but continuous work like pressing the pedal of a sewing machine for hours, or standing for hours behind a counter." (*Ib.*) Devas gives a very interesting description (borrowed from the *Tablet*, March 4th, 1882), of a farm of some 300 acres entirely worked by the girls of a reformatory, at Dartnetal near Rouen. Two men are employed to look after the horses (there are twenty-five of them) at night. Everything else, including carting, ploughing, road-making, etc., is done, and well done, by the girls under the direction of the nuns. Apparently there are, or at least were at the beginning of the present century (before the impious laws against religious associations were put into force), many other such female agricultural colonies in France, flourishing under the superintendence of the nuns. In Belgium also there is a very highly developed system for the training and employment of women in agricultural and technical, as well as domestic, employments. The great Agricultural College of Hevelé near Louvain directed by nuns and State-aided, is one of the best examples of this. Even in 1909 a second great Congress of women farmers was held in Namur, at which 41 associations were represented and about 600 women delegates attended (Cf. Fletcher, *op. cit.*, p. 76).
  It is high time that rural orphanages, reformatories and even penitentiaries organised with a view to rural and agricultural training be started in Ireland. How practical such a scheme is, and how easily it could be made to succeed, have been demonstrated by the success with which a small farm of about thirty acres at Killester, Co. Dublin, was reclaimed, and worked at a good profit, during the European War by women from the slums of Dublin under the charge of a stewardess. The women gladly came out from the city every morning for work. The influence of open-air work and country life upon these poor women was most salutary. The work, which had been undertaken in 1915, as a temporary expedient under the auspices of a war-relief committee, was discontinued about the year 1919.

Art. 2—*The Social Status of Women in Historical Times.*

Women in Non-Christian Nations.—In no nation known to history did the woman enjoy her natural rights previous to the advent of Christianity,[1] or occupy the position of dignity and influence in social life which is her due. " The world-wide story," writes the Bishop of Northampton, " of woman's oppression and degradation by man reads like a nightmare. . . . Slaves to man's brute force, or objects of man's brute desires, generations upon generations of women, with here and there a rare exception, have passed away without education, without rights, without honour and without virtue. Valued only for their physical beauty or their capacity for drudgery, they sank wholesale into a servile condition and contracted the proverbial duplicity and other vices of servitude.[2]

This is partially true even of the Jews, with whom, however, the woman had a much better status than in contemporary Gentile nations. Notwithstanding the prestige attaching to the names and memory of several celebrated Jewish women, such as Miriam, Deborah, Judith, and Esther, the Jewish woman was far from enjoying the position she occupies in Christian society. Marriage was her sole calling in life ; and neither inside nor outside the married state did the law secure her the same personal rights as the man.

It is not true to assert, as some have done, that even in non-Christian nations the progress of civilisation tends to emancipate woman from slavery and improve her social position. This contention " is refuted by the fact that in Rome and Greece woman's position deteriorated in proportion as civilisation and culture—taking these in their commonly accepted sense—advanced. At the time of Homer and under the Roman kings, woman occupied a respectable position ; but when pagan civilisation reached its climax, she became a slave. In ancient Egypt, too, and in China, the progress of civilisation was marked by the degradation of the female sex. And even to-day among

---

[1] Cf. Belliot, *op. cit.*, p. 528.
[2] *Christian Womanhood* (C. T. S., London, p. 2). Cf. also D'Azambuja, *op. cit.*, pp. 18–67, for an excellent sketch of the degraded position of women in non-Christian society ancient and modern.

those nations that have shut themselves off from the influence of Christianity, the status of woman is no better than it was in pagan antiquity. Especially Mohammedanism, in spite of all the external culture which it produced at one time in Spain and Arabia, has degraded woman to the rank of a slave."[1] On the same subject, De Maistre truly says: " In every country where Christianity does not prevail, a certain tendency towards the degradation of woman is to be found."[2]

Church's Influence on the Woman's Status.—In the early ages of Christianity, when its principles and ideals were pitted against the ingrained prejudices, and customs as well as the laws of the Roman Empire, still semi-pagan, and again, after the sixth century, when the Teutonic princes and nations were nominally converted to Christianity, the Church had to maintain a protracted struggle in defence of the dignity and personal rights of womanhood.[3] At the same time she took care to enforce the principles of womanly decorum and modesty which she raised among the barbarian nations, as she had previously done in the Roman Empire, to the highest degree of delicacy.

---

[1] Cathrein, S.J.—*Moral Philosophie*, vol. ii (5th edit.), pp. 409 ff, cited in Koch Preuss, *Handbook of Moral Theology*, vol. v, pp. 500, 501.

[2] Du Pape, liv. 3, chap. ii, p. 304.   The following extract from the letter of an Irish Missionary Priest in China, dated Jan. 29th, 1929, illustrates this :

" One cannot realise what Christianity has done for the world, and especially for women ; nor understand what paganism means till one sees it ' at home.'   Not to speak of the unnatural custom so prevalent here of selling girl children into slavery, and the wretched position of the wife or concubine in the pagan family, the lot of women in China is an unhappy one.   I could illustrate this in dozens of ways.   *On last Christmas Day* (which happened to be also a Sunday), when returning from a walk into the country, we came on a batch of women coolies working (for they alas ! knew nothing of Sunday nor what Christmas Day meant to us), and working, too, in a manner that no man or woman is ever asked to work in Europe.   Earth had to be carted up a long and rather steep slope on the mountain side.   A light railway was laid down for the purpose, but there was no engine.   Human labour is cheaper.   The heavy truck loads of clay were pulled up the hillside by the poor women.   Three women with ropes passing over their shoulders pulled each truck, evidently straining every nerve and muscle in the effort while three men pushed the truck *leisurely from behind*.   The hire of the women coolies is between 6d. and 8d. per day."

[3] The admiring exclamation of the heathen : " What women there are among the Christians ! " is an eloquent testimony to the power of Christianity in this regard.   Cf. *Cath. Encycl.*, *loc. cit.*

The influence upon the mind of Christendom of the prerogatives of the Virgin Mother[1]—the ideal of Christian
womanhood, and worshipped by all Christians as the Queen
of Angels and of men—the position secured in society as
well as in the home to the Christian wife by the sanctity,
the unity and the perpetuity of Christian marriage ; the
freedom allowed to every Christian maiden by the Church's
teaching and practice to dedicate her life to God in the
state of perpetual virginity ; and last, but not least, the
superior character of the typical Christian woman as compared with her non-Christian sisters, all contributed to
raise the woman's prestige, and secure for her a position
of influence and dignity in the family and in society immeasurably beyond anything she knew before the advent of
Christianity. Ample provision was made for the education
of the daughters as well as sons ; and when the guilds arose
with the rise of the cities after the 11th century women
were not excluded from them.

But just as in other aspects of mediæval Christian society
so also in regard to the social status of women, some remnants of the pagan tradition of woman's essential inferiority
still lived on ; and even in the centuries of the golden age
of Christianity women suffered from not a few disabilities,
especially before the law, which always remained deeply
impregnated with the tradition and spirit of the old Roman

---

[1] Even Lecky, who was a Rationalist, bears eloquent testimony to the
influence of the Catholic cult of the Blessed Virgin in raising the prestige
and elevating the character of the Christian woman : " For the first time
the woman was elevated to her rightful position. . . . No longer the slave
or toy of man, no longer associated only with ideas of degradation and of
sensuality, woman rose in the person of the Virgin Mother into a new
sphere, and became the object of a reverential homage of which antiquity
had no conception. Love was idealised. The moral charm and beauty
of female excellence were fully felt. A new type of character was called
into being : a new kind of admiration was fostered. Into a harsh and
ignorant and benighted age this ideal type infused a conception of gentleness and of purity unknown to the proudest civilisations of the past. . . .
In the millions who in many lands and in many ages have sought with
no barren desire to mould their character into her image, in those holy
maidens, who for the love of Mary have separated themselves from all
the glories and pleasures of the world to seek in fastings and vigils and
humble charity to render themselves worthy of her benediction, in the
new sense of honour, in the chivalrous respect, in the softening of manners,
in the refinement of tastes, displayed in all walks of society : in these and
in many other ways we detect its influence. All that was best in Europe
clustered around it, and it is the origin of many of the purest elements of
our civilisation."—*Rationalism in Europe*, vol. i, chap. iii, pp. 213, 214.

law of pagan times. These disabilities would doubtless
have gradually disappeared under a normal process of
evolution if the Christian social development had not been
violently disturbed.

Influence of Protestantism.—As a result of the Protestant
Revolt of the 16th century, and especially under the influence of Calvinism, the tendency towards the oppression
and degradation of women quickly reappeared in European
society.   The prestige of the woman suffered an incalculable
disaster by the abolition under Protestantism of the venera-
tion and cult of the Mother of God.   With the disappearance
of conventual life women were again shut out from a recognised status in social life outside the married state which
the religious life had previously afforded them.   Again,
while lay institutions, such as the English Grammar schools,
took the place of the Catholic monasteries and other ecclesiastical institutions for the education of boys, practically
nothing was done up to the 19th century to replace the
Convent schools for the literary training of girls.   Furthermore, the attitude of the husband towards the wife
naturally tended, once the Church's authority was removed
and Christian principles obscured, to return to the pagan
ideal of a master and an owner, rather than a loving friend,
companion and protector.

Clear evidences of the sad deterioration of the woman's
prestige can be seen in the English literature of the 17th
and 18th centuries, when the withering effects of Protestantism on social life had begun to be felt in full.   The
chivalrous regard and respect for her who to every Christian
mind owns a certain dignity reflected from the peerless
glory of the Queen of Heaven disappeared from English
literature as it had departed from Protestant social life.
The woman was now again valued only for her sex ; and
the one who did not, or had ceased to, exercise sex
attraction was too often made the target of coarse jest so
repulsive to the truly Christian mind.

Women in Modern Industrial Life.—In the industrial
centres of modern times, especially in the non-Catholic
countries, the lot of women of the poorer class has become
peculiarly hard.   One would expect that the discoveries of

science and the great progress in machinery would, by
relieving the tension of human labour and giving easier
access to the world's wealth, have the effect of releasing
women from the need of much industrial occupation outside
the home. But the very reverse has occurred. Owing to
the unchristian character of modern industrialism the
workers have not benefited by the discoveries of science.
Their lot is in fact harder than it was under the conditions
of Christian mediæval life. And this fact has affected very
much the life and social condition of the women. They are
compelled commonly enough to bear the double burden of
rearing a family and working for a livelihood oftentimes
under oppressive and tyrannical conditions,[1] which are
little, if at all, better than their lot in pre-Christian times
or in professedly pagan countries.

Characteristics of the Christian Woman.—The special
characteristics of the Christian woman are well known.
Although the type varies a good deal in non-essentials,
notably in the nature of her industrial activities and in the
degree of her literary culture, and although contact with
non-Christian manners, such as has occurred during the
past thirty years in Ireland, often causes deterioration, the
Christian woman has retained her distinctive character in
every country, and at every period of history.

Modesty, piety, self-sacrifice, devotedness to the duties
of the home and to all works of charity, are the main
attributes that mark her off from all other types of womanhood.

" The normal and characteristic Christian woman," writes
C. S. Devas, " appears as a constant type under varying external
circumstances, whether as a religious or a lay woman, from the
cottage to the throne, alike in the days of Tertullian or of St.
Ambrose, among the Teutonic invaders of the Roman Empire,
in the Christian Middle Ages, in the age of St. Francis of Sales
and St. Vincent of Paul, and among the Christians of our own
day, ever the same, frequenting the churches, ministering to the
necessities of the saints, serving the poor, tending the sick,
visiting the prisons, instructing the ignorant, training little

---

[1] Even at present it is an ascertained fact that some 70 per cent. of
the women workers receive less than a living wage, cf. *The Christian
Democrat*, Nov., 1930, p. 167.

28

children, carrying on a hidden apostolate . . . the servants of One who has chosen ' *the weak things of this world to confound the strong.*' "[1]

Religious Congregations of Women.

—These words apply, though not in like measure, to the Christian women living in the world as to the religious. Both belong in fact to the same general type. The importance of the religious orders of women and their influence on Christian society can scarcely be exaggerated. Not to speak of their educational work, and of the elevating effect upon social ideals of their lives of self-denial and prayer, which are well known, the study of the Sacred Scriptures during the Middle Ages flourished in the convents ; and next to the clergy, the women were during that period the representatives of learning and education.[2]

At every period of the history of the Church women have played a leading part in works of mercy. During the past century, the number and the wide diffusion of congregations of nuns devoted to all branches of Christian charity, and to the alleviation of every form of human misery have surpassed all previous records. Some 80,000 sisters were engaged in these works in France alone at the end of the 19th century, and there were proportionally the same number in every Catholic country of Europe. Considerably more than 50,000 sisters now labour in the pagan missions, for the permanent success of which their co-operation is essential.

---

[1] *Studies of Family Life*, p. 149.

[2] C. S. Devas (*Studies of Family Life*, p. 157) has the following interesting note illustrating the attitude of the Church towards the higher education of women. The substance of the note is borrowed from an article in the *Catholic World* (New York), June, 1875 : " A woman, St. Catherine of Alexandria, was the patroness of learning and eloquence ; her statue was in the old universities and schools. The papal university of Bologna can show the names of many women illustrious in canon law, medicine, mathematics, art, and literature, and not merely were they learners, taking their degrees, as late as the 18th century, in jurisprudence and philosophy, but teachers also. Anna Mazolina in the year 1758 was professor of anatomy ; Maria Agnesi was appointed by the Pope professor of mathematics ; Novella d'Andrea taught Canon Law for ten years, and a woman succeeded Cardinal Mezzofanti as professor of Greek. Remember, among painters, Sister Plautilla, a Dominican, Maria Tintoretto, and Elizabeth Sirani ; and that a woman, Plautilla Brizio, was an architect at Rome in the 17th century, building a palace and the chapel of St. Benedict."

Art. 3—*The Feminist Movement*

Its Aims.—The modern feminist movement aims at a so-called " Emancipation " of women, or in its Christian aspects at a fuller recognition of woman's personal equality with man and a widening of the sphere of her social activities.

Its Causes and Genesis.—Its rise in modern times is due partly to a growing realisation of the unjust lowering of woman's prestige and status already referred to as resulting from the Protestant Revolt, partly to the new non-Christian ideals of social life ; and in no small measure to the changes in social conditions caused by the industrial revolution. It may be held, too, that the exigencies of modern social life and the gradual evolution of the ideals contained in the Christian revelation imply or call for a wider participation by women in social activities. This is in fact suggested by the extraordinary multiplication in our own times of the religious congregations of women dedicated to all kinds of social work and the ever-increasing number of women saints inscribed in the Calendar of the Church.

(a) **Individualistic Concept of Society.**—The modern ideals of social life above referred to as one of the causes of the existing feminist movement in its unchristian aspects are founded on a false concept of liberty and human dignity and on the equally false principles of individualism which are associated with unchristian Liberalism. The doctrine of individualism as propounded by Rousseau in his *Contrat Social* (1762) and by Montesquieu in *l'Esprit des Lois* (1784), according to which the human person, and not the family, is the direct and immediate unit in the civil organism, as well as the later theories of the Socialists, setting aside in favour of an all-absorbing State the natural and organic unity of the family, are radically opposed to the Christian concept of society ; and they imply or logically lead to the complete equalisation or confusion of the sexes not only in civil, but also in domestic life.

It was in accordance with these principles that some leading French women demanded that the " Rights of

Women " (namely, the principle of their complete political and social equality with men) be incorporated in the " Declaration of the Rights of Man " which was adopted by the French Constituent Assembly in 1789. Their demand was in fact logical. For if every man by reason of his human personality has an innate right to a voice in the government, such a right cannot be denied to women. Besides, if the essential guarantee of the justice and equity of human law (namely, its need in order to be valid of being in conformity with the law of God) be removed, and if the only sanction of law consists in the consent of the multitude that are bound by it, it is clear that one half of the population cannot be justly denied the right to secure by their votes that they be not oppressed by the tyranny of the other half. The revolutionary leaders, however, while maintaining their false principles refused to abide by the logical consequences of them and rejected the women's demand.

(b) **Changes in Modern Social Conditions.**—The main causes, however, of the great and sudden expansion of the feminist movement in the 19th century are similar to those that have been the driving forces in the modern democratic and socialist uprisings. The false philosophy and irreligion by which both movements have been too often influenced and partially led astray, do not account for the strength and universality of the movements themselves. These would not have affected the masses of the people, were it not that the people were suffering from real grievances which called for a remedy. The changed conditions of modern life and altered methods of modern industry, consequent upon scientific discoveries, utilised largely in the interests of unchristian capitalism, have caused a considerable change in the relative spheres of men's and women's activities in industrial employment.

Women of the poorer classes now work extensively in factories and in other kinds of industrial labour outside the home, and often, too, under the most unjust conditions. This has come about partly because the home industries have been crushed out by the big factories, partly because the wife has frequently to supplement by her labour the family income for which the husband's earnings are not sufficient. Again, owing to the stress of economic conditions, men especially of the well-to-do classes, being unable to support a family, marry late in life, or do not marry at all; and thus a larger number of women than heretofore are left unmarried and have to earn their own living by such occupations as teaching, nursing, clerical work, commercial employment of various kinds. Finally, in non-Catholic countries the large number of girls who in Catholic countries would enter religious life remain in the ordinary life of the world, thus still further increasing indirectly the number of unmarried women, who have to earn their own living.

Owing to the presence of such large numbers of women in industrial life, special protection for women's peculiar interests has become more necessary than before; and the whole question of woman's education, her legal status, her political rights, has assumed a new importance. The question has usually been more urgent in non-Catholic than in Catholic countries. For in the former the relative number of women employed outside the home or outside the protection of conventual life is much larger; and besides, the woman's position is more difficult owing to the lesser influence of Christian principles, which always afford a certain protection to the weaker members of the social body.

Its Development and Organisation.—The definite organisation of the movement first assumed shape in the United States of America, where the earliest convention for the assertion of Women's Rights was held at Seneca Falls, July 14th, 1848. This was followed by a few other general conventions in different States; and these gradually developed into regular annual meetings. About the same time, or a little later, similar movements arose in Germany, England and the Protestant States of North-western Europe, as well as in Russia. France came into the field somewhat later; and the first French feminist congress met at Lyons in 1909.

The more advanced and radical sections of the feminists are closely allied with Freemasonry and with the Socialists of the Marxian school; and, like them, have an international organisation. August Bebel, the Socialist leader, has championed the claims of this party in his book, entitled *Die Frau und der Socialismus* (The Woman and Socialism), which was translated into fourteen different languages, and went through fifty-two editions during the period 1879–1910.[1]

Again, Mdlle. Maria Desraines, a woman Freemason and the founder of the modern Co-Freemasonry (1893), figured as one of the principal leaders of extreme or Revolutionary Feminism in the last quarter of the 19th century.[2] It is well known, too, even from the openly-declared policy of Masonic leaders, that one of their objects is to capture the feminist movement, and utilise it for the break up of the Christian family, and the destruction of the Christian social organisation ; for they realise that the woman is the mainstay and centre of the Christian home ; and that she also (as a Masonic leader expresses it) is " the last fortress which the spirit of Obscurantism [namely Catholicism] opposes to human progress."[3]

J. S. Mill was a very prominent supporter of the women's movement in England ; and Miss Florence Nightingale was one of the best-known names among the English women leaders in the second half of the 19th century. In 1869, Mill published his book, entitled *The Subjection of Women*, which is accepted as a standard authority by the non-Catholic promoters of the movement in Britain. In this book, Mill advocates a type of feminism which is often at variance with Christian principles ; for he ignores some of the natural inter-relations of the sexes, even in the family, and aims at their complete equalisation ; or the confusion of their functions in domestic as well as civil life.

The movement has spread more or less into every country inhabited by Europeans ; but it has taken strongest hold in the United States of America, and in the English-speaking countries of the British Empire. Its influence is felt least in the Catholic countries of Europe, and perhaps, least of all in Italy and Spain.

Liberal Feminism.—This non-Christian element in the feminist movement seems to have split up into two sections more or less distinct—the revolutionary or radical Feminist

---

[1] Cf. MacMahon, S.J., *op. cit.*
[2] Cf. Fletcher, *op. cit.*, p. 79 ; also Cahill—*Freemasonry*, etc. (2nd edit.), pp. 239, 240.
[3] Cf. Deschamps—*Sociétés Secrètes*, vol. ii, pp. 484 ff.   *See* also Cahill, *op. cit.* (Cf. Index *sub verbo*, " Women.")

party, and the moderate section. The former openly advocate such things as "free love," the "right of abortion," and the promiscuity of the sexes in almost every phase of social life. The moderate party, while opposed to these views, aim at the abolition of all legal discrimination between men and women in industrial, political and social life.

Although some of their principles and aims can hardly be reconciled with Christian teaching, this party have succeeded in accomplishing very much useful philanthropic work, especially for the material betterment of women and children. Their general outlook, however, is largely naturalistic, and, as their associations are what is called undenominational, religious motives and religious interests are practically outside their sphere. Seeing that most of the problems which call for solution are closely connected with religion or the moral law, it is clear that undenominational bodies with naturalistic principles can make little effective progress towards a real solution.

The central organisation of the Liberal Feminist movement is the International Council of Women which was established in 1888, and holds its congress every five years in different cities. The national organisations of some twenty-four different countries in all parts of the world are affiliated to it, including, apparently at least, some of the Revolutionary groups.[1] The members of the governing committee also include some Catholic women. The "National Union of Women Workers" of England is affiliated to it. The "Irish Women Workers' Union," which, like the latter, is undenominational, and more or less Liberal in general character and outlook, is not, apparently, formally affiliated to the International Council of Women.

Christian Feminism.—Side by side with the development of the Liberal and Revolutionary section, a strong Catholic

---

[1] Cf. Fletcher, *op. cit.*, chap. v ; *Cath. Encyclop.*, *loc. cit.*, 692, 693. The Headquarters of the Council are at 117 Victoria Street, London, S.W., where the *Bulletin*, which is the official organ of the Council, is published. Among the affiliated associations are : " The International Alliance of Women for Suffrage and Equal Citizenship " and The " Open Door " Association, also international, whose object is to obtain absolute equality of conditions of work for both sexes (Cf. *International Labour Conference*, Geneva, 1930, part i).

feminist movement, as a distinct element of Feminism, has been in progress since the opening years of the present century. In fact it forms an important element in the Catholic social movement of the present day.

In 1900, Mdlle. Mangeret brought about a federation of already existing Catholic Women Societies in France, under the title of the *Federation Jeanne d'Arc*. The first Congress, at which the Cardinal Archbishop of Paris presided, was held that same year. Since that time the movement towards the organisation of Catholic women has gone on apace in most countries of Europe and America.[1] In Germany and Italy the beginning of the movement was hastened by the need of counteracting the dangerous influence of the Liberal feminists.

In 1910 a great congress of the different national leagues was held at Brussels under the patronage of Cardinal Mercier and the Cardinal Archbishop of Paris. At this Congress the International Union of Catholic Women's Leagues (to which the English Catholic Union called St. Joan's Social and Political Alliance is affiliated) was founded. Its Constitution was approved by Pius X in 1910. The Pope nominates the President of the Union. Its fifth international Congress was held at Rome in 1922.[2]

Extension of the Women's Franchise.—Owing mainly to the strengh of the Feminist movement, the Women's franchise has been very much extended during the past thirty years, and very many of the other civil disabilities of women have been totally or partially removed. Since the European War women exercise the full political franchise in some thirty different countries. These include the United States of America (at least most States of the Union) ; nearly all the countries of the British Empire, as well as Ireland ; and all the predominantly Protestant countries of Europe, including Germany ; also Soviet Russia, Austria, Portugal,

---

[1] So far there is no Catholic Women's Union in Ireland, although there are National Catholic Women's Leagues for specific purposes, such as the Modesty Crusade, The League of St. Brigid, The Legion of Mary, etc.

[2] *The Catholic Citizen*, published on 15th of each month, is the official organ of the association. Cf. Fletcher, *loc. cit.*, also *International Handbook of Catholic Organisations*, 1924, pp. 71, 72. In this latter work the names (with a brief account of each) are given of over 40 distinct Unions of Catholic Women in Europe and America, exclusive of the associations for purely religious or charitable purposes such as those affiliated to the St. Vincent de Paul associations.

Hungary, Czecho-Slovakia, Rumania, and the States such as Poland, cut off after the European War from the old Russian Empire. Women do not enjoy the political franchise, at least except to a very limited extent, in Belgium, France, Spain, Italy, and the South American Republics. In some countries in which women have not the full franchise, they have in recent years obtained lesser civil rights, such as active and passive voices in the municipal and local bodies, and the right of entrance to the learned professions.

Removal of Civil Disabilities of Women.—In England (and in Ireland, too) practically all legal discrimination between the sexes has been abolished since 1919. Even the position of the married woman in regard to property is, except for a few particulars, the same as that of her husband, and is quite independent of him. The old principle founded on Christian teaching that the husband and wife form one moral person, of whom the husband is by divine appointment the official head, and between whom the State does not interfere except in extreme cases, has practically disappeared from British law ; and as all the laws which have brought about the change predate 1920, these laws, with the exception of the law of divorce, also hold in Ireland. What has been said of England applies also to the United States and to most of the British Colonial States.[1]

---

[1] The writer of the article in the *Encyclopædia Britannica* on the legal status of women thus explains the principles that underlie the recent changes in the laws of the United States of America ; and his words equally apply to Britain : " With the progressive breaking down of the legal conception of the household as an entity ruled from within by a head . . . it became necessary to give legal recognition and protection to the individual interests of women in domestic relations, which at common law were [previously] supposed to be secured through the internal economy of the household ; or were left unsecured in view of a paramount social interest in the household as a social institution " (*Encyclop. Britt.*, (edit. 1922), vol. 32, p. 1043). Again, speaking of the now antiquated legal disabilities of married women, the same writer says : " Some of these disabilities were rested on a fiction of the legal unity of the husband and wife, derived from the position of the husband, as guardian of the dependent members of the household, [a position which obtained] in the old German policy, and [which was] reinforced by certain texts of Scripture whose authority was decisive in the Middle Ages " (*Ib.*, p. 1044). All this, which, it must be remembered, is true also of British law, and therefore of the laws which at present obtain in Ireland, implies a definite break with the Christian concept of the family. The family is no longer regarded in British law—as it is in the Divine law—as " an entity ruled from within " ; nor as " a social institution " of " paramount interest " to society.

Although some of the aims and achievements of the feminist movement are worthy of condemnation, as being out of harmony with true Christian principles, many, on the other hand, are reasonable, while not a few are urgently needed, especially in the circumstances of modern life. Some, too, that may be out of place in countries where the Christian tradition is still strong, are necessary or desirable in the countries in which social life is practically de-christianised. It may occur, too, that claims which are reasonable in themselves are put forward by feminists of the Liberal school as deductions from a false philosophy, owing to which the claim is perhaps unfairly prejudiced in the minds of many Christians. Hence the proper attitude to adopt is to judge each claim on its objective merits, and in reference to the political constitution and social circumstances of the country concerned.

Art. 4—*Some Social Aspects of Feminism*

Tendency of Christianity Regarding Women.—The Christian ideal of womanhood is eminently sane and balanced, being equally removed from the degraded principles of paganism and the naturalistic ideal of modern times. The steady trend of Christian action in raising woman's social status has been always in one direction—not to make women manly, but to evolve more and more fully the special gifts and characteristics which enable woman to help man and be assisted by him in the duty incumbent equally on both of developing their faculties and carrying out God's designs in the creation of the world. This ideal must be kept in view in appraising the tendencies of the modern Feminist movement in woman's domestic, social and political life.

Feminism and the Married Woman.—By marriage a wife voluntarily accepts partnership with her husband, under conditions as already explained[1] which are laid down by the natural law and confirmed in the Christian revelation ; and which in no way detract from the wife's dignity, or suggest moral inferiority. " *Let women,*" says St. Paul, " *be subject to their husbands as to the Lord, because the husband is the head of the wife, as Christ is the Head of the Church.*"[2]

---

[1] See *supra*, chap. xix, art. i.   [2] *Eph.* v. 22, 23.

Besides, the same Christian law that confers headship on the husband gives the wife absolute equality with him in all the primary rights and obligations of marriage ; and requires that the husband's authority be not that of a master, but rather of a partner and protector ; and be tempered by reverence and love : " *Husbands love your wives,*" again writes St. Paul, " *as Christ also loved the Church, and delivered Himself up for it. . . . So also ought men to love their wives as their own bodies. He that loveth his wife loveth himself.*" [1]

Thus the wife's sacrifice of independence or freedom (the sacrifice in fact is mutual) is compensated by the gain of protective love. The wife, too, is raised, if need be, in social status to the husband's rank and shares his social privileges. Anything which would tend even remotely to undermine or weaken this organic unity of husband and wife is fundamentally opposed to the Christian ideal of social life. Such tendencies appear more or less marked in certain sections or aspects of the modern feminist movement. We have already referred to the tendency of modern law-making, especially in the English speaking countries to legislate as it were *between* husband and wife as independent units in the State, rather than *around* them as forming only one moral person.

Again, many of the claims now put forward by some of the British and International women's associations, seem to betray the same tendencies. As examples we may mention the demand that the wife be no longer held in law as assuming by the fact of marriage her husband's nationality ; and again, the demand that the State in regulating conditions of labour should for the future abstract from or ignore the circumstances of wifehood and motherhood.[2]

Women in Political Life.—Whatever may be said of universal suffrage as a political system, consistency and good sense seem to require, where such a system actually exists, that the woman as such have the same franchise as the man. Above all, in the conditions of modern life

---

[1] *Eph.* v. 25, 28.
[2] These demands are put forward, or at least supported, not only by the International Council of Women, but even by some British Catholic Women's Associations (Cf. *The Catholic Citizen*, March 15th, 1930, pp. 20 ff.)

where the social organisation is so complex, and such large numbers of women are engaged in industrial or other work outside the home, it is of the highest importance for safeguarding the interests of women and children and for the well-balanced conduct of public affairs that women's influence be felt in public life and women's peculiar talent be utilised. This is particularly true in the municipal administration where the woman's rôle is specially important owing to her superior grasp of details and her greater knowledge of many subjects such as destitution and housing, with which the municipal councils have to deal. The same is also true, though not in like measure, of the work of legislation and political administration, although in this department men are usually superior to women.

It is probable indeed that in the modern democratic State, women, and especially well-educated Catholic women, have a very important role to fulfil in raising social ideals in purifying the legal and especially the criminal code, in securing a purer and more just administration of public affairs, in getting rid of many social monstrosities such as the shameful traffic in women and children,[1] the double standard of public morality, the sweating system,[2] the neglect of infant life, and the city slums,[3] which at present, unfortunately, are outstanding evils in many countries. It seems, also, specially desirable for many reasons that in criminal cases of all kinds in which women and children are concerned, the services of some mature and properly qualified women be always secured on the juries.

Seeing, however, that in the Christian concept of social life as opposed to the Liberal and unchristian theory of individualism, the family, and not the individual (except where the individual is not an organic part of an existing family), is the social unit in the State, it seems clear that the family in its external social relations and activities should be treated as an indivisible whole. Hence the family vote should, according to the Christian ideal, be indivisible,

---

[1] Cf. *Report of the Special Body of Experts on the Traffic in Women and Children* (Publications of the League of Nations, Geneva, 1927).

[2] Cf. Wright—*Sweated Labour and the Trade Boards Act,* 2nd edit (King and Son, London, 1913).

[3] Cf. Toke—*The Housing Problem* (King, London, 1913), and Parkinson—*Destitution and Suggested Remedies* (King, London, 1911),

and should be exercised in the name of the family by its official head. The latter, as already shown, is the husband and father, or if he be dead or absent, the wife and mother. The matter is all the more important by reason of the closeness of the ties which, according to Christian teaching, unite the members of the family with one another ; and of the perils to all the best interests of the community, which are inherent in every tendency towards the disintegration of the home. The family vote should, of course, be accorded a special value in excess of the vote of the individual. It should have double or treble, or even more value in accordance with the size of the family. Even though such a system may seem to include certain difficulties, or even incongruities, these are to be accounted rather a result of the principles of universal suffrage, than of the family vote which is in fact the system advocated by some of the standard Catholic authors as reconciling the principle of universal suffrage with Christian ideals.[1]

Women in Industrial Life.—A practical consequence of the excessively large number of women, married and unmarried, in industrial occupations, is that while many women are over-worked, and their home duties neglected, numbers of able-bodied men are left idle, employers preferring the cheaper labour of women.

Another consequence of the same, and one which threatens seriously the interests of the home, is that while women crowd into occupations for which they are not suited or less suited than men, there is a growing dearth of women who are willing and able to undertake the work which they alone can do. Girls, attracted by the more showy, more exciting and freer life of the factory hand, the shop assistant, and the accountant, are less willing to undertake such work as the nursing of children, cookery, and general household work. In the United States, where exaggerated feminism has run riot, the difficulty of obtaining suitable household service is one of the principal causes which have led to the general abandonment of home life, among large sections of the people, an abuse that must eventually prove disastrous to the nation.

It is the duty of a Christian State to remedy, by prudent

---

[1] Cf. Vermeersch, *op. cit.*, nn. 521.

legislation, the abuses which have driven an excessive number of women into industrial employment outside the home. For this end the Government should procure, of far as possible, that all the men have an opportunity as work, and of earning by their labour a sufficient family income, thus obviating the need for women's work in industrial life at least outside the home. Meanwhile, existing facts have to be faced ; and women who need to work outside the home should have fair access to all employments suitable for their sex.

How far the State or municipality should interfere to define the occupations which are to be reserved for men or for women respectively, it is difficult to define in the concrete. The following general principles may be laid down as consonant with Christian ideals : In a Christian State women should be excluded even by law from occupations unbecoming or dangerous to their modesty. The employment of wives or mothers in factories or outside their own household should be strictly limited by legislation. Girls should not be employed away from their homes or in work other than domestic until they have reached a sufficiently mature age ; so that they be not exposed too soon to external dangers to their modesty ; and that they have sufficient time before leaving home to become acquainted with household work. Competition between men and women in the same employment should not be permitted ; it is unfair to both, and contrary to the intention of nature. It should be illegal to employ men and women together in the same factory.[1] It should be made a criminal offence for an

---

[1] An esteemed correspondent, who is a strong advocate of " Women's Rights," puts forward the following view on this many-sided question : " Women are confessedly superior to men in what concerns the inner or spiritual life. Seeing that the interests of the latter are paramount, woman's influence is desirable everywhere and in every department of social activity—in the legislature, the administration, in industrial life, etc., as well as in the home, which is her most important sphere. The good woman has always a restraining and elevating influence. Segregation of women leads to brutality, profanity and ribaldry in public life, where men have a monopoly of work or sport. The policy of sheltering a certain number of women means sacrificing the rest (who, especially in modern conditions, form the majority) to coarse contacts, and the partial relinquishment of an important portion of women's natural functions, namely, imparting to social life the needed element of self-restraint, refinement and courtesy. Remember that the women of the Gospel, including Her who is the perfect model of the Christian woman, shared in the Public Life of Our Divine Saviour and His disciples."

employer to abuse in any way or permit the abuse of the dependent position of women who are in his service.

Special inducements should be held out to encourage girls needing outside work to engage in the type of work which is most suitable to their sex. Thus the profession of domestic service could be made sufficiently attractive if training schools were established for women,[1] guilds formed, and suitable rules drafted for that profession which is so important, and at the same time so suitable for women. The salary should be fixed at such a scale that it would enable a girl to have laid aside sufficient after about ten years' service (when she would have reached the age of twenty-six or twenty-seven years), to provide her with a marriage portion. Arrangements could, perhaps, be made (for instance, by a suitable system of insurance, or by associating the guild or some appointed guardians in the control of the girls' surplus earnings during these years) to provide against her squandering her money to the injury of her future prospects.

The " Modern " or " Emancipated " Woman.—The indiscriminate employment of women associated or in competition with men in occupations and duties outside their natural sphere ; the loosening of family ties by the operation of unchristian laws and the gradual obscuring of the Christian ideals of womanly modesty and decorum, all of which are outstanding features of the modern semi-pagan civilisation, now threaten the very foundation of Christian social life in many countries. The following extracts referring to the United States of America, in the opening years of the present century will help to illustrate this.

" The girls almost entirely disregard parental control. In many places they are educated with the boys. They attend

---

[1] Cf. the important recommendations of the Gaedhealtacht Commission in favour of training young Irish-speaking girls to become nursery maids and domestic servants. The special course recommended, which would last about ten months, includes special training in hygiene, children's clothes (their washing, care and mending), the feeding of infants and young children, simple cooking for children, recreation (stories, first lessons, etc.), simple study of child mentality, treatment of sick children (Cf. *Coimisiún na Gaeltachta Report*, p. 55 (Eason, Dublin, 1926). The suggestions here made for the children of the Gaedhealtacht contain principles upon which a revision of the present system of primary education for girls could be profitably modelled.

the same classes, choose their own [boy] companions for their walks and their recreations, without any comment being excited thereby. . . .

" A very large number of families live in hotels, with private rooms, but with meals and recreations in the common rooms. The separate home which forms the mainstay and the charm of family life in Europe is becoming rarer and rarer in the towns, which are specially afflicted with the scourge of this unnatural feminism. . . .

" American society is agitated by a multitude of feminist diseases, such as Spiritism, Free-love associations, Anti-matrimonial and Anti-maternity clubs. . . . Divorce has reached alarming proportions. . . . The duties of maternity are shirked more and more. There is a ' horror of children.' Infanticide is common ; and artificial sterility is systematically practised. Hence the native American population is diminishing. The increase in the population has been maintained by the immigrants and the children of immigrants. . . .

" Although these deplorable phenomena of moral and social disorder are due in good measure to the vices of the men, they must be accredited in even still greater degree to the pest of radical feminism. Thus the greater number of the divorces, which are far more numerous than anywhere else in the world, are granted at the demand of the wife." [1]

Education of Women.—It is quite in accordance with Catholic principles that women should be well educated. Even from the days of the early Fathers, when Tertullian wrote his treatise, *De Cultu Feminarum* (On the Education of Women), and when St. Jerome formed at Jerusalem a kind of school of Theology and languages for Christian matrons, down to our own day, the Church has always encouraged and patronised the education of women as well as of men ; and has advocated even a liberal education for girls whose circumstances and means allow it. It is not by the Catholic Church, but by the enemies of Christianity, that unseemly ridicule has been cast on the learning of women. This prejudice against the intellectual culture of women was, says Bishop Dupanloup, " One of the most evil inventions

---

[1] Castelein, S.J., *op cit.*, pp. 543–545. The notes are borrowed mostly from E. de Varigny's book, *La Femme aux Etats Unis* and that of C. Janet—*Etats Unis*, both published in the closing year of the 19th century. The present conditions in Soviet Russia show a further and fuller development of the social tendencies which are here described. Cf. Dillon—*Russia To-day*, chap. viii (See *supra*, chap. xii, art. 4).

of the 18th century, that century of impiety and licentious-
ness. . . . It was useful to all those husbands without
virtue to have wives without worth. . . . For a man has
to give some account of himself to a woman who is
cultivated."[1]

For their own sake and in the interests of the home the
character and tone of which depend principally upon the
wife and mother, women should be well educated. It is
specially important for all social interests, seeing that the
formation of the minds and characters of the younger
generation devolves principally upon the women, that they
be well grounded in the practice of piety, and be thoroughly
trained in religious knowledge. Hence it is more imperatively necessary for girls even than for boys that religious
doctrine, Holy Scripture, Catholic Philosophy, Church
History, and even to a certain extent sacred music and
liturgy should have a prominent place in their education.
Furthermore, it is also necessary, in view of the numerous
occupations of different kinds outside the home which
women are nowadays competent to take up, that they be
fitted for them by a suitable training.

Not the Same as for Men.—Owing, however, to the
different characteristics of the sexes, the difference in their
physical strength, and the varying nature of their vocations
in life, boys and girls should not be trained according to
the same methods, or follow the same programmes, except
in their very early years.

Besides such common subjects as reading, writing and
arithmetic, all girls should be trained in domestic science,
elementary hygiene, simple book-keeping, and in those
handicrafts, such as needlework, which it befits a housewife
to know. It is also particularly fitting that women, whose
special function it is to contribute an element of brightness
and beauty to the home, should have some knowledge of
the fine arts, such as music and painting.

Girls who receive a more liberal education should study
literature, history, geography, and elementary science.
Modern languages and Latin are specially suitable, the
latter by reason of its use in the liturgy of the Church. The

---

[1] Bishop Dupanloup—*Femmes Savantes et Femmes Studieuses* (6th edit.,
1868), pp. 21, 22, quoted in Devas's *Studies of Family Life*, p. 158.

more abstract sciences, such as Metaphysics, Jurisprudence, Political Economy, and the more advanced stages of physical science are less suitable and less useful for women's life.

Distinct University Courses.—That women in the more advanced stages of their education should attend the public university discourses with the men, and compete with the latter, take part in their debates, and even use the same play-grounds (as is now becoming customary in Ireland even in the case of Catholic girls), is manifestly out of harmony with Christian ideals, and contrary to Catholic tradition.   It must needs be dangerous or positively harmful to the Christian ideals of womanly decorum.   Besides, the girl is, normally, not capable of enduring the same strain of intellectual activity as the youth ; and the methods of education that are best for the one do not suit the other. Hence, if women be admitted to academic degrees—and there seems to be no valid reason for excluding them, at least from degrees in such subjects as literature, history, pedagogy, geography, the fine arts, etc.—facilities should be afforded for university courses suited to women, which the latter could follow separately from men.   For this purpose colleges for women should be established in connection with the universities and endowed with the privileges of recognised or constituent colleges.

CHAPTER XXIII

THE STATE[1]

Introductory Note.—Having treated of the material elements which constitute the State or Civic Community, we have now to discuss that community itself as a moral whole. We use the term *State*, as meaning not merely the governing power, but the whole civic community organised with a view to the temporal good of its members.

The State is in practice made up of three elements—its members, a certain territory, and the mutual rights and duties which unite the members into one whole. It is distinguished from other societies belonging to the temporal order by its greater extent and its higher aims. It comprises, and within certain limits its central authority governs families, municipalities and townships, and all kinds of lesser institutions within it, such as professional and educational organisations, industrial and trading societies, social unions, and literary and artistic associations.

The object of the State is to secure and promote the temporal well-being or the common good of its members. We have already said that it is, like the Church, a perfect or supreme society in the sense that it is sovereign in its own sphere and does not depend in any way upon a super-state or any other higher power except God alone, although it has relations of inter-dependence with the Church and with other states. These relations are regulated by the divine law and the natural laws of Justice and Charity.

---

[1] Leo XIII—*Diuturnum Illud*, 1881 (" On the Origin of Civil Power ") ; *Immortale Dei*, 1885 (" On the Christian Constitution of States ") ; Pius XI—*Quadragesimo Anno*, 1931 (" On the Social Order ") ; *A Code of Social Principles*, nn. 32–54 ; Ryan and Millar—*State and Church*, chaps. i–x ; Antoine, *op. cit.*, 1^{iere} part., chaps. i–iii ; Meyer, *op. cit.*, pars. ii, sec. iii, lib. i (" Jus Civile Publicum Internum "), pp. 240–726 ; Donat, *op. cit.*, secs. 10, 111 (De Statu, pp. 91–281) ; Costa-Rosetti, *op. cit.*, Theses 149–165 ; *Cath. Encyclop.*, arts. " Civil Allegiance," " Authority," " State and Church," etc. ; Rickaby—*Moral Philosophy*, chap. viii ; Balmes, *op. cit.*, chaps. 49–51 ; Cronin—*The Science of Ethics*, vol. ii, chap. xvi ; Koch-Preuss, *op. cit.*, vol. v, part ii, chap. iii ; Cuthbert—*Catholic Ideals in Social Life*, chap. ii.

We shall first explain the fundamental concept of the State in Christian teaching as contrasted with the errors of the non-Christian schools. We shall then briefly treat each of the following questions, viz. : the origin of the State and the source of civil authority ; the essential functions of the State ; the general principles of civil organisation, or the component parts of which the State is made up ; and, finally, the different systems of government.

Art. 1—*Nature of the State*

Different Types of State.—From the historical summary given in Part I, it may be gathered that all the different types of civic union, so far known in Europe, may be roughly divided into four general classes, namely, the ancient Pagan State, the Christian State, the Liberal State, and the Socialist State. Although most existing states present features belonging to more than one type, their prevailing characteristics, as shown in their constitutions and laws and the tendency of their public policy, sufficiently indicate the class to which each one on the whole belongs.

Thus the States of the Russian Soviet Union, or at least their present government and laws are mainly Socialistic ; those of Spain (viz., before the revolution of 1931), Italy, Hungary, Poland and Belgium are predominantly Christian ; while France, Great Britain, the British Dominions, and the United States of America are mostly of the Liberal type.

The Pagan State.—In the ancient Pagan State, the element of religion in public life, albeit the religion was a false one, and the dependence of the State upon the Deity were recognised. Indeed, the fundamental laws of the old Roman Republic were regarded as gifts or deposits from the gods. Hence they were divine, and no human authority could change them. Later on under the Roman Empire, while the same principle still remained in theory, it was in practice disregarded ; for the Emperor's authority was absolute, and not limited even by the fundamental laws of the old Roman constitution. Since it was clear, however, even to the ancient pagans that a human authority which recognises no limitations to its competence, not even those set by a natural or divine law, cannot logically be reconciled with the recognition of a Supreme Being distinct from that authority, the ancient Romans met the difficulty by the crude expedient of deifying the Emperor who was regarded as the sole source of all law, and who, therefore, was honoured as a god. Another consequence of the supposed all-competence of the governing power was that the essential dignity and rights of human personality were totally disregarded. Again, in the Pagan State the privileges and rights of citizenship were a monopoly of a small ruling caste, the rest of the people being regarded almost as chattels.

The Pagan State gradually disappeared under the influence of Christianity. Most of its objectionable characteristics, however, have reappeared in modern times under the influence of materialistic, pantheistic and rationalistic philosophy. Thus the teachings of Hegel, according to which man is identified with the Deity, and civil society, the highest and most perfect manifestation of the divinity, leads to the deification of the State and the denial of essential personal rights, as well as of the rights and authority of a divinely constituted Church independent of the State. Again, the principle that " the King can do no wrong " implying, as it does that the existing civil law is the norm of morality and is always essentially valid and binding, even when it clashes with divine law or essential personal rights is founded on the same pagan ideal of the deification of the ruler.[1]

The Liberal State.—The Christian type of State prevailed over all Europe in mediæval times, and down to the Protestant Revolt in the 16th century. As a result of tho Revolt most of the governments of Europe gradually fell under the influence of Liberalism. Religion and everything supernatural were eliminated little by little from public life. The " Rights of Man " were substituted for the rights of God. All social rights and duties were regarded as of purely human institution ; and a materialistic individualism and egoism prevailed more and more in every section of the social organism.

In the theory of the Liberal State, personal human rights

---

[1] Cf. Donat, *loc. cit.*, pp. 142, 143 ; Ryan and Millar, *loc. cit.*

are acknowledged, and indeed exaggerated, for they are regarded as paramount, the rights of God and the limitations set by the divine law being disregarded. In actual practice, however, all individual rights are merged in or made subservient to the power of a majority, by which the actual government of the State is set up. Hence the governing authority again becomes omni-competent, although this omni-competence is upheld in virtue of a title different from the title of a deified emperor or a civil body identified with the deity.

Again, although in the Liberal theory of civil organisation, all the members of the social body have civic rights, these rights not being regarded as of divine institution may be over-ridden by a majority. Furthermore, seeing that the powerful frequently are able to secure in their own favour the decision of the majority, through the operation of finance and of the press, personal rights have in practice little more security in the Liberal State than under the old pagan régime. Thus arise the exploitation of the poor and the tyranny of the monied interest.

The Socialist State.—The Socialist type of State, which has arisen in modern times, is akin to the Liberal State in its repudiation of Divine authority ; and to the Pagan State in its claim to subordinate personal and family rights to the unlimited authority of the governing power. In this latter particular it goes further even than the Pagan State ; for it denies to its members the natural right to acquire or hold the ownership of productive property, which lies at the root of real liberty and personal responsibility.

Hence, in the Socialist State the omni-competence of the civil power is recognised in its most complete and tyrannical form. For the governing authority holding all the productive property, as well as the executive machinery under its control, can exercise an absolute despotism over the members who depend upon the government for the very necessaries of life. Moreover, in the Socialist State neither personal nor family rights, nor the rights of the Church are recognised. Even the children belong to the State, which also claims the power to arrange the education and to regulate the work of each member, and to control everything connected with his spiritual as well as his material well-being.

Christian Concept of the State.—In marked contrast with non-Christian theories and avoiding the extremes of each, stands the Christian teaching on the origin, nature and purpose of civil society. Christians agree with Pagans, Liberals and Socialists in asserting that the immediate purpose of the State is to promote the temporal good and happiness of the people [1] But in Christian philosophy in contrast with most non-Christian schools man's temporal good is taken to include his moral and intellectual interests as well as his material well-being ; and is regarded as subordinate to the eternal happiness which is man's ultimate end.

Again, according to the Christian concept of the State, the members come before the State itself, which can never override men's inalienable rights, nor limit any of their natural rights, except for a sufficient cause connected with the public good. For the State as a corporate body comes into being solely with a view to the good of the members, and has no interests or rights of its own which are not founded upon the rights and interests of the families and individuals that compose it. Hence all the activities and laws of the ruling authority must be directed solely to promote the public good of the citizens. In so far as they clash with that, they are unlawful and invalid.

Furthermore, instead of being meant merely for a certain section of the people, the State, according to Christian teaching, is for the good of all, and must defend and assist each and every individual living within it, " Jew or Gentile, bondman or free," rich or poor, in proper order and in proportion to each one's needs.

Again, the State is not something apart from its members as the ancient pagans implied : nor is it a conventional society as the Liberals assert ; neither is it the result of blind physical evolution, as the Socialists teach ; but it is a union of families and individuals held together by reciprocal rights and duties. It is ordained by the natural

---

[1] The Liberals of the older schools usually assert that the purpose of the State is merely the safeguarding of rights. They deny that it has to assist the members by positive measures to realise their happiness. This theory put forward by the economists of the " classical " school and utilised in support of the capitalist owners was never consistently followed out in practice. Cf. Donat, *loc. cit.*, p. 141.

law, which has determined its structure, its functions, and the extent and limitations of its powers. Its purpose is to supplement not to override, personal endeavour and the helps of family life.

The State includes the whole organised nation with all the living forces that compose it. The central authority is only one element in it (albeit the most important one), and must not absorb the activities of other lesser forces or organisations, but should foster private initiative whether individual or collective, while directing it along lines conducive to the public good.

Again, the State is subject to the same moral law as the individual person : and the government of the State in dealing with its own members as well as with other corporate bodies or individuals is bound by the laws of justice, charity and religion. The actual government or central authority in the State is also usually bound by positive laws—the fundamental laws of the constitution—which it cannot change without the clear consent of the people.

Finally, the State cannot interfere with the legitimate action of the Church to which God has committed the duty of guiding and assisting men in the pursuit of their eternal happiness. The State might conceivably have been so constituted as to satisfy completely all that is required to supplement individual and domestic activities ; and thus might have been the only type of a perfect and supreme society. But as a matter of fact, God has instituted the Church, another society equally perfect and supreme, and committed to it the care of man's eternal interests, which are thus withdrawn from the control of the State.

Hence, although it is the natural function of the State to promote men's good and happiness, there are whole spheres of activity—religious, personal and domestic—reserved from its control, but, even in these, the State is bound to afford protection and assistance where required.

Art. 2—*Origin of the State*

Necessary for Human Well-being.—From the beginning the family union was ordained by God to assist the individual person in striving after happiness, and realising a more complete fullness of life. In the initial stages of the

race, the family union was by itself sufficient for the purpose.
But as men multiplied on earth, other needs inevitably
arose to provide for which family co-operation is not
sufficient. To meet these needs the natural law has
ordained Civil Society, which therefore equally with the
family is a natural unit.

Men might subsist and multiply at least for a while even
if families lived in segregated units without any civic
organisation. But it is clear that the life of man in such
a case would not at best be normal nor prosperous ; nay,
with a numerous population on earth family co-operation
could scarcely supply even the helps that are essential.
Man requires peace in his possessions and adequate protection for his rights. These cannot ordinarily be secured
without the assistance and co-operation of a considerable
number of people. The very food a person eats, the clothes
he wears, the house that shelters him, to say nothing of
countless material comforts more or less necessary, cannot
be obtained, except in a crude and very imperfect way, by
the skill and labour of a single household. Roads, railways,
postal services, facilities for exchange and trade, books,
adequate means of education, all most useful for man's
proper development, can be procured only by the co-
operation of groups much greater than the largest families.

And in Accordance with Men's Faculties and Tendencies.—
Furthermore, nature has evidently fashioned man with a
view to membership of a civic body. It has given him the
power of speech, which enables him to communicate easily
and naturally with his fellows. It has implanted in his
soul the natural desire for such communication, so that
he normally requires companionship and friendship, and
tends to become unhappy without them. It has fitted him
for them by endowing him with qualities of mind and heart
by which he can appreciate the standpoint of others and
sympathise with their needs. He can understand, too,
the meaning of the common good, and can even employ his
energies with enthusiasm in the service of the community
to which he belongs. For nature has implanted in his soul
the strong instinct of patriotism or devotion to the public
weal, which so often impels the noblest of the race to work

and suffer, and even to sacrifice life itself, for the good of
their fellow-citizens.

Finally, an innate tendency or instinct of human nature
impels men to form themselves into groups more or less
elaborately organised in which the needs for which family
co-operation is insufficient can be provided for, and in which
families and individuals will find means and opportunity
for the full development of all their natural capabilities.
Even in the lower order of creation a similar instinct is sometimes found. Bees, for example, ants, and some other
species of insects can live and thrive only by co-operating
in large multitudes for mutual protection and assistance.
And just as an unreasoning instinct forces these creatures
to form a type of association which is suitable to their
nature and their needs, so a strong natural inclination,
operating under the guidance of reason, impels men to
organise themselves in the civil union called the State.

Again, everywhere and in all ages men have lived in civil
society of one kind or another ; and this society is found
to be more perfect and highly developed in proportion to
the intellectual culture, moral standards and religious spirit
of the people.

Hence a Natural Society.—All these considerations—man's
natural fitness for association with others, his innate tendency and desire for such association, his needs, which can
be satisfied only by the helps that civil society gives, his
powers and faculties which can find means for exercise and
development only in large civil associations—all these
influences show that nature intends man to live as a
member of an organised society much more extensive and
wide-embracing than mere family life. They prove, in
other words, that the State like the family is a creation of
nature, intended and ordained by God. Thus, the scope
of the State like that of the family, its fundamental structure
and the principal rights and duties of its members are
ordained by the natural law and cannot be altered by any
human enactment. A further deduction is that the State
being formed by the natural law to provide for certain needs
of the individual person and to supplement the aids afforded
by family life comes after the individual person and the
family. Hence, it cannot abrogate essential personal rights

nor override nor interfere with the functions and privileges already committed to the family by the natural law.[1]

How States are Formed.—Whereas all agree that the family though a natural society comes into existence in each individual case as a result of the marriage contract, Catholic authors are not in agreement as to the actual process by which individual States are formed. Some hold that the existence of a set of circumstances which make it essential for the public good that the individuals and families of a certain territory should unite to form a State is of itself sufficient to bring about the civil union ; and that, given these circumstances, the natural law imposes the duties and confers the rights of citizenship upon the people of such a territory[2].

What facts and circumstances would be necessary and sufficient for thus welding people into one civic body, it is difficult to determine with accuracy. They are generally said to include a unity of territory and of race, a common language, a similarity of customs, a community of interests and national aspirations, and, perhaps most important of all, a participation in common historical memories. Any such rule, however, must be regarded as loose and elastic, and as giving only a general indication of the working of natural tendencies. Each case must be judged in the concrete, and decided on its individual merits.

Another school of Catholic philosophy requires, in addition to such circumstances, the actual consent of the members— at least for the original formation of the State. This latter view was the ordinary teaching of Catholic philosophy up to the end of the last century ;[3] the other theory then became more popular, because it seems to make clearer and

---

[1] Cf. Antoine, *loc. cit.* ; Ryan and Millar—*The State and the Church*, chaps. ii and iii ; Castelein—*Droit Naturel*, Theses 19 and 20.

[2] Cf. Taperelli—*Droit Naturel*, liv. viii, chap. iii ; Cronin—*Science of Ethics*, vol. ii, chap. xvi ; Donat, *loc. cit.* ; Meyer—*Institutiones Juris Naturalis*, pars. ii, Theses xlii–xlv.

[3] Cf. Suarez—*Oper. Sex Dierum*, lib. v, c. vii ; and *Def. Fidei*, lib. iii, cap. ii ; Costa-Rosetti, *op. cit.*, Theses 158–160 ; Castelein, *op. cit.*, Theses 19, 20 ; O'Rahilly—*Some Theology about Tyranny* (article in *Irish Theological Quarterly*, vol. xv, 1920, pp. 301–320) ; also *Catholic Origin of Democracy* (article in *Studies*, vol. viii, 1919, pp. 1–18), and *The Democracy of St. Thomas* (*ib.*, vol. ix, 1920, pp. 1–19), and *The Sovereignty of the People* (*ib.*, vol. x, 1921, pp. 39–56 and pp. 277–287).

easier of defence against the Liberal school, the essential Catholic doctrine upon the natural origin and constitution of the State.

Upon the main position, however, which alone concerns us here, all Catholic authors are at one, namely, that when the State is once validly set up, the fundamental rights and obligations of the members are fixed by the natural law ; and that, so long as the conditions that led to the formation of the society substantially remain, these rights and obligations are beyond the control of any human authority to abrogate or alter ; just as in the matrimonial contract, once the parties become husband and wife, their conjugal obligations and rights and the permanent duration of the union itself are fixed by nature and the law of God.

Source of Civil Authority.[1]—We have already explained that the element of authority or governing power is essential to the very nature of human society.[2]   Hence the natural law, upon which the civil union is founded, confers upon society the power of governing its members within the limits which are defined by the objects of society itself. Consequently, the legitimate rulers of the State are invested with authority from God ; and while they act within the limits of their power, he who resists them disobeys the ordinance of God.

As in the preceding case, Catholic philosophers are divided as to the process by which the actual rulers of the State are determined.   Those who hold that the consent of the members is required for the original formation of the State also maintain that the authority to rule is originally vested in the State as a whole, and that the actual ruler holds his position by virtue of the consent of the members, expressed or implied.   Those, on the other hand, who say that the State may have been originally formed by a concurrence of natural circumstances, without the consent of the members being necessarily required, also maintain that a like con-

---

[1] For an excellent and comprehensive exposition and discussion of this whole question, see the pamphlet of Fr. Macksey, S.J.—*Sovereignty and Consent* (reprinted in Ryan and Millar, *op. cit.*, chap. iv, pp. 68–98).   Cf. also Ryan—*Catholic Doctrine on the Right of Self-Government* (Paulist Press, New York).

[2] Cf. *Supra*, part i, preliminary chapter.

currence of circumstances may, in a similar manner, mark
out a certain individual or set of individuals as the natural
and only persons capable of wielding supreme power ; and
that these become by that very fact the responsible rulers.

In *practical application* these views differ very little. For
where a concurrence of circumstances requires the formation of a State as essential for the public good, and
manifestly designates for the same end a certain individual
or set of individuals as the only persons in whom the ruling
authority can reside, it is certain that the implicit consent
of the people may always be presumed. On the other hand,
from the manifest and persistent withholding of such consent
by the people one can reasonably conclude that the required
natural conditions are also wanting.[1]

" Neither in theory nor in practice," writes F. C. Macksey, S.J.,
" will anything stay a resolute people who have the strength to
do so from readjusting their form of government, whether a
republic or a monarchy, except the fact that the government is
being properly and successfully conducted for the general welfare
with the protection of the rights of all, and the exclusion of none
from a fair opportunity to develop human life along the lines
indicated by the nature of man."[2]

These words have been so often verified that it is
unnecessary to stress their truth.

Art. 3—*Functions of the State*[3]

From the reasons put forward to prove the necessity and
natural origin of civil society we may easily deduce what its
scope and purpose are, and what are the limits to its
authority.

---

[1] From the fact that governing authority is an essential attribute of
civil society, it follows that when the natural conditions (whatever they
may be) exist, marking out the people of a certain territory as a distinct
nation or civil society, the governing power is conferred by the natural
law on that society. In other words, a nation's right to independence
from outside control is indefeasible, just like the individual's right to
personal liberty. In either case, however, the right may be temporarily
lost or suspended from accidental causes such as crime. Cf. Meyer, *op. cit.*,
Thesis 79 ; Costa-Rosetti, *op. cit.*, pars. v, pp. 839 ff ; Donat, *op. cit.*,
nn. 589–604.

[2] *Op. cit.*, p. 94.

[3] Cf. Antoine, *loc. cit.*, chap. iii ; Donat, *op. cit.*, sec. iii, cap. iii and v;
Costa-Rossetti, *op. cit.*, Thesis 165 ; Castelein, *op. cit.*, Theses 19 and 22 ;
Ryan and Millar—*The State and the Church*, chaps. vii–ix.

Limitations to State Authority.—The whole purpose of the State is to assist individuals and families in the pursuit of temporal happiness. Hence it cannot justly, or even validly, exercise its activities except for the good of the people. Consequently, it is a perversion and abuse of authority (which is usually called tyranny) if the rulers utilise their powers for personal advantage, or if they force or induce the nation to enter upon enterprises which, although calculated to increase the power or wealth of a certain class within the State, do not make for the greater happiness of the people at large. Nay, the same conclusion may hold true, even though the wealth and power of all the members of the social body be thereby promoted; for wealth and power are not the only or the most important means of realising temporal happiness.

Again, the government of the State cannot validly override the essential rights of the individual, nor violate the sacredness of family relations, nor encroach upon the domain of the Church; nor interfere unduly in the internal affairs of the other corporate bodies within the State. For the person and the family are prior to the State; and man's supernatural interests, which have been committed exclusively to the control of the Church, are more vital to the happiness of the individual than any temporal good; and finally, the same human needs and tendencies that lead to and justify the formation of the State also impel men to form other natural unions and associations which, though not perfect or supreme societies like the State, are useful and even necessary for men's well-being.[1]

In the spheres of action that properly belong to the individual, the family and the Church, the duty of the State is not to dictate or interfere, but to safeguard the rights of these bodies, and to render, as far as possible, whatever assistance may be necessary to enable them to exercise their own functions with efficiency. Again, seeing that the authority of the civil government is derived from God, it has no power to decree or approve any measure or policy contrary to God's law.

---

[1] Cf. Leo XIII—*Rerum Novarum*, p. 161; also Pius XI—*Quadragesimo Anno*, 1931 (C. T. S. edit., pp. 36–38).

The Public Good—(*a*) **Peace.**—Even within its own province the proper function of the State is supplementary, not primary. For the individual, being a person, is primarily responsible for his own well-being. In other words, the State's legitimate sphere of activity is confined to procuring what is technically called the *Public Good.* The public good is defined to mean *all those helps and facilities which are reasonably necessary for the temporal happiness of the individual, but which are unattainable without the assistance of the State.* It may be said to include two elements, namely, *Peace* and *Public Prosperity.*

Peace means security from violent interference with one's rights. This security can usually be assured only by the aid of the strong arm of public authority. For this aid each and every member of the community has an indefeasible claim upon the State. To secure peace to all is in fact the State's most important duty. This duty includes the essential function of defending the Commonwealth, and all interests and groups within it against unjust aggression from within or from without, and usually requires the maintaining of an army adequate for national defence, as well as a police force to secure internal order and tranquillity.

(*b*) **Public Prosperity.**—Prosperity, in general, means a sufficient supply of the means that the individual requires for his natural welfare and happiness. It includes such goods as bodily health, food, clothing, shelter, personal freedom, private property, good reputation, mental culture suited to one's station, and good moral and religious training. All these things it is the individual's own duty to strive after and secure by personal effort, helped by the family and the Church. As far as they are thus attainable, they are called *Private Prosperity.* Since the legitimate function of the State is secondary, and comes in only where private or family co-operation fails or is inadequate, the providing of Private Prosperity is not the State's direct or immediate duty.

It is clear, however, from what has already been said that there are many things necessary for temporal happiness, which the individual cannot secure without the assistance of the State. The means to meet these needs is what is technically known as *Public Prosperity,* which may therefore be defined as the *sum of the helps and facilities, which are required in order to place private prosperity within the reach of all.* Public prosperity is what the State has to provide for the citizens.

Concrete Examples of Public Prosperity.—For the present we can indicate, only in a general way, the principal matters coming within the range of this public prosperity. It will include State legislature, judiciary and executive, for the defining and adjusting in an equitable manner the mutual rights of the citizens. An element of primary importance in public prosperity is an impartial system of administering justice within easy reach of the poorest of the citizens. Public prosperity also includes such utilities as roads, railways, hospitals, public institutions of all kinds, *so far as these may be required to supplement private enterprise, whether individual or collective.* It includes, too, safe and equitable means of exchange and such a system of property laws as would normally secure to everyone an opportunity of procuring by his labour a sufficiency of material goods. Again, public prosperity requires that special provision be made for the weak, the poor, and those not endowed by nature with exceptional mental gifts, lest these be oppressed and enslaved by the wealthy and the strong.

As a portion of this latter provision, the governing authority is bound to see that no class within the community—whether it be warlike barons surrounded by armed retainers, or financial magnates exercising an undue control over the resources of the nation—become so powerful as to be a menace to the peace and safety of the people. Hence, the State is bound to secure, by means of good laws and a pure administration, an equitable distribution of the material resources of the nation, so that what nature meant for the good of all be not monopolised by a few.

The public good and public prosperity, however, include in their range a much wider sphere than man's material well-being : and extend to the intellectual and religious interests of the people. We have already discussed the functions of the State in regard to the intellectual good of its members.[1] Under the heading of Legal Justice we shall later on devote

---

[1] Chap. xx, art. 4.

a special article to the duties of the Government to safeguard and promote the people's material well-being.[1] We shall now discuss the important question of the functions of the State in connection with the people's moral and religious interests, which is of special urgency and importance at the present day.

Art. 4—*Functions of the State Regarding Religion and Morals*

Prevalent Non-Catholic View.—Non-Christian philosophers and jurists of different schools generally deny that the State has any function in regard to religion or morals. This view is held by the Liberals and Socialists, who maintain that "The State is Atheistic," or at least has no functions in regard to man's duties towards God, or towards the moral law, except in so far as the intervention of public authority may be needed for the preservation of peace and public order. Hence they will not, so far as their influence prevails, admit any public manifestation of religion in official and civil life. Under this heading they include even the public schools from which, therefore, religion is banished. Moreover, as the moral law rests essentially upon man's relations to God, that, too, is practically disregarded. As a result of this policy the government, the politics, and the international relations of modern states have become in large measure confessedly utilitarian ; and if diplomatists or statesmen do sometimes offer lip service to the moral law and the claims of right and justice, these professions are mostly regarded, and too often with good reason, as insincere. This policy is also largely accountable for the widespread immorality, irreligion and unrest, as well as for the material misery of the people. The principles of which we speak permeate more or less the laws and administrative policy of the dominions of the British Empire ; and are formally sponsored by most English and Anglo-Irish non-Catholic newspapers and reviews. Even Catholic writers and publicists too often show signs of being under their influence.

Catholic Teaching.—The Christian teaching on the natural duties of the State in regard to religion and morals may be summarised under two main headings.

---

[1] Chap. xxv, art. 3.

30

(a) **Public Recognition of God.**—The State (viz., the governing authorities of the State), is bound in its public and official capacity to acknowledge God as the supreme Lord and Creator and to offer to Him due worship and honour.

" Nature and reason," writes Leo XIII, " which command every individual to worship God in holiness because we belong to Him, and must return to Him, since from Him we came, bind also the civil community by a like law."[1]

The reason is that the duty of religion is founded upon man's nature, and attached to all his activities. Hence, it cannot be lawfully excluded from man's civil life. This reason is confirmed by the fact that the State is a moral person formed by the natural law ; and

" Society not less than individuals owes gratitude to God Who gave it being and maintains it, and Whose ever-bounteous goodness enriches it with countless blessings."[2]

Hence God should be formally acknowledged in the written laws and constitutions of the State as the sovereign Lord and Master of all. Sundays and the holydays of the Church should be observed as civil holidays and public work suspended. Public activities which tend to profane these days, such as horse-racing and profane cinema shows, should not be permitted in a Christian State. At suitable times and circumstances, such as the opening of State functions, the heads of the State should offer public worship to God ; and public thanksgiving to God and public supplication should be offered on occasions of rejoicing and of special national danger, respectively. The crucifix or some such religious emblem should be shown in the public places of assembly such as the Parliament houses, the law courts, and the municipal halls. Most important of all, the ruling authorities should take care that everything in the laws and administration of the State should be in harmony with the principles of true religion and morality. Most of these manifestations of a Christian régime are definitely prescribed in the laws and constitutions of those states of Europe and America which still retain their Christian character, and many of them are still upheld even in the

---

[1] *Immortale Dei*, 1885, p. 48.   [2] *Ib.*

states which have fallen partially under the influence of unchristian Liberalism.[1]

(b) Safeguarding the Religion and Morals of the People.—

Although the religion and morality of the citizens in so far as they are merely personal and do not affect others, are outside the immediate province of the civil power, the latter is bound, as one of its primary and most important duties, to safeguard the citizens against all public incentives to irreligion and immorality ; and to encourage and promote by all reasonable means true religion and good morals among the people.

Each one's religion and moral goodness, in so far as they do not affect others or influence the public good, are purely personal concerns between the individual soul and God. Besides, as they refer primarily to one's eternal interests, they come directly under the care of the Church. Activities, however, which are not merely personal or private, but which of their own nature tend to influence the religion and morals of the people, are within the province of the civil power to prevent or to promote. For the duty of the State is not merely to safeguard the peace and to uphold the rights of the citizens, but to aid and supplement, as far as may be required, the individual efforts of the latter in procuring and advancing their own temporal well-being.

Now, the temporal well-being, far from being confined to mere material interests, comprehends the good of the whole man, and, therefore, includes his intellectual, moral and religious interests ; for the intellect and will are man's noblest and most important attributes. Hence, the State is bound, as one of the primary objects of its existence, to help the individual, as far as the public authority can do so, to acquire, preserve and promote a spirit of true religion and habits of good morals.

" It is a public crime," again writes Leo XIII, " to act as though there were no God. So, too, it is a sin in the State not to care for religion as if it were something beyond its scope, or as of no practical benefit ; or out of many forms of religion to adopt the one which chimes in with the fancy ; for we are bound absolutely

---

[1] Cf. *infra.*, chap. xxix, art. 2.

to worship God in that way which He has shown to be His will.
All who rule, therefore, should hold in honour the holy name of
God ; and one of their chief duties must be to favour religion,
to protect it, to shield it under the credit and sanction of the
laws, and neither to organise nor enact any measure that may
compromise its safety."[1]

These functions of the State surpass in importance its
duties regarding the material well-being of the people, in as
much as good morals and true religion are more important
for all the best interests of the race than material comfort
or wealth or power. Besides, unless religious practice and
belief flourish among the people, every human interest will
inevitably suffer.

" The Government alone cannot govern."[2] It is only
religion can supply the helps and motives necessary to
restrain human passions and keep them within the bounds
of law. It alone can effectually inspire men, rulers as well
as subjects, to be faithful to their social duties of Justice
and Charity and Patriotism. Hence, although religion
and morals are always under the control and guidance of
the Church, the civil power has essential duties and responsibilities in their regard ; and even in the interest of self-
preservation it is bound to take all the measures within
its power to safeguard and promote the moral and religious
interests of the people.

Practical Application of Catholic Teaching.—Hence, the
civil authorities are bound to suppress or prevent public
scandals of any kind so far as is consistent with prudence
and due moderation—for cases will occur when evils and
abuses have to be tolerated lest worse evils may arise from
an attempt to suppress them. Irreligious or immoral propaganda by means of lectures, writings, theatrical exhibitions
or cinemas should be prohibited, and subversive and imported
publications, as well as foreign agitators and propagandists
of an undesirable character, should be rigorously excluded.
Public incentives to unchastity, intemperance, and gambling
should not be tolerated. The sanctity of marriage should

---

[1] *Immortale Dei*, p. 48 ; cf. also *supra*, chap. ix, art. 5.
[2] De Maistre—*Du Pape*, chap. ii.

be safeguarded. Secret societies of irreligious or immoral tendencies should be suppressed.[1]

The unnecessary intermingling of men and women in industrial work, as well as the conduct of places of public amusement such as dance halls, etc., should be carefully regulated. Facilities should be provided for the due practice of religious duties. The Government should see that public officials themselves give a good example of religious and moral observance, and men of scandalous life or bad reputation should not be retained in the public service. In a word, the ruling power of a State must consider it its first duty " to preserve unharmed and unimpeded religion, the practice of which is the link connecting man with his God."[2]

The Press, Cinema and Betting.

—Amongst the " enormous evils " which " a stern insistence on the moral law, enforced with vigour by civil authority, could have dispelled, or perhaps averted," Pius XI mentions

" the unscrupulous but well-calculated speculations of men, who, without seeking to answer real needs, appeal to the lowest human passions. These are aroused in order to turn their satisfaction to gain."[3]

Perhaps the most important matters calling for the interference of the civil authorities are the press, the cinema, and public incentives to betting and gambling. For while these agencies are or can be most productive of moral degradation, private effort is powerless to check their activities. The words of Pius VII, written more than a century ago, are of special application to-day :

" The licence of the press," he writes, " threatens the people with the greatest perils and with certain ruin. It is a fact demonstrated incontrovertibly by sad experience that this

---

[1] The Masonic or Orange societies are specially dangerous in this connection, as being linked up with the world-wide anti-Christian movement. Besides they form a kind of *Imperium in imperio*, and are akin to a spearhead or foreign body inserted into the body politic inevitably causing disease, corruption and unrest. " They form," says Leo XIII, " an invisible and irresponsible power and independent government as it were within the body corporate of the lawful state (Cf. Cahill, *op. cit.*, p. 159). Hence the repeated appeals of the Pope to have them suppressed, and their recent suppression in Italy and Hungary.

[2] Leo XIII, *ib.*, p. 49.

[3] *Quadragesimo Anno*, p. 60,

licence of the press has been the principal instrument which
has first depraved the people's morals ; then corrupted and
destroyed their faith ; and finally stirred up sedition, unrest
and revolution."[1]

These words of Pius VII have been again and again
confirmed by succeeding Pontiffs. Thus Leo XIII, writing
in 1897 on the Prohibition and Censorship of books, says :

" Most perilous of all is the uncurbed freedom of writing and
publishing noxious literature. Nothing can be conceived more
pernicious, and more apt to defile souls, through its contempt
of religion and its manifold allurements to sin. . . . The decline
and ruin of states commonly owes its origin and its progress to
bad books. . . . Worst of all, the civil laws not only connive at
this serious evil, but allow it the widest licence."[2]

Art. 5—*The Constituent Parts and Organisation of the State*[3]

The State being a union of several individuals, families
and other institutions co-operating for a definite purpose,
is made up of two main elements, namely, the material
element or the several units which compose it, and the

---

[1] *Post Tam Diuturnas*, 1814—Apostolic letter addressed to Mgr. Boulogne,
Bishop of Tours, concerning the new elements of Liberalism introduced
into the French constitution (reprinted in *Lettres Apostoliques de Pie IX,
Gregoire XVI, Pius VII, etc.*, published by " La Bonne Presse," Paris,
pp. 243, 244.)

[2] *Officiorum ac Munerum*, 1897 (cf. *Great Encyclicals of Leo XIII*,
pp. 407–410). In connection with this matter it is notorious that the
foreign press and cinema are amongst the worst and most destructive
agencies at present in Ireland making for the moral degradation of the
people. The character of both are completely out of harmony with the
moral standards and traditional culture of the nation, but both are so
powerful that private efforts are unable to check or counteract their
activities. Except the governing authorities deal drastically and effectively
with them (by prohibiting their activities, at least to the extent of rendering them harmless), it will have neglected a primary duty : and the neglect
imperils the most important and essential interests of the people.

The same applies to gambling and betting activities : which have a
notoriously demoralising influence upon the people. Hence all public
incentives to bet, such as the publication of betting tips and betting news,
should be effectually prohibited by public authority. The Licensed
betting booths recently introduced into the Irish Free State should be
abolished, or kept under very strict control, and the other safeguards
recommended by different Commissions put into force (*see* Appendix III).

[3] The substance of this article is borrowed from the Encyclical *Quadragesimo Anno* of Pius XI and the works already referred to of Fathers Donat
and Meyer. Cf. Donat, *loc. cit.*, cap. iv, pp. 145–178, and Meyer, *loc. cit.*,
caps. ii and iii, pp. 334–479.

formal element which is the force binding these units together. In the present article we treat primarily of the material element or the units which go to form the State.

The State a Natural Organism.—We have already indicated that the individual person forms and must form the fundamental element in the civil organism.[1] The rights and privileges of the family and of all other organisms within the State, as well as the constitution of the State itself, all rest ultimately upon the dignity of human personality, and the divinely implanted tendencies, needs and capabilities of the individual person. It does not follow, however, that the State is essentially an aggregation of isolated or unorganised individuals.

" As nature," writes Pius XI, " induces those who dwell in close proximity to unite into municipalities, so those who practise the same trade or profession, economic or otherwise, combine into vocational groups. These groups, in a true sense autonomous, are considered by many to be, if not essential to civil society, at least its natural and spontaneous development."[2]

The natural organism of the State may thus be compared in some respects to the composition of bodies. Even though it may be true that the atom is the fundamental unit in the composition of bodies, it does not follow that the human body is made up merely of a collection of atoms heaped mechanically together. The atoms first go to form cells of various kinds : from these cells, according to their different nature and constitution, the organs of the body are formed : and it is from the due union and disposition of the bodily organs, each in its own place, and adapted to fulfil its own peculiar functions that the human body is immediately composed.

So, too, in the properly constituted State, there are several organic units intervening between the individual person and the completely organised body, such as families, municipalities, and social or professional classes. These are natural institutions like the State itself. Some of them, such as the family, are more imperatively demanded by the natural law, and more important for human well-being

---

[1] Cf. *Supra*, chap. xvi, Introductory Note.
[2] *Quadragesimo Anno*, 1931, p. 38.

even than the State ; while others, such as municipalities, professional unions, etc., are founded like the State itself upon men's natural tendencies and needs, and although not so essential to the people's well-being as the State, are in accordance with the natural law.

Hence the properly constituted civil society will be made up of an organised union of these groups, held together by a common bond (viz., social Justice and Charity), with their social and economic activities duly co-ordinated by one governing authority : so that it should be possible to say of the State what the Apostle says of the mystical body of Christ : *The whole body, being compacted and fitly joined together by what every joint supplieth, according to the operation in the measure of every part, maketh increase of the body, unto the edifying of itself in charity.*[1]

Contrast Between the Christian and Liberal Ideals.—One of the fundamental points of difference between the Christian concept of the State and that of the Liberals as a whole, is the different attitude the two schools adopt towards the organic constitution of the State.   The Liberals generally, including the Socialists, in accordance with their philosophy of individualism, tend to regard the State as a collection of isolated or unorganised individuals, inhabiting the same territory, and bound together only by political ties.   Even the organism of the family is largely ignored.   This concept of the State, which is manifestly unnatural, usually results in a system of representation in which deputies are elected solely or mainly to represent certain numbers of individual citizens, even husbands and wives voting as isolated units. Another result of the system is the strong tendency of the Liberal State towards centralisation and bureaucratic despotism ; for the unorganised citizens are powerless against a highly organised bureaucracy controlling the whole machinery of government.   Thus Pius XI, referring to the individualism and bureaucracy which unhappily characterise so many modern States, writes :

" Things have come to such a pass that the highly-developed social life, which once flourished in a variety of prosperous institutions linked with each other, has been damaged and all but

---

[1] *Eph.* iv. 16.   Cf. Pius XI—*Quadragesimo Anno*, pp. 40–42.

ruined, leaving thus virtually only the individuals and the State. Social life lost its organic form. The State, which was now encumbered with all the burdens once borne by associations rendered extinct by it, was in consequence submerged and over-whelmed by an infinity of affairs and duties."[1]

This over-centralisation has paved the way (especially in modern times owing to the tyranny of the moneyed interest and the destructive influence of the Masonic or quasi-Masonic secret societies) to all kinds of corruption and abuse. Not only may a nation be enslaved by a bureaucracy but whole states, bureaucracies included, may fall under the controlling power of international financiers, who strive by this means to establish a practical hegemony over the civilised world.

Organism of the Christian State.—According to the Christian ideal, the State is made up essentially not of a multitude of individuals, or even of families, under one government, but it embraces within itself a whole variety of organised units, more or less self-contained.

" Just as it is wrong," writes Pius XI, " to withdraw from the individual and commit to the community at large what private enterprise and industry can accomplish, so too it is an injustice, a grave evil, and a disturbance of right order for a larger and higher organisation to arrogate to itself functions which can be performed efficiently by smaller and lower bodies."[2]

These smaller units are constituted in various ways according to natural needs and historical development, some founded upon a territorial basis like communes and munici-palities, some being professional unions, such as Lawyers' Guilds, Labour Unions, and Vocational Corporations ; each having its own privileges, rights and duties ; some being contained within larger units, such as a town guild within the municipality, or a Trade Union or Employers' Union, within a Vocational Corporation ; each exercising a certain measure of control within its own sphere ; but all chartered, protected and co-ordinated by the central authority in accordance with the common good of the whole. The power and jurisdiction of the central authority itself is, or should be, limited, not only by the divine and natural law, but

---

[1] *Ib.*, p. 36.   [2] *Ib.*, p. 37.

also by the fundamental laws and constitutions of the State, which should not be altered except with the consent of the whole people.[1]

Hence in building up the fabric of a Christian State, it is essential for its stability and for the well-being and safety of its members that it be instituted organically after the model of the natural living bodies and that facilities be afforded for the gradual formation within it of organic units more or less self-contained, whose object and constitution will naturally fit into and form a constituent part of the whole organism and be in accordance with the common good. " The State should leave to these smaller groups the management of business of minor importance ; it will then carry out with greater freedom, power and success the tasks belonging to it, because it alone can effectively accomplish these, directing, watching, stimulating and restraining, as circumstances suggest, or necessity demands."[2] These units should gradually become the basis at least of a considerable portion of the representation within the municipal bodies, which would themselves be strongly represented in the central governing authority.[3]

" Let those in power be convinced," again writes Pius XI, " that the more faithfully this principle is followed and a graded hierarchical order exists between the various subsidiary organisations, the more excellent will be both the authority and the efficiency of the social organisation as a whole, and the happier and more prosperous the condition of the State."[4]

Territory of the State.—The land, buildings, rivers, canals, harbours, etc.,[5] form an integral and important portion of the material elements of which the State is made up. Again, the sea within three (lately extended owing to the influence of U.S.A. to twelve) miles of the shore, and all ships of the fleet and mercantile marine, as well as air-craft, are regarded in international law as a portion of the territory of that State to which they belong. It is clear that a fixed territory

---

[1] Namely, by such a majority as may be regarded as morally the whole. Cf. Meyer, *loc. cit.*, Theses 48 and 49.
[2] Pius XI, *ib.*, p. 37.
[3] Cf. Meyer, *loc. cit.*, pp. 469, 480 ; Donat, pp. 165–170.
[4] *Ib.*, p. 37.
[5] Cf. Donat, *loc. cit.*, pp. 155–157.

is necessary for the well-being and due development of a nation.[1] The stability of the families, the progress of agriculture, industrial development, civic life, commerce, and the arts, are all closely associated with a fixed territory, while the quality of the soil, the nature of its surface (whether mountainous or flat), the climate and geographical position, exercise the deepest influence upon the character and customs of the people.

Proper Basis of Representation.—Hence, civil as well as ecclesiastical jurisdiction is usually affixed to a certain territory. Moreover, in the constitution of the State, and in the system of representation, the people themselves should be regarded in close association with their places of habitation. This principle, too, which is in accordance with the Christian concept of the State is out of accord with the tendency of the Liberal jurists to arrange representation in the governing bodies, not upon a territorial basis but rather upon the numbers of individuals, so that a single section of a large city may have more representatives than two or three whole counties. Such a system tends to disintegrate the State, detach it from its territory and throw the power into the hands of the more unstable elements.

Relations of the State to Its Territory.—The State is not the owner of the territory, which belongs to individuals or private corporations, but it can exercise with a view to the public good a certain type of jurisdiction (*altum dominium*) which is, however, quite distinct from ownership or property rights. Thus it can within certain limits impose taxes, enact laws of heredity, make regulations regarding the use of land, and forbid the cutting down of woods. We shall discuss later on[2] the functions of the Central authority to safeguard the territory of the State.

---

[1] A settled or definite territory with the accompaniments mentioned in the text cannot be said to be an *essential* portion of a State ; for there have been nomad states, such as the Israelites before their final settlement in the Promised Land. Some writers hold that the Hebrew race even to-day form a distinct, though only a partially organised State, as they confessedly are a distinct nation.

[2] Cf. *Infra.*, chap. xxv, art. 2.

Art. 6—*The Central Authority in the State*[1]

The Right to Rule and the Best Form of Government.— The Church condemns no governmental system as such provided the duties of government can be fulfilled under it. She does, however, reject certain false principles which are invoked in support of some of the different systems. Thus she rejects the claim that the ruling authority is, or ever was, attached by divine appointment (except in some exceptional and well known instances such as that of Moses, Saul, and David) to certain persons or families or groups (the interpretation sometimes given by royalists to the " Divine Right of Kings "). On the other hand, she condemns the Liberal theory that everyone has a natural and innate right to share at least by his vote in the government under which he lives, as if no one could be subject to the authority of another except by his own consent.

Every man and woman has a right to be justly governed, but no one has a *natural* right to share in the governmental authority. The decision as to who are to be the rulers and what is to be the system of government must be ultimately decided by the requirements of the public good, which is the object and purpose of civil society. Moreover, the relative merits of the monarchical, and the popular types of government depend upon concrete circumstances such as the degree of education, the national traditions, and racial characteristics of the people to be governed. Even the claims of a government set up originally by violence and injustice may be validated in time if and when the public good requires.

It is true, however, as already stated, that the best and surest indication of the real requirements of the common good in this matter is the persevering demand of the people for a certain type of government, or their persevering unwillingness to accept or submit to a government or a system which has been forced upon them.

Systems of Government.—The two main systems of government are the Monarchical and the Democratic. In the former the ruler holds his position for life and governs in

---

[1] Cf. Donat, *loc. cit.*, cap. iv, art 3, and Meyer, *op. cit., loc. cit.*, cap. iii, art. 3, pp. 447–479.

his own name, as being the actual depository of the supreme power. The essence of democracy consists in the fact that the people or the citizens of the State are the immediate depository of the supreme power.

Various Types of Monarchy.—There are at least three different types of monarchy known to history, viz., the Absolute Monarchy, the Limited or Constitutional Monarchy, and the Parliamentary Monarchy. The Absolute Monarchy is best exemplified in the old Roman Emperors, who not only controlled the administration, and the judiciary, but were the sole source of the law, the Emperor's power not being limited by any law of God or man or by the veto of any other body within the State. This type of monarchy disappeared under the influence of Christianity, but was partially revived in Europe for a time under the absolutism of the centuries following upon the Protestant Revolt of the 16th century.

The Constitutional Monarchy as now understood was the type of government that prevailed generally in mediæval Europe. The power of the Constitutional Monarch is limited by the fundamental laws of the State which bind king and subject alike, and also by the power (which, however, was only consultative) of the three privileged Classes or Estates, namely, the Clergy, the Nobility, and the Commons (viz., the representatives of the townspeople or municipalities).[1] The Parliamentary type of Monarchy developed originally in England. Under the influence of the Liberal movement it spread into several other European countries, including Spain, Italy and Belgium, during the past century and a half. In this system the king, while nominally appointing the ministers of the executive, can select only those whom the majority or the prevailing party in the parliament approve. Besides, owing to the control of the taxes and expenditure exercised by the parliament,

---

[1] The Pope as a spiritual ruler is a constitutional monarch, in the sense that he is bound by the fundamental laws of the Church as constituted by Jesus Christ. Thus he cannot abolish the Episcopal hierarchy, nor change the supreme position of the Papacy, nor alter the nature of the sacraments. He is an absolute monarch in the sense that his power as supreme legislator, administrator and judge in spiritual matters is not limited and cannot be vetoed by any other authority on earth within or without the Church.

or rather by the prevailing party in the parliament, the
latter are the real rulers and in practice exercise all or nearly
all the powers of an absolute monarch. The parliamentary
monarchy as a government system has not met with much
success outside of England, and the present generation is
witnessing a reaction against it.

Democracy and Its Types.—Democracy is of two main
types—the Direct Democracy (which prevailed more or
less in the city states of ancient Greece and Rome) and the
Representative Democracy, which alone is known in modern
times. In the former the body of the people themselves
exercised, or were supposed to exercise supreme governing
power through the medium of their popular assemblies in
which all the enfranchised citizens had a voice. Such a
system is possible only for a state of very small dimensions.
In the Representative Democracies the mass of the people
delegate all or nearly all their power to bodies of duly
elected representatives or deputies.

Again, there are two main systems of representative
democracy, namely, the American or *Constitutional* democracy, which also partially obtains in Switzerland ; and
the *Parliamentary* democracy which is exemplified in the
French Republican government, and to a certain extent in
the government of the Irish Free State. In the Constitutional democracy the Parliament controls only the
legislation, and even in that its power is kept in check by
certain reservations or limitations. Thus the people, at
least in Switzerland, reserve to themselves the right of
vetoing a law by means of the Referendum, and also the
right of initiating legislation even over the heads of the
elected deputies. Again, the President of U.S.A., who is
appointed not by the deputies but directly by the people
on a basis and system quite different from that adopted in
choosing the deputies, can veto any given law. Furthermore, the administrative power belongs almost entirely to
the President, who appoints independently all the ministers
of State. In the *Parliamentary* type of democracy the
parliament passes all laws by a majority (its power not
being limited even by any fundamental laws of the State) ;
it appoints the president and dominates the administration
through the ministers whom the president appoints, but

whom it has to approve. In this system the people exercise
no effective power in the Government except by recording
their votes at the elections; so that absolute control over
the whole State is thus committed to a bare majority of
the representatives.[1]

Suitable Systems of Government.—We may set aside the
system of absolute monarchy as incompatible with right
reason or the principles of Christianity. Parliamentary
Democracy is also unsatisfactory. Besides the fact that
the Parliament may discuss, and even pass laws at variance
with the divine law, the possibility of a bare majority of
representatives possessing unlimited power over the des-
tinies of the State, is manifestly fraught with danger. It
endangers the stability which is essential for prosperity :
and disaster is likely to occur sooner or later if parliament
is enabled by a majority of a single vote to come to a
decision or pass a law that may affect and disturb the very
foundations of the State.

Constitutional Democracy, on the other hand, or a Parliamentary Monarchy (at least in the country in which that
type of government is indigenous),[2] or a Constitutional
Monarchy is capable in normal circumstances of affording a
just and good form of government provided the particular
system chosen suits the nation, and is not forced upon it
by an outside power against the people's wishes. Another
essential proviso is that when a national crisis occurs, or
the need arises for the undivided exercise of the supreme
power, there be some one person or some moral body acting
as one person upon whom the power will automatically
devolve ; for no State " *divided against itself can stand.*"[3]

---

[1] In the Irish Free State there is at present no limitation to the absolute
authority of the majority of the Oireachtas. The limitations imposed by
Britain, including those contained in the Articles of Agreement with Great
Britain (1921), have ceased as a result of the Statute of Westminster
(1931), in which the sovereign status of the Irish Free State is virtually
recognised. The checks provided in the original Constitution upon the
absolutism of the Oireachtas majority have also become inoperative.
Thus the Constitution may at present be altered by a bare majority
vote; and the provision for a referendum to the people has been repealed.

[2] In England several elements concur to lend stability to the government
and limit the power of the parliamentary majority. These elements are
mostly wanting in the other countries which have copied her governmental
system (Cf. Barnes—*Universal Aspects of Fascism,* chap. iv—" Fascism
and Democracy.")

[3] Cf. Donat, cap. iv., art. 3.

Each of the systems we have named has its own special advantages and its own peculiar drawbacks. In modern times, owing to the more complicated elaboration of the social organism, the greater diffusion of literacy among the masses of the people, and above all, owing to the huge public burdens such as taxes that the people have now to bear, it is generally admitted that a democratic form of government of one kind or another (provided it be really democratic and not the despotism of a class operating under the cloak of democracy) is in normal circumstances usually the most suitable and the best adapted to promote general well-being and content. But the difficulties to be encountered are very great, especially in safeguarding the State aganist subversive forces and the intrigues and aggressiveness of the secret societies as well as in guarding the State from the dominance of the financial magnates. A strong central government such as a constitutional monarchy usually affords the people a much safer bulwark against subversive forces than a democracy. Hence it is that the secret societies have carried on so relentless a war against the monarchies of Europe during the last century.

General Principles Regarding Democratic Government.— The following general rules are put forward by some of the standard Catholic writers as usually conducive to the successful conduct of a democratic government. Their applicability will, of course, vary a good deal according to the different circumstances, character and tradition of each nation :

I. That the people may retain the real control of the State, it is essential that the municipal, industrial and professional units be strongly organised, and that the deputies for the governing assembly should at least to a considerable extent be the representatives of the organic units, of which the State is made up—viz., the municipalities, labour unions, etc.[1] It is essential, too, that these deputies be well instructed in Christian social principles, and that the people themselves be organised under such systems as now obtain in the countries in which Catholic Action is highly developed.

---

[1] Cf. Donat and Meyer, *loc. cit.*

II. All enfranchised citizens should be legally compelled to vote,[1] and the activities of electioneering propaganda be strictly limited by law.

III. A majority does not at best represent the State but only a section (albeit *perhaps* the larger section or portion of the State), and a majority of the representatives does not always represent even a majority of the citizens.[2] Hence, the power of the majority should be kept in check by constitutional provisions, so that the majority be forced, at least in case of fundamental issues, to compromise and make just concessions, and that the final decision, if a decision be taken, represent more or less the decision of the State as a whole.[3] This can be secured in various ways, as, for instance, by the fundamental laws of the Constitution; through the Referendum, and the initiative ; by the power of veto vesting in the President, or by means of a second chamber appointed directly by the people on a totally different basis. This latter body could very suitably be made up principally of the representatives of the Church, the Universities and higher schools (Ecclesiastical and lay), the Vocational Corporations or the labour unions, the agricultural interests, and the great national organisations.

IV. The holders of Legislative, Executive and Judiciary powers should be made independent of one another, possibly after the model of the Constitution of U.S.A., for there is always the danger that the Executive or administration may be able by the distribution of patronage and in other ways to control the other powers or make them subservient to its wishes.

V. The ministers of State should be made to render account of their administration before a competent tribunal, and be liable to punishment for illegal action or abuse of power.

---

[1] Cf. Donat and Meyer, *loc. cit.* This provision is now enforced with very satisfactory results in some countries, such as in the Federal Government of Australia.

[2] Cf. The words of Leo XIII referring to the principles of unchristian Liberalism : " The law . . . is at the mercy of a majority. Now this is simply a road leading straight to tyranny "—*Libertas, Præstantissimum,* p. 80.

[3] Cf. Donat, *loc. cit.,* n. 351 ; Meyer, *loc. cit.,* Thesis 49.

31

VI. The Party funds of the political party organisations,[1] if such exist, should be regularly audited by public authority ; and the accounts open to public inspection.

VII. The numbers and power of the permanent officials of the central government should be kept rigorously in check. The autonomy of the lesser bodies and local units in the State, such as the municipalities and vocational corporations, should be jealously guarded against the aggressiveness and interference of the central bureaucracy, which otherwise will become a despotism of a most dangerous type. All the higher officials should be required to have qualifications not merely in technical knowledge and experience, but, above all, in knowledge of Christian Ethics and the Christian principles of government and civic organisation. No public functionary should be retained in office if once found guilty of corruption or disreputable action.

VIII. Secret societies should be completely suppressed. Real democracy is incompatible with the presence and baneful influence of these associations.

IX. While the legitimate freedom of the people's Press should be safeguarded, the activities and power of the Capitalist Press (viz., the papers owned or controlled by wealthy syndicates or great financiers) as distinguished from the Free Press should be kept in check.[2] The foreign Capitalist Press and foreign controlled Press should be

---

[1] The Party System is a result of the individualistic system of representation. In proportion as the representation becomes organic, viz., based upon the organic units in the State, the Party System would tend to disappear. It does not now exist in Italy under the new system.

[2] This could be done, for instance, after the manner now obtaining in Italy (Cf. *Survey of Fascism*—Official Year-Book of the International Centre of Fascist Studies, 1928, pp. 170–189). The Italian reforms of Journalism include measures touching (*a*) the institution of responsible managers, (*b*) the juridical recognition of professional journalism, and (*c*) a series of regulations concerned with the financing of newspapers, and with offences committed by or through the press. Thus, before a candidate can be inscribed in the register of journalists he must give proof of sufficient education and of moral probity and must be an Italian citizen enjoying full civic rights. Again, various severe sanctions have been put in force with the object of protecting individuals from libel, and society in general from false, mendacious or dangerous propaganda calculated to corrupt morals and to disseminate scandal. For much useful and interesting matter regarding Democracy, and representation, etc., cf. Barnes —*Universal Aspects of Fascism*, chap. iv. " Fascism and Democracy."

excluded or rendered powerless. This may be practically secured by requiring registration for foreign publications before they are exposed for sale, and by the imposition of taxes, especially on foreign advertisements. Like the international secret societies, the foreign controlled Press is an unnatural and outside element, which, if allowed to operate freely within the organism of the body politic, will inevitably dominate the whole organism, or at least impede or destroy its healthy vital action.

CHAPTER XXIV

JUSTICE[1]

Introductory Note—The Social Bond.—We now come to analyse the formal element in the civil organism—the force, namely, which unites the different members of the State into one moral body. Reference has already been made more than once to the analogy which the Scholastic authors point out between a properly constituted State and the human body. The latter is an organic whole, and its parts, which are united to one another by physical contact, are so formed and arranged by nature that under the impulse of the vital principle all co-operate spontaneously for the well-being of the whole body, and each in turn participates in the life of the latter, receiving blood and vital energy in accordance with its own particular needs.

The State, too, forms a kind of organic whole, composed of various associations, families and unattached persons, who are its members or parts. These members are not united together by physical contact like the members of the human body. Each has, or is supposed to have, its own separate life and personality, which are incommunicable and independent. Hence they do not and cannot form one physical whole. Neither has the State a physical principle of life to secure the due interaction between its several parts. Nevertheless, each member of the State, without prejudice to its own separate rights and personality, belongs in a true sense to the civic body ; and just as in the case of the human body every member is meant by nature to co-operate for the good of the whole, and in turn, to receive from the whole its due proportion of the helps it needs for its own well-being and fuller development. Our present purpose is to analyse the force which binds these different members into one, assigning definite civic functions and securing certain helps and advantages to each.

This bond is not a substantial entity, like the human soul. It influences the members only through the medium of

---

[1] Cf. St. Thomas, 2ᵃ, 2ᵃᵉ, Q. 58. De Lugo—*De Justitia et Jure*, d. i, sec. i.

the human will and the laws of right and wrong. Justice is its main element ; for it is Justice that holds together the framework of the State, enabling it to function properly, and substantially to achieve its purpose. Hence Justice may be called in a certain sense the soul of the civic organism ; and its rôle and influence are paramount in all social and civic relations. The work of Justice is aided and supplemented by two other forces—those, namely, of Piety or Patriotism, and of Charity. These latter help to secure that the duties of social justice be carried out with smoothness and efficiency ; and in addition they meet many needs resulting from accidental causes (such as the weakness and vagaries of the human will) for which Justice may not sufficiently provide. This is the doctrine which Leo XIII outlines when he writes :

" It is clear and evident that the very notion of civilisation is a figment of the brain, if it rest not on the abiding principles of truth and the unchanging laws of virtue and justice ; and unless unfeigned love knit together the wills of men, and gently control the interchange and character of their mutual services."[1]

In the following chapters we shall first endeavour to analyse the nature and explain the different species of Justice, insisting especially on Legal and Distributive Justice which belong primarily to civic relations. Next we shall treat briefly of the virtues of Charity and Patriotism and their functions in social life.

Art. 1—*The Nature of Justice*

Meaning of Term.—The word *Justice*, if understood in its primary and original sense, would mean the exact agreement between one thing and something else with which it is meant to conform. Traces of this original meaning still survive in English in the verb to *adjust*. In its derived or metaphorical sense, the word *Justice* is sometimes used to mean the conformity or agreement between a man's acts and the moral law. In this sense Justice would be the sum of all the moral virtues. Thus, we read in Scripture of St. Joseph " *being* a just man."[2]

The term, however, is ordinarily used in a much more restricted sense. It refers to the mutual relations between

---

[1] *Inscrutabili*, p. 3. [2] *Matth*. i. 14.

two persons, and implies a conformity or agreement between the acts of one and the rights of the other. In this last sense, which is the ordinary one, and the one that alone concerns us here, we may regard Justice as a habit or virtue of the human will inclining one to act justly. Thus, St. Thomas defines Justice as : *A constant and permanent habit or intention to give each one his due.*

Objective Justice.—We may, however, look on Justice from another point of view, and consider it not as a virtue or habit of the will but rather as the reality outside the person (viz., the objective relations or proprieties) with which the virtue of the will must be in harmony. Justice considered from this standpoint (viz., *Objective Justice* as the Scholastics term it) may be defined as : *the relation of equality between two persons, in virtue of which one is bound to give the other his due (habitudo aequalitatis inter duos secundum debitum).* In other words Justice, regarded objectively, is nothing else than the law of nature, which demands that each person get his due or his rights from everybody else. It is with Objective Justice we are concerned here.

Objective Justice is based on what is called *personal equality.* Persons alone can possess rights, and all persons are equal in so far as the rights of all are inviolable. Hence, the acts or omissions of others, in order to be lawful, must be adjusted to be equal to or in conformity with these rights. This conformity or equation is Objective Justice.

We may note also that not only an individual, but also a moral body, such as the State or the Church, may be regarded as a person, and so have rights which are inviolable, just like the rights of individual persons. Such a moral person may also have duties in its corporate capacity. Thus, the relations with which Justice is concerned may apply not only to an individual person, but also to a moral unit like the State.

Essential Constituents of Justice.—Justice, whether as a virtue or an objective relation, has two essential constituents, namely, Distinction (*Altereitas*) and something due (*Debitum*). Both need further explanation.

(*a*) **Distinction of Persons.**—The law or virtue of Justice essentially implies two *distinct* persons ; and the goodness which Justice contains is founded upon the due relations of one with the other. Most other virtues, such as temperance, prudence, and fortitude, have reference to the right ordering of one's own acts, in accordance with the moral law without any reference to others. Even in these few virtues, such as charity, piety and obedience, which, like Justice, are concerned in some way with one's relations to others, the formal motives of the virtues do not rest on the fact that the persons concerned are distinct from each other, but rather that they are in some way, or to some degree, mutually identified. Thus, a man is bound to love his neighbour, not because the neighbour is a person distinct from himself, but because the neighbour has the same nature as he has, and is, like him, the child and friend of God. The direct and formal motive of Justice, on the other hand, is founded on the fact that the person towards whom the duty of Justice lies is distinct from and independent of the person who has the duty.[1]

The distinction of persons which Justice requires need not always be complete from every point of view. Thus, there can be real relations of Justice between an individual citizen and the State of which he is the member ; for the State, considered as a moral person has an end and purpose of its own (which is the common good) and, therefore, a distinct moral personality. In order to attain that end, it needs, and by the law of nature has a *right* to the co-operation of each of its members. In other words, the State has rights against its own members. The members, too, have rights against the State. For the citizen needs the help of the State, and has a *right* to that help. Now, these reciprocal rights and duties between the State and the individual citizens manifestly point to a distinction of personality sufficient for real relations of Justice.[2]

(*b*) **The Thing Due.**—It is the special characteristic of the virtue of Justice that it is concerned solely with acts that are *obligatory by reason of the rights of another*. In case of

---

[1] St. Thomas, *ib.*, a. 2. De Lugo, *ib.* n. 19.
[2] Cf. Vermeersch—*Questiones de Justitia*, cap. iii, p. 30.

all the other virtues, such as charity, fortitude and piety, there are many acts which belong to the virtue, and are, therefore, praiseworthy ; but which one may omit without sin or fault. In case of Justice this cannot occur, for every act of Justice is obligatory, and once an act ceases to be of obligation (once it ceases to be *due*), it is no longer an act of Justice, although it may be an act of charity, obedience, or liberality.

The idea expressed by the term ' one's due ' (*debitum*), or one's own (*suum*), is a correlative of that of right. A right as already explained[1] is the moral power which a person has and which every other person is bound to respect, to do something or to retain something, or to exact something from another. Now the *something*, which is the object of a man's right is said to be ' his,' ' his own,' or ' his due.' Thus, my horse is *my own*, hence, I have the right to the exclusive use of him ; again, the wages I have earned, but have not yet been paid, are *my due* : hence I have the right that my employer pay them to me.

A person comes to *have a right* to a thing (or in other words a thing comes to be *one's own*, or *one's due*) in two ways : First, one may have a natural personal connection with the thing. Thus, one has a right to one's life and to the free use of one's faculties. Or, secondly, some contingent fact may have occurred (such as occupation of the thing, productive labour, or inheritance) which establishes a natural connection with, and thus gives one a claim upon, the thing. Thus a person has a right to the fish he has caught, to the piece of land he has bought, to the property which his father has bequeathed him. In other words, these things are *his own* or *his due*.

Different Foundations of Dues and Rights.—Now, the idea of one's own, or one's due, and, therefore, the corresponding idea of right, admit of degrees, in the same manner as the idea of distinction, of which we have already treated. Some things are due to a person or belong to him by reason of some *immediate* connection between the thing and himself. Thus, the fish a man has caught is his, because of the immediate connection he has established (by the act of catching) between the fish and himself.

---

[1] Cf. *Supra*, chap. xvi, art. 2.

Other things are due to a man because he has an immediate or direct connection not with the things themselves ; but only with the persons to whom these things immediately belong. Hence his claim upon them is not *immediate* or *direct* (such as is the basis of property rights) but only indirect and mediate. It is in this way that a citizen has a certain claim on the goods of the State. In other words, these goods, or a certain participation in them, are *his due* not by reason of any direct and immediate connection between these goods and him, but because he is a member of the State, to which these things belong ; and the fundamental duty and object of the State is to utilize the goods or powers it has for the help and well-being of each of its members.

In a similar way, the State itself, considered as a moral person, has certain claims upon the goods and services of each of its members (in other words, these goods and services, or rather a certain participation in them, are *due* to the State) not on account of any direct connection of these things with the moral unit called the State, but because these things belong immediately and directly to one of the members of the State ; and the State has, from the natural law, a right, intimately connected with its very existence, that every citizen co-operate with or contribute to it in due proportion for the public good.

Hence, Three Distinct Classes of Rights and Dues.—From all this it follows that the meaning of the terms *one's due*, *one's own* (*debitum, suum*), may be realised in three[1] different ways :

(*a*) When an individual person or a society owns a thing directly, or has an exclusive right to use it for his own benefit. Thus, a man owns his house or the fish he has caught. Similarly, the whole State, considered as a moral person, owns the public revenues. This type of right is exemplified in the rights of ownership or property rights, also in one's right to life, liberty, etc., all of which we have already explained.[2]

---

[1] St. Thomas, 1ª, 2ᵃᵉ, Q. 96, a. 4 ; 2ᵈᵃ, 2ᵈᵃᵉ, Q. 58, a. 6 and 7 ; Q. 61, a. 1. Vermeersch—*Questiones de Justitia*, Q. 1, cap. ii, n. 22.
[2] Cf. chap. xvi, art. 2, and chap. xvii.

(*b*) When the State, regarded as a moral person, has a right to a certain proportion of the goods and services of each one of its members. For the whole has a right to participate in *due proportion* in the goods which belong directly to its parts, at least when the existence and the functions of that whole *have been ordained by the natural law ; and are impossible of realisation without the due co-operation of the parts.*

(*c*) When a person (or a society) has a right to a certain share of, or participation in the goods of the State of which he is a member : for a part has a right to its share of the things belonging to the whole, at least when *the whole is meant exclusively for the good and benefit of the parts.*

Indirect or Imperfect (but Strict) Rights and Dues.—It will be seen that, in the second and third case above, there is no immediate connection between the things or services in question and the person who has a right to them or to whom they are due. The connection is *indirect*, being established through the medium of the person to whom these things directly belong, who, in the second case, is the State considered as a moral person, and in the third case, is a unit or member of the State. Besides, in these two latter cases the rights are not absolute, as in the case of property rights, but relative, so that their extent cannot always be clearly defined. For they are limited and determined by the relative claims and capacities of the other members of the State. Hence, they are sometimes called *imperfect* rights, as contradistinguished from the first class, which are called *perfect* rights.[1]

These terms are not meant to imply that imperfect rights are not real (*strict*) rights, for, notwithstanding the difficulty of defining the exact extent of the obligation in each case, the claims of the State upon the citizen, and of the latter upon the State are things due (*debita*), and their neglect or violation constitutes real injustice. Usually, the extent of these claims is defined by civil law. Now and then they are so clear that they impose definite obligations independent

---

[1] It is well to note that the terms *Perfect* and *Imperfect* are also used in quite another sense, as indicated in chap. xvi, art. 2, to mark the distinction between rights that are inalienable or indefeasible and those that may for sufficient reason be limited or temporarily withdrawn.

of positive law ; sometimes, in the absence of positive law, the claim is not clear and definite enough to cause an obligation on the individual citizen to satisfy it, but quite sufficient to impose a definite obligation on the governing power of the State to provide for it by law or otherwise.

The three different types of dues and rights which we have just described form the foundation of the triple division of Justice into Commutative Justice, Legal Justice and Distributive Justice : of which we shall now treat.

Art. 2—*Commutative Justice*

Commutative Justice regulates the relations between two completely distinct persons, and has to do with rights which are perfect and clearly defined, being founded upon such an immediate connection between the person and the thing due that the former has a right to the latter for his own exclusive use or benefit. Commutative Justice is so-called from the Latin word *commuto*, to exchange, because it regulates in a special way contracts of exchange, such as buying and selling, lending, hiring, etc.

Definition and Nature.—Commutative Justice may be defined as *the relation of equality between two fully distinct persons in virtue of which each is bound to render to the other what is his due.* It may exist between individual persons or between individuals and societies, or between two societies with each other. Thus, if A. owes B. £20 ; if Mr. Rockfeller has lent to the English or French or American Government £5,000,000 ; if the British Government has overtaxed the Irish nation during the past century to the extent of £300,000,000 ; if any particular Government has inflicted a definite injury upon any of its own subjects ; all these debts and injuries and the obligations arising from them have to do with Commutative Justice. Commutative Justice has therefore to do with relations between person and person, abstracting from the question as to whether they are individual persons or moral units, and whether they are or are not members of the same civil body.

The Most Perfect Type of Justice.—All the elements which go to make up the idea of Justice are found in their most perfect form in Commutative Justice. Hence, we have here complete *distinction of persons*, perfection of *right* and fulness of *equality*, requiring that the payment or satisfaction of the claim be literally and *arithmetically* equal to the extent of the debt. The person's right to the thing due, which implies a corresponding obligation on the part of him who owes it, is indefeasible, and perseveres (unless freely surrendered or condoned) as long as the thing due is in being, or its equivalent obtainable. Therefore, Commutative Justice implies an obligation of restitution on the part of one who has violated it, whenever restitution is possible, that is when the thing due or its equivalent can be actually restored.

But Not the Proper Subject of Social Science.—Although Commutative Justice may be violated by the State in dealing with any of its members, or by one of the latter in his relations to the State, this can only occur in case of rights that the State and the citizen possess independently of each other. For instance, Commutative Justice would be violated by the Government which would unjustly seize the private property of one of its citizens or by a citizen who would embezzle public funds. The normal relations, however, between the State and its members, as such, are regulated not by Commutative Justice, but by Legal and Distributive Justice. Hence, these latter are the immediate province of Social Science, whereas, Commutative Justice belongs rather to the science of Ethics or Moral Theology, and is the ordinary subject-matter of the Theological treatises on Justice.

CHAPTER XXV

LEGAL JUSTICE[1]

Art 1—*General Principles*

Definition and Nature.—Legal Justice has to do with the second species of rights or debts referred to above, namely, to the right which the State possesses to the co-operation of each of its members for the common good. It is called *Legal* by reason of its close connection with the civil law, whose special function it is to determine the duties (including omissions as well as acts) to which the individual citizens are bound in view of the common good. As Legal Justice, however, is founded upon the law of nature, its scope is not confined within the limits of positive law and extends to matters which positive law may not have defined.

Legal Justice may be described as *the virtue or law of nature binding every member of the State to contribute his due share in safeguarding and promoting the common good.* The foundation of Legal Justice lies in the fact that the State is a creation of nature like the family, and needs the co-operation of its members in order to perform its essential functions (namely, to procure the common good), or even to exist. Hence, the members of the State are bound by the natural law to give that co-operation ; and the State has the duty and the right to exact it.

These mutual rights and obligations are something over and above the mutual duties and claims of Commutative Justice ; or the duties of Charity. These latter bind all men equally in their relations to one another, while the mutual rights and duties of the State and its members do not extend to those outside the State. They are the essential ties uniting the members of the State into one whole and differentiating them from others. These mutual rights and duties are what we call Legal Justice.

---

[1] Cf. St, Thomas, 1ª, 2æ, Q. 96, a. 4 ; 2ª, 2æ, Q. 58, a. 5 and 6. De Lugo *De Justitia et Jure*, dis. i, sec. iv ; Vermeersch—*Questiones de Justitia*, Q. 2, cap. i ; Costa-Rosetti, *op. cit.*, Theses 150–152 ; C. Macksey—*Argumenta Sociologica*, cap. ii, art. i.

Differs from Commutative Justice.—From the definition
it is clear that Legal Justice differs essentially from Commutative Justice. In the first place, the distinction between
the persons who are bound by the duties of Legal Justice
and the one towards whom the duties lie is not a *perfect*
distinction ; for the citizens who are bound by the duties
themselves make up the civil community towards which
the duties lie. In the second place, the rights conferred
by Legal Justice are not *perfect* rights, like those conferred
by Commutative Justice ; for the goods and powers accruing
to the State as a result of the co-operation of its members
are not meant for its own exclusive use, but for the common
good, that is, for the help of the individual members to
whom the State has to distribute them. Furthermore,
violations of Legal Justice, although against the moral
law, do not of themselves involve an obligation of restitution.

And from Distributive Justice.—These points of difference
between Commutative and Legal Justice apply also to
Distributive Justice, which differs from Commutative
Justice in the same manner as Legal Justice does. The
difference between Legal Justice itself and Distributive
Justice lies in the fact that whereas the former binds all
the members of the State, both rulers and subjects, to co-
operate for the common good, Distributive Justice applies
practically to the rulers alone, and binds them not merely
to seek the common good in exercising their public functions,
but to distribute its advantages equitably among all the
members of the State.[1]

And from Obedience, Patriotism, etc.—Legal Justice
differs also from the duty of *obedience* to the laws of
the State ; for the ultimate motive of obedience to the
law is the fact that all legitimate authority comes from
God ; whereas the motive underlying the duties of Legal
Justice is the natural relations of the part with the whole.
From these natural relations it follows that every member
of the civil body is bound to promote the good of the body
of which he is a part. Hence, Legal Justice is prior to and

---

[1] Cf. Costa-Rosetti, *op. cit.*, Thesis 152, pp. 544–546 ; Vermeersch, *op. cit.*,
Q. 2ª, cap. i, n. 44.

more comprehensive in its scope than civil law, and the latter, in order to be valid, must be in conformity with Legal Justice, that is, it must be ordained for the common good.[1]

Again, Legal Justice must not be confounded with such virtues as charity, patriotism, and liberality, although the proximate motive of some of the acts of these virtues may be the common good. For, unlike these virtues, the acts of Legal Justice are always of obligation ; otherwise they would not be acts of Justice ; and the foundation of the obligation is the *necessary* connection between the act and the common good, which the doer is bound to promote *at least to that extent*. Thus, if a person makes a voluntary sacrifice for the common good beyond what he is bound to do he may thereby perform an act of patriotism, of charity, of liberality, possibly of vanity, but his action is not an exercise of Legal Justice.

Doctrines of Liberals.—The existence of such an obligation as Legal Justice implies (namely, the duty of every member of the State to contribute towards the common good) is denied by the economists and jurists of the Liberal school, and is practically ignored by many others who are more or less influenced by Liberal principles. Denying, as the Liberals do, the natural or divine origin of Civil Society (which they say is the result of a free compact among men, like a trading company or a sporting club), they cannot logically admit, and, in fact, do not admit that a citizen has any duty towards his fellow-citizens except the duties of Commutative Justice and such duties as the civil authority may actually enforce. Further, they tend to confine the scope of the State's legitimate activities within the limits of preserving peace, and enforcing the claims of Commutative Justice.

" General Justice."—In the Catholic view, on the other hand, acts of any or of all the other virtues may become obligatory in virtue of Legal Justice, if such acts be commanded by a just law, or if, in a concrete case they are imperatively demanded in the necessary interests of the

---

[1] Cf. St. Thomas, 2a, 2æ, Q. 96, a. 94.

community. Hence it is, that Legal Justice is sometimes called General Justice.[1]

It should be noted, however, that since the individual and the family are prior to the State, no apparent public utility would justify a ruler in interfering with family relations or infringing the inalienable rights of the citizen, or curtailing unduly or without sufficient cause his ordinary natural freedom, or his right to form associations in accordance with the general good.[2]

Art. 2—*Obligations of Legal Justice*

Obligations Vary for Different Members.—As the duties of Legal Justice are directly founded, not upon personal independence and equality, as in the case of Commutative Justice, but rather upon the rights of a naturally constituted whole to the due co-operation of its several parts,[3] the type and degree of co-operation which each part is bound to give will vary in accordance with the natural capacity of that part, and the rôle it has to fulfil in the civil organism.

" Although all citizens without exception," writes Leo XIII, " can and ought to contribute to the common good, in which individuals share so advantageously to themselves, yet it should not be supposed that all can contribute in the like way or to the same extent."[4]

Just as in the domestic society the contributions to the good of the family due by the wife differ essentially from those of the husband, and may or may not be equal to his in difficulty or amount, so also in civil society, each unit is bound to do its share in accordance with its capacity and the function it has to fulfil and in proportion to the actual needs of the State.

Binds Rulers as Well as Subjects.—The duties of Legal Justice belong to the rulers of the State as well as to the

---

[1] St. Thomas, 2a, 2æ, Q. 58, a. 5 and 6 ; Vermeersch, *loc. cit.*, n. 43 ; cf. also St. Thomas, Ia, 2æ, Q. 96, a. 3, where he writes : " There is no virtue concerning whose acts, human law may not lay down precepts ; not indeed concerning all the acts of these virtues, but only concerning such as may affect the common good."

[2] St. Thomas, 2a, 2æ, Q. 104, a. 5.

[3] St. Thomas, 2da, 2dæ, Q. 58, a. 5.

[4] *Rerum Novarum*, p. 151.

subjects. In fact, they belong primarily to the rulers, as the latter have the most important function in the work of providing for the common good.

"Legal Justice," says St. Thomas . . . " resides in the ruler *principally*, as if he were the architect and director of the building : and in the subjects in a secondary way as if they were the assistants."[1]

In these pregnant words he compares the public good, which is the end and object of the State, to a great building or temple. The whole community or State regarded as a moral unit has from nature the right and the duty to build and maintain that edifice, and to exact from its several members the services and payments which are required for the work. Now, since the State as a whole cannot itself carry out the functions of planning the details of the building, supervising the construction, and allotting his proper function to each of the workmen engaged on it, it commits those duties to a certain person or persons (namely, the rulers) who exercise them in the name of the State, while it assigns to the other members (namely, the subjects) the rôle of carrying out the work under the direction of the rulers.[2]

It may be noted in this connection that the term Higher Dominion or Eminent Domain (*Dominium altum*) is sometimes applied to the authority which the State has from God over the person, the property and the activities of the citizen, and which it commits to the legitimate rulers.[3] This term has been used not infrequently as a pretext to legalise tyranny. For the words may suggest to the mind that the rulers are not bound by the duties of Legal Justice, and that these duties belong only to the subject. The very contrary, however, is the case. The duties of Legal Justice, although different for rulers and for subjects, belong to both, and are fully juridical in case of each. Hence, the State (the members taken in the aggregate) has the right to enforce even by physical coaction the fulfilment of their

---

[1] *Justitia Legalis* . . . *est in principe principaliter et quasi architectonice* ; in subditis autem *secundario* et quasi *administrative*, 2da, 2^{dae}, Q. 58, a. 6.
[2] Cf. Costa-Rosetti, *op. cit.*, pp. 547–548.
[3] Cf. Suarez-Opuscul—*De Justitia Dei*, sec. iv, n. 6.

duties from the rulers as well as from the subjects, and of punishing the violation or neglect of them.[1]

The duties of Legal Justice regularly bind in conscience. Otherwise they would not be duties of Justice. This is especially so, when the act or omission is imposed by the natural law, as being necessary for the public good, or when it is enforced by the executive authority of the State.

Duties of Subjects.—The duties of subjects, under the heading of Legal Justice, are mainly as follows :

I. The first and principal duty is to obey the just laws of the State, and to pay the taxes which are justly imposed.

II. In cases where the safety or some very important interests of the State are imperilled, individual citizens who see the danger and are able to avert it even at the cost of great personal sacrifice, would be bound by Legal Justice independently of all positive law to do so.[2]

III. Even in the absence of such urgent or immediate danger to the State, a citizen would be debarred by Legal Justice from many things which may not otherwise be unlawful. . . . Thus, voting for the less suitable candidate for a public office, indulging in certain types of political trickery, or in certain species of commercial speculation or commercial gambling, may well be so manifestly and gravely detrimental to the public good as to involve violations, possibly, even grave violations of Legal Justice, even though such practices be not forbidden by any positive law, nor imply any clear infringement of Commutative Justice.[3]

Duties of Rulers—(a) In Their Private Capacity.—All the duties of subjects referred to above apply also to the members of the ruling body in their *individual* capacity, for they as citizens are subject to the ordinary laws of the State, and are bound like the other members of the community to promote the common good.

---

[1] The fact that physical coaction is usually not lawful as against the ruling powers comes from the circumstance that it is usually impossible to employ it against the rulers without the risk of greater evil. Cf. Costa-Rosetti, *op. cit.*, Thesis 76, p. 221, and Thesis 152, pp. 549–551 ; also St. Thomas—*De Rege et Regno* (*De Regimine Principum*), lib. i, cap. 6.
[2] Cf. Macksey, *op. cit.*, cap. i, a. 1, pp. 30–34.
[3] Cf. Castelein, *op. cit.*, Thesis vi, p. 125.

In this connection it should also be noted that in a democratic form of government, which is the ordinary type in modern times, *all* the citizens who enjoy the franchise share to a certain degree in the responsibilities of the rulers. Thus, a citizen would violate Legal Justice should he cooperate even by his elective vote in perpetuating an unjust or inefficient régime, or should he in any way support a policy which is clearly out of harmony with the common good. This applies with special force to the citizens who, owing to their wealth, education, or social position, or the control they exercise over public opinion through the Press, have special influence in determining actions and policy of the ruling powers. Furthermore, in a democratic system of government all enfranchised citizens are bound in conscience to exercise the powers they have in so far as may be necessary or useful for the common good, lest a group of politicians or financiers or Press magnates be permitted to dominate public life to the injury or enslavement of the people. In this sense every citizen is bound to be a politician.[1]

(*b*) **In Their Capacity as Rulers.**—Over and above the duties that rulers share more or less with the subjects, they have duties which are peculiarly their own and which, seeing that they so deeply affect the well-being of the citizens, imply specially grave obligations. These we may summarise as follows :

General Principles.—I. The rulers, in their corporate capacity (viz., the legislative, Executive and judicial bodies), are bound to observe in their acts and decisions the precepts of the natural and divine law, as well as the fundamental laws of the constitution.[2] These latter are laid down or implied, by the natural law, or by custom, or in some cases by the written law of the State ; and it is outside the competency of any individual ruler or body of rulers to alter them, without the consent of the body of the people.[3]

---

[1] Cf. Cronin—*Primer of the Principles of Social Science*, pp. 30, 31.

[2] In the British constitution the Legislative authority is made up of the King, Lords and Commons. The King and his ministers (forming the Cabinet) are the heads of the Executive.

[3] Cf. St. Thomas, 1a, 2æ, Q. 90, a. 3 ; Q. 97, a. 3, ad. 3 ; *De Rege et Regno* (*De Regimine Principum*), cap. vi ; Costa-Rosetti, *op. cit.*, pp. 602–612,

Hence it is, that even hereditary kings and emperors usually have to swear before their accession to power to observe and uphold the fundamental laws of the realm and to respect the liberties of the people.

II. In the second place, rulers are bound to aim solely at the common good in all their legislative and administrative acts. Therefore, they violate Legal Justice if they utilise their position of authority for their own personal advantage, or for the special advantage of one class or section of the people at the expense of another : for this would be manifestly contrary to the common good.

" The rule of a tyrant is unjust," says St. Thomas, " because it does not aim at the common good, but at the personal advantage of the ruler."[1]

III. **Safeguarding the Territory and Industries of the State.**—We have already referred to the duty of the government to provide for national defence. Under the same heading comes its duty of preserving the integrity of the State and safeguarding its territory not merely against hostile armies, but (what is no less dangerous) against the peaceful penetration of foreign capitalists and syndicates. Hence, it is an elementary duty of the government of a State to safeguard for the people of the State the territorial waters, the land, the mines, the harbours, the fisheries, the waterways, the mills, the railways, etc., and prevent their coming under foreign control.

The same applies to the industries. For a State may suffer disintegration or lose its freedom no less really by economic than by military conquest. In fact, the disintegration which the States suffers by losing control of its fisheries, harbours, mines, mills, etc., is possibly a much more serious evil than the complete loss of a certain province whose people may find their material well-being as well cared under the new State to which they are assigned. But when alien control succeeds in penetrating into the bosom of the State, the public good and well-being of the whole nation is gravely imperilled ; and a way is opened for the enslavement of the people by foreign financiers, or even by a foreign State.

---

[1] 2a, 2æ, Q. 42, a. 2. Cf. also *De Rege et Regno* (*De Regimine Principum*), lib. i, c. iii.

IV. And the Rights of Each Individual Subject.—Rulers are bound to protect the rights of each and all of their subjects. The protection of these rights against unjust interference from any source is also a primary duty of the government. Hence, the rulers must secure for each the freedom to practise the true religion, personal liberty and safety, and the secure possession of his property.

Finally, the rulers are bound so to adjust the laws regulating public morality, family life, property rights, finance, industry and commerce, and so to regulate the administration of these laws that each and all of the subjects have a fair opportunity of securing temporal well-being in the physical, intellectual and moral order.

" Rulers are bound," writes Leo XIII, " to make sure that the laws and institutions and the general character of the administration shall be such as of themselves to realise public well-being and private prosperity. Now, a State chiefly prospers and thrives through moral rule, family life, respect for religion and justice, the moderate and equitable regulation of public taxes, the progress of the arts and of trade, the abundant yield of the land—through everything, in fact, which makes the citizen better and happier."[1]

V. And the Spirit of Union and Charity Among the Citizens.— A State divided against itself cannot flourish. Stability and social well-being are impossible while the citizens are split up into warring factions, with opposing interests and ideals. On the other hand, union is impossible except it is founded on the bedrock of Social Justice, and cemented by the forces of religion, charity and true patriotism. It is only on such a basis and by such influences that the " Peace of Christ in the Kingdom of Christ," which the Church desires to establish all over the world, can be realised in each individual State. Hence, it is a primary duty of the ruling authority of the State to eliminate all reasonable causes of division and antagonism among the different classes and sections of the people ; to remove occasions of irritation and unrest, and as far as possible win all round to the ideal of co-operating harmoniously for the common good. So important indeed and fundamental is this union and harmony within the State, that no effort should be

---

[1] *Rerum Novarum*, p. 150.

spared, nor any sacrifice deemed too great to secure it: for, as Pius XI truly lays down :

" This union of hearts and minds, binding men together, is the main principle of stability in all institutions no matter how perfect they may seem, which aim at establishing social peace and promoting mutual aid. In its absence, as repeated experience proves, the wisest regulations come to naught."[1]

VI. Regarding Religion, Morals and Material Well-being.—The duties above indicated, which are very comprehensive, include obligations as follows :

(a) To guard and promote the morals of the people, by encouraging religious practice and suppressing all public incentives to vice, as already explained.[2]

(b) To promote and encourage the proper and suitable education of the people, and above all, the due training of the children in religious knowledge, leaving, however, the control in the hands of the Parents and the Church.[3]

(c) To stimulate and protect productive industry and the development of the natural resources of the country so that the population may increase (for human life is the highest wealth of the State)[4] and all the citizens have a fair chance of living prosperously and happily in their own country.

" The ruler should secure by his efforts," writes St. Thomas, " that an abundance of the necessaries for becoming human life should be within the reach of all ; for the enjoyment of a sufficient supply of material goods is necessary for the practice of virtue."[5]

(d) To provide in a special way for the interests of the poorer classes.

VII. With Special Attention to the Interests of the Poorer Classes.—" Justice demands," says Leo XIII, " that the interests of the poorer classes be carefully watched over by the administration, so that . . . being housed, clothed, and enabled to sustain life they may find their existence less hard and more endurable."[6]

The reasons for the Government's special obligation in regard to the poor is, that this class usually forms by far

---

[1] *Quadragesimo Anno*, p. 64.   [2] Cf. Chap. xxiii, art. 4.
[3] Cf. Chap. xx, art. 4.   [4] Cf. *Code of Social Principles*, nn. 60 ff.
[5] *De Rege et Regno (De Regimine)*.   [6] *Rerum Novarum*, p. 152.

the more numerous portion of the population ; and, therefore, their well-being is most closely identified with the
public good. Besides, it is from the labour of the working-
class that the wealth of the State mostly comes ; and Justice
requires that they be allowed a fair participation in the
wealth which they produce. Finally, the poor, being
generally those who are most in need of the help and protection of the State, have the most urgent claims upon it,
seeing that the essential duty and the primary end of the
State are to supplement individual weakness.[1]

Hence, it may be taken for granted that the comfort,
prosperity and contentment of the working-classes are the
surest sign of good government ; while the absence of these
conditions, as evidenced by widespread pauperism, unemployment, forced emigration, discontent and unrest
point unmistakably to unjust or inefficient rule.

As the duties of the Government under the preceding two
heads are varied and comprehensive, we devote a special
article to them.

Art. 3—*Duties Regarding the People's Material Well-being*

Liberal and Socialist Extremes to be Avoided.—The
Laissez faire doctrine of the Liberals who would disallow
all interference of the State in economic affairs is out of
harmony with Christian teaching and is now generally discredited. On the other hand, the ideal of the Socialists
who would practically identify the State with the governing
authority, and concentrate all civic rights and duties in
the latter, is equally repugnant to Christian principles and
the common sense of mankind. Both extremes are to be
avoided.

Therefore, while taking care not to embarrass private
initiative, or the spontaneous action of individuals, or the
autonomous life of municipal or vocational groups, and
while avoiding undue interference with the freedom of the
citizens, the Government should stimulate, and as far as
possible co-ordinate the activities of all these, and when
necessary supplement and complete them. Again, while
respecting and safeguarding property rights, it must take
measures when necessary to prevent their abuse. Thus it

---

[1] *Ib.*, pp. 153, 154.

must prevent the exploitation or the oppression of the economically weak by the powerful and strong. It must foster and protect native industries. It must take care that the natural resources of the country are not held up by private individuals or syndicates, or diverted from their divinely ordained purpose of supplying the people's needs, into becoming merely or mainly a means of luxury for the few.

Should Imitate God's Government of the World.—The method here indicated of promoting the common good through the instrumentality of govermental action and guidance is in accordance with God's methods in the general government of the world, and is the one suited to man's nature. For the Creator, while forbidding the abuse of man's natural faculties and powers, enlists every force, including that of the free human will, and even natural ambition and human tastes and emotions, to assist His providential designs in leading men to their true happiness. In like manner, the Government of the State while keeping abuses in check should co-operate with all natural activities, according to a general policy or plan, whose main outlines it ought to fix, while leaving its execution as far as possible to be carried out by free associations and private individuals.

Directing but Not Absorbing Industrial Life.—It is in accordance with the principles just laid down that the Malines Union puts forward in the *Code of Social Principles* the following general rules, which are also quite in harmony with the teachings of Pius XI in his Encyclical on the Social Order.[1]

" The State, while in principle leaving to individuals the ownership and management of enterprises, lawfully interferes either to protect these enterprises against foreign competition . . . or to help them to enter foreign markets . . .

" It belongs to the State to give a general direction to the national economy, and for that purpose to set up a National Economy Council so as to enable the public authority to keep in close touch with qualified and competent representatives of every branch of production.

---

[1] *Quadragesimo Anno*, pp. 36–44.

" Special reasons may urge the State to take over the entire management of a State monopoly of certain industrial, commercial, or agricultural undertakings. But in general it should avoid absorbing the country's economical life in that way. If the nature of an enterprise requires that the undertaking be not wholly in private hands, the State should endeavour to retain a partial interest in it through some form of leasing out or granting concessions, rather than adopt the undesirable method of conducting it as a State concern."[1]

Nor Acting as if the Government were the State.—The central authority, in other words, should not act as if it were itself alone the State ; for the State is not the Government but the organised nation with all the living forces that compose it. The object of the Government should be to co-ordinate, for the general well-being, these voluntary forces through the operation of good legislation and well-directed administrative action. In great undertakings of public importance which tend to develop the national resources (such as the harnessing of water-power, the development of canals, harbours, mines, and the work of re-afforestation) this co-operation is particularly necessary, and every effort should be made within the limits of justice and natural freedom to bring it about. But to do so by making the undertaking a State monopoly is open to obvious objections. Among these are the increased expense and less efficient management, to which industrial enterprises worked directly by the State are liable ; and secondly, there is the danger of enabling a political party by means of these State monopolies to hold power unlawfully by bribery and patronage.

As it is outside our scope to enter into the details of this subject we shall indicate some particulars in which it is clearly the duty of the Government to interpose its authority in stimulating, checking, or co-ordinating the activities of private individuals or associations.

Safeguarding the Character of the State as a Perfect Society.—Since the State is a perfect society having full powers within its own sphere to safeguard and promote the temporal good of its members, it cannot validly abdicate its

---

[1] *Code of Social Principles*, pp. 28 and 52.

responsibilities. It is the duty of the Government to prevent outside interference in matters which are by the natural law within its own jurisdiction.[1] Thus it should not allow industrial unions within the State (such as Trade Unions, Employers' Unions, etc.), whose functions and activities are so closely and essentially connected with the common good of the whole State, to be under the jurisdiction of foreign and international committees. The only authority to which such unions are lawfully subject is that of the State and the Church.

Securing the Proper Control of Credit.—For similar reasons the Government should not hand over to any outside power the control of Credit and Currency, which nowadays form the ordinary means of exchange. They practically control industry ; and the whole economic life of the nations largely depends on them. Of the two, the issue of credit commonly called bank loans, is the more important. It is vital to the public interest, therefore, that the Government should secure that the issue of credit be not abused in the interest of private individuals, or worse still, fall under the control of the great international financiers.[2]

On the other hand, it is desirable for many reasons, that the bank or banks which issue fiduciary money should be distinguishable from the Government : hence, banks should be established, which, while enjoying independent management, would act under the supreme direction not of any outside power, but of the Government of the country and in accordance with a policy shaped solely with a view to the needs and interests of the people.[3]

Preventing the Holding Up of Natural Resources.—The natural resources of the country include the land, and the other elements naturally connected with it, such as mineral

---

[1] This is the fundamental reason why a State cannot consistently allow the existence within it of such associations as the Masonic and Orange Societies, or other secret associations of a similar character.

[2] At present (1931), the Bank of England practically controls the issue of credit for the Irish Free State, whose banks are forced automatically to follow the policy dictated by the Bank of England. This means that the economic life of the country is practically controlled from London. Cf. chap. x, art. 2 ; also McKenna—*Post Banking Policy* (*passim*).

[3] Cf. *Code of Social Principles*, nn. 108, 132 ; also McKenna, *op. cit.*, pp. 79 ff.

wealth, fisheries, waterways, water-power, the natural harbours, and the coastal waters. These are the ultimate source from which the citizens of the State have to be maintained. They are, in other words, the basic material upon which the people have to labour in order to earn their bread. For, as Leo XIII writes :

" It may be truly said that all human subsistence is derived either from labour on one's own land, or from some toil, some calling which is paid for either in the produce of the land itself, or in that which is exchanged for what the land brings forth."[1]

Now, the system of private property according to which private individuals may become owners of some of these natural resources has been ordained by the Law of the Nations (*Jus Gentium*) only as a means to an end. The end aimed at is to secure in the most effectual manner that the design of the Creator Who gave the earth and its resources to satisfy the needs of all be realised. The system of private ownership, when hedged round with the safeguards required by Christian teaching and tradition, generally speaking, secures this end better than any other method. But since the means must be subordinated to the end, it is clear that the system must be so worked that the use of property rights be subservient to the original design of the Creator in assigning the earth for the good of all.[2]

Consequently, the Government of the State, whose function it is to adjust and co-ordinate the different claims and rights of the citizens, is bound to take measures that property rights be not abused to such an extent that while numbers have no means of earning a becoming livelihood, and are compelled to live in excessive poverty or emigrate, certain individuals are allowed in virtue of their property rights to hold up the country's natural resources and prevent them from being duly developed and utilised for the general good.[3]

According to the Teaching of the Malines Union.—In connection with this important subject, the *Code of Social Principles*, to which we have just referred and which, next

---

[1] *Rerum Novarum*, p. 137.
[2] St. Thomas, 2a, 2æ, Q. 66, a. 2 and 7 ; Q. 32, a. 5, ad 2um ; cf. also Garriguet, *op. cit.*, pp. 158–164, and pp. 197–207.
[3] Cf. Devas—*Political Economy* (3rd edit.), pp. 201–205.

to the Papal Encyclicals, is the most authoritative expression of the Catholic attitude in social matters, has the following striking passages :

" Under the influence of various factors such as geographical position, the nature of the soil and subsoil, industrial technology, custom, laws, and so on, private ownership can take on different forms ; have wider or narrower applications ; and be subject to certain restrictions. In proportion as legislation and private initiative can exert effective influence, they should strive to set up that form of private ownership which brings out best its inherent advantages.

" In certain countries in particular there has arisen a rural problem under circumstances such as the following, namely— (a) the existence of estates untilled or under-tilled whose use and improvement are indispensable to the common good ; (b) cultivation which, though technically satisfactory, has by its mass production led to the use and growth of a rural proletariat *in great poverty* who are forced to leave the land, to emigration, or to some other alternative hurtful to the common good.

" In all such cases the State has the right, when less radical means have failed, *to decree the division of cultivation*, and if need be *of properties*. The exercise of the right is always subject to the granting of a just and well-considered indemnity to all those whose legitimate rights would be injured by the measures taken towards division."[1]

The principles here enunciated for land would apply equally to the other natural sources of wealth, such as the great fisheries of the country, the canals, the water-power, the harbours, etc.[2]

And the Example of the Popes.—A well-known example of drastic action taken by a Christian Government in this matter is that indicated in the series of laws made for the Papal States by several successive Popes—Clement IV (1241), Sixtus IV (1474), Clement VII (1523), Pius VI (1783), and Pius VII (1804). These laws empowered *anybody who may wish to do so* to enter upon and break up for his own use (in some cases a certain portion of the produce was reserved for the State or for the lord of the soil) any portion up *to a third part* of any estate, ecclesiastical or otherwise,

---

[1] nn. 77, 78, p. 39.
[2] Cf. also Devas—*Political Economy*, bk. i, chap. ii, n. 15.

which the owners persistently refused or neglected to cultivate. By some of these enactments the incoming cultivator was allowed to graze his working cattle on the lord's estate, during the time of cultivation, and to use the stables of the latter. Instruments of agricultural labour were exempt from seizure for debt.[1]

The multiplication of small proprietors, especially of land, is strongly insisted upon by Leo XIII, in the *Rerum Novarum*, as of the first importance in this connection. By such a policy, he adds, the excessive disparity between rich and poor will be moderated; industry and production will be increased; and the emigration of the people from their country will be checked.[2]

Fostering Native Industries.[3]—As the people's temporal well-being is closely associated with productive industries, and the trade and commerce of the nation, it is one of the functions of the Government to protect and foster native production, to promote such trade and commerce as may be necessary or reasonably useful, and to prevent such trade as may be harmful to the common good. Thus, while large numbers of the citizens of the nation are in want regarding the necessaries of life, it is manifestly injurious to the common well-being that food and other necessaries be exported in exchange for imported luxuries. In such circumstances both the import and the export should be kept in check by the central authority.

In modern times, especially owing to the facility of inter-communication with foreign countries and the activities of the international capitalists and financiers who subordinate the people's interests to their own personal gain, it is essential to the public safety and the stability of the economic life of the State that the people be safeguarded against the interference of outside capitalists and monopolists. Above

---

[1] Cf. L. Garriguet, *op. cit.*, pp. 199–203.
[2] *Rerum Novarum*, p. 159. It is well known and recognised that a farm of, say, 500 statute acres of good grazing land in Ireland, which, as a grazing farm, now maintains only the owner and two or three labourers with their families, would, if properly cultivated, easily maintain four or five, possibly even ten, times that number of peasant farmers in comfortable conditions. (Cf. Devas, *op. cit.*, pp. 201, 202. See also *supra*, chap. xviii, art. 2.)
[3] Cf. Devas, *op. cit.*, bk. ii, chap. v.

all, the people's food and all the other essential elements such as clothing, building materials, even the necessary weapons of defence, should be produced within the State : otherwise the State is not effectively independent.

Besides, without flourishing home industries, which can always be stimulated and protected by reserving the home market for home produce, the native population cannot find in their own country the opportunity of remunerative labour to which they have a natural claim, and so are unjustly forced to emigrate.[1]

Preventing Gambling on the Stock Exchange, Cornering, and Fictitious Companies.[2]

Speculation in stocks and shares means broadly an attempt to make profit out of changing prices, and like other forms of gambling, is not in itself unlawful. But without being in any way useful to the community, this type of activity is specially liable to abuse and in many of its forms is immoral and unjust. Thus, speculating and making profits from speculation in stocks by means of faked news and lies is definitely unjust. So also is the concerted buying or selling of goods or stocks with the object of raising or lowering prices to levels not corresponding with their real value.

Another type of speculation which is mostly unjust, and almost always injurious to the public interest, is the fictitious

---

[1] Cf. Devas, *loc. cit.*, pp. 297 ff, where this subject is specifically treated. The matter is specially applicable to Ireland, where the natural resources are abundant, and the people, nevertheless, probably the most impoverished in Europe. Not only the land but also the mineral resources (such as coal, peat, marble, slate, cement, etc.) could be developed under a system of suitable laws and the fostering aid of an enlightened and sympathetic government. The land as well as mineral and other natural resources is largely neglected. This neglect is due partly to the unnatural monopolies of native and foreign owners, partly to want of the required government protection, partly to difficulties in finding capital (which difficulties are rooted in the foreign control of credit), partly to the absence of the necessary training of those that should naturally exploit and develop these resources. The same applies even with greater force to the fisheries and to the industries naturally connected with local agriculture. All these could be revived if safeguarded by suitable protective laws which now exist in various forms suiting the different countries in almost every State, large and small, of Continental Europe and America.

[2] Cf. Devas—*Political Economy* (3rd edit.), pp. 392–398 ; also Ryan— *Distributive Justice*, pp. 262–277, and pp. 257–290.

buying and selling of what are called " futures,"[1] " options,"[2] and " margins."[3] This type of transaction has the effect of creating immense quantities of fictitious produce and thus lowering the prices to the producer without in any way lessening, and sometimes even increasing considerably the cost to the consumer. The profits go to the group of parasitical speculators who live on the toil and grow rich on the losses of others. Thus, it is said that not more than five per cent. of the transactions on the London Stock Exchange are *bona fide* transactions, the rest being fictitious or speculative buying of this kind without any intention of accepting delivery of the goods or supposed goods. It is to transactions of this type that Pius XI specially refers when he writes :

" Easy returns, which an open market affords to anyone, lead many to interest themselves in trade and exchange, their one aim being to make clear profits with the least labour. By their unchecked speculation prices are raised and lowered out of mere greed for gain, making void all the most prudent calculations of manufacturers . . .

"A stern insistence on the moral law, enforced with vigour by civil authorities could have dispelled, or pehaps averted, these enormous evils. This, however, was too often lamentably wanting."[4]

---

[1] Dealing in " futures " means the buying up of a crop or the produce of a mine long before it is actually realised. If the seller really means to deliver the goods and the buyer to receive them at some future specific time, and if besides, there is no intention of setting up a monopoly, the transaction, although containing an element of chance or gambling, would be lawful. But, as a matter of fact, the sale is usually fictitious : for neither buyer nor seller has any intention of giving over or receiving the goods in question of which they know little or nothing.

[2] " Options " differ from " futures " in that no actual sale of crop or produce is usually contemplated The person buying an option pays a certain amount to a broker, and in return obtains the right to purchase by a certain date the commodity mentioned. He has, however, no intention of accepting delivery, and the deal is just a gamble on the future price. It has been reckoned that in America, the quantity of wheat thus fictitiously sold every year, is more than a hundred times the quantity that is actually produced !

[3] " Margins " are of the same general nature as " options." The transaction may be thus described. Let us suppose that a person wishes to gamble on a " margin " to the extent of £50. He pays this sum to his stockbroker *plus* whatever commission the latter charges. The broker acquires stock to the value of a much larger amount. As long as this does not depreciate below £50, he holds it, but when it drops below this figure the client has to pay an amount representing the extent of the fall or lose his existing interest in the transaction. If the value of the stock rises the client can sell and make a profit.

[4] *Quadragesimo Anno*, p. 66.

Another well known type of fraud is the promotion of worthless or bogus companies. The public subscribe under the delusion (which the promoters bring about by publishing false news, bribing the Press, and fictitious buying and selling) that they are investing in a real business enterprise. In the end the promoter disappears with the money which has been subscribed.

It is the duty of government to suppress or keep in check by penal enactments, such as exist in Quebec,[1] rigorously enforced, all these fraudulent activities which are disastrous to the public good.

Safeguarding Human Life and Securing It Fair Conditions.—Perhaps the most important duty of the Government is the protection of human life. Under this heading comes legislation for labour so as to ensure proper wages, to limit the length of the working day, to provide for Sunday rest, hygiene, and security of employment. Consumers, and especially the poor, should be protected against fraud, profiteering, and usury, especially in regard to essential commodities such as food. The housing of the poor in country and towns is an essential subject of State solicitude. For, without proper housing, temporal well-being is impossible. It is desirable, too, that there should be a system of household exemption laws ensuring the poor man the inalienable possession of his home and the necessary implements of labour.[2] With the same end in view commercial and industrial companies and syndicates should be prevented from overproduction, causing crises and unemployment.

Protecting the Small Owners and Encouraging Co-operation.—Smaller firms and enterprises should be safeguarded against being absorbed or destroyed by the action of the more powerful.[3] Finally, legislation could profitably be made, as opportunity arises, facilitating and encouraging co-operative industry, granting special protection and special exemptions to all enterprises, whether agricultural or industrial, of a co-operative character : facilitating the

---

[1] Cf. Devas, *op. cit.*, p. 398.   [2] Cf. chap. xviii, art. 2.

[3] Cf. Macksey, *op. cit.*, pp. 276–294, for an excellent treatment of the dangers and injustice connected with " trusts " and private *monopolia.* Cf. also Vermeersch, *op. cit.*, n. 354, and Antoine , *op. cit.*, pp. 283 and 374 ff.

acquisition of land for rural co-operative colonies and for the gradual formation of city gardens.[1]

In a word, the policy of both legislature and administration should be shaped and adjusted so as gradually to realise the ideal of a Christian democracy, or co-operative commonwealth, in the true and only realisable sense, founded, namely, upon the principles of Christian teaching, upon ownership widely diffused, personal independence, self-contained, corporate bodies linked up under the protection of a central authority, whose duty it would be to protect their independence and safeguard their rights without any tendency towards absorption or undue centralisation.

---

[1] *Code of Social Principles*, nn. 60, 63, 72, 89, 97, 98, 128–130 ; also Devas, *op. cit., passim.* " Twenty men," writes Henry George, " working together where nature is niggardly will produce more than twenty times the wealth that one man can produce where nature is most bountiful." (cited by C. Gide—*History of Economic Doctrines*, p. 564, n. 2.)

33

CHAPTER XXVI

DISTRIBUTIVE JUSTICE[1]

Art. 1—*General Principles*

Nature and Definition.—Distributive Justice has reference to the third type of right mentioned above,[2] namely, to the indirect right which the individual citizen has, in virtue of his citizenship, to his due participation in the goods and advantages controlled by the State. These goods and advantages are the means which the State has (as a result of the co-operation of its members) of securing peace and prosperity for the citizens. The function of Distributive Justice is to provide for their equitable distribution amongst the latter. Hence, Distributive Justice may be defined as *The law of nature by which the State is bound to secure for each of the citizens his due and proportionate share of the advantages and helps which are the end and purpose of civil society ; and to allot the public burdens in due and equitable proportion.*

Distributive Justice is similar to Legal Justice in so far as the duties and rights to which both refer are founded upon the essential relations between the State considered as a moral unit and its individual members. Legal Justice imposes duties on the members (whether rulers or subjects) towards the State ; while the duties of Distributive Justice are those of the State towards the members. But as the rulers of the State control the full powers of the latter in all matters with which Distributive Justice has to do, its duties in practice belong to the rulers alone. Hence, over and above the obligations which rulers have in virtue of Legal Justice to govern in accordance with the general interest and procure the common good, they are bound by Distributive Justice to secure for every member of the

---

[1] St. Thomas, Iᵃ, 2ᵃᵉ, Q. 60, a. 3 ; 2ᵃ, 2ᵃᵉ, Q. 61 ; De Lugo—*De Justitia et Jure*, D. i, sec. iii, and D. xxxiv, secs. i and ii ; Costa-Rosetti, *op. cit.*, Thesis 153 ; Vermeersch, *op. cit.*, Q. 2, cap. ii ; Castelein, *op. cit.*, Thesis 19.
[2] Cf. chap. xxiv, art. 1.

State that fair and proportionate share of the advantages which the common good includes.

We have already treated of the advantages and helps it is the function of the State to secure for its members. They are made up of what is usually termed Peace and Public Prosperity, and include not only the safeguarding of the citizens' rights against unjust interference, but also such assistance and protection as the individual or family needs and which the State alone can give for the attainment of a due standard of moral and intellectual development, and of material well-being. The rulers of the State are bound by the duties of Distributive Justice to distribute these helps and advantages to the citizens equitably—namely, in accordance with each one's just claims.

As the public advantages included under the term Prosperity are in practice modified by one's obligations to share in the necessary public burdens (such as taxation, and military service), Distributive Justice also implies an equitable distribution of these.

Liberal and Socialist Theories.—Those who, like the Liberals, deny that the State is a natural society, reject the concept of Distributive Justice even more completely than they reject Legal Justice. According to the Liberals the duty of rulers is confined to defending the subjects against violence and enforcing the claims of Commutative Justice. Hence, there is no room for the claims of the subjects graduated in proportion to their needs which Distributive Justice implies.

The Socialists, on the other hand, who hold that all the goods of the State belong primarily to the community, and that all the working powers of the citizens are completely subject to the rulers of the State, make the duties and rights of Distributive Justice directly applicable to the private property and the personal productive labour of the citizens. Thus, according to the Socialists, the function of Distributive Justice is to secure that the rulers of the State exact labour from each member in proportion to his capacity, and distribute the fruit of the labour and the goods of the State to all in accordance with each one's needs. In other words, the Socialists conceive the State as a huge family, and would have it organised and ruled more or less after

the model of a religious community, in which all the property
is held in common and administered by the superior, who
also assigns to each member the work he is to do. We
have already shown that the Socialists' theory of the State
and, consequently, of Distributive Justice is false.

Hence, Distributive Justice refers only to the goods and
advantages (coming from taxes, etc.) which belong directly
to the State, or which the State controls, and to the services
which the citizens render for the common good. It does
not refer *directly* to the private property or the personal
activities of the citizens, except in so far as the State may
legitimately attach certain definite obligations to them,
such as taxes or military service.

How the Distribution is to be Determined.—The principle
to be followed in distributing the public advantages and
allotting the public burdens is altogether different from
that which trading and commercial societies justly adopt
towards their shareholders. In these societies the advantages or profits are distributed to the members in proportion to the share which each one bears of the common
burdens of the society—that is, in proportion to each one's
contribution to the company's capital and work. In the
social organism, on the other hand, the main considerations
determining the distribution must be partly the public good,
which is the *raison d'etre* of civil society and, subservient
to this, the relative capacity and the normal needs of the
members.

The reason of the difference lies in the fact that the State
is a natural society ; and the helps and advantages which
it brings are *necessary* for the *essential* well-being of its
members. Because it is a natural society, the fundamental
rights and duties of the members are arranged by the
natural law, and are independent of contract. And because
these rights and duties are needed for man's natural well-
being, they must depend at least to some extent upon the
relative extent of these needs. In a similar way, the just
share of the goods and advantages of the domestic society
due to each member does not depend upon the extent of
the burden which that member has to bear. The wife
cannot justly complain if the advantages she enjoys are less
pleasing, or the duties she is meant by nature to perform

are more onerous than those of her husband. Each has to do and to receive his or her own part as nature has ordained. So also in a State : each member is bound to contribute his just share to the common good, and the extent of his obligation must be determined in part at least by his capacity. Each member, too, has a claim to his rightful share of the advantages, and that share must be determined at least in some degree by the need he has of the assistance and protection of the State.

Its Duties Juridical.—The rulers' duties under Distributive Justice are *Juridical*—that is, they imply corresponding rights in those towards whom they lie. Hence, the individual members of the State have each and all the *right* that the rulers deal equitably with them in distributing the advantages and allotting the burdens of citizenship. The rights of the citizen in this matter are not *perfect* rights, as they cannot be always clearly defined, and besides they belong to the citizens not so much for the exclusive benefit of the latter as for the common good. Therefore, the violation of these rights, although in all cases unjust, does not necessarily imply an obligation of restitution, unless Commutative Justice be also violated. Rulers may, however, as we shall see later, violate Commutative as well as Distributive Justice by imposing unjust and unfair burdens upon the citizens or upon certain classes of citizens ; and if that occurs they would, strictly speaking, be bound to restitution. From these principles, which are generally admitted, the following conclusions may be deduced :

I. **Rights of Protection.**—All the citizens have exactly the same right to Peace—that is, to security against violent interference with their rights. It is a primary duty of the State to defend and uphold by just laws, fairly administered, and by an impartial administration of justice (sufficiently cheap and expeditious to be within the reach of the poorest citizen), the personal safety, the inalienable rights, the liberty and the property rights of *every one* of the citizens.

II. **And of Access to the Public Utilities.**—The use of the public utilities which the State provides, or indirectly subsidises, from the public funds—roads, railways, postal service, public hospitals, etc.—should be equally open to all. This principle is crystallized in such phrases as : " the King's highway," which implies that the public highway is owned by the King (or by the State) in trust for all the people, and cannot be monopolised by any individual or class.

III.—Taxes Should Not Infringe upon Necessaries of Life.

No public burdens (such as taxes) should infringe upon the necessaries of life : for, ordinarily, a man's first duty is to himself and his family. These needs should therefore be supplied before he can be justly compelled to contribute by taxes and services to the public good.

Hence, too, indirect taxes should, as a rule, fall upon purely superfluous property rather than upon such as is required to supply conventional needs, and upon the latter rather than upon the necessaries of life.[1] For, if commodities such as tea, sugar, tobacco, which are largely and almost equally used by all classes, are taxed, even the poorest of the community may be compelled to bear an altogether disproportionate share of the burdens of the State, and their essential right to provide, in the first place, a decent subsistence for themselves and their families may thus be unjustly interfered with.

IV. All Should Have a Fair Opportunity of Securing Necessaries.[2]—The Government is bound so to adjust the laws regulating property rights that every citizen of normal[3]

---

[1] *Conventional* needs refer to what one reasonably requires to maintain the standard of life belonging to his social station ; *absolute* needs refer to what is absolutely required by all to support human life, viz., proper food, clothing and shelter. (Cf. Devas—*Political Economy*, bk. i.) Note, too, in this connection that the Government is bound in a special way to protect the people from the losses consequent upon the changing value of the purchasing power of money. If the Banks withdraw money from circulation (viz., by lessening the bank loans), the real value or the purchasing power of a given sum of money will be very much increased to the injury of those who are indebted and the gain of creditors. It is a portion of the duties coming under Distributive Justice to prevent this : and especially to take measures against the Banks forcing debtors by such action to pay back more than they really owe. (Cf. Macksey, *op. cit.*, Thesis xxvii.) St. Thomas, 2a, 2ae, Q. 32, a. 6.

[2] The matter referred to in this paragraph has been already treated under the heading of Legal Justice. Whether or how far it belongs to Legal or Distributive Justice depends on the point of view from which it is considered and need not be discussed here.

[3] The State cannot in its general laws take account of exceptional circumstances, such as weak health or deficient mental capacity. Such cases must be provided for by special legislation, in so far as the resources of private charity are insufficient. In a Christian community these needs are usually met by efforts of private charity.

capacity and industry may have a fair opportunity of securing by honest labour a tolerable degree of human happiness and well-being. The providing of such an opportunity for its members is one of the essential ends and purposes of civil society ; and as the poor and weak are more in need of protection and assistance in this regard than the wealthy, Distributive Justice demands that their needs be specially attended to.

" When there is a question," writes Leo XIII, " of defending the rights of individuals, the poor and badly off have a claim to special consideration . . . the mass of the poor have no resources of their own to fall back upon and must depend chiefly upon the assistance of the State."[1]

It should be remembered, too, that the claims of the poor to this assistance are claims of Justice, not of Charity, and that " Charity cannot take the place of Justice unfairly withheld."[2] Hence, if these rights of the poor are denied or violated, they are the victims of injustice. Treating of this subject, Pope Pius XI writes :

" Such economic and social methods should be set up in the State as will enable every head of a family to earn as much as according to his station in life is necessary for himself, his wife, and for the rearing of his children. . . . To refuse this, or to make it less than is equitable is a *grave injustice*, and is placed by Holy Writ among the greatest sins. . . . Wherefore, those who have the care of the State and of the common good . . . must in making the laws and in disposing of the public funds do their utmost to relieve the penury of the needy, considering such as one of the most important of their administrative functions."[3]

Less Definite Rights and Duties.—In addition to these essential elements of due distribution there are others in which the measure of equality or the rule of due proportion as between different classes of the population is more difficult to determine. Among such are : the levying of taxes ; the distribution of patronage (viz., the appointment to offices in the service of the State) ; and the subsidising of particular undertakings or institutions. In so far as no principle of Commutative Justice is at stake, the fundamental rule of guidance in these matters is the public good ;

---

[1] *Rerum Novarum*, pp. 153, 154.
[2] Pius XI—*Quadragesimo Anno*, p. 64.
[3] *Casti Connubii* (Dec., 1930), p. 60.

and subordinate to this, much will depend upon the relative
needs, the customs of the country, the principles of the
constitution, which will vary according as the Government
is monarchical or democratic.[1]

Thus it is usually for the good and honour of the State
that the supreme ruler of a country have many privileges
and honours, and if he be a hereditary king, that many of
his privileges be shared by his relatives. Again, it is necessary that learning and art be fostered, and that public
merits be duly rewarded. In some countries, too, fathers of
large families are justly exempted from all taxes ; so also
are those who devote their lives to the service of others,
such as religious orders devoted to works of charity. All
these and other such considerations may justly influence
the distribution of public advantages, and the allotment of
public burdens. The question of taxes, however, as well
as that of the appointment to public offices, which are both
of primary importance, and directly pertain to Distributive
Justice, call for a somewhat fuller treatment here.

Art. 2—*Taxes*[2]

Nature of Taxes.—Since the State, like the family, is a
creation of nature, and depends for its existence, and its
power to function upon the co-operation of its members,
it has the right to exact that co-operation, and the members
are bound by the *natural* law to give it. Contributions to
the public revenues enabling the Government to fulfil its
duty of safeguarding and promoting the public good are
usually in modern times the most important element of this
co-operation. These contributions are what are called
Taxes. The citizens' obligations to pay such taxes and
the correlative right of the rulers to exact them rest on the
natural law, which imposes the duty on both rulers and
citizens to co-operate in promoting the common good of
the natural body to which they belong. From this it
follows that taxation does not bear directly on property
but upon the owner. In other words, it is a *personal* charge

---

[1] Cf. Macksey, *op. cit.*, Thesis xxvii.
[2] Cf. Vermeersch, *op. cit.*, Q. 3, cap. ii ; Bastable—*Public Finance*
(London, 1922) ; Devas—*Political Economy*, bk. iv ; Palgrave, *op. cit.*,
art. " Taxation."

upon the citizen, and represents an important element of the co-operation towards the common good which he is bound to give.

Not Payment for Services Rendered nor Rent.—Hence, taxes are not given by the citizen in payment for the services he receives from the State, like the annual subscription given by a member of a club to the common fund of the association. The wealthy citizen is bound to a much greater contribution in taxes than the poor citizen, although the latter's right to the State's protection and assistance are usually much greater, owing to his greater need, than that of the former.

Neither have public taxes any real analogy with the rent paid to the landlord by the tenant living on his estate. The rulers who impose taxes are not in any sense the owners of the private property of the citizen; and the taxes which they assess and with whose administration they are entrusted are not their own. They have no power to impose them except in accordance with principles of Legal and Distributive Justice ; and no right to utilise the revenues coming from them or any other portion of the property of the State except for the purpose of the common good and in accordance with the just laws of the State.

General Principle of Just Assessment.—In accordance with the analogy of all other natural units, whether physical (such as the human body) or moral (such as the family), in relation to their members, the extent and nature of the co-operation which may be justly required from each member of the State, and therefore the amount of tax that may be justly exacted from him must be measured by the needs of the State and the relative capacity of the particular member.[1] Again, since the citizen's rights and obligations to provide for himself and his family are prior to and ordinarily more urgent than his duty to co-operate for the common good, he cannot justly be forced to pay taxes that infringe upon the necessaries of life.

Unjust Taxation.—Leo XIII refers more than once to the injustice and evils of excessive taxation. Thus, after enumerating the good results that would follow from a

---

[1] St. Thomas, 2a, 2æ, Q. 61, a 1 and 2.

wider distribution of the ownership of the land, he goes on to say :

" These important benefits, however, can be reckoned on only on condition that a man's means be not exhausted and drained by excessive taxation. The right to possess private property is derived from nature, not from man ; and the State has the right to control its use only in the interests of the public good, but by no means to absorb it altogether. The State would therefore be unjust and cruel if, under the name of taxation, it were to deprive the private owner of more than is just."[1]

Again, in his Encyclical, concerning the evils of modern society, which was issued thirteen years previously, the Pope enumerates among the outstanding evils of modern times

" the reckless mismanagement, waste and misappropriation of the public funds, the shamelessness of those who full of treachery make semblance of being champions of country, of freedom, and of every kind of right."[2]

Malice of Unjust Taxation.—In modern States practically all the public revenues come from taxes which the rulers of the State exact from the people (as being necessary for the common good). If, therefore, the rulers mismanage or devote any portion of these funds to purposes other than the common good, they are guilty not only of violating Legal Justice, but also of exacting money from private individuals on false pretences, which is robbery or *rapine*, and they abuse a public trust in doing so which is *embezzlement*.[3] Furthermore, if rulers impose taxes in excess of what is needed for the common good or beyond what the individual citizen is justly able to pay, they are likewise guilty of injustice and fraud. Hence, in all such cases not only the persons primarily responsible for the injustice but all those who co-operate in it are bound to restitution[4] in accordance with the principles laid down in Moral Theology. This is outside our present scope to explain in detail.[5] On this subject St. Thomas writes in his usual uncompromising and impersonal style :

" If rulers exact from their subjects what the latter are bound to give for the safeguarding of the public good, such action is

---

[1] *Rerum Novarum*, p. 159.   [2] *Inscrutabili*, 1878, pp. 1, 2.
[3] St. Thomas, 2a, 2æ, Q. 66, a. 8, ad 3um.   [4] *Ib.*
[5] Cf. Genicot—*Theolog. Mor.*, vol. i, nn. 535–550.

not rapine (*Rapina,* that is robbery accomplished by violence) even though force be used. If, however, any ruler forcibly exact what is not due according to the principles of Justice, their action is rapine, just like highway robbery. Hence, St. Augustine says : ' If Justice be not present what are States (*regna*) but associations for brigandage on a large scale (*magna latrocinia*).[1] In the book of *Ezechiel* also it is written : *Her rulers are in her midst like wolves carrying off their prey.*[2] Hence, such rulers are bound to restitution in the same way as highway robbers. Nay, their crime is greater than that of ordinary brigands, in as much as it is fraught with greater danger, and causes more far-reaching injury to the rights of the community with the guardianship of which they have been entrusted."[3]

Principles of Just Taxation.—From what has been said regarding the general nature of taxation and its connection with the essential constitution and purpose of the State, the general rules of Distributive Justice regarding taxation may be deduced. These rules are generally set down as follows :

(*a*) **Must be Necessary and Imposed by Legitimate Authority.**—Taxes can be imposed only by legitimate authority, and must be really necessary for the common good of the community ; otherwise[4] they are against Commutative Justice, and would imply obligations of restitution. Hence, for instance, taxes imposed to provide naval or military equipment beyond what is required for reasonable defence, or to finance activities of any kind not necessary or proportionally useful for the common good, or to support more public officials, or to pay them higher salaries than is necessary for securing efficient public service, would imply a violation of Commutative Justice.

(*b*) **And Within Limits of Taxable Capacity.**—Taxes that are out of proportion to the wealth of the country or infringe upon the necessaries of life are unjust. Leo XIII, in the passage quoted above, refers to the injustice and cruelty of which governments may be guilty under this head. " From the sad pages of history," writes Devas, " we can learn that the unjust overburthening of private resources

---

[1] *De Civ. Dei,* cap. iv, col. 115, Thesis 7.   [2] *Ezech.* xxii. 27.
[3] 2a, 2æ, Q. 61, a. 7, ad 3um.
[4] Cf. De Lago, *op. cit.,* tome viii, d. 26, n. 1.

by public force has been in fact one of the chief causes of misery and ruin ; and its prevalence is attested by the prevalence of the popular view that to evade the payment of taxes is neither dishonourable nor wrong."[1] As examples of grossly excessive and unjust taxation, Devas mentions the later Roman Empire, modern Italy (before the great war), and modern France. Taxation in the Roman Empire of the 5th century A.D. was so heavy that Roman citizens not infrequently fled away to live among the barbarians in order to escape the crushing burdens. In Italy the taxation reached some 14 per cent. of the gross annual income about the year 1890 ; and cases are cited of families of very moderate income (about £100 per annum) having to pay over £24 in taxes of all kinds.

Besides the vast sums now expended in many countries in military equipment,[2] another principal source of excessive taxation is the unnecessary multiplication of State officials (of which France and Great Britain and both Governments in Ireland afford glaring modern examples) and a scale of salaries beyond what the State can bear or the circumstances of the people warrant. The limits of just taxation depend upon what is called the *taxable capacity* of the people ; and it is a generally acknowledged principle that "whenever taxation instead of being drawn from superfluities makes an encroachment on absolute or conventional necessities and threatens to lower the standard of life, the people are taxed above their taxable capacity."[3]

Generally speaking, a rate of taxation which corresponds to about 5 or 6 per cent. of the gross national income is reckoned as light : that which is about 8 per cent. is fair. If it reaches 10 per cent. it is usually considered heavy taxation ; and if it exceeds 14 per cent. it is immoderate and excessive.[4] The figures, however, presuppose that a

---

[1] *Pol. Economy*, bk. iv, chap. i, n. 8.

[2] The British people at present pay in taxes some £400,000,000 a year to meet the interest of a war debt of about £8,000,000,000, besides paying over ninety millions annually for military and naval equipment in preparation for, or forestalment, of future wars.

[3] Devas, *loc. cit.*, n. 9.

[4] Cf. Vermeersch, *op. cit.*, Q. 3, cap. ii, n. 100.   Cf. also Bastable, who writes : " It is plain that the agreement of the writers referred to above (viz., Just, Hock and Leroy-Bealieu) supports the belief that 15 per cent. of the national income is too large an amount to appropriate for State objects, except in very exceptional cases." *Op. cit.*, bk. i, chap. viii, p. 137.

normal number of the population are of taxable capacity, that is, have incomes greater than are required for the absolute and conventional necessities of life. For, in a very poor country such as India or Ireland, a rate of 10 per cent. may well be much more burdensome than 30 per cent. in England or the United States.[1]

(c) **And be Equitably Distributed.**—Taxation should be equitably distributed among the citizens. The equality demanded is not *arithmetical*, but proportional or *geometrical* equality.[2] " So that those who have greater capacity may contribute more, and those of lesser capacity contribute less. Otherwise the common burdens are not distributed with *formal*, but only with *material* equality, which in reality is the height of inequality, and would be just as if a child and a full-grown man were compelled to carry the same weight on their shoulders."[3] Modern economists, even of the Liberal school, admit this principle at least in theory. They acknowledge that real equality of taxation implies " equality of sacrifice." Hence, " people should

---

[1] Cf. Bastable, *op. cit.*, pp. 131 ff. The pre-war rate of taxation of the United Kingdom, which was under 10 per cent. of the gross annual income, was accounted quite tolerable for Great Britain, but excessive for Ireland. The Belgian rate at that time was about 6 per cent. Again, the Childer's Commission of Financial Relations (1896) declared that Ireland's taxable capacity was only about one-twentieth of that of Great Britain, whereas her relative gross income would seem to represent a very much larger fraction, as she was taxed in the proportion of one to eleven.

It seems impossible to obtain accurate figures from any published documents to represent the present gross national income of all Ireland or to estimate with any degree of accuracy its present taxable capacity. It is certain that the latter, owing to the poverty of the people, is very low, as compared with the gross income. Calculating roughly from figures given in Mulhall's *Dictionary of Statistics* (Webb's Edition, 1911) representing the gross income of the United Kingdom (1906–1907), the amount of that income assessed to tax, the amount of Irish income assessed to tax during the same year, and finally the " index figures " of relative money values then and now, one may gather that £160,000,000 per annum would be a very high estimate of the present gross annual income of all Ireland. If that be so, it may be taken as certain that 10 per cent. of that income, or £16,000,000 a year, for *all* Ireland would be the highest State tax commensurate with national prosperity or reconcilable with the standard laws of Commutative and Distributive Justice. It seems very probable, however, that such a figure is far too high. The actual taxation of Ireland at present (1931) is more than double that sum and nearly four times what it was in 1896 when the country was declared to be taxed beyond its taxable capacity !

[2] St. Thomas, 2da, 2dæ, Q. 61, a. 2.

[3] De Lugo, *op. cit.*, d. xxxvi, n. 23.

be taxed, not in proportion to what they have, but to what they can afford to spend."[1]

Proportional, Progressive and Digressive System of Taxation.—How to secure this equality of sacrifice consistently with other important public interests is a difficult and much-disputed question. All seem to agree that the necessaries of life should not be encroached upon, and that superfluous property alone should be considered in estimating relative taxable capacity. But the agreement ends there. Some are in favour of *Proportional* Taxation. In this system each citizen contributes the same percentage of his gross income so far as the latter exceeds the amount necessary for his reasonable needs. But this system does not realise equality of sacrifice. For a tax of £20 a year is a much greater burden for a man with a gross annual income of £400 than a tax of £500 for one with a yearly income of £10,000.

Hence, others advocate the principle of the *Progressive* Tax. In this system the *percentage* of taxation rises in proportion to the increase of the income. Thus, a man of £400 a year may contribute 2 per cent. of his income (viz., £8), a man of £800, 4 per cent. (£32), and so on. The principal objection against this system is that very high incomes would be completely absorbed by the taxes ; and incomes higher still would imply the absurd obligation on the owner to pay in taxes even more than his gross income. This difficulty can be got rid of by limiting the increase of percentage at a certain point beyond which the increase ceases, or the rate of increase gradually lessens. This system, which is a variant of the Progressive Tax, is sometimes termed the *Digressive* or *Progressional* system of taxation.

In theory the ideal system of taxation would probably be a single Progressive tax (modified as suggested after the Progressional system) on income. *Direct* taxation of that kind has the further advantage of asking from the citizen a conscious sacrifice, which gives him an interest in public affairs. *Indirect* taxation, however (viz., taxation on articles of use), is usually accepted more willingly, and

---

[1] J. S. Mill—*Pol. Economy*, bk. v, chap. ii, n. 4. (Cf. Palgrave, *op. cit.*, *loc. cit.*, pp. 158 ff, " Taxation.")

when the necessaries of life are not taxed, does not so easily become oppressive. Hence, it is in practice found necessary to obtain at least some portion of the needed public revenue through indirect taxation.[1]

Economic and Political Principles of Taxation.—Besides the essential rules of Justice, which we have so far considered, there are economic and political considerations which will justly influence the distribution of taxes. Varying circumstances will call for varying methods of adjusting actual taxation to the principles of Distributive Justice. The following principles, however, are of general application :

I. Taxes Should Tend to Stimulate Home Industry.— Taxes ought to be so distributed as to encourage, rather than check, home industry ; to secure as far as possible that the natural resources of the country be developed to the utmost, and to reserve the home market for home production. Economists differ as to the best methods of securing these results. Most, however, will agree on the following general rules :

(a) In dealing with the necessaries of life, such as food, and clothing, direct prohibition of unnecessary imports combined with control of prices is usually a safer system than that of tariffs which frequently play into the hands of monopolists.

(b) Taxes on natural resources and unearned increment should be encouraged rather than taxes on necessary buildings and productive industry. It may even be desirable in certain circumstances to tax natural resources in proportion to their potential, rather than their actual, productivity, so that the owners may be thus forced to develop them, as far as the public good may require.

(c) Heavy tariffs on imported luxuries should be encouraged.

(d) Taxes on dividends from foreign investments, on foreign insurances, etc., are also usually helpful.

II. Public Contentment and Morality to be Considered.— Taxes should, as far as possible, affect more or less all the

---

[1] Cf. Vermeersch, *loc. cit.*, nn. 101, 102 ; Bastable, *op. cit.*, *loc. cit.*, chap. ii ; Fallon—*Principes d'Economie Sociale*, part iv, sec. ii, chaps. i–iii ; *Code of Social Principles*, nn. 124, 125 ; Devas, *op. cit.*, bk. iv, chaps. iii and v.

citizens who exercise the franchise : so that all may have an interest in promoting good and pure administration. Taxes should also, as far as possible, be of such a nature as not to arouse discontent. Again, taxes that easily admit of fraud ought to be avoided, as they tend to injure the public good by encouraging habits of evasion.[1]

Again, sumptuary taxes—namely, those which fall on luxuries, or tend to check undue extravagance, ought to be encouraged ; for even though their results in public revenue be not great, the moral lessons they teach, enlighten the public conscience and thus serve the common good. On the other hand, taxes which imply, or may seem to imply, an official approval of harmful public activities should be avoided. They mislead the public conscience, and are a temptation to the rulers of the State to permit for the sake of revenue the growth of practices which should be suppressed or kept in check by direct repressive legislation. This applies to such taxes as those on betting, gambling houses, cinemas and shows.

III. **Taxes Should Not Develop into Confiscation.**—Very high taxation on legacies, or excessive death duties, though justifiable in exceptional circumstances, tend to undermine the principle of property. They scarcely differ from confiscation and hinder the building up of natural reserves.[2] When an undue proportion of the national wealth becomes unnaturally concentrated in the possession of a small minority, as has occurred in Britain, very heavy death duties are made use of as a means of equalising the balance. The method, however, is not always a wholesome one, and should not be used except it tends in *the actual results* towards a much wider diffusion of ownership among the people.

Art. 3—Taxing of Land Values[3]

- **Existing Prejudices Against the Proposal.**—We have already referred[4] to the Single Tax system in connection

---

[1] Cf. Palgrave, *loc. cit.* ; Bastable, *op. cit.*, bk. iii, chap. vii ; *Code of Social Principles, loc. cit.*
[2] Cf. *Code of Social Principles*, nn. 124–127.
[3] Cf. Wright—*Single Tax* (Daniel Co., London, 1923) ; Gide—*History of Economic Doctrines*, bk. v, chap. iii ; Palgrave, *op. cit.*, art. " Single Tax " ; Ryan—*Distributive Justice*, chaps. iii, iv, viii.
[4] Cf. *Supra*, chap. xvii, art. 2.

with Henry George's theories regarding the ownership of land. The case for the taxation of land values (which may be truly considered as a partial application of the Single Tax system) as a means of raising a portion of the needed revenues for the State, has been much prejudiced in many people's minds by the fact that the advocates of it frequently advance inconclusive arguments in its favour, or strive to rest it on ethical principles which are unsound. Sometimes, too, they associate it with unacceptable doctrines of ownership and of land nationalisation with which it has no necessary connection ; and, finally, while making exaggerated claims in its favour as a panacea for almost all modern economic abuses, they propose in some cases, to put it in force in a manner that would be revolutionary or unjust. It is possible, however, to consider the essential elements of the proposed method in itself, as applicable at least partially and gradually, where circumstances are favourable.

What the Taxation of Land Values Means.—In the Single Tax system, if adopted in its entirety, all the revenues needed for the public services (namely, the whole income of the State) would be obtained by appropriating to the public treasury the *Economic Rent* of all the land, mines, water-power, fisheries, and of all the other natural resources of the country. All taxes would then be removed from industry and buildings, and from all other activities or persons in the State.

The Economic Rent includes two things—viz. : (*a*) the estimated yearly value of the natural productivity of the land, the mines, etc., apart from buildings, drainage, fences, roads, and all the other improvements resulting from the owner's labour ; and (*b*) the estimated yearly value of the *unearned increment.* This latter means the additional value accruing to the natural productivity by reason of adventitious circumstances produced by the community as a whole : such circumstances would be increased population, the neighbourhood of a town or railway station, or electric power-house. In other words, the Economic Rent means, roughly, the annual interest on the current market value of the land, mines, etc., apart from the build-

34

ings and fixtures erected by the present owner or his predecessors.[1]

It is clear that natural resources and unearned increment could be taxed at a rate much less than the Economic Rent, while taxes are at the same time removed, at least partially, from industries, houses and the necessaries of life. This is what is called the Taxation of Land Values.

Special Reasons for Taxing Land Values, etc.—Land and the other natural resources of the earth are essentially different in several particulars from every other species of property. While limited in amount, they are the ultimate source from which everything must come that is required to supply the people's physical needs.[2] Hence, those who control these sources of supply dominate, to a large extent, the whole economic life of the country.

Again, the ownership of these resources confers on him who possesses it, benefits of an accumulative character, which belong to no other species of property, and which do not come in any way from the owner's labour. The extension of cultivation, the increase of population, the growing demand for commodities which the land alone can produce, and the progress of science and invention (none of which is necessarily due in any degree to the initiative or intelligence of the owner), all tend to enhance the value of the land he holds, so that he may come after a time to be owner of immense values really created by the community.

" Suppose," says Mill, " that there is a kind of income which continually tends to increase without any exertion or sacrifice on the part of the owner, these owners constituting a class in the community whom the natural course of things progressively enriches consistently with complete passiveness on their own part. In such a case, it would be no violation of the principles on which private property is founded, if the State should appropriate this income as it arises. This would not properly be taking anything from anybody : it would merely be applying an accession of wealth created by circumstances to the benefit of

---

[1] *Economic Rent* must be carefully distinguished from the *Commercial Rent*, which would include the estimated value of the yearly productivity of the land, *as it now is*, including, namely, not merely its natural productivity and the increased value produced by the community, but also the *improvements* made by the owner.

[2] Leo XIII—*Rerum Novarum*, p. 137.

society instead of allowing it to become an unearned appendage to the riches of a certain class. Now, this is actually the case with rent."[1]

Hence, there are deeply-rooted convictions, which have been embodied more or less in the ordinary constitutional law of Europe, that the community has some sort of natural rights or common interest in the land of the country ; and that, while individual ownership of land is lawful, and even within certain limits, necessary for the general well-being, the land should not pass into the *complete control* of private individuals, in the same way as movable property.[2]

Advantages Claimed from Taxation of Land Values.—The advantages claimed for the taxation of land values in so far as it could be enforced without injustice, or undue hardship on individuals, are as follows :

1. The removal of the burden of taxation or a larger share of that burden from industry and buildings, on to the natural resources of the country, would render it unprofitable for a person to retain the possession of large tracts of uncultivated or unused lands or other natural resources. The owner would be forced either to exploit or sell them.[3]

---

[1] *Principles of Pol. Econ.*, bk. v, chaps ii and v (cited in Gide, *op. cit.* p. 562). The same idea, and especially the extent to which undue land monopoly tends to strengthen a parasitical class, are thus graphically illustrated by George : " Here is a small village ; in ten years it will be a great city—in ten years the railroad will have taken the place of the stage-coach, the electric light, of the candle : it will abound with all the machinery and improvements that so enormously multiply the effective power of labour. Will interest in ten years be any higher ? You answer ' No.' Will the wages of the common labourer be any higher ? ' No.' ' What then will be higher ? ' ' Rent : the value of land. Go : get yourself a piece of ground and hold possession . . . you may sit down and smoke your pipe : you may lie down like the *lazzaroni* of Naples or the lepers of Venice : you may go up in a balloon or down a hole in the ground : and without doing a stroke of work, without adding one iota to the wealth of the community, in ten years you will be rich ! In the new city you may have a luxurious mansion, but among the public buildings there will be an almshouse.' " (Cf. *Progress and Poverty*, bk. v, chap. ii).

[2] This is specially true of English law, in which no absolute ownership of the land, except the ownership of the Crown (namely, of the State) is recognised. Cf. Gide, *op. cit.*, p. 559. *See* also *supra*, chap. xvii, art. 2.

[3] It is said that at present some 70 people own about half of Scotland, and some 2,200 people own half the cultivable area of England. Millions of acres of land are devoted to the preserving of game : there are many millions more whose potentialities are only partially developed. The same thing applies to Ireland in an increasing degree. Cf. Wright, *op. cit.*, pp. 56–60.

This would tend to that increase in the number of small peasant owners, which is so strongly advocated by Leo XIII, and so much desired by almost all statesmen.

II. Taxation of the small land owners, on the other hand, would not be increased ; for, although they would now have to pay a land tax, their houses and farm-buildings would be untaxed, and the tax on the necessaries of life would be lessened.

III. By making land more easily available for the landless, and also by affording more employment owing to the increased cultivation, the system would check the present fatal tendency towards urbanisation.

IV. The lightening of the burden of taxation on industry, whether agricultural or otherwise, would provide a useful stimulus, and would make the necessaries of life more plentiful.

V. The housing problem for both town and country would become much easier of solution. Sites and plots would be available at reasonable prices, and the owner of the new house would not be confronted with the burden of a new tax.[1]

History of Land Taxation.—The idea of taxing land values is much older than the time of Henry George or the modern Single taxers. Whereas at the present day industries as distinct from natural resources are made to bear the main burden of taxation, it was not so formerly. In ancient and mediæval times the greater part of public expenditure was borne in one shape or another, by the land. This remained true even after a flourishing industrial life had already arisen.[2] Again, the Physiocrats of the 18th century advocated a tax on the rent of land, and the abolition or practical abolition of all other taxes, on the ground that, as the land was the ultimate source of all other values, the simplest and most convenient method of raising the necessary revenues would be to make it the only object of taxation.[3] In the 19th century, J. S. Mill and H. Spencer also

---

[1] Cf. Ryan, *op. cit.*, p. 52, and chap. viii, pp. 94–133 ; Palgrave, *loc. cit.* p. 404.

[2] Cf. Bastable, *op. cit.*, bk. iv, chap. i ; also Wright, *op. cit.*, chap. ii, and Palgrave, *op. cit.*, art. " Taxation," pp. 517, 518.

[3] Cf. Bastable *op. cit.*, p. 34.

put forward similar proposals. Mill's proposal was, that while the Economic Rent (including unearned increment) already appropriated by individuals should not be interfered with, all future increase in unearned value should be taken over by the State.[1] George's proposals are more radical and sweeping. According to George, the Economic Rent (including the unearned increment) belongs inalienably by the natural law to the community, so that the appropriation of it by individuals is essentially unjust. Hence, the community (viz., the State) should resume possession of it forthwith and without compensation.

During the past thirty years or more, the question of the taxation of land values has been gradually forcing its way into practical politics in several countries, especially England, Germany, Denmark, Australia, New Zealand, Brazil, Canada, Transvaal, and some of the States of the North-American Union. In some of these countries the system is especially proposed as a means of breaking down the monopolies of lands, mines, etc., of stemming the rural depopulation and lowering the cost of the necessaries of life.[2] Again, numerous projects more or less successful have been launched to tax the surplus value of suburban lands, and thus make them cheaper and more easily obtainable for building.[3]

Denmark has been the first country to adopt the principle. By a law passed Aug. 4th, 1922, a moderate land tax (combined with partial exemption from taxes on buildings and other improvements) was put on all the land within the State. The law was the result of a persevering demand of the small farmers (some 120,000 in number) who had

---

[1] Cf. Gide, *loc. cit.*
[2] Cf. *Land and Freedom*, a propagandist bi-monthly, published at 150 Nassau Street, New York.
[3] This was one of the modes of contention in the famous English Budget of 1909, and the Finance Act of 1910, which aroused such fierce opposition from the landed proprietors, and brought to a head the constitutional struggle of the Liberal Party with the House of Lords (Cf. Ryan, *op. cit.*, pp. 114–120 ; Gide, *op. cit.*, pp. 569, 570). Partly owing to this opposition such conditions were inserted into the provisions of the Act that the measure proved a failure. (Cf. Paper No. 11—*The Lloyd George Finance Act*, 1910—issued by the International Union for Land Value Taxation, 11 Tothill, London, S.W.). These Papers were issued in connection with the International Conference to Promote Land Value Taxation, held in Edinburgh, 1929

been agitating for it since 1902. Again, in the new constitution of the German Republic, the provision is made that :

" All the increase in land values not due to the expenditure of capital and labour must be used for communal purposes."

In New South Wales, also in New Zealand and in parts of Brazil, the legislatures have partially adopted the principle in varying degrees.[1]

Critique of the Single Tax System and the Taxation of Land Values.—I.

Henry George's proposal that the State should take over, without compensation, the whole economic rent of all the natural resources of the country and the unearned increment, need not be discussed here. Such a measure would be grossly unjust, seeing that most of the present owners of these values have acquired them by purchase or own them by good and valid titles. Besides, such a revolutionary measure would destroy the stability of the State.[2]

II. That the State should acquire even compulsorily after compensating the present owners in accordance with the principles of Commutative and Legal Justice, the values corresponding to the present Economic Rent (including value of unearned increment) ; and should take over without any compensation future accessions as they arise, would not be unjust.

Neither would such measures be against the teaching of Leo XIII on the rights of private property.[3] For all the elements of ownership which he demands, namely, secure possession, the usufruct of the property, independent management, full ownership of the improvements and the power to transmit, would be assured to the individual while still leaving to the State such rights as that of the Economic Rent. Similarly, in mediæval times private ownership in the Christian sense was maintained notwithstanding the fact that the king (viz., the State) held certain rights as supreme suzerain over all, or practically all, the land of the

---

[1] Cf. The *Transaction of the Fourth International Conference to Promote Land Value Taxation and Free Trade*, published at 11 Tothill, London, S.W.1.

[2] Cf. Gide, *loc. cit.*, p. 567 ; Ryan, *loc. cit.*, pp. 33, 34.

[3] Cf. *Rerum Novarum*, pp. 134–140.

country. When Leo XIII condemns, as he does condemn, the assertion that it is against Justice for a private person *ever* to own land outright or in full ownership, he does not assert that a positive[1] law or custom against such complete ownership existing in certain countries is unjust or invalid. All he asserts is that it is possible for a person to acquire by a just title, the complete ownership of land where there is no previous right of another, or valid law, which may prevent him from doing so.[2]

III. Whether the advantages of such a measure would outweigh the disadvantages, may be questioned,[3] and the true solution would probably depend upon the different circumstances and traditions of the particular country.

IV. It may be a very useful measure, at least in some countries, to put on a moderate land tax on the capitalised value of the Economic Rent for all the land and other natural resources of the country, while lessening at the same time the taxes on houses and industries as has been done in Denmark and New South Wales. The practical method recommended by the promoters of the idea would be to put a tax, say, of 3d. in the pound or more on the present market value of all the land *minus* the improvements.[4] Besides, the State could take over by taxes, all, or a substantial portion of, the future accessions of unearned values as they arise.[5] Such measures should facilitate the wider diffusion of proprietorship in land. They would tend to prevent the holding up of the natural resources of the country, would obstruct or check the rise of harmful monopolies, and facilitate the solution of the housing problem where such a problem exists.[6]

Art. 4—*Appointment to Public Offices*

Public Appointments and Distributive Justice.—Catholic authors generally hold that the just allotment of public offices by the rulers of the State appertains to Distributive

---

[1] *Ib.*, pp. 137, 138.   [2] Cf. Ryan, *op. cit.*, pp. 44, 45.   [3] Cf. Ryan, *ib.*
[4] Cf. Paper 11 (Lloyd George Finance Act, 1910), cited above.
[5] Justice would probably demand that in some cases at least moderate compensation should be made to the owner (Cf. Ryan, *loc. cit.*).
[6] Cf. Ryan, *op. cit.*, pp. 100-104, for a useful and interesting discussion on this subject, in its social, economic and moral aspects.

Justice.[1] The law of nature demands that just proportion
of parts, and the beauty of good order be preserved in the
organisation of the State and the conduct of public
administration. This principle is violated if officials are
appointed not by reason of their fitness for the particular
office, but from such motives as private interest, membership of a secret society, friendship, or family relationship.
Besides, a fair chance of obtaining these offices and appointments may be regarded, especially in modern times, as one
of the normal advantages of citizenship, so that he who is
unfairly shut out is more or less the victim of injustice.
Again, the honour and emolument which the possession of
one of these offices brings with it is not infrequently meant
to be, in part at least, a reward for public merit, and a
stimulus to other members of the community to work for
the public good. Hence, it is but right that all citizens
who are suitable have a fair chance of obtaining these
offices, and that in the selection of candidates nothing but
the merits of the case be allowed to weigh.[2]

Legal and Commutative Justice also Concerned.—There
are still weightier reasons resting on motives of Legal
Justice, why merit and suitability should be the only considerations in making public appointments. For the character and suitability of public officials affect public interests
very much for good or for ill. Furthermore, all authorities
agree that the person who knowingly appoints or votes for
a really unsuitable candidate violates, or may violate Commutative Justice, and is so far personally responsible for
all the injuries that the community may thereby suffer.[3]

Respect of Persons.—St. Thomas applies the term *accep-
tatio personarum* (respect of persons) to the action of the

---

[1] The rights and duties here discussed apply with equal force to municipal
appointments such as those of medical officers, engineers, etc., and to the
allocation of public contracts with builders, purveyors, etc. When these
appointments and allocations are made by boards of electors, the duties
of each member of the board to vote only for suitable or for the most
suitable candidates are quite similar to the duties of rulers which are
discussed in the text.

[2] Cf. Costa-Rosetti, *op. cit.*, Thesis 153, pp. 552–554 ; also Vermeersch,
op. cit., nn. 64, 67, 68, 75.

[3] Cf, De Lugo, *op. cit.*, d, xxxvi, nn. 9, 10,

ruler or superior who selects candidates for an office, not
for reasons founded upon the necessities or proprieties of
the case, but from such motives as interest or friendship
or kinship. He adds, that this *respect for persons* is a
violation of Distributive Justice, and is sinful.[1]

Even De Lugo, who holds (against the common view as
he himself admits) that in civil, as opposed to ecclesiastical,
appointments, rulers and electors are, in theory, only bound
to appoint or vote for a sufficiently suitable candidate,
substantially agrees with the more ordinary opinion. For
he admits that in practice there is a strict obligation of
appointing and voting for the most suitable candidate,[2]
not, indeed, by reason of any right the candidate may have,
but on account of the grave evils which commonly result
to the common weal if it were lawful for a ruler or voter
to lower his standard, and appoint or vote for a candidate
whom he knows to be less suitable than his competitors.

These evils and dangers are all the more serious if the
ruler or elector accepts a bribe, even though the candidate
he selects be not altogether unsuitable. For, if money
becomes the best means of obtaining public appointments,
the whole public service will quickly become corrupted and
its efficiency lowered.[3]

Specially Dangerous in Democratic States.—Whatever may
be said of the question in the circumstances of the time in
which the great scholastic authors wrote, it is certain that
in our days and under the present system of democratic
government, the interests of the public good imperatively
demand the strictest impartiality and uprightness in the
matter of public patronage.

It is well known and admitted that "favouritism,"
"graft," and "jobbery," in the public administration have
the most prejudicial effects on the whole life of a nation,
and are, perhaps, the greatest perils to which democratic
government is exposed. When these abuses once get a
foothold in the administration, corruption and injustice

---

[1] 2a, 2æ, Q. 63, a. 1.
[2] De Lugo, *loc. cit.*
[3] *Ib.*, n. 5. Cf. also Ballerini-Palmieri—*Opus Theologicum Morale*,
vol. ii, tr. vi, sec. iv, pp. 589, 590 (2nd edit., 1892), where the opinion
given in the text is upheld as the only safe one in practice.

of all kinds quickly spread into every department of the State, and even into the whole public and private life of the people.

The imminence of this danger is one of the many reasons why the existence of such influences as Freemasonry and kindred associations in the administration of any country is practically incompatible with just government or national well-being.

CHAPTER XXVII

CHARITY[1]

Introductory Note—Justice and Charity.—Although Justice is in a certain sense the soul of the social organism, and its obligations the most important and fundamental of civic duties, Justice alone will not suffice to secure the objects of civil society. For, as Pius XI teaches :

" Justice alone, even though most faithfully observed while removing the cause of social strife, can never bring about a union of hearts and minds. Yet this union binding men together is the main principle of stability in all institutions, no matter how perfect they may seem, which aim at establishing social peace and promoting mutual aid."[2]

On the other hand, in the words of Leo XIII :

" Justice and Charity mutually conjoined, according to the equal and gentle law of Christ, maintain in a wonderful way the bonds of human society and providently lead every member to cater for his own and the common good."[3]

Hence, in order to secure social well-being, Justice and Charity must go hand in hand. Charity without Justice is unreal. Justice without Charity has too little of the " milk of human kindness " to respond to the actual needs of men.

The duties of Charity are not juridical like those of Justice. By Justice we render to another that which is in some sense already his ; by Charity we give him what is absolutely our own. Accordingly, the neglect or violation of Charity does not imply an obligation of restitution once the circumstances that called for its exercise have ceased to exist, whereas a violation of at least one species of Justice (namely, Commutative Justice) does.

---

[1] Cf. St. Thomas, 1ma, 2æ, Q. 26–28 ; 2a, 2æ, Q. 26–28, 30–33 ; *Quæstiones Disputatæ, De Caritate,* Suarez, tom. xii, *De Caritate,* disp. i, iv, v, vii, ix ; Costa-Rosetti, *op. cit.,* Thesis 29 ; *Dictionnaire de Theologie Catholique,* art. " Charité," *Cath. Encyclopedia,* art. " Charity."
[2] *Quadragesimo Anno,* p. 64.   [3] *Graves de Communi,* p. 176.

But, although duties of Charity are in that respect less urgent than those of Justice, the rôle which Charity has to play in actual social life is all-important ; and indeed may be regarded in a certain sense as the most important of all.

" In its absence," writes Pius XI,[1] " as experience proves, the wisest regulations come to nothing.   Then only will it be possible to unite all in harmonious striving for the common good, when all sections of society have the intimate conviction that they are members of a single family and children of the same Heavenly Father, and further, that they are *one body in Christ, and everyone members one of another,*[2] so that *if one member suffer anything, all members suffer with it.*"[3]

Unless men aim seriously at fulfilling their duties of Charity as understood in the Christian law, even Justice will soon be disregarded.   The virtue of Charity, especially when practised from supernatural motives, tends to elevate every other virtue, including that of Justice, to a higher plane.   Acts of Justice are made easier and more perfect when the motives of Justice are reinforced by those of Charity.   Moreover, since the latter are more comprehensive and far-reaching than the motives of Justice, obligations of Charity extend to countless cases of human need which Justice will not reach.   Finally, in addition to the duties that Charity imposes as necessary and binding, the motives which underlie it, especially the supernatural ones, as understood in the law of Christ, supply a stimulus towards works of beneficence and self-sacrifice far beyond the limits of what any virtue could impose as obligatory.

Thus, Charity strengthens the whole social organism, rendering its working smoother and more efficient.   It perfects and intensifies the moral beauty of the wondrous mechanism of social life as God and Nature have designed it.   Charity is justly considered the foundation of Christian life, the " Queen of the Virtues," the abridgment of the law.[4]

In the present sketch we shall discuss, first, the general nature and motives of the virtue of Charity : next, the Precept of Almsgiving, which is for our purpose its most important application ; and finally, the discipline and traditional practice of the Church in its regard.

---

[1] *Quadragesimo Anno*, p. 64.   [2] *Rom.* xii. 5.   [3] I *Cor.* xii. 26.
[4] Cf. St. Thomas, 2a, 2æ, Q. 23, a. 6, 7 and 8.

Art. 1—*Nature and Motives of the Virtue of Charity*

General Idea of Charity.—Charity in its general sense
means love for others, but it includes the idea of esteem
and appreciation in addition to that of love. Hence,
Charity can have for its object only rational beings ; for,
although one may in a certain sense love even the lower
animals, as a man be said to love his horse or his dog,
nobody will assert that these can be the objects of an act
of charity.[1]

Charity as a Moral or Natural Virtue.—Man is bound by
the natural law to love God with a supreme love, as the
Author of his life and the first principle of all being.[2] As
a consequence he is bound to love in a certain degree all
rational creatures whom God loves. Man, besides, has an
instinctive tendency to love other men by reason of their
natural likeness to himself, and their connection with him
as members of the same human race.[3] The tendency is
stronger in proportion to the extent of the likeness or the
nearness of the connection. Seeing that this instinctive
love for others, like all natural tendencies, comes from God,
it must be reasonable and praiseworthy.[4] The fact that
man is intended by nature to live as a member of organised
society, and thus to assist others by co-operating with them
for the common good, is a further proof of the reasonableness
of man's natural love for his fellow-men. It is this love
which supplies the basis of a moral virtue. That virtue is
what is called Charity or Philanthropy. It may be defined
as a *love of benevolence for others*.[5] Although Charity includes man's natural love of God and of the angels, as well
as his love of his fellow men, it is only with this last that
we are concerned here, seeing that it alone has a direct
bearing on social well-being.

The virtue of Charity resides in the will and not in the
sensitive appetite ; and it aims at the good of the person
beloved rather than the gratification of the lover. It is
thus distinguished from the love of concupiscence, which

---

[1] *Ib.*, Q. 22, a. 1, and Q. 25, a. 2.   [2] *Ib., Quodlibeta,* i, a. 8.
[3] *Ib.*, 1ª, 2æ, Q. 27, a. 3.   [4] *Ib., Quodlibeta,* i, a. 8 (*corp.*).
[5] *Ib.*, 2æ, 2ª, Q. 23, a. 1.

has for its object the good or satisfaction of the person who loves. For, as St. Thomas says :

" The love of concupiscence is that by which we are said to love what we wish to use or enjoy. The love of friendship (or benevolence) is that by which we are said to love a friend whose good we desire."[1]

Its Duties.—According to the natural law, the moral virtue of Charity or benevolence should result in interior acts of love when circumstances require as well as in those other interior dispositions of the soul that flow from the love of others—viz., *Joy, Peace,* and *Compassion.*[2] Above all, the virtue of Charity should express itself in acts. To assist others in their spiritual and corporal needs is the practical application of the virtue of Charity. In fact, all the duties of supernatural Charity as taught, and practically enforced by, the Catholic Church, including even the love of one's enemies, are founded upon the natural law, and are obligatory independently of any positive precept either human or divine.[3]

Its Effective Strength.—Charity like material forces acts in a kind of inverse ratio to the distance of the object to which it refers. When other considerations are equal, the intensity of one's love for others increases in proportion to the closeness of their connection with one or the greatness of their likeness. Nearness and likeness go further than excellence in winning one's love. This tendency, too, is quite in accordance with right reason.[4]

It is clear, however, that the natural virtue, although like all moral virtues capable of being strengthened by repeated acts, will remain, except in the case of very noble souls, comparatively weak. In practice it is quite inadequate to meet the needs of social life. Its motives are not strong or urgent enough to resist effectually the tendencies of indolence and selfishness so deeply engrained in man's nature. Thus, we find how comparatively inoperative

---

[1] *Quodlibeta,* i, a. 8 *(corp.)* ; cf. also 1ª, 2ᵃᵉ, Q. 26, a. 4 ; and 2ª, 2ᵃᵉ, Q. 31, a. 1.
[2] *Ib.,* Q. 28–30.
[3] *Ib.,* Q. 31 ; cf. also 1ª, 2ᵃᵉ, Q. 108, a. 4 ; and Suarez, *loc. cit.,* disp. i, sec. v, n. 4.
[4] *Ib.,* Q. 26, a. 6 and 7.

was the virtue of Charity in the ancient pagan world, and how inoperative it remains even to-day, except where assisted by the driving force of supernatural motives, such as the Christian revelation supplies.

Non-Christian Charity.—In the highly developed civilisation of the ancient Greeks and Romans, the very idea of Charity, as we have defined it, did not exist. Neither Roman nor Greek recognised the inherent worth of human personality, which lies at the foundation of the virtue of Charity. Hence, among them, just as in modern neo-pagan society, the poor and defenceless, especially the slaves, were despised or treated with a pity akin to contempt. Whatever mercy or consideration was shown them was founded upon self-respect, or upon natural shrinking from the sight of suffering. The sentiments of a cultured Greek or Roman towards his slave would be akin to those of a Christian towards the lower animals. It seems certain that no public institution for the treatment of disease existed in Rome or Greece before the Christian era.[1]

Of the other non-Christian religions of the world, the nearer any of them approaches to the true religion, the more living is the spirit of Charity among its votaries. Thus, Buddhism inculcates a certain duty of Charity, and imposes even a limited love of one's enemies ; but the motives put forward are utilitarian and selfish. The Mohammedans, while regarding Charity, and especially almsgiving towards their co-religionists, as a fundamental duty, do not recognise any such duties towards their fellowmen of other religions. Indeed, the systematic cruelty and injustice which they have usually practised towards their political or religious opponents, have scarcely any parallel among Christian nations.

Jewish Charity.—The type of Charity inculcated in the Old Testament, and practised among the Jews until the people fell away from the ideals of their faith, was of a very high order ; and, so far as it went, differs little from Christian

---

[1] The motives of the doles which were distributed in Rome to the poor by the State or by wealthy citizens were not charitable, but purely political. Doles were usually given to secure the goodwill of the citizens, or to keep them quiet, and thus preserve domestic peace.

Charity. Jewish Charity, however—at least in so far as it was enforced by the Law—referred only to fellow-Jews, and did not extend even to strangers dwelling in the country, much less to enemies. We shall treat this more fully under the heading of Almsgiving.

Christian Charity.—It remained for the Christian religion to elevate the whole concept of Charity to a higher plane, and to cause the virtue to be practised more widely and with greater perfection than was previously known. Further, by its counsels of perfection the Catholic Church has in every age induced immense numbers to aim at ideals of love and benevolence far beyond the limits of what is strictly obligatory according to the natural or even the Christian law itself. The realisation of the Christian ideal is in fact rendered possible only by the assistance of super-natural grace, aided by the example and appeal of Him who, though the God of glory, "*emptied Himself, taking the form of a servant*" for love of man, and even laid down His life for His enemies.

"Christianity for the first time," writes Lecky, "made Charity a rudimentary virtue. . . . It effected a complete revolution in this sphere by regarding the poor as the special representatives of the Christian Founder, and thus making the love of Christ rather than the love of man the principle of Charity. . . . No achievements of the Christian Church are more truly great than those it has effected in the sphere of Charity. For the first time in the history of mankind, it has inspired many thousands of men and women at the sacrifice of all worldly interests, and oftentimes under circumstances of extreme discomfort and danger, to devote their entire lives to the single object of assuaging the sufferings of humanity. It has covered the globe with countless institutions of mercy absolutely unknown to the pagan world. It has indissolubly united in the minds of men the idea of supreme goodness with that of active and constant benevolence."[1]

We shall, therefore, explain briefly the motives, obliga-tions and practice of Charity as understood and inculcated in Christian teaching. As we are concerned only with the social aspects of the subject, we omit entirely several

---

[1] Cf. *History of European Morals*, bk. ii, pp. 79–85 (3rd edit.).

questions that would necessarily enter into an adequate treatment of the theological virtue of Charity.

Its Nature.—For our present purpose, Christian Charity may be defined as *a supernatural virtue which disposes us to love God above all for His own sake, and ourselves and others for the love of God*. The motive of our love of others under the Christian law is not alone their likeness to us or the closeness of the natural bonds that may unite us with them. It is not merely that they and we are the creatures of the same God, as known to us by the light of reason, and therefore, the servants of the same Lord ; although all these and other natural motives may exist as subsidiary and subordinate.[1] The primary motive of Christian Charity is God Himself as revealed to us by faith. The act of Charity by which we love God efficaciously includes love of all those who are the special friends or children of God, those whom God loves, and with whom He shares or desires to share His own happiness and glory by the gift of sanctifying grace and eternal life. Thus, Christian Charity includes within its object and scope all human beings, without exception, seeing that God loves all, and the Divine Saviour died for all, and desired to share with all His gifts of the natural and supernatural order.

The life and teaching of our Divine Saviour contain all these motives in their strongest and most appealing form. It is the personal love of Him that is most efficacious in producing works of self-sacrificing beneficence. Every Catholic is constantly reminded that Our Lord died for all without exception ; that He longs to share with everyone the riches of His eternal glory ; that He nourishes each with His own most precious Body and Blood, or desires to do so ; that He bequeathed to all His own Blessed Mother to be the mother of each one ;[2] that He has decreed in the most express and unmistakable terms that one's effective

---

[1] Cf. St. Thomas—*Quæstiones Disput., De Caritate*, a. 7 (*corp.*) : " The love of supernatural Charity includes within itself all kinds of human love, except such as are based on sin. . . . Hence, the mutual love of relatives or fellow-countrymen, or of travelling companions, or of any other such persons can rest ultimately upon Charity and be meritorious. But a mutual love founded upon common participation in robbery or adultery cannot be based on Charity, nor be meritorious." Cf. also Suarez, *loc. cit.*, disp. i, sec. iii.

[2] *John* xix. 26, 27.

35

love of Him will be measured by one's charity towards others : *As long as you did it to the least of these My brethren you did it to Me* ;[1] that this love of others is His own special precept, solemnly repeated at His last meeting with His Apostles before His Passion ;[2] that this love is the peculiar mark of His true followers, and the surest guarantee of final union with Him.[3]   Therefore, Charity and beneficence will flourish in a Christian community in proportion to the strength of the people's faith in Christ, and the intensity of the Christian spirit among them.   On the other hand, where faith in Christ is weak, and love of Him languishes, true Christian Charity gradually disappears ; and avarice, indolence and self-seeking, gain the upper hand.

Order of Charity.—It is true that, just as in the case of the natural virtue of Charity, a due order should be observed in the intensity of one's supernatural love for others, and in the practical acts of beneficence that naturally flow from that love.   Well-ordered Charity should begin at home. Where other considerations are equal, it will impel us to prefer those who are more closely connected with us to those that are further removed.[4]   It is true also that when the precept of Christian Charity commands us to love the wicked, and even to love our enemies, it does not imply that we are not to hate their wickedness and their unjust hostility, and even defend ourselves and others against them.[5]

Its Effective Strength.—Notwithstanding this, however, Christian Charity is a living force, showing itself in active, warm benevolence towards persons united to one by no natural tie, and even towards those who are naturally hostile and distasteful.   It does literally regard all as

---

[1] *Matth.* xxv. 40.   [2] *John* xiii. 34, 35.   [3] *Matth.* xxv. 34–46.
[4] St. Thomas, 2a, 2æ, Q. 26, a. 6 and 8 (*corp.*).
[5] " Everything naturally abhors that which is opposed to itself.   Now, enemies are opposed to us, in so far as they are our enemies.   Hence, thus far we ought to hate them (*hoc debemus in eis odio habere*), for the fact that they are our enemies ought to displease us.   But, in so far as they are men and capable of heavenly glory, they are not opposed to us, and thus far we ought to love them."   *Ib.*, 2a, 2æ, Q. 25, a. 8 ad 2um. Cf. also *ib.*, a. 6 and 8 (*corp.*).   *See* Suarez (*loc. cit.*, disp. v, sec. v, n. 1 and 2) for the sense in which one may lawfully wish temporal evil (not, however, eternal perdition) to one's enemies, and, therefore, in a certain sense *hate* them.

brothers in Jesus Christ ; and its motives are sufficiently strong and appealing to reach out effectively to those who are farthest removed in natural connection, no matter how hostile they may be, or how great their physical or moral degradation. Besides, in addition to the duties it imposes as obligatory, Christian Charity contains the strongest and most appealing motives, urging one constantly to acts of supererogation, in generous and even heroic beneficence. Hence it is, that this virtue, in its supernatural form, influences profoundly the whole character and tone of Christian society.

Practice of Christian Charity.—We have already said that the virtue of Charity will express itself in the first place in the love of benevolence,[1] and the interior acts and dispositions of the soul that flow from it. St. Thomas enumerates these latter as : *Joy* at the success or happiness of others ;[2] *Peace* of the soul resulting from substantial agreement of one's will with others ;[3] and *Compassion* or *Mercy*, which implies sorrow for the misfortune of another, accompanied by the efficacious desire to relieve it as far as one can.[4]

Besides these *interior* acts and dispositions (with which we are not directly concerned here), Charity implies the exterior acts which are the natural expression of the interior. St. Thomas treats especially of three types of the exterior acts of Charity—viz., *Beneficence, Almsgiving,* and *Fraternal Correction.* This last, namely, Fraternal Correction, which is directed towards preventing or remedying the moral delinquencies of others,[5] seems to differ little from the *Spiritual Works of Mercy,* which we shall touch on in the next article. *Beneficence* includes all acts by which one assists or serves another from motives of Charity. *Almsgiving* is a species of Beneficence, but implies that the person assisted is in need of help. This last is the most important of the exterior acts of Charity, as it is principally through almsgiving that Charity towards others exercises such great influence on Christian society. The subject therefore requires a somewhat fuller treatment.

---

[1] St. Thomas, 2a, 2æ, Q. 27, a. 7 and 8.   [2] *Ib.,* Q. 28.
[3] *Ib.,* Q. 29.   [4] *Ib.,* Q. 30.   [5] *Ib.,* Q. 33.

Art. 2—*The Precept of Almsgiving*[1]

Definition and Nature of Almsgiving.—The term *Almsgiving* includes every species of activity, not already obligatory under the virtue of Justice, that springs from a motive of genuine Charity and is directed towards helping others in their spiritual, mental and material needs. Hence, Almsgiving may be defined as *acts of mercy done from love of God by which one assists others who are in need* ("opus quo datur aliquid indigenti ex compassioné propter Deum.") [2]

Assistance given to another solely with a view to gain his friendship or to win public esteem, or from a wish to be rid of the sight of human misery, although such motives may not be blameworthy, would not be an exercise of Almsgiving. Acts of beneficence which are not Almsgiving may, however, be inspired by unworthy motives such as vanity or ambition, and thus be vitiated at their source. Thus it is, that loudly-trumpeted charitable displays, advertised in the newspapers and supported by large contributions from ambitious persons, frequently inspire nothing but envy and hatred in the hearts of those who are the objects of the so-called charitable efforts. Christian Charity must in some way establish a bond of union and equality between giver and receiver reminding both of their equal human dignity, their common sonship of God, and their mutual brotherhood in Jesus Christ. Further, in order that Almsgiving be in the full sense an act of true Christian Charity, its motives must include the supernatural love of God in the sense already explained.

---

[1] Cf. St. Thomas, 2a, 2æ, Q. 32, a. I, 2, 5, 6, 10. *Quodlibeta* viii, a. 12, and vi, a. 12, *In IV. Dist.* xv, Q. 2 ; Billuart—*Summa St. Thomae*, tom. v, disert. v. *De Eleemosyna.* Cajetanus, Bannes and Sylvius—*Commentaria* in 2am, 2æ, *Sti. Thomae*, Q. 32 (*De Eleemosyna*). Suarez—*Opera*, tom. xii. " De Caritate," disp. vii, secs. i, ii, iii, iv ; De Lugo—*Opera*, tom. vi. " De Justitia et Jure," disp. xvi, sec. 7 ; St. Alphonsus Liguori—*Theolog. Mor.*, lib. iii, trac. iii. dub. iii ; Lacroix—*Theol. Mor.*, tom. i, lib. ii, dub. iii, and Addenda ; Ballerini-Palmieri—*Theol. Mor.*, vol. ii, tract. v, sec. iii, cap. ii, dub. iii ; Vermeersch—*Theol. Mor.*, vol. ii, lib. i, trac. iii, tit. iii, cap. iii, art. ii ; Costa-Rosetti—*Phil. Mor.*, th. 29 and Schol. i, and ii, pp. 289–295 ; *Dictionnaire de Théologie Catholique*, " Aumone " ; Antoine—*Cours d'Economie Sociale*, Première Partie, chap. v, arts. 3 and 4 ; Deuxième Partie, chap. xx ; Palgrave—*Dictionary of Political Economy*, " Property " ; *Catholic Encyclopedia*, " Alms " and " Charity " ; Dr. J. A. Ryan—*Distributive Justice*, chap. xxi (" The Duty of Distributing Superfluous Wealth ").

[2] St. Thomas, 2a, 2æ, Q. 32, a. I (*corp.*).

Again, if the person have a right in justice to the thing given, even though the right be not strict or clearly defined, as happens in the case of Legal and Distributive Justice, the service is no longer an alms. Thus, when the rulers of the State make just laws to secure that the honest workman have a fair opportunity of remunerative labour, or subsidise from the resources of the State those who through no fault of theirs are deprived of such an opportunity, their action is not Almsgiving but an exercise, or an attempted exercise, of Legal Justice ; for all the citizens normally have a right to be allowed a fair chance of earning a becoming livelihood by their labour.

Neither are the contributions exacted by the State or the municipal authorities for poor relief, alms, although they may indirectly affect the extent of one's obligations of Almsgiving by lessening the poverty that needs relief or diminishing one's superfluous goods.

Different Species of Almsgiving.—The division of Almsgiving into what are ordinarily called the *Spiritual Works of Mercy* and the *Corporal Works of Mercy* is well known. Almsgiving of the former class is directed to the spiritual or supernatural needs of others ; the latter to the relief of their material wants. In illustration of some of the different acts of Almsgiving belonging to both of these classes, St. Thomas quotes the following passage from the Homilies of St. Gregory the Great :

" Let the man that has mental gifts beware of burying them in useless silence ; let him who enjoys an abundance of material goods take heed that he grow not slack in distributing them liberally to the needy ; let the one that has ability in the management of business be most careful to share with his neighbour the advantage of his skill ; let him that has influence or intimacy with the great, fear eternal perdition for the sin of hiding his talent, if he fail to protect the poor man's interests when he is able to do so."[1]

We are here principally concerned with the corporal works of mercy, and especially with those referring to food, clothing and shelter. For it is a fundamental element of social well-being that all the members of the civic body

---

[1] 2a, 2æ, Q. 32, a. 2 (*Sed contra*).

have the means of securing these primary essentials for human life.

Attitude of Materialists, Liberals and Socialists.—Many sociologists of the non-Christian type reject the practice of Almsgiving as pernicious or undesirable, or as out of harmony with human dignity, and the essential equality of men. Some also, who would repudiate the imputation of being non-Christian, practically deny the *obligation* of Almsgiving on the principle that a man is master of his own property. Herbert Spencer and his disciples of the Materialistic school openly attack the practice of Almsgiving as being contrary to the designs of the Author of nature, Who has ordained misery and poverty as an essential element in the order of the universe. Thus, Spencer writes :

" The poverty of the incapable, the distress of the improvident, the nakedness of the idle, the crushing of the weak in conflict with the strong, which leaves so great a number of people in the depths of misery, have all been ordained by a mighty and far-seeing Providence."[1]

Similar ideas appear more or less explicitly in the writings of other English and French moralists. The attitude of modern plutocratic society towards the poor and wretched is practically in accordance with these principles of materialism.

" This hideous concept of society," writes Father Antoine, " the outcome of materialistic philosophy, is devoid of all serious foundation. Man's struggle for existence is within the domain of the moral law ; and its results depend upon the exercise of man's free will."[2]

In other words, even though it be true, as Spencer implies, that the natural law does ordain a certain struggle for existence, it is equally true that that struggle, in case of free and responsible agents, must be carried on in accordance with the laws of Justice and Charity which always safeguard individual rights and human dignity.

Moralists of the Liberal school, according to whose economic principles social well-being is best attained by

---

[1] Quoted in French by Antoine, *op. cit.*, chap. xx, art. 3.
[2] *Dictionnaire Apologétique de la Foi Catholique*, art. " Aumone," col. 324.

every individual seeking exclusively his own aggrandisement, naturally tend to adopt Spencer's attitude towards
the poor. Hence, not only do they deny or minimise the
duty of the State, to protect the poor and weak, but many
even condemn the practice of private Almsgiving, as if it
tended necessarily to lessen in the poor the sense of personal
responsibility, and encourage improvidence. It is manifest
that this is true only of such Almsgiving as is excessive or
imprudent.

Finally, the Socialists, who hold that everyone has a
right under Distributive Justice to receive from the State
all he needs, condemn Almsgiving as an outrage on the
dignity of man ; and proclaim that, even though it contained
an efficacious remedy for the social evils of the present day,
they would still continue to protest against it.[1] But, independently of the fact that the Socialists' concept of
Distributive Justice is false, as already pointed out,[2] it is
plain that their objections do not hold against Almsgiving,
as understood by Christians, which is founded upon the
principle of human equality, and the mutual brotherhood
in Jesus Christ of the giver and the receiver.

"So far from its being unbecoming to anyone," writes
Leo XIII, " it [viz., almsgiving] rather fosters the good fellow-
ship of human association by fostering the obligation of mutual
service. There is no one so rich as to have no need of anyone
else ; none so poor that he cannot do his neighbour some good
turn ; it is human nature that we should confidently ask for and
charitably afford assistance one with another."[3]

Christian Teaching on Almsgiving.—The Christian doctrine
of Almsgiving is in striking contrast with these non-Christian
theories. The duty of Almsgiving is one of the fundamental
laws of Christianity, and its practice has always been an
outstanding feature of the Catholic religion. The traditional
teaching of the Church on the subject may be summed up
in the two following propositions :

I. Almsgiving is a duty imposed not only by divine
precept, but also by the law of nature. The obligation is
of its own nature grave, although actual violations may
sometimes be venial owing to levity of matter.

---

[1] Cf. C. B. Malon, *Le Socialisme Intégral*, part ii, p. 150 (cited) *ib.*
[2] Cf. *Supra*, chap. xxvi, art. 1. [3] *Graves De Communi*, p. 176.

II. Those to whom alms are to be given include all who are in need, whether relatives or strangers, good or bad, friends or enemies : but when one cannot meet the needs of all a due order of preference should be observed. This order depends partly upon the closeness of one's connection with the person in need and partly upon the seriousness of the need itself.

We are not directly concerned here with the latter principle, which belongs rather to the domain of Ethics and Moral Theology, and we shall confine ourselves for the present to the former. The natural obligation of Almsgiving is a necessary corollary and corrective of the right of private ownership. From the exercise of that right the division of the human race into rich and poor—the " haves " and the " have nots "—will inevitably arise—" *The poor you have always with you.*"[1] What provision has the Creator made for the propertyless or the poor when remunerative work cannot be found, or is insufficient, or, owing to illness or other causes, is impossible ? The obligations of the State under Legal Justice (even though these obligations were fulfilled) do not fully meet the difficulty. In the ultimate resort no answer can be found, except that those who possess superfluous means are bound to share with those in need. The principle, which is fundamental in Christian teaching, that human ownership is only a stewardship, and that the possessor of superfluous goods is bound to administer them for the needs of others, as well as his own, is clearly implied in Sacred Scripture, and has always been upheld by the Church.

Sacred Scripture on Almsgiving.—The precept of Almsgiving is included in that of fraternal charity, as laid down by Our Divine Lord : " *Thou shalt love thy neighbour as thyself.*"[2]

" Love," says St. Thomas, " includes benevolence, by which one *wishes good* to the person that one loves. But wishes, if efficacious and real, result in action when the occasion arises. Hence, active beneficence towards others flows as a necessary consequence from one's love of them."[3]

The ideas of love, benevolence and beneficence (or service of others) are so closely connected with one another that

---

[1] *Matth.* xvi. 11.   [2] *Matth.* xxii. 39.   [3] 2a, 2æ, Q. 31, a. 1.

they cannot in practice be separated. Now, of all acts of service or beneficence, that of Almsgiving (where the person is in need of one's service) is clearly the most essential.[1] Hence, St. John writes : " *He that hath the substance of this world, and shall see his brother in need, and shall shut up his bowels from him ; how doth the charity of God abide in him* ? "[2]

Besides being essentially included in the general precept of fraternal charity, the duty of Almsgiving is directly inculcated again and again in the Old and New Testaments,[3] and that, too, so clearly and forcibly, that the serious nature of the obligation cannot be called in doubt, and even pertains to divine faith.[4] The neglect of this duty is the only reason assigned by Our Lord for the eternal punishment of the damned in the parable of the rich man who died and was buried in hell,[5] and still more clearly in the account of the Last Judgment.[6] Again, St. James writes : "*Judgment to him that hath not done mercy.*"[7]

The Fathers on Almsgiving.—The Fathers of the Church insist upon the grave duty of Almsgiving in the most uncompromising terms : St. Basil of Cæsarea lays down that the superfluous goods of the wealthy belong to the poor, and that the person who withholds them is a robber.

" Are you not then a miser and a robber, you who keep to yourself what you have received to share with others ? If he that steals a dress is called a thief, does that person merit any other name who, while able to clothe the poor without subjecting himself to real want, nevertheless allows them to go naked ? The bread that you keep to yourself, although not required for the needs of your family, belongs to the poor who are perishing of hunger.[8]

---

[1] *Ib.*, Q. 32, a. 1 (*corp.*). [2] 1 *John* iii. 17.
[3] The following are smoe Scriptural Texts on the duty of almsgiving : *Tobias* iv. 7–13 and 17, 18 ; *Eccles.* iv. 1–11 ; *Isaias* lviii. 7 and 10 ; *Matth.* xxv. 41–46 ; *Luke* x. 30–37 ; xi. 41, xii. 33, xvi. 19–30 ; *Acts* xv. 31–33 ; 2 *Cor.* viii and ix ; 1 *Tim.* vi. 17–19 ; *James* ii. 13.
[4] Cf. Suarez, *loc. cit.*, sec. i.
[5] *Luke* xvi. This is the interpretation usually given by the Fathers and the great mediæval theologians of the parable of Dives and Lazarus. Dives, namely, was condemned owing to his neglect of Almsgiving.
[6] *Matth.* xxv. 41–44. [7] *James* ii. 13.
[8] S. Basilii—*Ascetica—Sermo de Eleemosyna*, col. 1158 (Migne, *P.G.*).

St. Ambrose writes in a similar strain :

" Consider, you rich man, into what a furnace of fire you are plunged. It is you that speak these words ' *Father Abraham, bid Lazarus to dip the tip of his finger in water to cool my tongue.*'[1] . . . It is not from your own property that you contribute to the poor man's needs. You only restore him part of what already belongs to him. For you usurp for your own single use what has been given for the use of all. The earth belongs to all—not to the rich alone. But those that do not enjoy what really is theirs are fewer than those that do. Therefore [in giving alms] instead of giving what is not due you only repay a debt."[2]

Again, St. Augustine writes :

" What has the Scripture said ? ' *Judgment without mercy to him that hath not done mercy.*' Even though we retain only what is necessary, we have many things we can do without. . . . For the widow two mites were sufficient to enable her to do a work of mercy in order to buy the heavenly kingdom. . . . Find out how much God had given you, and from it take what you need ; the remainder which you do not require is needed by others. The superfluities of the rich are the necessities of the poor. Those who retain what is superfluous possess the goods of others."[3]

St. Gregory the Great, directing pastors and preachers how to deal with the different classes of the faithful, says that robbers and plunderers are not to be admonished in quite the same terms as the wealthy who, while abstaining from covetousness and plunder, omit to give alms. To the latter he directs the pastors to point out that :

" The earth from which they were made is the common property of all, and therefore produces nourishment for all in common. It is vain for a man to regard himself as innocent while he usurps for his own use the gifts of God, which belong in common to all. Those who do not distribute what they have received are wading in the life blood of their brethren. Every day they murder as many of the poor, who are dying of hunger, as might be saved by the means which they keep to themselves. For when we distribute to the poor whatever they need, we are not giving what belongs to us; we merely pay them back

---

[1] *Luke* xvi. 24.
[2] S. Ambrosii—*Opera Omnia*, tom. i, par. 580. De Nabute (Migne, *P.L.*).
[3] August—*Opera Omnia*, tom. v (Enarrat. in *Psalm* cxlvii), col. 1922 (Migne, *P.L.*, vol. 37).

their own. We are paying a debt of justice rather than fulfilling a work of mercy."[1]

From the many passages of St. Jerome's writings that bear on the same subject we select the following. St. Jerome is writing from his home near Bethlehem to Hedibias, a wealthy matron of western Gaul, who had applied to him for direction. Hedibias was a widow and was childless. Of the twelve parts or chapters into which Jerome's letter is divided, the first is taken up wholly with the question of alms. Here are a few extracts :

" The Saviour did not say, ' Give to your children, or to your brother or to your relatives,' but ' *Give to the poor!* . . . That is, give to Christ, who is fed in the persons of the poor, who when He was rich became poor for our sakes, and who speaks in the thirty-ninth Psalm, ' *I am a beggar, and a poor man.* . . .' The Lord says, ' *How hard it is for a rich man to enter into the Kingdom of Heaven* ' (Matth. xix. 13). He did not say *impossible*, but *hard*, although the illustration He gives suggests impossibility, viz., ' *It is easier for a camel to pass through a needle's eye than for a rich man to enter the Kingdom of Heaven.*' Now, this is impossible rather than difficult.[2] . . . ' *He who has two coats let him give one to the person that has not* ' (Luke iii. 11). . . . As much as can suffice for our bodily weakness, seeing that nature has sent us naked into the world, that is to be understood as *one coat* ; and whatever is required for our immediate wants, that is called *the food of one day*. Hence, we are told, ' *Take not thought of the morrow* ' (Matth. vi. 13), that is of the future. The Apostle also says : ' *Having food and raiment, with these let us be content* (1 Tim. vi. 8). If you have more than you need for food and clothing, give it in alms, and know that you are bound to do so. . . . How a widow ought to live is summarized by the Apostle, when he says, ' *A widow that lives in luxury is dead while she is alive.* ' " (1 Tim. v. 6).[3]

Such extracts might be multiplied, for nearly all the Fathers, including Tertullian, treat of the Christian duty

---

[1] S. Gregorii Magni—*Reg. Pastor*, cap. xxi, p. 66 (Migne, *P.L.*, vol. 77).

[2] St. Clement of Alexandria (*circ.* A.D. 200), in his well-known treatise *Quis Dives Salvetur*, discusses and explains the sense in which riches constitute an immediate danger to salvation : " Wealth should not be cast away imprudently, seeing that it can prove useful to one's neighbour. . . . Wealth is an instrument. If you use it under the guidance of justice and reason, it will assist you in fulfilling your duties. If you reject this guidance, it becomes an instrument of wickedness."—Clem. Alex—*Opera, Quis Dives Salvetur*, cap. xiv (Migne, *P.G.*, vol. ix, col. 618).

[3] S. Hieronymi—*Opera*, tom. i, col. 983–986 (Migne, *P.L.*, vol. 22).

of Almsgiving ; and all, both the Greek and the Latin
Fathers, write in the same strain. Several of the Fathers,
including St. Cyprian of Carthage, St. Gregory of Nyssa,
St. Gregory Nazianzen, St. Ephrem, St. Leo the Great, have
special treatises on the subject.

Reasons for Their Uncompromising Attitude.—The universal corruption which then prevailed in public life, the
extravagance and oppression of the officials, the grinding
usury of the capitalist money-lenders, combined with the
frequent wars caused by the barbarian inroads, had produced in the Roman Empire widespread wretchedness and
poverty, probably not unlike what similar causes have
produced in so many countries to-day. This partially
explains the continued insistence of the Fathers of these
centuries (the third to the sixth) on the duty of Almsgiving.

As the Fathers were intent upon emphasising the obligations of the rich, and do not profess to speak with scientific
exactitude, passages, such as those quoted, will not prove
conclusively, as at first sight they would seem to do, that
the rich were bound not merely in Charity, but in strict
justice to contribute their superfluous goods to the poor ;
much less do they prove that the Fathers favoured communism. But they do make clear the attitude of the
Fathers and of the early Church on the nature of ownership,
and the grave obligations which ownership implies of sharing
with the poor what one does not require for one's own
reasonable needs. Whether the duty is to be classed under
the heading of Justice or of Charity is a matter of secondary
importance, which it was outside their scope to determine.

The Theologians on Almsgiving.—The teaching of St.
Thomas and the great Catholic theologians on the duty of
Almsgiving is in harmony with that of the early Fathers.[1]
Their doctrine is briefly this : The material goods of the
earth are, by the natural law, meant primarily to supply
the needs of all.[2] On the other hand, the ownership of
these goods by individuals is in practice necessary for the
proper conduct of human life.[3] In order to reconcile these
two principles, St. Thomas, who is followed by all the great

---

[1] Cf. *Supra*, chap. vi, art. 1 ; chap. xvii, art. 3.
[2] St. Thomas, 2a, 2æ, Q. 66, a. 7.   [3] *Ib.*, a. 2.

mediæval and 17th century theologians, draws the celebrated distinction between the *dominion* of property and *its use*.

" Two things may belong to a person in regard to material goods : one is the power of procuring [or exploiting] and distributing them [viz., the dominion or ownership] and, in as far as that power goes, a man may possess things as his own. . . . The other thing, that may belong to one in regard to material goods, is the *use* of them ; and, as far as that is concerned, a man must not possess things as his own, but as common to all, so that, namely, he is ready to share them with others that need them."[1]

From the principles here laid down, the duty of sharing with others what one can reasonably spare is an obvious conclusion. It follows also that the duty is in the highest degree serious, and is closely connected with the right of ownership. The fundamental principle underlying the teaching of St. Thomas and that of other great mediæval writers on such questions as justice, theft, alms, etc., is that the goods of the earth are meant by Providence for the support of all men, and hence, no human institution, such as the actual division of property, can lawfully contravene that primal decree.[2] Consequently, the exercise of ownership must be so limited and hedged round by safeguards, that it does not shut out anyone from a fair opportunity of supporting himself and his dependents upon the earth's bounty. Thus, to the current argument against the strict obligation of giving alms, namely, " One may use one's own or keep it to one's self," St. Thomas replies :

" The temporal goods, which Providence gives, belong to one as regards ownership ; but as regards their use they belong not to one's self alone, but also to others who can be supported from what one does not need for one's own use."[3]

And he quotes the words of St. Ambrose :

" Feed him that is perishing of hunger ; if you fail to do so you are guilty of his death."[4]

---

[1] *Ib.*
[2] Cf. St. Thomas—Cajetan, Sylvius, Banes, Suarez, Lugo, Billuart, *loc. cit.* and *passim.*
[3] 2a, 2,æ Q. 32, a. 5.
[4] *Ib.*, Q. 66, a. 7 ; cf. also *Quodlibeta* viii, a. 8.

Again, discussing the question as to how far a needy person is justified in appropriating the property of another, St. Thomas writes :

" Human institutions cannot contravene the natural or divine law. Now, according to the law of nature, instituted by Divine Providence, the goods of the earth are designed to supply the needs of men ; and hence, the division of goods and their appropriation by individuals which result from men's arrangement, must be of such a nature as not to contravene this purpose. Consequently, the goods which a man does not require for his own needs are due, by the natural law, for the sustenance of the poor."

And he again quotes with approval the words of St. Ambrose :

" The bread which you retain belongs to the hungry, the dress that you lock up is the property of the naked, and the money which you hide in the earth is due for the redemption and freedom of the wretched."

Finally, he adds these pregnant words :

" The apportioning of one's goods to the particular needs of the individuals in want of them is usually to be left to the discretion of the owner. If, however, the need be evidently urgent, . . . in such case a person may relieve it by seizing another's property, either openly or secretly."[1]

From this and other passages we gather the exact meaning of St. Thomas's principle that the use of, or revenues from, superfluous goods is *due* to the needy. The owner's obligation of giving them is not one of *strict* justice, except in case of extreme or quasi-extreme (*evidens et urgens*) need, seeing that it is only in such a case that he allows the needy person to seize the goods without the owner's permission. But the lawful exercise of the owner's rights over his own superfluous goods in the face of the needs of others is limited to his right of deciding as to what particular needy person or class of persons he will assign them. It is in fact by explaining in this sense the strong expressions of the Fathers that he saves the latter from the imputation of communism.

" When St. Ambrose says, speaking of the material goods of the earth : ' *Let no man call his own what is the property of all,*'

---

[1] 2a, 2æ, Q. 66, a. 7 ; cf. also *Quodlibeta*, viii, a. 12.

he condemns only personal appropriation as regards the use of superfluous goods; for he adds: '*What is superfluous for one's needs is to be regarded as plunder* [if one retains it for oneself].' "[1]

Leo XIII on Almsgiving.—The doctrine of the Fathers and the great theologians on the duty of Almsgiving and the limitations to the lawful exercise of private ownership, is confirmed by the teaching of Leo XIII, who writes:

" Nor does she [viz., the Church] omit solicitude for the poor, or fail to provide for their needs; . . . nay, . . . she takes thought to have erected in every land in their behalf homes and refuges, where they can be received, nurtured, and tended, and takes these charitable foundations under her protecting care. . . . Moreover, she lays the rich under strict command to give their superfluous means to the poor,[2] impressing them with the fear of divine Judgment which will exact the penalty of eternal punishment unless they succour the wants of the needy."[3]

Again, speaking of the rights and duties of ownership, he says:

" If the question be asked, ' How must one's possessions be used ? ' the Church replies without hesitation in the words of the same holy Doctor : ' Man should not consider his outward possessions as his own, but as common to all, so as to share them without hesitation when others are in need.' Hence, the Apostle saith ' *Command the rich to apportion largely.*' True, no one is commanded to distribute to others that which is required for his own needs and those of his household ; nor even to give away what is reasonably required to keep up becomingly his condition in life. ' For no one ought to love otherwise than becomingly ' (St. Thomas, 2ᵃ, 2ᵃᵉ, Q. 32, a. 6). But when all that necessity demands has been supplied, and one's standing fairly taken thought of, it becomes a duty to give to the indigent out of what remains over. ' *Of that which remaineth give alms* ' (Luke xi. 41). It is a duty not of justice (save in extreme cases), but of Christian Charity—a duty not enforced by human law.

[1] *Ib.*, Q. 66, a. 2 ad 3.
[2] *Ut quod superest pauperibus tribuant*, literally, " that they should give to the poor what remains over." In the translation, as given in *The Pope and The People*, " to give of their superfluities to the poor," the limiting preposition *of* is inserted, which does not seem to be contained or necessarily implied in the Latin text.
[3] *Quod Apostolici Muneris*, pp. 19, 20.

But the laws and judgments of men must give place to the laws and judgments of Christ—the true God."[1]

Art. 3—*The Church's Practice and Discipline*

In the matter of Almsgiving and kindness to the poor the Church's tradition has been uniform and unbroken. For almost two thousand years she has always regarded the relieving of distress as a portion of her essential functions. The duty was regarded as an essential one, even in the Old Law ; but has been enforced more clearly and strongly under the Christian dispensation.

Almsgiving Among the Jews.—According to the Old Testament law no unrelieved poverty was allowed to exist among the Jews. "*There shall be no poor or beggar among you,*"[2] and again : "*There will not be wanting poor in the land of thy habitation ; therefore, I command thee to open thy hand to thy needy and poor brother that liveth in the land.*"[3] Widows, orphans, the blind and the lame, received special assistance. The poor had many legal privileges. Thus, they had a right to the gleanings of the cornfields.[4] The spontaneous growth of the land every seventh year (when by Jewish law the land had to lie fallow) was the property of the poor.[5] On the same occasion, the Jew who had been compelled to sell himself into slavery was released ; and his master had to provide him with a homestead.[6]

---

[1] *Rerum Novarum*, p. 145. The translation in *The Pope and The People* of the words of the original text *Officium est de eo quod superest gratificari indigentibus* (" it is a duty to give to the indigent *out of* what remains over ") is literal. Whether it is an accurate rendering of the sense is disputed. It is maintained by some such as Bouquillon (*De Virtutibus Theologicis*, pp. 332–348, referred to by Dr. Ryan) and by Dr. Ryan (*op. cit.*, pp. 309, 310) that the text does not mean (as the translation " *out of* what remains over " suggests) " to give some of what remains to the indigent " : but rather " to assist the indigent *out of* what remains over," implying that the duty of assisting the indigent continues as long as there are superfluous goods to draw from. The French translation given in the edition of the works of Leo XIII, published by " La Bonne Presse " of Paris (" C'est un devior de verser le superflu dans le sein des pauveres ") is in accordance with this latter view (Cf. *Actes de Leon XIII*, vol. iii, p. 37), which is also borne out by the parallel passage from *Quod Apostolici Muneris* quoted above.

[2] *Deut*. xv. 4.

[3] *Ib*. xv. 11 ; cf. also *Exod*. xxxviii. 5–9 ; *Deut*. xxii. 1–4.

[4] *Lev*. xix. 9, 10 ; *Deut*. xxix. 19–21.

[5] *Exod*. xxiii. 11 ; *Lev*. xxv. 4, 5.

[6] *Lev*. xxv. 47–53 ; *Deut*. xv. 12–15.

Jewish workmen had to be paid daily.[1] No interest on borrowed money could be charged to Jews.

These laws were generally well observed, at least while the people remained faithful. Hence, as a rule, the only type of poverty to be found among the Jews of those times was such as arose from accidental causes, and was what is usually designated as ordinary or common poverty. The poor consisted mostly of orphans, widows, the infirm, the lazy, the stupid, etc., and every Jew was bound to come to the relief of his fellow-Jew who had thus become the victim of distress.[2] The Jewish duties of charity, however, in so far as they were enforced by positive law, referred solely to fellow-Jews.[3]

Changes Wrought by Christianity.—The Jewish Church was essentially national, and outsiders were not regarded as brethren. Under the Christian dispensation such barriers are removed, and the Christian must regard everyone as his neighbour, and assist every child of God as one of his brethren, although those bound to one by closer ties have the prior claim. No history can be more inspiring than that of the Charity of the Catholic Church.[4]

Charity of the Early Christians.—The Charity of the Christians of the early ages surpassed anything the world has witnessed before or since. The duty of providing for the poorer brethren, so strongly emphasised by the New Testament writers, was definitely recognised and insisted upon. It was a universal rule for those who had wealth to divide it among the needy brethren, and alms were constantly sent for distribution among the poor even of far distant places. " *Their possessions and goods they sold and divided them to all according as everyone had need.*"[5] And again : " *Neither did anyone say that aught of the things he had was his own, but all things were common unto them. . . . Neither was there anyone needy among them.*"[6]

This custom of providing for the wants of all the needy

---

[1] *Lev.* xix. 13. [2] *Ib.*, xv. 10, 11.
[3] Cf. Vigouroux—*Dict. de la Bible*, art. " Pauvres " (Paris, 1908).
[4] Dr. Ryan's excellent article on " Charity " in the *Catholic Encyclopedia* (12 pp.) is taken up mainly with this history.
[5] *Acts* ii. 45. [6] *Ib.*, iv. 32–34.

36

brethren was the occasion of the first appointment of deacons in the early Church.[1]

The Christians of the generations immediately following, and of the early centuries of the Church, maintained the same tradition. Thus, in the *Didache* or *Teaching of the Twelve Apostles*, drawn up probably about A.D. 70, and purporting to contain a summary of the duties of Christian life, no obligation is more strongly emphasised than that of Almsgiving. Thus we read :

" Do not hesitate to give, nor murmur when thou dost so. Thou shalt not turn away from him that is in need, but shalt share all things with thy brother, and shalt not say that they are thine own, for if ye are sharers in that which is everlasting, how much more in those things that are perishable."[2]

In the *Pastor of Hermas* also, a document belonging to about a century later, the obligation of Almsgiving as an essential Christian duty is very strongly insisted on.[3]

Second to Fifth Centuries.—The *Apostolic Constitutions*, which belong to the 3rd or 4th century, are full of the same doctrine ; and the Fourth Book is entirely devoted to Almsgiving. The care of the poor was in a special way a portion of the functions of the Bishop whose duty, according to these Constitutions, it is to exhibit :

" To the orphans the care of parents ; to the widows the care of husbands . . . to procure work for the artificer, to provide food for the hungry, drink for the thirsty and clothing for the naked, to visit the sick, assist the prisoners."[4]

We find the clearest evidence of the same tradition (viz., that the Christians regarded it as a strict duty to provide for the poorer brethren) in the Canons of several of the early Councils. Thus, it is provided in a 5th-century decree that in every town a special officer be appointed by the ecclesiastical authorities who would live near the church, or in the

---

[1] *Acts* vi. 1–6.
[2] Cf. *The Didache* in *Patres Apostolici*, vol. i, p. 51 (Bibliotheca S.S. Patrum, Romæ, 1901).
[3] *Ib.*, vol. v, p. 189.
[4] *The Apostolical Constitutions*, bk. iv, chap. ii, p. 108 (Ante-Nicene Christian Library, vol. xvii, p. 262, Edinburgh, 1870).

public hospital, and whose special function would be to see
to the wants of the poor, the suffering, and the prisoners.[1]
In the Council of Gangra (*circ.* A.D. 350) those are anathematised who ridicule the custom of inviting the poor to
the houses of the rich.[2] Again, in the *Statutes of the Ancient
Church*, which are often cited as the Canons of a (pseudo)
Fourth Council of Carthage, and which belong, probably,
to the 4th century, the 83rd Canon orders that " in the
Church, the poor, and the aged are to be honoured more
than the others."[3]

Fifth to Eighth Centuries.—When the freedom of the
Church was declared (A.D. 315) by the decrees of
Constantine, its property gradually accumulated as a result
of grants and bequests which were made in its favour by
the Emperor and other wealthy Christian proprietors.
Towards the end of the 6th century (namely, under Gregory
the Great), the total area of the Church lands in Italy,
Africa, Gaul, Dalmatia, etc., was probably little less than
20,000 square miles. The Church possessions were generally
referred to as the "Patrimony of the Poor."

" Your duty," writes Gregory to the administrators of the
Church's property, " is to be our agents, and to pay less attention
to the material gain of the Church than to the relief and
amelioration of misery."[4]

The Church revenues were usually divided into four
parts. Of these one remained under the personal administration of the Bishop, one went to the support of the
clergy, a third was devoted to the maintenance of public
worship, Church buildings, etc., and a fourth was set apart
for the relief of the poor. But the clergy were bound,
besides, to distribute to the poor what could be spared from
their own share ; and in time of distress Bishops did not

---

[1] This is provided for in the 80th decree of the Arabic version of the
Canons of the Council of Nicæa (A.D. 325). *See* Harduin—*Acta Concili-
orum*, vol. i, col. 478. Cf. also Hefelé—*Histoire des Conciles*, tom. i,
Prèmière Partie. Liv. ii, chap. ii, sec. 42, pp. 503–528.
[2] *Can.* ii. Cf. Hefelé, *op. cit.*, tom. i, 2ième, Partie, p. 1037.
[3] *Ib.*, tom. ii, 1ère Partie, p. 119.
[4] *Epist.*, lib. i, n. 36, col. 490, 491 (Migne, *P.L.*, vol. 77) ; cf. also Lecky—
Rationalism in Europe, vol. ii, pp. 243 ff, for striking testimony borne by a
rationalist in regard to the charity of the Church (See *Supra*, chap. iii,
art. 5).

hesitate to sell even the sacred vessels in order to provide relief for the sufferers.[1] In the decrees of the provincial Councils of these centuries, the subject of Almsgiving constantly occurs. Now and then we find decrees ordering the clergy to visit the prisons, and supply the prisoners' wants out of the funds of the Church.

In the Mediæval Times.—In the 8th century and after, when Christian life became concentrated round the monasteries, the main work of relieving the poor mostly passed on to the monks and the nuns. It was principally they who fed the hungry, reared the orphans, cared for the sick, and afforded refuge and consolations to the wretched and miserable. At the monastic schools, rich and poor were treated alike. Besides the monasteries, the Mediæval Guilds also had the responsibility of caring for all their own needy members and for the families and dependents of their deceased associates.[2] Even the municipalities of the free cities and towns also took a leading part under the inspiration and guidance of the diocesan clergy in relieving the poor, the helpless, and the stranger, while in the country districts the feudal lords recognised their duty of attending to the wants of all the people of their manorial estates. Usury, too, was kept in check. Later on the *Montes Pietatis* were established, mostly by the Franciscan Friars, in order to enable the poor who needed money to borrow it at practically a nominal interest.

Modern Times.—As a result of all these agencies, there was usually no unrelieved poverty either in city or country while the influence of the Catholic Church was predominant :

" The spectre of the modern proletariat wretched, debased, with no definite place in the social organism, and no definitely recognised claim upon any group or institution, had no counterpart in the municipal life of the Middle Ages."[3]

The degrading poverty which now prevails among large sections of the people, began after, and was partly the result

---

[1] Cf. Sozom—*Hist. Eccl.* iv. 25, and *passim.* Cf. also Socrates—*Hist. Eccl.* vii. 25 and *passim* (Select Library of the Nicene and Post-Nicene Fathers, Oxford, 1891).

[2] Cf. Gasquet—*Eve of the Reformation*, chap. xi ; Husselein—*Democratic Industry* ; Ashley—*English Economic History*, vol. i, p. 1, cap. ii, and vol. i, p. 2, cap. 1 and 2.

[3] Dr. Ryan—*Cath. Encyclop.*, " Charity," p. 599.

of, the plunder of the Church in the 16th century, and the transference of the *Patrimony of the Poor* to the capitalist proprietors.[1]

Down to our own day, however, the practice of Almsgiving occupies the same place as ever in the life of the Church.[2] Under the charge of the Church there are institutions for the relief of well-nigh every type of human suffering—hospitals, reformatories, and asylums of all kinds, and to-day as ever the faithful are taught that their generosity in Almsgiving is the surest index of the reality and thoroughness of their Christian Faith.

Art. 4—*Practical Application of the Church's Teaching*[3]

One's obligation to assist others is measured in practice by two things, namely, the urgency of their needs and the extent of one's ability to relieve them.

Nature and Extent of Poverty.—The different degrees of human needs are illustrated in the following passage of Suarez :

" The needs of one's neighbour may be of three different kinds. The first is called *common* (or ordinary) need, such as exists in the case of the ordinary poor. The second is *grave* need, as when a person is in such straits that he cannot, without assistance, escape from a serious injury to his spiritual interests or his reputation or property. The third is *extreme* need, which in this connection usually refers to an evident peril to one's life, or to the danger of losing a limb, or being deprived of one's reason, or of losing completely one's reputation or property."[4]

It is apparently to the ordinary poor our Divine Lord specially refers in the oft-quoted passage : *The poor you*

---

[1] Before this robbery of the Church took place the ecclesiastical bodies controlled probably almost one-fourth of the whole wealth of England and Scotland, and possibly the same proportion in Ireland. The surplus revenues of this property were mostly used in the service of the poor and in education.

[2] Cf. Plater—*Catholics and Social Action* (C. T. S. edit.).

[3] In addition to works already referred to in article 2. Cf. Parkinson, *op. cit.*, part iv, " Poverty " ; Garriguet, *op. cit.*, chap. lx ; B. S. Rowntree—*Poverty: A Study of Town Life* (Macmillan, London, 1902, 4th edit.), chaps. lv and lx ; Smith—*Dict. of Christian Antiquities,* " Alms," " Poverty," " Pauperism."

[4] *Loc. cit.*, sec. i, n. 4 ; cf. also St. Thomas, 2ª, 2ᵃᵉ, Q. 32, a. 6. St. Thomas does not distinguish clearly between *grave* and *extreme* need.

have always with you.[1] The ordinary poor are not devoid
of the necessaries of life, namely, sufficient food, clothing
and shelter, but they find it difficult to obtain them, and
as a result of their poverty are exposed to constant suffering
and inconvenience. Even in normal circumstances ordinary
poverty is very widespread in Great Britain, Ireland and
U.S.A., while grave, and even quasi-extreme, want are all
too common. These conditions have been much intensified
in recent years owing to the unprecedented extension of
unemployment, which at present (1931) affects directly
some 10,000,000 or more workers in the countries just
referred to, without computing their dependents, who have
to suffer owing to the failure of the family income. Again,
large masses of the population of the Irish cities and towns,
and even a considerable percentage of the rural population,
especially in the Gaedhealtacht, normally live in a state of
grave or semi-grave and sometimes even of extreme want.[2]

Superfluous Goods.—One's ability, and consequently one's
obligations to relieve the wants of others depend upon the
possession of *superfluous* goods. For no one is bound
(except, perhaps, in very rare and exceptional cases in which
the public good or the defence of religion is intimately

---

[1] *Matth.* xxvi. 18.

[2] S. Rowntree (*op. cit.*) gives the results of an exhaustive investigation,
which he made about the year 1906, into the conditions of the poorer
classes in the city of York. He had chosen that city " as being fairly
representative of the conditions then existing in many, if not in most, of
the provincial towns of Britain " (Introduction, p. viii). By poverty he
means an absence of the conditions in food, clothing and housing, which
secure the " minimum necessary for the maintenance of merely physical
health " without taking any account of what may be " needful for the
development of the mental, moral and social side of human nature "
(chap. iv, p. 87). In other words, he applies the term poverty to what
Catholic theologians describe as *grave* need. The results of his investiga-
tions go to show that out of a total population of 75,812 persons, which
the city then contained, 20,362 persons (viz., 43.4 per cent. of the wage-
earning class, or 26.85 per cent. of the whole population) were living in
permanent want, more or less grave, of the very necessaries of life
(pp. 117, also 133–137). The writer touches upon some of the effects
produced by these dreadful conditions upon the physical life of the people,
" the high death-rate among the poor, the terribly high infant mortality,
the stunted stature and the dulled intelligence." In Ireland the emigration, the dwindling population, the extraordinarily low marriage rate,
the bad housing conditions in the cities and the high rate of infant
mortality, all point to a degree of poverty among the masses of the people
which is probably much worse than that which existed in the English
cities when Rowntree wrote. See *infra*, Appendix III.

concerned) to give to others what is needed to supply the necessaries of life for one's self and dependents.

In relation to men's needs, moralists distinguish three classes of goods—viz., *necessaries of life, conventional necessaries*, and what is simply *superfluous*. The first type includes sufficient food, clothing and shelter for one's self and one's dependents. The second class (viz., conventional necessaries) is described by St. Thomas as

" those goods which are needed to enable one's self and one's dependents to live becomingly in accordance with one's state and condition of life."[1]

Hence, goods of that class are superfluous in relation to the necessaries of life, but relatively necessary for that person's reasonable expenses. Completely superfluous goods are those which are over and above what can be considered reasonably necessary, even for the becoming maintenance of the individual or family to whom they belong.

Obligations of Almsgiving.—No one is bound, in order to relieve the *ordinary* need of others, to deprive himself or his dependents of the necessaries of life, or even of conventional necessaries. On the other hand, one is certainly bound to relieve the extreme or quasi-extreme needs of others, not only at the cost of sacrificing one's superfluous goods, if one have such, but even to the extent of foregoing for the purpose, at least within reasonable limits, what may be required to meet the needs of one's state in life. The like is true, although not to the same extent, nor under equally strict obligations, when there is a question of the grave need of one's neighbour. Finally, theologians usually lay down that one is bound even under sin to do one's share in proportion to one's means in relieving ordinary poverty.

Case of Extreme Need.—The obligation of relieving extreme need includes a duty of Justice as well as Charity.[2] For in *extreme* need the rights of individual ownership no longer hold, in so far as they may prevent a person in extreme need from obtaining what he requires to meet it.

---

[1] 2a, 2ae, Q. 32, a. 6 (*corp.*).
[2] Cf. Leo XIII—*Rerum Novarum*, p. 145.

" When one's neighbour is in extreme need," says St. Thomas,
" all things become common as far as he is concerned. Hence
he would not commit sin even by seizing them violently or
stealing them."[1]

This principle is not recognised at least explicitly in
British law in the application of which an exaggerated and
false view of private ownership is assumed. Thus, instances are quoted in which some of the starving poor were
hanged for the so-called offence of " stealing " in order to
avert starvation.[2] Again, in the middle of the 19th century
in Ireland millions were forced to starve within sight of
rich cornfields and herds of fat cattle, more than sufficient
to supply their wants. This implied a legalised violation
of Commutative Justice. No positive law can validly override the law of nature, according to which everyone has
an inalienable right to take what is required for his *essential*
needs.

Limits to Conventional Needs.—The following proposition
was condemned by Pope Innocent XI in 1679 :

" It is scarcely possible to find among laymen, even among
kings, goods that are superfluous to one's state. Therefore,
hardly anyone is bound to give alms on the score of possessing
such goods."

The condemned proposition is little more than the assertion
of a theory of life which is in accordance with the materialistic spirit of the present day. " Those who acquire," writes
Dr. Ryan, " a surplus over their present absolute and conventional needs generally devote it to an expansion of their
social position. They move into larger and more expensive
houses, thereby increasing their requirements, not merely
in the matter of housing, but as regards food, clothing,
amusements, and the conventions of the group with which
they are affiliated. . . . It is commonly assumed that life
to be worth while must include the indefinite growth and
variation in the means of satisfying them."[3] Most of these

---

[1] In IV, d. 15, Q. 2, a. 1 ; Q. 4, ad 2um. Cf. also 2a, 2æ, Q. 66, a. 7, ad 2um.

[2] Cf. Dickens in the Preface to *Barnaby Rudge*, where the pathetic story
is told of the execution (for attempted theft) of Mary Jones at Tyburn
about the year 1770. She was a young mother with infant children, whose
husband had been forcibly conscripted for the navy. She and her children
were starving.

[3] *Op. cit.*, p. 315.

increased wants and enjoyments refer to the gratification of the senses. The Christian view of life is quite opposed to this doctrine of materialism. Hence, a limit should be fixed beyond which no Christian and no Christian family could go in catering for their so-called conventional needs. The limits will, of course, vary with the reasonable habits and social standing of the particular persons. But the maximum limit is probably below what is nowadays not infrequently assumed even by practical Catholics to be not extravagant. Dr. Ryan would place it between £1,000 and £2,000 a year, even for the wealthier classes in U.S.A.,[1] where the normal standard of living is much higher than in Ireland, as the well-to-do classes are in fact much wealthier.

Different Forms of Almsgiving.—Almsgiving, properly so-called, is of two kinds—viz., *Individual* or *Occasional* and *Organised* or *Permanent*. The former, in which a person helps or relieves the individual who begs his assistance, or with whom he has some personal relations, is always necessary, even in the best organised social conditions. For there will always exist special needs which no organisation can reach, and which individual charity alone can effectually relieve. Individual or Occasional Almsgiving will not, however, suffice. It is of its nature uncertain and transitory, and can reach only an inconsiderable fraction of existing needs. Besides, it usually only deals with distress that actually exists, and does not attack the evil in the root by prevention. Hence it is, that the organisation of charitable effort is so important. The bulk of one's Almsgiving will usually be best devoted to the foundation and upkeep of some of the numberless charitable institutions which tend to multiply in every Catholic country under the patronage and direction of the Church : schools, hospitals, homes for the aged and poor, and for the mentally or physically incapable, asylums and hostels for widows and for girls out of employment, savings banks and insurance societies.

Again, moralists and economists of all schools agree on the principle that the most recommendable form of assistance for the distressed is that given through the medium

---

[1] *Ib.*, pp. 317, 318.

of work or employment.   When the needy person is capable of work, employment ensuring a suitable wage saves him from the dangers of idleness, and safeguards his self-respect by enabling him to gain his livelihood by his own efforts.

The State and Poor Relief.—Although the duties of the State in regard to the poor come under the virtue, not of Charity, but of Legal Justice, a few points regarding such duties may be mentioned here. As the legitimate functions of the State in social life are essentially supplementary, they have place only where private effort fails, or is manifestly inadequate.   Thus, it would be an act of unlawful usurpation for the State to attempt to supplant private charity, as is being attempted under the existing unchristian régime in France.   The normal duties of the State in regard to the poor are :

(*a*) To eliminate, as far as possible, by wise laws and a just administration, the radical causes of excessive poverty.

(*b*) To protect and encourage private effort on behalf of the poor.

(*c*) To supplement the same as far as is found necessary, especially by subsidising and assisting religious and charitable organisations.

In modern times, however, and especially in Britain, Ireland, and the United States of America, as well as in some continental countries, such as France, Prussia and Saxony, in which the principles of unchristian Liberalism specially prevail, poverty and destitution have reached dimensions far beyond the power of private charity to cope with ; and direct action on the part of the State is needed. This is in accordance with the principle laid down by Leo XIII :

" Whenever the general interest or any particular class suffers, or is threatened with mischief, which in no other way can be met or prevented, the public authority must step in to deal with it."[1]

We are familiar with several forms of State intervention for the relief of poverty, which are more or less useful and successful.   Among these are : the Old Age Pensions, Out-

---

[1] *Rerum Novarum*, p. 155.

door Relief, Health Insurance, Public Hospitals, Asylums for the Mentally Affected, Orphanages and Industrial Schools.

It is generally admitted that the *direct* relief of poverty from State resources (as distinguished from remedial or preventative measures, and from State help for private charitable organisations) should, as a rule, be confined to cases of destitution, namely, want of the necessaries of life, or of serious illness. Hence, the main efforts of the State should be directed to such remedial measures as would place within the reach of all a fair opportunity of realising a becoming livelihood by their own labour, and thus eliminate preventable misery.

The Christian Attitude in Poor Relief.—Any element in poor relief, whether public or private, which tends to humiliate the poor or otherwise runs counter to natural right and personal dignity, is foredoomed to failure. A classical example of this is the English (and Irish) poorhouse system, already referred to.[1] Whatever may be said of the general character of the English poor laws and the extent to which regulations which are apparently harsh may be needed to prevent abuse, it is certain that the system in its actual working had a humiliating and degrading effect on the poor owing to the absence of religion and a spirit of true Christian charity in its administration.

The unnatural and humiliating conditions even still required in order to secure a place in an orphanage for a destitute child, namely, that the child should be convicted of some legal offence, such as begging, is indefensible for similar reasons. The tendency of Christian charity is to encourage hopefulness, and foster self-reliance and self-respect in those who, for the time being, have been worsted in the race of life.

Private Efforts Better than State Relief.—As a general rule, the less the State intervenes in the actual management and administration of charitable as well as educational enterprises the better for all parties concerned. In the case of direct State management it is well known that the

---

[1] Cf. *Supra*, chap, viii, art. 4.

administrative expenses usually absorb an excessive proportion of the resources, and the actual results obtained are
mostly inadequate and unsatisfactory.   Besides, under a
secular administration, the poor are unfairly humiliated
and embittered, and the element of religious and supernatural love, which constitutes the soul of charity, is too
often wanting.   Above all, secular officials are usually un-
suited to the task of healing the moral ills and miseries which
so often accompany or are the results of destitution.   None
but the respresentatives of Him who was " the Father of
the Poor " and the " Friend of Publicans and Sinners "
can influence for good the seared and embittered heart of
the wretched.   Hence, in a Catholic country, where religious
bodies are willing and able to undertake the management
of all manner of charitable institutions, governments will
be well advised to entrust to these bodies the administration
of the greater part of the public funds set apart for the
different forms of poor relief.   The public money will thus
be spent to better advantage, and the work will be incomparably better done.   In this way the taxpayer's burden will
be lightened, and the poor at the same time better provided
for.

CHAPTER XXVIII

PATRIOTISM[1]

Art. 1—*Introductory*

Relations of Patriotism to Justice and Charity.—We have said that while Justice is the main element in well-ordered civic life, it has to be supplemented by other forces, of which Charity and Patriotism are the chief. Patriotism fulfils a function in the social organism not unlike what we have already ascribed to Charity. Within its own sphere it supplements Justice, facilitating and perfecting the activities of the latter, and constantly urging one on to acts of benevolence and self-sacrifice far beyond the limits of what Justice or any other virtue could impose under strict obligation. Patriotism, however, is much more restricted than Charity in the range of objects to which it refers, bearing somewhat the same relation to Legal and Distributive Justice as Charity does to Commutative Justice. For while Charity includes within its scope one's relations to all men, as Commutative Justice does, Patriotism, like Legal and Distributive Justice, refers to one's fellow-countrymen alone ; and just as these latter virtues, having to do only with men's civic relations, are not quite so essential for the well-being of society as Commutative Justice, which regulates all of men's dealings with one another, so also Patriotism is not so fundamental or far-reaching in its influence upon man's social life as Charity, which is the Queen of the Virtues. This is probably one of the reasons why St. Thomas and the other great Catholic theologians, while laying down clearly enough the principles which

---

[1] Cf. St. Thomas, 1a, Q. 60, a. 5 ; 2a, 2æ, Q. 80, a. 1 ; Q. 101, a. 1 and 3 ; Q. 31, a. 3 (*corp.*) ; Q. 26, a. 3 (*corp.*) ; *Quodlibeta*, i, a. 8 (*corp.*) ; Abbé Paulin Giloteaux—*Patriosme et Internationalisme* (Tequi, Paris, 1927) ; Taparelli—*Droit Naturel* (translated from the Italian), liv. 4, chap. iv, sec. 3 ; Chateaubriand—*Genie du Christianisme*, liv. 5, chap. xiv ; K. Digby —*Mores Catholici* or *Ages of Faith*, vol. iii, chap. ix ; Koch-Preuss—*Handbook of Moral Theology*, vol. v, part ii, chap. iii ; Godts—*Scopuli Vitandi*, chap. xxviii ; Ryan—*The State and the Church*, chaps. xiii and xvii.

underlie the virtues of Legal and Distributive Justice and of Patriotism, do not treat these virtues with the same fulness of detail as Charity and Commutative Justice receive.

Its Special Importance at the Present Day.—Nevertheless, Patriotism, as well as Legal and Distributive Justice, have very important functions to fulfil in social life.   Owing to the special needs of modern society and the enhanced importance of all civic relations, these virtues are now receiving more attention from Catholic writers than formerly. For the same unchristian social reformers, especially those identified with extreme Liberalism and Revolutionary Communism, who would disintegrate the family, and abrogate the privileges and reasonable autonomy of the local and professional units within the State, concentrating in a bureaucracy all civic and even domestic authority, deny also the virtue of Patriotism.   They reject and repudiate national and civic ties and obligations as being opposed to their false theories of humanitarianism and internationalism, or the so-called " Solidarity of Labour." In place of the natural and traditional virtue of devotion to one's own country they wish to substitute a colourless and ineffective love of humanity and a so-called " Patriotism of the world," or " International Patriotism."[1]

Again, Pius XI speaking of another section of these opponents of the Christian virtue of Patriotism, those, namely, who are identified with the forces of international finance, writes :

" As regards the relations of peoples among themselves, a double stream has issued from this one fountain-head : on the one hand economic Nationalism, or even economic Imperialism ; on the other, a not less noxious and detestable Internationalism or international Imperialism in financial affairs, which hold that where a man's fortune is, there is his country."[2]

Division of Subject.—In the present sketch we shall treat first of the nature and foundation of the virtue of Patriotism ; secondly, of its place in the Christian law, and finally, of its practical applications in social life.

---

[1] Cf. Giloteaux, *op. cit.*, pp. 190 ff.
[2] *Quadragesimo Anno*, p. 48.

Father F. X. Godts, C.S.S.R., in the volume of instructions
already referred to, addressed to the clergy of Belgium on
the best means of dealing with the present social evils,
insists strongly on the essential need of inculcating the love
of country on the children. "Just as the nature of God,"
he writes, "is charity or love, so that of Socialism is hatred—
hatred towards the earthly country . . . whose very name
they desire to blot out; hatred especially towards the
heavenly country, the hope and knowledge of which they
are striving to filch away from the unhappy labourers in
this land of exile. Hence, the Socialists reject the national
flag which each country has made its own; and they adopt
instead a red flag, the symbol of death and destruction.
Hence, too, they take the name of 'Internationalists,'
boasting that they have no country and no fellow-countrymen. . . . Their unholy doctrine is as much opposed to
nature as it is to religion."[1]

Art. 2—*Virtue of Patriotism*

Instinctive Love of Country.—Love of the environment
and society amidst which one has been born and grown up
is founded upon natural tendencies and needs, and, like
parental affection and filial love, it exists as an unreasoning
instinct, even in the lower animals. As man's upbringing
and growth take a longer time than the growth of the lower
animals, and include the development of mind and will,
as well as of bodily organism, this natural tendency is,
perhaps, stronger and more deeply rooted in men than in
other creatures. Just as parents gladly sacrifice their own
interests and ease for the future well-being of their children,
so men willingly labour and suffer for the future safety
and prosperity of their country. They grieve, too, over
the evils which they foresee may overtake it after they
themselves have passed away, and they find consolation
in its future welfare and happiness.[2]

"Nature," writes a well-known seventeenth century author,
"has implanted so deeply the love of country in the hearts of
men, that . . . we cannot restrain our thoughts from turning

---

[1] F. X. Godts, C.S.S.R.—*Scopuli Vitandi* (3rd edit., Bruges, 1896),
chap. xxvii, p. 292.
[2] Cf. Cicero—*Tuscul. Quaest.*, lib. i, nn. 38, 39.

fondly and continually to the concerns of the fatherland. Like the sun-flower, which constantly looks towards the sun, turning with him every hour of the day, even when the clouds obscure his rays, so are we all impelled by an instinct of nature to centre all the affections of our souls on the land that gave us birth."[1]

The natural love of the surroundings of one's childhood includes in its object not only the material place, its scenery and climate, but still more the persons associated with these, the civic institutions, the language and traditions with which one's early years have been familiarised, and which must have played each its part in shaping one's character and tastes. This instinctive love, like all other natural tendencies, comes from the Author of nature, who is God, and so must in itself be good and useful to the human race.

Its Utility for Social Well-being.—This natural love of country acts upon a man as a kind of magnetic force, tending to retain him in his own country, and if he is absent to recall him to it. Without some such force there would be a perpetual flow of the human race towards the more temperate climes and the more fertile lands, with the result that the more barren as well as the excessively hot and cold portions of the globe would be deserted, to the great detriment of the human race. It seems to be a law of man's nature that neither harshness of climate nor barrenness of soil, nor the fact that he suffers hardships or persecution in his native land lessens his love for it.[2]

Furthermore, and of still greater importance for the

---

[1] Lynch—*Cambrensis Eversus*, vol. i, cap. i, p. 106 (Dublin, 1848).
    Cf. also   " Me natale solum quadam dulcedine tangit
            Semper et immemorem non sinit esse sui."
            My native land with rapture stirs my heart
            Nor lets its charms from remembrance part.
                    Peter of Blois, *Ep.* 160 (quoted by K. Digby, *loc. cit.*)

[2] Cf.   The shuddering tenant of the frigid zone
        Boldly proclaims the happiest spot his own ;
        .   .   .
        The naked negro, panting at the line,
        Boasts of his golden sands and palmy wine
        Basks in the glare, or stems the tepid wave,
        And thanks his gods for all the goods they gave.
        Such is the patriot's boast, wher'er we roam,
        His first, best country ever is at home.
                    Goldsmith—*The Traveller.*

interests of the human race, the natural love of country assists the due relations of social life. Just as the natural love between husband and wife and between parents and children facilitates the mutual co-operation of the members of the family, so also the love of country, by closely uniting the families and individuals of a nation in bonds of a common affection and common ideals promotes the harmonious and efficient working of the State. Thus, when controlled and guided by right reason, this instinctive love of country becomes the foundation of a moral virtue.

Virtue of Patriotism—A Portion of Piety.—The virtue of Patriotism is a branch or subdivision of Piety. Piety is the virtue which inclines one to render due honour and service to those who are the source of one's being, and the agents or authors of one's upbringing and education. Now, since God is the primary source of man's being and of all the good he has, the first duties of piety are towards God. These duties, however, by reason of their transcendent excellence, are usually classed apart, under the special name of *Religion*, and the term Piety is confined to one's obligations towards those who are the secondary or immediate source of one's being and education. Principal among these are one's parents and the country or civil society amid which one was born and brought up.

"Our parents and our country," writes St. Thomas, "are the sources of our being and education (*gubernationis*). It is they that have given us birth and nurtured us in our infant years. Consequently, after his duties towards God, man owes most to his parents and his country. One's duties towards one's parents include one's obligations towards relatives, because these latter have sprung from [or are connected by ties of blood with] one's parents . . . and the services due to one's country have for their object all one's fellow-countrymen and all the friends of one's fatherland."[1]

Hence, obligations of piety extend in due proportion, directly or indirectly, to parents, relatives, fellow-countrymen, and to all persons closely connected with these. For the present we are concerned only with that branch of piety which refers to one's countrymen, and which is called *Patriotism*.

---

[1] 2a, 2æ, Q. 101, a. 1 (*corp.*).

37

Patriotism may be defined as *the virtue which inclines one to love and serve the country to which one belongs.* The existence of the strong natural instinct already described, which God has implanted so deeply in the human heart, goes far to show that man is bound by the natural law to love and serve the civil society with which he is naturally identified, just as he is bound to love and, when necessary, to assist his parents and his own immediate family.

Moral Relations of the Part with the Whole.—Besides the ties of origin upon which the virtue of Patriotism primarily rests, there are other kindred relations between a citizen and his country to which St. Thomas frequently refers, in connection with the civic virtues (*Virtutes Politicæ*), which latter he identifies, at least partially, with the virtue of Patriotism. His doctrine is briefly this : The part tends instinctively to seek the good of the whole to which it naturally belongs, rather than its own. This tendency, which belongs to all creatures, points unmistakably, in the case of rational beings, to a dictate of the natural law, and hence it may be taken as the guide in determining the citizen's duty of service to his country. For, the State is, or may be, a natural whole of which citizens or members are the parts.

" The tendencies of nature [he writes] are perceived in actions which are done without deliberation. . . . Now, we see that every part strives spontaneously and according to natural inclination to procure the good of the whole, even at the cost of its own peril or loss. Thus, a person exposes his hand to the sword-cut to defend his head, for upon the latter the safety of the whole body depends. Hence, it is a tendency of nature that each part should in its own way love the whole to which it belongs more than itself. Consequently, it is in accordance with the dictates of social virtue that a good citizen should expose himself to death for the common good."[1]

In another passage St. Thomas explains that the whole, for whose good the part has a natural inclination to sacrifice itself, must be a *natural* whole, one, namely, founded upon natural ties, as distinct from artificial arrangement, or mere positive law.

" Everything [he writes] that *by its nature and being is a part of another* has a stronger and more deeply-rooted inclination

---

[1] *Quodlibeta* i, a. 8 ; cf. also 2a, 2æ, Q. 26, a. 3, and Q. 32, a. 6.

in favour of the whole to which it belongs than of itself. . . . And since reason copies nature, we find such an imitation in the civic virtues. For it is the duty of a good citizen to expose himself to the danger of death for the safety of the whole State. And if the citizen be a natural part of the State, this tendency would be natural to him."[1]

One's birth and education in a certain family, and in the midst of a particular society, together with all the associations that accompany or result from these facts, are the usual foundation of the natural union of which there is question here. But even in after life quasi-natural ties may arise, as when an immigrant becomes by long association, practically identified with the civil society into which he has been adopted.

"Fellow-citizens," writes Cicero, "have many things in common, their places of public assembly, their temples, their public halls, their highways ; they have the same constitutions, the same laws, the same courts of Justice. They vote according to the same system, follow the same social customs, and have numberless bonds of friendship, of interest and of business dealing."[2]

It is clear, however, from what we have already explained of the natural foundations of the virtue of Patriotism that when all natural and quasi-natural ties are wanting, one cannot have duties of Patriotism towards a State, although duties of Legal Justice and of Charity may exist.

The Civic Union a Natural Society.—Seeing that the virtue of Patriotism rests essentially upon natural civic ties, it will be well to analyse more fully the meaning of these latter. According to the ordinary Catholic teaching the State or Nation[3] is a *natural* society. This means, according to the

---

[1] Ia, Q. 60, a. 5 (*corp.*).   [2] *De Officiis*, lib. i, cap. xvii.

[3] The terms *Nation* and *State* are sometimes used synonymously. This, however, is incorrect. The former properly refers to a civil community held together by *natural* ties, such as are explained in the text ; the latter term (*respublica*) means such a nation as enjoys its natural right of independent self-government, or a group of nations or parts of nations which, as a result of treaty or conquest, or some other artificial arrangement, just or otherwise, are united together into a single political whole. Patriotism, being founded on natural ties, refers only to the nation ; Legal Justice to the State. A political union, however, that in the beginning was purely artificial, may, in lapse of time, owing to change of circumstances, become natural, and thus come within the scope of the virtue of Patriotism.

designs of Providence as manifested in human nature, man is meant to live as a member of an organised civil union, the purpose of which is to assist the members to attain temporal happiness. The general structure, functions and powers of the civil union are determined by the natural law ; just as the same natural law determines the functions of the matrimonial union and the general nature of the marriage contract.[1] It does not, however, follow that the natural law directly ordains that any particular group of families and individuals are bound together into one nation or State.

The formation of the State depends upon certain contingent facts, given which there arises a natural inclination or need for these families and individuals to coalesce into an organised State. When the natural tendency is strong, permanent, and clearly defined, and when its realisation will not interfere with the rights of any other group, or with any vital interest of the community at large, it is clearly a dictate of the law of nature, which ordains that men should enjoy reasonable freedom in pursuing their own happiness, that no outside individual or group should prevent such a natural inclination from being gratified. Moreover, no *fait accompli*, resulting from coercive force, can of itself justly override or invalidate such a fundamental right. The case is to a certain extent on a par with a man's natural right to choose his own partner in life. When a young man and woman have a desire, founded perhaps upon natural sympathy or mutual suitability, to get married, no one has a right to interfere, at least as long as there exists no legal impediment, and the just claims of no third party will be violated by the union.

The Natural Civic Ties.—That sets of historical facts and concrete circumstances may in actual fact bind together certain groups of individuals, families and social units into a naturally constituted whole united with one another by ties closely connected with the virtue of Patriotism, few will seriously deny, except under the influence of political prejudice. If, as a result of the great European war (1914–18), Germany were to have forcibly annexed France,

---

[1] See *supra,* chap. xviii, art. i.

or Holland, or England, to the German Empire, disregarding all the cherished aspirations of the people, their historical traditions, their natural sympathies, their racial characteristics and antipathies, their just and reasonable national pride, the action would be unjust, and would be condemned by all as a gross violation of the natural and divine law. The continued enforcement of such a union would still remain unjust, even after the first victims of the wrong had passed away. If the time ever came when such a union would cease to be unjust and unnatural, that could only be when the natural bonds of union, such as the racial characteristics of the nations concerned, their sympathies and antipathies, and their reasonable national aspirations, had in the evolution of time become so altered that these countries could no longer be regarded as distinct natural units, different from the German nation. It is only in such a sense that prescriptive titles can heal the original injustice of a forcible conquest or annexation.

Although most authorities agree in asserting the existence of natural civic ties, even Catholic writers are not always at one in specifying exactly what these ties are ; and still greater differences cf opinion sometimes exist in the application of the general principles to concrete cases. Is such a group to be regarded as a distinct nation or not ? Granted that such another group was once a separate nation, has it now, as a result of changed circumstances, lost its national individuality ? The former question may arise in regard to such groups as the Flemish or the Basques of Northern Spain, the latter concerning groups like the Welsh or the Scotch.

Among the natural ties usually enumerated are : a certain unity or convenient contiguity of territory, unity of race, a common language, a similarity of customs, identical national aspirations, a certain community of economic interests ; and, most important of all, a participation in common historical memories and associations.[1] Such an enumeration, however, must be regarded as only indicating in a general way the main constituents of the national unit. How far any one or more of the conditions named is to be considered essential to the idea of nationhood, or how far

---

[1] See *supra, chap*. xxiii, art. 2.

the absence of some may be counterbalanced by the presence of others in a more intense degree, it would be impossible to determine in the abstract. Each case must be examined separately. The element of size has also to be considered ; for the unit should be large enough to constitute an independent and self-sufficing State ; and this again has to be judged in the light of several other circumstances. Thus, in ancient and mediæval times, a single city, with a moderate amount of surrounding territory, might more easily form an independent economic unit than it could to-day, when increased facilities of intercommunication, intensified economic activity and the custom of mass production require larger bodies of producers and consumers and a much more complex organisation.

The consent or wishes of the people, whether essential or not in itself as a constituent part of the ties that go to make a natural unit, is evidently the strongest and most important indication of the actual presence or absence of those ties. For no people will persevere in wishing and striving after a certain political ideal unless the latter is founded upon natural requirements.

The Subject of Patriotism.—We may now analyse the virtue of Patriotism a little more closely. The *subject* of the virtue (those, namely, that are bound by its duties) include all the individual and corporative members of the naturally constituted civic body, whether the latter be actually organised, as normally it should be, into a unified and self-governing State like France, England, or Spain, or is subject to another State, as Czecho-Slovakia was before the great European war, or is partitioned up, like Poland before the same war, among several different empires. Such a temporary incompleteness of development or artificial division, caused by unjust aggression or similar accidental causes, does not of itself essentially alter the force of the natural ties that bind the members together, nor invalidate the rights of the people to their independence and natural unity. As long as the common characteristics remain which make the people a distinct nation, the different parts and members of the partitioned or conquered country are still to be regarded as one nation, towards which all its own members are bound by the duties of Patriotism. These members normally include all who have been born and brought up among the inhabitants of the nation or who, owing to long continued and voluntary residence among them and mutual exchange of services, have contracted with them mutual ties, founded upon friendship, congeniality of tastes and opinions, identity of interests and aspirations.

Its Term or Object.—The *term* or *object* of the virtue of Patriotism (those, namely, towards whom its duties and activities are directed), is primarily the naturally constituted nation to which one belongs, and which may or may not be an organised State, with a legitimate government of its own. The nation means the families and individuals composing it, as they exist in the concrete, namely, with the national characteristics that differentiate them from all others, and the natural ties that bind them together, and make them one moral whole. Hence, these latter, as well as the persons of the nation, enter essentially into the term or object of the virtue of Patriotism. In other words, seeing that the virtue refers primarily to the nation as a distinct unit, it must imply a special reference to the natural ties which hold the parts of that unit together, and make them one moral body.[1]

" Love of Country."—Consequently, the national characteristics of the people, their common historical traditions, their legitimate national aspirations and social customs, and the national language, all enter more or less into the object of Patriotism. Even the material soil which one's countrymen inhabit, and which holds their national monuments, the tombs of their ancestors, and the battle-grounds on which their predecessors fought in defence of the nation's liberties, tends to become, owing to its close connection with the nation, an object of the patriot's devotion.

This is why the virtue of Patriotism is so frequently referred to as *love of country*. This phrase, when used as a synonym of the virtue of Patriotism, does not merely mean

---

[1] " People's charitable activities towards one another are to be exercised in accordance with the varying nature of the ties that unite them. For to each one must be given the service which belongs to the special nature of his connection with him that gives it."—St. Thomas, 2ª, 2ᵃᵉ, Q. 31, a. 3 (*corp.*) ; cf. also Taparelli, *loc. cit.*

love of the dead land, or the natural scenery and climate of the country ; for such an affection, in so far as it may exist, belongs to the natural instinct upon which the virtue of Patriotism is founded, not to the virtue itself. Love of country means rather a love of benevolence for one's countrymen as such, implying an efficacious desire to promote their interests along the lines of the national characteristics, such as the legitimate aspirations and traditions of the people, which latter are, as a rule, closely connected with the land which they inhabit.

Patriotism and Legal Justice.—From what has been said it follows that although the virtue of Patriotism coincides partly with that of Legal Justice, which also rests upon relations between the part and the whole of a civic unit,[1] there is a clear distinction between the two. Patriotism is independent of positive law and artificial arrangement, whether the latter be just or unjust. It rests solely upon natural ties, and refers to the naturally constituted national unit, whether it is or is not an organised State. Legal Justice refers only to the organised State,[2] which may include members who are not connected with it by any natural tie, and exclude others who are so connected. This actual or legal connection, in so far at least as it is just, implies certain moral obligations to do one's just share in promoting the good of the body to which one belongs. Nay, duties of Legal Justice may exist, even though the formation and continued existence of the State be morally indefensible. For, if a State be actually set up and working peacefully, the citizens are usually bound by Legal Justice to perform the usual civic duties, in so far at least as such co-operation does not lend unlawful support or moral sanction to an unjust or usurping régime.

Hence, if owing to the unjust action of a conquering power or other accidental causes, the actual civic organisation does not include the whole nation, as nature has formed it, or embraces, under pressure of coercive forces, nations or communities that do not naturally belong to it, the

---

[1] Cf. *Supra*, chap. xxiv., art. I.

[2] Cf. St. Thomas, 2a, 2æ, Q. 101, a. 3 ad 3um ; Costa-Rosetti, *op. cit.*, Thesis 152, p. 546.

duties of Patriotism still refer to all the members of the natural unit, and to none else. The duties of Legal Justice, on the other hand, such as the obligation to pay taxes and to obey just laws, refer to the actual civil organisation, and to it alone. Thus, in the existing political arrangement in Ireland the Munsterman's duties of Legal Justice would have little or no reference to the people of Derry, Armagh or Belfast, whereas, his duties of Patriotism would extend to them as well as to the citizens of Galway or Cork, seeing that they all equally belong to the naturally constituted national unit.

Again, duties of Legal Justice bind all the actual members of the civic union, even natives of another country, who are naturalised citizens, and within certain limits, even those living in the State without being legally naturalised. The duties of Patriotism, on the other hand, which are independent of all positive law, bind only those naturally identified with the country. Thus, a native of Ireland who has emigrated in adult age to England or the United States has duties of Legal Justice to his adopted country, but no duties of Patriotism, at least until by continued residence he has grown more or less identified with it. Again, one may have duties of Legal Justice to an artificial union of countries like the British Empire (in so far at least as such a union is founded upon just laws and morally valid ties), but it would be a misuse of terms to refer to such obligations as duties of Patriotism, except in so far as their fulfilment may react indirectly upon the community or nation to which one naturally belongs.

Acts of Legal Justice are always obligatory, otherwise they would not be acts of Justice ; those of Patriotism, while always praiseworthy and sometimes obligatory, are not necessarily always so, for Patriotism, like Charity, inclines one to go far beyond the limits of strict obligation. Again, duties of Patriotism, unlike those of Justice, are not juridical. In other words, they do not imply a strict right on the part of the persons towards whom they lie. Neither may they be enforced by coercive laws, except they come under the virtue of Legal Justice.

Influence of Patriotism on Mankind.—Next to religion, Patriotism has probably been the greatest force in shaping the history of mankind. Bound up inextricably with the whole civilisation of the ancient Greeks and Romans, it breathes as a dominating influence through all their literature and art, and was the principal driving force in most of their public achievements. The same may be said of the Jews, in whose minds the motives of religion and Patriotism were so closely associated as almost to become identical. A similar spirit, but modified by Christian influence, is to be found in the extant literature and the national character-istics of the ancient and mediæval Irish. In fact, love of country is the dominant note and the main inspiration of Irish poetry.

During the Middle Ages, it is true the patriotic motive appears less prominent in the history of continental Europe. This was due in large part to the fact that during the centuries of upheaval and general unrest which followed the dismem-berment of the Roman Empire, the newly-formed nations of Europe had not yet sufficiently coalesced to possess a self-conscious national life. As the centuries advance, how-ever, and the peoples of modern Europe gradually develop their own language and national culture, the spirit of Patriotism reappears in all its former vigour.

Although not infrequently distorted by exaggeration and excess, and too often made the pretext for injustice and crime,[1] the virtue of Patriotism has a wonderful efficacy in elevating individual character, and developing the best capabilities of a people.

"Patriotism," writes Lecky, "has always proved the best cordial of humanity, and all the sterner and more robust virtues are matured in the highest degree by its power. In nations that have been long pervaded by a strong and continuous political life . . . habits of self-reliance are formed which enable men to confront death with a calm intrepidity, and to retain a certain sobriety of temperament amid the most trying vicissitudes. A capacity for united action, for self-sacrifice, for long and per-severing effort, becomes general. . . . The spirit [of Patriotism]

---

[1] Cf. Johnson's saying : " Patriotism is the last refuge of the scoundrel " (Boswell's *Life of Johnson*, chap. xi). It may have been true in England in Johnson's time (and for that matter may be true in England, or even in Ireland to-day) that the virtue of Patriotism was the best disguise for the scoundrel to assume in order to cover up his wicked designs. The cloak of religion is all too frequently utilized for the same purpose ; just as in the days of the Crusades the best and most effectual disguise was, presumably, zeal for the liberation of the holy places.

has often infused into society a heroism and a fortitude that have proved the invariable precursors of regeneration."[1]

In the next article we shall touch briefly on the perverted idea of Patriotism, sometimes termed *Nationalism*, which should not be confounded with the sane and well-balanced concept of the virtue as understood by Catholic writers.

Art. 3—*Patriotism and the Christian Law*

The excellence of Patriotism has always been well recognised in the common estimation of mankind. Poets of all nations and every age have sung its praises ; and many of the best and noblest men and women that the world has known have consecrated its practice by their example. In the Sacred Scriptures also the virtue of Patriotism is frequently referred to, with strong commendation expressed or implied.

Patriotism in the Old Testament.—The whole religion of the Jews was closely bound up with devotion to their country's interests, and zeal for their national institutions and traditions. According to the divine promises contained in the Old Law, which were again and again literally fulfilled, the fidelity of the people to their religious obligations was to be the measure of their national prosperity.

The literature of mankind probably possesses no better or more touching example of patriotic poetry breathing a most intense love of country than the 136th Psalm : "*Upon the rivers of Babylon there we sat and wept, when we remembered Sion.*" Again, in the books of the Machabees, the inspired writer relates with approval the most stimulating examples of patriotic heroism and zeal. Judas Machabeus exhorts his men to gird themselves for battle against the nations that were assembled to destroy their people and their sanctuaries : "*For it is better for us*

---

[1] *Rationalism in Europe*, vol. ii, chap. v. Lecky's statement that Patriotism " has proved the best cordial of humanity " is an exaggeration ; or applies only to some of the non-Christian nations. The Christian religion has always been " the best cordial of humanity," wherever it is accepted and practised. True Patriotism, like filial piety and parental love, develops under its influence. And where religion and Patriotism go hand in hand according to Christian ideals, the best type of national character will be produced.

to die in battle," he adds, voicing a sentiment familiar to the patriots of every country and age, *" than to see the evils of our nation."*[1] Again, when the youngest of the seven brothers who were martyred before their mother's eyes, was about to die, the boy proclaimed in the tyrant's presence that he died for his country : *" I, like my brethren, offer up my life and body for the laws of our fathers, calling upon God to be speedily merciful to our nation.*[2]

It is true that there were special reasons for the attachment of the chosen people to their own laws and institutions, which were so closely bound up with their religion. Besides, they knew from divine revelation that God wished their national institutions and unity to be preserved, and desired that the nation be free from foreign interference. But the mere fact that God did, in the case of the Jews, so closely connect their religion with their patriotic instincts seems to imply a strong commendation of the virtue of Patriotism.

In the New Testament.—In the New Testament also we find sanction and approval of the virtue of Patriotism. St. Paul acknowledges that he had a special obligation towards the Jews, and a special love for them, because they were his own countrymen. *" I speak the truth in Christ,"* he says, *" that I have great sadness, and continual sorrow in my heart. For I wished myself to be anathema from Christ for my brethren, who are my kinsmen according to the flesh."*[3] In another place he writes : *" Hath God cast away His people ? God forbid ! For I also am an Israelite of the seed of Abraham, of the tribe of Benjamin."*[4] Here, too, the great Apostle, whose heart was all on fire with zeal for the salvation of souls, gives evidence of that special love for his own fellow-countrymen which is the essence of the virtue of Patriotism.

Our Divine Lord Himself, who possessed all virtues in perfection, must have had in His human soul the virtue of Piety in all its fulness. Consequently, just as He had an intense filial affection for His Blessed Mother and for His foster-father, St. Joseph, and just as He must have loved in a special way His cousins, who are called in the Gospel

---

[1] 1 *Machab.* iii. 59.   [2] 2 *Machab.* vii. 37.   [3] *Rom.* ix. 1–3.
[4] *Rom.* xi. 1.

history the " Brethren of the Lord," so also there can be
no doubt that He cherished with a peculiar love the Jewish
nation, in whose bosom He was born and grew to manhood.
He burst into tears on one occasion when, seeing the beauty
and grandeur of the city of His people, He thought of the
awful fate that would overtake it. *" Seeing the city, He
wept over it.* . . . *' For the days shall come upon thee,'* He
cried, *' and thy enemies shall cast a trench round about thee
and compass thee round, and straiten thee on every side, and
beat thee flat to the ground, and shall not leave in thee a stone
upon a stone.' "*[1] Again He cries : *" Jerusalem, Jerusalem,
how often have I wished to gather thy people, as a hen doth
gather her chickens under her wings, and thou wouldst not."*[2]

It is true that our Divine Lord's special grief for the
obstinacy and consequent destruction of the people of
Jerusalem may be explained by the fact that He saw in
Jerusalem a type of the human soul hardened in sin ; but
it is also reasonable to hold that in the words and incidents
here referred to, He gives expression to a special love for
the Jewish nation, founded upon natural human ties, a
type of love which he wishes not to be destroyed, but
elevated and sanctified by supernatural motives.

Hence, when St. Paul says that in the Church *" there is
neither Gentile nor Jew . . . Barbarian or Scythian, bond
or free, but Christ, all in all ; "*[3] or, again : *" there is neither
Jew nor Greek, there is neither bond nor free, there is neither
male or female,"*[4] he does not imply that the Church wishes
to abolish or ignore the natural ties which bind individuals
to their own country, no more than she would wish to
abolish family ties or distinction of sex, or even reasonable
distinctions of class, all of which are necessary for the good
of the human race. He means rather, that just as the
Church, while consecrating and upholding domestic ties
and obligations, nevertheless, receives equally into her fold
the members of every family, so also she receives and
cherishes impartially the citizens of all nations, for all are
equally dear to her Founder.

Leo XIII on Patriotism.—Leo XIII, voicing the official
teaching of the Catholic Church, inculcates the duty of

---

[1] *Luke* xix. 41–44. [2] *Matth.* xxiii. 37. [3] *Col.* iii. 11.
[4] *Gal.* iii. 28.

Patriotism and love of country, as one of the fundamental Christian virtues.

" The natural law [he writes] enjoins us to love devotedly and to defend the country in which we had birth and in which we were brought up, so that every good citizen hesitates not to face death for his native land. . . . We are bound then to love dearly our country, whence we have received the means of enjoyment which this mortal life affords. . . . .

" Moreover, if we judge aright, the supernatural love of the Church and the natural love of our country proceed from the same eternal principle, since God Himself is their Author and originating cause."

Again, explaining the subordination of the love of country to one's obedience and devotedness to the Church, he says :

" Wherefore, to love both countries, that of earth below and that of heaven above, yet in such mode that the love of our heavenly surpass the love of our earthly home, and human laws be never set above the divine law, is the essential duty of Christians, and the fountain head, so to speak, from which all other duties spring."[1]

On the same subject Cardinal Mercier truly writes :

" The religion of Christ makes Patriotism a positive law; and there is no perfect Christian who is not a perfect Patriot."[2]

Christian and Non-Christian Patriotism (Nationalism).— The Christian concept of Patriotism, however, differs essentially from the false and exaggerated Nationalism which is sometimes called by the same name. In the Christian teaching duties of Patriotism come after religious obligations ; and are, besides, subject to the principles of Justice, and the obligation of charity towards all ; for, by the Christian law all are brothers in Jesus Christ. In the non-Christian concept there is a tendency to regard the State or the Nation as the highest object of devotion,[3] as if it were an end in itself : and not an institution arranged by

---

[1] *Sapientiæ Christianæ*, pp. 110, 111.

[2] *Patriotism and Endurance* (Pastoral Letter of Cardinal Mercier, Christmas, 1914, pp. 16–19).

[3] Cf. for instance, Cicero's advice to his friend : " I exhort and implore you, my dear Plancus . . . to apply all the energies of your soul to public affairs. Nothing can be more fruitful in glory to yourself, nor is there anything in human life more praiseworthy or excellent than to promote the interests of the State." *Ep. ad Fam.*, lib. i, n. 5.

Providence to assist its members towards their temporal and eternal happiness. Hence, the votaries of this false Nationalism tend to measure virtue and vice only in relation to the supposed public good, and to ignore not only the claims of religion, but also the duties of Justice and Charity as between one's own country and a foreign nation. These tendencies, which were a natural outcome of the pagan philosophy of ancient Greece and Rome, reappear in modern semi-pagan ideals and sometimes even in the attitude of those who are otherwise good Catholics. The sentiments formally expressed in the well-known words of the American jingo patriot are not infrequently adopted in practice even when not so clearly expressed : " Our country, in her inter-course with foreign nations, may she be always right ! but our country ! right or wrong."[1]

Again, Patriotism of the non-Christian type tends to regard the citizens of other nations with contempt, if not hostility. Even amongst the Jews, whose religion was national, this tendency was strongly marked. It appears still more prominently among the Greeks and Romans, who referred to all foreigners as barbarians, and regarded them as essentially inferior. This, too, is opposed to the Christian spirit, and is not an expression of true Patriotism.

Christian Patriotism and True Internationalism.—In the Christian concept the relations of one's country or nation to other nations are akin to the mutual relations of different families, so that the nation's place in the universal society of mankind is somewhat like the position of the family within the nation itself. Just as one's family affections do not exclude a due regard and real love for members of other families and for the nation at large, so neither does Christian patriotism, even in its most intense form, exclude love and due appreciation of other nations, or zeal for the good of the human race. In fact, these latter are the natural develop-ment of a true love for one's own country, just as the domestic virtues and affections are the natural foundation of Patriotism itself.[2]

---

[1] Spoken by Stephen Decatur at a toast given at Norfolk, in Virginia, U.S.A., April, 1816. Decatur was one of the American naval commanders in the war with Britain (1812–1815).
[2] Cf. Giloteaux, *op. cit.*, pp. 149–200.

Hence, we often find the most intense love of country in persons who devote all their energies to the service of other nations, or of mankind at large. Thus, an intense love of Ireland was an outstanding characteristic of the early Irish missionary saints who worked in Britain and continental Europe ;[1] and an intense and almost exaggerated love of France and appreciation of her greatness usually characterises the French missionaries of modern times.

Art. 4—Duties of Patriotism

Appreciation, Love and Service.—The virtue of Patriotism, like the other branches of piety, comprises the duties of honour or appreciation (*cultus*) and those of actual service (*obsequium*).[2] The former imply not merely a due attitude of mind and will towards one's own country, but also the reasonable outward manifestation of the same when occasion requires. Thus, to love with a reasonable well-ordered love one's own countrymen, because they are one's own, and therefore nearer to one than foreigners, to think and speak kindly of them, to regard with a friendly eye and judge with a kindly disposition all that appertains to them would belong to the virtue of Patriotism.

Often Outweigh Other Duties of Piety.—The obligation of service (*obsequium*) requires a more elaborate treatment. St. Thomas teaches that the child's duties towards his parents do not, other things being equal, take precedence of his duties to himself, because since identity is a closer bond than union, one's self is nearer to one than one's parents.[3] Again, the same teacher lays down that the services due to one's parents under the obligation of piety take priority over those due to one's relatives, because a person's connection with his relatives and with his country is usually established through his birth from his parents; and, therefore, the latter touch him more closely than the former.[4] One might infer from these principles that a man's duties

---

[1] Cf. for instance, Mrs. Concannon's *Life of St. Columban* (Dublin, C. T. S. edit., 1915).

[2] 2a, 2æ, Q. 101, a. 2 ; cf. Pearse's analysis of the duties of Patriotism, which, he says, include a *Faith* and a *Service* (*Political Writings of Patrick Pearse*, Dublin, 1922).

[3] Cf. 2a, 2æ, Q. 60, a. 4.   [4] *Ib.*, Q. 122, a. 5 ad 2um.

to self, to parents, and to relatives normally outweigh his obligations to his country.

The inference, however, has to be modified by another consideration. One's duties to one's country are founded not merely on the relations of origin and close association as in the case of one's duties towards parents and relatives. They are founded also, and indeed mainly upon the fact that one is a member or a part of the nation to which one belongs ; and, as already shown, " it is a tendency of nature, and consequently, in accordance with the natural law that the part should love the whole more than itself."[1] Besides, seeing that the interests of the nation are identified with the good of all its members, its claims upon each of the latter may outweigh the claims of any particular individual. Hence, duties of Patriotism may sometimes claim preference to one's duties towards one's nearest relatives and even towards one's self, at least to the extent that one is justified, and does a praiseworthy act in sacrificing one's own temporal interests and those of one's nearest relatives for the sake of the common good.

" Seeing that the common good," says St. Thomas, " is to be preferred before one's own, it would be praiseworthy to expose oneself and one's family, even to the danger of death, in order to serve another on whose safety the interests of the Church or State depend."[2]

Again, explaining the seeming anomaly that a soldier in war is bound to aid a fellow-soldier of his own side, who may happen to be a complete stranger, rather than a near relative that belongs to the opposing army, he writes :

" It is in accordance with the divine law to seek the good of the many rather than that of a single individual. Hence, it is an act of virtue to expose one's life to peril for the spiritual or temporal good of the State. . . . Now, the soldier who aids a fellow-soldier in war does so for the sake of the whole State. Hence, it is no wonder that in such cases he prefers a stranger before one who is connected with him by ties of blood."[3]

Special Duties of Patriotism.—Since the virtue of Patriotism is so closely connected with the natural ties binding the citizen to his country, and uniting the in-

[1] St. Thomas—*Quodlibeta* i, a. 8 ; cf. *supra*, art. 2.
[2] 2a, 2æ, Q. 32, a. 6 (*corp.*).
[3] 2a, 2æ, Q. 31, a. 3 ad 2um.

38

dividuals of the nation into a distinct civic unit, its duties will refer primarily, on the principles already explained, to the interests and rights of the nation as a whole.

Defence of the Freedom and Integrity of the Nation.—

Among these the integrity, the political unity and the independence of the nation have the first place. They are the primary rights of a nation, and the violent invasion of them by a foreign power has always been recognised by the common consent of mankind as the greatest national evil that a people can suffer. For, as with the individual, so also with the nation, slavery is justly regarded as an evil and a degradation, which no earthly advantage can outweigh. To be deprived of its independence has always been looked upon as a greater disaster for a nation than any loss of material resources, no matter how severe, greater even than the destruction of the flower of the nation's manhood in the horrors of war.

Besides, forced subjection to a foreign power is, or inevitably tends to become, the parent of a whole train of degrading evils. The first care of the master State usually will be to make sure of its hold upon the subject nation, even at the cost of the gravest moral and material injury of the latter. Thus, dissensions and domestic strife are fostered, education is perverted for political ends, the virtue of true Patriotism is regarded by the governing power as dangerous and seditious. Even the nation's material advancement is sometimes deliberately obstructed or destroyed, lest a too strong subject become a peril to the master's control or a rival to the master's trade.

" The rule of a tyrant," says St. Thomas, " aims not at the good of the community, but at the private advancement of the ruler . . . who encourages dissensions and sedition in the nation subject to him in order to maintain his own control with more safety. For this is tyranny, since it aims at promoting the interests of the ruling power to the detriment of the nation."[1]

---

[1] 2a, 2æ, Q. 42, a. 2 ad 3um. In this passage St. Thomas adds the pregnant words which summarize his own attitude and that of the great scholastic writers on the question of submission to unjust or unlawful rule : " The overthrowing of such a rule is not seditious [or sinful] unless, perchance, when the effort to do so is so ill-timed or out of place (*inordinate*) that the subject people suffer more injury from the supervening confusion than from the tyrant's rule." Cf. also Costa-Rosetti, *op. cit.*, Thesis 164, pp. 661, 662.

Hence it is, that in the universal judgment of mankind the defence of the nation's freedom and integrity has always been closely associated with the virtue of Patriotism ; and the names of most of the great heroes of Patriotism are associated with the defence of their country's freedom or integrity. So it is with the names of William Tell, Wallace, St. Joan of Arc, John Sobieski, Kosciusko, Andreas Hofer, George Washington, Abraham Lincoln, and hosts of others, whose memory is honoured and revered, not only by their own fellow-countrymen, but by the world at large. This judgment is in accordance with Christian principles and with the best traditions of mankind.

" It is considered a glory for the individual," says St. Ambrose, " to expose himself to peril for the peace and safety of the community, and one is always better pleased to have averted the ruin of one's country, than to have saved oneself from danger."[1]

" And for one's country 'tis a bliss to die,"[2] sang Homer, more than a thousand years earlier. " *For it is better to die in battle*," says the Jewish patriot, " *than to behold the evils of our nation*."[3] Cardinal Mercier only followed the lines of the highest Christian and human traditions when, in 1914, he praised in such magnificent terms the sacrifice of the Belgian soldiers

" who fought, who suffered, who fell . . . so that Belgium might keep her independence, her dynasty, her patriotic unity,"[4]

and he does not hesitate to compare their sacrifice even to that of martyrdom for the Christian Faith.

And of the National Traditions and Culture.—The freedom and integrity of one's country include, when properly understood, much more than mere exemption from forcible subjugation or dismemberment. A nation may be practically destroyed or broken up without the actual application of physical force. Thus, as already explained,[5] a nation may be effectually disintegrated and enslaved as a result of economic peaceful penetration. Again, if the people lose their national traditions and aspirations and abandon their

---

[1] *De Officiis Ministrorum*, lib. iii, cap. iii, n. 23.
[2] *Iliad*, bk. xv, 1, 583.   [3] 1 *Machab*. iii. 59.   [4] *Ib*., p. 5.
[5] Cf. *Supra*, chap. xxiv, arts. 2 and 3.

national customs, above all, if the native language ceases
to be used, and the native literature and history to be
studied, the people may disappear as a distinct unit, and
get absorbed into the life of another State. So in ancient
times the old Etruscan, Gallic, and Spanish peoples, as well
as most of the North African nations, lost their distinctive
identity, their national aspirations, their native language
and traditions, and got completely merged into the system
of Imperial Rome.[1] So, in modern times, the people of
Scotland have practically lost their national distinctiveness
and become a province of Britain.

One need not, and perhaps could not, maintain that such
an absorption or cessation of the national life is always an
unmixed calamity ; for certain advantages for the conquered peoples, or for the human race at large, may some-
time accompany or accidentally result even from the destruction of the life of a nation. The Spanish and Portuguese colonial conquests are the outstanding examples that
may be quoted. The Spaniards who destroyed the native
civilisations of Mexico and Peru brought these nations the
priceless gift of the Christian Faith, and gave them a profoundly Christian civilisation. These advantages which the
conquerors brought go far to extenuate the wrongs they
inflicted, but do not change the wrong into right. These
native American nations might have been made Christian
while still possessing their own national civilisation, which
would then develop and grow along more natural and
healthier lines. As a rule denationalisation means injury
and degradation. In the case of the destruction of a
Christian civilisation that will invariably be the case.

" When vice and corruption," writes Taparelli, treating of
this subject, " begin to find entrance into the national outlook
of a people, the latter deteriorate. They lose that unity of ideas
and tendencies [which form what is called the ' national spirit '] ;
and wish to abandon the ways of their forefathers. As if aiming
at a more intimate union with the universal society of men the
nation changes its own self into that of another, and becomes

---

[1] Cf. St. Augustine—*Civitas Dei*, lib. xix, cap. vii : " Opera data est
ut imperiosa civitas non solum jugum verum etiam linguam suam domitis
gentibus imponeret " (It was the imperial policy of Rome not only to
subjugate by force, but also to impose its language and civilisation upon
the conquered nations).

the pitiable and slavish admirer of certain exotic customs which, are valueless and unsuitable to it The people adopt opinions, [or an outlook on life] which constitute a veritable national apostasy. These opinions are, after a while, expressed in action ; and the upshot is a radical change in the ancient manners of the nation. The last century presents a sad example of this corruption of the national spirit in certain countries. . . . How many nations, in the slavish imitations of others, have made shipwreck not only of their religion, but of their nationality, their language, and their national institutions."[1]

Patriotism the Foundation of True Internationalism.— Just as one's natural attachment to one's own family traditions and to one's own immediate relatives are the foundation which Nature has supplied for sympathy and benevolence towards one's fellow-citizens, so, too, the citizen of each nation, in order to attain to true cosmopolitan virtues and well-ordered zeal for the good of the race, must have as the foundation of these virtues that love and devotion to his own country which the law of nature and right-ordered charity demand. True charity and true piety must begin at home.

In the same way the higher and more perfect culture of a people, if it be real perfection and not a degradation or deterioration, must develop along the lines of the national characteristics and traditions. A declassed man or woman, who, owing to worldly training or a false ambition for social advancement, has come to disregard or despise his or her own immediate family, forfeits the respect of right-thinking men ; and from such a one nothing great or generous may be hoped. The same applies substantially to the more or less degraded citizen, who has lost or never possessed the love and appreciation of the nation to which he belongs, and to which he is bound by the closest natural ties. It is in this sense that Chateaubriand, the Catholic apologist and historian writes : " We doubt whether it is possible for a man to possess any real virtue, any real talent or ability, without love of country."[2]

---

[1] *Op. cit.*, pp. 411, 412. Taparelli's book on the *Natural Law*, from which these words are quoted, and which laid the foundation of the modern science of Catholic Sociology, was published in 1857.

[2] *Op. cit.*, *loc, cit,*

Special Importance of the National Language.—The native language and literature of a country are usually bound up very intimately with the whole national spirit, and with almost every aspect of the national life. This is specially true of a literary language like Greek or Irish, which contains the native history, the national laws and institutions, and enshrines the traditional ideals and aspirations of the people. In such a case, at least, the preservation of the native language may be regarded as essential for the continued existence of the historic nation itself. The truth of Davis' oft-quoted words cannot be seriously questioned :

" A nation should guard its language more than its territories, 'tis a surer barrier and more important frontier than fortress or river."[1]

Devotion to All Civic Duties.—It would be a mistake, however, to suppose that the virtue of Patriotism can appear only in its war paint, or is confined to the duty of defending or regaining the freedom of one's country, or saving the nation from extinction. A person manifestly owes many other services to his country, which, though more ordinary and commonplace, are, at least, in normal circumstances, more practical, and sometimes little less heroic. The spiritual, intellectual, and material interests of the nation need the services of each of its members. The object of the civil union with which Patriotism is so closely connected, is to assist the members each and all towards the highest development of their faculties, moral, intellectual, and physical. Hence, the patriot will do his part to procure for the country the benefit of good laws, to check the spread of vice, above all, to secure that the most worthy are chosen for the public offices ; in a word, all the duties already referred to under the heading of Legal and Distributive Justice are also included in those of Patriotism.

Even to the Material Interests of One's Country.—Even the material interests of the country deserve the patriot's attention. Swift's exaggerated saying contains (or suggests) a kernel of truth :

He gave it as his opinion that whosoever could make two ears of corn or two blades of grass to grow upon a spot of ground

---

[1] *Prose Writings of Thomas Davis*—" Our National Language."

where only one grew before, would deserve better of mankind, and do more essential service to his country than the whole race of politicians put together.[1]

A certain measure of material prosperity is as essential to the well-being of the nation as of the individual. For extreme poverty or destitution is the source of many evils in the case of both.

Among the national evils that may result from excessive poverty is that of forced emigration. De Maistre discusses the question as to whether a person is ever justified, consistently with his duties of Patriotism, in exiling himself permanently, and transferring his allegiance to another country. He is willing to allow it only in very rare and altogether exceptional cases.[2] However this may be, it is certain that, in normal circumstances, it is in accordance with the ordinary providence of God, who has implanted the love of country as an invincible instinct in the heart of man, that people should live in their own country, and increase and multiply there. In order that this be possible it is necessary that the material resources of the country be duly developed. In no country is this truer than in Ireland, where, for several generations, emigration has been one of the principal national evils, imperilling even the very existence of the nation.

True Patriotism Unselfish.—In connection with the services of Patriotism, we shall conclude with one remark. The true patriot serves his country as the dutiful and affectionate son shows kindness to his parents, from motives not of interest but of love. Hence, he will not seek or expect payment or reward, save the consciousness of having done his duty ; for the proposition may be accepted as substantially true that the man who demands gratitude from his country as his due, rarely gets it, and still more rarely deserves it.

---

[1] *Gulliver's Travels*, part ii, chap. viii.
[2] Cf. *Œuvres*, vol. xi, *loc. cit.*, pp. 484, 485.

CHAPTER XXIX

Introductory Note.—The Science of Sociology, being founded on the natural law, is not concerned *directly* with the Church, nor with the truths of revelation of which the Church is the custodian and authentic teacher. The Church, however, and divine revelation, are realities which cannot be ignored. Catholics have rights and duties with regard to the Church which the State cannot lawfully override. Again, the truths of revelation cannot be lost sight of in any scientific enquiry, and, least of all, by the student of Social Science. For these truths confirm and supplement the conclusions of reason, and safeguard the jurist, the statesman, and the social worker against danger or error in many all-important matters. Moreover, the State, in carrying out its proper function of promoting the temporal well-being of its members, has certain duties in regard to religion, morals and education which by divine law are directly under the guidance and control of the Church. Hence, it is essential for the student of Social Science to understand the rôle of the Church as well as of the State in regard to these matters and the rules which regulate their mutual relations. Furthermore, as is well known from experience, the State cannot effectually promote even the physical and material well-being of the people without the co-operation of the Church and the aid of the powerful influences, internal and external, which the Church dispenses and controls.

In the present chapter, we shall first strive to explain the prerogatives and position of the Church in the social organism and the due relations between Church and State. We shall then discuss the Church's influence upon social well-being and the means it has at its disposal for promoting it.

Art. 1—*Prerogatives of the Church*[1]

Religion and Morals Protected but Not Controlled by State.—We have treated of the duties of the State in reference to religion and morality. These duties would be incumbent on the State, although there were no divine revelation, and even if the human race were not raised to the supernatural order, nor redeemed by the merits of the Incarnate Son of God. One must not, however, infer that the control of the religion and morals of the people belongs to the civil power. Such an inference would be false. For civil society is directly concerned only with the temporal interests of the citizens, whereas religious observance and obedience to the moral law, although necessary for temporal well-being and happiness, have a direct and immediate bearing upon the life to come ; and the interests of the latter being eternal would not normally be under the control of an authority whose immediate purpose is confined to man's temporal welfare. Hence, even if there were no divine revelation, the local or national organisations that would then exist for promoting the worship of the Creator would or might be at least partially independent of the State, seeing that the end and purpose of each would be in part different. But the civil power would still be bound to encourage these religious organisations and to uphold their rights, as long as their constitution and activities were in harmony with the natural law.

Man's Elevation to the Supernatural Order.—In point of fact, however, God has raised man to a supernatural order. He has accorded him a divine revelation containing truths which are impervious to human reason or beyond man's unaided power to attain to. With that revelation God has imposed on man new obligations in addition to

---

[1] Cf. *Immortale Dei* (" The Christian Constitution of States "), Nov., 1885 ; *Sapientiæ Christianæ* (" The Chief Duties of Citizens as Christians "), Jan., 1890 ; Leo XIII—*Præclaræ Gratulationis Publicæ* (" The Reunion of Christendom "), June, 1894 ; J. Donat, S.J., *op. cit.*, sec. iii, cap. v, art. 2 ; Th. Meyer, S.J., *op. cit.*, Theses 70–74 ; Costa-Rosetti, *op. cit.*, Theses 170–174 ; Ch. Antoine, S.J., *op. cit.*, chap. vi ; *Cath. Encyclop.*, arts. " Church," secs. v, vii, ix, xiii, and " State and Church " ; Finlay, S.J. —*The Church of Christ* ; Ryan and Millar—*The State and the Church* ; *Code of Social Principles*, nn. 53–56 ; C. S. Devas—*Key to the World's Progress*.

those of the natural law. He has, besides, endowed him with privileges and given him hopes immeasurably beyond anything to which man might naturally aspire. For the supernatural life after death, and the gift of sanctifying grace which fits the human soul to enter into that life, are privileges greater than man could merit by his own efforts and higher than any created intellect can ever fully understand.

Man's elevation to the supernatural order, and the privileges which that elevation implies, have culminated in the mystery of the Incarnation of which the inspired Prophet wrote some five centuries before the coming of Jesus Christ : " *From the beginning of the world they have not heard ; nor perceived with their ears ; the eye hath not seen O God, besides Thee, what things Thou hast prepared for those that wait for Thee.*"[1]

Church in Supreme Control of Religion and Morals.—The Incarnation and the mission of Christ on earth now dominate the whole question of religion and morals and the State's relation to them. For Christ founded on earth a society destined to last to the end of time, to which He committed the supreme and undivided control of religion and of everything pertaining to the supernatural and eternal life of man. To this society, too, He gave infallible authority to interpret the divine law both natural and revealed. And since Christ is God, every person and every human organisation, including the State, are bound by His laws.

It is outside our present scope to prove the divinity of Christ's mission or to describe in detail the constitution and distinguishing marks of the society to which are confided the execution of His decrees, the control of His religion, and the practical application of the fruits and merits of His life on earth. These questions belong to the domain of Dogmatic Theology and Christian Apologetics.[2] Our present purpose is to indicate briefly the prerogatives of this society, its position in the social organism, and the relations which should exist between it and the State.

---

[1] *Isaias* lxiv. 4.
[2] For clear and succinct treatment of these subjects, cf. Rev. P. Finlay, S.J., *Church of Christ*, and Dr. Sheehan, *Apologetics and Catholic Doctrine*.

Its Authority Denied by Modern Governments.—The rulers of the Protestant nations which revolted against the Church in the 16th century completely deny the Church's authority and prerogatives. The Liberal Governments, too, of most of the countries of Europe, even of those which still substantially retain the true faith, refuse to concede to the Church more than a fraction of her just claims, while extreme Liberal or Masonic Governments, such as those of Mexico, Russia and France, aim at suppressing all real religion and destroying the organisation of the Catholic Church. Uneducated Catholic opinion, in many countries, and even in Ireland, is considerably influenced in these matters by Liberal and non-Catholic principles owing to the powerful and insidious press propaganda by which such principles are supported.

Founded by Jesus Christ the Son of God.—From the Gospel history we know that Jesus Christ, the Eternal Son of God, established on earth one universal society for assisting and guiding men in the due service of God and the pursuit of supernatural happiness. It can be shown by arguments clear and conclusive enough to convince an impartial enquirer that that society is the Catholic Church alone. The Catholic Church may be described in Bellarmine's well-known words as :

" A society founded by Jesus Christ composed of the faithful living on earth who profess the same faith, partake of the same Sacraments, and, under the government of their lawful pastors, are subject to the supreme rule of the Roman Pontiff, who is the centre of Catholic unity."

A Society Permeating All Others, and Potentially Universal in Its Membership.—The Church, therefore, is a society composed, like the State, of individuals joined together by visible bonds of union. But it differs essentially from the State in the fact that the purpose and scope of the latter are man's temporal well-being, while those of the Church are his spiritual and eternal interests.

" The Church," writes Leo XIII, " is a society perfect in its kind, whose office and mission it is to school mankind in the precepts and teaching of the Gospel, and by safeguarding the integrity of morals and the exercise of Christian virtue to lead men to that happiness which is held out to everyone in Heaven."[1]

In its scope and membership the Church is universal. While remaining one society, organised under the government of a single supreme ruler, the Church embraces the whole world, and transcends all distinctions of race, or nation, or class, or sex. For in her " *there is neither Jew nor Greek, there is neither bond nor free, there is neither male nor female. For . . . all are one in Jesus Christ.*"[2] All are invited, and by God's positive command all are bound to belong to the Church, though many live and die in inculpable ignorance of that obligation.

" The Church rules peoples," writes Leo XIII, " scattered through every portion of the earth, differing in race and customs, who, living under the laws of their respective countries, give obedience alike to the civil and religious authorities."[3]

A Perfect Society.—Like the State, the Church is a *perfect* society. In other words, it comprehends in its scope all of men's interests that have to do with their eternal salvation, and is supreme within its own sphere. Hence, it is subject to God alone and does not borrow its authority or sanction from any created person or body outside itself.

" It is," again writes Leo XIII, " a society chartered as of right divine, perfect in its nature and its title, to possess in itself and by itself, through the will and loving kindness of its Founder, all needful provision for its maintenance and action."[4]

Thus, the Church is in no sense inferior to the civil power nor in any way dependent upon it, and, because its end and object are the greatest of all, so also its authority is the most exalted. The Church, therefore, has its own supreme ruler, its own code of laws, its own sanctions, its own punishments for transgressors, its executive officers, and its ceremonial observances.

" Jesus Christ," again writes Leo XIII, " gave to His Apostles unrestrained authority in regard to things sacred, together with

---

[1] *Præclaræ Gratulationis*, 1894. " The Reunion of Christendom " (cf. *The Great Encyclicals of Leo XIII*, Benziger, New York, 1908, p. 312). See also *Sapientiæ Christianæ*, pp. 121, 122, and Pius XI—*Ubi Arcano*, 1922, pp. 243, 244.
[2] *Gal.* iii, 28.   [3] *Sapientiæ Christianæ*, p. 121.   [4] *Immortale Dei*, p. 50.

the genuine and truest power of making laws ; as well as the twofold right of judging and punishing which flows from that power."[1]

This power extends to everything in which religion is concerned. It includes the right to teach all nations and to propagate the Christian Faith in every country. The Church need not wait on the behest of the civil power in any country to preach freely among the people and to govern in religious matters the baptised citizens of that country. For she has got from Christ the charge " of administering freely and without hindrance in accordance with her own judgment all matters that fall within her competence."[2]

Rights Violated, but Virtually Acknowledged.

—These indefeasible rights of the Church and the independent sovereignty over all its members which belongs to its supreme ruler are denied by non-Catholic and Liberal governments of the present day, just as they were denied by the pagan emperors of ancient Rome.

The Church, however, has never ceased to claim them and even to exercise them openly in despite of civil laws to the contrary which are essentially invalid. Thus, seeing that Christian marriage, being in its essence a Sacrament, is directly under the control of the Church, she proclaims as null and void the so-called civil marriages of Catholics which unchristian governments uphold and approve ; and in many cases she recognises, as valid and binding, marriages which the State regards as null. She has never ceased to protest against the usurpation by the State of her authority regarding education. She maintains, often against the express prohibition of the State, her right to own corporate property, and to found and charter religious orders. Christian princes and Christian States have always recognised the independent sovereignty of the Church ; and even non-Catholic and non-Christian rulers, while denying it in word and opposing it when they can, are in practice often forced to acknowledge it ; whereas every other so-called Church is either an annex of the civil power like the

---

[1] *Ib.* [2] *Ib.*, p. 51.

Anglican, the Presbyterian, and the Lutheran churches, or is practically ignored by the ruling authorities.

" It cannot be called in question," writes Leo XIII, " that in the making of treaties, in the transaction of business matters, in the sending and receiving of ambassadors, and in the interchange of other kinds of official dealings, princes and all invested with ruling power have been wont to treat with the Church as with a supreme and legitimate power."[1]

Pope's Temporal Sovereignty.—The object of the temporal sovereignty of the Popes over the Papal States was to symbolise and safeguard this independent status of the Church. For " it was not without a singular disposition of God's providence that the Church was provided with a civil sovereignty as the surest safeguard of her independence,"[2] and that Rome, " once the capital of an empire large indeed, but limited, became the capital of the whole world, the seat of a sovereignty or divine principality, which embraces all peoples and nations."[3]

It is necessary in the interests of civil society, as well as in the spiritual interests of the people, that the Church should enjoy the fullest liberty, and that her sovereign ruler on earth be subject to no earthly power.   For, as Pope Pius XI again writes :

" The Divine origin and nature of this (viz., the Church's) sovereignty require, and the inviolable right arising from the universality of the faithful of Christ spread throughout the world, demands that this sacred sovereignty shall not appear to be subject to any human power, to any law, even such law as might profess to secure the liberty of the Roman Pontiff with certain safeguards and guarantees, but must be an absolutely independent sovereignty and must manifestly appear as such."[4]

For these reasons the Popes never ceased to protest against the unjust violation of the Papal States in 1870 until the Treaty of the Lateran, 1929, by which the Pope was re-established as an independent temporal sovereign, with his rights as such internationally recognised.

---

[1] *Ib.*, p. 51.   On this whole question, cf. Ryan—*The State and the Church*, pp. 39 ff.
[2] *Ib.*   [3] Pius XI—*Ubi Arcano*, 1922, p. 251.
[4] *Ib.*, pp. 251, 252.

Art. 2—*Relations Between Church and State*

The Law of Christ and the Canon Law.—Seeing that Christ is God and Christ's laws are meant for all men, and that He established His Church as the guardian and interpreter of these laws, every State and every civil government are bound by the laws of Christ as interpreted by the Church. Hence, the State is bound to rule the people in accordance with Christian principles, even though it be true that the members as well as rulers of many States may be inculpably ignorant of that obligation. Moreover, the rulers of the Church have the right and sometimes the obligation to point out to temporal rulers the duties which the Christian law imposes on them ; to urge them to the faithful discharge of these duties, and, if necessary, even to denounce their injustice or negligence.

Again, since the Church is supreme in all that concerns man's spiritual interests, it can itself make laws concerning matters appertaining to these interests ; and the State, although independent of the Church in purely temporal matters, is bound by these laws no less than the individual citizen. Furthermore, the civil power in carrying out its own duty of worshipping and obeying God and protecting and promoting religious observance and good morals among the people must conform to the directions of the proper ecclesiastical authorities, and especially to those of the Sovereign Pontiff who reserves the cognizance of the more important questions (*causæ majores*) to his own tribunal.

State Bound to Protect and Assist Church.—Finally, as a result of the duty of the State to safeguard and uphold religious interests, it is bound to extend protection and all reasonable assistance to the Church in the exercise of her own proper functions. Thus, the State is bound to afford the ministers of the Church all needed facilities to teach, preach and administer the Sacraments. Again, the civil government is bound to respect and safeguard Church property and to uphold, as far as may be necessary, ecclesiastical laws and to facilitate their observance. Hence, a Christian Government will safeguard the observance of the Lord's Day and the holydays of the Church, by removing from the people's way the need, or temptation, to violate them.

State Supreme in Temporal Affairs.—The rights and prerogatives of the Church do not nullify or lessen the just claims of the State, which is supreme within its own sphere, just as the Church is supreme within its sphere.

" The spiritual and the secular power," writes St. Thomas,[1] " each rests upon divine authority. Hence, the secular power is subject to the spiritual power only in as far as it has been made subject to it by God, namely, in matters appertaining to eternal salvation. In these, therefore, one has to obey the spiritual power rather than the secular. But in matters which have to do with temporal goods one must obey the secular power rather than the sporitual, according to the words : *' Render to Cæsar the things that are Cæsar's, and to God the things that are God's !* ' "[2]

On the same subject Leo XIII writes :

" The Almighty . . . has appointed the charge of the human race between two powers, the Ecclesiastical and the Civil, the one being set over divine, and the other over human things. Each in its kind is supreme, each has fixed limits within which it is contained, limits which are defined by the nature and special province of each."[3]

State Assisted by the Church.—Churchmen no less than others are bound by the just laws of the State in all matters that relate to the temporal sphere.

Furthermore, the Church is bound in accordance with the natural and divine law, to assist the State in promoting the true temporal welfare of the citizens, for this is an important means of carrying out her own duty of safeguarding and advancing the people's spiritual interests. Hence it is, that the Church uses her influence with the people, which in a Catholic country is always very great, to promote the observance of just laws, to inculcate peaceful submission and obedience to legitimate authority, and to encourage the spirit of true Christian patriotism. She exhorts the rulers to govern with righteousness and to seek constantly the good of their subjects ; while to rulers and subjects alike she ceases not to preach justice, charity and forbearance and a cordial union among all in working for the common good.

So powerful, and at the same time so neceesary, are the Church's influence and teaching and the religious helps,

---

[1] 2 *Sent.*, D. 44, Q. 2, a. 4.   [2] *Matth.* xxii.   [3] *Immortale Dei*, p. 51.

both external and interior, which she administers and controls, that it may be safely said that without the aid of a living spirit of religion (which the Catholic Church alone can impart and maintain) among the people, no State can be permanently prosperous and happy. On the other hand, religion, and consequently, the influence of the Church, are the most powerful of all means in the work of safeguarding and promoting true social well-being.

Mixed Questions.—Besides the purely spiritual matters which belong exclusively to the Church, such as dogmatic teaching, the sacraments and the training of the clergy, and the purely temporal affairs which are under the supreme control of the State, such as national defence, the police, and hygiene, there exists a fairly wide zone of mixed questions, in which both spiritual and temporal interests are concerned and are more or less indivisibly intermingled. Matters of this kind are education, marriage and family life, ecclesiastical property and pious bequests and civil laws which indirectly affect the people's religious interests.

Church's Role Predominant.—In questions of this type, although, since they are partly temporal, the State has certain duties and certain functions in their regard, her rôle is in a certain sense and to a certain degree subject to the direction and control of the Church.

This principle, which is of paramount importance, may be thus explained : The end and purpose of the State, namely, man's temporal good, is subordinate to that of the Church, which has for its ultimate object man's supernatural union with God for ever. For, although the individual and the State have the right and, within certain limits, a duty to seek after temporal happiness and prosperity, this right and duty are limited by the obligation of abstaining from anything that may be inconsistent with man's eternal welfare. Hence, in a clash, or apparent clash, between the interests of the Church and the State (which would in fact be a conflict between man's eternal and his temporal welfare), the latter is bound to give way. And as the Church is the authentic and divinely appointed teacher and judge of moral obligation and duty, with power to decide questions with infallible authority, it is clear that

39

the rulers of the State must, in the ultimate resort, abide by the decision of the Church. In this sense, and to this extent, the civil power may be said to be subject to the Church, even in matters that do not appertain directly or solely to the sphere of religion or morals.

Concordats.—It is such mixed questions which most frequently lead to serious difficulty and misunderstanding, and it is specially in connection with such that *Concordats* are made. These are specific agreements between the temporal rulers and the Sovereign Pontiff concerning the points which may prove contentious. In these Concordats the Pope not infrequently makes important concessions to the temporal rulers in things which are not deemed essential to the Church's interests, on condition that the State allow the Church freedom and the necessary protection in essential matters.

The actual relations at present existing between Church and State, whether arranged by Concordat or otherwise fall more or less within one of the three following divisions :

Union of Church and State.—The first is that of a harmonious union between the two, analogous to the union between husband and wife, or to that between the body and soul by which the complete man is formed. The Church and State recognise each other's prerogatives. The State (while allowing freedom of conscience and thus tolerating such non-Catholic religions as may exist within its territory), itself publicly professes the Catholic faith. It recognises also the higher importance of the Church's functions and engages to fulfil its own part in the union according to the Christian principles, which we have already explained. This system existed over all Europe before the 16th century. It is broadly speaking (for actual arrangements vary in accordance with different Concordats) the system which exists at present in Italy, Spain (viz., before the Revolution of 1931), Belgium, Poland, as well as in the Argentine Republic, Bolivia, Costa Rica, Paraguay, Peru, Ecuador, and practically in Colombia.

The system is that most in accord with the divine law ; and the nearer the actual arrangements approach it the better for the spiritual interests of the people and for their peace and well-being even in temporal matters.

Persecution of the Church by the Civil Power.—The second type of relation is the exact opposite of the first. In it the temporal rulers claim a complete authority even in spiritual affairs, and not only ignore the Church's rights, but positively persecute it. This was the position in the British Isles, Holland, Prussia and Denmark, up to the 19th century. It exists in Russia to-day, and in other countries such as Mexico and France, in varying degrees, and seems to be the position towards which the present (1931) Republican Government of Spain is tending.

Separation of Church and State.—The third class, which is at present, the most numerous, includes those countries in which neither the Church nor her prerogatives are specially recognised in the Constitution of the State or in the legal system and administration. The Church is allowed, however, the more or less generous treatment accorded by the ordinary law of the land to all associations that are not deemed detrimental to the public peace. She is classed as a religious association and on a par with other religious or pseudo-religious bodies, including the non-Christian as well as the heretical sects. Thus, any one of the fundamental rights or laws of the Church, such as on the question of divorce or birth control, may at any time be discussed and voted upon in the legislative bodies.

This class admits of two main sub-divisions, namely : (*a*) the States such as England, Scotland, Finland, Norway, Denmark, Greece and Roumania, in which a religion other than the Catholic is the professed religion of the State ; and (*b*) those which have no State religion but tolerate all equally, such as the United States of America, Germany, Holland, Ireland (both Governments), Czechoslovakia, Cuba and Chile. Several of the States belonging to this class have made special Concordats with the Holy See, by which some at least of the Catholic claims are conceded, and secured by the Constitution.

Critique of Preceding System.—This system is manifestly not the ideal, as it is not founded upon true principles, and ignores some of the most important facts of life, such as the

Incarnation. Furthermore, it postulates, or presupposes "separation between Church and State," which is in practice impossible. For the two societies, Church and State, rule the same subjects on the same territory, and both have authority and interests in certain indivisible matters of essential importance, such as education and marriage. Consequently, where such a system obtains, clashes and friction are inevitable if Catholic principles are insisted on. This is especially so in education. It is especially unnatural and anomalous that a predominantly Catholic State should allow the true religion of Christ to be placed on a par with Methodism, Judaism, Theosophism or Christian Scientism. Pope Pius XI deplores this in his Encyclical instituting the Feast of Jesus Christ the King.

" The plague of the age," he writes, " is what is called secularism with all its attendant errors and impious purposes. . . . The rule of Christ over mankind has been denied, the Church has been refused the right to make her own laws. . . . Little by little the Christian religion has been made the equal of other and false religions and has been lowered to their level."[1]

More than a century before, Pius VII wrote in still stronger terms, complaining of the new French Constitution, in which

" the Catholic religion is passed over in silence. There is no mention of the Omnipotent God by Whom kings reign and princes command, and . . . the Catholic religion of France finds itself smitten by a mortal wound. . . . Truth is confounded with error. The holy and spotless Spouse of Christ, the true Church . . . is degraded to the same rank as the heretical sects, even that of the perfidious Jews."[2]

Popes' Exhortation Towards Union of Church and State.— Hence, in a predominantly Catholic State, in which it may be found impossible, owing to accidental or temporary causes, to establish a union of Church and State after the manner of the Catholic countries belonging to the first class

---

[1] *Quas Primas*, 1926 (Cf. *Encyclicals of Pius XI*, edited by J. H. Ryan : Herder, London, p. 147).

[2] *Post tam Diuturnas*, 1814 (Cf. Lettres Apostoliques de Pie IX, Gregoire XVI, Pie VII, etc., published by La Bonne Presse, Paris, pp. 243, 244).

mentioned above, it would seem desirable, and the modern tendency is, that a Concordat be made between the ruling authorities and the Holy See, in which the Catholic Church is accorded a special status, her fundamental laws and rights secured by the civil constitution and a basis arranged upon which contentious questions may be satisfactorily settled.

" If the civil power," writes Leo XIII, " combines in a friendly manner with the spiritual power of the Church, it necessarily follows that both parties will greatly benefit. The dignity of the one (viz., the civil power) will be enhanced, and with religion as its guide there will never be a rule that is not just ; for the other (viz., the Church) there will be at hand a safeguard and defence which will operate to the public good of the faithful."[1]

Pius XI urges the same in the strongest terms :

" We earnestly exhort in the Lord all those who hold the reins of power that they establish and maintain firmly harmony and friendship with the Church of Christ in order that through the united activity and energy of both powers the tremendous evils may be checked which menace civil society as well as the Church. . . . For at present there are those who think that whatever is permitted by the laws of the State, or at least is not punished, is allowed also by the moral law. . . . Hence, often they bring ruin on themselves and on many others."

Then, after referring to the recent solemn convention between the Holy See and the Kingdom of Italy, " quite in accordance with right order and in complete conformity with the law of Christ," the Holy Father goes on to say :

" This arrangement might well be an example and proof to all even in this our day (when, sad to say, the absolute separation of the civil power from the Church, and indeed from every religion is so often taught), that one supreme authority can be united and associated with the other without detriment to the rights and supreme power of either, and with the greatest advantage to the highest interest of both."[2]

---

[1] Leo XIII—*Arcanum Divinæ*, p. 41. Cf. also *ib. Libertas, Præstantissimum*, pp. 83 ff ; also *Immortale Dei*, pp. 52 ff.
[2] *Casti Connubii*, 1930 (C. T. S. edit.), pp. 63, 64.

Art. 3—*The Church and Social Well-being*[1]

Within the Church's Sphere.—Social well-being, as already explained, has reference not merely to the material or physical welfare of the people, but also to their moral and intellectual interests. While the two latter come directly within the sphere of the Church's functions, the material interests of the people do not, but are very closely connected with them. Hence, even the science of Political Economy, which is concerned with the material prosperity of the State, has moral aspects, and is not, like Mathematics or Chemistry, outside the purview of an authority, whose *immediate* sphere is confined within the domain of religion and morals.

The view of the economists of the " Classical School," once shared even by some Catholic writers, that the sole aim of Political Economy is the greater prosperity of the State ; and that Political Economy has no immediate bearing on the well-being of the masses of the people cannot be sustained and is now generally abandoned. The view has become discredited with the discrediting of the economic doctrines (associated with the " Manchester School ") on which it was founded.[2] Since the State is made up of persons, and is meant essentially for the good of its members, its prosperity cannot be regarded as something apart from the prosperity of its members. Hence, the science of Political Economy, which has to do with the material prosperity of the State, must, if its principles be true, have an immediate bearing on the material well-being of the people of whom the State is composed.[3] Now, moral and religious considerations cannot be entirely eliminated from questions whose direct and immediate object is man's material well-being. Man is not merely a producer and

---

[1] Cf. C. Plater, S.J.—*The Priest and Social Action* (Longmans, London 1914) ; Ryan and Husselein—*The Church and Labour* ; Husselein—*Democratic Industry* and *The World Problem* ; Ryan—*Social Reconstruction* (Macmillan, New York, 1920) ; Dardano, *op. cit.*, Introduction, pp. ix–xv ; Lugan—*Social Principles of the Gospel*, translated from the Italian (Macmillan, New York, 1928) ; Devas—*Key to the World's Progress* ; Schmidt, *op. cit.* (Preliminary Essay by R. T. Dale) ; Chateaubriand—*Génie du Christianisme* ; Balmes—*European Civilisation.*

[2] Cf. *Supra*, chap. ix, arts. 6 and 7.

[3] Cf. Devas—*Political Economy* (3rd edit.), Epilogue, part i ; Plater, *op. cit.*, chap. i ; Antoine, *op. cit.*, Introduction.

consumer. He is by his very nature a human person and a social being. He has personal rights and duties which are inalienable. He is, or may be, a member of a family and a citizen, and these aspects of his nature and the needs to which they give rise cannot be made subservient to so-called "Economic Laws," or disregarded in discussing economic questions. Now, all Catholics admit that ethical or moral questions come even directly within the scope of the Church's authority and activities.

Furthermore, the material conditions of the people react strongly on their moral and spiritual welfare ; for, as St. Thomas says : "the use of bodily and external commodities is necessary to virtuous action."[1] Besides all this, the precepts and example of the Divine Founder of the Church " *Who went about doing good,*" make it obligatory upon the Church and upon its pastors and priests to strive in due measure for the material welfare of the people.

"It must not be supposed," writes Leo XIII, "that the solicitude of the Church is so taken up with the spiritual concerns of her children as to neglect their temporal or earthly interests. Her desire is, that the poor, for example, should rise above poverty and wretchedness, and better their conditions in life ; and for this she earnestly strives. . . . Herein she has always succeeded so well as to have even extorted the praise of her enemies."[2]

Church's Aid Necessary for Social Well-being.—Again, Leo XIII constantly insists on the principle that the State cannot be permanently prosperous without the aid of the Church. Thus he writes :

"If society is to be healed now, in no other way can it be healed save by a return to Christian life and Christian institutions."[3]

And again :

"No solution of the social question will be found apart from the intervention of religion and the Church."[4]

The Pope's reasoning is as follows : European society was formed and moulded upon the teachings of Christianity, by which it was in the Middle Ages " brought back from

---

[1] *De Regimine Principum* i, 15.
[2] *Rerum Novarum*, pp. 148, 149.   [3] *Ib.*, p. 148.   [4] *Ib.*, p. 141.

death to life, and so excellent a life that nothing more
perfect had been known before, or will come to be known
in the ages that have yet to come." The general decadence
dates from the 16th century, when the unity of Christendom
was broken, and the countries began, one after another, to
abandon Christian principles in their civil and social life.
Therefore, for their renovation and cure they must return
to those principles.   For

" when a society is perishing, the wholesome advice to give to
those who would restore it is to recall it to the principles from
which it sprang. . . . To fall away from its former constitution
implies disease ; to go back to it, recovery."[1]

Since Religion is Necessary for It.—Leo XIII gives a
further reason why the Church's influence and assistance
are necessary for the task of solving the social question.
He says :

" Without the instincts, which the Christian religion implants
and keeps alive, without providence, self-control, thrift, endurance and other natural qualities, you cannot secure real
prosperity however hard you may try. That is the reason
why . . . associations for the assistance of the poor or . . .
other schemes of the kind must not be attempted without the
sanction of religion, without its inclusion and aid."[2]

In another Encyclical he writes on the same subject :

" Since religion alone can avail to destroy the evil at its root,
all men should rest persuaded that the main thing needed is to
return to real Christianity, apart from which all the plans and
devices of the wisest will prove of little avail."[3]

Teaching of Pius XI.—Pius XI also insists on the necessity
of restoring Christian standards in public and private life,
as the one sure means of attaining temporal well-being

" when once men recognise," he writes, " both in private and
public life that Christ is King, society will at last receive the
great blessings of real liberty, well-ordered discipline, peace and
harmony."[4]

Again, in his Encyclical on the Social Order, he writes :

" There can be no other remedy [viz., for the social evils from
which modern States suffer] than a frank and sincere return to

---

[1] *Rerum Novarum*, p. 148.   [2] *Graves de Communi*, 1901, p. 174.
[3] *Rerum Novarum*, p. 163.
[4] *Quas Primas* (Cf. Encyclicals of Pius XI, edited by J. H. Ryan, p. 142).

the teachings of the Gospel. . . . All those versed in social matters demand a rationalisation of economic life, which will introduce sound and true order. But such an order . . . will necessarily be quite faulty and imperfect, unless all men's activities harmoniously unite to imitate, and as far as is humanly possible, attain the marvellous unity of the Divine plan . . , which places God as the first and supreme end of all created activities, and regards all created goods as mere instruments under God to be used in so far as they help towards the attainment of one supreme end. . . .

"If these principles be observed . . . not merely the production and acquisition of goods, but also the use of wealth, now so often uncontrolled, will within a short time be bought back again to the standards of equity and just distribution. Mere sordid selfishness, which is the disgrace and the great crime of the present day, will be opposed in very deed by the kindly and forcible law of Christian moderation."[1]

The Church Alone Teaches True Social Principles.—The Church, and she alone, can teach with infallible authority and with definite clearness and consistency the principles of the moral law, regulating social conduct and men's relations with the Creator and with one another. These principles include the obligations of religion, the duties of Justice, the privileges of human personality, the mutual rights and duties of rulers and subjects, the obligation of self-sacrifice, the call of charity, of filial affection, and of Patriotism. All these principles and teachings proved from reason and confirmed by divine revelation, are founded upon man's nature and the circumstances of his creation and preservation by God. Unless these truths are known and followed, it is clear that God's designs in creating man for happiness and instituting human society to aid him in attaining it, will not be realised.

She Alone Can Secure Their Adoption.—Again, the Church, and she alone, has at her disposal the means of securing that the principles which she inculcates will become effective in social life. For such a purpose it is essential that rulers as well as subjects, the wealthy as well as the poor be responsive to conscientious obligations. Without that, principles and duty have no meaning, and all men alike are swayed only by passion and self-interest.

---

[1] *Quadragesimo Anno*, pp. 62, 63.

" The Government alone cannot govern," says De Maistre. " It has the further need of an essential support, either of slavery, which lessens the number of wills that can effectually oppose the government, or of some spiritual force which, by a kind of divine graft, destroys the waywardness of these wills and gets them to act in harmony."[1]

The Church, by her religious teaching, her moral code, and the sanctions by which this code is upheld ; her sacraments, and the practice of prayer upon which she insists, permeates the people at large with a sense of religion and respect for duty which no other influence can impart. She has an ecclesiastical organisation which is the most powerful and highly-developed in the world. Her ministers and clergy have the functions not merely of carrying out divine worship, but of striving incessantly to make the principles of Christianity operative in men's lives.

Christianity Secures even Temporal Happiness.—Thus it is, that notwithstanding the fact that the Church's mission is to save and sanctify souls : she actually, although incidentally, does far more. Solomon's praises of divine wisdom : " *All good things came to me together with her ; and innumerable riches through her hands,*"[2] even as applied to temporal blessings and true material well-being, have been verified of the Church in every country and every age. Consequently, wherever the Church is free, and her members numerous enough to dominate public life, the social question, as it presents itself in modern times, will not arise. And in proportion as a State or Government comes under the influence of Christianity, in that proportion will social injustice be eliminated and preventable human misery disappear.

" Caring little," says Balmes, " whether such and such political forms are established in a country, she [the Church] has ever addressed herself to man, seeking to enlighten his understanding and purify his heart, fully confident that when these objects are attained, society will naturally pursue a safe course."[3]

That the efforts of the Church to lead men to eternal happiness should also result in promoting their temporal

---

[1] *Du Pape*, liv. iii, chap. ii.   [2] *Wisdom* vii. 11.
[3] *Op. cit.*, cap. 57, p. 321.

welfare is in accordance with the promise of her Divine Founder : " *Seek ye first the Kingdom of God and His justice and all these* [other] *things shall be added unto you.*"[1]

Art. 4—*The Priest and Social Action*[2]

It has sometimes been argued even by priests that social and economic activities such as the establishing of agricultural colonies or co-operative and mutual benefit societies, or labour associations, or Raiffeisen banks, etc., form no part of a priest's functions, and that his time would be better and more suitably spent in the duties which refer exclusively to the spiritual interests of his people.

Social Action Closely Connected with the Sacred Ministry.— It is true indeed that the priest's primary duty refers to purely spiritual interests. But, closely connected with these very interests there is a whole multitude of other questions, which cannot be regarded as outside the priest's sphere. His very zeal for the people's spiritual welfare must make him solicitous about almost every phase of their social life. The material conditions and social environment of the faithful, the munieipal organisation, the social customs, the amusements of the people, the literature they read, the houses they live in, the economic conditions in which they have to work, all have a bearing more or less direct upon their moral and religious life. Hence, those to whom the care of the spiritual interests is committed cannot afford to be indifferent to material affairs. The peculiar circumstances of our own time and the pressing nature of the many social problems which cannot be solved without the active co-operation of the Church render that co-operation all the more necessary. It may be added that at the present day, when the social question looms so large in European life, when, as Leo XIII so truly says : " The momentous gravity of the state of things now obtaining fills every mind with painful apprehensions, so that there is no other question which has taken deeper hold of the public

---

[1] *Matth.* vi. 33.
[2] Cf. Plater, *op. cit.* ; Antoine, *op. cit.*, chap. vi, art. 6 ; Godts, *op. cit.* ; Dardano, *op. cit.* (Introduction, pp. ix–xv) ; O'Riordan—*Catholicity and Progress in Ireland* (Kegan, Paul, London, 1906), chap. xi.

mind,"[1] the duty of social action and of a deep interest in every aspect of social science is especially incumbent upon Catholics, and above all, on the clergy.

Exhortations of Popes and Bishops.—Besides all these reasons, the Holy See and a very large and increasing number of Bishops in every country advocate in the clearest and most urgent terms this active co-operation of the clergy in social organisation and reconstruction.

" Every minister of holy religion," writes Leo XIII, " must bring to the struggle the full energy of his mind and all his power of endurance. Moved by your authority, Venerable Brethren, and quickened by your example, . . . they must by every means in their power strive to secure the good of the people."[2]

And again :

" In any enterprise of the kind [viz., establishing Catholic associations for the betterment of the people] . . . it is clear that the priesthood ought to be concerned throughout, and that it may assist in many ways by its learning, its prudence and its charity."[3]

The Ecclesiastical Seminaries.—In the splendid Encyclical, on the Training of the Clergy and the exercising of the Sacred Ministry, which Leo XIII addressed to the Bishops of Italy a short time before his death, he, while insisting on the fundamental need of forming the young ecclesiastics to habits of prayer and self-denial, and of grounding them thoroughly in the Sacred Sciences during their years of preparation, adds these words which are apropos of our present subject.

" It is clear, Venerable Brethren, that all we have so far enjoined not only does not imply anything contrary to the social activity of the clergy, which we have so often recommended as a need of our age, but rather tends to promote it in the highest degree. For, in exacting the faithful observance of the rules we have laid down, we are helping to promote that which ought to be the life and soul of such activities. Let it therefore be here again repeated with greater emphasis : the clergy must go to the Christian people now surrounded on all sides by snares and allured by all sorts of false promises and especially by socialism . . .

---

[1] *Rerum Novarum*, p. 176.   [2] *Ib.*, pp. 167, 168.
[3] *Graves de Communi*, 1901, p. 179.

" For this purpose we desire that the aspirants to the Priesthood, while abstaining . . . from all participation in actual movements outside, should towards the end of their seminary course, be duly instructed in the Papal documents which have to do with the social question and Christian Democracy. Later on, when advanced to the Priesthood, let them employ themselves with the people who at every period have been the special object of the Church's most affectionate care. To rescue the children of the people from ignorance of spiritual and eternal interests . . . to promote among the Catholic laity those organisations which are recognised as truly efficacious for their moral and material betterment ; above all, to defend the principles of justice and Christian charity in which all the rights and duties of civil society find a fair and equitable balancing, such in its outstanding characteristics is the grand duty and object of the social activities."[1]

Pius X.—Pius X followed closely on the footsteps of his predecessor. Thus in the letter which he addressed (Feb. 20th, 1907) to the Provincial Directors of the recently-founded *Catholic Social Economic Union* of Italy, he writes :

" The most suitable institutions for the Union to foster will be, as it seems to us, these which are called *Professional* [viz., *Trade*] *Unions*. We again earnestly recommend you to be solicitous for their foundation and progress. . . . The co-operation of the clergy will be very helpful in this matter. Herein they will find fresh means of rendering their sacred ministry more efficacious. Workingmen thus trained will not only become good trade unionists, but also sturdy auxiliaries of the priest in the diffusion and defence of the practice of Catholic Teaching."[2]

Again, speaking in a private audience to the Abbé François of the diocese of Cambrai (March, 1907), he is reported as saying :

" Tell your venerable Archbishop of the great satisfaction with which I learn that he has appointed two priests to devote themselves particularly to the farmers and their labourers. I wish that those matters which interest the peasantry were as well known by the rural clergy as their theology. They can never do too much to show how the Church loves the working classes."[3]

---

[1] Encyclical (Dec. 8th, 1902) to the Bishops of Italy on the education of the Clergy and the Sacred Ministry. Cf. *Actes de Leo XIII* (La Bonne Presse, Paris), vol. viii, p. 147.
[2] *Actes de Pius X* (La Bonne Presse, Paris), tome iii, pp. 38, 39.
[3] *Actes Sociaux* (published by *L'Action Populaire*, nos. 49–50, p. 44), quoted in Plater, *op. cit.*, p. 256.

Pius XI.—Our present Holy Father touches briefly on this same matter in the very first Encyclical of his Pontificate. After commending in magnificent terms the various activities and organisations of clergy and laity which have sprung up in our time over the whole Church to promote Christ's Kingdom on earth, he adds :

" We include among these fruits of piety the whole group of movements, organisations and works so dear to our Fatherly heart which passes under the name of " Catholic Action " and in which we have been intensely interested. All these organisations and movements . . . ought to be developed more and more. . . . Since such work is vitally necessary it is without question an essential part of our Christian life and of the sacred ministry. Tell your clergy, therefore, Venerable Brothers, who we know have laboured so devotedly in these different fields of activities whose work we have seen at close range and have even shared . . . that when they co-operate with you they are united with Christ and guided by Him through you ; that at the same time they also co-operate with Us, and that we bless them with our fatherly blessing."[1]

These exhortations have been repeated and emphasised again and again by the Holy Father during the past nine years. He has indeed made the promotion of " Catholic Action " one of the outstanding features of his Pontificate. He, furthermore, includes social and economic organisation among the principal elements of Catholic Action, and intimates that in this social and economic organisation of Catholics the clergy are to be the leaders under the guiding control of the Bishops. Above all, in his Encyclical on the Social Order, from which we have quoted so profusely in the present work, the Pope makes very urgent appeals to the Bishops and Clergy to be zealous and unremitting in their efforts to promote Social Action among the faithful as the great need of the present day.

" We must gather," he writes, " and train from amongst their very ranks [viz., of the men themselves] auxiliary soldiers of the Church. . . . Undoubtedly the first and immediate apostles of the workingmen must themselves be workingmen, while the apostles of the industrial and commercial world should themselves be employers and merchants.

---

[1] *Ubi Arcano* (Cf. Ryan—*Encyclicals of Pius XI*, London, 1927, pp. 37, 38).

" It is your chief duty, Venerable Brethren, and that of your clergy . . . to select prudently and train fittingly these lay apostles amongst workingmen and amongst employers. . . . Wherefore all candidates for the sacred priesthood must be adequately prepared . . . by intense study of social matters. . . .

" We earnestly exhort in the Lord the beloved sons who are chosen for this task to devote themselves whole-heartedly to the formation of the men entrusted to them. In the execution of this most priestly and apostolic work, let them make opportune use of the powerful resources of Christian training by instructing youth, by founding Christian associations, by forming study-circles on Christian lines. Above all, let them hold in high esteem and employ with diligence for the benefit of their disciples the Spiritual Exercises, a most precious means of personal and of social reform."[1]

The Irish Bishops.—These precepts and exhortations of the Sovereign Pontiffs are emphasised and confirmed by the Bishops of Ireland in the Plenary Synod of Maynooth, 1927. Thus we read :

" We exhort in the Lord all both clergy and laity to promote Catholic Action which in repeated exhortations the Sovereign Pontiffs have recommended. . . . Particular care should be paid to the working class, lest lured by the promises and deceived by the frauds of the Socialists it lose its ancestral faith.

" Parish priests and other priests should teach employers by word and by example that a just and decent wage must be paid to workers and that more labour must not be imposed on them than was settled by fair agreement, or their sex or age has strength for. . . .

" Parish priests should encourage organisations of farmers and workers in conformity with Catholic principles, and should expound and defend their rights and duties. . . .

" Clergy and laity should strive to promote Economic Action also, which directly concerns temporal welfare, but indirectly the welfare of religion also."[2]

---

[1] *Quadragesimo Anno*, pp. 67, 68.

[2] The quiet but effective work of priests like the late Father M. Aherne, P.P., of Coachford, in the diocese of Cloyne, Co. Cork (*d.* 1928), illustrates what a zealous priest with practical ability can accomplish even in the matter of social and economic reconstrucion. While a curate in Youghal in the early years of the century, and later on in Gortroe, a parish situated a few miles from Youghal, Fr. Aherne organised in connection with the Youghal branch of the League of the Cross a Workman's Club, with lecture hall ; a co-operative society, by means of which the members were enabled to procure necessaries at greatly reduced prices ; a Land

Finally, in the last section of the Chapter on Catholic Action the Bishops have inserted the following important provision :

" In the more important towns let associations be organised with the approval and under the control of the Bishop. These associations will be made up principally of priests that are specially skilled in this matter ; and their object shall be the study and investigation of social and economic questions and the promotion of social and economic activities ; and especially such as tend to promote industrial peace and harmony. . . . "[1]

Social Action a Proof of the Church's Mission.—So urgent and of such dominating importance is the modern social question that it may be taken as certain that the truth of the Church's mission and the sincerity and efficiency of her ministers will in our day be rightly or wrongly measured in large degree by the vigour and success with which they deal each in his own sphere with the social question.

" God Almighty," writes Cardinal Capecelatro, " has so constituted Christian life that in every age . . . it appears with a new *Apologia* due to the new conditions of the race. Now in our day, if I am not deceived the new *apologia* will be the product of the social question ; and progress in that question will most certainly be made in the name of Jesus Christ living in the Church. To the classic defences of the past, to martyrdom, to the more perfect sanctity of the Church, to the doctrine of the Fathers, to the monastic life, to the overthrow of barbarous

---

Bank through which the peasant farmers of Gortroe could, when necessary, obtain advances of money at very low interest. He also founded the Youghal Art Metal Works, which operated very successfully as long as he was there. His co-operative society was able to charter a special vessel to convey coal from the pit-head to Youghal Harbour, and sell it to the members at about half the current retail prices. At Gortroe he organised the peasant cottiers into a co-operative society by means of which they were enabled to market their produce more easily and favourably, to establish their own Land Bank, and above all, to found the industry (which still flourishes) of raising early potatoes for the English and Scotch markets. These potatoes were bought up eagerly by English and Scotch traders at prices varying from £20 to £30 per ton. Not infrequently, a farmer disposed of a whole field of potatoes while still in the ground at a rate of £300 (three hundred pounds) per acre. Through the skilled instructors whom the society (or Fr. Aherne) employed, the cottiers were taught to sow the land with turnips or other suitable crop immediately after the potatoes were taken up, so that the large profits which the potato crop brought in were a source of revenue over and above the cottiers' usual income.

[1] Cf. *Conc. Plen. Mayn* (1927)—*Acta et Decreta*, pp. 88–91.

powers, to Christian art and literature, to the new poetry, to the harmony of science and faith, to the new forms of charity of the last two centuries—to all these will be added this fresh *apologia*—a solution of the social question by Catholicism and the science which Catholicism inspires."[1]

Ireland a Most Promising Field.—In Ireland the social question is awaiting solution. Probably in no country of the world is there a more promising field, or greater possibilities of immense and far-reaching good for the interests of Christ's Kingdom on earth than there is at present in Ireland. The good which may be looked for as a result of solving triumphantly Ireland's social evils will not be confined to the country itself. It will react and make its lessons felt among the many millions of people in Europe and America, not of the Irish race alone, among whom Ireland and the inspiration of her story and example are still a great moral force.

---

[1] *Christ, the Church and the Man* (London, Burns, Oates and Washbourne), quoted in Plater, *op. cit.*, p. 16.

40

APPENDICES

APPENDIX I

SOCIAL LIFE IN MEDIÆVAL IRELAND[1]

Peculiar Character of the Irish Social System.—The social organisation of ancient Ireland differed in many ways from that of mediæval Europe, although both were influenced deeply by the same Christian principles. Hence, it will be useful to supplement the sketch of mediæval society given in the First Part of this work[2] by some notes on the peculiar features which distinguished the Christian social organisation in Ireland from that of other countries of Christendom.

The difference between Ireland and the rest of Western Europe is rooted in the fact that Ireland was never incorporated into the system of imperial Rome ; nor affected by the general upheaval consequent upon the break up of the Western Empire in the 5th century. Irish civilisation developed on its own lines for more than a thousand years, without being much affected by any outside influence except Christianity. In Ireland, Latin never became, as it did over most of Europe, the sole or indeed, the principal, medium of instruction and literary expression. Neither did the Irish ever adopt Roman law, which during the middle ages imposed itself upon almost every other European country.

Historical Outline.[3]—Although Christianity was introduced into Ireland, probably about the beginning of the 5th century or a little earlier, the national movement towards the true

---

[1] Cf. Green—*History of the Irish State to* 1014 (Macmillan, 1925) ; and *Making of Ireland and Its Undoing,* chaps. i–vi and xii. MacNeill—*Phases of Irish History,* chaps. viii and x ; and *Celtic Ireland,* chaps. vi, vii, ix and x. Gougaud—*Les Chrétiéntés Celtiques,* chaps. iii, viii, x ; Sigerson—*Irish Land Tenures ;* Joyce—*Social History of Ireland* ; Ryan—*Ireland from the Earliest Times to* 800 *A.D.* (Browne and Nolan, Dublin, 1927), chap. ix ; and *Irish Monasticism* (Talbot Press, Dublin, 1931). O'Sullivan—Introduction to O'Curry's *Manners and Customs of the Ancient Irish* ; Curtis—*History of Mediæval Ireland*—Introduction, and chaps. viii, xii, xv ; Butler—*Gleanings from Irish History.*

[2] Chaps. iii–vii.

[3] *See* Ryan, *op. cit.,* and *Ireland from A.D.* 800 *to A.D.* 1600 (Browne and Nolan, Dublin, 1927).

629

faith only began after the arrival of St. Patrick in 432 A.D. We may perhaps fix the middle of the 6th century, when the great monasteries rose into prominence as the point at which the Christian religion had already gained definite mastery in the country. This was nearly two centuries after it had secured predominance in the Roman Empire. Ireland was then, and remained long after, the only country (except Armenia) outside the Roman Empire which had definitely embraced Christianity.

The Christian development in Ireland met no serious interruption until the 9th and 10th centuries, the period of the Norse and Danish inroads. The country then experienced its full share of the confusion and destruction and foreign and domestic strife by which all Europe was desolated. There was a certain recovery in the 11th and 12th centuries after the Norsemen had been driven out, or partially absorbed into the Christian life of the nation. The process of reconstruction, however, which went on for about a century and a half, was still incomplete when the Anglo-Norman and English invaders arrived (1169). These proved more fatal to Irish progress even than their Norse and Danish predecessors.

All the horrors of the wars that had desolated most of Europe during the 9th and 10th centuries were now renewed in Ireland. Within about seventy years from the beginning of their inroads, the Norman and English invaders had nominally established their feudal sway over the greater part of the country. They broke up completely for the time being the political and social organisation. They seized the land, perpetrated many massacres on the people, overturned large numbers of the churches and schools, or converted them into military fortresses, destroying their literary and artistic treasures. As a result of the Anglo-Norman invasion the development of Irish literature, architecture and art came to a sudden standstill. Architecture and art never afterwards recovered.[1]

Before the middle of the 15th century, however, the native

---

[1] Cf. Petrie—*Round Towers*, p. 320 and *passim* ; also Hyde—*Literary History of Ireland*, pp. 460–466, and Ryan—*Ireland from A.D. 800 to A.D. 1600*, pp. 137–139. For a contemporary account of the excesses of the Anglo-Normans in Ireland, *see* in McGeoghegan's *History of Ireland* O'Neill's *Letter to Pope John XXII* (1316).

Irish princes had reconquered most of the territories they had lost. Where the Anglo-Normans outside the towns still retained their foothold, they had mostly adopted the native civilisation and customs which were now re-established, with many alterations however, over most of the country. A district of about a thousand square miles around Dublin, as well as most of the principal seaports and some of the inland towns, still remained strongholds of the English power, and were ruled and organised after the manner of the English and continental mediæval cities.[1]

These conditions continued without substantial change until the English conquest, which began in the middle of the 16th century. This finally put an end to the mediæval Christian organisation over the whole of Ireland. Irish law was suppressed in the beginning of the 17th century, and in the course of the same century practically all the Irish owners were dispossessed of their lands and property, which were seized by the Protestant and Presbyterian planters.

Hence, the fairest fruits of Christian civilisation, which in Britain and continental Europe are to be looked for in the 12th and 13th centuries, are best exemplified in Ireland during the period lying between the 6th and 9th centuries.

Ireland's Golden Age.[2]—Christian principles and ideals then permeated the whole social life of the country (although in Ireland as in continental Europe, even during the golden age of Christianity, some unchristian customs and principles inherited from paganism still lived on). This was the era of Irish monasticism, of the great Irish missionary movement, and of the great schools. It was then that Ireland earned the title of the "Island of Saints," by which it was known in Europe at least as early as the 11th century. It is generally admitted that the Irish people of that period attained a height of Christian fervour which has probably never been exceeded and rarely equalled by any other country or at any other period of history.

"Such a flowering of holiness," writes Dom Gougaud, the French Benedictine historian, "persevering over a period of

---

[1] Cf. Ryan—*Ireland from A.D. 800 to A.D. 1600*, chaps. vii, viii; also MacNeill—*Phases of Irish History, loc. cit.*

[2] Cf. Ryan—*Irish Monasticism.*

three or four centuries, is a spectacle which does honour to human nature. It shows to what heights Christianity may raise a people through the workings of Divine grace."[1]

Readjustment of Irish Law.—Even in the 5th century, as soon as a considerable number of the Irish princes and of the literary class had become Christian, the legal system of the country, which was still in a crude stage, was readjusted and brought into harmony with the principles of Christianity. Of this readjustment, the ancient Irish chronicles give the following accounts, embodying a tradition which dates at least from the 7th century:

" The Seanchus Mór and Feinechus of Ireland were purified and written, the writings and old books of Ireland having been collected to one place at the request of St. Patrick."[2]

Again : " What did not clash with the Word of God in the written law and in the New Testament and with the consciences of the believers, was confirmed in the laws of the Brehons by Patrick and the ecclesiastics and the chieftains of Erin . . . and this is the Seanchus Mór."[3]

Even though one may reject the tradition which these entries record (viz., that a formal recodification of Irish law was made in the 5th century by a commission appointed for the purpose and comprised of rulers, ecclesiastics and lawyers), the main facts which the tradition enshrines are quite certain. These facts are that a readjustment of the pre-Christian Irish law took place in the 5th century, and that then and in the following centuries the Irish law developed under a prevailing Christian influence.[4]

Compared with the Christianisation of Roman Empire.— Hence, the fundamental code of Irish law, known as the *Feinechus* or *Seanchus Mór*, is a blend of the old pre-Christian laws and customs with the law of Christ. We do not fully know what were the special particulars in which the pre-Christian customs of the Irish were at variance with the teaching of the Gospel. It may, however, be safely presumed—and the presumption is confirmed from several

---

[1] *Op. cit.*, pp. 105 and 377.
[2] *Four Masters*, vol. i, *sub anno* A.D. 438.
[3] *Ancient Laws of Ireland*, vol. i, p. 17 (Rolls Series).
[4] Cf. MacNeill—*Celtic Ireland*, pp. 173 ff.

isolated indications—that the transition from pagan to Christian civilisation in Ireland followed in its broad outlines the same course of development as in Britain and continental Europe. The main differences are rooted in the fact that the Irish pre-Christian civilisation, as compared with the Hellenic and Latin culture of the Roman Empire, was in a relatively undeveloped state at the introduction of Christianity, and the morals of the nation far less corrupt than those of Rome. Therefore, the existing social organism was more quickly and more easily attuned to Christian principles. Thus, we find in the case of Ireland's conversion to Christianity the unique phenomenon that the transition from paganism to Christianity was accomplished without the blood of martyrs. Moreover, practically the whole of the higher cultural development in Ireland took shape under the influence of Christianity.

Effects of Christianity on the National Character and Customs.—The first effect of the new ideals was a profound change in the national outlook of the people. The establishment of Christianity in the 5th century marks the termination of foreign warlike expeditions.[1] Furthermore, the new era of peace and religious fervour witnessed not only an extraordinary missionary activity but also a very remarkable intellectual movement, great progress in industry and agriculture, and abundant material prosperity, the last three of which continued on to the Norse invasions.

During the Christian period, although wars (or, rather battles, for war in Ireland usually meant a single battle)[2] were frequent, as indeed they were in most countries of Europe, wars between reigning kings were rare and were mostly undertaken for some such purpose as that of enforcing a decision of the courts. War could not be declared without the consent of the ruling assembly of the *Tuath*, or principality. In war not only were the obligations of the Peace of God observed, as in mediæval continental countries, but in addition the persons and property of the *literati* were sacrosanct and inviolable. Above all, there was no revolt

---

[1] Cf. MacNeill—*Phases of Irish History*, pp. 227–229. The Venerable Bede, writing about the middle of the 8th century, refers to the Irish as a " harmless people who had never injured the English " (Cf. *ib.*, pp. 159, 160).
[2] *Ib.*, p. 228.

of the people against their hereditary rulers ; there was no
" Peasant War," nor any rising against the established law
to which the people clung with unshakable fidelity.[1]

Stability of the Kingdom of Ireland.—Notwithstanding
the numerous dynastic disputes, the traditional lines of
succession were preserved with very little interruption
during all the Christian period ; and the average length of
the reigns compare favourably with other European
countries. The relative stability of the Irish dynastic line
of High Kings may be illustrated by a comparison with the
English monarchy, which was perhaps the most stable in
Europe. From the first establishment of the descendants
of Niall at Tara in A.D. 483 down to the final downfall of
the High Kingship with the death of Malachy in 1022 (a
period of 539 years), the sceptre remained with Niall's
direct descendants, except for an interruption of twelve
years under Brian Boru (1002–1014). Forty-one High
Kings reigned during that period, the average reign being
thirteen years.

From the establishment of the Kingdom of England under
Athelstan, A.D. 937, until the death of Edward IV in 1488
(a period of 546 years), twenty-nine kings, *belonging to three
different dynasties*, reigned in England, an average of
eighteen and a half years for each reign. This very high
average, in the case of England, is partly due to the fact
that the three kings, Henry III, Edward III, and Henry VI,
whose reigns cover in all a period of 147 years, succeeded
to the throne while still infants or minors. This could not
occur in the case of the Irish kings, who were appointed
by election.

Prevailing Influence of the Church.—The representatives
of the Church had great influence even in the political life
of the country.[2] Thus we find that Colmcille, " the most
far-sighted political thinker of his time,"[3] was summoned
back to Ireland by the political rulers twelve years after

---

[1] Cf. Green—*History of the Irish State*, pp. 270–274.

[2] Cf. Ryan—*Irish Monasticism*, pp. 313 ff. It may be noted that the
influence of the Church, though very great, was not always able to secure
the abandonment of some ancient customs not reconcilable with the
Christian law, especially those governing marriage.

[3] Green—*History of the Irish State*, p. 133.

his departure to Iona, to take part in the great convention of Druim Ceat (575). Among the questions to be discussed at the Convention were the future relations between Ireland and Scotland and the reorganisation or abolition of the native bardic class. Both questions were decided in accordance with Columba's advice and authority.[1]

Later on we find evidence of a similar influence exercised by St. Adamnan (Columba's ninth successor as Abbot of Iona) in the famous Assembly held at Birr (697), to which he was summoned by Loingsech, the High King. It was under his advice that the " Law of Innocents " was enacted —the " first law made in heaven and on earth for women and their emancipation." Although the official history of the Synod, which was signed by forty-seven kings and a long roll of ecclesiastics, has not yet been adequately studied, we know that its enactments include provisions for the protection of women, children, and young clerical students.[2]

Irish Monasticism.[3]—In Ireland monasticism played even a more decisive part than in mediæval Europe in developing Christian civilisation. Irish monasticism from the 6th to the 8th century accomplished a work similar to that of the Benedictine and Columban monks in mediæval Europe. The monasteries were from the beginning homes of peace and schools of religious fervour and learning. It was in them that the art of illumination developed with such extraordinary perfection. The Irish monastic schools attracted crowds of students from Britain and continental Europe. These the Irish monks entertained and instructed free, and supplied gratis with books.

The monasteries also led the way in the industrial development of the nation. The example of the monks impressed upon the people and their leaders the dignity of manual toil, and broke down gradually the traditional prejudices " of a class whose white hands never suffered the degradation of axe and spade." The social conventions against manual labour could not long survive when in the monastery, which was the centre of the populous life and

---

[1] Green—*History of the Irish State*, pp. 148–155.   [2] *Ib.*, p. 300.
[3] Cf. Ryan—*Irish Monasticism*.

activity of the district, "abbots and bishops sometimes of kingly race, were seen sowing, reaping, planting fruit trees, carrying sacks of corn on their backs to the mill, working as smiths, etc."[1] In the monasteries a tradition of highly skilled agriculture and handicraft soon grew up, and from the monasteries these arts gradually spread among the people.

Abolition of Slavery and of All Impassable Distinction of Caste.—We have evidence that slavery disappeared as Christian influence gained the upper hand. Personal dignity and personal responsibility were recognised, and all impassable barriers between the different social classes were suppressed. Mrs. Green, in her study of Irish social life, refers frequently to this last characteristic, namely, "the opportunity which runs through all the Irish laws for the man of ability and industry to enter the rank above his own, and the liability of an unworthy man to lose his social rank."[2] Dr. MacNeill quotes passages from a 7th century tract which seem to indicate that these social reforms, including the practical abolition of slavery, were brought about while Christianity was still young in the country.[3]

Again, according to Irish Law, "learning in every degree and skill in any art or craft entitled one to the full rights of citizenship."[4] This feature of the Irish social system was peculiar to itself. In the old Roman Empire several of the founders of the Latin literature were slaves or the sons of slaves ; and even in early mediæval Europe skilled craftsmen were usually serfs.

Social Position of Women.—We have referred more than once in the present work to the influence of Christianity in raising the social status of women in mediæval Europe. It is true, however, that European laws and customs had not,

---

[1] Green, *ib.*, pp. 241–246.
[2] *Ib.*, pp. 201, 216, etc.
[3] *Celtic Ireland*, chap, x, p. 173. Again, the same author writes (*ib.*, p. 110) : "Apparently numerous in heathen times, slaves diminished in number in the early Christian period, but became numerous once more [after 8th century] owing to the slave traffic carried on by the Norse settlers." The so-called "unfree classes" which formed a portion of the agricultural population were not slaves. Cf. *ib.*, pp. 108–111 ; also Sigerson, *op. cit.*, chap. i.
[4] MacNeill—*Celtic Ireland*, pp. 107 ff.

even in mediæval times, completely divested themselves in this regard of pre-Christian prejudices inherited from the old Roman law. Thus, women, whether married or not, were still incapacitated by law for independent ownership of property ; and had but very limited rights of independent action.[1] Outside of Italy women rarely received higher education ; nor were they admitted to the learned professions.[2]

Irish laws and customs present in this matter a striking contrast to those of feudal Europe. According to Irish law, even in the 6th and 7th centuries, women were nearly on a par with men in all social rights. Furthermore, after marriage a woman could remain the sole owner of the property she possessed before the marriage';[3] and the rights of husband and wife in the joint property of the family were both fully recognised. The consent of both was required for its disposal.

Again, women had free access to higher education. Thus, we have proof in the ancient lives of the Irish saints that young women frequented the great monastic schools of the 6th and 7th centuries, or received an education similar to that given in these schools. The unique position in the Irish Church accorded to women like St. Brigid and her successors who exercised a certain control or authority over a monastery of men in the 6th century, is a very remarkable phenomenon and in some respects quite unparalleled in Europe.

In the Annals of the *Four Masters* there are very frequent entries in the early centuries, recording the activities or the death of distinguished Irish women, some " renowned for hospitality and piety," some described in some such terms as " Nurse of all the poets and strangers and all the learned." Under the date A.D. 932 is recorded the death of Ullach, daughter of Muimhnecan, " Chief Poetess of Ireland," which seems to imply that women poets were then not uncommon in Ireland. Panegyrics of noble or generous women frequently occur in the fragments of early

---

[1] Cf. Maine's *Ancient Law* (edit. 1885), pp. 152–160.
[2] Cf. Walshe, *op. cit.*, chap. xx.
[3] Cf. Joyce—*Social History of Ireland*. *See* index under " Woman " for full references. *See* also *The Ancient Laws of Ireland* (Rolls Series)— the index of each volume under " Woman."

Irish literature that have been published.[1]   All this points
to the conclusion that from the early Christian times women
held a position of independence and social prestige in
Ireland very much in advance of that held by them in
Continental Europe even in mediæval times.

Irish Principles Regarding Property Rights.—Another
peculiarity of Irish law, a result doubtless of Christian
influence, was the *legal* aspect of ownership, which seems
to have been almost fully in accord with Christian principles.
In continental Europe, although the actual practice was
probably much the same as in Ireland, the prevailing codes
of law did not lay down the limitations and safeguards which
Christian principles include.   In Ireland the fundamental
right of everyone to an opportunity of labour and to a
sufficient access to the goods of the earth was safeguarded
by law.   Everyone, or practically everyone, was attached
to some family or group upon which he had claims for
reasonable help and protection.

We shall refer below to the limited nature of the ownership the Irish law allowed in the case of land and the safeguards which it furnished against the undue accumulation
of land in the possession of individuals.   Besides these
provisions certain common rights were reserved to the
community in all land.   For instance, in every appropriated
woodland

" a right was reserved for the people to the wild animals of the
forest, to a night's supply of kindling, to sticks for cooking a
meal, a fistful of nut gathering, timber for a yoke and a plough,
for a bier, for a churn staff, hoops for a barrel," etc. . . . " One
salmon of the place " was common property, and one cast of the
net in every stream.[2]

Even in the case of movable private property there were
certain limitations to the use of ownership founded upon
the natural law and formally expressed in the Irish code.
According to this latter the rights of the private owner gave

---

[1] Cf. for instance *The Circuit of Ireland*, by Muircheartach Mac Neill, a
10th century Irish poem, edited by O'Donovan, with English translation,
and published in the I. A. S. series.   It contains splendid panegyrics on
several noble women who apparently were specially generous and
hospitable.

[2] Green, *op. cit.*, p. 244 ; cf. also MacNeill—*Celtic Ireland*, pp. 167–169.

way in the case of certain things to the claims of "every condition of person that stand in need of them." Special mention is made of wild herbs for flavouring, the leavings of various industrial operations, etc.[1] All of these characteristics of Irish law took shape between the 6th and 9th centuries, when Irish society was largely dominated by Christian and monastic influences. They disappeared after the 16th century under the régime of the Protestant and Presbyterian planters.

Material Well-being of the People.—Although the material conditions of the mass of the people from the 6th to the 9th century have not yet been adequately studied, there is sufficient evidence to show that the country was then comparatively prosperous. There were, of course, richer and poorer classes, and almsgiving is constantly inculcated in the ascetical writings of the time, but the poor of whom there is question seem to be the ordinary poor, whom, as Our Lord says, we have always with us, whose poverty results from accidental, and more or less, exceptional causes. There is no indication in the extant literature or records of that period of the existence of any social class like the modern proletariat whose reasonable needs were not sufficiently supplied. Ireland was during that period probably the most prosperous country in Western Europe, as it was also the most religious and the most advanced in Christian culture.[2]

Agriculture flourished in proportion as war had declined ; "on all sides fertile soil was reclaimed for tillage, partitioned, mered and fenced in rectangular strips."[3]

The recorded wise sayings of the period indicate the trend of the national energy. Thus we read :

" Three slender things that best support the world, the slender stream of milk from the cow into the pail, the slender blade of green corn upon the ground, the slender thread over the hand of a skilful woman."[4]

There was an elaborate system of farm law which provided,

---

[1] MacNeill, loc. cit.
[2] There was also a high degree of Christian culture in Spain during the 7th century—viz., immediately before the Saracen or Moorish invasions.
[3] Green, op. cit., p. 241.
[4] Ib.

amongst other things, for the legal rights of groups of farmers, who tilled, harvested, and ground their grain according to a well-defined co-operative system. These co-operative groups, which were a prominent feature of Irish rural life, probably grew out of the joint families. Such matters as the distribution, fencing, tilling of the soil, keeping it free from debt or injury, the care of the country roads and of the mill-streams, the charge of the sick and aged were committed by law to the joint families among whom the soil was divided and to the large agricultural communities already referred to.

There are abundant indications in the laws and records of the time of widely diffused comfort and plenty. The houses of the well-to-do farmers were well and usefully furnished :

"Good were their houses, rich their threshing floors, large their families, many their well-born, complete their waggon harness ; their gifts are herds of cattle, few their undesirables."[1]

The wealthier proprietor had his enclosed garden for vegetables, his lawn or pleasure ground, his field of sanctuary or protection. He owned ploughs and ox-teams, milch cattle, sheep, swine, horses for work, as well as for chariot and saddle, and stocks of poultry, while the poorest peasant, living in his wattled booth or cabin, and tilling his small farm in partnership with others of his own class, was legally protected against all injury or defamation and against eviction. The precinct round his house was sacrosanct and inviolable, in which slaying, wounding or quarrelling, was an offence against the owner's status. Within these limits he could give protection to strangers of his own rank, and it was a penal offence to interfere with any of these rights.[2] What a contrast between the position of the poor man under these ancient laws and customs of the Irish Christian period and that of the Irish peasant of the 18th and 19th, and even the 20th century ! In the latter period under an unchristian legal system he was left isolated and unprotected, a tenant at will of an absentee landlord, oppressed by unjust laws and partial administration, impoverished by rent and taxes, and with

---

[1] Green, *op. cit.*, p. 200.   [2] *Ib.*

no means of providing for his growing family, who were too often forced to leave their homes and go into exile as soon as they were capable of productive labour !

Differences Between the Irish and the Feudal Social Systems.—As it is outside our present scope to analyse the structure of the Irish mediæval State except in so far as may be necessary in order to convey a just idea of the social condition of the people, we shall, in order to complete this short sketch, only touch on a few additional features in which the Irish organisation differed from the feudal type :

(*a*) **Slavery and Serfdom.**—The feudal organisation of mediæval Europe, with its outstanding features of a small but highly organised military caste, ruling over a population of servile workers who, whatever their actual social conditions, had no political status, nor any legal ownership of the land, was an intermediate stage between the servile State of pagan Rome and the free civic communities of later mediæval Europe. In Ireland, slavery was never a very important factor in the social organism. The slaves that did exist in those early Christian times were comparatively few. The agricultural serfs who appear later seem to have been a result of the centuries of turmoil, or of the Norman feudal system which took root here and there. The so-called unfree classes were not slaves, nor apparently even serfs in the ordinary sense, but freemen with a limited franchise, who could by several paths pass into the ranks of the free classes ; for, according to the principle of Irish law : " A man is better than his birth."[1]

(*b*) **Position of the Ruling Class.**—The relations of the local chiefs to the provincial kings and of these latter to the High Kings were in many respects not unlike the interrelations of the feudal nobles of different grades in Britain and continental Europe. Like the feudal rulers, too, the Irish princes were the supreme arbiters in the civil and criminal courts, the heads of the administration and the leaders in war. But in some respects their position differed profoundly from that of the feudal rulers.

---

[1] MacNeill—*Celtic Ireland*, chap. vii.

41

In Ireland, at least at that period, the different social classes were not contained in water-tight compartments. Thus, the nobility or ruling class did not form an exclusive caste. It has been aptly described as an "elastic aristocracy,"[1] into whose ranks a way was open through merit to the members of the lower social grades, while nobles could forfeit their rank by ceasing to fulfil the required conditions.

Again, the kings and higher nobility were not, even in legal theory, absolute rulers nor the owners of the land. They had, indeed, certain well-defined claims to rent and taxes and some other services. But these claims did not rest on ownership as in the case of the feudal lords. They were political and not economic.[2] The Irish lords had no power of eviction nor of alienating the rights they possessed, for they had only a life interest in them. The actual cultivators were for the most part the real owners of the soil.

Even the political authority of the king was strictly limited by law. A large section of the people had, as in modern times, through the great assemblies, a voice in the government, in the election of rulers, the making of laws, and the declaration of war. Hence, the Irish social and political organisation was much more democratic than the feudal system, and was better adapted for agricultural and industrial life than for warfare.

(c) **Land Tenure and the Deirbfhine.**—In Ireland the manor organisation did not exist, at least to any great extent. The family estate was held and worked by a family group called the *deirbfhine*. The latter included all the members of the family for four generations, namely, from great-grandparents to great grand-children inclusive. Every member had an inalienable right to protection and support from the *deirbfhine*, which, like the manorial group in the feudal system, was the ordinary unit in the social and economic organisation of the State. It was responsible as a whole for the taxes, fines or imposts due to the administrative authorities, and even for the debts due by individual members of the *deirbfhine* to members of another group.

---

[1] Cf. Ryan—*Ireland from Earliest Times to A.D. 800*, p. 162.
[2] Cf. MacNeill—*Phases of Irish History*.

Besides the communal property of the *deirbfhine*, including pasturage, forest and bogland, in which all shared as in the case of the common lands of the European manor, each individual or family had his or its own allotment. These allotments or farms, as well as the burdens attached to them, were determined and assigned by the head or patriarch of the group according to a system which the law regulated in its minutest details. When a man died, his property and the land he held went to his children probably in equal shares. If he had no children all the members of the *deirbfhine* were his heirs. No one could sell or alienate his land outside the *deirbfhine*, without the consent of the latter, which had to be given by the members in an assembly presided over by the patriarch or chief. As the whole *deirbfhine* had these claims on all the family land, and were responsible to outsiders for the legal liabilities of each member, the governing assembly and the chief exercised pressure upon each land-holder to care his land properly, and keep out of debt. It is clear that in this system the Christian principle of solidarity, communal rights and mutual support is secured even more completely than in the feudal organisation, and that it is farther removed than the latter from the modern individualistic spirit.

From what has been said one can see the difference between the Irish conceptions of ownership as applied to land and as applied to movable property, a distinction which did not exist in Roman law. Ownership of movable property was not usually shared by one's *deirbfhine*, and was absolute except for the legal limitations already referred to.[1] It was not so in the case of land. The occupier or owner of a farm of land, although he had fixity of tenure and could not be evicted in any circumstances, had only a life interest. Hence, he could not sell the land, for the *deirbfhine* had certain definite claims upon it. This made the alienation of land very difficult and helped to prevent the undue accumulation of land in the hands of individuals, which is one of the great evils of modern times.

General Critique of the Irish Social System.—The Irish social organisation had some drawbacks, and in one respect at least, namely, the method of dynastic succession was

---

[1] Cf. *Supra.*

gradually changed as a result of the Anglo-Norman invasion. On the other hand, it had many advantages which have scarcely ever been surpassed. The fact that it subsisted for nearly two thousand years without any revolutionary change, without ever experiencing a revolt of the people against it or against the rulers who administered it, is a rare if not unique phenomenon in European history. The passionate attachment of the people to their own customs and laws was so great that they clung to them and mostly followed them in their own social dealings for centuries after the power that governed the country had abolished them by law.

Again, the reverence for law which the Irish system produced among the people, as contrasted with their instinctive suspicion of the civil authority that prevailed in Ireland since the 17th century, points conclusively to the equity and even-handed justice which marked the old Christian law of Ireland.

" For there is no nation under the sun," wrote the English Attorney-General, Sir John Davies, in 1612, " that doth love equal and indifferent justice better than the Irish or will rest better satisfied with the execution thereof although it be against themselves."[1]

---

[1] *Discovery of the True Cause*, etc. (Cf. Morley's *Ireland Under Elizabeth and James I*, p. 212). The English judge, Sir Edward Coke, in 1640, confirms the statement of Davies : " There is no nation of the Christian world, that are greater lovers of justice than they [the Irish] are, which virtue must of necessity be accompanied by many others " (Quoted in *Hardiman's Statutes of Kilkenny*, p. x, I.A.S. publications). The English planter, Robert Payne, who led a colony of English settlers in the confiscated Desmond lands about 1590, writes in the same sense : " They are obedient to the laws, so that you may travel through all the land, without any danger or injury offered of the very worst Irish, and be greatly relieved of the best." (Payne's *Description of Ireland*, London, 1590, p. 3, I.A.S. publications). Such testimonies from foreign visitors or settlers regarding the Irish of that period could be multiplied.

APPENDIX II

HISTORICAL BACKGROUND OF THE SOCIAL QUESTION IN IRELAND

Introductory Note.—Owing to its geographical position and historical causes, already referred to, Ireland differs in many special ways from the other countries of Europe. Its social history and conditions are in fact unique. Hence, as in the case of the sketch of social conditions in mediæval Europe, our general account of the social decadence of the last three centuries[1] needs to be supplemented in a special notice giving a brief review of the historical causes which produced the present abnormal social conditions in Ireland.[2]

Bird's-eye View of Irish History (1600-1900).—We have said[3] that the old Gaelic and Catholic régime in Ireland came to an end with the Tudor Conquest of the 16th century, which culminated in the battle of Kinsale (1601). The confiscations and persecutions and general policy of destruction which accompanied and followed the Tudor wars

---

[1] Cf. *Supra*, chaps. viii–xiv.

[2] Cf. Lecky—*History of Ireland in the Eighteenth Century* (London, 1893) ; Mitchell—*History of Ireland* (vol. ii, Dublin, 1869) ; Prendergast—*Cromwellian Settlement* (Dublin, 1870) ; MacCaffrey—*History of the Catholic Church from the Renaissance to French Revolution* (Dublin, 1915), vol. ii, chaps. vii–x ; O'Brien—*Economic History of Ireland in the Seventeenth Century* (Dublin and London, 1919) ; *Economic History of Ireland in the Eighteenth Century* (Dublin and London, 1918) ; and *The Economic History of Ireland from the Union to the Famine* (Longmans, London, 1921) ; Burke—*Outlines of the Industrial History of Ireland* (Dublin and Belfast, undated, circ. 1921). Beaumont—*L'Irlande Sociale, Politique et Religieuse* (Paris, 1839) ; Cf. especially, pp. 187–412 ; Cardinal Perraud—*Etudes sur L'Irlande Contemporaine*, 2 vols. (Paris, 1862) ; Dubois—*L'Irlande Contemporaine* (Paris, 1907), translated into English and published under title *Contemporary Ireland* (Dublin, 1911). This trilogy on Ireland by three French writers contains the best balanced and most complete account of the sources of the modern Irish social conditions. Atkinson—*The Penal Times* (Introduction to S. Atkinson's *Life of Mary Aikenhead* (Dublin, 1879) ; Sigerson—*History of the Land Tenures and Land Classes of Ireland* (London and Dublin, 1861). This latter is the best book on this subject it deals with. Butler—*Confiscations in Irish History* (2nd edit., Dublin, 1918) ; Mgr. P. F. Walsh—*William J. Walsh, Archbishop of Dublin* (Dublin, 1928).

[3] Cf. *Supra*, Appendix I.

were renewed in an intensified form under the Puritans in the middle of the 17th century. For, both the Elizabethan and Puritan wars in Ireland were wars of extermination rather than conquest.[1] Finally, after the Jacobite war, which was brought to a close by the famous Treaty of Limerick (1691), the Irish nation entered upon two centuries of oppression and degradation which make its history unique in the annals of modern Europe.

The suppression of the Irish law (1607), the spoliation and displacement of the Irish landowners, and the complete break up of the religious, social, and educational organisation which took place during the 17th century prepared the way for the impoverishment, enslavement, and degradation of the native population which characterised the English policy of the 18th century. The famines and " clearances " of the 19th century, facilitated by the state of villenage to which the people were reduced;[2] the setting up of an unCatholic and unIrish educational system ; the well-nigh total destruction of the national language and tradition, and the steady draining away of the old Irish population, which is still in progress, were results, or constituent parts, of a policy which the English Parliament and, with the exception of one short period, the Irish Colonial Parliament as well, consistently followed in regard to Ireland.

The Religious Persecution (1540-1900)—(a) **Its Inauguration.**—The break-up of the religious and ecclesiastical organisation of the country commenced when the English King, Henry VIII, was declared King of Ireland, and head of both Church and State (1537–1541). As a fitting and significant inauguration of the new régime, the most venerable Catholic relics in Ireland, associated in the people's minds with an unbroken Catholic tradition of a thousand years, were publicly desecrated and destroyed. The famous statue of the Blessed Virgin at Trim, as well as the Holy Rood at Ballybogan, Co. Meath, were pulled down ; and

---

[1] Cf. Lecky, *op. cit.*, vol. ii, chap. vi : " The oppression of the native race was carried on with a ferocity which surpassed that of Alva in the Netherlands, and was hardly exceeded by any page in the bloodshed annals of the Turk." See *Cambrensis Eversus*, vol. i, for a contemporary account by Father Quin, S.J., of the workings of the Puritan Policy in the 17th century.

[2] Cf. Sigerson—*Land Tenures*, chap. x ; and *Modern Ireland*, pp. 67, 68.

the venerable staff of Jesus in Christ Church, Dublin, which, according to Irish tradition, St. Patrick had received from our Divine Lord when embarking on his Irish mission, was publicly burned in High Street. The shrines and tombs of Saints Patrick, Brigid, and Columcille at Down were desecrated and pillaged, and the sacred relics scattered to the winds. At the same time the English garrison at Athlone sacked and razed to the ground the magnificent cathedral of Clonmacnoise.

(*b*) **Its Fierceness.**—In the course of the 16th and 17th centuries all the monasteries and religious houses (some 550 in number)[1] were pillaged and broken up in every part of the country : their lands were seized, and the churches and conventual buildings secularised or destroyed. The parochial and cathedral churches were also seized, and the buildings and revenues applied to the purposes of the heretical creed.

A religious persecution of unexampled ferocity was instituted which continued, with a few brief interruptions and some short periods of relaxation, for more than two centuries. Priests and religious were banished or put to death ; every public manifestation of the Catholic faith was suppressed ; shrines and religious emblems were destroyed or removed ; Catholic holydays were secularised ; the wearing in public of the religious dress was prohibited ; the celebration of Mass even in private was made a criminal offence.[2] Those who refused to conform to the heretical sect were harassed, impoverished, and degraded by a series of laws and a system of administration which have gained a unique notoriety in the history of the world.

" The simple profession of the Catholic faith," writes Lecky, " excluded a man from every form of political and municipal power ; from all the learned professions except medicine ; from almost every means of acquiring wealth, knowledge, dignity or influence. It subjected him at the same time to unjust and oppressive taxation, deprived him of the right of bequeathing

---

[1] Cf. De Burgo—*Hibernia Dominicana*, pp. 726–750, for a list of the pre-Tudor religious houses in Ireland. He enumerates 513 of men and 43 of women, every one of which was suppressed in the course of the 16th and 17th centuries.

[2] Cf. Burke (from p. 235)—*Irish Priests in the Penal Times* (Waterford, 1914) ; S. Atkinson, *op. cit.* ; Lecky, *op. cit.*, vol. ii.

his property and managing his family as he pleased ; enabled any Protestant who was at enmity with him to injure and annoy him in a hundred ways, and reduced him, in a word, to a condition little better than that of absolute serfdom."[1]

Edmund Burke, in an oft-quoted passage, describes the Penal Code as

" a machine of wise and elaborate contrivance as well fitted for oppression, impoverishment and degradation of a people and the debasement in them of human nature itself, as ever proceeded from the perverted ingenuity of man."

Unlike other religious persecutions, which are usually of comparatively brief duration, and mean the oppression and persecution of a minority within the State, the Irish persecution continued for nearly three centuries, and was directed against the overwhelming majority of the nation. Even when the policy of open persecution was abandoned, as it was in the last quarter of the 18th century, the laws and the civil and municipal administration of the State still continued hostile to the Catholic religion. Thus, Edmund Burke, writing to Dr. Hussey on the occasion of the proposed establishment of a Catholic college in 1794, used these significant words :

" Be well assured that they [the Anglo-Irish Government] never did and never will consent to give one shilling of money for any other purpose than to do you mischief. If you consent to put your clerical education, or any part of your education, under their direction or control, you will have sold your religion for their money."[2]

Replaced by Liberalism.—In the 19th century religious persecution was replaced by the more dangerous and insidious policy of secularism or unchristian Liberalism. Of the public institutions set up by the Government, or under government patronage, some, such as the Royal Dublin Society and the Royal Irish Academy, were predominantly Protestant, and, consequently, anti-Catholic ; while even such institutions as public hospitals, asylums, poorhouses and prisons, were given a secularist character when it was not an anti-Catholic one. This was done partly

---

[1] *Op. cit.*, vol. ii, p. 199.
[2] *Burke's Correspondence*, vol. iii, p. 274 (cited in Dr. Healy's *Centenary History of Maynooth College*, p. 101).

under the pretext of the inmates being of mixed religion. But under one pretext or another the Church was effectually prevented from exercising her legitimate influence on the character and working of these institutions. The Crucifix and all religious emblems were excluded from them ; as they were from the public schools, at least during the ordinary school hours. It is easy to understand how this policy tended to dechristianise public life, and to confine to the domain of private life the exercise of religion, which, according to Catholic teaching, should permeate all activities.

Although most of the original Penal Laws ceased to be enforced in the 19th century many were not repealed, and several new penal enactments against religious were made as a counterpoise to the Catholic Relief Bill of 1829 ; and down even to the end of the 19th century and later, the spirit of which these laws were the expression continued to be active. This was exemplified in the attitude assumed by the Government on the question of a Catholic university,[1] and again in the provision inserted in the Local Government Act of 1898, excluding priests from membership of the county and municipal councils.

Effects of the Religious Persecution.—The purely religious persecutions of the 17th and 18th centuries considered apart from the destructive war against education and nationality were, on the whole, beneficial to religion. The religious and national interests of the people, assailed by the same enemy, became identified. The administration and government of the Catholic Church in Ireland was rid for the time being of the baneful effects of the English State interference. Thus the persecutions produced the unforeseen result of enlisting the full strength of the national and patriotic sentiment on the side of religion and welding priests and people into one.

Hence, during the period of persecution, the influence of the clergy was one of the main bulwarks of the Irish language and national spirit. Every rank and grade in the Church was purified in the fires of suffering and poverty. The people's faith was intensified and elevated, and the spirit of self-sacrifice and Christian heroism called into action among every section of the community.

---

[1] Cf.Walsh, *op. cit.*, chaps. vi, xviii and xx.

Educational Persecution—Period of Destruction.—It was far otherwise, however, with the English economical and educational policy in Ireland. The nation has not so far recovered from the disastrous effects of the English educational and economic régime of more than three and a half centuries.

The Irish educational policy of the British Government followed the same general lines of development as its religious policy. There was first a long period of destruction and open persecution,[1] which was succeeded in the 19th century by one of partial reconstruction. But the latter was conceived and carried out largely on secularist and Liberal lines. It excluded, as far as the Government could exclude them, the essential elements of religion and Christian patriotism.[2]

During the period of destruction all the existing educational institutions, both religious and secular, were completely destroyed and the revenues seized. The same fate awaited the professional schools conducted by the Irish *literati* or bardic class as befell the private schools and those attached to the monastic and ecclesiastical institutions. The whole class of *literati*, one of the chief mainstays of the national spirit and tradition, was marked out for destruction. All the bardic schools were broken up ; Irish books, manuscripts and even musical instruments were destroyed.[3] Before the " law " the activities of the Irish teacher were no less criminal than those of the priest.[4] The repeated attempts which were made during the 16th and 17th centuries by the Irish leaders under the direction of the Church to found an Irish Catholic University were foiled.[5]

---

[1] Cf. Corcoran—*State Policy in Irish Education from* 1536 *to* 1816 (Dublin, 1916) ; Healy—*Maynooth College Centenary History* (Dublin, 1885), chaps. ii–iv ; Mahaffy—*An Epoch in Irish History* (London, 1903) ; Atkinson, *loc. cit.*

[2] Cf. Archbishop Walsh—*Statement of the Chief Grievance of Irish Catholics in Education* (Dublin, 1890) ; O'Riordan—*Catholicity and Progress in Ireland* (London, 1906), pp. 420–506 ; Hyde—*Literary History of Ireland* (London, 1899), chaps. xliii and xliv ; Dubois, *op. cit.*, part ii, chap. xii.

[3] Cf. Green—*The Making of Ireland and Its Undoing*, chaps. ix and x ; O'Sullivan—Introduction to O'Curry's *Manners and Customs of the Ancient Irish*.

[4] Cf. Atkinson, *op. cit.*, pp. 44 ff.

[5] Cf. Mahaffy—*An Epoch of Irish History*, pp. 48 ff ; Corcoran, *op. cit.*, pp. 72–74 ; Healy, *op. cit.*, pp. 29–31.

Reconstruction on Secularist Lines—Trinity College.—In 1592 Trinity College was founded under Royal Charter on the grounds of the suppressed monastery of All Saints, Dublin. It was richly endowed mainly from grants of the Irish confiscated lands.[1] The original object of the foundation (to which Trinity College has remained faithful for more than three centuries) was to secure an intellectual stronghold of Protestantism as well as of English power in Ireland. For this purpose it developed a school of Economics and of Irish History, calculated to support the English Protestant domination. With the same object in view it set itself from the outset to train up a middle class and a professional class, who would be " good Protestants and sincere in the English interest." For nearly three centuries it was closed to Catholics who refused to abjure their faith. Except that a course in Irish was instituted for proselytising purposes, the Irish language (spoken by the vast majority of the people) as well as the Irish literature were ignored in this so-called Irish University.

New Policy of Liberalism in Education.—In the 19th century, in accordance with the altered policy of the English Government, the Queen's Colleges were established under a secularist and Liberal constitution ; and Trinity College itself was opened to all without religious tests. This changed the character of the latter from a Protestant University into a secularist institution like the Queen's Colleges. The people under the Church's guidance still steadily refused to make use either of Trinity College or the Queen's Colleges, and themselves established a Catholic University in Dublin (1854). The English Government, however, refused to recognise the latter, and established the Royal University of Ireland, which in 1910 was merged in the National and Queen's Universities which were set up that year. Both of these were constituted on more or less secularist and undenominational principles, but accompanied by such circumstances that Catholics are permitted to frequent them.[2]

---

[1] Cf. Mahaffy, *op. cit.* ; Stubb's *History of the University of Dublin* (1889) ; Heron—*Constitutional History of Trinity College.* The Irish estates of Trinity College, according to the Commission of 1853, comprised 200,000 acres—about one per cent. of the whole land of Ireland—valued at £92,000 a year. Cf. O'Riordan, *op. cit.*, pp. 486 ff.
[2] Cf. Walsh, *op. cit.*, chap. xx.

Primary and Secondary Schools.—In connection with Trinity College a whole network of primary and secondary schools were established[1] during the 17th and the two following centuries. These, like Trinity College itself, were definitely English and Protestant. The people, however, some five-sixths of whom were Catholics and Irish, refused to send their children to these institutions and organised their own schools in the early 19th century. Some of these were a continuation of the illegal " hedge schools " of the preceding century. Others were conducted by the newly-founded religious teaching Congregations such as the Christian Brothers, the Presentation and Patrician Brothers, the Sisters of Mercy, and Sisters of Charity. Such schools, however, received no help or encouragement from the Government ; and the latter established the " National " schools in 1831. These, like all the Anglo-Irish institutions of the 19th and 20th centuries, were by law undenominational and Liberal in character, but their rules allowed religious knowledge to be taught outside school hours, and permitted the local Parish Priest to be manager with the power of appointing and dismissing the teacher.

Although the worst dangers of the " National " school system were counteracted by the watchfulness of the clergy and the Catholic faith of the lay teachers, their evil influence has been very great. They are largely accountable for the ruin of the Irish language during the second half of the 19th century. Again, such unnatural features of the " National " school programme as the elimination from the regular school course of all things Irish and Catholic, has weakened and confused the whole mental outlook of the present generation.

Economic Persecution—(a) Its General Character.—The English economic policy in Ireland, like the religious and educational policy, was, at least in its tendency and results, directly opposed to Irish interests. As a result of the Tudor wars and the after-war policy of the conquerors, the social and economic life of Ireland, including its agricultural and industrial organisation, were completely destroyed.[2]

---

[1] Cf. O'Riordan, *loc. cit.*, for a brief account of the principal Anglo-Irish schemes for Irish Education down to the 19th century.

[2] Cf. O'Brien—*Economic History of Ireland in the Seventeenth Century.*

In the 17th century the old Irish nobility and middle class
were banished, put to death or reduced to beggary ; and
Scotch and English colonists of the Puritan type, who were
fanatically opposed to everything Irish and Catholic, in-
stalled in their place as the ruling and propertied class.
The native Irish population were henceforward regarded in
law (much as the South African Kaffirs or Australian
aborigines are regarded in English colonial administration)
as an inferior race unworthy of serious consideration. A
political theory was adopted that Ireland (represented by
the Protestant colonists) was a colony of England and that,
consequently, its own immediate interests were to be subordinate to those of the " Mother Country." The English
policy regarding the native population was " to make them
poor and keep them poor," thus rendering them helpless
as potential enemies.[1]

(b) **Oppression of the Rural Population.**—The ancient
system of Irish land tenure was abolished ; and between the
16th and the first quarter of the 19th century the legal
ownership of the land was gradually transferred from the
people to the landlord class who as a body still remained as
alien to the life of the nation as the British colony in India
is to-day. The Irish agricultural population was degraded
through successive stages to the position of tenants at will,[2]
ground down under a weight of rack rents and excessive
taxes, deprived of the means of education and oppressed
by all manner of tyrannies, petty and otherwise, which
rendered their condition probably unparalleled in European
History of any known period.[3]

The rack-rents besides paralysing the peasantry, impoverished the nation as a whole : for they went in large
measure to enrich an absentee class, and so were in reality
a tribute levied by an imperial conqueror upon a subject
nation. Even after the ownership of the land was transferred, as it was by the various Land Acts of the past
half-century, to the present occupiers (who are in the main

---

[1] Cf. O'Brien, op. cit., pp. 116, 118, 223–225.
[2] Cf. Sigerson—*Irish Land Tenure*, chaps. ix and x ; also *Modern
Ireland*, pp. 57–137.
[3] Cf. O'Brien, op. cit. ; Beaumont, op. cit., chap. ii, pp. 211–343 ;
Lecky, op. cit., vol. i ; Atkinson, op. cit. ; Dubois, op. cit., pp. 1–89.

a remnant of the former agricultural class) the tribute still remained.[1]

(c) **Strangling of Irish Industry and Commerce.**—But economic oppression was not confined to agriculture. By a series of Acts passed in the English Parliament between the middle of the 17th and that of the 18th century practically all Irish industries were crushed. When the restrictive laws were removed in 1778 under pressure from the Irish Volunteers there was a marvellous industrial revival which continued to the " Union " (1800). After the Union the needed protection for the still infant industries was withdrawn, and industrial Ireland, still comparatively weak and undeveloped, was suddenly exposed to the full brunt of foreign competition.

Industrial weakness was accentuated by several other unfavourable elements, rooted in centuries of oppression. Among these may be mentioned the presence of a powerful alien element in the bosom of the nation ; the lack of a native Irish educated class ; the steady pressure of partial laws ; the stranglehold of a whole network of institutions—educational, financial and commercial—which were set up under the influence of the colonial principle that Ireland's interests were to be subordinated to those of England.

Effects on the Social and Economic Life.—As a result of all these causes Ireland entered after 1800 on a downward course of economic decay, accelerating as the disastrous years and decades sped on. Manufactures, mining, fisheries, commerce have been almost completely ruined. Agriculture is fast following in their wake. Ireland's mercantile marine has disappeared. Famines and emigration have reduced the population by almost fifty per cent. since the middle of the last century, while that of every other European country has increased.

---

[1] Cf. Wakefield—*Ireland, Statistical and Political* (London, 1912). *Report of the Recess Committee*, 1896 (new edit., 1907) ; Lough—*England's Wealth Ireland's Poverty* (Ponsonby, Dublin ; *Blue Book—Commercial and Financial Relations Between England and Ireland* (London, 1903).

Even though the people have now secured a considerable measure of autonomy for more than two-thirds of the country, the effects of the centuries of persecution have penetrated so deeply into almost every detail of the national life, that the ultimate recovery of the country will be at best a slow and difficult process. This will appear more clearly from the detailed description of the present social evils of Ireland which forms the subject-matter of Appendix III.

APPENDIX III

Protestant Civilisation and Environment.—In Ireland we are confronted with the anomaly of a profoundly Catholic people devoid of many of the external features of a Catholic civilisation and suffering from all the material and many of the mental defects which usually result from an unchristian social régime. The explanation of this abnormal condition has been given in Appendix II. The social system in which the Irish people live is not of their own making. It is a result of centuries of oppression and is fashioned after an English Protestant model.

Contrast with Other Countries.—In this respect the position of the Irish nation differs profoundly from that of the Catholic populations of Italy and Spain and the more or less Catholic countries of Continental Europe and South America. Although these have all felt the effects of the non-Christian or anti-Christian movement of the past three centuries, the old Catholic tradition in public life was never completely broken. Their civilisation and culture still rest largely upon a Catholic basis ; their best literature and art, their legal system and social customs, are more or less permeated with the Catholic spirit. It is far otherwise with the countries of the English civilisation. The institutions and ideals of these latter in morals, laws and administration, their literature and art all spring from the Protestant England of the 17th century and repose upon a non-Catholic or anti-Catholic basis. Therefore, for a nation like Ireland, whose civilisation as it now exists belongs in large measure to the Protestant culture, a return to Catholic standards in public life is a much more difficult process than for Catholic nations of the Continent.

The difficulties are increased by the many ties—political, economic and even racial (for the greater part of the Irish race now live in the United States of America and the British Dominions), binding the modern Irish nation to the English-speaking world. A further, and perhaps more serious, obstacle to the restoration of Catholic principles and ideals in the public life of Ireland is the presence in

---

[1] Cf. the booklet, *Ireland's Peril*, by the present writer (Gill, Dublin, 1930), of which the present article is a summary.

the bosom of the nation itself of a strongly organised party closely allied with the British Imperial party and with Anglo-American Freemasonry. This party, which is anti-Catholic and anti-Irish in its general outlook and tendency, formed up to quite recently the dominant and governing class in the country, and still retains its ascendancy and control in the North-Eastern counties of Ireland.

Prevalence of False Principles.—The results of these conditions are to be seen in many ways. Unchristian principles and ideals are not unfrequently championed (sometimes even by practical Catholics) in the press, on the platform, and sometimes even in the legislature itself. The principles of unchristian Liberalism are too often accepted as criteria in determining such questions as the rights and duties attaching to the ownership of property, the duties of Civil Government in safeguarding the religion and morals of the people, the due relation between Church and State, the duties and rights of the Church, and the parent and the civil power in the matter of Education.

Summary of the Social Evils.—The prevalence of unchristian principles in public life, and the undue influence of the non-Catholic and unchristian forces in the country are the greatest obstacles in the work of healing the social evils that afflict Ireland to-day. The widespread and excessive poverty, side by side with extravagance and luxury and the maintenance of two huge armies of State officials ; the restlessness and disinclination for serious work that now affect almost all classes ; the general craze for pleasure and excitement ; the abnormal emigration from an already under-populated country ;[1] the enforced idleness of multi-

---

[1] Ireland, although one of the richest countries of Europe in the fertility of her soil and other natural advantages, is the most sparsely populated of all European countries, except Scandinavia and parts of Southern Spain. The following table, taken from the *Census of the Irish Free State, Preliminary Report*, 1926, page 6, will be of interest in this connection :

POPULATION PER SQUARE MILE OF SOME EUROPEAN COUNTRIES

England and Wales	.. 649	Holland	.. ..	545
Belgium	.. 635	Italy (pre-war area)	..	338
Germany	.. 328	IRELAND—The Free State ..		112
Czecho-Slovakia ..	.. 251	The six N.E. Counties		240
Denmark	.. 197	Spain ..	.. ..	110
France	.. 184	Sweden ..	.. ..	34
Scotland	.. 161	Norway ..	.. ..	21

42

tudes in presence of abundant natural resources, which are left undeveloped ; the uncultivated lands ; the neglected fisheries ; the dwindling population, are all the natural results of an unchristian social régime, and can be healed only by a complete social reconstruction on a Christian basis. The same applies to the excessive drink traffic ; the destructive betting and gambling activities now actively propagated by the Press and other agencies to the remotest parts even of the rural districts ; the multiplication of debasing amusements ; the obscuring of the Catholic tradition regarding the safeguarding of Christian modesty. These and such like evils, which now threaten the very life-springs of the nation, would never have reached their present proportions among such a profoundly Catholic people as the majority of the Irish are, if the social organisation were national and Catholic, as in normal circumstances it undoubtedly would be.

Among the evils enumerated and the problems connected with them, some are of special urgency, such as the emigration question, the desertion of the land, the problem of the Gaedhealtacht, the betting evil, the unchristian Press and Cinema, and the absence of Catholic industrial organisation. We treat briefly of each of these in order :

I. **Emigration.**[1]—The evils of emigration and urbanism are of such importance in the Irish social question, threatening, as they do, the very existence of the Irish Catholic nation, that emigration and urbanism may be at present regarded as the central social evils in Ireland, in reference to which almost every other public question has to be considered. An abnormal or forced emigration, resulting from misgovernment and social injustice, has been an outstanding phenomenon in Irish life ever since the ill-starred Flight of the Earls after the Tudor Conquest of Ireland in the beginning of the 17th century. It is only since the middle of the 19th century, however, that the evil has attained the proportions of a national exodus.

---

[1] These notes were written before the interruption of the Irish emigration movement caused (1930–31) by the unemployment and the anti-immigration regulations in U.S.A. and Great Britain. This interruption has come solely from the present unfavourable conditions of these latter countries.

(a) **Exodus of the Irish Nation.**—The number of Irish emigrants since 1847 would reach a total of about one and a-half the present population of Ireland. While the population of every other country in Europe has increased, and in the case of many has been doubled or trebled, during the last eighty years, that of Ireland, though one of the richest of all in natural resources, has been reduced to about half of what it was in 1847, and, probably, to much less than one-third or one-fourth of the number that the country could, in normal conditions, easily maintain.[1]

Of the Irish-born men and women now living, about one-third are in exile. This makes the case of Ireland quite unique among the countries of the world and unparalleled in the History of Europe. Norway, whose number of exiles is about 14 per cent. of the home population, is the nearest approach to Ireland.[2]

---

[1] Cf. G. O'Brien—*The Economic History of Ireland from the Union to the Famine* (Longmans, 1921), pp. 74–86, and *passim*. On the showing of Dr. O'Brien it would appear that the land of Ireland could easily maintain more than four times its present population on agriculture alone.

[2] The following table, arranged from figures given in the *Preliminary Report of Census of Irish Free State,* 1926 (pp. 8, 9), shows the unique position of Ireland in regard to emigration. The figures represent the number of exiles from each country as per cent. of the home population :

COUNTRY OF BIRTH AND NUMBER OF EXILES AS PER CENT. OF THE HOME POPULATION

France	..	..	..	0.5	Italy	.. ..	.. 8.4
Belgium	..	..	..	1.0	England and Wales	..	6.3
Holland	..	..	..	2.1	Scotland ..	..	.. 14.1
Germany		..	..	2.9	Norway ..	..	14.8
Spain	..	..	..	5.2	IRELAND	..	.. 43.0

The following tabulation will convey a succinct idea of the state of the emigration question up to recent years :

YEARS		ANNUAL EMIGRATION	
1891–1900	..	.. 43,352	⎫ Average for the ten years
1901–1910	..	.. 34,906	⎬ (Cf. *Thom's Directory*)
1911–1925	..	.. 33,468	⎭
1926 ..	..	.. 43,751	
1927 ..	..	.. 44,890	
1928 ..	..	.. 41,931	

These figures represent (approximately) the total number of emigrants, including emigrants to Great Britain, *which have not been included in the ordinary official returns since* 1922. For fuller explanation and details cf. *Ireland's Peril*, pp. 7, 8 ; also *The Statistical Abstract*, published 1931 by the Department of Industry and Commerce, Dublin.

(*b*) **Ruinous Results of the Exodus.**—When we bear in mind that over 85 per cent. of these emigrants leave Ireland between the ages of seventeen and forty-five, and that about 80 per cent. are drawn from the agricultural population,[1] we can understand something of the disastrous results of such a drain. First there is the purely economic loss. It is estimated that a full-grown healthy man or woman normally represents in merely economic value to the nation anything between £300 and £600. On this estimate the yearly emigration from Ireland of some 40,000 of the very best and most vigorous of her sons and daughters would represent, in mere economic loss, an annual drain upon the national resources of anything between £12,000,000 and £24,000,000 ! The sums sent home every year by the exiled Irish (although a certain recoupment as far as they go), represent at most only a very small fraction of this yearly loss.

The economic loss is not, however, the principal one. The physical health and strength of the home population must, necessarily, be depressed to a lower standard owing to the constant drawing off of so many of the best of the younger generation The people's interests tend to be diverted from their own country. Energy, enthusiasm and the spirit of joyousness and hope so essential to the nation's welfare are damped, and discouragement and pessimism tend to prevail.[2]

---

[1] Cf. Lists in *Irish Catholic Directory*, 1929, pp. lx–lxi.

[2] Another consequence of the exodus of the Irish from Ireland is that the *extinction of the whole Irish race* is definitely threatened. On this subject (which is perhaps outside our present scope) cf. a series of articles by M. V. Kelly, entitled " The Suicide of the Irish Race," published in *America*, November 17th, November 18th, and December 1st, 1928. On the same subject see in *Studies*, vol. v (1916) an article by Austin O'Malley, M.D., etc., entitled " The Effects of the American Climate on the European Emigrants," also vol. vii (1918), an article by the same writer, entitled " Irish Vital Statistics in America " ; and, finally, an article by J. J. Walsh, M.D., etc., in the same review, vol. x (1921), entitled " Irish Mortality in New York and Pennsylvania." The conclusions from these and other writings seem to be that : (*a*) the actual mortality of the Irish in New York (and still more in the other great cities of U.S.A.) is more than double the home mortality, and much higher than that of any other section of the American population ; (*b*) an Irish man or woman sacrifices on an average, at least ten years of his or her natural life by emigrating to America ; and, finally (*c*) the Irish in America are not increasing at anything like the normal rate, and in fact seem doomed to extinction.

(c) **The Low Marriage and Birth Rates.**—Another result of the abnormal emigration and of the economic conditions which are its main cause is that the marriage rate in Ireland is *much less than half* the normal marriage rate of the other European countries. According to censuses taken in twenty-one different European countries during the years 1900 to 1911, Ireland presents, in the small percentage of its married men, a strange and very striking contrast with every other European country. The figures refer to men between the ages of 25 and 34. Of the total number of men of that age living in ten different countries, the following percentages were married:

In Serbia	.. 84.1	In England and Wales	60.6
In Spain	.. 72.1	In Austria	.. 60.1
In France	.. 65.0	In Scotland	.. 51.4
In Germany	.. 63.3	In Sweden	.. 49.9
In Italy	.. 63.1	In IRELAND	.. 29.2 [1]

The unnatural and unwholesome conditions and economic stagnation which such a low marriage rate implies and intensifies do not need to be emphasised. As a result of the low marriage rate, the birth-rate (about 21 per 1,000), although fair in proportion to the marriage rate, is, absolutely speaking, one of the lowest in the world.[2]

Hence, the population is steadily declining. Between 1841 and 1926 it had fallen from 8,196,547 to 4,229,124. A year later (1927) it had again declined to 4,208,000, showing a diminution of over 20,000 in one year.[3]

---

[1] These figures have been supplied by the Irish Free State Department of Industry and Commerce. Since 1921 the marriage rate in Ireland has declined still further. Cf. *Census of Population (Saorstat Eireann)*, vol. v (Eason, Dublin, 1929).

[2] The absolute birth-rates in England (16.0), France (18.2), and Switzerland (18.2), are now lower than that of Ireland. The decline in these countries is mainly due to a cause which does not operate, or operates comparatively little, in a country like Ireland, where the vast majority of the people are practising Catholics.

[3] The diminution of the population is actually *very much greater* than the figures here given, which are taken from the Registrar-General's Annual Report, where no account seems to be taken of the yearly emigration to Great Britain. The actual diminution is probably about 30,000. Owing to the interruption of the emigration movement since 1929–30, the population of Ireland now (1931) begins to show an increase for the first time since 1841.

II. **Urbanism.**—Side by side with the emigration movement there is a growing tendency among the rural population to abandon the land, and migrate to the towns. Thus, in the twenty-six counties now comprising the Irish Free State, the rural districts have lost *nearly two-thirds* of their population since 1841. The " country " population of these counties, which was 5,281,000 in 1841, had fallen to 1,878,000 in 1926.[1] Some rural parishes have actually lost more than five-sixths of their population[2] since the middle of the last century. On the other hand, the cities of Dublin, Cork, Limerick, Galway and twenty-five other towns, have increased in population although their industries have mostly decayed, the increase having been brought about by the absorption of the distributing trade of the smaller towns and villages.

(*a*) **Its Ruinous Effects.**—As a result of this unnatural and abnormal migration of the people into the larger towns, which have no industries to maintain them, the numbers engaged in the distributive occupations, and the more or less parasitical employments have grown beyond all proportion. The prices of the necessaries of life are excessive ; for, besides the fact that an increasing crowd of middlemen have to be maintained from trading profits, prices especially of bread, milk and meat are too often swollen by arbitrary and unjust profiteering, the effects of which fall especially upon the poor.[3] Very great numbers are unemployed.[4] The housing

---

[1] *Preliminary Report of Census of Irish Free State*, 1926, p. 2.

[2] In a census of the parish of Cappagh and Nantenan, Co. Limerick, which was recently taken (1928) by the Parish Priest (Rev. P. Woulfe), it was found that the population of the parish, which had been about 4,500 in the year 1841, had fallen to 653 in 1927. There is no reason to regard this case as exceptional. The land, which half a century ago was mostly under tillage, is now nearly altogether in pasture, and the rural industries which then existed have completely disappeared.

[3] Cf. *Report of the Commission on Prices* appointed by the Irish Free State Executive, 1926 ; also a valuable series of articles published in *The Nation* (Dublin), 1929, Sept. 7th, Sept. 21st, and Oct. 12th.

[4] In April, 1926, the date of the last Census, the unemployment figures for the Irish Free State were 78,071 (Cf. *Census of Population* 1926). There are no reliable figures obtainable of the present extent of unemployment in the Irish Free State. It is admitted, however, by those in the best position to judge (such as those engaged in social or charitable work amongst the poor) that it has reached unprecedented dimensions. The

accommodation is quite inadequate ; and extreme poverty, probably unequalled in any other country in Europe, prevails.

(*b*) **Deplorable Conditions of the Urban Population.**— Among the evidences of the excessive poverty of the town population of Ireland, perhaps the most striking are the badness of the housing accommodation and the high rate of infant mortality. Taking Dublin as an example, we find that the total population of the Borough of Dublin at the last census (1926) was 316,693. Of these, 23,665 families, including 78,920 persons (viz., 27.8 per cent. of the whole), lived in one-room tenements, and 63,458 more lived in two-room tenements. These two classes include little less than half the total population ! [1] Of these dwellings very many are cellars ; and more than 10 per cent. were declared more than ten years previously to be unfit for human habitation. Again, even before 1912, when conditions of unemployment and over-crowding were not nearly as bad as they are at present, more than a thousand children under five years of age died every year in Dublin as a result of insufficient nourishment, deficient clothing and unsanitary housing. [2] Similar conditions, though not always quite so bad, prevail in other towns, especially in the industrial towns of the four north-eastern counties.

(*c*) **Threatened Extinction of the Irish Race and Nation.**— Meanwhile, as the rural districts are becoming deserted, the land, which is the main basis of the economic life of

---

numbers of unemployed in the six N.E. Counties was over 50,000 in 1929, and well over 70,000 in 1931. Although the number of unemployed in the Free State is now probably less in proportion to the population than in the six N.E. Counties, it seems safe to assert that the complete unemployment figures for all Ireland would be over 150,000.

[1] *Census of Population—Saorstat Eireann*, 1926, vol. iv, p. 4 (Stationery Office, Dublin).

[2] This is according to the report drawn up (1912) by Sir Charles Cameron, who was Medical Superintendent Officer of Health in Dublin for thirty-five years. Cf. Hughes—*Poverty in Dublin* (*Irish Messenger* series) ; McSweeney O.P.,—*Poverty in Cork* (University and Labour series, Cork) ; also Rowntree, *op. cit. See* also *Census of Population*, 1926, vol. iv. It may be noted that this poverty-stricken population of Dublin is made up in large part of the descendants of the rural cottiers who were driven from their holdings in the rich plains of central Ireland during the 19th century.

the nation, is steadily going out of cultivation.[1] The result of this last movement on the national prosperity may be gathered from the recognised fact that the food product from uncultivated but arable land is less than one-third or one-fourth of what the same land yields by suitable cultivation.[2]

At present, considerably less than three-quarters of a million of people in the Irish Free State, of both sexes, including boys and girls under eighteen years of age, are engaged in agriculture,[3] while the total population is little short of three millions. Hence, seeing that agriculture is practically the only productive industry of Ireland, the land, which is largely uncultivated, has to maintain more than three times the number of people employed on it. Again, since town families do not usually survive beyond the third generation, even when they have plenty of work, food and housing, which they have not in Ireland, this migration to the town is nearly as fatal to the vitality of the nation as emigration itself. Both are leading directly towards the final extinction of the historic Irish nation, which is now menaced with the same fate as has already overtaken the Highland Scotch.

(d) **Causes of the Rural Depopulation.**—That the root causes of emigration and urbanisation are economic, is beyond doubt. Among these causes are excessive taxation ; an unsuitable financial system ;[4] the concentration of the

---

[1] The cultivated area of the twenty-six counties of the Irish Free State, which was in round numbers 3,509,000 statute acres in 1851, had dwindled to 1,551,447 statute acres in 1926—being in the latter year less by about 100,000 acres than in 1909, which was the lowest record previously reached. Cf. *Agricultural Statistics*, compiled for the Department of Industry and Commerce (Stationery Office, Dublin, 1928), pp. xxix, xxx–xxxii. The cultivated area has shrunken still further by over 126,000 acres during the past five years (1926–1931), so that in 1931 the total area under tillage is set down at 1,425,021 statute acres.

[2] Cf. *Labour and Agriculture*, p. 10 ("Labour Policy Pamphlets," Dublin, 32 Lower Abbey Street, 1926).

[3] In 1912, the number of persons engaged in agriculture in all Ireland was 1,074,485, of whom 861,994 were in the counties of the present Irish Free State, and 212,491 in the six N.E. Counties. (Cf. *Agricultural Statistics*, 1847 to 1926, p. 160). Since then the "country" population of the Free State has fallen by about 167,000 (*ib.*, p. xxix).

[4] Owing to its monetary system being tied on to that of Great Britain, and to the absence of adequate protection for native industries, Ireland and Great Britain form one and the same economic unit (cf. *Post-War Banking Policy*, by Rt. Hon. R. McKenna, pp. 74 ff and 137 ff, where this fact is made plain), whereas the circumstances and needs of the two countries are entirely different.

most fertile land in the ownership of the great ranchers, who do not cultivate it ; the practical cessation for the past fifteen years of the building of labourers' cottages, to which small allotments of land are attached ; insufficient protection for native productive effort and the excessive importation of luxuries in exchange for exported food. Until these causes are removed, there can be no well-grounded hope of real and permanent improvement.

There are besides many subsidiary causes at work, which tend to grow rather than diminish in proportion to the increasing weakness of the national vitality. Among such may be mentioned : an entirely unsuitable educational system ;[1] the increasing dreariness of rural life, which is intensified by the exodus of the younger generation ; the absence of laws needed to stabilise the agricultural population ; the lowering prestige of manual labour ; the prevailing restlessness and craving for excitement and change ; the inducements to emigration held out by relatives already in exile ; the complete absence of Catholic rural organisation such as now exists in most of the Catholic countries of Continental Europe.

III. **Problem of the Gaedhealtacht.**[2]—The evils of pauperisation and emigration have reached their climax in the Gaedhealtacht. The conditions prevailing there, which are growing steadily worse since 1901, are heading fast towards

---

[1] The system of Primary education in Ireland tends to impart to the children a distaste for Irish rural life, while a very large percentage of the secondary school pupils and of the University graduates leave Ireland to seek a livelihood elsewhere. The sums of public money spent on the education of these latter is only one element and the smallest element of the loss thereby sustained by the nation itself. Trinity College, which is un-Irish and un-Catholic is a permanent source of difficulty and danger. Its influence has always tended to pervert the Irish Educational system to ideals that are opposed to the spiritual and temporal interests of the nation at large. Cf. *Secondary Schools for Rural Ireland*, by the present writer (*Irish Messenger* Series, 1919).

[2] The term Gaedhealtacht is used here to denote those districts of Ireland in which Irish is the spoken language of all, or of a considerable section of the inhabitants. Cf. *Coimisuin na Gaedhealtachta—Report*, pp. 5-10 (Eason, Dublin, 1926). The Gaedhealtacht Commission was appointed in 1926 by the Irish Free State Government to investigate the Gaedhealtacht question and suggest means to deal with it. The *Report*, issued July, 1926, contains an excellent survey of the situation and a set of important proposals for dealing with it, practically none of which has so far (1931) been put into execution.

the final extinction of the Irish-speaking population. From the Report of the Gaedhealtacht Commission the following general conclusions may be drawn :

(a) **Paramount Importance of the Gaedhealtacht Population.**—The people of the Gaedhealtacht (in 1925 they numbered a little less than a million, of whom about 300,000 spoke Irish as their native language) are the main repositories of the old Irish Catholic tradition.[1] Furthermore, " the future of the Irish language and its part in the future of the Irish nation depend, more than on anything else, on its continuing in an unbroken tradition as the language of Irish homes. This tradition is the living root from which *alone* organic growth is possible."[2] If the Irish language disappears from the Gaedhealtacht as a living speech, the prospect of its revival as the spoken national language of Ireland will, to put the matter mildly, have been considerably lessened ; and if the native language dies, the salvation of the distinct nationality of the Irish people will become humanly-speaking, impossible. On the other hand, " given a State policy . . ." and a State attitude to the language such as is outlined in the *Report* of the Gaedhealtacht Commission " . . . then the National language can be maintained in unbroken continuity as the traditional language of a considerable number of existing Irish homes, and passed on therefrom to the nation."[3]

Hence, the people of the Gaedhealtacht, besides being amongst the very best of the Irish race physically and morally, are of incalculable importance to the future of the Irish nation. Besides, the old Catholic Irish tradition of the Gaedhealtacht, where alone the Irish Catholic tradition now lives, is one of the nation's best bulwarks against the materialism of the English-speaking world by which it is surrounded.

(b) **Their Present Wretched Condition.**—The Gaedhealtacht population are at present living in conditions of destitution and material misery which, probably, have no parallel in

---

[1] *Ib.*, p. 42.
[2] *Ib.*, p. 3. Extract from the letter of the President of the Executive Council of the Free State to the Chairman of the Gaedhealtacht Commission.
[3] *Report*, p. 57.

Europe—at least among rural communities. It is probable indeed, that no like conditions can be found in any other civilised country of the world, except, perhaps, among the expiring remnants of the Red Indians of the United States of America, or in portions of British India. " In a bad year they are saved from extreme privation [viz., starvation] only by relief measures." Again, " the surplus population has continually to look for a living outside, while those who remain at home live in grinding poverty."[1] The rateable value of the farms and houses on which they are forced to live is less than an average of thirty shillings for each person, which is less than one-third of what would be needed to enable a family to live in any kind of becoming human condition.[2] This state of affairs, which is at its worst in the district where the Irish language survives most fully,[3] is a result of the oppression and social injustice of the past two centuries. For these people are, " to a large extent the wrecks of past racial, religious, agrarian and social storms . . . and of famine catastrophies."[4] Thus, they are correctly designated in the *Report* as the " Evicted Tenants of the Race." They are, in other words, the surviving remnants of the old Irish nation, whose forefathers were disinherited, and driven from their lands.

Their condition *has deteriorated still further* during the past six or seven years (1923–30). This deterioration has been produced by a succession of exceptionally bad seasons ; the abolition of the Congested Districts Board in 1923 ; the collapse of the fishing industry about the same time ; the crushing out of the few surviving rural industries ;[5] the high taxation, and the general depression in agriculture.

(c) **The Resulting Danger of Their Final Extinction.**—As a consequence of these conditions the Gaedhealtacht population is now in immediate danger of final extinction. The total population of the Gaedhealtacht fell during the fourteen years, 1911–1925, from 1,121,354 to 975,371, being a decrease of 145,983 or 13 per cent. of the whole. The percentage of decrease during the preceding ten years (1901–1910) was

[1] *Ib.*, pp. 36, 37.   [2] *Ib.*, pp. 40, 41, 123, 133.
[3] *Ib.*, pp. 40, 41 ; also Appendix v, pp. 123, 124.
[4] Words of the Royal Commission of 1908. Cf. *Report*, p. 36.
[5] *Ib.*, pp. 47, 48.

only about half of the above, so that the *rate of decline is increasing rapidly*. Seeing that the decline of population in all Ireland during the years 1911–26 was only 161,095, it follows that more than five-sixths of the total loss fell upon the Gaedhealtacht.[1] This decline is due almost entirely to emigration.

The growing decrease of population in the Gaedhealtacht affects the Irish-speaking families of these districts most of all, for they are in fact the poorest.[2] The Irish-speaking population, which numbered 436,758 in 1911, had actually declined to 299,249 in 1925, thus losing 137,000, or nearly 33 per cent. of the whole, in fourteen years.[3]

(*d*) From the preceding one may infer that a very large proportion of the emigrants from the Irish Free State comes (or rather came up to 1930) from the Gaedhealtacht. Of the total yearly toll of emigration from Ireland (about 40,000) probably about one-half (20,000), at a conservative estimate, comes from these districts. Hence, the Irish-speaking population, which was a little less than 300,000 in 1925, is manifestly doomed to disappear within the lifetime of the present generation, unless drastic and effective measures are adopted to save it before it is too late. The core of the problem in its acutest aspects is in the economic conditions and the outflow of emigrants.[4] These call for immediate remedies, which must be drastic if they are to be effective.

IV. **The Unchristian Press and Cinema.**—Several of the forces which are among the contributing causes of emigration and urbanisation, such as the morbid restlessness and discontent with rural agricultural life, are intensified by the unchristian Press and cinema, and by the vice of betting and gambling, which has become so prevalent over the whole country in recent years.

The books and papers which the people read are too often saturated with materialism, and still oftener are devoid

---

[1] Cf. *Report*, p. 9 ; also *Preliminary Report of Census of Population of Irish Free State*, pp. 1, 4, 6. The figures in the two Reports show discrepancies, but these do not impair the main conclusion.
[2] *Report*, p. 140.   [3] *Ib.*, p. 9.
[4] The interruption (already referred to) of the emigration movement seems to afford an opportunity of inaugurating a successful effort to save the Gaedhealtacht population.

of a Catholic outlook. A very large proportion, probably more than one-half of the papers, magazines and reviews circulating in Ireland, are British publications of the purely materialistic type.[1] The quantity of debasing literature of all kinds sold in Ireland *is on the increase.*[2] The circulation of Sunday papers is probably over half-a-million. Of these even the least harmful is unfit for a Catholic country, while very many are positively bad, some being English Sunday papers of the very worst type.

The cinema is, as a rule, almost equally debasing, and, to say the least, is as far removed from the Christian character as the foreign non-Catholic Press. It is well known that the general tendency of the ordinary cinema shows even when they are not openly suggestive or debasing, as they too frequently are, is definitely unchristian. Like the unchristian Press the cinema tends gradually to demoralise and wean the mind of the spectator from his moral convictions, and from the Christian outlook and tradition.

In the matter of the unchristian Press, the position of Irish people is quite different from that of the Continental Catholic countries, and calls for much more efficient and drastic safeguards than would be needed in the case of these latter. In Spain, Italy and Poland, the mass of the people are protected by the language barrier, and to a certain extent by their national sympathies and outlook from the evil literature of countries other than their own. The Irish people, on the other hand, owing to their knowledge of English and the partial denationalisation resulting from the destruction of their own language and civilisation are completely exposed to the corrupting influence of the Press and literature of Great Britain and the United States of America.

---

[1] On the whole question of Evil Literature in Ireland, which is at present one of the worst and most destructive of all the social evils afflicting the country, cf. *Evil Literature*, by Rev. R. Devane, S.J. (Browne and Nolan, Ltd., Dublin, 1927) ; also *Report of the Committee on Evil Literature* (Stationery Office, Dublin, 1926).

[2] The Board of Trade returns for 1930 reveal the fact, that the imports of books and newspapers into the Irish Free State, which for the year 1929 represented a value of £622,189, increased for the year 1930 to £652,207, implying an advance of £30,018 in one year. During the same period the value of exports of books and newspapers from the Irish Free State fell from £226,564 to £189,370.

V. The Betting Evil.—Betting (that is the staking of money or other value on an event of doubtful issue which none of the parties concerned has the power to control) is not in itself morally wrong. As in the case of alcoholic drink, the evil of betting arises from excess or other accidental circumstances—such as loss of time, demoralisation of character, and the fact that the money is needed for one's family. It is notorious, however, that the practice of betting is peculiarly liable to degenerate into a vice, and that it exerts a very dangerous fascination, especially in modern times, upon those who indulge in it to any extent. Owing to this fact, and owing to the many social evils attendant upon the practice, betting activities are usually controlled by law in most modern States.

In Great Britain and Ireland the practice of betting and gambling, as well as the affording of facilities for or offering inducements to such practices, were strictly controlled by a series of laws enacted in the British Legislature between the years 1845 and 1920. Thus, all cash betting was illegal, except on race courses. Betting houses of all kinds were forbidden, and for the offence of keeping such a house a person was liable to fine or imprisonment. Furthermore, the circulation of betting news or of information or advice which might induce others to bet was strictly prohibited. It was, besides, a serious offence against the law to carry out a betting transaction of any kind with persons under sixteen years of age.[1]

Changes Wrought by the Betting Act of 1926.—Unfortunately, however, these laws were not always strictly enforced, especially since the period immediately before the European War. By the Betting Act, enacted for revenue purposes in the Irish Free State Legislature in 1926, betting houses were legalised on condition of their being registered, and a tax was put upon the betting transactions carried out in them. By this law there is no limitation enforceable upon the number of betting houses, so that they are increasing beyond all proportion. No restriction now exists, or at least none is enforced, upon the

---

[1] Cf. *Report of the Joint Commission on the Betting Act of* 1926, pp. 2–6 (Eason, Dublin, 1929).

advertisement and circulation of betting news and of all
kinds of information calculated to induce people to bet.

Present Magnitude of the Betting Evil.—Even before the
European War the vice of betting and gambling, notwithstanding the restrictive laws, was a great social evil in
Ireland, being, in the opinion of many competent judges,
scarcely less destructive and harmful than the drink evil.
As a result of the general decadence of public morality
consequent upon the War, the betting evil grew worse.
With the passing of the Act of 1926 by the Irish Free State
Legislature, legalising betting houses in the twenty-six
counties of the Free State, the evil has attained unprecedented proportions, and is at present one of the worst and
most demoralising of the many social ills which afflict the
country.[1]

The evidence given before the Joint Commission appointed
by the Free State Executive to examine into the working
of the Betting Act of 1926 conveys some idea of the nature
and extent of the betting evil in the Irish Free State.
Perhaps the worst effect of the facilities for betting afforded
by the Act of 1926 has been the widespread demoralisation
of women, children, and the poor, especially in the cities.[2]
Besides the valuable information on the subject contained
in the evidence just referred to, a considerable amount of
useful knowledge may be had from *The Report of the Select
Committee of the House of Lords*,[3] which led to some useful
anti-betting legislation in the early years of the present

[1] Thus, for the financial year ending March 31st, 1928, the Betting turn-
over on which Betting Duty is paid was between £5,000,000 and £6,000,000
for the Irish Free State, whose total population is only about 3,000,000.
The corresponding amount for Great Britain, with a population nearly
thirteen times as great, was about £80,000,000 so that at present the
Betting evil is as intense in the Irish Free State as in Great Britain.

[2] Cf. *Ireland's Peril*, pp. 23–25, where extracts are cited from the *Report
of the Joint Commission*, 1929.

[3] Cf. *Report from the Committee of the House of Lords on Betting* (London :
H. M. Stationery Office, 1901–1903). The Committee attributes the
increase of betting mainly to the increased facilities afforded by the Press.
It condemns very strongly the " advertisements of the sporting tipsters."
According to the *Report* the information given in these advertisements, if
true, is usually obtained by fraud and corruption, and they are forbidden
by law in France. The Committee recommends that betting be allowed
only in *the places* (and only in special portions of these places) *where the
sport is carried on ;* and that effective sanction, including even imprisonment, be attached to the existing and proposed Betting Laws.

century.   From these and other sources of reliable authority
one may get an idea of the grave and destructive nature of
this vice which is becoming daily more and more widespread
among the people.

It is also certain that the evil is due, at least in its intensified form, to the increased facilities now afforded, and
the inducements held out, and to the propaganda carried
on by the Press in so many different forms.   By the with-
drawal of these facilities, and the prevention by State action
of the inducements referred to, the betting habit could, in
a short time, be reduced to moderate proportions.

VI. Absence of Catholic Organisation.—One of the baneful
results of the Penal Laws and of the severance of Ireland
from contact with the Continent, has been the tardiness to
form Catholic lay organisations for social and industrial
purposes.   Such organisation now so widespread in Continental Europe, is recognised as one of the great needs of
the hour.   In Ireland there are so far no unions of Catholic
employers, and the Employers' Unions that do exist are
dominated largely by non-Catholics, and are too often
marked by the want of a Christian outlook.

Special Need of Catholic Workers' Associations.—Catholic
Workers' Associations, for both town and country, are
possibly a still more pressing need, especially as more than
95 per cent. of the Irish working class, at least of the Free
State, are practical Catholics, who, probably, are not surpassed by any Catholics in the world in the vigour of their
Catholic faith, and their responsiveness to religious motives.

It may be true, indeed, that it would be difficult if not
impossible, at the present time to organise Catholic Trade
or Labour Unions of the ordinary kind, seeing that the
field is already occupied by neutral organisations.   But it
would be quite feasible to form Catholic associations of
workingmen (like the *Katholische Arbeitervereine* of Germany)
whose scope would include the large range of interests, such
as intellectual and religious education, workers' banks,
housing, co-operative marketing, etc., which are not provided for by the existing Trade and Labour Unions.   These
associations, while in no wise clashing with the existing
unions or hindering their effectiveness in their own sphere,

would serve to supplement them to the immense benefit of the workingmen and the whole cause of labour ; and above all they would eliminate the many elements of danger which the existing unions now contain.[1]

VII. **Conclusion.**—From all the above it is clear that the seriousness and pressing nature of the social question in Ireland can hardly be exaggerated. The question is one which affects the highest interests of the whole English-speaking world and even of the Catholic Church itself.

Although the English-speaking countries now contain between 25,000,000 and 30,000,000 Catholics, Ireland is the only country among them (if we except the French-speaking provinces of Canada) that contains a practically homogeneous Catholic population with an historical past. That Catholic population, now in such peril, is one of the main sources of supply of priests and religious of both sexes for the whole English-speaking world. It is in a sense, and to a certain extent, the very centre and source of the Catholic life of a scattered Catholic population of more than 25,000,000 souls. Its failure, or serious weakening, would be a disaster to them and to the Catholic Church.

To rescue the Irish Catholic nation from the perils by which it is now menaced a new social system organised in accordance with Catholic principles and tradition must be gradually built up ; and it is at this objective rather than at applying palliatives here and there, that the social reformer in Ireland should consistently direct his efforts. For it is certain that nothing else and nothing less can ultimately save the nation, and at the same time preserve intact the wondrous faith and substantial goodness of the people. The faith and religious fervour of the Irish people (probably unsurpassed in any country of the world) forms the great counterbalancing element in the present depressing situation. For their Catholic faith is still apparently as strong as ever, and the traditional habit of fidelity to religious duties has not so far been affected.

The people have now substantially regained the ownership

---

[1] Pius X—*Singulari Quadam*, Sept., 1912. Cf. Ryan and Husselein—*Church and Labour* (Harding and More, London, 1920), pp. 122–132. For a summary of this important Encyclical, cf. *Ireland's Peril*, pp 26–28.

43

of the land of Ireland. Under the new political conditions the Catholic Irish, over the greater portion of the country, have secured, besides, substantial control of the civil administration. Hence, what was impossible during the last four centuries has now become feasible—namely, to inaugurate a social reconstruction upon an Irish Catholic basis. A national movement for such a reconstruction could in a comparatively short time change the whole national outlook and usher in a new era of prosperity and social peace.

INDEX

INDEX

Germany, 70, 72, 83, 87, 88, 89, 94,
95, 97, 108, 110, 124, 149, 157,
167, 174, 177, 186, 195, 198, 199,
226, 240, 248, 255, 256, 259, 260,
261, 265, 266, 268, 273, 318, 389,
411, 417, 437, 440, 533, 580, 581,
611, 672.
Gerrard, 313.
Gide, C., 15, 123, 126, 127, 156,
159, 162, 163, 309, 513, 533, 534.
Gierke, Otto, 31.
Giovanni Dominici, 351.
Giloteaux, Abbé Paulin, 573, 574,
591.
Girls, training of, 374, 447–50.
Gladiators' contests, 9.
Glorification of Athletics, 375.
Gnostic Philosophy, 112.
Gnosticism, 111.
Gnostics, 222.
Godden, G. M., 208.
God's poor, 101.
Godts, Rev. F. X., 573, 575.
Godwin, 167.
Golden Age, the, 24 ; Ireland's, 163.
Goldsmith, 332, 576.
Gompers, Samuel, 205.
Goode, W. T., 214.
Gortroe, 623, 624.
Goths, the, 14.
Gougaud, Dom, 15, 18, 631.
Governing authority, xi.
—— Council of Guilds, 75.
Government, best form of, 476.
—— functions, 147, 153. See
Duties, State.
Graft, 537.
Grand Architect, the, 224.
Grand Lodges : Belgium, Brazil,
Denmark, Dublin, Egypt,
France, Greece, Holland, Italy,
Mexico, Portugal, South America,
Spain, Switzerland, 228, 229.
Graves de Communi, 551, 620.
Great Britain, 141, 143, 149, 177,
178, 179, 228, 229, 369, 412, 452,
524, 525, 566, 658, 669, 670, 671,
See Britain.
Great War, 204, 348. See European
War.
Greece, its arts, 18 ; 221, 280, 429,
611.
Greeks, 291, 347, 543, 586, 589,
591, 604.
Green, Mrs., 29, 636.
Gregory VII, 14, 26, 56.
—— X, 48.

Gregory XVI, 122.
—— St. (Nazianzen), 556.
—— St. (Nyssa), 556.
—— the Great, 549, 554, 555.
Grundlach, 253.
Guilds : their Christian and democratic character, 71–72 ; their
destruction, 80 ; their equipment,
74 ; their grades—apprentices,
journeymen, masters, 75 ; their
independence, 74; their industrial
protection and control, 77 ; their
municipal authority, 74 ; their
organisation, 75 ; their origin,
71 ; their religious character, 79 ;
social and economic policy, 77 ;
trades (different), 74 ; their
wealth, 74. See Mediæval.
Guitton, Père, 260, 404.
Guizot, 19.
Gurewitch, 206.

Haeckel, 110.
Hall, C., 167.
—— Rev. H. T., 422.
Hallam, 19, 33.
Harduin, 563.
Harmel, Leon, 260.
—— silk factory, 404.
Harmonists, 160.
Havas, 241.
Haywood, W., 158.
Health insurance, 571.
Healy, Most Rev. John, 648, 650.
Hebrew race, 475.
Hedge schools, 652.
Hedibias, 555.
Hedley, Dr., 357.
Hedweg of Poland, 25.
Hefelé, 563.
Hegel, 110, 170, 453.
Helleputte, M., 271.
Helot slaves, 159.
Henry II of England, 31.
—— III, 634.
—— IV of Germany, 56.
—— VI, 634.
—— VIII, 99, 646.
Herile Society, the, 378, 379 ff.
Heriot, 64, 66.
Hermeticism, 232.
Hermits of St. Augustine, 27.
Herriot, 186.
Hevelé, 428.
Hickey, Rev., xxvi
Higher dominion, 497.

M. H. GILL AND SON, LTD., PRINTERS, DUBLIN.